THE MILITARY
BALANCE
1993-1994

Published by BRASSEY'S for

**THE INTERNATIONAL
INSTITUTE FOR
STRATEGIC STUDIES**
23 Tavistock Street
London WC2E 7NQ

THE MILITARY BALANCE 1993–1994

Published by Brassey's (UK) Ltd. for
The International Institute for Strategic Studies
23 Tavistock Street, London WC2E 7NQ

Director

Dr Bo Huldt

**Assistant Director
for Information**

Col. Andrew Duncan

Information Officers:

Ground Forces
Philip Mitchell

Aerospace
Wg Cdr Kenneth Petrie RAF

Naval Forces
Cdr Geoffrey Bryant RN

Defence Economist
Nicolas Protonotarios

Editorial:
Victoria Fisher

Production:
Rosalind Winton
Clare Wilkes

This publication has been prepared by the Director of the Institute and his Staff, who accept full responsibility for its contents. These do not, and indeed cannot, represent a consensus of views among the worldwide membership of the Institute as a whole.

First published October 1993

ISBN 1 85753 038 1
ISSN 0459-7222

Military Balance (ISSN 0459 7222) is published annually by Brassey's (UK) Ltd, 165 Great Dover Street, London SE1 4YA. All orders accompanied with payment should be sent directly to Turpin Distribution Services Ltd, Blackhorse Road, Letchworth Herts SG6 1HN, UK. 1993 annual subscription rate is UK and overseas £35.00, single copy £36.00. North America $58.00, single copy $60.00. Airfreight and mailing in the USA by Publications Expediting Inc, 200 Meacham Avenue, Elmont, New York 11003, USA.
USA POSTMASTER: send address changes to Military Balance, Publications Expediting Inc, 200 Meacham Avenue, Elmont, New lYork 11003, USA. Application to mail at second-class postage is pending at Jamaica, New York 11431. All other despatches outside the UK by Printflow Air within Europe and Printflow Airsaver outside Europe.

PRINTED IN THE UK by Halstan & Co. Ltd, Amersham, Bucks.

CONTENTS

THE MILITARY BALANCE 1993–1994
LAYOUT AND PRINCIPLES OF COMPILATION

The Military Balance is updated each year to provide a timely, quantitative assessment of the military forces and defence expenditures of over 160 countries. The current volume contains data as of 1 June 1993. This chapter explains how *The Military Balance* is structured and outlines the general principles followed. The format for country entries remains the same as in the 1992–93 edition.

The break-up of the Soviet Union necessitated a re-evaluation of the way in which *The Military Balance* divides the world into geographical sections. Russia is both a European and an Asian state and is given a separate section. *The Military Balance* assumes that Russia has taken on all former USSR overseas deployments unless there is specific evidence to the contrary. We have shown all the strategic nuclear forces of the former Soviet Union in the Russian section as there still appears to be an attempt at joint control under the aegis of the Commonwealth of Independent States (CIS), although this becomes more doubtful every day. Those forces located in other republics are listed again in the relevant country entry. The future of these nuclear forces is discussed in the essay 'Nuclear Developments'. The section on 'Non-NATO Europe' now includes the Baltic Republics, Belarus, Ukraine, Moldova and the three Transcaucasian republics (Azerbaijan, Armenia and Georgia). The latter have been included in Europe as signatories of the Conventional Armed Forces in Europe (CFE) Treaty. Bosnia-Herzegovina, Croatia, Macedonia and Slovenia are listed as independent, while Serbia and Montenegro are shown in a single entry as the follow-on states to the Federal Republic of Yugoslavia. There are now two Asian sections. 'Central and South Asia' covers the five Central Asian republics of the former Soviet Union (Kazakhstan, Kyrgyzstan, Tajikistan, Turkmenistan and Uzbekistan), Afghanistan, Bangladesh, India, Myanmar (Burma), Nepal, Pakistan and Sri Lanka. The remaining Asian countries are in the 'East Asia and Australasia' section (with China no longer receiving individual section status).

GENERAL ARRANGEMENT

There are two parts to *The Military Balance*. The first comprises national entries grouped by region; the Index on p. 12 gives the page reference for each national entry. Regional groupings are preceded by a short introduction describing the strategic issues facing the region, and significant changes in the defence postures, economic status and military aid arrangements of the countries concerned. Inclusion of a country or state in no way implies legal recognition or IISS approval of it.

The second section contains more general analysis and tables, and includes two descriptive pieces. The first examines nuclear weapons developments: the future of nuclear weapons in the republics of the former Soviet Union; the significance and implications of the START II Treaty; nuclear testing and a Comprehensive Test Ban Treaty; and nuclear proliferation. A table gives details of the strategic nuclear weapons of the US and the former Soviet Union: in 1993; after the implementation of START I; and a possible deployment after START II. The second essay covers all other aspects of arms control including: the CFE Treaty one year after it came into force; the new UN Register of Conventional Weapons; the 1993 Chemical Weapons Convention; and up-to-date information on supplier-group controls. Tables provide information on nuclear delivery means, and a comparison of the defence expenditure and military manpower of all the countries listed in *The Military Balance*. There is also a summary of the composition of all United Nations and other peacekeeping forces, together with a short description of their missions.

At the back of the book there is a list of the type, name/designation, maker and country of origin of all aircraft and helicopters mentioned in *The Military Balance*, and a list of all the abbreviations and symbols used is printed on a card which can be detached from the book for easier use. A wall-map covering Asia from Pakistan in the west to Japan and Australia in the east is provided as a loose insert. It illustrates the changes in armaments holdings and in defence spending in the region over the last ten years.

ABBREVIATIONS AND DEFINITIONS

Space limitations necessitate the use of abbreviations. The abbreviation may have both singular or plural meanings, e.g., 'elm' = 'element' or 'elements'. The qualification 'some' means *up to*, whilst 'about' means *the total could be higher than given*. In financial data, the $ sign refers to US dollars unless otherwise stated; the term billion (bn) signifies 1,000 million (m). Footnotes particular to an entry in one country or table are indicated by letters, while those which apply throughout the book are marked by symbols (i.e., * for training aircraft counted by the IISS as combat capable, and † where serviceability of equipment is in doubt).

NATIONAL ENTRIES

Information on each country is given in a format as standard as the available information permits: economic and demographic data; military data, including manpower, length of conscript service, outline organisation, number of formations and units; and an inventory of the major equipments of each service, followed where applicable by a description of their deployment. Details of national forces stationed abroad and of foreign stationed forces are also given.

GENERAL MILITARY DATA

Manpower

The 'Active' total comprises all servicemen and women on full-time duty (including conscripts and long-term assignments from the Reserves). Under the heading 'Terms of service' only the length of conscript service is shown; where service is voluntary, there is no entry.

In *The Military Balance* the term 'Reserve' is used to describe formations and units not fully manned or operational in peacetime, but which can be mobilised by recalling reservists in an emergency. Unless otherwise indicated, the 'Reserves' entry includes all reservists committed to rejoining the armed forces in an emergency, except when national reserve service obligations following conscription last almost a lifetime. Then *The Military Balance* strength estimates of effective reservists are based on the numbers available within five years of completing full-time service, unless there is good evidence that obligations are enforced for longer. Some countries have more than one category of Reserves, often kept at varying degrees of readiness; where possible these differences are denoted using the national descriptive title, but always under the heading of Reserves, so as to distinguish them from full-time active forces.

Other Forces

Many countries maintain paramilitary forces whose training, organisation, equipment and control suggest they may be usable in support, or in lieu, of regular military forces. These are listed, and their roles described, after the military forces of each country; their manpower is not normally included in the Armed Forces totals at the start of each entry. Home Guard units are counted as paramilitary. Where paramilitary groups are not on full-time active duty, the suffix (R) is added after the title to indicate that they have reserve status. When internal opposition forces are armed and appear to pose a significant threat to the security of a state, their details are listed separately after national paramilitary forces.

Equipment

Numbers are shown by function and type and represent total holdings, including active and reserve operational and training units and 'in store' stocks. Inventory totals for missile systems (e.g., SSM, SAM, ATGW, etc.) relate to launchers and not to missiles.

Stocks of equipment held in reserve and not assigned to either active or reserve units are listed as 'in store'. However, aircraft, in excess of unit establishment holdings, held for such purposes as to allow repair and modification or the immediate replacement of established aircraft, are not shown 'in store' and this accounts for apparent disparities between unit strengths and aircraft inventory strength.

Operational Deployments

The Military Balance does not normally list short-term operational deployments, particularly where military operations are in progress. We make an exception to this rule in the case of peacekeeping operations. The contribution or deployment of forces on operations are normally covered in the text preceding each regional section.

GROUND FORCES

The national designation is normally used for army formations. The term 'regiment' can be misleading. In some cases it is essentially a brigade of all arms; in others, a grouping of battalions of a single arm; and lastly (the UK and French usage) a battalion-sized unit. The sense intended is indicated. Where there is no standard organisation the intermediate levels of command are shown as HQs, followed by the total numbers of units which could be allocated between them. Where a unit's title overstates its real capability, the title is put in inverted commas, and an estimate of the comparable NATO unit size in parentheses: e.g., 'bde' (coy).

Equipment

The Military Balance uses the same definitions as those agreed to at the Conventional Armed Forces in Europe (CFE) negotiations. These are:

Battle Tank (MBT): An armoured tracked combat vehicle weighing at least 16.5 metric tonnes unladen, maybe armed with a 360° traverse gun of at least 75mm calibre. Any new wheeled combat vehicles entering service which meet these criteria will be considered battle tanks.

Armoured Personnel Carrier (APC): A lightly armoured combat vehicle designed and equipped to transport an infantry squad, armed with integral/organic weapons of less than 20mm calibre. Versions of APC converted for other uses (such as weapons platform, command post, communications terminal) which do not allow the transporting of infantry are considered 'look alikes' and are not regarded as treaty-limited equipment (TLE), but are subject to verification.

Armoured Infantry Fighting Vehicle (AIFV): An armoured combat vehicle designed and equipped to transport an infantry squad, armed with an integral/organic cannon of at least 20 mm calibre. There are also AIFV 'look alikes'.

Heavy Armoured Combat Vehicle (HACV): An armoured combat vehicle weighing more than six metric tonnes unladen, with an integral/organic direct-fire gun of at least 75mm (which does not fall within the definitions of APC, AIFV or MBT). *The Military Balance* does not list HACV separately, but under their equipment type (light tank, recce or assault gun), and where appropriate annotates them as HACV.

Artillery: Systems with calibres of 100mm and above, capable of engaging ground targets by delivering primarily indirect fire, namely guns, howitzers, gun/howitzers, multiple-rocket launchers (MRL) and mortars.

Weapons with bores of less than 14.5mm are not listed, nor, for major armies, are hand-held ATK weapons.

Military Formation Strengths

The manpower strength, equipment holdings and organisation of formations such as brigades and divisions differ widely from state to state. Where possible, we give the normal composition of formations in parentheses. It should be noted that where divisions and brigades are listed, only separate brigades are counted and not those included in divisions. We have discontinued the table which showed the manpower and equipment strength of divisions as this is under review and being restructured in most countries as a result of the end of the Cold War.

NAVAL FORCES

Categorisation is based partly on operational role, partly on weapon fit and partly on displacement. Ship classes are identified by the name of the first ship of that class, except where a class is recognised by another name (e.g. *Krivak, Kotlin*, etc.). Where the class is based on a foreign design, the original class name is added in parentheses.

Each class of vessel is given an acronym designator based on the NATO system. All designators are included in the list of Abbreviations on the perforated card inserted in the book.

The term 'ship' is used to refer to vessels of over both 1,000 tonnes full-load displacement and 60 metres overall length; vessels of lesser displacement, but of 16m or more overall length are termed 'craft'. Vessels of less than 16m overall length have not been included.

The term 'commissioning' has different meanings in a number of navies. In *The Military Balance* we use the term to mean that a ship has completed fitting out, initial sea trials, and has a naval crew; operational training may not have been completed, but in all other respects the ship is available for service. By 'decommissioning', we mean a ship has been removed from operational duty and the bulk of its naval crew transferred. De-storing and dismantling of weapons may not have started.

Classifications and Definitions

To aid comparison between fleets, naval entries have been subdivided into the following categories, which do not necessarily agree with national categorisation:

Submarines: Submarines with SLBM are listed separately under 'Strategic Nuclear Forces'.

Principal Surface Combatants: All surface ships with both 1,000 tonnes full-load displacement and a weapons system other than for self-protection. They comprise aircraft carriers (with a flight-deck extending beyond two-thirds of the vessel's length), battleships (armour-protected, over 30,000 tonnes, and with armour-protected guns of at least 250mm bore); cruisers (over 8,000 tonnes) and destroyers (less than 8,000 tonnes), both of which normally have an anti-air warfare role and may also have an anti-submarine capability; and frigates (less than 8,000 tonnes) which normally have an anti-submarine role.

Patrol and Coastal Combatants: All ships and craft whose primary role relates to the protection of the sea approaches and coastline of a state. Included are: corvettes (600–1,000 tonnes and carrying weapons systems other than for self-protection); missile craft (with permanently fitted missile launcher ramps and control equipment); torpedo craft (with an anti-surface-ship capability). Ships and craft which fall outside these definitions are classified as 'patrol'.

Mine Warfare: This category covers surface vessels configured primarily for mine-laying or mine countermeasures, which can be minehunters, mine-sweepers or dual-capable vessels.

A further classification divides both coastal and patrol combatants and mine-warfare vessels into: offshore (over 600 tonnes), coastal (300–600 tonnes) and inshore (less than 300 tonnes).

8

Amphibious: Only ships specifically procured and employed to disembark troops and their equipment over unprepared beachheads have been listed. Vessels with an amphibious capability, but which are known not to be assigned to amphibious duties, are not included. Amphibious craft are listed at the end of each entry.

Support and Miscellaneous: This category of essentially non-military vessels provides some indication of the operational sustainability and outreach of the navy concerned.

Weapons Systems: Weapons are listed in the order in which they contribute to the ship's primary operational role. After the word 'plus' are added significant weapons relating to the ship's secondary role. Self-defence weapons are not listed. To merit inclusion, a SAM system must have an anti-missile range of 10km or more, and guns must be of 100mm bore or greater.

Aircraft: The CFE definition of combat aircraft does not cover maritime aircraft. We include all armed aircraft including anti-submarine warfare and some maritime reconnaissance aircraft as combat aircraft in naval inventories.

Organisations: Naval groupings such as fleets and squadrons are often temporary and change-able; organisation is only shown where it is meaningful.

AIR FORCES

The following remarks refer to aviation units forming an integral part of ground forces, naval forces and (where applicable) Marines, as well as to separate air forces.

The term 'combat aircraft' comprises aircraft normally equipped to deliver ordnance in air-to-air or air-to-surface combat. In previous editions of *The Military Balance* reconnaissance aircraft were not counted as combat but, as the CFE Treaty counts some types as combat-capable, we have attempted to differentiate between combat-capable types (Su-24, RF-4, etc.) and non-combat types (TR-1). Most air forces therefore show an increase in the number of combat aircraft held. The 'combat' totals include aircraft in operational units (OCU) whose main role is weapons training, and training aircraft of the same type as those in front-line squadrons and assumed to be available for operations at short notice. (Training aircraft considered to be combat-capable are marked by an asterisk: *.) Where armed maritime aircraft are held by air forces we do not include these in combat aircraft totals.

Air force operational groupings are shown where known. Squadron aircraft strengths vary; attempts have been made to separate total holdings from reported establishment strength.

The number of categories of aircraft listed is kept to a minimum. 'Fighter' is used to denote aircraft with the capability (weapons, avionics, performance) for aerial combat. Dual-capable aircraft are shown as FGA, fighter, etc., according to the role in which they are deployed. Different countries often use the same basic aircraft in different roles; the key to determining these roles lies mainly in air-crew training. For bombers, long-range means having an unrefuelled radius of action of over 5,000km, medium-range 1,000–5,000km and short-range less than 1,000km; light bombers are those with a payload of under 10,000kg (which is no greater than the payload of many FGA).

The CFE Treaty lists three types of helicopters: attack (one equipped to employ anti-armour, air-to-ground or air-to-air guided weapons by means of an integrated fire control and aiming system); combat support (which may or may not be armed with self-defence or area suppression weapons, but without a control and guidance system); and unarmed transport helicopters. *The Military Balance* uses the term 'attack' in the CFE sense, and the term 'assault' to describe armed helicopters used to deliver infantry or other troops on the battlefield. Except in the case of CFE signatories, *The Military Balance* continues to employ the term 'armed helicopters' to cover those equipped to deliver ordnance, including ASW ordnance.

ECONOMIC AND DEMOGRAPHIC DATA

Economic Data

Figures for Gross Domestic Product (GDP) are provided, but Gross National Product (GNP) and Net Material Product (NMP) are used when necessary (GNP equals GDP plus net income from abroad; NMP equals GNP minus non-earning state services). GDP figures are quoted at current market prices. Where available, published sources are used, but estimated figures are used when data is incomplete. GDP/GNP growth rates cited are real growth in real terms. Inflation rates are based on available consumer price indices and refer to annual averages. 'Debt' means gross foreign debt and includes all long-, medium- and short-term debt, both publicly and privately owed; no account is taken of similar debt owed to the country in question by others. For some developed economies we have introduced a more appropriate indicator: 'Public Debt' means gross public debt and is expressed as a percentage of nominal GDP.

Wherever possible, the UN System of National Accounts, based on the latest available International Monetary Fund (IMF) *International Financial Statistics* (*IFS*), has been used. Other sources include data from *Economic Survey of Europe 1992–1993* (New York: UN, 1993), *World Economic Outlook* (Washington, DC: IMF, May 1993), *World Debt Tables* (1992–1993): *External Debt of Developing Countries* (Washington, DC: World Bank, 1991) and *Key Indicators of Developing Asian and Pacific Countries,* vol. 23 (Asian Development Bank, 1992). For African countries we have used issues of *Africa Research Bulletin* and *Marchés Tropicaux et Méditerranéens*. For 1991 data on the states of the former Soviet Union we have used IMF Economic Review papers, and for the former states of Yugoslavia and the Balkans, the *Southeastern European Yearbook* (Athens: Hellenic Foundation for Defence and Foreign Policy, 1992).

Defence Expenditure

The latest defence expenditure or budget data available as at 1 June 1993 is quoted. Some countries include internal and border security force expenditures in their defence budgets; where separate budgets exist they are indicated in footnotes. Figures may vary from previous years, often because of updates made by the governments themselves.

NATO uses a 'standard definition' of defence expenditure which includes all spending on regular military forces, military aid (including equipment and training) to other nations, military pensions, host government expenses for NATO tenant forces, NATO infrastructure and civilian staff costs; but excludes spending on paramilitary forces. Both the nationally calculated defence expenditure and the NATO definition are shown.

Foreign Military Assistance (FMA) figures are included where these exceed $US1m, with other economic data in country entries. The total of FMA received from the US is shown. FMA includes both cash grants and credits; it may also include the cost of military training.

Currency Conversion Rates

National currency figures have been converted into $US to permit comparisons. The rate is averaged for the national financial year (for 1993–94 figures, the mid-1993 rate is used). Wherever possible, exchange rates are taken from *IFS*, though they may not be applicable to commercial transactions. Plan Econ PPP (Purchase Power Parity) estimates have been used for some economies, and exchange rates have been adjusted accordingly. Where appropriate, the interpretation of national currencies has departed significantly from the official one, when this would have resulted in a meaningless figure. In some cases, in an effort to make $US figures more relevant for international comparisons, a different set of exchange rates has been used to calculate national accounts and defence spending, reflecting the differences in Purchase Power Parity terms between the civilian and military sectors.

Population

All population data is taken from: the latest census data available in *World Population Projections 1992–93* (Baltimore and London: Johns Hopkins University Press for the World Bank, November 1992); the *1989 Demographic Yearbook* (New York: UN, 1991; latest national statistics where available, as well as calculated trends and projections.

WARNING

The Military Balance is a quantitative assessment of the personnel strengths and equipment holdings of the world's armed forces. It is in no way an assessment of their capabilities. It does not attempt to evaluate the quality of units or equipment, nor the impact of geography, doctrine, military technology, deployment, training, logistic support, morale, leadership, tactical or strategic initiative, terrain, weather, political will or support from alliance partners.

Nor is the Institute in any position to evaluate and compare directly the performance of items of equipment. Those who wish to do so can use the data provided to construct their own force comparisons. As essays in many editions of *The Military Balance* have made clear, however, such comparisons are replete with difficulties, and their validity and utility cannot but be suspect.

The Military Balance provides the actual numbers of nuclear and conventional forces and weapons based on the most accurate data available, or, failing that, on the best estimate that can be made with a reasonable degree of confidence – this is not the number that would be assumed for verification purposes in arms-control agreements, although we attempt to provide this information as well.

The data presented each year in *The Military Balance* reflects judgments based on information available to the Director and Staff of the Institute at the time the book is compiled. Information may differ from previous editions for a variety of reasons, generally as a result of substantive changes in national forces, but in some cases as a result of our reassessment of the evidence supporting past entries. Inevitably, over the course of time we have come to believe that some information presented in earlier versions was erroneous, or insufficiently supported by reliable evidence. Hence, it is not always possible to construct valid time-series comparisons from information given in successive editions, although in the text which introduces each regional section we do attempt to distinguish between new acquisitions and revised assessments.

CONCLUSION

The Institute owes no allegiance to any government, group of governments, or any political or other organisation. Our assessments are our own, based on the material available to us from a wide variety of sources. The cooperation of all governments has been sought and, in many cases, received. Not all countries have been equally cooperative, and some of the figures have necessarily been estimated. We take pains to ensure that these estimates are as professional and free from bias as possible. The Institute owes a considerable debt to a number of its own members and consultants who have helped in compiling and checking material. The Director and Staff of the Institute assume full responsibility for the facts and judgments contained in this study. We welcome comments and suggestions on the data presented, since we seek to make it as accurate and comprehensive as possible.

Readers may use items of information from *The Military Balance* as required, without applying for permission from the Institute, on condition that the IISS and *The Military Balance* are cited as the source in any published work. However, reproduction of major portions of *The Military Balance* must be approved in writing by the Deputy Director of the Institute, Colonel Michael Dewar, prior to publication.

October 1993

1

_____

COUNTRIES

INDEX

The United States

Political Developments

In the last months of the Bush administration two major developments took place. Following the adoption of UN Security Council Resolution 794, which authorised member-states to 'use all necessary means' to create a secure environment in Somalia in which humanitarian relief operations could be successfully undertaken, President Bush deployed in December 1992 considerable forces to Somalia for *Operation Restore Hope*. In January 1993 Presidents Bush and Yeltsin signed a treaty, commonly known as START II, under the terms of which strategic nuclear forces would be further reduced to roughly one-quarter their current levels by the year 2003.

However, both this major arms-control agreement and the unilateral attempt at peacekeeping came too late to restore President Bush's popularity and credibility; on 4 November 1992 a Democratic president was overwhelmingly elected to office by the American people. During the election campaign the Democratic candidate Bill Clinton pledged to devote himself primarily to achieving economic reform and to solving domestic problems. He maintained that the cuts in force posture and defence expenditure set in train by the Bush administration did not go deep enough. At the same time he argued that the US should play a more positive role, not excluding the use of force, to bring an end to the conflict in Bosnia. Shortly after his election President Clinton repeated his campaign promise to allow homosexuals to serve openly in the armed forces. After a generally hostile reception, a decision was reached that applicants to the services are not to be questioned on their sexual orientation. The strength of feeling on the matter can be judged by the incessant press coverage it has received; the compromise solution is unlikely to be welcome to either side.

Defence Policy

In his Annual Report to the President and Congress given in January 1993 US Secretary of Defense Dick Cheney stated that there were four critical elements of strategy which would guide plans for force posture and shape regional defence policies. The first was Strategic Deterrence and Defense which required the US to maintain a balanced deterrent force with both strategic and tactical offensive capabilities. Strategic Defense was to be based on developing systems to protect both the US, its forces, allies and friends from a ballistic missile attack of up to 200 re-entry vehicles. The second, Forward Presence, which covered activities such as exercises, periodic deployment, exchanges and visits, as well as forward-basing and prepositioning, was essential as a demonstration of commitment. The third, Crisis Response, involved the capability to react simultaneously to crises in widely separated regions and required the maintenance of highly ready and rapidly deployable forces. Crisis Response also required the capability for the rapid movement of forces. The fourth element, the capability for Reconstitution of both military forces and defence industry, was necessary as an insurance against a future threat of global dimension.

In response to the changed world situation the Bush administration planned to implement a 25% reduction in active forces by 1995. The Army would reduce from 18 to 12 divisions, the Navy from 530 ships to 430 (including a reduction from 15 carrier battle-groups to 13) and the Air Force from 22 fighter wings to 15.

The new Secretary for Defense, Les Aspin, has presented his first budget (for FY 1994) to Congress. In requesting a Budget Authority (BA) of $263.4 billion (bn) (including the Department of Energy) the new administration plans to spend approximately $10bn less than had been appropriated by Congress for FY 1993. The budget contains several new initiatives: $448m has been requested to cover Peacekeeping, Disaster Relief, Humanitarian Assistance and the Promotion of Democracy; $400m, in addition to that already authorised, is requested to assist in the elimination of nuclear and chemical weapons of the former Soviet Union and $40m for efforts to counter the proliferation of weapons of mass destruction. Force reduction will be accelerated, and Secretary Aspin has announced his goal of reducing active duty strength to 1.4m (200,000 less than the Bush administration's target). No details of cuts beyond those already planned have been announced. The

Secretary also announced the holding of a 'bottom-up' review of defence needs and programmes to be completed by late summer 1993 (thus too late to be covered by this edition of *The Military Balance*).

Operations

The last act of the Bush administration was to order an attack by *Tomahawk* sea-launched cruise missiles (SLCM) on 15 January 1993, on the plant at Zaafaraniyah in Iraq, which had been proven to be involved in the Iraqi nuclear-weapons programme. The raid was ordered becauseIraq was constantly defying the UN, both by its activities in the DMZ on the Kuwait border and by obstructing the work of the United Nations Special Commission (UNSCOM). The first similar act of the Clinton administration was to order an SLCM attack on 27 June 1993 on the intelligence complex in Baghdad, after it had been reliably claimed that Iraqi intelligence was behind the plot to assassinate former president Bush during his visit to Kuwait in April 1993. The plot was uncovered, an explosive-filled vehicle was discovered and a number of Iraqi and Kuwaiti nationals arrested. The use of SLCM as opposed to manned aircraft avoids the possibility of being refused the use of allied airfields and of being given over-flying permission (which was refused by several NATO countries when US aircraft raided Libya in 1986).

During the past 12 months US forces, together with those of its allies, have taken part in a number of peacekeeping and other operations; most are still in progress.

Iraq

Operation Provide Comfort II / Poised Hammer. This operation, involving the US, British and French air forces based in eastern Turkey, provides aircraft to enforce the no-fly zone over the Kurdish area of northern Iraq. Further details are given on p. 62.
Operation Olive Branch. U-2 aircraft carry out reconnaissance sorties over Iraq to assist UNSCOM in its task of locating and destroying all elements of Iraq's nuclear, chemical and ballistic missile programmes.
Operation Southern Watch. Together with British and French aircraft, the US Air Force and Naval Aviation enforce the no-fly zone, which was declared in August 1992 as a means of halting the air attacks on the Shi'i population in southern Iraq, from bases in Saudi Arabia and an aircraft carrier in the Persian Gulf.

Somalia

Operation Restore Hope. On 9 December 1992 US Marines began the deployment into Somalia of a US-led coalition force (Unified Task Force (UNITAF)) whose aim was to ensure that the delivery of humanitarian aid was achieved throughout the country. At its peak the US force numbered some 25,000 men, including naval units offshore. The US Command handed over to a new UN force (UNOSOM II) on 4 May 1993. A strong US contingent forms part of UNOSOM II, with the role of a rapid reaction force. It has already been in action against General Aideed, the warlord in Mogadishu, when his followers ambushed UN troops, causing heavy casualties. The UN responded with a series of air attacks carried out by special forces aircraft and attack helicopters, backed up by ground operations by US and other UN forces. Further details of UNITAF and UNOSOM are given in the essay 'Peacekeeping Operations'.

Former Yugoslavia

UNPROFOR II. The US Army has deployed a field hospital to Croatia in support of UNPROFOR I. Apart from this relatively small contribution to the UN forces in former Yugoslavia, the US has consistently maintained a policy of not deploying ground troops to the region. However, in June 1993 it was decided to send 300 troops to Macedonia to reinforce the Scandinavian battalion there.
Operation Deny Flight. While a no-fly zone was declared over Bosnia in October 1992, it was only in April 1993, following the adoption of a further UN Resolution, that enforcement was authorised.

US air forces, along with aircraft from France, the Netherlands, Turkey and the UK, patrol Bosnian airspace from bases in Italy.

Operation Disciplined Guard. The US has deployed Air Force, Navy and Marine Corps aircraft to air bases in Italy in readiness to implement *Operation Disciplined Guard* should this be authorised. The operation is designed to provide air cover for UN troops in Bosnia should they be attacked, and to attack those responsible should the strangulation of Sarajevo and other areas continue.

Operation Provide Promise. The airlift of humanitarian aid carried out by the US and Allied aircraft into Sarajevo airport commenced in July 1992. This operation was extended to cover the parachute drop of supplies by US and German aircraft to the Bosnian Muslims besieged in enclaves in eastern Bosnia which began on 28 February 1993. Supply drops were carried out from a height far above that normally chosen in order to avoid the risk of losing aircraft to air-defence fire. As a result, a high proportion of the supplies did not reach those for whom they were intended.

Operation Sharp Guard. The US Navy contributes to the NATO naval force which is monitoring shipping and enforcing the economic sanctions imposed by the UN on Serbia and Montenegro and the arms embargo on the whole of the former Yugoslavia.

Nuclear Developments

On 2 October 1992 President Bush signed the Energy and Water Development Appropriations Act which introduced a number of restrictions on nuclear testing in the US. A nine-month moratorium on US testing took effect on 1 October; at the end of the moratorium testing would be restricted to a maximum of 15 safety-related tests (five per reporting year, of which one may be carried out by the UK). A maximum of one additional reliability-related test per year may take place if the President certifies that this is necessary. After 30 September 1996 no further tests are to take place unless a foreign state conducts a test after this date. Whether or not the Clinton administration chooses to resume testing in 1993, it does not seem willing to challenge the complete ban after 1996.

The US Senate ratified the START I Treaty on 1 October 1992. Congress has so far approved $800m to help the four former Soviet nuclear republics (Belarus, Kazakhstan, Russia and Ukraine) to dismantle and store nuclear warheads, and the FY 1994 budget request includes a further $400m for this purpose. In April it was reported that $458m had so far been spent or earmarked. In February 1993 the US signed an agreement with Russia to negotiate the purchase of weapons-grade uranium over a 20-year period; up to 500 tons could be involved at a probable total cost of nearly $8bn.

Strategic Forces

A follow-on treaty to the Strategic Arms Reduction Treaty (START) was signed by Presidents Yeltsin and Bush on 3 January 1993. It is based on the joint understanding reached at the Washington Summit meeting of June 1992. The effect of START II on US strategic deployment is to require the down-loading of *Minuteman* III ICBM from three warheads to one, the elimination of all MX *Peacekeeper* ICBM, and a reduction in the number of SLBM warheads deployed to no more than 1,750. The total number of strategic warheads that can be deployed may not exceed 3,500. The counting rules for air-delivered warheads have been changed from those agreed for START I, and the US plans to restrict its bomber force to 95 B-52H carrying ALCM or advanced cruise missiles (ACM), and 20 B-2s. The details of START II are analysed in the essay 'Nuclear Developments'. Under the terms of START II the B-1B bomber force will be re-oriented to the conventional role.

The reduction in US strategic forces has continued despite the failure of Ukraine to ratify START I. Approximately 189 *Minuteman* II ICBMs have been removed from their silos; as yet no missiles or silos have been destroyed and still remain START-countable. The deactivation began in October 1991 and is scheduled to be complete by the end of 1995. The remaining silo-based *Minuteman* II have been taken off alert. There are now 507 *Minuteman* III ICBM deployed; there has been no change to MX *Peacekeeper* deployment of 50 ICBM. Of the ten *Poseidon* C-3-equipped SSBN withdrawn from patrol in 1992, one remains commissioned (until November 1993), two have recommissioned as dry-dock shelters; these and four decommissioned SSBN remain START-countable. One *Franklin*-class and one *Madison*-class *Trident* C-4-armed SSBN have decommissioned and a further *Madison* decommissions in October 1993. Some 52 B-52G have been withdrawn from service and now await elimination at Davis-Monthan Air Force Base in Arizona.

A sixth *Ohio*-class SSBN armed with *Trident* D-5 SLBM has commissioned. Plans to procure D-5 SLBM through to FY 1999 are under Congressional question. The Navy is asking for 133, bringing its total holding to 428. Opponents of D-5 production would terminate the programme, leaving the Navy with some 250 missiles, insufficient to meet plans to deploy ten SSBN in the Atlantic Fleet with 24 SLBM each. The Navy appears to have abandoned reluctantly its plan to retrofit D-5 SLBM in Pacific Fleet SSBN. The first two operational B-2 bombers have been delivered and two more B-2 have joined the test flight (they are not START-countable). One B-1B has crashed.

Strategic Defense Initiative

The change in emphasis in anti-ballistic missile defence which began in 1992 when Congress reduced the SDI budget request for FY 1993 from $5.4bn to $3.04bn, plus just over $1bn for theatre missile defence, has been continued and accelerated by the new administration. Congress also overturned the plans for a ground-based national missile defence as required by the Warner–Nunn Act of November 1991 which called for the development of such a system by 1996. The SDI budget request for FY 1994 is $3.76bn, not much more than that eventually authorised for FY 1993 but $2.54bn or roughly 40% less than that planned by the Bush administration. As well as a major change in emphasis in the programme the SDI has been renamed the Ballistic Missile Defense Office.

Of the two main projects within BMDO, Theater Missile Defense (TMD) has been given the higher priority and the larger share of the budget ($1.8bn). It includes: Theater High Altitude Area Defense (THAAD); improvement to the *Patriot* missile system; and a naval version of TMD. The second project, National Missile Defense, for which $1.19bn is requested, still aims to install a ground-based system (probably at Grand Forks in North Dakota), which complies with the Anti-Ballistic Missile (ABM) Treaty, but not until the year 2004. *Brilliant Pebbles*, which envisaged the deployment of 1,000 space-based interceptors, is now just a development project and only $75m is requested for continued research and development.

Conventional Forces

Ground Forces

The reduction in the number of active army divisions to the 'base force' level of 12 has been completed, with the deactivation of two light infantry divisions. Seven of the remaining divisions (including one based in Germany) have their order of battle completed with a third 'Round-Out' National Guard (ARNG) or Army Reserve (AR) brigade. The third brigade of the other division based in Germany is, in peacetime, located in the US. Active manpower strength has been reduced by 100,000 to 575,000, of which 20,000 were from posts in Germany. Two ARNG infantry divisions and one armoured cavalry regiment (ACR) have been deactivated, and ARNG manpower strength reduced by 30,000. One AR infantry brigade and roughly half the AR artillery and engineer battalions have been deactivated. AR manpower has been drastically reduced from 681,000 to 260,000.

There have been both increases and decreases in equipment holdings, the latter mainly through the 'cascading' to European allies of tanks, APC and artillery in excess of the CFE Treaty limits. Overall tank strength has dropped by around 1,150, including the 639 M-47 tanks previously stored in Italy which have been destroyed. M-1/-1A1 *Abrams* tank holdings have increased by about 130. Other increases in Army equipment holdings include: some 500 *Bradley* AIFV, 56 MLRS (80% of MLRS are now ATACMs capable) and 56 M-54/M-48 *Chaparral* SP SAM. All *Lance* SSM launchers have now been destroyed.

The US Marine Corps has suffered far less from force cuts than the other services. Three active divisions are to be maintained plus one reserve division, albeit at a slightly reduced strength. Active manpower strength has dropped by 10,000. There have been no significant changes in equipment holding. The February 1993 report by the Chairman of the Joint Chiefs of Staff, 'Roles, Missions and Functions of the Armed Forces of the United States', recommends that MLRS and additional tank support should be provided by the Army (subject to further validation).

Air Forces

The reorganisation of the Air Force into two commands came into effect on 1 June 1992. Air Combat Command (ACC) comprises five numbered air forces: one commands all ICBM units; another reconnaissance and associated tanker assets; and three are made up of bomber/tanker and fighter/FGA wings. The Air Division level of command has been eliminated. Air Mobility Command (AMC) comprises three numbered air forces: one commands all air-refuelling assets; the other two transport units are split between East- and West-Coast orientated air bases. Both Commands contain units of the active Air Force, Air National Guard (ANG) and Air Force Reserve (AFR). Five numbered air force HQ are deployed overseas.

Some aircraft have been added to the inventory in the last 12 months, these include nine more EC-135 command aircraft, some 60 F-16 FGA aircraft, and 15 MC-130 E-H special operations aircraft. Many more older types have been withdrawn from squadron service and put into store. The most significant withdrawals (other than strategic aircraft) are: 30 RF-4C reconnaissance aircraft (only the ANG holds these in squadron service); some 40 F-15A fighters; some 120 F-111-A/-D/ and -G fighter bombers; only F-111 E/-F remain in squadron service; 100 A-7 fighter-bombers; some 80 A-10A anti-tank aircraft and around 30 KC-135 tankers. Air Force active manpower strength has been reduced by some 50,000, of which 11,000 were serving overseas.

During the FY 1993 budget process the Department of Defense was severely criticised for planning to develop three new aircraft: F-22 for the Air Force and F/A-18E/F and A/F-X for the Navy. Congress ordered a further review of the tactical aircraft requirement and restricted spending to 65% of the funds authorised until the review was completed. In the event, Congress authorised $1.9bn for F-22 research and development, $820m to procure an additional 24 F-16 aircraft and $2.2bn for R & D and procurement of six C-17 transport aircraft. For FY 1994 the Air Force has requested $2.25bn for F-22 R & D, $914m for a further 24 F-16 aircraft and $2.5bn for the C-17, including procurement of six more aircraft.

There have been some changes to overseas deployment. A total of some 70 combat aircraft have been withdrawn from Europe; 110 F-111E/F and 60 A-10 from the UK, but numbers in Germany have increased (50 F-16C/D, 24 A-10/OA-10, most F-4G have been withdrawn). Manpower strength in Europe has dropped by around 11,000. As a result of the withdrawal from the Philippines, Air Force numbers in Japan and South Korea have risen by some 5,000 men and additional special operations, AWACS and tanker aircraft.

The C-17 transport aircraft built by McDonnell Douglas is a four-engine aircraft designed to deliver up to 102 paratroopers or 110,000lbs of air-drop cargo or 172,200lbs of air-landed cargo over intercontinental distances landing at small austere airfields near the battle zone. The original requirement was for 210 aircraft, but current plans are for 120 aircraft at a cost of about $40bn. The first squadron of 12 was due in service in 1992, but the C-17 programme has been considerably delayed because of technical and cost problems. A series of initiatives has been launched to get the programme back on track, while at the same time looking at three alternatives: reopening the Lockheed C-5 *Galaxy* line; rewinging existing Lockheed C-141 and extending their service life; and acquiring commercial aircraft to meet a portion of the military airlift requirement. The C-17 programme faces termination in August 1993 unless there are concrete assurances from the Air Force, McDonnell Douglas and an independent review team that costs and technical problems are manageable.

The replacement aircraft for the McDonnell Douglas F-15 *Eagle* was required to have incorporated low observable technology (*Stealth*) and supercruise (supersonic cruise without afterburners) capability. In April 1991 the Lockheed YF-22 prototype won the competition against the Northrop YF-23 prototype. In August 1991 engineering and manufacturing development authority was given for 11 development aircraft to be built with a first flight in mid-1994 and entry to service in 2002. It was planned to acquire 648 aircraft but this number has been revised downwards to about 440.

Budget shortfalls have forced the USAF to rephase its development programme, dropping two of the aircraft types and delaying the first flight until 1996. The first production aircraft is now due in 2000 and as a decision on high-rate production has been delayed until July 2001 the entry to service date is also likely to be put back.

While the report 'Roles, Missions and Functions' concludes that all four services require their own ground-attack capability (the Army only having attack helicopters), naval and Marine Corps aviation assets are both being reduced and becoming less independent. All aircraft procurement budgets show a significant drop in FY 1994 from FY 1992 (Army 42%, Air Force 27%, Navy and USMC 12%). Although the number of carrier air wings has been maintained (11 active, 2 reserve) the number of active squadrons has been reduced (by one F-14, five A-6E, all six A-7E, two EA-6B (ECM) four P03B/C(MR)). In the Naval Reserve Aviation both A-6E and A-7E have been withdrawn and replaced with F-14 aircraft. The USMC has deactivated one A-6E squadron and in the USMC Reserve F-4S has been replaced by F-18A and two squadrons of A-4M have been disbanded. Some USMC squadrons, other than those with VSTOL aircraft and helicopters, are to be integrated into carrier air wings.

Naval Forces

The US Navy is scheduled to take large force reductions; from a 466-ship battle force in FY 1992 it will reduce to a 413-ship force in FY 1994. The shipbuilding procurement budget of $8.7bn in FY 1992 is reduced to $4.3bn in FY 1994. Manpower strength was 542,000 in FY 1992 and will come down to 480,000 in FY 1994.

During the past 12 months a number of ships have decommissioned including: two *Sturgeon-* and one *Permit*-class attack submarines; one *Forrestal*-class aircraft carrier; three *Coontz-* and five *Adams*-class destroyers; and eight *Knox*-class frigates with a further eight relegated to a training-ship role. However, a number of modern ships have commissioned: three improved *Los Angeles*-class attack submarines; four *Ticonderoga*-class, *Aegis*-equipped, cruisers; and one *Arleigh Burke* destroyer. Two further *Spruance*-class destroyers have been fitted with the Vertical Launch System (VLS).

The Navy's aim is to maintain as many as 12 aircraft carriers despite their large operating costs (estimated at $350m a year). To achieve this the two remaining *Forrestal*-class carriers will decommission in FY 1993; one was roled as a training carrier and this role will have to be rotated amongst operational carriers. No doubt the argument over the number of carriers to be kept in service will continue for some time; justified during the Cold War as the prime means of maintaining control of the high seas and taking the war to the Soviet Union, they are now being more clearly seen as, what in fact they always were, the prime weapon in power projection. There have been changes also in the mine countermeasures and amphibious fleets. Three more *Avenger*-class offshore mine counter-measure ships have commissioned, while four *Aggressive*-class offshore mine-sweepers have been retired, as have the five MSB-15 inshore mine-sweepers. A second *Wasp*-class LHA has commissioned which can embark 2,000 marines and 20 VTOL aircraft. Three more *Wasps* are under construction, with one to be completed during FY 1993. Two *Iwo Jima*-class LPH, one *Raleigh*-class LPD and four *Newport*-class LST have been retired.

This year the entry for Strategic Sealift has been renamed Military Sealift, which we feel is more accurate.

The US Navy's withdrawal from the Subic Bay base in the Philippines was completed in November 1992. The Navy has negotiated use of facilities in all other ASEAN countries.

Defence Spending

In 1990 President Bush proposed an FY 1993 budget request of $291bn; by 1992 this request had been reduced to $274 bn. The last $7bn reduction came entirely from defence appropriations, leaving the amounts requested for military construction ($8bn) and nuclear weapons funded through the Department of Energy ($12bn) intact.

The main loser in the FY 1993 budget cuts was SDI whose request for $5.4bn was slashed to $3.04bn. For the first time in 20 years Congress cut the Operations and Maintenance request by some

$6bn, the bulk of which will come from savings achieved by not replacing spare parts and supplies. Some $700m was saved on manpower costs, with the loss of some 99,000 posts.

Funding was reduced for only a few major weapons systems: the C-17 strategic transport aircraft (two aircraft and $700m); fast cargo ships ($600m); F/A-18 Navy fighters (12 aircraft and $460m); R & D for F/A18 E and F models ($400m). As usual, Congress reinstated some of its favourite projects which the Department of Defense had planned to terminate: Advanced Cruise Missile ($127m); M-1 tank upgrade ($160m); the Bell model 406 Army Helicopter Improvement Program (AHIP) US Army designation OH-58D *Kiowa Warrior* ($225m); procurement of an extra JSTARS intelligence collection aircraft ($200m); and, of course, the USMC *Osprey* tilt-rotor aircraft ($755m).

The total national defence budget request for FY 1994 is $263.4bn, $8.5bn lower than the FY 1993 budget authority and $12bn less than that planned by the Bush administration for FY 1994. The planned cut for FY 1994 through to FY 1997 is $88bn less than the previous administration's proposal. When adjusted for inflation the FY 1994 request is 5% below that for FY 1993 and 24% below that for FY 1990. It is forecast that by 1997 the cumulative real decline in defence spending since FY 1985 will be over 41%. As a share of GDP, defence expenditure is expected to fall to 3% in FY 1998, compared with double that figure in the mid-1980s.

Two areas in the FY 1994 budget proposal show a real increase: Operations and Maintenance (1.2%) and Military Construction (25%). There is to be only one reduction in the key operational training rates: Air Force tactical flying hours per month are down from 19.8 to 19.5. Army ground operations and tactical flying hours, and Naval steaming days and flying hours have not been affected by the cuts. The main savings come from personnel costs (down 9.2%) and procurement (17%). The priority given to Research and Development, as promised by Secretary Cheney, has been maintained with a budget of only 1.1%.

US Defence Budgets

Explanatory Note:
Each year the US government presents its Defense Budget to Congress for the next two fiscal years, together with a long-term spending plan covering a further three years. Until approved by Congress, the Budget is referred to as the Budget Request, after approval it becomes the Budget Authority (BA), and authorises funds for immediate and future disbursement. The term Total Obligational Authority (TOA) represents the value of direct defence programmes for each fiscal year regardless of financing (i.e. from previous fiscal years and receipts from earned income or interest). The term 'outlay' represents actual expenditure; each year the government estimates what the outlay will be, the difference between this and the BA providing for contingencies. However, moneys authorised, particularly in the procurement and construction areas, are rarely all spent in the year of authorisation, though contracts are signed which commit the government to payment in future years. On average, carried forward authorities constitute some 40% of each year's outlay, while similarly some 40% of each year's BA will be carried forward to future years.

Table I: Selected Budgets 1988–94 ($bn)[a]

FY 1 Oct– 30 Sept	National Defense Function[b] (BA)	(outlay)	Department of Defense (BA)	(outlay)	Atomic Energy Defense Activities (outlay)	Inter- national Security Assistance (outlay)	Veterans Admin- istration (outlay)	Total Govt Exp (outlay)	Total Govt Budget Deficit (outlay)
1988	292.008	290.361	283.755	281.935	7.913	4.500	29.428	1,064.051	155.090
1989	299.567	303.559	290.837	294.880	8.119	1.467	30.066	1,144.064	153.400
1990	303.263	299.331	292.999	289.755	8.988	8.652	29.112	1,251.778	220.470
1991	303.574	273.292	290.904	262.389	10.004	9.823	31.349	1,323.011	268.746
1992	295.070	298.350	282.127	286.892	10.619	7.490	34.133	1,380.860	290.400
1993 (administration request)	272.768	290.617	258.869	277.185	11.664	7.915	35.620	1,467.639	322.000
1994	263.363	276.869	250.745	264.152	11.505	6.777	37.918	1,515.318	264.100

[a] Data is from *Budget of the United States Government* – Fiscal Year 1994. All categories include off-budget items.
[b] The National Defense budget function includes DoD Military Activities, Department of Energy Atomic Energy Defense Activities, and smaller support agencies such as the Federal Management Agency, the Selective Service System and the General Services Administration Stockpile of Strategic Materials, National Defense Function. *NOT* included are: International Security Assistance, Veterans Administration and spending by NASA and the Coast Guard.

THE UNITED STATES

GDP   1991: $5,677.5bn
         1992: $5,945.7bn
Growth   1991: –1.2%   1992: 2.1%
Inflation 1991: 4.3%   1992: 3.0%
Publ debt 1992: 63.2%
Def exp 1992: BA $282.13bn, Outlay $286.89bn
Def bdgt 1993: BA $258.87bn, Outlay $277.19bn
Request 1994: BA $250.75bn, Outlay $264.15bn
NATO defn 1992: $314.32bn

Population: 257,143,800

	13–17	18–22	23–32
Men	8,931,300	9,067,600	20,632,300
Women	8,541,200	8,698,900	20,096,900

TOTAL ARMED FORCES:
ACTIVE: 1,729,700 (203,100 women) (excl Coast Guard).
RESERVES:
READY RESERVE: 1,842,200 Selected Reserve and Individual Ready Reserve to augment active units and provide reserve formations and units:
NATIONAL GUARD: 527,600. Army (ARNG) 410,000; Air (ANG) 117,600.
RESERVE: 1,314,600. Army 725,600; Navy 281,800; Marines 110,800; Air Force 196,400.
STANDBY RESERVE: 24,900. Trained individuals for mob: Army 1,000; Navy 9,800; Marines 500; Air Force 13,600.
RETIRED RESERVE: 182,400. Trained individuals to augment support and training facilities: Army 92,000; Navy 28,800; Marines 7,200; Air Force 54,400.

US STRATEGIC COMMAND: (US STRATCOM)
HQ Offut Air Force Base, Nebraska
(manpower incl in Navy and Air Force totals).

NAVY: 480 SLBM in 23 SSBN.
[Plus 128 *Poseidon*-C3 START-accountable launchers in 7 non-operational SSBN]
SSBN
14 *Ohio*
  6 (SSBN-734) with 24 UGM-133A *Trident* D-5 (144 msl)
  8 (SSBN-726) (includes 1 in refit) with 24 UGM-93A *Trident* C-4 (192 msl)
5 *Franklin* (SSBN-726) with 16 *Trident* C-4 (80 msl)
4 *Madison* (SSBN-627) with 16 *Trident* C-4 (64 msl)
(excludes 1 taken out of service 7 July 1993).

AIR FORCE (from Air Combat Command (ACC)).
ICBM: 818: 6 strategic msl wings (2 with 20 launch control centres, 4 with 15) (2 wings being deactivated, 1 trg wing with 13 silo launchers).
  261 *Minuteman* II (LGM-30F) (undergoing deactivation).

507 *Minuteman* III (LGM-30G).
50 *Peacekeeper* (MX; LGM-118A); in mod *Minuteman* silos.
AIRCRAFT: 238 hy bbr (553 START-countable);
OPERATIONAL: 15 bbr sqn (9 B-52, 6 B-1B).
6 sqn with 94 B-1B.
6 sqn with 94 B-52H (with AGM-86B ALCM).
3 sqn with 36 B-52G: (conventional only).
Plus 2 B-2A.
FLIGHT TEST CENTRE: 12: 4 B-52B/G/H, 2 B-1B, 6 B-2A (not START-countable).
AWAITING CONVERSION/ELIMINATION: 327 B-52; -C 29, -D 87; -E 49; -F 52; -G 110 (80 ALCM capable).

STRATEGIC RECCE/INTELLIGENCE COLLECTION (SATELLITES)
IMAGERY: KH-11: 160–400-mile polar orbit, digital imagery (perhaps 3 operational). KH-12 (*Ikon*): 1 launched 1989. AFP-731: Optical imaging satellite with sensors operating in several wavebands. 203-km orbit, at approx 60° inclination; to replace KH-11. *Lacrosse* radar-imaging satellite.
OCEAN SURVEILLANCE (OSUS): 4 satellite-clusters to detect ships by infra-red and radar.
NAVIGATIONAL SATELLITE TIMING AND RANGING (NAVSTAR): 24 satellites, components of global positioning system.
ELINT/COMINT: 2 *Chalet (Vortex)*, 2 *Magnum*, 2 *Jumpseat*; 'Ferrets' (radar-monitoring satellites).
NUCLEAR DETONATION DETECTION SYSTEM: Detects and evaluates nuclear detonations. Sensors to be deployed in NAVSTAR satellites.

STRATEGIC DEFENCES:
US Air Force Space Command: (HQ: Peterson AFB, Colorado).
North American Aerospace Defense Command (NORAD), a combined US–Canadian org (HQ: Peterson AFB, Colorado).

EARLY WARNING:
DEFENCE SUPPORT PROGRAMME (DSP): infra-red surveillance and warning system. Approved constellation: 3 operational satellites and 1 operational on-orbit spare.
BALLISTIC MISSILE EARLY WARNING SYSTEM (BMEWS): 3 stations: Clear (Alaska); Thule (Greenland); Fylingdales Moor (UK). Primary mission to track ICBMs and SLBMs. Also used to track satellites.
SPACETRACK: USAF radars Pirinçlik (Turkey), Eglin (Florida), Clear, Thule and Fylingdales; optical tracking systems in New Mexico, Choejong-San (S. Korea), San Vito (Italy), Maui (Hawaii), Diego Garcia (Indian Ocean).
USN SPACE SURVEILLANCE SYSTEM (NAVSPASUR): 3 transmitting, 6 receiving sites field stations in south-east US.

PERIMETER ACQUISITION RADAR ATTACK CHARACTERISATION SYSTEM (PARCS): 1 north-facing phased-array system at Cavalier AFS (N. Dakota); 2,800-km range.
PAVE PAWS: phased-array radars in Massachusetts, Georgia, Texas, California; 5,500-km range.
MISCELLANEOUS DETECTION AND TRACKING RADARS: US Army: Kwajalein Atoll (Pacific). USAF: Ascension Island (Atlantic), Antigua (Caribbean), Kaena Point (Hawaii), MIT Lincoln Laboratory (Massachusetts).
GROUND-BASED ELECTRO-OPTICAL DEEP SPACE SURVEILLANCE SYSTEM (GEODSS): Socorro (New Mexico), Taegu (S. Korea) and Maui (Hawaii), Diego Garcia (Indian Ocean).

AIR DEFENCE:
RADARS:
OVER-THE-HORIZON-BACKSCATTER RADAR (OTH-B): 1 in Maine (limited operation, 40 hrs per week). 1 in Mount Home AFB, Montana, (mothballed). Range 500nm (minimum) to 2,000nm.
NORTH WARNING SYSTEM: to replace DEW line. 15 automated long-range radar stations now operational. 39 short-range (110–150km) stations due in service by 1994.
DEW LINE: 31 radars: Alaska (7), Canada (20) and Greenland (4) roughly along the 70°N parallel from Point Lay, Alaska to Greenland (system being deactivated, completion by September 1993).
AIRCRAFT:
ACTIVE: 48: 3 sqn:
2 with 36 F-15C/D (Alaska).
1 with 12 F-15C/D (Iceland).
ANG: 216: 12 sqn:
2 with 36 F-15A/B.
10 with 180 F-16A/B.
Augmentation: ac on call from Navy, Marine Corps and Air Force.
AAM: *Sidewinder*, *Sparrow*, AMRAAM.

ARMY: 586,200 (72,000 women).
5 Army HQ, 4 Corps HQ (1 AB).
3 armd div (3 bde HQ, 5 tk, 4 mech inf, 3 SP arty bn, 1 MLRS bty, 1 AD bn; 1 avn bde) (incl 1 ARNG bde in 1 div).
4 mech div (3 bde HQ, 4 tk, 5 mech inf, 3 SP arty bn; 1 MLRS bty; 1 AD bn; 1 avn bde) (incl 1 ARNG bde in 4 div).
1 inf div (3 bde HQ, 2 air aslt, 4 mech inf, 2 tk, 4 arty bn, 1 MLRS bty, 1 AD bn; 1 avn bde) (incl 1 ARNG bde).
2 lt inf div (3 bde HQ, 9 inf, 3 arty, 1 AD bn; 1 avn bde) (incl 1 ARNG, 1 AR bde in 2 div).
1 air aslt div (3 bde HQ, 9 air aslt, 3 arty bn; avn bde (7 hel bn: 3 ATK, 2 aslt, 1 comd, 1 med tpt)).
1 AB div (3 bde HQ, 9 para, 1 lt tk, 3 arty, 1 AD, 1 cbt avn bn).
2 indep armd bde (2 tk, 1 mech inf, 1 SP arty bn) (2–3 ARNG bn).
2 inf (theatre def) bde (3 inf, 1 lt arty bn).

1 inf, 1 AB bn gp.
7 avn bde (1 army, 4 corps, 2 trg).
3 armd cav regt.
7 arty bde.
1 theatre AD comd.
9 *Patriot* SAM bn: 4 with 3 bty (all to form 6 bty as eqpt becomes available).
6 *HAWK* SAM bn.

READY RESERVE:
ARMY NATIONAL GUARD (ARNG): 410,000 (32,200 women): capable after mob of manning 8 div (3 armd, 1 mech, 3 inf (2 cadre), 1 lt inf); 20 indep bde (5 armd, 6 mech, 9 inf (3 lt) incl 7 'Roundout' (1 inf, 1 armd, 4 mech, 1 lt inf) for Regular Army div; 1 armd cav regt; 1 inf gp (Arctic recce: 4 scout bn); 16 fd arty bde HQ. Indep bn: 5 tk, 3 mech, 1 mtn inf, 50 arty, 17 AD (3 *HAWK*, 8 *Chaparral*, 6 *Stinger* SP), 62 engr.
ARMY RESERVE (AR): 725,600 (126,500 women): 9 trg div, 2 trg bde (no cbt role). 3 indep bde: 1 mech, 1 inf (theatre def), 1 lt inf ('Roundout'); 3 arty bde HQ, 60 indep bn.

EQUIPMENT:
MBT: some 15,120: 890 M-48A5, 1,581 M-60/M-60A1, 4,821 M-60A3, 7,828 M-1/M-1A1 *Abrams*.
LIGHT TANKS: 900 M-551 *Sheridan*.
RECCE: 55 *Fuchs*.
AIFV: 6,329 M-2/-3 *Bradley*.
APC: some 28,400, incl 5,100 M-577, 12,346 M-113.
TOWED ARTY: 2,506:
105mm: 538 M-101, 513 M-102, 230 M-119;
155mm: 550 M-114, 675 M-198.
SP ARTY: 3,471:
155mm: 2,442 M-109A1/A2/A6;
203mm: 1,029 M-110A1/A2.
MRL: 227mm: 491 MLRS, incl some 397 ATACMS capable.
MORTARS: 107mm: 2,585 (incl some 500 SP); 120mm: some 69.
ATGW: 15,336 *TOW* (incl 36 M-113, 5,776 *Hummer*, 3,195 M-901, 6,329 M-2/M-3 *Bradley*), 6,140 *Dragon* launchers.
RL: 84mm: AT-4.
RCL: 1,827, incl 84 mm: 27 *Carl Gustav*; 1,800 90mm and 106mm.
AD GUNS: 20mm: 63 M-167 *Vulcan* towed, 135 M-163 SP.
SAM: FIM-92A *Stinger*, 114 *Avenger* (vehicle-mounted *Stinger*), 396 M-54 and M-48 SP *Chaparral*, 233 *Improved HAWK*, 482 *Patriot* launchers.
AMPHIBIOUS: 40 ships:
5 *Frank Besson* LST: capacity 32 tk.
35 *Runnymede* LCU: capacity 7 tk.
Plus craft: some 124 LCM, 26 ACV.
AVIATION: incl eqpt in store.
AIRCRAFT: Some 404, incl 67 OV-1D, 38 RC-12D/G/H/K, 29 RU-21, 13 RV-1D, 119 C-12D, 16 C-23A/B, 114 U-21, 6 UV-18A, 2 UV-20A.

HELICOPTERS: some 8,013 (1,682 armed hel): 875 AH-1S, 754 AH-64A, 53 AH-6/MH-6, 2,598 UH-1 (being replaced), 3 EH-1H (ECM), 1,173 UH/MH-60A, 66 EH-60A (ECM), 420 CH-47D, 193 OH-6A, 1,543 OH-58A/C, 335 OH-58D.

NAVY (USN): 510,600 (56,500 women): 4
Fleets: 2nd (Atlantic), 3rd (Pacific), 6th (Mediterranean), 7th (W. Pacific) plus Military Sealift Command.
SUBMARINES: 110:
STRATEGIC SUBMARINES: 23: (see p. 20).
TACTICAL SUBMARINES: 87: (incl about 8 in refit).
SSGN: 21:
13 imp *Los Angeles* (SSN-751) with 12 x *Tomahawk* SLCM (VLS), 533mm TT (Mk 48 HWT, *Harpoon, Tomahawk*).
8 mod *Los Angeles* (SSN-719) with 12 x *Tomahawk* SLCM (VLS); plus 533mm TT (Mk 48 HWT, *Harpoon, Tomahawk*).
SSN: 66:
31 *Los Angeles* (SSN-688) with Mk 48 HWT, plus *Harpoon, Tomahawk* SLCM.
32 *Sturgeon* (SSN-637) with Mk 48 HWT; plus *Harpoon*, 21 with *Tomahawk* SLCM. (Incl 10 capable of special ops).
2 *Permit* (SSN-594) with Mk 48 HWT, plus *Harpoon*.
1 *Narwhal* (SSN-671) with Mk 48 HWT, *Harpoon, Tomahawk*.
SUBMARINES, OTHER ROLES: nil:
[2 ex-SSBN (SN 642 & 645) (Special ops) by October 1993].
PRINCIPAL SURFACE COMBATANTS: 161:
AIRCRAFT CARRIERS: 12 (excl 1 in long refit/refuel).
CVN: 6 (plus *Enterprise* in long refit/refuel)
6 *Nimitz* (CVN-68) (96/102,000t).
CV: 6:
3 *Kitty Hawk* (CV-63) (81,000t).
1 *Kennedy* (CV-67) (79,700t).
2 *Forrestal* (CV-59) (79,250/81,100t).
AIR WING: 13: (11 active, 2 reserve). The average mix of type and numbers of ac assigned to an Air Wing:
2 ftr sqn with 20 F-14A.
3 FGA/attack sqn:
    2 lt with 20 F/A-18A.
    1 med with 10 A-6E.
2 ASW sqn:
    1 with 6 S-3B ac; 1 with SH-3H hel.
1 ECM sqn with 4 EA-6B.
1 AEW sqn with 4 E-2C; 4 KA-6D tkr.
CRUISERS: 52 (incl some 8 in refit):
CGN: 9:
4 *Virginia* (CGN-38) with 2 x 2 SM-2 MR SAM/*ASROC* SUGW; plus 2 x 4 *Tomahawk* SLCM, 2 x 4 *Harpoon*, SH-2F hel (Mk 46 LWT), 2 x 3 ASTT, 2 x 127mm guns.
2 *California* (CGN-36) with 2 x SM-2 MR; plus 2 x 4 *Harpoon*, 1 x 8 *ASROC*, 2 x 3 ASTT, 2 x 127mm guns.

1 *Truxtun* (CGN-35) with 1 x 2 SM-2 ER SAM/*ASROC*; plus 2 x 3 ASTT, 1 x SH-2F hel, 1 x 127mm gun.
1 *Long Beach* (CGN-9) with 2 x 2 SM-2 ER; plus 2 x 4 *Tomahawk*, 2 x 4 *Harpoon*, 1 x 8 *ASROC*, 2 x 3 ASTT, 2 x 127mm guns.
1 *Bainbridge* (CGN-25) with 2 x 2 SM-2 ER, plus 2 x 4 *Harpoon*, 1 x 8 *ASROC*, 2 x 3 ASTT.
CG: 43:
25 *Ticonderoga* (CG–47 *Aegis*):
    5 Baseline 1 (CG-47–51) with 2 x 2 SM-2 MR/*ASROC*; plus 2 x 4 *Harpoon*, 2 x 1 127mm guns, 2 x 3 ASTT, 2 x SH-2F or SH-60B hel.
    20 Baseline 2/3, (CG-52) with 2 x VLS Mk 41 (61 tubes each) for combination of SM-2 ER, and *Tomahawk*. Other weapons as Baseline 1.
9 *Belknap* (CG-26) with 1 x 2 SM-2 ER/*ASROC*; plus 2 x 3 ASTT, 2 x 4 *Harpoon*, 1 x 127mm gun, 1 x SH-2F hel.
9 *Leahy* (CG-16) with 2 x 2 SM-2 ER/*ASROC*; plus 2 x 3 ASTT, 2 x 4 *Harpoon*.
DESTROYERS: 38: (incl some 6 in refit).
DDG: 7:
2 *Arleigh Burke* (DDG-51 *Aegis*) with 2 x VLS Mk 41 (32 tubes fwd, 64 tubes aft) for combination of *Tomahawk*, SM-2 ER and *ASROC*; plus 2 x 4 *Harpoon*, 1 x 127mm gun, 2 x 3 ASTT, 1 x SH-60B hel.
4 *Kidd* (DDG-993) with 2 x 2 SM-2 MR/*ASROC*; plus 2 x 3 ASTT, 2 x SH-2F hel, 2 x 4 *Harpoon*, 2 x 127mm guns.
1 *Coontz* (DDG-37) with 1 x 2 SM-2 ER; plus 1 x 8 *ASROC*, 2 x 3 ASTT, 1 x 127mm gun, and with 2 x 4 *Harpoon*.
DD: 31: *Spruance* (DD-963) (ASW):
13 with 1 x 8 *ASROC*, 2 x 3 ASTT, 1 x SH-2F hel; plus 2 x 4 *Harpoon*, 2 x 127mm guns; 7 with 2 x 4 *Tomahawk*.
18 with 1 x VLS Mk 41 (*Tomahawk*), 2 x 3 ASTT, 1 x SH-60B hel; plus 2 x 127mm guns, 2 x 4 *Harpoon*.
FRIGATES: 59: (incl some 7 in refit).
FFG: 51:
51 *Oliver Hazard Perry* (FFG-7), (16 in NRF) all with 2 x 3 ASTT; 24 with 2 x SH-60B hel; 27 with 2 x SH-2F hel; all plus 1 x SM-1 MR/*Harpoon*.
FF: 8:
8 *Knox* (FF-1052) with 1 x 8 *ASROC*, 1 x SH-2F hel, 4 x ASTT; plus *Harpoon* (from *ASROC* launcher), 1 x 127mm gun (excl 8 *Knox*-class trg).
ADDITIONAL IN STORE: 1 CV, 4 BB, 9 DDG, 14 FF.
PATROL AND COASTAL COMBATANTS: 28:
Note: Mainly responsibility of Coast Guard.
MISSILE CRAFT: 6 *Pegasus* PHM with 2 x 4 *Harpoon*.
PATROL, COASTAL: 2 *Cyclone* PFC (by August 1993).
PATROL, INSHORE: 20 .
MINE WARFARE: 18:
MINELAYERS: None dedicated, but mines can be laid from attack submarines, aircraft and surface ships (limited).

MINE COUNTERMEASURES: 18:
1 *Osprey* (MHC-51) MHC.
11 *Avenger* (MCM-1) MCO.
6 *Aggressive* (MSO-422)/*Acme* (MSO-509) MCO (6 with NRF).
AMPHIBIOUS: 56:
COMMAND: 2 *Blue Ridge*: capacity 700 tps.
LHA: 7:
2 *Wasp*: capacity 1,900 tps, 60 tk; with 6 AV-8B ac, 12 CH-46E, 4 CH-53E, 4 UH-1N, 4 AH-1W hel; plus 12 LCM-6 or 3 LCAC.
5 *Tarawa*: capacity 1,700 tps, 100 tk, 4 LCU or 1 LCAC, 6 AV-8B ac, 12 CH-46E, 4 CH-53E, 4 UH-1N, 4 AH-1T/W hel.
LPH: 5 *Iwo Jima*: capacity 1,750 tps, 12 CH-46E, 4 CH-53E, 4 UH-1N hel, 4 AH-1T/W.
LPD: 11: 11 *Austin*, capacity 930 tps, 4 tk, 2 LCAC.
LSD: 13:
8 *Whidbey Island* with 4 LCAC or 21 LSM: capacity 450 tps, 40 tk.
5 *Anchorage* with 4 LCAC or 15 LCM: capacity 350 tps, 38 tk.
LST: 15 *Newport* (3 NRF): capacity 400 tps, 10 tk.
LKA (amph cargo ships): 3 *Charleston* (3 NRF): capacity 360 tps, 10,000 tonnes stores.
CRAFT: some 97:
About 60 LCAC: capacity 1 MBT.
About 37 LCU-1610: capacity 3 MBT.
Numerous LCVP, LCU, LCM.
SUPPORT AND MISCELLANEOUS: 158:
(Total includes 78 USN ships, 77 ships of the Military Sealift Command Fleet Auxiliary Force, and 5 AGOR owned by the US Navy, but operated by civil research institutes.)
UNDERWAY SUPPORT: 50:
AO: 24: 5 *Cimarron*, 5 *Wichita*, 12 *Henry Kaiser* (MSC), 2 *Neosho* (MSC).
AOE: 4 *Sacramento*.
AE: 13: 1 *Kilauea* (MSC), 7 *Butte*, 5 *Suribachi/Nitro*.
AF: 9: 6 *Mars* (2 MSC), 3 *Sirius* (MSC).
MAINTENANCE AND LOGISTICS: 58:
8 AD, 9 AS, 1 AR, 12 AT (7 MSC), 14 AOT (MSC), 2 AH (MSC), 12 salvage/rescue (2 NRF).
SPECIAL PURPOSES: 16:
1 *Forrestal* avn trg, 8 *Knox* FFT (NRF), 2 comd, 5 technical spt (4 MSC).
SURVEY AND RESEARCH: 34:
14 *Stalwart* AGOS (towed array) (MSC).
4 *Victorious* AGOS (SWATH) (MSC).
7 AGOR (2 MSC), 9 AGHS (MSC).

MILITARY SEALIFT:

Military Sealift Command operates and administers 296 strategic sealift ships in addition to the 77 ships of the Fleet Auxiliary Force.
ACTIVE FORCE: About 37:
15 dry cargo (incl 2 ro-ro veh and 4 ro-ro container) and 22 tankers.
STANDBY FORCE: 259:
AFLOAT PREPOSITIONING FORCE: 25:
13 maritime prepositioning ships in 3 sqn (MPS) (each to support a MEB)

12 prepositioning ships (3 tankers, 7 cargo/ ammunition, 1 heavy lift, 1 hospital)
FAST SEALIFT: 8:
1 fast sealift ship sqn of 8 ro-ro, (30 knot) ships at 4 days' notice.
NATIONAL DEFENSE RESERVE FLEET (NDRF): 226:
READY RESERVE FORCE (RRF): 96 regularly maintained ships:
51 bulk cargo, 17 Ro-Ro, 11 tankers, 8 crane ships, 7 barge lift, 2 troop ships.
(30% at 5 days' reactivation notice, remainder at 10 to 20 days).
NAVAL INACTIVE FLEET: About 130:
Includes about 50 'mothballed' USN ships, incl 1 CV, 4 battleships, plus about 25 dry cargo, 10 tankers and some 60 'Victory' WW II cargo. (60 to 90 days' reactivation notice, but many ships very old and of doubtful serviceability).
AUXILIARY STRATEGIC SEALIFT:
About a further 300 US-flag and effectively US-controlled ships potentially available to augment these holdings.

RESERVES:
NAVAL RESERVE SURFACE FORCES: 34 ships: 16 FFG, 8 FF (trg), 4 MCMV, 3 amph and 3 spt/misc vessels. Incl in main Navy entry. Crewed by about 70% active USN and 30% NR.
COMBAT SUPPORT FORCES (provision of units for MCM, underwater ops, ashore construction, cargo handling).
AUGMENT FORCES (provision of additional manpower to regular org).

NAVAL AVIATION: (91,000) incl 13 carrier air wings.
AIRCRAFT:
FIGHTER: 21 sqn: 13 with F-14A, 4 with F-14B, 4 with F-14D.
FGA/ATTACK: 33 sqn:
11 with A-6E.
2 with F/A-18A.
20 with F/A-18C/N.
ELINT: 4: 2 sqn with EP-3, 2 sqn with ES-3A.
ECM: 11 sqn with EA-6B.
MR: 18 land-based sqn, 6 sqn with P-3CII, 12 sqn with P-3CIII.
ASW: 18 sqn with S-3A, 9 with S-3B.
AEW: 2 sqn with E-2C.
COMD: 2 sqn with E-6A (TACAMO).
OTHER: 6 sqn: 1 with C-130F, 1 with LC-130, 1 with EC-130G, 3 with C-2A.
TRAINING:
5 'Aggressor' sqn with F-5E/F, T-38, A-4, F-16N.
14 trg sqn with T-2C, T-34C, T-44, T-45A.
HELICOPTERS:
ASW: 28 sqn:
10 with SH-60B (LAMPS Mk III).
5 (3 NR) with SH-2F (LAMPS Mk II).
13 with SH-60F/HH-60H.
MCM: 3 sqn with MH-53E/CH-53E.

MISC: 4 sqn with SH-3, 5 with CH-46, 2 with CH-53E.
TRG: 2 sqn with TH-57B/C.

RESERVES:
FIGHTER ATTACK: 4 sqn with F-18.
ATTACK: 2 sqn with A-6E.
FIGHTER: 4 sqn with F-14.
AEW: 2 sqn with E-2C.
ECM: 2 sqn with EA-6B.
MPA: 2 wings of 13 sqn with P-3B/C.
FLEET LOGISTICS SUPPORT: 1 wing with 11 sqn with C-9B/DC-9, 2 sqns with C-130T.
HELICOPTERS: 1 wing with 5 ASW sqn with SH-3H and SH-2F/G, 2 MCM sqn with MH-53E, 2 HCS sqn with HH-60H.
EQUIPMENT: (incl NR)
1,688 cbt ac; 474 armed hel.
AIRCRAFT:
F-14: 428. **-A:** 300 (ftr, incl 48 NR) plus 58 in store; **-A plus:** 70 (ftr) **-D:** 58 (ftr).
F/A-18: 474. **-A:** 159 (FGA, incl 36 NR); **-B:** 29* (trg); **-C:** 245 (FGA); **-D:** 41* (trg).
F-5E/F/T-38: 26 (trg).
F-16: 26. **-N:** 22 (trg); **TF-16N:** 4 (trg).
A-4: 245 (trg). **-E/-F:** 39 (trg); **-M** 20; **TA-4F/J:** 186 (trg) (plus in store -M: 8; TA-F/J: 67).
A-6: 461. **-E:** 332 (FGA, incl 20 NR); **EA-6B:** 107 (ECM, incl 4 NR); **KA-6D:** 22 (tkr incl 8 NR).
E-2C: 110. 108 (AEW, incl 10 NR); **TE-2B:** 2 (trg).
P-3: 375. **-B:** 69 (MR, NR) (plus 25 in store); **-C:** 252 (MR, NR); **EP-3:** 17 (ELINT); **RP-3A/D:** 12 (survey); **U/VP-3A:** 14 (VIP); **TP-3A:** 11.
S-3 134. **-A/B:** 113 (MR/ASW) (plus 16 in store); **-ES-3A:** 16 (ECM); **-US-3A:** 5 (tpt).
C-130: 27. **-F/LC-130F/R:** 13 (misc), **-TC-130 G/Q:** 2; **-C-130T:** 12 (NR); (plus **EC-130Q:** 10 (comd) in store).
CT-39: 9 (misc). **C-2A:** 39 (tpt) (plus 6 in store). **C-9B:** 17 (tpt).
T-2B/C: 142 (trg) (plus 47 in store). **US-3:** 5 (tpt). **T-39D/N:** 18 (trg).
TA-7C: 9 (trg) (plus 21 in store). **T-44:** 57 (trg). **T-45:** 30 (trg). **T-38A/B:** 7. **T-34:** 369. **-B:** 51; **-C:** 318.
TC-4C: 8.
C-20D: 2 (VIP). **DC-9-30:** 10 (tpt). **U-6A:** 3 (utility). **NU-1B:** 1 (utility). **UC-12:** 67. **-B:** 51; **-F:** 6; **-M:** 10.
HELICOPTERS:
HH-1N: 38 (attack, NR).
RH-53D: 10 (MCM); **MH-53E:** 31 (MCM, incl 12 NR), **CH-53G:** 17.
SH-60: 211 **-B:** 140 (ASW); **-F:** 71 (ASW).
HH-60H: 18 (cbt spt, NR).
SH-2F/G: 76 (ASW, incl 24 NR).
SH-3G/H: 149 (ASW/SAR incl 12 NR).
CH-46D/F: -30 (tpt, trg)
UH/HH-46D: 47. **TH-57:** 139. **-B:** 50; **-C:** 89. **VH-3A:** 5 (VIP).
MISSILES:
AAM: AIM-120 AMRAAM being delivered. AIM-7 *Sparrow*, AIM-54A/C *Phoenix*, AIM-9 *Sidewinder*.
ASM: AGM-78D *Standard* ARM, AGM-45 *Shrike*, AGM-88A *HARM* (anti-radiation); AGM-84 *Harpoon*, AGM-119 *Penguin* Mk-3.

MARINE CORPS: 183,000 (8,100 women).
GROUND: 3 div (2 with 3 inf regt (9 bn), 1 tk, 1 lt armd inf (LAV-25) bn, 1 with 2 inf regt (4 bn); all with 1 arty regt, 1 recce, 1 aslt amph, 1 cbt engr bn). 3 Force Service Support Groups.
1 bn Marine Corps Security Force (Atlantic and Pacific).
Marine Security Guard Bn (1 HQ, 7 region coy).
RESERVES (MCR):
1 div: (3 inf (9 bn), 1 arty regt (5 bn); 2 tk, 1 lt armd inf (LAV-25), 1 aslt amph, 1 recce, 1 cbt engr bn). 1 Force Service Support Group.
EQUIPMENT:
MBT: 221 M-1A1 *Abrams,* 16M-60A1 (plus 618 M-60A1 in store).
LAV: 415 LAV-25 (25mm gun), 200 LAV (variants, excl ATGW).
AAV: 1,323 AAV-7A1 (all roles).
TOWED ARTILLERY: 105mm: 335 M-101A1; 155mm: 584 M-198.
SP ARTILLERY: 155mm: 131 M-109A3.
MORTAR: 81mm: 656.
ATGW: 1,300 *TOW*, 1,978 *Dragon*, 95 LAV-*TOW*.
RL: 84mm: AT-4.
RCL: 83mm: 1,919.
SAM: 1,929 *Stinger*.

AVIATION: 41, 900 (2,200 women), 3 active air wings.
AIR WING: (no standard org but a notional wing is shown below): 148 fixed-wing aircraft, 152 hel: 48 F/A-18, 10 A-6, 60 AV-8B, 6 EA-6B, 12 OV-10, 12 KC-130, 60 CH-46, 44 CH-53, 24 AH-1, 24 UH-1.
AIRCRAFT:
FIGHTER/ATTACK: 10 sqn with F-18A/C.
FGA: 8 sqn:
7 lt with AV-8B.
1 med with A-6E.
ECM: 4 sqn with 20 EA-6B.
FAC: 2 sqn with 19 OV-10A/D.
COMD: 4 sqn with 48 F/A-18D.
TANKER: 3 sqn with KC-130F/R.
TRAINING: 3 sqn.
HELICOPTERS: 30 sqn:
ARMED: 6 lt attack/utility sqn with AH-1/UH-1N.
TRANSPORT: 15 med with CH-46E, 9 hy with CH-53 (4 with -A/-D, 5 with -E).
TRAINING: 4 sqn.
SAM:
2 bn (4 bty) with phase III *HAWK*.
2+ bn (5 bty) with *Stinger*.

RESERVES 5,300 (300 women) (MCR): 1 air wing.
AIRCRAFT:
FIGHTER/ATTACK: 4 sqn with 48 F-18A.
FGA: 2 sqn with 24 A-4M.

FAC: 1 sqn with 12 OV-10A.
TANKER: 2 tkr/tpt sqn with 22 KC-130T.
HELICOPTERS:
ARMED: 2 attack sqn with 27 AH-1J.
TRANSPORT: 3 sqn (2 med with 24 CH-46E, 1 hy with 12 CH-53A).
UTILITY: 3 sqn with 24 UH-1N.

EQUIPMENT (incl MCR): 551 cbt ac; 96 armed hel.
AIRCRAFT:
F-18A/-B/-C/-D: 288 (FGA incl 48 MCR, 33* trg).
AV-8B: 219. 183 (FGA), 18* (trg); **TAV-8B:** 18* (trg).
A-4M: 34 (incl 24 MCR).
A-6: 35. **-E:** 10 (attack); **EA-6B:** 25 (ECM).
OV-10A/D: 36 (FAC, incl 12 MCR), plus 14 in store.
F-5E/F: 13 (trg, MCR).
KC-130: 73. **-F:** 37 (OCU); **-R:** 14; **-T:** 22 (tkr, MRC).
HELICOPTERS:
AH-1J/T/W: 141 incl 96 (armed, incl 27 MCR), 18 trg, plus 43 in store.
UH-1N: 109 (incl 24 MCR, 12 trg).
CH-46D/E: 238 (tpt, incl 24 MCR, 6 HMX, 20 trg).
CH-53A/-D/-E: 180 (tpt, incl 12 MCR, 20 trg), plus 17 in store.
RH-53D: 6 (MCR) plus 1 in store.
VH-60A: 8 (VIP tpt).
VH-3D: 11 (VIP tpt).
MISSILES:
SAM: 48 phase III *Improved HAWK* launcher, *Stinger.*
AAM: *Sparrow, Sidewinder.*
ASM: *Maverick.*

COAST GUARD (By law a branch of the Armed Forces; in peacetime operates under, and is funded by, the Department of Transportation. Budgets are not incl in the figures at p. 19):
Budget   1992: BA $3.57bn.
                1993: BA $3.665bn.
                1994: Request $3.812bn
Strength: 39,100 (includes 2,400 women).
PATROL VESSELS: 142:
PATROL, OFFSHORE: 48:
12 *Hamilton* high endurance with HH-65A LAMPS *Dolphin* hel, 2 x 3 ASTT, 4 with 1 x 76mm gun, 3 with *Harpoon* SSM (4 in refit).
13 *Bear* med endurance with 1 x 76mm gun, HH-65A hel.
15 *Reliance* med endurance with 1 x 3 inch gun, hel deck (excl 2 undergoing modernisation).
8 other med endurance cutters.
PATROL, INSHORE: 94:
49 *Farallon*, 3 *Sea Hawk* SES, 42 *Point Hope*⟨.
SUPPORT AND OTHER: 12:
2 icebreakers, 9 icebreaking tugs, 1 trg.
AVIATION: 77 ac, 152 hel.
FIXED WING: 25 HU-25A, 7 HU-25B, 9 HU-25C, 1 EC-130V, 30 HC-130H, 1 CA-21, 2 RG-8A, 1 VC-4A, 1 VC-11.
HELICOPTERS: 36 HH-3F (being replaced with HH-60J), 20 HH-60J, 96 HH-65A.

COAST GUARD RESERVE: 18,500.
Selected: 10,000; Ready 7,800; Standby 640.

AIR FORCE: 449,900 (66,500 women); Air Combat Command (ACC): 5 air force (incl 1 ICBM), 36 ac wing. Air Mobility Command (AMC): 3 air force, 21 ac wing.
STRATEGIC:
TACTICAL: 57 tac ftr sqn (sqn may be 18 or 24 ac):
16 with F-15.
7 with F-15E.
22 with F-16C/D (incl 3 AD).
4 (2 trg) with F-111.
5 with A-10.
1 *Wild Weasel* with F-4G.
2 with F-117.
SUPPORT:
RECCE: 3 sqn with U-2R and RC-135.
AEW: 1 Airborne Warning and Control wing; 7 sqn (incl 1 trg) with E-3.
EW: 2 sqn with EC-130, EF-111.
FAC: 8 tac air control sqn:
7 mixed A-10A/OA-10A.
1 with OA-37B (test).
SPECIAL OPERATIONS (5,900): 1 wing plus 2 groups, 12 sqn (see pp. 27).
TRAINING:
1 'Aggressor' sqn with F-16.
31 trg sqn with F-16, T-37, T-38, T-39, T-41, T-43, UV-18, Schweizer 2-37, C-5, C-12, C-130, C-141 ac and HH-3, HH-53, HH-60, U/TH-1 hel.
TRANSPORT: 45 sqn:
16 strategic: 5 with C-5; 11 with C-141.
16 tac airlift with C-130.
Units with KC-10, C-135, VC-137, C-140, C-9, C-12, C-20, C-21.
TANKER: 29 sqn:
23 with KC-135, 6 with KC-10A.
SAR: 9 sqn (incl STRATCOM msl spt), HH-1, HH-3, HH-60 hel.
MEDICAL: 3 medical evacuation sqn with C-9A.
WEATHER RECCE: 1 sqn with WC-135.
TRIALS/weapons trg units with A-10, F-4, F-15, F-16, F-111, T-38, C-141 ac, UH-1 hel.

RESERVES:
AIR NATIONAL GUARD (ANG): 117,600 (15,800 women).
24 wings, 100 sqn;
FIGHTER:
12 AD sqn (see pp. 21).
FGA: 33 sqn;
1 with A-10, OA-10.
6 with A-7D/K
2 with A-10.
20 with F-16.
4 with F-15A/B.
RECCE: 4 sqn with RF-4C.
EW: 1 sqn with EC-130E.
FAC: 1 sqn with OA-10.
TRANSPORT: 22 sqn:

19 tactical (1 trg) with C-130A/B/E/H.
3 strategic: 1 with C-5; 2 with C-141B.
TANKER: 17 sqn with KC-135E/R.
SAR: 3 sqn with HC-130 ac, MH-60G hel.
TRAINING: 7 sqn.
AIR FORCE RESERVE (AFR):
21 wings, 61 sqn (40 with ac);
FGA: 12 sqn:
8 with F-16; 4 (incl 1 trg) with A-10.
TRANSPORT: 19 sqn:
13 tactical with C-130B/E/H;
1 weather recce with WC-130E/H.
5 strategic: 2 with C-5A, 3 with C-141B.
TANKER: 4 sqn with KC-135E/R.
SPECIAL OPERATIONS: 1 sqn (AFSOC):
1 with AC-130A.
SAR: 3 sqn (AMC) with HC-130H ac, HH-60 hel.
ASSOCIATE: 21 sqn (personnel only):
4 sqn for C-5, 13 for C-141, 1 aero-medical for C-9
3 sqn for KC-10.

EQUIPMENT:
LONG RANGE STRIKE/ATTACK: 226 cbt ac, plus 8
test ac (plus 327 in store).
B-52: 130: **-G:** 36 conventional only, test; **-H:** 94strike
(with AGM-86 ALCM) (plus in store B-52: 327 -C:
29, -D: 87, -E: 49, -F: 52, -G: 110).
B-1B: 96 (strike, test).
B-2: 8 (strike, test).
RECCE: U-2R/RT: 16; RC-135: 19
COMMAND:
E-3: 34.**E-4B:** 4.**EC-135:** 20.
TACTICAL: 3,451 cbt ac; (incl ANG, AFR plus 1,452
in store); no armed hel.
F-4: 167. **-E:** 17 (FGA); **-G:** 53 (incl 6 ANG (*Wild
Weasel*)); **RF-4C:** 97 (recce: 4 USAF, 93 ANG). Plus
831 in store (incl 159 RF-4C).
F-15: 824: **-A/B/C/D:** 505 (ftr incl 146 ANG); 130
(OCU, test) **-E:** 194 (FGA). Plus 65 F-15A in store.
F-16: 1,910, **-A:** 606 (incl ftr 206 ANG, FGA ,118
AFR, 264 ANG) **-B:** 110 (incl ftr 19 ANG, FGA 16
AFR, 51 ANG) **-C:** 1,006 (incl 69 AFR, 247 ANG) -
D: 188 (incl 8 AFR, 48 ANG).
F-111: 152. **-E/F:** 152 (FGA); (incl 23 OCU); plus
172 in store, **EF-111A:** 41 (ECM) plus 2 in store.
F-117: 55. 46 (FGA), 9* (trg), plus 1 test.
A-7: 60 (ANG); plus 211 in store.
A-10A: 135 (FGA, incl 75 ANG, 60 AFR) plus 171 in store.
OA-10A: 148 (FAC incl 38 ANG)
EC-18B/D: 6 (Advanced Range Instrumentation).
E-8A: 2 (JSTARS ac).
WC-135B: 7 (weather recce).
AC-130: 124: **-A:** 10 (special ops, AFR); **-H/U:** 14
(special ops, USAF). **HC-130N/P:** 52 (22 special ops;
30 SAR incl 12 ANG, 11 AFR); **EC-130E/H:** 28
(special ops incl 8 ANG); **MC-130E/H:** 37 (special
ops); **WC-130E/H:** 12 (weather recce, AFR).
OA-37B: 2 (FAC, plus 19 in store).
TRANSPORT:
C-5: 126. **-A:** 76 (strategic tpt; incl 12 ANG, 32
AFR); **-B:** 50 (incl 6 OCU).
C-141B: 269 (212 strategic tpt, 16 OCU, 16 ANG, 25

AFR) plus 10 in store.
C-130: 527. 496 (tac tpt, incl 202 ANG, 114 AFR);
31 (trg, incl 9 ANG), plus 57 in store.
C-135A/B/C/E: 10.
VC-137B/C: 7 (VIP tpt).
C-9A: 20. (19 medical, 1 cmd spt).
C-12: 85 (liaison, incl 12 ANG).
C-17A: 7 (flt test).
C-22A/B: 4 (ANG).
C-23A: 3.
VC-25A1: 2.
C-26A/B: 27 (tpt incl 13 ANG).
C-27A: 10 (tpt).
C-29A: 6 (cal).
T-43A: 4 (tpt ANG).
TANKERS:
KC-135: 587 (356 USAF, 177 ANG, 54 AFR), plus
45 in store.
KC-10A: 59 tkr/tpt.
TRAINING:
MiG-21: 24. **MiG-23:** 4. **T-37B:** 575 (plus 21 in store).
T-38: 691 (plus 29 in store).
T-39: 8. **T-41A/C:** 100. **T-43A:** 12. **TC-135S:** 1. **TC-
135W:** 1. **UV-18B:** 2. **Schweizer 2-37:** 17. **T-1A:** 43.
HELICOPTERS:
CH/HH-3: 7. Plus 22 in store.
MH-53-J: 41 *Pave Low* (special ops).
HH-60G: 64 (incl 9 AFR, 15 ANG).
MH-60G: 30.
HH-1H: 23. **UH-1N:** 68.
MISSILES:
AAM: AIM-9P/L/M *Sidewinder*, AIM-7E/F/M
Sparrow, AIM 120, A/B AMRAAM.
ASM: 1,300 AGM-69A SRAM; 1,666 AGM-86B
ALCM; 26,000+ AGM-65A/B/D/G *Maverick*;
5,904 AGM-88A/B *HARM*; AGM-84A *Harpoon*;
AGM-86C ALCM; 86 AGM-142A/B/C/D *HAVE
NAP*.
CIVIL RESERVE AIR FLEET (CRAF): 442
commercial ac (numbers fluctuate):
LONG-RANGE: 408
262 passenger (Boeing 747, L-1011, DC-8/-10),
146 cargo (Boeing 707, 747, DC-8/-10).
SHORT-RANGE: 34 (Boeing 727, 737, 757).

SPECIAL OPERATIONS FORCES:
Units only listed – manpower and eqpt shown in
relevant single service section.
ARMY: (15,000):
5 SF gp (each 3 bn).
1 Ranger inf regt (3 bn).
1 special ops avn regt (3 bn).
1 Psychological Operations gp (5 bn).
1 Civil Affairs bn (4 coy).
1 sigs, 1 spt bn.
RESERVES: (3,000 ARNG, 11,000 AR):
2 ARNG SF gp (6 bn).
1 ARNG avn bn.
2 AR SF gp (6 bn).
3 AR Psychological Operations gp.
12 AR Civil Affairs HQ (3 comd, 9 bde).

24 AR Civil Affairs 'bn' (coy).
NAVY: (3,400):
1 Naval Special Warfare Command.
2 Naval Special Warfare Gps.
4 Naval Special Warfare units.
7 Sea-Air-Land (SEAL) teams.
2 SEAL delivery veh teams.
3 Special Boat units.
4 amph tpt submarines.
6 Drydeck shelters (DDS).
RESERVES: (1,400):
6 Naval Special Warfare gp det.
2 Naval Special Warfare unit det.
5 SEAL team det.
2 Special Boat sqn.
4 Special Boat unit.
1 engr spt unit.
2 cbt spt special hel sqn.
AIR FORCE: (6,000)
1 air force HQ, 3 wings, 13 sqn:
5 with MC-130.
1 with AC-130.
3 with HC-130.
3 with MH-53 hel.
1 with MH-60 hel.
RESERVES: (1,200)
3 sqn (AFSOC):
1 with 9 AC-130A/H (AFR).
1 with 5 MH-60 hel (AFR).
1 with 8 EC-130E (ANG).

DEPLOYMENT:
Commanders' NATO appointments also shown
(e.g., COMEUCOM is also SACEUR).

EUROPEAN COMMAND (EUCOM): some
183,000: HQ Stuttgart-Vaihingen (Commander is
SACEUR).
ARMY: HQ US Army Europe (USAREUR),
Heidelberg.
NAVY: HQ US Navy Europe (USNAVEUR),
London (Commander is also CINCAFSOUTH).
AIR FORCE: HQ US Air Force Europe (USAFE),
Ramstein (Commander is COMAIRCENT).
GERMANY:
ARMY: 98,000.
V Corps with 1 armd, 1 mech inf div, 1 armd cav
regt, 1 arty, 1 AD (1 *Patriot* (6 bty), 1 *Chaparral*
bn), 1 engr, 2 avn bde.
Army AD Comd (1 bde with 2 bn *Patriot* (6 bty)).
1inf bde: (Berlin).
Prepositioned equipment (POMCUS) for 3 div and 1
armd cav regt configured in 6 bde sets (3 armd, 3
mech). Approx 70% stored in Ge.
EQUIPMENT (incl POMCUS in Ge, Be and Nl):
Some 3,213 MBT, 1,820 AIFV, 2,020 arty/MRL/
mor.
AIR FORCE: 25,400, 182 cbt ac.
2 air force HQ: USAFE and 17th Air Force.
3 tac ftr wings: 9 sqn (2 with 54 F-16C/D, 4 with 80

F-16C/D, 2 with 48 F-15, 1 with 18 A-10 and 6 OA-
10).
1 cbt spt wing, 1 air control wing.
1 tac airlift wing: incl 16 C-130E and 4 C-9A.
BELGIUM:
ARMY: 1,200. Approx 15% of POMCUS stored in
Be.
NAVY: 100.
AIR FORCE: 600.
GREECE:
ARMY: 50.
NAVY: 200. Base facilities Soudha Bay. Makri
(Crete).
AIR FORCE: 600, 1 air base gp. Facilities at
Iraklion (Crete).
ITALY:
ARMY: 3,500. HQ Vicenza. 1 AB bn gp, 1 arty bty.
Equipment for Theatre Reserve Unit/Army Readiness
Package South (TRU/ARPS) incl 133 MBT, 194
AIFV, 42 arty/MLRS.
NAVY: 6,000. HQ Gaeta, bases at Naples, La
Maddalena, 1 MR sqn with 9 P-3C at Sigonella.
AIR FORCE: 3,400: 1 ftr wing (ac on det only).
MEDITERRANEAN:
NAVY: Some 15,500; incl 2,000 marines.
Sixth Fleet: typically 4 SSN, 1 CVBG (1 CV, 6–8
surface combatants, 2 fast support ships), 1 URG (4–
6 support ships, 2 or 3 escorts), 1 amph ready gp (3–
5 amph ships), 4 depot ships.
MARINES: Some 2,000: 1 MEU (SOC) embarked
aboard Amph Ready Gp ships.
NETHERLANDS:
ARMY: 600. Approx 15% of total POMCUS is
stored in Nl.
AIR FORCE: 1,800: 18 cbt ac.
1 ftr gp with 18 F-15A/B.
NORWAY: Prepositioning for 1 MEB (24 arty, no
aviation assets).
PORTUGAL: (for Azores, see Atlantic Command).
NAVY: 400.
AIR FORCE: 1,100.
SPAIN:
NAVY: 3,400, base at Rota.
1 MR sqn with 9 P-3C.
AIR FORCE: 500.
TURKEY:
ARMY: 600.
NAVY: spt facilities at Iskenderun and Yumurtalik.
AIR FORCE: 3,200, facilities at Incirlik.
1 tac gp, 2 air base gps (ac on det only). Some 57 ac:
F-15, F-16, F-111F, EF-111, F-4G.
Installations for SIGINT, space tracking and seismic
monitoring.
UNITED KINGDOM:
NAVY: 2,400. HQ London, admin and spt facilities,
1 SEAL det.
AIR FORCE: 14,400: cbt ac.
1 air force HQ: 4 ftr wings, 1 air base gp: 4 sqn, 48
F-15E.
1 special ops wing with 5 MH-53 J, 4 MC-130H.
1 SAR sqn with 4 HC-130, 5 MH-53.
1 air refuelling wg with 9 KC-135.

PACIFIC COMMAND (USPACOM):
HQ: Hawaii.
ALASKA:
ARMY: 9,400. 1 lt inf div (2 inf bde, 2 arty bn, 1 avn bde).
AIR FORCE: 10,900. 1 air force HQ; 3 sqn (2 with 36 F-15C/D, 1 with 18 F-15E).
HAWAII:
ARMY: 18,800. HQ US Army Pacific (USARPAC). 1 lt inf div.
1 ARNG inf bde.
AIR FORCE: 4,800. HQ Pacific Air Forces (PACAF).
1 air base wing, 1 tac ftr sqn with 24 F-15A/B (ANG), 1 comd/control sqn with 2 EC-135.
NAVY: 12,000. HQ US Pacific Fleet. Homeport for some 17 submarines, 16 PSC and 10 spt and misc ships.
MARINES: 8,900. HQ Marine Forces Pacific, 1 MEB.
SINGAPORE:
NAVY: About 100, log facilities.
AIR FORCE: 40 det spt sqn.
JAPAN:
ARMY: 1,900.
1 corps HQ, base and spt units.
AIR FORCE: 15,600: 1 air force HQ: 78 cbt ac.
2 wings (6 sqn) with 36 F-15C/D, 24 F-16, 18 F-15E, 7 C-12F, 2 C-21A ac, 3 UH-1N hel.
1 sqn with 3 E-3 AWACS.
1 tac tpt gp with 20 C-130 (ANG).
1 sqn with 15 KC-135 tkr (ANG).
1 SAR sqn with 6 HC-130, 3 MC-130 ac, 4 HH-60 hel (ANG).
NAVY: 7,300: Bases: Yokosuka (HQ 7th Fleet). Homeport for 1 CV, 8 surface combatants. Sasebo. Homeport for 3 submarines, 3 amph ships.
MARINES: 18,300: 1 MEF.
SOUTH KOREA:
ARMY: 26,000.
1 Army HQ (UN command).
1 inf div (2 bde, (6 bn)), 2 SP arty, 1 MLRS, 1 AD bn.
AIR FORCE: 9,500: 1 air force HQ: 2 wings, 84 cbt ac.
3 sqn with 72 F-16.
1 tac control sqn with 12 OA-10.
1 SAR sqn with 4 MH-60G hel.
1 recce det with 3 U-2, 2 C-12.
GUAM:
AIR FORCE: 2,500: 13 AF HQ.
NAVY: 4,600, MPS-3 (4 ships with eqpt for 1 MEB). Naval air station, comms and spt facilities.
AUSTRALIA:
AIR FORCE: 300.
NAVY: some 100: comms facility at NW Cape, SEWS/SIGINT station at Pine Gap, and SEWS station at Nurrungar.
DIEGO GARCIA:
NAVY: 900, MPS-2, (5 ships with eqpt for 1 MEB). Naval air station, spt facilities.

US WEST COAST:
MARINES: 1 MEF.
AT SEA:
PACIFIC FLEET: (HQ Pearl Harbor).
Main base: Pearl Harbor.
Other bases: Bangor (Washington); San Diego and Long Beach (California).
Submarines: 7 *Ohio* SSBN, 5 SSGN, 29 SSN.
Surface Combatants: 6 CV/CVN, 29 CG/CGN, 2 DDG, 15 DD, 12 FFG, 4 FF.
Amphibious: 1 comd, 3 LHA, 3 LPH, 7 LPD, 6 LSD, 6 LST, 2 LKA.
Surface Combatants divided among two fleets:
3rd Fleet (HQ San Diego): covers Eastern and Central Pacific, Aleutians, Bering Sea, etc. Typically 4 CVBG, 4 URG. Amph Gp.
7th Fleet (HQ Yokosuka, Japan): covers Western Pacific, Japan, Philippines, ANZUS responsibilities, Indian Ocean. Typically 1 CVBG, 1 URG, amph ready gp (1 MEU embarked).
INDIAN OCEAN: (det from 7th/2nd Fleets).

CENTRAL COMMAND (USCENTCOM):
Takes command of deployed forces in its region.
HQ USCENTCOM. MacDill AFB, Florida.
AT SEA:
Joint Task Force Middle East.
1 comd ship, 1 LPD, 6 PSC, 3 MCO.
1 CVBG in N. Arabian Sea. (1 MEU (SOC) in AOR). Forces provided from Atlantic and Pacific.
KUWAIT:
ARMY: Prepositioned eqpt for 6 coys (3 tk, 3 mech), 1 arty bty incl 44 MBT, 44 AIFV, 8 arty.
SAUDI ARABIA:
AIR FORCE: Units on rotational detachment, numbers vary (incl: F-4G, F-15, F-16, F-117, C-130, KC-135, U-2, J-STARS). 1 *Patriot* bn.

SOUTHERN COMMAND (USSOUTHCOM):
HQ USSOUTHCOM, Quarry Heights, Panama.
PANAMA:
ARMY: HQ US Army South, Fort Clayton, Panama: 7,400.
1 inf bde (2 inf bn), 1 avn bde.
NAVY: HQ US Naval Forces Southern Command, Fort Amador, Panama: 500.
Special boat unit, fleet support.
MARINES: 200.
AIR FORCE: 2,100.
1 air div: 2 C-130, 1 C-21, 9 C-27, 1 CT-43.
HONDURAS:
ARMY: 300.
AIR FORCE: 35.

ATLANTIC COMMAND (USLANTCOM):
HQ: Norfolk, Virginia (Commander is SACLANT).
US EAST COAST:
MARINES:
1 MEF.
NAVY:
MPS-1 (4 ships with eqpt for 1 MEB)

BERMUDA:
NAVY: 800.
CUBA:
NAVY: 1,900 (Guantánamo).
MARINES: 400 (Guantánamo).
ICELAND:
NAVY: 1,800. 1 MR sqn with 9 P-3.
AIR FORCE: 1,200.
1 AD sqn with 12 F-15C/D, 1 comd/control
sqn with 2 E-3, 1 SAR sqn with 4 HH-3.
MARINES: 100.
PORTUGAL (AZORES):
NAVY: 10.
Limited facilities at Lajes.
AIR FORCE: 1,100.
1 SAR det.
UK:
NAVY: 150.
Comms and int facilities, Edzell, Thurso.
AT SEA:
ATLANTIC FLEET: (HQ Norfolk, Virginia).
Other main bases: Groton (Connecticut); Charleston
(S. Carolina); King's Bay (Georgia); Mayport
(Florida).
Submarines: 6 *Ohio*, 9 other SSBN, 16 SSGN, 37
SSN.
Surface Combatants: 6 CV/CVN, 23 CG/CGN, 5
DDG, 16 DD, 23 FFG, 4 FF.
Amphibious: 1 LCC, 2 LHA, 4 LPH, 6 LPD, 5 LSD,
6 LST, 1 LKA.
Surface Forces divided into two Fleets:
2nd Fleet (HQ Norfolk): covers Atlantic, both north
and south. Typically 4–5 CVBG, Amph Gp, 4 URG.
6th Fleet (HQ Gaeta, Italy): Mediterranean. Under op
comd of EUCOM. See EUCOM entry for typical
force levels.

CONTINENTAL UNITED STATES
(CONUS): Major units/formations only listed.

FORCES COMMAND: (FORSCOM): 222,700:
ARMY: provides general reserve of cbt-ready
ground forces for other comd.
Active: 4 Army HQ, 3 Corps HQ (1 AB), 2 armd,
3 mech, 1 lt inf, 1 AB, 1 air aslt div; 2 armd,

6 arty bde; 2 armd cav regt.
Reserve: ARNG: 2 armd, 2 mech, 5 inf, 1 lt inf div;
20 indep bde, 1 armd cav regt. AR: 3 indep bde.

US STRATEGIC COMMAND
(USSTRATCOM):
See entry on p. 20
AIR COMBAT COMMAND (ACC):
Responsible for provision of strategic AD units and
of cbt-ready Air Force units for rapid deployment.

US SPECIAL OPERATIONS COMMAND
(USSOCOM): HQ MacDill AFB, Florida. Has under
comd all active, reserve and National Guard special
ops forces of all services based in CONUS. See pp.
26–27.

US TRANSPORTATION COMMAND
(USTRANSCOM): Responsible for providing all
common-user airlift, sealift and land transportation
to deploy and maintain US forces on a global basis.
AIR MOBILITY COMMAND (AMC):
Responsible for providing strategic, tac and special
op airlift, aero-medical evacuation, SAR and weather
recce.
MILITARY SEALIFT COMMAND
See entry on p. 23.

UN AND PEACEKEEPING
CAMBODIA (UNTAC): 49 Observers.
CROATIA (UNPROFORII): 290, field hospital.
EGYPT (MFO): 500, 1 inf bn.
IRAQ/KUWAIT (UNIKOM): 14 Observers.
ITALY *(Disciplined Guard)*: 12 A-10, 14 F/A-18, 4
AC-130.
MACEDONIA: 300, reinforced inf coy gp
MIDDLE EAST(UNTSO): 36 Observers
SOMALIA: (UNOSOM II): 4,100, incl elm 10 mtn
div, plus attack hel and log spt. Not incl Marines
offshore.
WESTERN SAHARA (MINURSO): 29 Observers.

PARAMILITARY:
CIVIL AIR PATROL (CAP): 68,000 (27,500
cadets); HQ, 8 geographical regions, 52 wings, 1,881
units, 579 CAP ac, plus 8,465 private ac.

NATO

NATO has begun to implement its plans for the reorganisation of its command structure; in the Central Region the arrangements for creating more multinational formations are being clarified. The civil war in Bosnia-Herzegovina has led to the first NATO-sponsored peacekeeping effort.

NATO Reorganisation

The reorganisation of NATO's command structure, announced in November 1991, has started. On 1 July 1993 Northern and Central Army Groups and 2nd and 4th Allied Tactical Air Forces (ATAF) were stood down and their assets transferred to two new commands: Allied Land Forces Central Europe (LANDCENT); and Allied Air Forces Central Europe (AIRCENT). The latter is a renamed Allied Air Forces Central Europe (AAFCE). Also on 1 July 1993 Allied Forces Baltic Approaches (BALTAP) was transferred from Allied Forces Northern Europe (AFNORTH) to Allied Forces Central Europe (AFCENT). Considerable progress has been made towards the establishment of multinational corps in the LANDCENT area. Details of the future organisation of these corps are on page 47 in a diagram primarily designed to show the future organisation of the German Army.

The next round of organisational changes will take place on 1 July 1994 when responsibility for NATO's northern flank will be transferred from AFNORTH (which will be disbanded) to the new Allied Forces North West Europe (AFNORTHWEST) whose HQ and those of its Naval and Air components will be in the UK, while its ground force HQ will remain in Norway. At the same time, Allied Command Channel (ACCHAN) will be eliminated and its area absorbed by Allied Command Europe (ACE). During the next 12 months, it is planned to establish as part of Allied Forces Southern Europe (AFSOUTH) two new principle subordinate commands in Greece: Allied Land Forces South Central Europe (LANDSOUTHCENT); and 7th ATAF.

Peacekeeping

NATO is now playing a major role in peacekeeping activities in the former Yugoslavia. On land, United Nations Protection Force II (UNPROFOR II) is manned primarily by NATO troops, with one Egyptian and one Ukrainian battalion at Sarajevo airport under its command. Its HQ is provided by elements of HQ Northern Army Group (with no German staff but with personnel from the non-NORTHAG countries contributing to UNPROFOR II) and its first commander was a French general. Apart from the Sarajevo airport garrison, which also includes two French battalions, there are four groups each based on a mechanised infantry battalion provided by Canada, France, Spain and the UK. Belgium, Denmark, the Netherlands, Norway and Portugal have contributed support and logistic units and detachments. The US has provided a Mobile Army Surgical Hospital.

NATO also made plans to take on the provision and command of any new peacekeeping force for Bosnia (possibly with Russian and other non-NATO elements) had a permanent cease-fire and a political settlement (such as the Vance–Owen plan) been reached. No details have been announced of its possible composition, which was expected to include a significant US contribution, nor of the command arrangements (which could have involved HQ Allied Rapid Reaction Corps (ARRC) and HQ AFSOUTH).

Monitoring and, since April 1993, enforcement of the air-exclusion zone over Bosnia-Herzegovina has been carried out by NATO air units. Monitoring of both the ban on military flights over Bosnia and of flights which could violate either the arms embargo enforced on all of the former Yugoslavia or the economic sanctions imposed on Serbia and Montenegro has been carried out by airborne early-warning aircraft of the United Kingdom air force and the NATO AWACS squadron. German air crews, despite heavy domestic political pressure, were not withdrawn from NATO AWACS aircraft when the enforcement of the air-exclusion zone was authorised. Air Force units from France, the Netherlands, Turkey and the UK based at Italian airfields, and US Navy aircraft from the carrier *Theodore Roosevelt* (when it is in the Adriatic), have patrolled Bosnian airspace since 12 April 1993.

Economic sanctions were imposed on Serbia and Montenegro by UN Security Council Resolution 757 on 30 May 1992. Resolution 787 authorised the interdiction of shipping in the Adriatic. Initially two separate naval forces operated in the Adriatic, first monitoring and then enforcing the sanctions regime: one was under NATO command; the other under the Western European Union (WEU). At a joint session of the North Atlantic Council and the Council of the WEU on 8 June 1993 it was agreed that the two operations would be combined, with operational control delegated to NATO's Commander Allied Naval Forces Southern Europe (COMNAVSOUTH). NATO has also provided the aircover to protect UNPROFOR II should it be attacked as authorised by UNSC Resolution 836.

European Pillar
Western European Union

The WEU planning cell was established in Brussels on 1 October 1992, and the WEU Secretariat moved there from London in January 1993. In April 1993 the WEU Satellite Centre of Torrejón, Spain, was inaugurated. Initially the centre is to train analysts in satellite imagery interpretation using existing commercial imagery and later that gained by the French/Italian/Spanish *HELIOS* programme.

The expansion of WEU membership, agreed in June 1992, with Greece joining as a full member, Iceland, Norway and Turkey as associates, and Denmark and Ireland as observers, has not been formally completed, as the Greek government has not yet ratified the agreement. Meanwhile Ireland has said it will not become an observer until the Treaty of European Unity (Maastricht) has been fully ratified.

The WEU has been active in assisting in the monitoring and enforcement of UN economic sanctions imposed on Serbia and Montenegro. A WEU-coordinated naval force was operating in the Adriatic until 8 June 1993 when it was agreed that it should merge with a similar NATO squadron to form a joint naval force with operational control exercised by NATO's COMNAVSOUTH.

The WEU has established a mission, based at Calafat in Romania, to assist in monitoring traffic on the River Danube. The mission comprises civil police and customs officers. The WEU has also expressed a wish to contribute a force to form part of any new peacekeeping operation established to implement a political settlement in Bosnia-Herzegovina. The Secretary-General of the WEU has suggested the force should have its own sector and would prefer this to be the city of Sarajevo.

Member-states have begun to declare forces available to the WEU. So far three multinational forces have been declared:
- The Eurocorps (see below)
- The Multinational Division (Central) which also forms part of NATO's ARRC and comprises Belgian, British, Dutch and German air-mobile forces.
- The UK/Netherlands Amphibious Force of marines which also has a NATO role reinforcing northern Norway.

A number of other responsibilities are being transferred to the WEU. In December 1992, defence ministers of the 13 nations forming the Independent European Programme Group (IEPG) agreed that the IEPG should be incorporated into the WEU to form its European Armament Agency. NATO's Eurogroup, in an effort to economise and avoid duplication, is negotiating to transfer some of its activities to the WEU. Of five sub-groups it is already agreed that the communications sub-group and the publicity function should go to the WEU. Negotiations continue regarding the long-term planning and logistics sub-groups. The future of the medical sub-group is less certain, but has been offered to NATO while the fifth, which is responsible for training in cooperation with US forces, was transferred to NATO in April 1993.

The Eurocorps

More information is now available on the composition of the Eurocorps. The Corps HQ is located at Strasbourg and will be fully operational by July 1994. The two main components are the French 5th Armoured Division stationed in Germany and the German 10th Armoured Division in south-west

Germany. Belgium announced in June 1993 that it was prepared to make a mechanised division of some 12,000 men available to the Corps. An important development has been the decision that the Eurocorps could be made available to NATO for peacekeeping missions or should one of its members be attacked.

European Community

The work of the European Community Monitor Mission (ECMM) in the former Yugoslavia is little publicised. It was established in July 1991, initially with the task of easing the withdrawal of the Yugoslav National Army (JNA) from Slovenia, and comprises some 200 monitors (mainly diplomats or military officers) and a further 200 support staff. All 12 EC partners are represented, together with personnel from Canada, the Czech Republic, Poland, Slovakia and Sweden. All ECMM monitors are unarmed, although on occasion they are escorted by UNPROFOR troops, and wear distinctive white uniforms. Later the ECMM monitored cease-fires and provided a neutral presence in Croatia until UNPROFOR took on responsibility for the UN Protected Areas (UNPAs). ECMM still has responsibilities in Croatia (including monitoring at military airfields) and is deployed on monitoring and humanitarian duties in the part of Bosnia-Herzegovina not controlled by Bosnian Serbs.

Nuclear Forces

There have been few developments concerning **French** and **British** nuclear forces. Neither has carried out a nuclear test in the last 12 months. The UK has been constrained by the US moratorium on testing which expired on 1 July 1993. France declared its own moratorium in April 1992 to last until the end of that year; it has not been formally extended, but neither has testing resumed. After the July 1993 Franco-British summit it was announced that the Franco-British Joint Commission on Nuclear Policy and Doctrine, first set up in autumn 1992, was to become a permanent standing body. The objective of the Commission is to coordinate approaches to deterrence, nuclear doctrines, anti-missile defences, arms control and non-proliferation.

The **British** strategic nuclear force will still comprise four *Vanguard*-class SSBN equipped with the US-made *Trident* II (D5) SLBM armed with a British warhead. The first *Vanguard* is due to commission after completing its sea trials in August 1993; the keel of the fourth was laid down in February 1993; the second is due to be 'rolled out' in September 1993. Despite much criticism, the government has never committed itself to any limit on the number of warheads it will produce or deploy, other than to say that 'the number deployed may in certain circumstances be substantially less than the maximum' (which is 512). The UK is in something of a dilemma; to maintain a credible deterrent it should be capable of penetrating whatever ABM defences may be deployed. The US was aiming for a system capable of intercepting up to 200 incoming warheads. To guarantee to penetrate the defence of a potential enemy deploying a similar system would require two fully armed SSBN. At the same time, the government needs to be seen to be reducing its capability rather than increasing it. There have been press reports of plans to arm some *Trident* SLBM with only one warhead and to employ these as a sub-strategic weapon instead of replacing the Royal Air Force's free-fall nuclear bombs with an expensive stand-off weapon. In the 1993 Defence Estimates, the government confirmed its commitment to maintain a sub-strategic nuclear capability.

Denmark has announced that it is to form a 4,550-strong reaction brigade which will be operational by the end of 1995. The brigade will be earmarked for NATO's ARRC but will also be able to operate independently, at short notice, in a wide range of peacekeeping operations.

In December 1992 the **French** government approved the design of a new strategic missile, the M5-S5, with which it will progressively arm the SSBN force from about the year 2000. M5-S5 missiles could also replace the land-based S-3D IRBM should this ever be considered necessary. In June 1993 the new Defence Minister confirmed that he would shortly order the third *Triomphant*-class SSBN. The first *Triomphant,* which was 'rolled out' on 13 July 1993, is expected to join the fleet in 1996. The *Pluton* SSM held by the Army have been withdrawn, *Pluton* units are being disbanded and the SSM eliminated. The replacement, SSM *Hadès*, of which 15 launchers have been produced, is not to be deployed. Expenditure on nuclear forces has been reduced by 17% compared to that in 1990.

Conventional Forces

The majority of NATO members are reducing the manpower strength of their armed forces; a number are considering increasing the proportion of 'career' volunteers to conscripts, and some are considering the abolition of conscription. Announced manpower reductions and current manpower levels are shown in the table below.

	1992 (000s)	1993	Planned by 1997
Belgium	81	81	40
Canada	84	80	76
Denmark	29	28	25[a]
France	432	411	371
Germany	447	408	300
Greece	159	159	159
Italy	354	325	287
Luxembourg	0.8	0.8	0.8
Netherlands	93	74	70
Norway	33	29	25[a]
Portugal	58	58	No information
Spain	217	201	170–190
Turkey	560	480	360[a]
UK	293	259	241
US	1.914m	1.730m	1.355m

[a] Based on army cuts only, final strengths could be smaller.

There are both advantages and disadvantages in abandoning conscript service. The advantages include: more proficient units; reduced training overheads; less unit turbulence by not having to cope with large-scale annual/biannual turnover of manpower; more flexibility with regard to UN and out-of-area operations. The disadvantages are: increased manpower costs; and possible difficulty in raising sufficient volunteers to man adequate reserves.

The **Belgian** government has announced its long-term plans to be fully implemented by 1997. Conscription is to end after the 1993 intake and an all-volunteer force will be limited to 40,000 men; until then the length of conscript service has been shortened to only eight months (six if serving in Germany). The army will comprise a para-commando brigade, available for rapid reaction and committed to the multinational air-mobile brigade, and one mechanised division which will require mobilisation to bring it to operational strength. The reservists to meet this commitment, approximately 30% of the division's manpower, will be volunteers from recently discharged soldiers. All Belgian land forces are likely to be made available to the Eurocorps. A new volunteer reserve force of around 30,000 will be raised for territorial defence. Air Force strength will be reduced to two wings with 72 F-16 aircraft (plus operational reserve aircraft) and a transport force of C-130 aircraft whose in-service life is to be extended. The Navy will be reduced to 16 ships, of which three will be frigates (with perhaps only one operational), the remainder being either mine warfare or command ships. Defence expenditure is to be held at Bfr 98bn until 1997, plus whatever is raised by the sale of equipment, land and property. The planned purchase of *Agusta* A-109 attack helicopters is not affected.

While **Canada's** active force strength is to be cut, there will be an increase in reserve numbers. The Army is to retain its divisional HQ, but will be reduced to only three brigade groups, plus one airborne battalion group. A number of brigade units will become joint active/reserve units; three infantry battalions will have only 10% of their strength in active manpower, while in each of three armoured regiments one squadron will be predominantly manned by reservists. Although Canada's permanent presence in Europe has now been withdrawn, it remains committed to providing an infantry battalion group to either AMF(L) or the NATO composite force for Norway. Canada will also make available to NATO, in the event of crisis in Europe, one brigade group and two squadrons of CF-18 aircraft. The Army has increased its air defence capability, acquiring more ADATS and *Javelin* SAM. The Navy has commissioned two more *Halifax*-class and one *St Laurent*-class, and two *Mackenzie*-class frigates have been retired. A very high proportion of Canadian forces are deployed on UN peacekeeping operations with infantry battalions in Bosnia, Croatia and Somalia; the Cyprus commitment, which in recent years has been met mainly by reservists, has been given up.

The new **French** government has indicated its intention of playing a greater role in NATO without altering its policy of not putting its armed forces under the integrated military command. It is expected that France, like Spain, will take part in meetings of the Defence Planning Committee (DPC) and Nuclear Planning Group (NPG). France has already agreed to participate in UN peacekeeping operations organised and commanded by NATO. The French have also announced their intention to continue with conscription, although a larger number of units will be manned by a combination of professionals and long-term volunteer conscripts. At present, the majority of units in the divisions (except the mountain division) of the Force Action Rapide (FAR) are manned in this way and so are ready for service abroad. The Army HQ is to be disbanded at the end of August 1993 leaving the ground forces divided between: FAR; a corps of three armoured and one infantry division; and the Eurocorps, which includes one French armoured division and the Franco-German brigade. One active infantry division has been disbanded, as has the reserve division whose task was to defend strategic nuclear forces, while the Rhine division, which was mainly composed of engineers, has been reduced to brigade status and no longer has an active component. Equipment holdings generally have been reduced (including 340 AMX-30 tanks, all 140 AMX-13 light tanks and some 80 artillery pieces). There have been some increases, including the first *Leclerc* MBT, 30 more 155mm TR-F-1 towed artillery and 13 MLRS. The Navy has commissioned a sixth *Rubis*-class nuclear-powered attack submarine and two more *Floréal*-class frigates (a third is to commission in October 1993), while one *Commandant Rivière*-class has been retired. There has been a change in the Air Force command structure with all fighter units being transferred to the Tactical Air Force, leaving Air Defence Command with only ground-based air-defence units. The Air Force has received small numbers of additional *Mirage* 2000B/C and 2000N aircraft and its first five 2000D out of the order for 90. The order for the production of *Rafale* has been placed; the first delivery will be made in 1996. The Air Force is to have 235 *Rafale* aircraft, the Navy 86.

Germany has announced yet another plan to reorganise the armed forces: *Bundeswehrplan* 94. A diagram on page 47 shows the new organisation of the army and the affiliation of units to multinational formations. At present, the field army still has 12 divisions, to be reduced to six by the end of 1994 with 20 brigades to be reduced to 17. The Territorial Army has been reduced to only eight infantry regiments, one for each of the divisions/districts under the new plan. There has been no change to the organisation of ground forces in Eastern Command (two divisions/districts with six brigades). In the new organisation only seven brigades, plus the Franco-German brigade, will be fully manned in peacetime. The other brigades, which have two armoured and two mechanised infantry battalions, will have both active and reserve units (currently planned to be two active battalions, one armoured, one infantry; this ratio could be altered if further manpower cuts are ordered). Two fully manned brigades (the mountain and one airborne) are to be prepared for UN peacekeeping and humanitarian operations. The overall strength of German armed forces is to be reduced to 300,000 from its current level of 408,000, a reduction of 40,000 from the 1992 manning level. Large quantities of army equipment, mainly belonging to the former East German Army are being destroyed; the only weapon increase of note is that of 33 MLRS. The Navy has retired two Type 205 SSC tactical submarines. The bulk of former East German naval ships are in the process of being sold to Indonesia (but no transfers have yet taken place) or are about to be transferred without charge to the three Baltic Republics. At the end of 1993 some 40 *Tornado* aircraft will be transferred from the Navy to the Air

Force. The Navy has formed a helicopter transport squadron equipped with Mi-8 helicopters. The Air Force is phasing out its RF-4E reconnaissance aircraft which are to be replaced by *Tornado* aircraft. One wing of *Alpha Jet* FGA aircraft has been deactivated and the remaining two are due to be deactivated by the end of 1993. The *Alpha Jet* will be retained as a training aircraft. One fighter squadron has been formed and equipped with MiG-29 aircraft. All other aircraft of the former East German Air Force are due to be destroyed by the end of 1994.

The German government is often criticised for failing to amend the constitution to allow a greater and unchallenged contribution to UN peacekeeping operations. However, as the entry on page 48 demonstrates, Germany is already making a significant contribution. Not shown is the German component to the NATO AWACS squadron employed in monitoring the no-fly zone over Bosnia-Herzegovina, which was not withdrawn as had been forecast, when enforcement of the zone was authorised.

The **Greek** Army has benefited greatly from NATO's policy of 'cascading' equipment above CFE limits and has received 590 M-60 and a further 170 *Leopard* tanks, and 70 M110 203mm SP guns. The Navy, too, has been considerably strengthened by taking delivery of: three more US *Adams*-class destroyers (three US *Gearing*-class and one US *Sumner*-class have been retired); one German-built MEKO frigate (another of this class is under construction in Greek shipyards); the first of three more *Kortenaer*-class frigates from the Netherlands; and three US *Knox*-class frigates (on lease), while two US *Cannon*-class frigates have been retired. The Navy has also received a further three German *Thetis*-class ASW corvettes. Air Force aircraft numbers are hardly changed, but there have been some squadron changes with two F-104 squadrons being disbanded and one *Mirage* 2000 E/D squadron formed. Greece and Bulgaria have signed an agreement on a programme of military cooperation which includes provisions for confidence-building measures (CBM) of a more stringent nature than those required by the Vienna Document. Observers must be invited to exercises and other military activities involving 9,000 (CSCE 12,000) troops, 250 (300) tanks and 200 (250) pieces of artillery. In addition, observers will be invited to one battalion-level exercise each year.

The **Italian** armed forces have dropped in strength by some 30,000, mainly from the Army. The Army has taken delivery of 90 *Centauro* B-1 armoured reconnaissance vehicles, four more MLRS and 15 more A-129 attack helicopters. The Navy has commissioned one more *Pelosi*- (improved *Sauro*) class submarine and a second *Luigi Durand de la Penne*-class destroyer. Two *De Cristofaro*-class frigates have been retired. The Air Force has taken delivery of some 30 more AMX FGA aircraft. Its fighter aircraft, the F-104S, is obsolescent and the Air Force is looking to fill the gap until the Eurofighter comes into service in 2000 by leasing air-defence fighters. It is reported that the British government has been approached to lease Italy a number of *Tornado* F-3 fighters. The armed forces are to be reorganised, further reduced in strength and modernised over the next ten years. The ratio of volunteers to conscripts will be changed, the latter cut to around 123,000, which will represent only 43% of the total force of about 287,000. There will be three categories of unit: rapid-reaction forces at 100% operational readiness; secondary or principal forces at around 50% of full strength; and reserve or mobilisation forces.

The Defence White Paper published by the **Netherlands** government in January 1993 announces major reductions in the armed forces spread over the next five years. It is planned to end conscription in 1998, but parliament has asked for a feasibility review every two years. Conscription is to be reduced from 12 to 9 months in 1994. Parliament is divided into those who believe the cuts go too deep and those who maintain they do not go deep enough. The Army is bearing the brunt of the cuts and will be reduced from its 1992 organisation of a corps with three divisional HQ and ten brigades to one division of three brigades (to form part of a German-commanded corps), and an air-mobile brigade forming part of the multinational division. The future of further cadre brigades is not yet decided. A number of army equipments have been disposed of, including 170 *Leopard* 1 tanks and 100 M-113 APC. The Navy has commissioned a third *Zeeleeuw*-class submarine and two more *Karel Doorman*-class frigates. The remaining *Dolfijn*-class submarine, one *Kortenaer*-class frigate and five *Dokkum* coastal minesweepers have already been retired.

The **Norwegian** Army has taken delivery of more than 60 additional *Leopard* 1 tanks, 130 M-113 APC and some 200 RBS-70 SAM. The Navy has commissioned a sixth *Ula*-class submarine, and five *Storm* missile craft have been retired. Overall manpower strength has dropped by about 3,000, but the ratio of volunteers to conscripts has altered and the number of volunteers has risen by 4,000. Norway has recently published details of its plans for a restructured war force posture to be operational by the year 2000. A new division with three brigades will be established and the number of independent brigades reduced to three. There will also be a reduction in the number of missile boats, coastal artillery and air-defence batteries, while both missiles for coastal and short-range defence will be introduced.

The **Portuguese** Army has received 80 M-60 tanks under the 'cascading' scheme.

The **Spanish** Army has received 310 M-60 tanks, 100 M-113 APC and 24 203mm M-110 SP guns from the US under NATO's 'cascading' scheme. The *Skyguard/Aspide* SAM programme is now complete with 36 systems in service. 36 *Mistral* SAM firing posts have been received. The Air Force has retired over 40 aircraft (F-5A, RF-5A, *Mirage* 111D/EE).

A major reorganisation of the **Turkish** Army is in progress: the command level of division is being replaced, with a few exceptions, by brigades. At the same time, manpower strength has been reduced by some 80,000. Equipment holdings have risen drastically: over 700 M-60 tanks, about 20 *Leopard* 1 tanks, 72 M-110 203mm SP guns (all under the 'cascading' scheme) and also some 60 UR-416 APC, 15 AH-1 *Cobra* attack helicopters and 40 S-70 (UH-60) utility helicopters. It now appears that the Navy has a total of nine US *Guppy*-class submarines, all of whose serviceability is doubtful. A number of Air Force squadron changes have taken place, not all in the last 12 months. There are now three (rather than five) with F-5A/B, eight (four) with F-4E, six (three) with F-16 and two (five) with F/TF 104 G (FGA role). The aircraft inventory has been increased by some 26 F-16 FGA aircraft.

The armed forces of the **United Kingdom** have continued to reorganise, restructure and disband as required by the 'Options for Change' report. There have been several changes to this plan. The first, announced in February 1993, halted the amalgamation of four infantry battalions; added 3,000 to the manpower ceiling; and transferred a further 2,000 troops from support duties to combat units. The second, on 17 June 1993, announced cuts to naval and air force reserves. The Royal Naval Reserve (RNR) is to be cut by 1,200 reserves, half its shore training stations are to close and the *River*-class minesweepers, whose crews are from the RNR, retired. The Royal Naval Auxiliary Service, responsible for the organisation of merchant shipping movement in wartime, is to be disbanded. The RAF Regiment Auxiliary Reserve is to lose one anti-aircraft squadron and one ground-defence squadron, while two active regiment *Rapier* SAM-equipped squadrons will be manned jointly by regulars and reservists. It was also announced that arrangements were being made for the reinforcement of active forces by Territorial Army soldiers in peacetime, for example on UN peacekeeping missions.

During the year the Army has reorganised its two remaining divisions, one in Germany and one in the UK. It has continued to receive new weapons including: some 70 *Warrior* AIFV, 80 *Saxon* wheeled APC, 16 MLRS and the first eight 155mm AS-90 SP guns. The Navy has retired two *Oberon*-class submarines (with the last of this class to be retired in 1993), and four *Leander*-class frigates (one of which is being kept on stand-by for rapid reactivation), and six *Amazon*-class frigates are to be retired and sold to Pakistan (the first was handed over in July 1993). Two *Duke*-class frigates have commissioned and an order for a 20,000-tonne helicopter carrier has been placed. Originally this project was termed an Aviation Support Ship with a rather less amphibious role than the carrier which will operate 12 assault helicopters and can embark several hundred troops. The Air Force disbanded four squadrons (one *Tornado* FGA, two *Phantom* fighters and one *Nimrod* maritime reconnaissance).

The UK government's statement on the 1993 Defence Estimates – 'Defending Our Future' – was released on 5 July 1993. It contains a far more detailed description of the UK's defence commitments than previous annual statements. Three defence roles are identified: *i*) Military aid to the civil power in the UK (including Northern Ireland and anti-terrorist operations). This role includes the peacetime safeguarding of the UK, its airspace and territorial waters, and the provision of the independent nuclear deterrent. It also includes the protection and security of the UK's dependent territories. *ii)* The threat of a large-scale attack against NATO (for which considerable warning can be expected) and a limited regional conflict in which a NATO ally is involved and calls for assistance. *iii)* A serious conflict elsewhere which threatens European security or British interests, and other military assistance to support international order and humanitarian principles (probably under UN auspices). Or put more simply: home defence; NATO operations; and 'out-of-area' operations. The statement goes on to elaborate some 50 military tasks within these three roles, and assesses the forces needed for each. It also considers which tasks are unlikely to have to be met simultaneously and thus where double earmarking can take place. From this study the overall structure can be decided upon (but this is not easily apparent from the many tables provided in the statement). The only contingency which has not been catered for is the unexpected. What new force cuts, apart from those announced in 'Options for Change', are being made? The Navy is to lose its diesel submarine force or four *Upholder*-class, the number of destroyers and frigates will be reduced by four or five (the remaining *Leander* and Type 21 *Amazon*-classes) and mine countermeasure forces will lose the older *Waveney* and *Tom* classes (12 ships), but production of *Sandown*- and *Hunt*-class will continue until 25 are completed by the end of the century. The Air Force is to disband one *Tornado* F-3 fighter squadron. The project to develop a medium-range surface-to-air missile to replace the already retired *Bloodhound* SAM has been abandoned. The Army has suffered no further cuts on this occasion. Manpower strengths in 1995 are to be: Army 119,000 (as already announced, but 3,000 more than allowed by 'Options for Change'); Navy 32,500 (a new cut of 2,500); and Air Force 70,000 (a new cut of 5,000).

European Fighter Aircraft

A requirement to replace European obsolescent and obsolete fighter aircraft in the 1990s to counter the threat of MiG-29 (*Fulcrum*), Su-27 (*Flanker*) and their derivatives resulted in France, Germany, Italy, Spain and the United Kingdom agreeing in 1983 to produce an outline European Staff Target for a future European Fighter Aircraft (EFA). France pulled out of the project in 1985 as it considered that the specifications were not suited to French requirements. It was decided that the work and cost would be shared as a proportion of the number of EFA the countries would order: Germany and the UK taking 33% and 250 aircraft each, Italy 21% and 165, Spain 13% and 95. In 1992 the German Defence Minister raised doubts about the costs of EFA and proposed scrapping EFA for a 'cheaper fighter'. In December 1992 a study not only forsaw a 30% reduction in costs, but also the provision of an alternative range of offensive and defensive equipment options for the now politically renamed Eurofighter 2000. Nations that did not want to include all the options in their aircraft could have a cheaper but less capable aircraft.

The UK has maintained its requirement for 250 aircraft, while Germany has reduced its to 140, Italy to 130 and Spain to 82. This has resulted in renewed discussions on development and production work-share to reflect potential orders, and also, equally important, on the need to keep costs from escalating. The first flight of the aircraft is now scheduled for September 1993, about 18 months behind schedule. The main reason for the delay is the programme's work-share agreements. The aircraft's flight software development and other key activities are carried out by contractors in four different countries.

Progress towards an in-service date of 2000 is unlikely to be smooth as governments may see the project as a target for further cost reduction or even cancellation. This would have a disastrous effect not only on re-equipment programmes of the four air forces, but also on the aircraft industries, their suppliers and sub-contractors. Meanwhile Russia will continue its vigorous marketing of highly sophisticated fighter aircraft which other current European fighters may not match.

BELGIUM

GDP	1991:	fr 6,877bn ($201.4bn)	
	1992:	fr 7,186.5bn ($223.53bn)	
Growth	1991:	2.6%	1992: 1.6%
Inflation	1991:	3.2%	1992: 2.4%
Publ Debt	1992:	135.2%	
Def bdgt	1992:	fr 101.70bn ($3.16bn)	
	1993:	fr 99.00bn ($2.95bn)	
NATO defn	1992:	fr 130.94bn ($4.07bn)	
$1 = fr	1990:	33.418	1991: 34.148
	1992:	32.150	1993: 33.602

fr = Belgian francs

Population: 10,033,000

	13–17	18–22	23–32
Men	315,800	338,600	765,000
Women	301,600	324,400	738,900

TOTAL ARMED FORCES:
ACTIVE: 80,700 (incl 5,000 Medical Service); 2,950 women; 28,600 conscripts.
Terms of service: 8 months in Belgium or 6 months in Germany. Conscription ends after 1993.
RESERVES: Total Reserve Status: 228,800 (Army 139,100; Medical Service 36,800; Navy 12,400; Air Force 40,500). With service in past 3 years: ε146,000.

ARMY: 54,000 (23,300 conscripts). Both figures incl Medical Service.
1 Corps HQ.
1 armd bde (2 tk, 2 mech inf, 1 SP arty bn, 1 ATK coy).
2 mech inf bde (each 1 tk, 2 mech inf, 1 SP arty bn, 1 ATK coy).
1 para-cdo regt (3 para-cdo bn, armd recce sqn, ATK coy, arty bty).
1 indep recce bn.
2 SP arty bn.
3 AD bn: 2 *HAWK*; 1 *Gepard* AA.
3 engr bn (2 fd, 1 bridge).
3 lt avn sqn.
RESERVES: some on immediate recall status; 1 armd bde (2 tk, 2 mech inf, 1 SP arty bn, 1 ATK coy).
1 mot inf bde (2 mot inf, 1 SP arty bn, 1 ATK coy, 1 recce sqn).
1 para cdo, 1 *Gepard* AA, 1 engr (eqpt) bn.
Territorial defence: 11 lt inf regt, 4 lt inf bn.
EQUIPMENT:
MBT: 334 *Leopard* 1, 25 M-41.
LIGHT TANKS: 133 *Scorpion*.
RECCE: 153 *Scimitar*.
AIFV: 514 AIFV-B.
APC: 1,362: incl 509 M-113, 266 *Spartan*, 510 AMX-VCI, 77 M-75 to be sold/scrapped.
TOTAL ARTY: 376 (60 in store).
TOWED ARTY: 105mm: 21 M-101.

SP ARTY: 207: 105mm: 28 M-108; 155mm: 41 M-109A3, 127 M-109A2; 203mm: 11 M-110.
MORTARS: 107mm: 130 M-30 (incl some SP); 120mm: 18. Plus 81mm: 285.
SSM: 5 *Lance* launchers (in store).
ATGW: 420 *Milan* (325 veh-mounted), 43 *Striker* AFV with *Swingfire* (in store).
ATK GUNS: 80 JPK-90mm SP (to be scrapped).
AD GUNS: 20mm: 36 HS-804, 100 M-167 *Vulcan*; 35mm: 54 *Gepard* SP.
SAM: 39 *Improved HAWK*, 22 *Mistral*.
AIRCRAFT: 10 BN-2A *Islander*.
HELICOPTERS: 43 SA-318, 18 A-109.

NAVY: ε4,400 (ε1,000 conscripts).
BASES: Ostend, Zeebrugge.
FRIGATES: 3 *Wielingen* with 2 x ASTT (Fr L-5 LWT), 1 x 6 ASW mor; plus 4 x MM-38 *Exocet* SSM, 1 x 100mm gun and 1 x 8 *Sea Sparrow* SAM.
MINE WARFARE: 13 MCMV:
4 *Van Haverbeke* (US *Aggressive* MSO).
9 *Aster* (tripartite) MHC.
SUPPORT AND MISCELLANEOUS: 3:
2 log spt/comd with hel deck, 1 research/survey.
HELICOPTERS: 3 SA-318.
(By 1994 a further 1 FF, 1 MSO and 2 MHC are expected to have paid off.)

AIR FORCE: 17,300 (4,300 conscripts).
FGA: 4 sqn with F-16A/B.
FIGHTER: 2 sqn with F-16A/B.
RECCE: 1 sqn with *Mirage* 5BR.
TRANSPORT: 2 sqn: 1 with 12 C-130H; 1 with 2 Boeing 727QC, 3 HS-748, 5 *Merlin* IIIA, 2 *Falcon* 20.
TRAINING: 5 sqn: 3 with *Alpha Jet*; 1 with SF-260, 1 with CM-170.
SAR: 1 sqn with *Sea King* Mk 48.
EQUIPMENT: 122 cbt ac (plus 74 in store), no armed hel.
AIRCRAFT:
Mirage **5BR:** 15 (recce); plus 47 in store (37-BA, 10-BD).
F-16: 107: **A/B:** 72 (FGA), 35 (ftr); plus 27 in store.
C-130: 12 (tpt).
Boeing 727: 2 (tpt). **HS-748:** 3 (tpt). **CM-170:** 18 (liaison). **SF-260:** 28 (trg). *Alpha Jet:* 31 (trg).
HELICOPTERS:
Sea King: 5 (SAR).
MISSILES:
AAM: AIM-9 *Sidewinder*.

FORCES ABROAD:
GERMANY: 19,000;
1 corps HQ, 1 armd bde; 2 arty, 1 *Gepard* AA, 2 SAM, 2 engr bn; 3 hel sqn.
UN AND PEACEKEEPING:
BOSNIA (UNPROFOR II) 100: 1 tpt coy.
CAMBODIA (UNTAC): 2 Observers.

CROATIA (UNPROFOR I): 702, 1 inf bn, plus 6 Observers.
INDIA/PAKISTAN (UNMOGIP): 2 Observers.
MIDDLE EAST (UNTSO): 6 Observers.
SOMALIA (UNOSOM): some 940, 1 AB bn.
WESTERN SAHARA (MINURSO): 1 Observer.

FOREIGN FORCES:
NATO:
HQ NATO Brussels. HQ SHAPE Mons.
WEU:
Military Planning Cell.
US:
Some 1,900, Army (1,200); Navy (100+); Air (600).

CANADA

GDP	1991: $C 674.39bn ($US 588.63bn)
	1992: $C 687.33bn ($US 568.65bn)

Growth	1991: -1.7%	1992: 0.9%
Inflation	1991: 5.6%	1992: 1.5%
Publ Debt	1992: 83%	
Def bdgt	1992: $C 12.46bn ($US 10.31bn)	
	1993: $C 11.96bn ($US 9.60bn)	
NATO defn[a]	1992: $C 13.72bn ($US 11.35bn)	
$ 1 = $C	1990: 1.1668	1991: 1.1457
	1992: 1.2087	1993: 1.2464

Population: 27,347,000

	13–17	18–22	23–32
Men	941,100	965,100	2,249,200
Women	898,500	927,800	2,209,800

[a] Canadian fiscal year is 1 April–31 March. NATO data refer to calendar year.

Canadian Armed Forces are unified and are organised in functional commands. Mobile Command commands land combat forces, and Maritime Command all naval forces. Air Command commands all air forces, but Maritime Command has operational control of maritime air forces. Mobile Command has operational control of Tactical Air Group. This entry is set out in the traditional single service manner.

TOTAL ARMED FORCES:
ACTIVE: 78,100; 8,700 women; of the total strength some 25,000 are not identified by service.
RESERVES: Primary 37,200. Army (Militia) (incl comms) 28,400; Navy 6,500; Air 2,300. Supplementary 39,000.

ARMY (Land Forces): 20,000.
1 Task Force HQ:
3 mech inf bde gp, each with 1 armd regt, 3 mech inf bn, 1 arty, 1 engr regt, 1 AD bty.
1 AB bn gp.
1 indep AD bty.
1 indep engr spt regt.
RESERVES: Militia: 18 armd, 18 arty, 52 inf, 11 engr, 20 spt bn level units, 12 med coy.
Canadian Rangers: 3,100: 109 patrols.
EQUIPMENT:
MBT: 114 *Leopard* C-1.
RECCE: 174 *Lynx*, 195 *Cougar*.
APC: 1,404: 881 M-113 A2 (136 in store), 55 M-577, 269 *Grizzly*, 199 *Bison*.
TOWED ARTY: 255: 105mm: 12 Model 44 (L-5) pack, 189 C1 (M-101); 155mm: 54 M-114 (in store).
SP ARTY: 155mm: 76 M-109.
MORTARS: 81mm: 150.
ATGW: 150 *TOW* (incl 64 M-113 SP).
RCL: 84mm: 780 *Carl Gustav*.
AD GUNS: 35mm: 20 GDF-005; 40mm: 57 L40/60.
SAM: 36 ADATS, 111 *Blowpipe*, 110 *Javelin*.

NAVY (Maritime Forces): 12,500.
SUBMARINES: 3 *Ojibwa* (UK *Oberon*) SS with Mk 48 HWT. (Equipped for, but not with, *Harpoon* USGW).
PRINCIPAL SURFACE COMBATANTS: 17:
DESTROYERS: 4
DDG: 4 *Iroquois* ex-FFH (2 in conversion refit/post-refit trials) with 1 x Mk-41 VLS for 29 SM-2 MR, 2 CH-124 *Sea King* ASW hel (Mk 46 LWT), 2 x 3 ASTT, plus 1 x 76mm gun.
FRIGATES: 13:
FFH: 7:
3 *Halifax* with 1 CH-124A *Sea King* ASW hel (Mk 46 LWT), 2 x 2 ASTT; plus 2 x 4 *Harpoon* and 2 x 8 *Sea Sparrow* SAM.
2 *Annapolis*, 2 *St Laurent* with 1 *Sea King* hel, 2 x 3 ASTT, 1 x 3 ASW mor; plus 2 x 76mm gun.
FF: 6:
4 Improved *Restigouche* with 1 x 8 *ASROC*, 2 x 3 ASTT, 1 x 3 ASW mor, plus 2 x 76mm gun.
2 *Mackenzie* with 2 x 3 ASTT, 2 x 3 ASW mor, plus 4 x 76mm gun (excl 1 paid off August 1993).
PATROL AND COASTAL COMBATANTS: 12:
6 *Fundy* (ex MSC) PCC (trg).
5 *Porte St Jean* PCC, 1 PCI((reserve trg).
MINE WARFARE: 2:
2 *Anticosti* MSO (converted offshore spt vessels) (reserve trg).
SUPPORT AND MISCELLANEOUS: 8:
2 *Protecteur* AO with 3 *Sea King*, 1 *Provider* AO with 2 *Sea King*, 1 AO, 3 AGOR, 1 diving spt.

DEPLOYMENT AND BASES:
ATLANTIC: Halifax (HQ) (Maritime Commander is also COMCANLANT): 3 SS, 2 DDG, 5 FFH, 2 FF, 2 AO, 1 AGOR. 2 MR plus 1 MR (trg) sqn with CP-140 and 3 CP-140A, 1 ASW and 1 ASW (trg) hel sqn with 26 CH-125 hel.
PACIFIC: Esquimalt (HQ): 2 FFH, 5 FF, 6 PCC, 1 AO, 1 AGOR. 1 MR sqn with 4 CP-140 and 1 ASW hel sqn with 6 CH-124 hel.

RESERVES: 6,500 in 24 divisions: Patrol craft, MCM, Naval Control of Shipping, augmentation of regular units.

AIR FORCE: 20,600.
FIGHTER GROUP:
FIGHTER: 5 sqn (1 trg) with CF-18.
1 sqn with CF-5.
EW: 2 sqn with CE-144 (CL-601), CT-133.
EARLY WARNING: Canadian NORAD Regional Headquarters at North Bay. 47 North Warning radar sites: 11 long-range, 36 short-range; Region Operational Control Centre (ROCC), (2 Sector Operational Control Centres SOCC).
4 Coastal Radars and 2 Transportable Radars.
MARITIME AIR GROUP:
MR: 4 sqn (1 trg) with CP-140 *Aurora*;
ASW: 3 hel sqn (1 trg) with CH-124, *Sea King*.
TACTICAL AIR GROUP (TAG):
HELICOPTERS: 11 sqn: 3 with CH-135, 2 with CH-135 and CH-136; 5 reserve sqn with CH-136,1 test with CH-135 and CH-136.
AIR TRANSPORT GROUP:
TRANSPORT: 6 sqn:
4 (1 trg) with CC-130E/H *Hercules*.
1 with CC-137 (Boeing 707).
1 with CC-109, CC-144.
SAR: 4 tpt/SAR sqn (1 with twinned reserve sqn) with CC-115, CC-130, CC-138 ac; CH-113/-113A hel.
LIAISON: 3 base hel flt with CH-118, CH-135.
TRAINING: (reports direct to HQ Air Comd).
2 flying schools with CT-114 ac; CH-139 hel.
1 demonstration sqn with CT-114.
EQUIPMENT: 198 (incl 18 MR) cbt ac (plus 62 in store); 128 armed hel.
AIRCRAFT:
CF-18: 123: **-A:** 84; **-B:** 39 (plus **-A:** 2 in store).
CF-5: 57: **-A:** 26; **-D:** 31 (plus **-A:** 55, **-D:** 5 in store).
CP-140: 18 (MR).
CP-140A: 3 (environmental patrol)
CC-130E/H: 30 (25 tpt, 5 AAR/tpt).
CC-137: 5 (3 tpt, 2 tkr/ tpt).
CC-109: 7 (tpt). **CC/E-144:** 16 (6 EW trg, 3 coastal patrol, 7 VIP/tpt). **CC-138:** 7 (SAR/tpt). **CC-115:** 10 (SAR/tpt). **CT-133:** 51 (EW trg/tpt plus 9 in store).
CT-114: 108 (trg). **CC/T-142:** 6 (2 tpt, 4 trg).
HELICOPTERS:
CH-124: 31 (ASW, afloat); plus 3 in store.
CH-135: 43 (36 tac, 7 SAR/liaison). **CH-136:** 63 (61 tac, 2 test/trg). **CH-113:** 14 (SAR/tpt). **CH-118:** 9 (liaison). **CH-139:** 14 (trg).

FORCES ABROAD:
NORWAY: prepositioned TLE: 6 arty, 14 ACV.
UN AND PEACEKEEPING:
BOSNIA (UNPROFOR II): 1,043: 1 inf bn gp, 1 engr sqn, 15 Observers..
CAMBODIA (UNTAC): 207.
CROATIA (UNPROFOR I): 1,222: 1 inf bn, 1 engr bn, 45 civ pol .

EGYPT (MFO): 27.
EL SALVADOR (ONUSAL): 4.
IRAQ/KUWAIT (UNIKOM): 5.
MIDDLE EAST (UNTSO): 13.
MOZAMBIQUE (ONUMOZ): 15 Observers.
SOMALIA (UNOSOM): 5.
SYRIA/ISRAEL (UNDOF): 176 (log).
WESTERN SAHARA (MINURSO): 17 plus 15 Observers.

PARAMILITARY:
COAST GUARD: 6,400 (civilian-manned); some 89 vessels including: 1 heavy icebreaker/cable ship,7 heavy, 6 medium and 5 light icebreakers; 14 large SAR cutters/tenders; 5 hovercraft; plus 1 DC-3 ac, 1 S-61, 5 Bell 212, 5 Bell 206L, 2 Bell 206L-1, 16 Bo 105 hel.

DENMARK

GDP	1991:	kr 833.30bn	($130.28bn)
	1992:	kr 857.50bn	($142.06bn)
Growth	1991: 1.2%	1992: 1.1%	
Inflation	1991: 2.4%	1992: 2 %	
Publ Debt	1992: 62.4%		
Def bdgt	1992:	kr 16.85bn	($2.79bn);
	1993:	kr 14.23bn	($2.21bn)
NATO defn	1992:	kr 16.84bn	($2.79bn)
$1 = kr	1990: 6.189	1991: 6.396	
	1992: 6.036	1993: 6.254	

kr = Danish kroner

Population: 5,168,200

	13–17	18–22	23–32
Men	162,000	184,600	401,000
Women	155,200	177,300	385,300

TOTAL ARMED FORCES:
ACTIVE: 27,700 (9,100 conscripts, 1,000 women).
Terms of service: 9–12 months (up to 27 months in certain ranks).
RESERVES: 70,000: Army 54,000; Navy 5,000; Air Force 11,000. Home Guard (*Hjemmevaernet*) (volunteers to age 50): Army 54,500; Naval 4,000; Air Force 10,700.

ARMY: some 16,900 (7,700 conscripts, 400 women):
1 op comd, 1 mil region, 1 land comd (east).
1 mech inf div (recce bn, 3 mech inf bde, div arty (reserve)).
2 mech inf bde each 2 mech/mot inf, 1 tk, 1 arty bn.
1 regt cbt gp (1 mot inf bn).
1 recce bn.
Army avn.
RESERVES:
6 mil region.

4 regt cbt gp incl 2 inf, 4 arty bn.
1 tk, 2 inf, 3 arty bn.
EQUIPMENT:
MBT: 462: 230 *Leopard* 1A3/4, 179 *Centurion*, 53
M-41DK-1.
APC: 643 M-113 (incl variants).
TOTAL ARTY: 565.
TOWED ARTY: 317: 105mm: 184 M-101; 155mm: 24
M-59, 97 M-114/39; 203mm: 12 M-115.
SP ARTY: 155mm: 76 M-109; 203mm: 12 M-110.
MORTARS: 120mm: 160 Brandt. Plus 81mm: 388
(incl 55 SP).
ATGW: 140 *TOW* (incl 56 SP).
RCL: 84mm: 1,117 *Carl Gustav*; 106mm: 150 M-40.
AD GUNS: 40mm: 36 L/60.
SAM: *Hamlet* (*Redeye*).
AIRCRAFT: 8 SAAB T-17.
HELICOPTERS: 13 Hughes 500M/OH-6, 12 AS-
550C2.

NAVY: 4,500 (incl 200 women, 700 conscripts).
BASES: Copenhagen, Korsør, Frederikshavn.
SUBMARINES: 5:
3 *Tumleren* (mod No *Kobben*) SSC with Sw FFV
    Type 61 HWT.
2 *Narhvalen*, SSC with FFV Type 61 and 41 HWT
FRIGATES: 3:
3 *Niels Juel* with 2 x 4 *Harpoon* SSM.
PATROL AND COASTAL COMBATANTS: 35:
MISSILE CRAFT: 10 *Willemoes* PFM with 2 x 4
Harpoon.
PATROL: 25:
OFFSHORE: 5:
1 *Beskytteren*, 4 *Thetis* PCO all with 1 *Lynx* hel.
COASTAL: 10:
7 *Flyvefisken* (Stanflex 300) PFC.
3 *Agdlek* PCC.
INSHORE: 10: 9 *Barsø*, 1⟨.
MINE WARFARE: 9:
MINELAYERS: 6: 4 *Falster* (400 mines), 2 *Lindormen*
(50 mines).
MCMV: 3 *Alssund* (US MSC-128) MSC.
SUPPORT AND MISCELLANEOUS: 7:
2 AOT (small), 4 icebreakers (civilian-manned), 1
Royal Yacht.
HELICOPTERS: 8 *Lynx* (up to 4 embarked).

COAST DEFENCE: 2 coastal fortresses; 150mm
guns; 40mm AA guns. Coastal radar.
RESERVES (Home Guard): 37 inshore patrol craft.

AIR FORCE: 6,300 (700 conscripts, 400
women).
TACTICAL AIR COMMAND:
FGA/FIGHTER: 4 sqn: with F-16A/B.
FGA/RECCE: 1 sqn with RF-35 *Draken*.
TRANSPORT: 1 sqn with C-130H, *Gulfstream* III.
SAR: 1 sqn with S-61A hel.
TRAINING: 1 flying school with T-17.
AIR DEFENCE GROUP:
AD: 2 SAM bn: 8 bty with 36 *Improved HAWK*, 129

40 mm L/60, 28 40 mm/L70.
CONTROL/REPORTING GROUP: 5 radar
stations.
EQUIPMENT: 71 cbt ac, no armed hel.
AIRCRAFT:
F-16A/B: 63 (FGA/ftr).
RF-35: 8*.
C-130H: 3 (tpt). **Gulfstream III:** 3 (tpt). SAAB T-17:
29 (6 liaison, 23 trg).
HELICOPTERS:
S-61: 8 (SAR).
MISSILES:
ASM: AGM-12 *Bullpup*.
AAM: AIM-9 *Sidewinder*.

FORCES ABROAD:
UN AND PEACEKEEPING:
BOSNIA (UNPROFOR II): 186 spt unit.
CROATIA (UNPROFOR I): 975: 1 inf bn, 15
Observers, 39 civ pol.
CYPRUS (UNFICYP): 4.
INDIA/PAKISTAN (UNMOGIP): 6 Observers.
IRAQ/KUWAIT (UNIKOM): 6 Observers, 46 spt
personnel.
MACEDONIA (UNPROFOR M): 83, plus 12
Observers.
MIDDLE EAST (UNTSO): 11 Observers.

FOREIGN FORCES:
NATO:
HQ Allied Forces Baltic Approaches (BALTAP).

FRANCE

GDP	1991: fr 6,750.4bn ($1,196.43bn)		
	1992: fr 7,114.9bn ($1,270.5bn)		
Growth	1991: 1.2%	1992: 2.1%	
Inflation	1991: 3.1%	1992: 2.8%	
Publ Debt	1992: 51.6%		
Def bdgt	1992: fr 195.27bn ($34.87bn);		
	1993: fr 197.92bn ($35.83bn)		
NATO defn	1992: fr 241.42bn ($43.11bn)		
$1 = fr	1990: 5.45	1991: 5.64	
	1992: 5.60	1993: 5.523	

Population: 57,169,000

	13–17	18–22	23–32
Men	1,974,500	2,103,200	4,328,500
Women	1,881,500	2,007,800	4,231,500

TOTAL ARMED FORCES:
ACTIVE: some 411,600 (incl 16,400 women,
190,400 conscripts) incl 5,200 Central Staff, 8,600
(2,300 conscripts) Service de santé, 400 Service des
essences not listed below.
Terms of service: 10 months (can be voluntarily
extended to 12–24 months).

RESERVES: Earmarked for mob: 379,800; Army 280,000, Navy 29,800, Air 70,000. Potential: 1,353,700; Army 915,000, Navy 259,200, Air 179,500.

STRATEGIC NUCLEAR FORCES:
(17,000; some 1,700 Army, 5,000 Navy, 9,700 Air Force, 600 Gendarmerie).

NAVY: 80 SLBM in 5 SSBN.
SSBN: 5:
1 *L'Inflexible* and 4 mod *Le Redoutable* with 16 M-4/TN-70 or -71; plus SM-39 *Exocet* USGW.

AIR FORCE:
IRBM: 18 SSBS S-3D/TN-61 msl in 2 sqn. (Test centre: 4 silos.)
BOMBERS: 2 sqn with 15 *Mirage* IVP (*ASMP: Air-Sol, Moyenne-Portée* nuclear ASM), plus 13 in store, 3 sqn with 45 *Mirage* 2000N (ASMP)
TRAINING: 5 *Mirage* IIIB, 1 *Mystère-Falcon* 20P, 1 *Alpha Jet*.
TANKERS: 1 wing:
2 sqn with 11 C-135FR.
COMMUNICATIONS: 4 C-160 *ASTARTE* airborne comms centres.
RECCE: 3 *Mirage* IVP.

'PRESTRATEGIC' NUCLEAR FORCES:
(1,400).
ARMY (1,200): 15 *Hadès* SSM launchers (in store).
NAVY (190): 38 *Super Etendard* strike ac (*ASMP* nuc ASM); plus 19 in store.
Eqpt also listed with Service sections.

ARMY: 241,400 (7,900 women, 138,000 conscripts).
Note: regiments are normally of bn size.
1 corps with 3 armd, 1 inf div.
1 corps with 1 armd div (in Eurocorps from January 1994)
1 Fr/Ge bde (2,100: Fr units incl 1 lt armd, 1 mot inf regt; 1 recce sqn).
Summary div cbt units:

11 armd regt	1 lt armd regt
8 mech inf regt	3 mot inf regt
9 arty regt	6 ATK sqn.

Corps units: 1 armd recce, 1 para (SF), 1 mot inf, 1 MLRS, 3 *Roland* SAM (each of 4 bty), 2 *HAWK* SAM regt (each 30 SA-330, 20 SA-341/-342 ATK, 15 SA-341 gunships), 3 engr, 2 EW regt.
Rapid Action Force (FAR): 51,200.
1 para div: 6 para inf, 1 armd cavalry, 1 arty regt. 1 air portable marine div: 2 inf, 2 lt armd, 1 arty, 1 engr regt.
1 lt armd div: 2 armd cavalry, 2 APC inf, 1 arty, 1 engr regt.
1 mtn div: 5 mtn inf, 1 lt armd, 1 arty regt; 1 engr bn.
1 air-mobile div: 1 inf, 4 cbt, 1 comd, 1 spt hel regt.
(Total 274 hel: 80 SA-330, 90 SA-342/*HOT*, 104

SA-341 (30 gun, 74 recce/liaison).)
Corps units: 1 MLRS, 1 *Roland* SAM, 1 *HAWK* SAM, 1 engr regt.
Foreign Legion (8,500): 1 armd, 1 para, 6 inf, 1 engr regt.
11 Marine inf regt (overseas).
RESERVES:
2 lt armd div (based on inf and armd schools): cbt units: 3 tk, 3 inf, 1 arty, 1 engr regt.
1 territorial bde (Rhine) (reserve: 1 engr, 2 inf bn).
Individual reinforcements for 2 corps (incl Eurocorps) and FAR (92,000).
Territorial def forces: 75 regt
EQUIPMENT:
MBT: 1,000 AMX-30 (658 -B2), 13 *Leclerc*.
RECCE: 325 AMX-10RC, 192 ERC-90F4 *Sagaie*, 588 AML-60/-90 (perhaps 300 in store), 584 VBL M-11.
AIFV: 816 AMX-10P/PC.
APC: 124 AMX-13 VTT, 3,975 VAB (incl variants).
TOTAL ARTY: 1,435.
TOWED ARTY: 401: 105mm: 116 HM-2; 155mm: 180 BF-50, 105 TR-F-1.
SP ARTY: 351: 155mm: 253 AU-F-1, 98 F-3.
MRL: 227mm: 57 MLRS.
MORTARS: 120mm: 370 RT-F1, 256 M-51.
ATGW: 200 *Eryx*, 1,400 *Milan*, *HOT* (incl 135 VAB SP).
RL: 89mm: 11,200; 112mm: *APILAS*.
AD GUNS: 1,242: 20mm: 105 53T1, 775 53T2; 30mm: 362 towed.
SAM: 449: 69 *HAWK*, 180 *Roland* I/II, 200 *Mistral*.
HELICOPTERS 683: 22 AS-332M, 123 SA-313/-318, 5 AS-555, 63 SA-316/-319, 133 SA-330, 153 SA-341F/M (16 with *HOT*, 67 gun-armed, 70 utility), 184 SA-342M (154 with *HOT*, 30 utility).
AIRCRAFT: 5 MH-1521, 3 Reims-Cessna 406, 6 PC-6.

NAVY: 65,400 incl 11,000 Naval Air, 6,000 Marines (2,500 women; 19,700 conscripts).
COMMANDS: 1 strategic sub (ALFOST), 2 home (CECLANT, CECMED), 2 overseas: Indian Ocean (ALINDIEN), Pacific Ocean (ALPACI).
BASES: *France:* Cherbourg, Brest (HQ), Lorient, Toulon (HQ). *Overseas:* Papeete (HQ) (Tahiti); La Réunion; Nouméa (New Caledonia); Fort de France (Martinique).
SUBMARINES: 19.
STRATEGIC SUBMARINES: 5 SSBN (see above).
TACTICAL SUBMARINES: 14:
SSN: 6 *Rubis* ASW/ASUW with F-17 HWT, L-5 LWT and SM-39 *Exocet* USGW (incl 1 commissioning July 1993).
SS: 8:
4 *Agosta* with F-17 HWT and L-5 LWT; plus *Exocet* USGW.
4 *Daphné*, with E-15 HWT and L-5 LWT; (plus 4 in store).
PRINCIPAL SURFACE COMBATANTS: 42:
CARRIERS: 2:

2 *Clémenceau* CVS, (33,300t) capacity 40 ac
(typically 2 flt with 16 *Super Etendard*, 1 with 6
Alizé; 1 det with 2 *Etendard* IVP, 2 *Super Frelon*,
2 *Dauphin* hel.
CRUISERS: 1:
1 *Jeanne d'Arc* CCH (trg/ASW) with 6 MM-38
Exocet SSM, 4 x 100mm guns, capacity 8 x *Lynx*
hel.
DESTROYERS: 4 DDG:
2 *Cassard* with 1 x 1 *Standard* SM-1 MR; plus 8 x
MM-40 *Exocet*, 1 x 100mm gun, 2 x ASTT, 1
Lynx hel (ASW/OTHT).
2 *Suffren* with 1 x 2 *Masurca* SAM; plus 1 *Malafon*
SUGW, 4 ASTT, 4 MM-38 *Exocet*, 2 x 100mm
guns.
FRIGATES: 35:
4 *Floréal* with 2 MM-38 *Exocet*, 1 AS-365 hel and 1
x 100mm gun.
7 *Georges Leygues* with 2 *Lynx* hel (Mk 46 LWT), 2
x ASTT; plus 5 with 8 MM-40, 2 with 4 MM-38
Exocet, all with 1 x 100mm gun.
3 *Tourville* with 2 x *Lynx* hel, 1 *Malafon* SUGW, 2 x
ASTT; plus 6 x MM-38 *Exocet*, 2 x 100mm guns.
1 *Aconit* with *Malafon*, 2 x ASTT; plus 8 MM-38
Exocet, 2 x 100mm guns.
3 *Commandant Rivière* with 2 x 3 ASTT, 1 x 12
ASW mor; plus 3 with 4 x MM-38 *Exocet*, all with
2 x 100mm guns.
17 *D'Estienne d'Orves* with 4 x ASTT, 1 x 6 ASW
mor; plus 6 with 2 x MM-38, 6 with 4 x MM-40
Exocet, all with 1 x 100mm gun.
PATROL AND COASTAL COMBATANTS: 23:
PATROL OFFSHORE: 1 *Albatross* PCO (Public
Service Force).
COASTAL: 20:
10 *L'Audacieuse*.
8 *Léopard* PCC (trg).
1 *Sterne*, 1 *Grebe* PCC (Public Service Force).
INSHORE: 2 *Athos* PCI.
Plus: 4 *Patra* PCI, 1 *Lt Combattante* PCI, 5 PCI⟨.
(manned by Gendarmarie Maritime).
MINE WARFARE: 21.
MINELAYERS: Nil, but submarines and *Thetis* (trials
ship) have capability.
MINE COUNTERMEASURES: 20:
9 *Eridan* tripartite MHC.
5 *Circé* MHC.
2 *Ouistreham* (US *Aggressive*) MSO.
4 *Vulcain* MCM diver spt.
AMPHIBIOUS: 9:
1 *Foudre* LPD, capacity 450 tps, 30 tk, 4 *Super
Puma* hel, 2 CDIC LCT or 10 LCM.
2 *Ouragan* LPD: capacity 350 tps, 25 tk, 2 *Super
Frelon* hel.
1 *Bougainville* LSD: capacity 500 tps, 6 tk, 2 AS-
332 hel: (assigned to spt DIRCEN nuclear test
centre South Pacific).
5 *Champlain* LSM (*BATRAL*): capacity 140 tps, tk.
Plus craft: 6 LCT, 24 LCM.
SUPPORT AND MISCELLANEOUS: 37:
UNDERWAY SUPPORT: 5:
5 *Durance* AO.

MAINTENANCE/LOGISTIC: 21:
1 AOT, 1 *Jules Verne* AR with 2 SA-319 hel, 4 *Rhin*
depot/spt, 1 *Rance* med and trg spt, all with hel; 8
tpt, 6 ocean tugs (3 civil charter).
SPECIAL PURPOSES: 5:
2 msl trials, 1 electronics trials, 1 *Thetis* mine
warfare trials, 1 div trials.
SURVEY/RESEARCH: 6: 5 AGHS, 1 AGOR

NAVAL AIR FORCE: (11,000).
NUCLEAR STRIKE: 3 flt with *Super Etendard* (AN-52
nuclear weapons).
FIGHTER: 1 flt with F-8E (FN) *Crusader*.
ASW: 2 flt with *Alizé*.
MR: 6 flt, 4 with *Atlantic*, 2 with *Gardian*.
RECCE: 1 flt with *Etendard* IVP.
OCU: *Etendard* IVM; *Alizé*; *Zéphyr*.
TRAINING: 5 units with N-262 *Frégate*, Piper
Navajo, EMB-121 *Xingu*, MS-760 *Paris*, Falcon
10MER, *Rallye* 880, CAP 10, *Zéphyr*.
MISCELLANEOUS: 4 comms/liaison units (1 VIP)
with *Falcon* 10MER, *Alizé*, N-262, EMB 121,
Xingu, Navajo.
1 trial unit with *Atlantique* 2, MS-760 *Paris*.
2 lt ac units with 12 *Rallye* 880, 6 CAP-10.
ASW: 2 sqn with *Lynx*.
COMMANDO: 2 aslt sqn with SA-321.
TRAINING: SA-316.
MISCELLANEOUS: 2 comms/SAR units with SE-
3130, SA-316, 1 trials unit with SE-3130, SA-319,
Lynx, SA-321.
EQUIPMENT: 107 cbt ac (plus 43 in store); 40
armed hel (plus 14 in store).
AIRCRAFT:
Super Etendard: 38 (strike); plus 19 in store. Total of
48 to be mod for *ASMP*.
Etendard: IVP: 8 (recce); Plus 7 in store.
Crusader: 12 (ftr) plus 7 in store. 18 of these
undergoing modification to extend in service life).
Alizé: 19 (18 ASW, 1 trg) plus 6 in store.
Atlantic: 16 (MR), plus 12 in store.
Atlantique: 9 (MR).
Gardian: 5 (MR).
Zéphyr: 12 (trg). **Nord 262:** 23 (13 MR trg, 10 misc).
Navajo: 6 (2 trg, 4 misc). ***Xingu***: 17 (10 trg, 7 misc).
Rallye 880: 14 (4 trg, 10 misc). **CAP-10:** 8 (misc).
MS-760: 7 (trg). **Falcon 10MER:** 5 (3 trg, 2 misc).
HELICOPTERS:
Lynx: 28 (ASW). **SA-321:** 12 (12 ASW) plus 5 in
store. **SA-313:** 8 (2 trg, 6 misc). **SA-316/-319:** 29 (6
trg, 23 misc). **AS-365:** 6 (SAR).
MISSILES:
ASM: AS-12/-20/-30, *Martel* AS-37, *Exocet* AM-39.
AAM: R-530, R-550 *Magic*, AIM-9 *Sidewinder*.

MARINES: (6,000).
COMMANDO UNITS: (600).
4 Assault gp.
1 Attack Swimmer unit.
1 HQ section.
NAVAL BASE PROTECTION: (2,000).
FUSILIERS-MARIN: (3,400)

PUBLIC SERVICE FORCE: Naval personnel, performing general coast guard, fishery, SAR, anti-pollution and traffic surveillance duties: 1 *Albatros*, 1 *Sterne*, 1 *Grebe* PCC, 4 N-262 ac, 3 SA-365 hel (ships incl in naval patrol and coastal totals). Command exercised through 'Maritime Prefectures' (Premar): Manche (Cherbourg), Atlantique (Brest), Mediterranee (Toulon).

AIR FORCE: 90,600 (6,000 women, 32,700 conscripts), incl strategic and prestrategic forces.
AIR DEFENCE COMMAND (CAFDA):
CONTROL: automatic *STRIDA* II, 10 radar stations, 1 wing with 4 E3F.
SAM: 12 sqn (1 trg) with 24 *Crotale* bty (48 fire, 24 radar units).
4 sqn *Mistral*.
AA GUNS: 300 bty (20mm).
TACTICAL AIR FORCE (FATAC):
9 wings, 31 sqn.
FIGHTER: 4 wings, 11 sqn.
5 with *Mirage* F-IC. 6 with *Mirage* 2000C.
FGA: 11 sqn:
1 with *Mirage* 2000N. 2 with *Mirage* IIIE.
2 with *Mirage* IIIBE/*Mirage* VF.
5 with *Jaguar* A.1 with *Mirage* F1-CT.
RECCE: 1 wing, 3 sqn with *Mirage* F-1CR.
TRAINING: 1 OCU sqn with *Jaguar* A/E.
1 OCU sqn with F1-C/B,
1 OCU sqn with *Mirage* 2000/BC.
EW: 2 sqn: 1 with C-160 ELINT/ESM ac, AS-330 hel; 1 with DC-8 ELINT.
HELICOPTERS: 1 sqn with SA-313, SA-319.
AIR TRANSPORT COMMAND (COTAM):
TRANSPORT: 19 sqn:
1 hy with DC-8F;
5 tac with C-160/-160NG/C-130H;
13 lt tpt/trg/SAR with C-160, DH-6, EMB-121, *Falcon* 20, *Falcon* 50, *Falcon* 900, MS-760, N-262.
TRAINING: 1 OCU with N-262, C-160.
HELICOPTERS: 5 sqn with AS-332, AS-355, SA-313/-316/-319, SA-365.
TRAINING: 1 OCU with SA-313/-316, SA-330.
TRAINING COMMAND (CEAA): (5,000).
TRAINING: *Alpha Jet*, CAP-10B/-20, CM-170, EMB-121, TB-30.
EQUIPMENT: 796 cbt ac, no armed hel.
AIRCRAFT:
Mirage: 486: F-1B: 18 (OCU); F-1C: 98 (ftr); F-1CT: 22 (FGA); F-1CR: 51 (recce); IIIE: 30 (FGA); IIIB/BE: 9* (trg); -5F: 30 (FGA); IVP: 19 (bbr); -2000B/C: 132 (112 -C, 20 -B); -2000N: 72; -2000D: 5.
Jaguar: 151: -A: 117 (strike, FGA, trg); -E: 34* (trg).
Alpha Jet: 159* (trg).
E-3F: 4 (AEW).
DC-8: 4.
C-130: 12. -H: 3 (tpt); -H-30: 9 (tpt).
C-135F/FR: 11 (tkr).
C-160: 77 (2 *Gabriel* ELINT/ESM, 4 *ASTARTE* comms, 40 tac tpt, 9 OCU, 22 -NG tac tpt).

CN-235M: 6 (tpt).
N-262: 24 (21 lt tpt, 2 trg, 1 trials).
Falcon: 20: -20: 14 (7 tpt, 7 misc); -50: 4 (tpt); -900: 2 (tpt). MS-760: 40 (misc). DHC-6: 10 (tpt). EMB-121: 25 (4 tpt, 21 trg). TB-30: 148 (trg). CAP-10B/230: 52 (trg). TBM-700: 6.
HELICOPTERS:
SA-313: 19 (incl 9 OCU) (*Alouette* II).
SA-319: 35 (*Alouette* III).
SA-330: 28 (25 tpt, 3 OCU) (*Puma*).
SA-365: 1 (tpt) (*Dauphin*), 2 (tpt) (*Cougar*)
AS-332: 6 (tpt) (*Super Puma*).
AS-350: 6 (*Ecureuil*).
AS-355: 34 (tpt) (*Fennec*).
MISSILES:
ASM: AS-30/-30L, *Martel* AS-37.
AAM: *Super* 530F/D, R-550 *Magic* 1/II.

DEPLOYMENT:
NAVY:
Atlantic Fleet: (HQ, Brest): 5 SSBN, 6 SS, 1 CCH, 16 FF, 2 MSC, 11 MHC, 2AO.
Channel Flotilla: (HQ, Cherbourg): 2 patrol combatants.
Mediterranean Fleet: (HQ, Toulon): 6 SSN, 2 SS, 2 CV, 4 DDG, 12 FF, 3 MCMV, 3 amph, 2 AO.

FORCES ABROAD:
GERMANY: 16,000; 1 corps HQ, 1 armd div; Gendarmerie (260).
Berlin: (2,700); 1 armd regt, 1 mot inf regt.
ANTILLES-GUYANA (HQ Cayenne): 8,400; 2 marine inf, 1 Foreign Legion regt, 1 spt bn, 8 ships (incl 1 log spt and 1 amph), 1 *Atlantic* ac (Dakar, Senegal), 1 air tpt unit (2 C-160 ac); Gendarmerie (1,400).
INDIAN OCEAN (Mayotte, La Réunion): 3,400; incl 1 marine inf regt, 1 spt bn, 1 Foreign Legion coy, 1 air tpt unit (2 C-160 ac, 2 SA-355 hel); Gendarmerie (700).
NAVY: Indian Ocean Squadron, Comd ALINDIEN (HQ afloat): (1,400); 4 FF, 2 patrol combatants, 2 amph, 3 spt (1 comd), 1 *Atlantic* ac.
NEW CALEDONIA (HQ Nouméa): 3,700; 1 marine inf regt; some 10 AML recce, 5 105mm arty; 1 air tpt unit, det (2 C-160, 1 *Gardian* MR ac, 2 SA-319, 7 SA-330 hel). Navy: 2 P-400 PCC. Gendarmerie (1,100).
POLYNESIA (HQ Papeete): 4,000 (incl Centre d'Experimentations du Pacifique); 1 marine, 1 Foreign Legion regt, 1 air tpt unit (3 SE-210, 1 *Gardian* ac; 3 AS-332, 3 SA-319 hel), Gendarmerie (350).
PACIFIC NAVAL SQUADRON (comd, ALPACI, HQ Papeete) (700); 3 FF, 5 patrol and coastal, 3 amph, 1 AOT, 2 survey, 5 *Gardian* MR ac.
CENTRAL AFRICAN REPUBLIC: 1,200:
GARRISON: 1bn gp incl 1 motor coy; 1 pl AML armd cars (6); spt coy with O-1E lt ac, 120mm mor, *Milan* ATGW.

FROM FRANCE: 1 AML armd car sqn and 1 tp (10 AML), 2 inf coy, 1 arty bty (105mm), 1 avn det (4 SA-330 hel); air elm with 5 *Jaguar*, 3 C-160 ac.

CHAD: 750; 2 inf coy, 1 AML sqn (-), AA arty units; 3 C-160 ac.

COTE D'IVOIRE: 500; 1 marine inf regt (10 AML-60/-90, 5 AMX-13); 1 AS-355 hel.

DJIBOUTI: 4,000; 1 marine inf(-), 1 Foreign Legion regt(-); 36 ERC-90 recce, 5 155mm arty, 16 AA arty; 3 amph craft, 1 sqn with 10 *Mirage* F-1C, 1 C-160 ac, 1 SA-319, 2 AS-355 hel.

GABON: 500; 1 marine inf regt (5 AML-60); 1 C-160, 1 *Atlantic* ac, 1 SA-355 hel.

RWANDA: 400; 2 inf coy.

SENEGAL: 1,200; 1 marine inf regt (10 AML-60/-90); Atlantic MR ac; 1 air tpt unit (1 C-160 tpt ac; 2 SA-316/-319 hel).

UN AND PEACEKEEPING:
ADRIATIC: About 2 FF to NATO/WEU (*Sharp Guard*).

BOSNIA: (UNPROFOR II) 3,096; 3 inf, 1 engr bn, 1 hel sqn (5 AS-332, 4 SA-316); Gendarmerie (20).

CAMBODIA (UNTAC): 1,293; 1 mot inf bn, 3 C-160 ac; Gendarmerie (141), plus 45 Observers.

CROATIA (UNPROFOR I): 2,239; 1 inf bn, 1 log bn; 1 ALAT det; Gendarmerie (22), plus 12 Observers.

EGYPT (MFO): 40; incl 1 DHC-6.

EL SALVADOR (ONUSAL); Gendarmerie (17).

FORMER YUGOSLAVIA (*Provide Promise*); 3 C-130.

IRAQ/KUWAIT (UNIKOM): 15 Observers.

ITALY (*Deny Flight*): 160; 10 *Mirage* 2000C, 4 *Mirage* FI-CR, 1 DHC6.

LEBANON (UNIFIL): 441; 1 log bn; Gendarmerie (11).

MIDDLE EAST (UNTSO): 17 Observers.

SAUDI ARABIA (*Southern Watch*): 130; 9 *Mirage* 2000C, 1 C-135, 1 N-262.

SOMALIA (UNOSOM): 1,083; 1 mot inf bn, 1 engr, 1 log coy, 6 SA-330, 6 SA-341 hel.

TURKEY (*Provide Comfort*): 100; 4 *Mirage* F1-CR, 4 *Jaguar*, 1 C-135.

WESTERN SAHARA (MINURSO): 30 Observers (Gendarmerie).

PARAMILITARY:
GENDARMERIE: 96,300 (2,600 women, 12,200 conscripts, plus 980 civilians); incl: *Territorial* (58,500); *Mobile* (17,200); *Schools* (5,700); *Republican Guard* (3,200); *Overseas* (3,200); *Maritime* (1,200); *Air* (1,100); *Air Tpt* (1,200); *Arsenals* (400); *Administration* (4,600); *Reserves* (115,600).
EQUIPMENT: 121 AML, 28 VBC-90 armd cars; 33 AMX-VTT, 155 VBRG-170 APC; 278 81mm mor; 10 PCIs (listed under Navy),plus 11 other patrol craft and 4 tugs. 6 Cessna 206C ac, 3 SA-316, 9 SA-319, 29 AS-350 hel.

GERMANY

GDP	1991:	DM 2,612.6bn ($1,574.3bn)	
	1992	DM 2,772.0bn ($1,774.9bn)	
Growth	1991: 3.6%	1992: 0.5%	
Inflation	1991: 3.5%	1992: 4.1%	
Publ Debt	1992: 43.2%		
Def bdgt	1992:	DM 52.13bn ($33.38bn);	
	1993:	DM 50.80bn ($31.20bn)	
NATO defn	1992:	DM 66.143bn ($42.35bn)	
$1 = DM	1990: 1.6157	1991: 1.6595	
	1992: 1.5617	1993: 1.6281	

DM = Deutschmark

Population [79,753,000]

	13–17	18–22	23–32
Men	2,090,000	3,011,000	6,858,000
Women	1,979,000	2,874,000	6,458,000

TOTAL ARMED FORCES:
ACTIVE: 408,200 (176,300 conscripts; 1,000 active Reserve trg posts, all Services).
Terms of service: 12 months.
RESERVES: 696,600 (men to age 45, officers/NCO to 60): Army 592,000, Navy 16,650, Air 87,950.

ARMY: 287,000 (140,400 conscripts); and incl 8,800 staff not listed below.
FIELD ARMY: (170,300) 3 Corps, 12 div.
I Corps: 3 armd, 1 armd inf div.
II Corps: 1 armd, 1 armd inf, 1 AB, 1 mtn div.
III Corps: 2 armd, 1 armd inf div.
1 armd inf div (LANDJUT).
(These 12 div will be reduced to 6 by end 1994. In 1993 they command and control 9 armd, 7 armd inf, 1 mtn and 3 AB bde, of which 7 are fully manned, the remainder being mixed active and reserve units.)
(For cbt spt a total of 9 armd recce bn, 6 arty regt (each 24 FH-70, 6 110mm MRL, 18 MLRS), 3 mixed AD regt (each 21 *Roland* and 21 *Gepard*), 5 AD regt (each 42 *Gepard*) and 12 avn sqn are available.)
Corps Tps: 3 avn comd each 1 lt (48 UH-1D), 1 med tpt (32 CH-53), 1 ATGW hel (56 Bo-105 *HOT*) regt.
TERRITORIAL ARMY (cadre; 69,100 in peacetime); Command Structure: 3 Territorial Comd, 5 Military Districts, 28 Military Regions, 76 Sub-regions: Units (eqpt holding only unless stated).
1 German/French bde (Ge units incl 1 mech inf, 1 arty bn; 1 SP ATK coy).
8 inf regt; 11 mot inf bn.
EASTERN COMMAND (38,700):
1 Corps/Territorial Cmd HQ, 2 Military Districts/div HQ, 14 Military Regions, 45 Sub-Regions.
6 Home Defence bde; 3 inf, 4 arty bn.
EQUIPMENT:
MBT: 4,778: 649 M-48A2G, 2,007 *Leopard* 1A1 (1,258 upgraded to A5), 2,122 *Leopard* 2 (253 to be upgraded).

RECCE: 408 SPz-2 *Luchs*, 95 TPz-1 *Fuchs* (NBC), 115 *Wiesel* (*TOW*).
AIFV: 3,096: 2,073 *Marder* A1/A2 (to upgrade to A3), 1,023 BMP-1A1.
APC: 3,117: 294 TPz-1 *Fuchs* (incl 83 EW variant), 2,600 M-113 (incl 426 arty obs), 223 M-577.
TOTAL ARTY: 2,601
TOWED ARTY: 429: 105mm: 27 M-56, 190 M-101; 155mm: 212 FH-70.
SP ARTY: 794: 155mm: 569 M-109A3G; 203mm: 225 M-110A2.
MRL: 363: 110mm: 206 *LARS*; 227mm: 157 MLRS.
MORTARS: 1,015: 120mm: 410 Brandt, 110 Tampella, 495 Tampella on M-113.
ATGW: 1,971 *Milan*, 198 *TOW*, 337 RJPz-(*HOT*) *Jaguar* 1, 162 RJPz-(*TOW*) SP.
ATK GUNS: 90mm: 118 JPz-4-5 SP.
AD GUNS: 2,410: 20mm: 1,988 Rh 202 towed; 35mm: 422 *Gepard* SP.
SAM: 658 *Fliegerfaust* 1 (*Redeye*), 141 *Roland* SP.
HELICOPTERS: 205 PAH-1 (Bo-105 with *HOT*), 180 UH-1D, 110 CH-53G, 97 Bo-105M, 120 *Alouette*.
MARINE: (River Engineers): 36 LCM, 12 PCI (river).
EQUIPMENT OF FORMER GDR ARMY: (in store).
MBT: 1,788: 6 T-54, 1,455 T-55, 327 T-72M.
LIGHT TANKS: 140 PT-76.
RECCE: 1,262 BRDM-1/-2.
APC: 4,504: 711 BTR-40, 144 BTR-50, 1,150 BTR-60, 1,250 BTR-70, 520 BTR-152, 729 MT-LB.
TOWED ARTY: 516: 122mm: 167 D-30, 172 M-1938 (M-30); 130mm: 172 M-46; 152mm: 5 D-20.
SP ARTY: 396: 122mm 314 2S1; 152mm: 82 2S3.
MRL: 265: 122mm: 223 Cz RM-70, 42 BM-21.
MORTARS: 120mm: 209 M-120, 26 2B11.
ATGW: AT-3 *Sagger* (incl BRDM-2 SP), AT-4 *Spigot*, AT-5 *Spandrel*.
ATK GUNS: 85mm: 64 D-48; 100mm: 267 T-12.
AD GUNS: 670: 23mm: 295 ZU-23, 131 ZSU-23-4 SP; 57mm: 244 S-60.
SAM: 226 SA-4/-6/-7/-8/-9.
HELICOPTERS: 8 Mi-2, 29 Mi-8 (T/TB), 7 Mi-9, 49 Mi-24.

NAVY: 31,200 incl naval air (5,700) and conscripts (6,900).
Fleet Command organised into 7 type commands: Frigate; Patrol Boat; MCMV; Submarine; Support Flotillas; Naval Air; Naval Comms and Electronics Commands.
BASES: Glücksburg (Maritime HQ) and four main bases: Wilhelmshaven, Kiel, Olpenitz and Warnemünde. Other bases with limited support facilities: Baltic: Eckernförde, Flensburg, Neustadt. North Sea: Emden.
SUBMARINES: 20:
TACTICAL SUBMARINES: 20:
18 Type 206/206A SSC with *Seeaal* DM2 533mm HWT (12 conversions to T-206A complete).
2 Type 205 SSC with DM3 HWT.
PRINCIPAL SURFACE COMBATANTS: 14:
DESTROYERS: 6:

DDG: 3 *Lütjens* (mod US *Adams*) with 1 x 1 SM-1 MR SAM/*Harpoon* SSM launcher, 2 x 127mm guns; plus 1 x 8 *ASROC* (Mk 46 LWT), 2 x 3 ASTT.
DD: 3 *Hamburg* (ASUW) with 2 x 2 MM-38 *Exocet*, 4 x 533mm TT (SUT), 3 x 100mm guns.
FRIGATES: 8:
8 *Bremen* with 2 *Lynx* hel (ASW/OTHT), 2 x 2 ASTT; plus 2 x 4 *Harpoon*.
PATROL AND COASTAL COMBATANTS: 38:
MISSILE CRAFT: 38:
10 *Albatros* (Type 143) PFM with 2 x 2 *Exocet*, and 2 x 533mm TT.
10 *Gepard* (T-143A) PFM with 2 x 2 *Exocet*.
18 *Tiger* (Type 148) PFM with 2 x 2 *Exocet*.
MINE WARFARE: 41:
MINELAYERS: 1 *Sachsenwald* (600+ mines), mine transport but can be used for minelaying.
MINE COUNTERMEASURES: 40:
10 *Hameln* (T-343) comb ML/MCC.
6 *Lindau Troika* MSC control and guidance, each with 3 unmanned sweep craft.
10 converted *Lindau* (T-331) MHC.
3 *Frankenthal* (T-332) MHC.
10 *Frauenlob* MSI.
1 MCM diver spt ship.
AMPHIBIOUS: Craft only: some 11 LCU/LCM.
SUPPORT AND MISCELLANEOUS: 40:
UNDERWAY SUPPORT: 2:
2 *Spessart* AO.
MAINTENANCE/LOGISTIC: 25:
1 *Rhein* SS/MCMV spt, 2 *Elbe* spt, 4 small (2,000t) AOT, 6 *Lüneburg* log spt, 2 AE, 8 tugs, 2 icebreakers (civil).
SPECIAL PURPOSE: 9:
3 AGI, 2 trials, 3 multi-purpose (T-748), 1 trg.
RESEARCH AND SURVEY: 4:
1 AGOR, 3 AGHS (civil-manned for Ministry of Transport).

NAVAL AIR ARM:
4 wings, 8 sqn, 1 Transport Gp.
2 wings with *Tornado*.
1 MR/ASW wing with *Atlantic*, *Lynx*.
1 SAR/liaison wing with Do-28, *Sea King*.
1 Transport Gp with 1 sqn Mi-8.
FGA/RECCE: 2 sqn with *Tornado*.
TRAINING: 1 sqn with *Tornado*
MR/ELINT: 1 sqn with *Atlantic*.
LIAISON: 1 sqn with Do-28/Do-228.
ASW: 1 sqn with *Sea Lynx* Mk 88 hel.
SAR: 1 sqn with *Sea King* Mk 41 hel.
TRANSPORT: 1 sqn with Mi-8.
EQUIPMENT: 115 cbt ac plus 3 in store, 19 armed hel.
AIRCRAFT:
Tornado: 101 (90 FGA, 11* trg) plus 3 in store.
Atlantic: 19 (14 MR, 5 ELINT).
Do-28: 11 (10 SAR, liaison; 1 environmental protection).
Do-228: LM: 1 (environmental monitoring).
HELICOPTERS:
Sea Lynx Mk 88: 19 (ASW). *Mi-8:* 10 (tpt).
Sea King Mk 41: 22 (SAR).

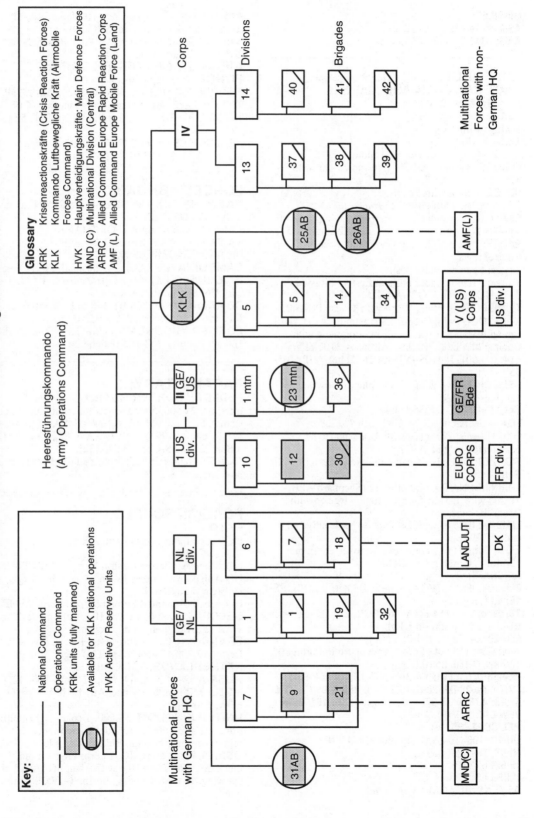

FUTURE GERMAN ARMY ORGANISATION Showing affiliations to multinational forces

Key:
— National Command
- - - Operational Command
KRK units (fully manned)
Available for KLK national operations
HVK Active / Reserve Units

Glossary
KRK Krisenreactionskräfte (Crisis Reaction Forces)
KLK Kommando Luftbewegliche Kräft (Airmobile Forces Command)
HVK Hauptverteidigungskräfte: Main Defence Forces
MND (C) Multinational Division (Central)
ARRC Allied Command Europe Rapid Reaction Corps
AMF (L) Allied Command Europe Mobile Force (Land)

Heeresführungskommando
(Army Operations Command)

Corps
Divisions
Brigades

Multinational Forces with German HQ

Multinational Forces with non-German HQ

MISSILES:
ASM: *Kormoran, Sea Skua.*
AAM: AIM-9 *Sidewinder.*

AIR FORCE: 90,000 (29,000 conscripts).
TACTICAL COMMAND (GAFTAC).
5 air div: 3 tac, 2 AD.
FGA: 8 wings, 15 sqn:
5 wings with *Tornado.*
1 with F-4F.
2 with *Alpha Jet* (deactivated end of 1993).
FIGHTER: 3 wings with F-4F (6 sqn), 1 sqn with MiG-29.
RECCE: 1 wing with RF-4E.
EW: 1 trg sqn with HFB-320 *Hansa Jet.*
SAM: 6 wings (each 6 sqn) *Patriot*; 6 wings (each 6 sqn) *HAWK*; 14 sqn *Roland*, 1 wing (2 sqn) SA-5.
RADAR: 1 tac Air Control Command, 2 tac Air Control regts.
7 sites; 5 remote radar posts.
3 sites; 8 remote radar posts in Eastern division.
TRANSPORT COMMAND (GAFTC).
TRANSPORT: 3 wings: 4 sqn with Transall C-160, incl 1 (OCU) with C-160, 1 sqn with Bell UH-1D, 1 sqn with Mi-8T, 1 special air mission wing with Boeing 707-320C, Tu-154, Airbus A-310, VFW-614, CL-601, L-410S (VIP); UH-1D hel (VIP), Mi-8S (VIP).
HELICOPTERS: 1 wing: 3 sqn; plus 1 det with UH-1D (liaison/SAR).
TRAINING COMMAND:
FGA: 1 det (Cottesmore, UK) with *Tornado*;
1 OCU (Beja, Portugal) with *Alpha Jet* (to be deactivated by end 1993).
FIGHTER: OCU (Holoman AFB, New Mexico) with F-4E.
TRAINING: NATO joint pilot trg (Sheppard AFB, Texas) with T-37B, T-38A; primary trg sqn with Beech-Bonanza.
LIAISON: base flt with Do-28D (to be deactivated by end of 1993).
EQUIPMENT: 617 cbt ac (42 trg (overseas)); plus 336 for disposal, no attack hel.
AIRCRAFT:
F-4: 193. **-F:** 143 (FGA, ftr); **-E:** 7 (OCU, in US); **RF-4E:** 43* (recce).
***Tornado*:** 237 (154 FGA, 36* ECR, 28* OCU, 19* in tri-national trg sqn (in UK)).
MiG-29: 24, 20 (ftr), **-UB:** 4 *(trg).
***Alpha Jet*:** 163 (148 FGA, 15* wpn trg in Portugal).
Transall C-160: 85 (tpt, trg).
Boeing 707: 4 (VIP).**A-310:** 3 (VIP, tpt) **CL-601:** 7 (VIP). **Do-28-D2:** 20 (tpt/liaison). **HFB-320:** 7 (tpt). **L-410-S:** 4 (VIP). **T-37B:** 35. **T-38A:** 41. **Tu-154:** 2 (tpt).
VFW-614: 3 (VIP). **An-26:** 1.
HELICOPTERS:
UH-1D: 108 (104 SAR, tpt, liaison; 4 VIP).
Mi-8T: 16 (SAR tpt).
Mi-8S: 6 (VIP).
MISSILES:
ASM: AS-20, AGM-65 *Maverick.*

AAM: AIM-9 *Sidewinder*, AA-10 *Alamo*, AA-11 *Archer* (AA-10, AA-11 for MiG-29).
SAM: 216 *Hawk* launchers; 95 *Roland* launchers. 288 *Patriot* launchers.
AIRCRAFT OF FORMER GDR AIR FORCE: (not being operated)
FIGHTER: 174 MiG-21; 44 MiG-23; 40 Su-22 (all TLE will be disposed of in accordance with CFE).
TRANSPORT: 3 Tu-134; 3 An-26; 8 L-410T; 52 L-39.
HELICOPTERS: 5 Mi-2 (20 in use for civilian rescue); 1 Mi-9; 14 Mi-14; 2 Mi-24.

FORCES ABROAD:
NAVY: 1 FF each with STANAVFORLANT and STANAVFORMED;
1 MCMV with STANAVFORCHAN;
3 MPA in ELMAS/Sardinia.
UN AND PEACEKEEPING:
CAMBODIA (UNTAC): 147 medical, 74 civ pol.
IRAQ (UNSCOM): 44: 2 C-160 ac, 3 CH-53 hel with UN Special Commission.
SOMALIA (UNOSOM II): 173 to be 1,650 from July 1993: 46 *Fuchs* APC, 5 UH-1D hel.
FORMER YUGOSLAVIA (*Provide Promise*): 3 C-160 (Frankfurt), 1 C-160 (Falconara, Italy).

===

PARAMILITARY:
FEDERAL BORDER GUARD (Ministry of Interior): 24,800; 5 cmd (constitutionally has no cbt status). Eqpt: 297 MOWAG SW-3/-4 APC (to be 100 by end of 1993); Hel: 32 SA-318C, 13 UH-1D, 8 Bell 212, 22 SA-330, 3 SA-332L.
COAST GUARD: 535; some 11 PCI, 1 inshore tug, plus boats.

===

FOREIGN FORCES:
NATO:
HQ Allied Land Forces Central Europe (LANDCENT).
HQ Allied Air Forces Central Europe (AIRCENT).
HQ Allied Land Forces Jutland and Schleswig-Holstein (LANDJUT).
HQ Allied Command Europe Mobile Force (AMF).
BELGIUM: 19,000; 1 corps HQ, 1 armd bde, 2 arty, 1 AA, 2 SAM, 2 engr bn, 3 hel sqn.
FRANCE: 16,000; 1 corps HQ, 1 armd div.
Berlin: (2,700), 1 armd, 1 mot inf regt.
NETHERLANDS: 3,700; 1 lt bde.
RUSSIA: 58,000. Army: 1 Gp, 2 Army HQ, 4TD, 2 MRD,1 MR bde, 6 arty bde. Air: 1 Air Army HQ; 2 FGA, 3 ftr regt.
UNITED KINGDOM: 53,600; 1 corps HQ (multina-tional), 1 armd div, 1 arty bde, 1 armd recce, 5 engr regt. 6 ac sqn, 1 hel sqn. Berlin: 1 inf bde.
US: 123,400. 1 army HQ, 1 corps HQ; 1 armd, 1 mech div; 2 air force HQ; with 9 sqn FGA/ftr, 1 cbt spt wing, 1 tac airlift wing. Berlin: (4,300), 1 inf bde.

GREECE

GDP	1991:	dr 12,863.4bn ($70.57bn)	
	1992:	dr 14,558.6bn ($76.37bn)	
Growth	1991:	1.8%	1992: 1.5%
Inflation	1991:	19.5%	1992: 15.8%
Publ Debt	1992:	92.4%	
Def bdgt	1992ε:	dr 838.80bn ($4.40bn)	
	1993ε:	dr 977.20bn ($4.41bn)	
NATO defn	1992:	dr 809.39bn ($4.25bn)	
FMA	1993:	$315.27m	
$1 = dr	1990:	158.51	1991: 182.27
	1992:	190.62	1993: 221.51

dr = drachmas

Population: 10,127,600

	13–17	18–22	23–32
Men	362,400	374,500	764,400
Women	339,400	351,800	723,900

TOTAL ARMED FORCES:

ACTIVE: 159,300 (122,300 conscripts, 5,900 women).

Terms of service: Army up to 19, Navy up to 23, Air Force up to 21 months.

RESERVES: some 406,000 (to age 50). Army some 350,000 (Field Army 230,000, Territorial Army/National Guard 120,000); Navy about 24,000; Air about 32,000.

ARMY: 113,000 (100,000 conscripts, 2,200 women).

FIELD ARMY (82,000): 3 Military Regions.
1 Army, 4 corps HQ.
2 div HQ (1 armd, 1 mech).
9 inf div (3 inf, 1 arty regt, 1 armd bn) 2 Cat A, 3 Cat B, 4 Cat C.
5 indep armd bde (each 2 armd, 1 mech inf, 1 SP arty bn) Cat A.
1 indep mech bde (2 mech, 1 armd, 1 SP arty bn), Cat A.
2 inf bde.
1 marine bde (3 inf, 1 lt arty bn, 1 armd sqn) Cat A.
1 cdo, 1 raider regt.
4 recce bn.
10 fd arty bn.
6 AD arty bn.
2 army avn bn.
1 indep avn coy.
2 SAM bn with *Improved HAWK*.
Units are manned at 3 different levels: Cat A 85% fully ready; Cat B 60% ready in 24 hours; Cat C 20% ready in 48 hours.

TERRITORIAL DEFENCE: (31,000):
Higher Mil Comd of Interior and Islands HQ.
4 Mil Comd HQ (incl Athens).
1 inf div.
1 para regt.
8 fd arty bn.

4 AD arty bn.
1 army avn bn.
RESERVES (National Guard): 34,000. Role: internal security.

EQUIPMENT:
MBT: 2,640: 396 M-47, 1,220 M-48 (299, 110 A2, 212 A3, 599 A5),591 M-60 (359 A1, 232 A3), 154 AMX-30 (in store), 279 *Leopard* (170 1A1,1091A3).
LIGHT TANKS: 67 M-24.
RECCE: 48 M-8.
AIFV: 96 AMX-10P.
APC: 2,165 (517 in store): 130 *Leonidas*, 114 M-2, 403 M-3 half-track, 372 M-59, 1,146 M-113.
TOTAL ARTY: 2,151.
TOWED ARTY: 875: 105mm: 18 M-56, 469 M-101; 140mm: 32 5.5-in; 155mm: 271 M-114; 203mm: 85 M-115.
SP ARTY: 371: 105mm: 76 M-52; 155mm: 48 M-44A1, 51 M-109A1, 84 M-109A2; 175mm: 12 M-107; 203mm: 100 M-110A2.
MORTARS: 107mm: 773 M-30, 132 M-106 SP. Plus 81mm: 690.
ATGW: 394: *Milan*, *TOW* (incl 36 SP).
RCL: 90mm: 1,057 EM-67; 106mm: 763 M-40A1.
AD GUNS: 20mm: 101 Rh-202 twin; 40mm: 227 M-1, 95 M-42A twin SP.
SAM: 42 *Improved HAWK, Redeye*.
AIRCRAFT: 2 *Aero Commander*, 2 *Super King Air*, 20 U-17A.
HELICOPTERS: 10 CH-47C1 (1 in store), 85 UH-1D/H/AB-205, 1 AB-212, 15 AB-206, 10 Bell 47G, 30 Hughes 300C.

NAVY: 19,500 (7,900 conscripts, 2,600 women);

BASES: Salamis, Patras, Soudha Bay.
SUBMARINES: 10:
8 *Glavkos* (Ge T-209/1100) with 533mm TT (1 with *Harpoon* USGW).
2 *Katsonis* (US *Guppy*) with 533mm TT (trg).
PRINCIPAL SURFACE COMBATANTS: 15:
DESTROYERS: 8:
4 *Kimon* (US *Adams*) with 1 x SM-1; plus 1 x 8 *ASROC*, 2 x 3 ASTT, 2 x 127mm guns, *Harpoon* SSM.
4 *Themistocles* (US *Gearing*) (ASW) with 1 x 8 *ASROC*, 2 x 3 ASTT, 1 with AB-212 hel; plus 3 x 2 127mm guns, 4 with 2 x 4 *Harpoon* SSM.
FRIGATES: 7:
1 *Hydra* (MEKO 200) with 2 x 3 ASTT; plus 2 x 4 *Harpoon* SSM and 1 x 127mm gun (1 SH-60 hel, 1 DC).
3 *Elli* (Nl *Kortenaer*) with 2 AB-212 hel, 2 x 3 ASTT; plus 2 x 4 *Harpoon*
3 *Makedonia* (ex-US *Knox*) (on loan) with 1 x 8 *ASROC*, 1 x SH-2F hel, 4 x ASTT; plus *Harpoon* (from *ASROC* launcher), 1 x 127mm gun.
PATROL AND COASTAL COMBATANTS: 40:
CORVETTES: 5:
5 *Niki* (ex-Ge *Thetis*) (ASW) with 1 x 4 ASW RL, 4 x 533mm TT.
MISSILE CRAFT: 16:

14 *Laskos* (Fr *Combattante*) PFM, 8 with 4 x MM-
38 *Exocet*, 6 with 6 *Penguin* 2 SSM, all with 2 x
533mm TT.
2 *Stamou*, with 4 x SS-12 SSM.
TORPEDO CRAFT: 10:
6 *Hesperos* (Ge *Jaguar*) PFT with 4 x 533mm TT.
4 No '*Nasty*' PFT with 4 x 533mm TT.
PATROL: 9:
COASTAL: 2 *Armatolos* (Dk *Osprey*) PCC.
INSHORE: 7: 2 *Tolmi*, 5 PCI .
MINE WARFARE: 16:
MINELAYERS: 2 *Aktion* (US LSM-1) (100–130
mines).
MINE COUNTERMEASURES: 14:
9 *Alkyon* (US MSC-294) MSC.
5 *Atalanti* (US *Adjutant*) MSC.
AMPHIBIOUS: 12:
1 *Chios* LST with hel deck: capacity 300 tps, 16 tk.
1 *Nafkratoussa* (US *Cabildo*) LSD: capacity 200 tps,
18 tk, 1 hel.
2 *Inouse* (US *County*) LST: capacity 400 tps, 18 tk.
4 *Ikaria* (US LST-510): capacity 200 tps, 16 tk.
4 *Ipopliarhos Grigoropoulos* (US LSM-1) LSM,
capacity 50 tps, 4 tk.
Plus about 65 craft: 2 LCT, 8 LCU, 13 LCM, some
42 LCVP.
SUPPORT AND MISCELLANEOUS: 14:
2 AOT, 4 AOT (small), 1 *Axios* (ex-Ge *Lüneburg*)
log spt, 1 AE, 5 AGHS, 1 trg.
NAVAL AIR: 12 armed hel.
ASW: 1 hel div: 2 sqn:
2 with 9 AB-212 (ASW), 2 AB-212 (EW), 2 SA-319
(with ASM).

AIR FORCE: 26,800 (14,400 conscripts, 1,100
women).
TACTICAL AIR FORCE: 8 cbt wings, 1 tpt wing.
FGA: 6 sqn:
2 with A-7H. 2 with A-7E.
1 with F-16. 1 with F-4E.
FIGHTER: 10 sqn:
2 with F-4E. 2 with F-5A/B.
1 with NF-5A/B, RF-5A. 1 with F-16 C/D.
2 with *Mirage* F-1CG. 2 with *Mirage* 2000 EG/BG.
RECCE: 1 sqn with RF-4E
MR: 1 sqn with HU-16B.
TRANSPORT: 3 sqn with C-130H/B, YS-11,
C-47, Do-28, *Gulfstream*.
LIAISON: 4 T-33A.
HELICOPTERS: 2 sqn with AB-205A, Bell 47G, AB-
212.
AD: 1 bn with *Nike Hercules* SAM (36 launchers). 12
bty with *Skyguard/Sparrow* SAM, twin 35mm guns.
AIR TRAINING COMMAND:
TRAINING: 4 sqn:
1 with T-41A; 1 with T-37B/C; 2 with T-2E.
EQUIPMENT: 384 cbt ac incl 5 MR (plus 77 in
store), no armed hel.
AIRCRAFT:
A-7: 92. **-H:** 38 (FGA); (plus 5 in store); **TA-7H:** 7
(FGA), **A-7E:** 40 (plus 15 in store); **A-7K:** 7.
F-5: 90. **-A:** 64, (plus 10 in store); **-B:** 8, plus 1 in store,

NF-5A: 11, **NF-5B:** 1. **RF-5A:** 6, (plus 3 in store).
F-4: 64. **-E:** 54, plus 19 in store; **RF-4E:**10 (recce),
plus 10 in store.
F-16: 35. **-C:** 29 (FGA/ftr), plus 3 in store; **-D:** 6.
Mirage F-1: **CG:** 26 (ftr), plus 3 in store.
Mirage 2000: 36. **-EG:** 32 plus 2 in store (ftr); **BG:** 4*
(trg).
F104G: 20 in store, **RF-104G:** 6 in store, **TF-104G:** 4 in
store.
HU-16B: 5 (MR). **C-47:** 4 (tpt). **C-130H:** 11 (tpt). **C-
130B:** 5 (tpt). **CL-215:** 11 (tpt, fire-fighting). **Do-28:**
12 (lt tpt). *Gulfstream* **I:** 1 (VIP tpt). **T-2:** 36* (trg). **T-
33A:** 30 (liaison). **T-37B/C:** 29 (trg). **T-41D:** 19 (trg).
YS-11-200: 6 (tpt).
HELICOPTERS:
AB-205A: 14 (tpt). **AB-212:** 3 (VIP, tpt). **Bell 47G:** 5
(liaison).
MISSILES:
ASM: AGM-12 *Bullpup*, AGM-65 *Maverick*.
AAM: AIM-7 *Sparrow*, AIM-9 *Sidewinder*, R-550
Magic.
SAM: 36 *Nike Hercules*, 40 *Sparrow*.

FORCES ABROAD:
CYPRUS: 2,250. 2 inf bn and officers/NCO
seconded to Greek-Cypriot forces.
UN AND PEACEKEEPING
IRAQ/KUWAIT (UNIKOM): 6 Observers.
WESTERN SAHARA (MINURSO): 1 Observer.
SOMALIA (UNOSOM II): 82.

PARAMILITARY:
GENDARMERIE: 26,500; MOWAG *Roland*, 15
UR-416 APC, 6 NH-300 hel.
COAST GUARD AND CUSTOMS: 4,000;
some 100 patrol craft, 2 Cessna *Cutlass*, 2 TB-20
Trinidad ac.

FOREIGN FORCES:
US: 850. Army (50); Navy (200) facilities at Soudha
Bay. Air (600) 2 air base gp.

ICELAND			
GDP	1991:	K 382.87bn ($6.49bn)	
	1992:	K 384.82bn ($6.69bn)	
Growth	1991:	1.5%	1992: -3.3%
Inflation	1991:	6.8%	1992: 4.0%
Debt	1991:	$3.52bn	
$1 = K	1990:	58.284	1991: 58.996
	1992:	57.546	1993: 64.487
K = Kronur			

Population: 263,400

	13–17	18–22	23–32
Men	11,000	11,000	22,000
Women	10,200	10,200	21,500

ARMED FORCES: None.

PARAMILITARY: 130
COAST GUARD: 130:
BASE: Reykjavik
PATROL CRAFT: 4:
3 PCO: 2 *Aegir* with hel, 1 *Odinn* with hel deck;
1 PCI⟨.
AVIATION: 1 F-27 ac, 1 SA-360.

FOREIGN FORCES:
NATO: Island Commander Iceland (ISCOMICE,
responsible to CINCEASTLANT).
US:
NAVY: 1,800: **MR:** 1 sqn with 9 P-3C.
AIR FORCE: 1,200: 1 sqn with 18 F-15C/D, 1
Comd/Control sqn with 2 E-3 ac, 1 SAR sqn with 4
HH-3.
NETHERLANDS:
NAVY: 30: 1 P-3C.

ITALY

GDP	1991:	L 1,426,580.0bn ($1,149.91bn)	
	1992:	L 1,507,190.0bn ($1,222.48bn)	
Growth	1991: 1.4%	1992: 0.9%	
Inflation	1991: 6.4%	1992: 5.4%	
Publ Debt	1992: 108.1%		
Def bdgt[a]	1992:	L 24,517.0bn ($19.89bn)	
	1993:	L 26,560.0bn ($16.50bn)	
NATO defn	1992:	L 30,250.0bn ($24.55bn)	
$1 = L	1990: 1,198.1	1991: 1,240.6	
	1992: 1,232.4	1993: 1,548.7	

L = lire
[a] Excl budget for Carabinieri.

Population: 57,831,000

	13–17	18–22	23–32
Men	1,881,600	2,191,400	4,664,800
Women	1,789,600	2,098,900	4,538,900

TOTAL ARMED FORCES:
ACTIVE: 344,600 (207,900 conscripts).
Terms of service: All services 12 months
RESERVES: 584,000. Army 520,000 (obligation
to age 45), immediate mob 240,000.
Navy 36,000 (to age 39 for men, variable for officers
to 73). Air 28,000 (to age 25 or 45 (specialists)).

ARMY: 223,300 (165,000 conscripts).
FIELD ARMY:
(Note: regt are normally of bn size).
3 Corps HQ (1 mtn):
1 with 1 mech, 1 armd bde, 1 armd cav bn,
1 arty, 1 AA regt, 2 avn sqn.
1 with 2 mech, 1 armd, 1 armd cav bde, 1 amph, 4
arty, 1 avn regt.
1 with 4 mtn bde, 1 avn, 1 armd cav, 2 hy arty, 1 AA
regt.
1 AD comd: 4 *HAWK* SAM, 3 AA regt.
1 avn gp (1 sqn AB-412, 2 sqn CH-47, 1 flt Do-228).
TERRITORIAL DEFENCE:
7 Military Regions.
8 indep mech, 1 AB bde (incl 1 SF bn, 1 avn sqn).
(Rapid Intervention Force (*FIR*) formed from 1
mech, 1 AB bde (see above), plus 1 Marine bn (see
Navy), 1 hel unit (Army), 1 air tpt unit (Air Force).
5 armd cav regt (1 recce).
1 inf regt.
4 engr regt.
5 avn units.
RESERVES: On mob: 1 armd, 1 mech, 1 mtn bde.
EQUIPMENT:
MBT: 1,210: 300 M-60A1, 910 *Leopard*.
RECCE: 150 *Centauro* B-1.
APC: 3,683: 1,821 M-113, 1,793 VCC1/-2, 44 Fiat
6614, 25 LVTP-7.
TOTAL ARTY: 2, 022.
TOWED ARTY: 944: 105mm: 357 Model 56 pack;
155mm: 164 FH-70, 423 M-114.
SP ARTY: 286: 155mm: 260 M-109G/-L; 203mm: 26
M-110A2.
MRL: 227mm: 18 MLRS.
MORTARS: 120mm: 774. Plus 81mm: 1,205.
ATGW: 432 *TOW* (incl 270 SP), 1,000 *Milan*.
RL: 1,000 *APILAS*.
RCL: 80mm: 720 *Folgore*.
AD GUNS: 25mm: 154 SIDAM SP; 40mm: 252.
SAM: 126 *HAWK*, 145 *Stinger*.
AIRCRAFT: 62: 47 SM-1019, 12 O-1E (target
acquisition/utility), 3 Do-228.
HELICOPTERS: 29 A-109, 12 A-129, 91 AB-205A,
136 AB-206 (observation), 14 AB-212, 23 AB-412,
30 CH-47C.

NAVY: 43,600 incl 1,500 air arm, 600 special
forces and 1,100 marines; (16,400 conscripts).
Commands: 1 Fleet Commander CINCNAV (also
NATO COMEDCENT): 6 Area Commands; Upper
Tyrrhenian; Adriatic; Lower Tyrrhenian; Ionian and
Strait of Otranto; Sicily and Sardinia.
BASES: La Spezia (HQ), Taranto (HQ), Ancona
(HQ), Brindisi, Augusta, Messina (HQ), La
Maddalena (HQ), Cagliari, Naples (HQ), Venice
(HQ).
SUBMARINES: 8:
2 *Pelosi* (imp *Sauro*) with Type 184 HWT.
4 *Sauro* with Type 184 HWT (includes 2 non-op,
  undergoing modernisation).
2 *Toti* SSC with Type 184 HWT.
PRINCIPAL SURFACE COMBATANTS: 28:
CARRIER: 1:
1 *G. Garibaldi* CVV with 16 SH-3 *Sea King* hel,
  4 *Teseo* SSM, 2 x 3 ASTT (has capability to
  operate V/STOL ac, acquisition in progress).

CRUISERS: 1:
1 *Vittorio Veneto* CGH with 1 x 2 SM-1 ER SAM, 6 AB-212 ASW hel (Mk 46 LWT); plus 4 *Teseo* SSM, 2 x 3 ASTT.
DESTROYERS: 4:
2 *Luigi Durand de la Penne* (ex-*Animoso*) DDGH with 1 x SM-1 MR SAM, 2 x 4 *Teseo* SSM, plus 2 x AB-312 hel, 1 x 127mm gun, 2 x 3 ASTT (incl 1 commissioning Summer 1993).
2 *Audace* DDGH, with 1 x SM-1 MR SAM, 4 *Teseo* SSM, plus 2 x AB-212 hel, 1 x 127mm gun, 2 x 3 ASTT.
FRIGATES: 22:
8 *Maestrale* FFH with 2 AB-212 hel, 2 x 533mm DP TT; plus 4 *Teseo* SSM, 1 x 127mm gun.
4 *Lupo* FFH with 1 AB-212 hel, 2 x 3 ASTT; plus 8 *Teseo* SSM, 1 x 127mm gun. (Note: 2 of 4 additional *Lupo* FF built for Iraq may be taken into service during 1993.)
1 *Alpino* FFH with 1 AB-212 hel, 2 x 3 ASTT, 1 x ASW mor.
8 *Minerva* FF with 2 x 3 ASTT.
1 *De Cristofaro* FF with 2 x 3 ASTT, 1 ASW mor (excl 1 paying off August 1993).
ADDITIONAL IN STORE: 1 CGH, 3 FF.
PATROL AND COASTAL COMBATANTS: 18:
CORVETTES: 2
2 *Albatros* with 2 x 3 ASTT.
MISSILE CRAFT: 6 *Sparviero* PHM with 2 *Teseo* SSM.
PATROL OFFSHORE: 6: 4 *Cassiopea* with 1 AB-212 hel.
2 *Storione* (US *Aggressive*) ex-MSO.
COASTAL: 4 *Bambu* (ex-MSC) PCC assigned MFO.
MINE WARFARE: 12:
MCMV: 12:
7 *Lerici* MHC.
5 *Castagno* (US *Adjutant*) MHC.
AMPHIBIOUS: 2:
2 *San Giorgio* LPD: capacity 350 tps, 30 trucks, 2 SH-3D or CH-47 hel, 7 craft.
Plus some 7 craft: about 3 LCU, 3 LCM and 1 LCVP.
SUPPORT AND MISCELLANEOUS: 42:
2 *Stromboli* AO, 8 tugs, 9 coastal tugs, 6 water tankers, 4 trials, 2 trg, 3 AGOR, 6 tpt, 2 salvage.
SPECIAL FORCES (600) (*Comando Subacquei Incursori* – COMSUBIN):
6 gp; 2 assigned aslt swimmer craft; 2 raiding ops; 1 underwater ops; 1 SF; 1 school; 1 research.
MARINES (San Marco gp) (800):
1 bn gp.
1 trg gp.
1 log gp.
EQUIPMENT: 30 VCC-1, 10 LVTP-7 APC, 16 81mm mor, 8 106mm RCL, 6 *Milan* ATGW.

NAVAL AIR ARM (1,500); 2 cbt ac, 30 armed hel.
FGA: 2* TAV-8B.
ASW: 5 hel sqn with 30 SH-3D, 59 AB-212.
ASM: *Marte* Mk 2.

AIR FORCE: 77,700 (26,500 conscripts).
FGA: 9 F FGA:
4 with *Tornado*;
1 with F-104 ASA.
1 with G-91Y.
3 with AMX.
CAS: 1 sqn:
1 lt attack with MB-339.
FIGHTER: 6 sqn with F-104 ASA.
RECCE: 1 sqn with AMX.
MR: 2 sqn with *Atlantic* (Navy-assigned).
EW: 1 ECM/recce sqn with G-222VS, PD-808.
CALIBRATION: 1 navigation-aid calibration sqn with G-222RM, PD-808, MB-339.
TRANSPORT: 3 sqn: 2 with G-222; 1 with C-130H.
TANKER: 1 sqn with 707-320.
COMMUNICATIONS: 2 sqn with *Gulfstream* III, *Falcon* 50, DC-9 ac; SH-3D hel.
TRAINING: 1 OCU with TF-104G;
1 det (Cottesmore, UK) with *Tornado*;
5 sqn with G-91T, MB-339A, SF-260M ac, NH-500 hel.
SAR: 1 sqn and 3 det with HH-3F.
6 det with AB-212.
AD: 8 SAM gp with *Nike Hercules*;
12 SAM bty with *Spada*.
EQUIPMENT: 385 cbt ac (plus 123 store), no armed hel.
AIRCRAFT:
***Tornado*:** 70 (66 FGA, 4* in tri-national sqn), plus 22 in store.
F-104: 120. **-ASA:** 99 (73 AWX, 26 FGA), plus 26 FGA, 18 AWX in store; **-G:** 8, **TF104G:** 13 plus 9 in store.
AMX: 72. 69 (FGA); **-T:** 3* (trg).
G-91: 58. **-Y:** 21 (FGA), plus 34 in store; **-T:** 37* (trg); plus 7 in store.
MB-339: 86 (15 tac, 62 (incl 50*) trg, 9 calibration), plus 7 in store.
***Atlantic*:** 18 (MR).
MB-326: 56 (liaison).
Boeing-707-320: 2 (tkr/tpt). **C-130H:** 12 (tpt). **G-222:** 42 (38 tpt, 4 calibration), plus **-GE:** 1 (ECM). **DC9-32:** 2 (VIP). ***Gulfstream* III:** 2 (VIP). ***Falcon* 50:** 4 (VIP). **P-166:** 14: (**-M:** 8, **-DL3:** 6 liaison and trg). **PD-808:** 18 (ECM, calibration, VIP tpt); **SF-260M:** 39 (trg). **SIAI-208:** 36 (liaison).
HELICOPTERS:
HH-3F: 28 (SAR).
SH-3D: 2 (liaison).
AB-212: 36 (SAR).
AB-47G: 6 (trg).
NH-500D: 50 (trg).
MISSILES:
ASM: AS-20, *Kormoran*, AGM-88 HARM.
AAM: AIM-7E *Sparrow*, AIM-9B/L *Sidewinder*, *Aspide*.
SAM: 96 *Nike Hercules*, 7 bty *Spada*, ASPIDE.

FORCES ABROAD:
UN AND PEACEKEEPING:
CAMBODIA (UNTAC): 75 civ pol.

EGYPT (MFO): 82; 3 PCC.
EL SALVADOR (ONUSAL): 10 civ. pol.
INDIA/PAKISTAN (UNMOGIP): 5 Observers.
IRAQ (UNSCOM): 1 Observer.
IRAQ/KUWAIT (UNIKOM): 6 Observers.
LEBANON (UNIFIL): 49. Hel unit.
MIDDLE EAST (UNTSO): 8 Observers.
MOZAMBIQUE (ONUMOZ): 1,042: 1 inf bn, 1 avn unit.
SOMALIA (UNOSOM II): 2,500: 1 AB bde, ac 2 G-222, hel 3 HH-3F.
WESTERN SAHARA (MINURSO): 6 Observers.

PARAMILITARY:
CARABINIERI (Ministry of Defence) 111,800: Territorial: 5 bde, 17 regt, 96 gp. Trg: 1 bde. Mobile def: 2 bde, 1 cav regt, 1 special ops gp, 13 mobile bn, 1 AB bn, avn and naval units.
EQUIPMENT: 48 Fiat 6616 armd cars; 40 VCC2, 91 M-113 APC; 24 A-109, 4 AB-205, 40 AB-206, 17 AB-412 hel.
PUBLIC SECURITY GUARD (Ministry of Interior): 80,400: 11 mobile units; 40 Fiat 6614 APC, 3 P-64B, 5 P-68 ac; 12 A-109, 20 AB-206, 9 AB-212 hel.
FINANCE GUARDS (Treasury Department): 64,100; 14 Zones, 20 Legions, 128 Gps; 15 A-109, 66 Breda-Nardi NH-500M/MC/MD hel; 5 P-166-DL3 ac; 3 PCI, 65 ; plus about 300 boats.
HARBOUR CONTROL (*Capitanerie di Porto*) (Subordinated to Navy in emergencies): Some 12 PCI , 130+ boats.

FOREIGN FORCES:
NATO:
HQ Allied Forces Southern Europe (AFSOUTH).
HQ 5 Allied Tactical Air Force (5 ATAF).
US: 13,000. Army (3,600); 1 AB bn gp; Navy (6,000); Air (3,400); 1 ftr wing (ac on det only).
OPERATION DENY FLIGHT:
FRANCE: 10 *Mirage* 2000C, 4 *Mirage* F1-CR, 1 DHC.
GERMANY: 1 C-160.
NETHERLANDS: 18 F-16.
TURKEY: 18 F-16.
UNITED KINGDOM: 8 *Tornado* F-3, 2 VC-10 (tpt), 3 E-3D *Sentry*, 2 *Nimrod* MPA ac.
OPERATION DISCIPLINED GUARD:
FRANCE: 8 *Jaguar*.
NETHERLANDS: 12 F-16.
UNITED KINGDOM: 12 *Jaguar*.
UNITED STATES: 12 A-10; 14 F/A-18; 4 AC-130.

LUXEMBOURG

GDP	1991:	fr 318.80bn ($9.34bn)		
	1992:	fr 339.30bn ($10.55bn)		
Growth	1991:	3.7%	1992:	2.4%
Inflation	1991:	3.1%	1992:	3.2%
Publ Debt	1992:	3.7%		
Def bdgt	1992:	fr 3.08bn ($95.93m)		
	1993:	fr 3.36bn ($98.94m)		
NATO defn	1991:	fr 3.61bn ($105.72m)		
NATO defn	1992:	fr 3.88bn ($120.75m)		
$1 = fr	1990:	33.418	1991:	34.148
	1992:	32.150	1993:	34.000

fr = Luxembourg francs

Population: 381,600 (104,000 foreign citizens)

	13–17	18–22	23–32
Men	11,000	11,700	28,500
Women	10,500	11,200	29,100

TOTAL ARMED FORCES:
ACTIVE: 800.

ARMY: 800.
1 lt inf bn.
EQUIPMENT:
APC: 5 *Commando*.
MORTARS: 81mm: 6.
ATGW: *TOW* some 6 SP (*Hummer*).
RL: *LAW*.

AIR FORCE: (None, but for legal purposes NATO's E-3A AEW ac have Luxembourg registration.)
1 sqn with 18 E-3A *Sentry* (NATO Standard), 2 Boeing 707 (trg).

FORCES ABROAD:
UN AND PEACEKEEPING:
CROATIA (UNPROFOR 1): 35.

PARAMILITARY:
GENDARMERIE: 560.

NETHERLANDS

GDP	1991:	gld 543.60bn ($290.74bn)		
	1992:	gld 570.79bn ($324.60bn)		
Growth	1991:	2.3%	1992:	1.2%
Inflation	1991:	3.9%	1992:	3.7%
Debt	1990:	$75.00bn		
Def bdgt	1992:	gld 14.09bn ($8.01bn)		
	1993:	gld 13.60bn ($7.34bn)		
NATO defn	1992:	gld 14.55bn ($8.28bn)		
$1 = gld	1990:	1.821	1991:	1.870
	1992:	1.759	1993:	1.852

gld = guilders

Population: 15,237,000

	13–17	18–22	23–32
Men	466,000	542,600	1,281,500
Women	446,000	518,700	1,222,300

TOTAL ARMED FORCES:
ACTIVE: 74,600 (incl 3,600 Royal Military Constabulary, 800 Inter-Service Organisation); 2,600 women; 30,050 conscripts.
Terms of service: Army and Air Force 12 months, Navy 12–15 months.
RESERVES: 150,300 (men to age 35, NCO to 40, officers to 45). Army 131,300 (some – at the end of their conscription period – on short leave, immediate recall), Navy some 9,000 (7,000 on immediate recall); Air Force 10,000 (immediate recall).

ARMY: 43,300 (24,700 conscripts).
1 Corps HQ, 3 mech div HQ.
4 mech inf bde.
1 lt bde.
1 airmobile bde.
2 fd arty, 1 AD gp.
1 army avn wing.
Summary of Combat Arm Units:
12 mech inf bn.	11 arty bn.
9 tk bn.	3 AD bn.
4 recce bn.	3 hel sqn (Air Force-manned).

RESERVES: cadre bde and corps tps completed by call-up of reservists.
Territorial Command (34,400 on mob): 4 bn, spt units, could be mob for territorial defence.
Home Guard: 3 sectors; inf weapons.
EQUIPMENT:
MBT: 743 (incl 163 in store): 298 *Leopard* 1A4, 445 *Leopard* 2.
AIFV: 984 (incl 246 in store): 718 YPR-765, 266 M-113C/-R all with 25mm.
APC: 1,759: 372 M-113, 1,120 YPR-765, 267 YP-408 (in store).
TOTAL ARTY: 653.
TOWED ARTY: 165: 105mm: 42 M-101 (in store); 155mm: 123 M-114.
SP ARTY: 298: 155mm: 222 M-109A3; 203mm: 76 M-110 (in store).
MRL: 227mm: 22 MLRS.
MORTARS: 107mm: 23 M-30 (in store); 120mm: 145 (incl 10 in store).
SSM: 7 *Lance* launchers (in store).
ATGW: 753 (incl 135 in store): 427 *Dragon*, 326 (incl 302 YPR-765) *TOW*.
RL: 84mm: *Carl Gustav*.
RCL: 106mm: 185 M-40 (in store).
AD GUNS: 35mm: 95 *Gepard* SP; 40mm: 131 L/70 towed.
SAM: 474 *Stinger*.
HELICOPTERS: 58 SA-316 (to be replaced), 28 Bo-105 (Air Force-manned).
MARINE: 1 tk tpt, 3 coastal, 15 river patrol boats.

NAVY: 14,900, incl naval air arm (830) and marines (3,250) (1,650 conscripts).
BASES: Netherlands: Den Helder (HQ); Vlissingen. Overseas: Willemstad (Curaçao), Oranjestad (Aruba).
SUBMARINES: 5:
3 *Zeeleeuw* with Mk 48 HWT; plus *Harpoon* USGW.
2 *Zwaardvis* with Mk 37 HWT.
PRINCIPAL SURFACE COMBATANTS: 17:
DESTROYERS: 4 DDG (NL desig = FFG):
2 *Tromp* with 1 SM-1 MR SAM; plus 2 x 4 *Harpoon* SSM, 1 x 2 120mm guns, 1 *Lynx* hel (ASW/OTHT), 2 x 3 ASTT (Mk 46 LWT).
2 *Van Heemskerck* with 1 SM-1 MR SAM; plus 2 x 4 *Harpoon*, 2 x 2 ASTT.
FRIGATES: 13:
4 *Karel Doorman* FF with 2 x 4 *Harpoon* SSM, plus 2 x 2 ASTT; 1 *Lynx* (ASW/OTHT) hel.
9 *Kortenaer* FF with 2 *Lynx* (ASW/OTHT) hel, 2 x 2 ASTT; plus 2 x 4 *Harpoon*.
MINE WARFARE: 21:
MINELAYERS: none, but *Mercuur*, listed under spt and misc, has capability.
MINE COUNTERMEASURES: 21:
15 *Alkmaar* (tripartite) MHC (6 in reserve).
6 *Dokkum* MSC.
AMPHIBIOUS: craft only; about 12 LCA.
SUPPORT AND MISCELLANEOUS: 13:
2 *Poolster* AOR (1–3 *Lynx* hel), 3 survey, 1 *Mercuur* torpedo tender, 2 trg, 1 aux, 4 *Cerberus* div spt.

NAVAL AIR ARM: (830);
MR: 1 sqn with F-27M (see Air Force).
MR/ASW: 2 sqn with P-3C.
ASW/SAR: 2 sqn with *Lynx* hel.
EQUIPMENT: 13 cbt ac, 22 armed hel.
AIRCRAFT:
P-3C: 13 (MR).
HELICOPTERS:
Lynx: 22 (ASW, SAR).

MARINES: (3,250).
3 marine bn (1 cadre). 1 spt bn.
RESERVE: 1 marine bn .
EQUIPMENT:
MORTARS: 120mm: 14.

AIR FORCE: 12,000 (3,300 conscripts).
FIGHTER\FGA: 8 sqn with F-16A/B (1 sqn is tactical trg, evaluation and standardisation sqn).
FIGHTER/RECCE: 1 sqn with F-16A.
MR: 2 F-27M (assigned to Navy).
TRANSPORT: 1 sqn with F-27.
TRAINING: 1 sqn with PC-7.
SAR: 1 flt with SA-316.
AD: 8 bty with *HAWK* SAM (4 in Ge).
4 bty with *Patriot* SAM (in Ge).
EQUIPMENT: 185 cbt ac, no armed hel.
AIRCRAFT:
F-16: 185. **-A:** 150 (123 FGA/ftr, 19 recce, 8* trg); **-B:** 35.

F-27: 14 (12 tpt, 2 MR).
PC-7: 10 (trg).
HELICOPTERS:
SA-316: 4 (SAR) to be replaced by 3 AB-412 SP.
MISSILES:
AAM: AIM-9/L/N *Sidewinder*.
SAM: 48 *HAWK*, 20 *Patriot*, 100 *Stinger*.
AD: GUNS: 25 VL 4/41 *Flycatcher* radar, 75 L/70 40mm systems.

FORCES ABROAD:
GERMANY: 3,700. 1 lt bde (1 armd inf, 1 tk bn), 1 recce bn, 1 engr bn, spt elm, 4 *HAWK*, 4 *Patriot* bty.
ICELAND: Navy: 30: 1 P-3C.
NETHERLANDS ANTILLES: 1 frigate, 1 amph cbt det, 1 MR det with 2 F-27MPA ac.
UN AND PEACEKEEPING:
ANGOLA (UNAVEM II): 6 Observers, 6 civ pol.
CAMBODIA (UNTAC): 807, 1 marine bn, 1 engr unit; 4 SA-316 hel, 2 civ pol.
CROATIA (UNPROFOR I): 925: 1 sigs, 1 tpt (Be/Nl) bn, 38 Observers.
EGYPT (MFO): 105: 5 sigs det.
ITALY *(Deny Flight)*: 18 F-16.
(Disciplined Guard): 12 F-16.
MIDDLE EAST (UNTSO): 15 Observers.

PARAMILITARY:
ROYAL MILITARY CONSTABULARY:
(*Koninklijke Marechaussee*): 3,600 (400 conscripts); 3 'div' comprising 10 districts with 72 'bde'.

FOREIGN FORCES:
NATO:
HQ Allied Forces Central Europe (AFCENT).
US: 2,700. Army 900; Air 1,800, 1 tac ftr gp.

NORWAY

GDP	1991:	kr 686.73bn ($105.93bn)	
	1992:	kr 721.07bn ($116.03bn)	
Growth	1991:	1.9%	1992: 2.0%
Inflation	1991:	3.4%	1992: 2.4%
Publ Debt	1992:	43.3%	
Def bdgt	1992:	kr 23.16bn ($3.73bn)	
	1993:	kr 22.72bn ($3.28bn)	
NATO defn	1992:	kr 23.76bn ($3.82bn)	
$1 = kr	1990:	6.2597	1991: 6.4829
	1992:	6.2145	1993: 6.9282
kr = kroner			

Population: 4,215,600

	13–17	18–22	23–32
Men	144,000	161,300	333,600
Women	137,000	153,000	315,500

TOTAL ARMED FORCES:
ACTIVE: some 29,400 (18,800 conscripts) incl 400 Joint Services org, 500 Home Guard permanent staff.
Terms of service: Army, Navy coast arty, Air Force, 12 months, plus 4 to 5 refresher trg periods; Navy 15 months.
RESERVES: 298,000 mobilisable in 24–72 hours; obligation to 44 (conscripts remain with fd army units to age 35; officers to age 55; regulars: 60).
Army: 159,000; Navy: 26,000; Air: 28,000.
Home Guard: War some 85,000.
Second-line reserves: 60,000 (all services).

ARMY: 12,900 (10,000 conscripts).
2 Commands, 5 district comd, 1 div, 15 subordinate comd.
STANDING FORCES:
North Norway:
1 reinforced mech bde: 2 inf, fd arty, 1 engr bn, 1 AD bty, spt units.
1 border garrison bn.
1 reinforced inf bn task force: inf, fd arty, AD bty.
South Norway:
1 inf bn (Royal Guard).
Indep units.
RESERVES: cadre units for mob: 1 div HQ, 2 mech, 12 lt inf bde, 22 inf, 6 arty bn; 60 indep inf coy, tk sqn, arty bty, engr coy, sigs units, spt.
LAND HOME GUARD: 80,000
18 districts each divided into 2–6 sub-districts and some 470 sub-units (pl).
EQUIPMENT:
MBT: 261: 144 *Leopard* 1, 55 M-48A5, 62 NM-116 (M-24/90).
AIFV: 53 NM-135 (M-113/20mm).
APC: 287 M-113.
TOTAL ARTY: 527.
TOWED ARTY: 105mm: 228 M-101; 155mm: 48 M-114.
SP ARTY: 155mm: 126 M-109A3GN SP.
MORTARS: 107mm: 97 M-30F1, 28 M-106A1 SP. Plus 456 81mm (12 SP).
ATGW: 292 *TOW*-1/-2, 97 NM-142 (M-113/*TOW*-2).
RCL: 84mm: 2,380 *Carl Gustav*.
AD GUNS: 20mm: 216 Rh-202.
SAM: 300 RBS-70.

NAVY: 8,300, incl 1,400 coastal artillery (4,500 conscripts).
8 Naval/Coast defence districts under 2 commands.
BASES: Horten, Haakonsvern (Bergen), Ramsund, Olavsvern (Tromsø).
SUBMARINES: 12:
6 *Ula* SS with Ge *Seeal* DM2A3 HWT.
6 *Kobben* SSC (with Swe T-612) HWT.
FRIGATES: 5 *Oslo* with 2 x 3 ASTT, 1 x 6 *Terne* ASW RL; plus 6 x *Penguin* 2 SSM.
PATROL AND COASTAL COMBATANTS: 30:
MISSILE CRAFT: 30:
14 *Hauk* PFM with 6 x *Penguin* 2, 2 x 533mm TT.

10 *Storm* PFM with 6 x *Penguin* 2.
6 *Snøgg* PFM with 4 x *Penguin* 2, 4 x 533mm TT.
MINE WARFARE: 8:
MINELAYERS: 2:
2 *Vidar*, coastal (300–400 mines).
Note: Amph craft also fitted for minelaying.
MINE COUNTERMEASURES: 6:
3 *Sauda* MSC, 1 *Tana* MHC.
2 diver spt.
AMPHIBIOUS: craft only; 5 LCT
SUPPORT AND MISCELLANEOUS: 2:
1 *Horten* sub/patrol craft depot ship.
1 Royal Yacht.
ADDITIONAL IN STORE: 1 *Sauda* MSC.
NAVAL HOME GUARD: 7,000. On mob assigned to
8 naval/coast defence comd.
2 LCT, some 400 fishing craft.
COAST DEFENCE: 26 fortresses:
75mm; 105mm; 120mm; 127mm; 150mm guns.
7 cable mine and 4 torpedo bty.

AIR FORCE: 8,200 (4,300 conscripts).
FGA: 4 sqn with F-16.
FIGHTER: 1 trg sqn with F-5A/B.
MR: 1 sqn with P-3C/N *Orion* (2 assigned to coast
guard).
TRANSPORT: 3 sqn:
1 with C-130.
1 with *Falcon* 20 (tpt, EW).
1 with DHC-6.
TRAINING: MFI-15.
SAR: 1 sqn with *Sea King* Mk 43.
COAST GUARD: 1 sqn with *Lynx* Mk 86.
TAC HEL: 2 sqn:
2 with Bell 412 SP.
AD: 22 lt AA arty bty.
(Being delivered: 6 bty NOAH SAM, 10 bty RB-70).
EQUIPMENT: 86 cbt ac (incl 4 MR) no armed hel.
AIRCRAFT:
F-5A/B: 22 (ftr/trg).
F-16: 60. **-A:** 48 (FGA), **-B:** 12 (FGA).
P-3: -C: 4 (MR); **-N:** 2 (coast guard).
C-130H: 6 (tpt).
Falcon **20C:** 3 (EW/tpt).
DHC-6: 3 (tpt); **MFI-15:** 18 (trg).
HELICOPTERS:
Bell 412 SP: 18 (tpt). *Lynx* **Mk 86:** 6 (coast guard).
Sea King **Mk 43:** 10 (SAR).
MISSILES:
ASM: *Penguin* Mk-3.
AAM: AIM-9L/N *Sidewinder*.
ADGUNS: 40mm: 64 L/70.
SAM: NOAH (Norwegian-adapted *HAWK*).
ANTI-AIRCRAFT HOME GUARD (on mob
under comd of Air Force): 3,000; 2 bn (9 bty) lt AA;
some Rh-202 20mm, 72 L/60 40mm guns (being
replaced by Rh-202).

FORCES ABROAD:
UN AND PEACEKEEPING:
ANGOLA (UNAVEM II): 5 Observers.

BOSNIA (UNPROFOR II): 35 hel unit.
CAMBODIA (UNTAC): 20 civ pol.
CROATIA (UNPROFOR I): 89 plus 24 Observers,
30 civ pol.
EGYPT (MFO): 3 Staff Officers.
EL SALVADOR (ONUSAL): 3 civ pol.
INDIA/PAKISTAN (UNMOGIP): 8 Observers.
IRAQ/KUWAIT (UNIKOM): 8 Observers, medical
unit (19).
LEBANON (UNIFIL): 866; 1 inf bn, 1 service coy,
plus HQ personnel.
MACEDONIA (UNPROFOR M): 139.
MIDDLE EAST (UNTSO): 15 Observers.
SOMALIA (UNOSOM II): 74.

PARAMILITARY:
COAST GUARD: 680:
PATROL OFFSHORE: 13:
3 *Nordkapp* with 1 x *Lynx* hel (SAR/recce), 2 x 3
ASTT, fitted for 6 *Penguin* Mk 2 SSM.
1 *Nornen*, 2 *Farm*, 7 chartered.
AIRCRAFT: 2 P-3N *Orion* ac, 6 *Lynx* hel (Air Force-
manned).

FOREIGN FORCES:
NATO:
HQ Allied Forces Northern Europe (HQ
AFNORTH).
US: Prepositioned eqpt for 1 MEB.
CANADA: Prepositioned 6 arty, 14 ACV.

PORTUGAL

GDP	1991:	esc 9,553.40bn ($66.12bn)	
	1992:	esc 11,268.9bn ($83.47bn)	
Growth	1991:	2.7%	1992: 1.3%
Inflation	1991:	11.4%	1992: 8.9%
Debt	1991:	$35.00bn	
Def bdgt	1992:	esc 224.60bn ($1.66bn)	
	1993:	esc 230.20bn ($1.51bn)	
NATO defn	1992:	esc 325.66bn ($2.41bn)	
FMA[a]	1993:	$91.0m	
$1 = esc	1990:	142.55	1991: 144.48
1992:	135.000		1993: 152.500
esc = escudos			

Population: 10,472,800

	13–17	18–22	23–32
Men	411,400	436,800	861,100
Women	393,300	421,000	847,500

TOTAL ARMED FORCES:
ACTIVE: 50,700 (17,600 conscripts).
Terms of service: Army: 4–8 months, Navy and Air
Force: 4–18 months.
RESERVES: 210,000 (all services) (obligation: to
age 35).

ARMY: 27,200 (15,000 conscripts).
5 Territorial Commands (1 mil governance, 2 mil regions, 2 mil zones).
1 composite bde (1 mech, 2 mot inf, 1 tk, 1 fd arty bn).
3 inf bde.
1 AB bde.
1 lt inf bde.
3 cav regt.
9 inf regt.
2 fd, 1 AD, 1 coast arty regt.
2 engr regt.

EQUIPMENT:
MBT: 209+: 43 M-47, 86 M-48A5, 80 M-60A3 (being delivered).
RECCE: 8 *Saladin*, 40 AML-60, 15 V-150, 21 EBR-75, 8 ULTRAV M-11, 30 *Ferret* Mk 4.
APC: 357: 276 M-113, 79 V-200 *Chaimite*, 2 EBR.
TOTAL ARTY: 305 incl:
TOWED ARTY: 142: 105mm: 54 M-101, 24 M-56; 140mm: 24 5.5-in; 155mm: 40 M-114A1.
SP ARTY: 155mm: 6 M-109A2.
MORTARS: 157: 107mm: 57 M-30 (incl 14 SP); 120mm: 100 Tampella.
COAST ARTY: 150mm: 15; 152mm: 6; 234mm: 6.
ATGW: 51 *TOW* (incl 18 M-113, 4 M-901), 65 *Milan* (incl 6 ULTRAV M-11).
RCL: 240: 90mm: 112; 106mm: 128 M-40.
AD GUNS: 105 incl 20mm: M-163A1 *Vulcan* SP; 40mm: L/60.
SAM: 12 *Blowpipe*, 5 *Chaparral*.

DEPLOYMENT:
Azores and Madeira: 2,000. 3 inf regt, 2 coast arty bn, 2 AA bty.

NAVY: 12,500 incl 1,850 marines (800 conscripts)
1 Naval area Cmd, with 5 Subordinate zone Cmds. (Azores, Madeira, North Continental, Centre Continental and South Continental).
BASES: Lisbon (Alfeite), Portimão (HQ Continental comd), Ponta Delgada (HQ Azores), Funchal (HQ Madeira).
SUBMARINES: 3:
3 *Albacora* (Fr *Daphné*) SS with EL-5 HWT.
FRIGATES: 11:
3 *Vasco Da Gama* (Meko 200) with 2 x 3 ASTT (US Mk-46), plus 2 x 4 *Harpoon* SSM, 1 x 8 *Sea Sparrow* SAM, 1 x 100mm gun (2 x *Super Lynx* hel on order).
4 *Commandante João Belo* (Fr *Cdt Rivière*) with 2 x 3 ASTT, 1 x 4 ASW mor; plus 3 x 100mm gun.
4 *Baptista de Andrade* with 2 x 3 ASTT; plus 1 x 100mm gun.
PATROL AND COASTAL COMBATANTS: 30:
PATROL OFFSHORE: 6:
6 *João Coutinho* PCO.
PATROL COASTAL: 10 *Cacine*.
INSHORE: 13 : 5 ARGOS , 8⟨.
RIVERINE: 1 *Rio Minho*⟨.

AMPHIBIOUS: Craft only; 3 LCU, 13 LCM
SUPPORT AND MISCELLANEOUS: 8:
1 AO, 1 AK, 3 AGHS, 3 trg.

MARINES: (1,850).
3 bn (2 lt inf, 1 police), spt units.
EQUIPMENT: *Chaimite* APC, mor.

AIR FORCE: 11,000 (1,800 conscripts) incl 1,700 AB tps listed with Army.
1 operational air command (COFA).
FGA: 3 sqn:
2 with A-7P;
1 with G-91R3/T1;
SURVEY: 1 sqn with C-212.
MR: 1 sqn with P-3P.
TRANSPORT: 4 sqn:
1 with C-130;
1 with C-212;
1 with *Falcon* 20 and *Falcon* 50.
1 with SA-316 hel.
SAR: 2 sqn, 1 with SA-330 hel, 1 with SA-330 hel and C-212.
LIAISON: 1 sqn with Reims-Cessna FTB-337G.
TRAINING: 2 sqn:
1 with T-38.
1 with SOCATA TB-30 *Epsilon*
EQUIPMENT: 99 cbt ac plus 6 MR ac, no attack hel.
AIRCRAFT:
Alpha Jet: 40 (FGA trg).
A-7: 37. **-7P:** 31 (FGA); **TA-7P:** 6* (trg).
G-91: 22. **-R3:** 18 (FGA); **-T3:** 4* (trg).
P-3P: 6 (MR).
C-130H: 6 (SAR, tpt).
C-212: 22. **-A:** 18 (12 tpt/SAR, 1 Nav trg, 2 ECM trg, 3 fisheries protection); **-B:** 4 (survey).
Cessna 337: 12 (liaison).
Falcon **20:** 1 (tpt, calibration).
Falcon **50:** 3 (tpt).
RF-10: 2 (trg). **T-37:** 23 (trg). **T-38:** 12 (trg). *Epsilon:* 16 (trg).
HELICOPTERS:
SA-330: 10 (SAR/tpt). **SA-316:** 21 (trg, utility).

FORCES ABROAD:
UN AND PEACEKEEPING:
CROATIA (UNPROFOR I): 9 plus 12 Observers, 35 civ pol.
MOZAMBIQUE (ONUMOZ): 282.

PARAMILITARY:
NATIONAL REPUBLICAN GUARD: 20,900;
Commando Mk III APC, 7 SA-313 hel .
PUBLIC SECURITY POLICE: 20,000.
BORDER SECURITY GUARD: 8,900.

FOREIGN FORCES:
NATO:
HQ IBERLANT area at Lisbon (Oeiras).

US: 1,500. Navy (400). Air (1,100) (incl Azores).
GERMANY: Air. OCU (Beja) with 18 *Alpha Jet*.

```
┌─────────────────────────────────────┐
│               SPAIN                  │
└─────────────────────────────────────┘
```

GDP   1991: pts 54,775.0bn ($527.14bn)
            1992: pts 59,212.0bn ($578.36bn)
Growth   1991: 2.4%   1992: 1.0%
Inflation   1991: 5.9%   1992: 6.0%
Publ Debt   1992: 51.9%
Def bdgt   1992: pts 785.88bn ($7.68bn)
            1993: pts 757.7bn ($6.5bn)
NATO defn   1991: pts 984.28bn ($9.61bn)
FMA   1990: $2.1m (US)
$1 = pts   1990: 101.93   1991: 103.91
            1992: 102.38   1993: 116.63

pts = pesetas

Population: 39,542,000

	13–17	18–22	23–32
Men	1,545,200	1,665,100	3,260,900
Women	1,456,300	1,577,600	3,147,200

TOTAL ARMED FORCES:
ACTIVE: 200,700 (133,500 conscripts (to be reduced), some 200 women) .
Terms of service: 9 months.
RESERVES: 498,000 (all services to age 38);
Immediate Reserve: 140,000:
Army 122,000; Navy 10,000; Air Force 8,000.

ARMY: 138,900 (100,000 conscripts);
8 Regional Operational Commands incl 2 Overseas:
1 armd div (1 armd inf, 1 mech bde, 1 arty, 1 lt armd cav, 1 engr regt).
1 mech div (2 mech bde, 1 arty, 1 lt armd cav, 1 engr regt).
1 mot div (2 mot, 1 mech bde, 1 arty, 1 lt armd cav, 1 engr regt).
2 mtn div (each 2 bde, 1 arty, 1 engr regt).
2 armd cav bde (each 1 armd, 2 lt armd cav, 1 arty regt).
1 air portable bde.
5 island garrison (bde).
6 special ops bn.
6 regional engr units.
General Reserve Force:
1 AB bde (3 bn).
1 AD comd (6 AD regt incl 1 *HAWK* SAM bn, 1 composite *Aspide* bn, 1 *Roland* bn).
1 fd arty comd (1 fd, 1 locating, 1 MRL regt).
1 engr comd (3 engr regt).
4 Spanish Legion regt (6,400):
  2 with 1 mech, 1 mot bn, 1 ATK coy;
  1 with 2 mot bn; 1 lt inf bn.
  1 with 1 mot bn, 1 special ops bn.
Army Aviation (FAMET) with:

1 attack hel bn.
1 tpt bn (1 med, 1 hy coy).
4 utility units.
1 Coast Arty Comd (6 mixed arty regt; 1 coast arty gp).
EQUIPMENT:
MBT: 1,148: 299 AMX-30 (60-EM2), 329 M-47E1, 46 M-47E2, 164 M-48A5E, 310 M-60 (50A1, 260A3).
RECCE: 340 BMR-VEC, 100 BMR-625.
APC: 2,000: 1,313 M-113, 687 BMR-600.
TOTAL ARTY: 1,291.
TOWED ARTY: 634: 105mm: 284 M-26, 170 M-56 pack; 122mm: 72 390-1; 155mm: 84 M-114; 203mm: 24 M-115.
SP ARTY: 180: 105mm: 48 M-108; 155mm: 96 M-109A1; 203mm: 36 M-110A2.
MRL: 140mm: 12 *Teruel*.
MORTARS: 120mm: 265 M-40, 192 M-106 SP, 8 BMR SP. Plus 81mm: 1,200 (incl 187 SP).
COAST ARTY: 6-in: 117; 305mm: 16; 381mm: 17.
ATGW: 443 *Milan*, 28 *HOT*.
RCL: 106mm: 654.
AD GUNS: 20mm: 329 GAI-BO1; 35mm: 92 GDF-002 twin; 40mm: 274 L/70.
SAM: 24 *Improved HAWK*, 18 *Roland*, 36 *Skyguard/Aspide*.
HELICOPTERS: 180 (28 attack): 3 HU-8, 51 HU-10B, 70 HA-15 (31 with 20mm guns, 28 with *HOT*, 9 trg), 6 HU-18, 14 HR-12B, 18 HT-21, 18 HT-17.

DEPLOYMENT:
CEUTA AND MELILLA: 10,000;
2 armd cav, 2 Spanish Legion, 2 mixed arty regt; 2 lt AD bn, 2 engr, 1 coast arty gp.
BALEARIC ISLANDS: 5,000;
1 inf regt: 2 mot bn. 1 arty regt: 2 fd arty, 1 coast arty; 1 engr bn, 1 special ops coy.
CANARY ISLANDS: 8,500;
2 inf bn, 1 Spanish Legion, 2 coast arty regt, 2 engr bn, 2 special ops coy.

NAVY: 32,000, incl 1,100 Naval Air, 7,000 Marines (18,000 conscripts).
5 Commands (Fleet, plus 4 Naval Zones: Cantabrian, Strait (of Gibraltar), Mediterranean and Canary (Islands)).
BASES: El Ferrol (La Coruña) (Cantabrian HQ), San Fernando (Cadiz) (Strait HQ), Rota (Cadiz) (Fleet HQ), Cartagena (Murcia) (Mediterranean HQ), Las Palmas (Canary Islands HQ), Palma de Mallorca and Mahón (Menorca).
SUBMARINES: 8:
4 *Galerna* (Fr *Agosta*) with F-17 and L-5 HWT plus possibly *Exocet* USGW.
4 *Delfin* (Fr *Daphné*) with F-17 and L-5 HWT.
PRINCIPAL SURFACE COMBATANTS: 16:
CARRIERS: 1 (CVV):
1 *Príncipe de Asturias* (16,200t). Air gp: typically 6 to 10 AV-8S/EAV-8B FGA, 4 to 6 SH-3D ASW hel, 2 SH-3D AEW hel, 2 utility hel.

FRIGATES: 15:
FFG: 9 (AAW/ASW):
4 *Santa Maria* (US *Perry*) with 1 x 1 SM-1 MR
SAM/*Harpoon* SSM launcher, 2 x SH-60B hel, 2
x 3 ASTT plus 1 x 76mm gun.
5 *Baleares* with 1 x 1 SM-1 MR SAM, 1 x 8
ASROC, 4 x 324mm and 2 x 484mm ASTT; plus 2
x 4 *Harpoon*, 1 x 127mm gun.
FF: 6 *Descubierta* with 2 x 3 ASTT, 1 x 2 ASW RL;
plus 2 x 2 *Harpoon* SSM.
PATROL AND COASTAL COMBATANTS: 28:
PATROL OFFSHORE: 5: 4 *Serviola*, 1 *Chilreu*.
COASTAL: 11:
1 *Cormoran*, 10 *Anaga* PCC.
INSHORE: 12:
6 *Barceló* PFI; 6 PCI⟨ (plus some 50 boats).
MINE WARFARE: 12:
MCMV: 12:
4 *Guadalete* (US *Aggressive*) MSO.
8 *Júcar* (US *Adjutant*) MSC.
AMPHIBIOUS: 4:
2 *Castilla* (US *Paul Revere*) amph tpt, capacity:
1,600 tps plus some 15 amph craft.
2 *Velasco* (US *Terrebonne Parish*) LST, capacity:
400 tps, 10 tk, or some 20 amph craft.
Plus 13 craft: 3 LCT, 2 LCU, 8 LCM.
SUPPORT AND MISCELLANEOUS: 28:
1 AO, 4 ocean tugs, 3 diver spt, 2 tpt/spt, 6 water
carriers, 6 AGHS, 1 AGOR, 1 sub salvage, 4 trg.

NAVAL AIR: 1,100
FGA: 2 sqn:
1 with AV-8S *Matador* (*Harrier*), TAV-8S.
1 with AV-8B.
LIAISON: 1 sqn with 3 *Citation II*.
HELICOPTERS: 4 sqn:
ASW: 2 sqn:
1 with SH-3D/G *Sea King* (mod to SH-3H stand-
ard).
1 with SH-60B (LAMPS-III fit).
AEW: 1 flt with SH-3D (*Searchwater* radar).
COMMAND/TRANSPORT: 1 sqn with AB-212.
TRAINING: 1 sqn with Hughes 500.
EQUIPMENT: 21 cbt ac, 28 armed hel.
AIRCRAFT:
EAV-8B: 11, **AV-8S:** 8, **TAV-8S:** 2 (trg).
Citation II: 3 (liaison).
HELICOPTERS:
AB-212: 10 (ASW/SAR).**SH-3D:** 12 (9 **-H** ASW, 3 **-D**
AEW). **Hughes 500:** 10 (trg). **SH-60B:** 6 (ASW).

MARINES: (7,000). (5,500 conscripts)
1 marine regt (3,500): 2 inf bty, 1 spt bn; 3 arty bty.
5 marine garrison gp.
EQUIPMENT:
MBT: 16 M-48E.
AFV: 17 *Scorpion* lt tk, 19 LVTP-7 AAV, 28 BLR
APC.
TOWED ARTY: 105mm: 12 Oto Melara M-56 pack.
SP ARTY: 155mm: 6 M-109A.
ATGW: 12 TOW, 18 *Dragon*.

RL: 90mm: C-90C.
RCL: 106mm: 52.
SAM: 12 *Mistral*.

AIR FORCE: 29,800 (15,500 conscripts).
CENTRAL AIR COMMAND (MACEN): 4 wings.
FIGHTER: 3 sqn:
2 with EF-18 (F-18 *Hornet*);
1 with RF-4C;
TRANSPORT: 7 sqn.
2 with C-212.
2 with CN-235, C-212.
1 with Boeing 707.
1 with *Falcon* (20, 50, 900).
1 with AS-332 (tpt).
SUPPORT: 4 sqn
1 with CL-215.
1 with C-212 (EW) and *Falcon* 20.
1 with C-212, AS-332 (SAR).
1 with C-212 and Cessna *Citation*.
TRAINING: 4 sqn.
1 with C-212.
1 with C-101.
1 with Beech (*Baron*).
1 with Beech (*Bonanza*).
EASTERN AIR COMMAND (MALEV): 2
wings.
FIGHTER: 3 sqn:
2 with EF-18 (F-18 *Hornet*)
1 with *Mirage* F1.
TRANSPORT: 2 sqn:
1 with C-130H.
1 tkr/tpt with KC-130H
SUPPORT: 1 sqn with C-212 ac, hel (SAR) AS-332.
GIBRALTAR STRAIT AIR COMMAND
(MAEST): 5 wings
FIGHTER: 2 sqn with *Mirage* F-1 CE/BE.
FGA: 3 sqn
2 with F-5B. 1 with C-101.
MR: 1 sqn with P-3A/B.
TRAINING: 6 sqn.
2 hel sqn with AB-205, *Hughes* 300C, S-76C.
1 with C-212. 1 with E-26 (*Tamiz*)
1 with C-101. 1 with C-212 and *Bonanza*.
CANARY ISLANDS, AIR COMMAND
(MACAN): 1 wing.
FGA: 1 sqn with *Mirage* F-1EE.
TRANSPORT: 1 sqn with C-212.
SAR: 1 sqn with F-27 ac, AS-332 hel (SAR).
LOGISTIC SUPPORT COMMAND
(MALOG):
1 sqn.
1 trials sqn with C-101, C-212, E-26.
EQUIPMENT: 150 cbt ac, no armed hel.
AIRCRAFT:
EF-18 A/B: 70 (ftr, OCU).
F-5B: 22. (FGA).
Mirage: 50. **F-1CE:** 30 (FGA); **F-1BE:** 3 (ftr);
F-1EE: 17 (ftr);
RF-4C: 8 (recce).
P-3: 7. **-A:** 2 (MR); **-B:** 5 (MR).

Boeing 707: 3 (tkr/tpt).
C-130H: 12. 7 (tpt); **KC-130H:** 5 (tkr).
C-212: 76. (32 tpt, 9 SAR, 6 recce, 25 trg, 2 EW, 2 trials).
Cessna *Citation*: 2 (recce).
C-101: 81 (trg).
CL-215: 21 (spt).
***Falcon* 20:** 5 (3 VIP tpt , 2 EW); ***Falcon* 50:** 1 (VIP tpt); ***Falcon* 900:** 2 (VIP tpt).
F-27: 3 (SAR).
E-26: 39 (trg).
CN-235: 18 (16 tpt, 2 VIP tpt).**E-20** (*Baron*): 5 trg, **E-24** (*Bonanza*): 27, trg.
HELICOPTERS:
AB-205/UH-1H: 7 (trg). **SA-330:** 5 (trg), **AS-332:** 16 (10 SAR, 6 tpt), **Hughes 300C:** 17 (trg), **S-76C:** 8 (trg).
MISSILES:
AAM: AIM-7 *Sparrow*, AIM-9 *Sidewinder*.
ASM: *Maverick, Harpoon, HARM*.

FORCES ABROAD:
UN AND PEACEKEEPING:
ANGOLA (UNAVEM II): 4 Observers.
BOSNIA (UNPROFOR II): 1,219, 1 inf bn gp, 10 Observers.
EL SALVADOR (ONUSAL): 15 Observers, 108 civ pol.
MOZAMBIQUE (ONUMOZ): 20 Observers.

PARAMILITARY:
GUARDIA CIVIL: 66,000 (3,000 conscripts); 9 regions, 20 inf *tercios* (regt) with 56 rural bn, 6 traffic security gp, 6 rural special ops gp; 12 BLR APC, 16 Bo-105, 7 BK-117 hel.
GUARDIA CIVIL DEL MAR: (340); about 13 PCIs.

FOREIGN FORCES:
US: 3,900. Navy (3,400), Air Force (500).

TURKEY

GDP	1991:	TL 467,258.6bn ($112.0bn)	
	1992:	TL 817,701.5bn ($118.9bn)	
Growth	1991:	0.3%	1992: 5.5%
Inflation	1991:	66%	1992: 72.0%
Debt	1991:	$49.21bn	1992: $56.10bn
Def bdgt[a]	1992ε:	TL 28,443.0bn ($4.14bn)	
	1993ε:	TL 46,948.0bn ($5.00bn)	
NATO defn	1992:	TL 38,738.5bn ($5.64bn)	
FMA[b]	1993:	$653.5m	
$1 = TL	1990:	2,608.6	1991: 4,171.8
	1992:	6,872.4	1993: 9,392.6

TL = Turkish liras
[a] Incl budget for Gendarmerie.
[b] Incl $200m as Economic Support.

An additional $4bn will benefit the national defence fund agreed by Saudi Arabia, Kuwait, UAE, US within the next five years. $743m were disbursed in 1992 and $760m in 1993.

Population: 59,255,400

	13–17	18–22	23–32
Men	3,015,600	2,935,600	5,214,100
Women	2,850,500	2,666,500	4,369,700

TOTAL ARMED FORCES:
ACTIVE: 480,000 (390,000 conscripts).
Terms of service: 15 months.
RESERVES: 1,104,000 to age 46 (all). Army 950,000, Navy 84,000, Air 70,000.

ARMY: 370,000 (320,000 conscripts).
4 army HQ: 9 corps HQ. (Reorganisation may not be complete.)
1 mech div (3 mech regt, 1 arty, 1 recce bn).
1 inf div.
15 armd bde (each 2 armd, 2 mech inf, 2 arty bn).
18 mech bde (each 1 armd, 2 mech inf, 1 arty bn, 1 recce sqn).
9 inf bde (each 4 inf, 1 arty bn).
3 cdo bde (each 3 cdo, 1 arty bn).
1 armd regt.
1 Presidential Guard regt.
5 coastal def regt.
10 coastal def bn.
RESERVES: 1 armd, 1 mech, 2 cde bde.
EQUIPMENT:
MBT: some 4,835: 766 M-47 (in store), 748 M-48A2C, 2,303 M-48T5/AST1/AST2, 706 M-60 (574 A3, 132 A1), some 312 *Leopard* 1A3.
AIFV: 65 AIFV.
APC: 2,896: 125 IAPC, 2,412 M-113/-A1/-A2, 300 BTR-60, 59 UR-416.
TOTAL ARTY: 4,551.
TOWED ARTY: 1,788: 105mm: 810 incl 640 M-101A1; 150mm: 128 Skoda; 155mm: 517 M-114A1\A2, 171 M-59; 203mm: 162 M-115.
SP ARTY: 696: 105mm: 364 M-52A1, 26 M-108; 155mm: 168 M-44; 175mm: 36 M-107; 203mm: 9 M-55, 93 M-110.
MRL: 227mm: 20 MLRS; plus 70mm: 12 RA-7040 40 tube, towed.
MORTARS: 2,035: 107mm: 1,457 M-30, M-106 SP; 120mm: 578. Plus 81mm: 1,500 incl SP.
COAST ARTY: 240mm: 20.
ATGW: 182 *Cobra*, 300 SS-11, 365 *TOW* SP, 392 *Milan*.
RL: M-72.
RCL: 57mm: 974 M-18; 75mm: 619; 106mm: 2,329 M-40A1.
AD GUNS: 1,870: 20mm: 577 GAI-DO1; 35mm: 224 GDF-003; 40mm: 877 L60/70, 192 M-42A1.
SAM: 12 *Rapier*, 108 *Stinger*, 789 *Redeye*.
AIRCRAFT: 269: 8 Cessna 206, 3 -421, 1 *Cherokee*, 40 *Citabria*, 1 DHC-2, 5 Do-27A, 29 -28D, 50 O-

1E, 5 B-200, 4 T-42A, 98 U-17, 25 T-41.
HELICOPTERS: 538: 40 S-70A, 21 AH-1W/P, 214
AB-204, 64 AB-205, 20 AB-206A, 2 AB-212, 29 H-
300C, 30 OH-13H, 3 OH-58, 70 TH-55, 30 UH-1D,
15 UH-1H.

NAVY: 50,000, incl marines (40,000 conscripts).
BASES: Ankara (Navy HQ and COMEDNOREAST),
Gölcük (HQ Fleet), Istanbul (HQ Northern area and
Bosphorus), Izmir (HQ Southern area and Aegean),
Eregli (HQ Black Sea), Iskenderun, Aksaz Bay,
Mersin (HQ Mediterranean).
SUBMARINES: 15 SS:
6 *Atilay* (Ge Type 209/1200) with SST-4 HWT.
7 *Canakkale/Burakreis*† (plus 2 non op) (US *Guppy*)
   with Mk 37 HWT.
2 *Hizirreis* (US *Tang*) with Mk 37 HWT.
PRINCIPAL SURFACE COMBATANTS: 19:
DESTROYERS: 11:
8 *Yücetepe* (US *Gearing*) (ASW/ASUW) with 2 x 3
   ASTT (Mk 46 LWT); 5 with 1 x 8 *ASROC*, 2 with
   Harpoon SSM, all with 2 x 2 127mm guns.
2 *Alcitepe* (US *Carpenter*) with 1 x 8 *ASROC*, 2 x 3
   ASTT, 1 x 2 127mm guns.
1 *Zafer* (US *Sumner*) with 2 x 3 ASTT, 3 x 2 127mm
   guns.
FRIGATES: 8:
4 *Yavuz* (Ge MEKO 200) with 1 x AB-212 hel
   (ASW/OTHT), 2 x 3 ASTT; plus 2 x 4 *Harpoon*
   SSM, 1 x 127mm gun.
2 *Gelibolu* (Ge T-120 *Köln*) with 4 x 533mm ASTT,
   2 x 4 ASW mor; plus 2 x 100mm gun.
2 *Berk* with 2 x 3 ASTT, 2 Mk 11 *Hedgehog*.
(Plus: 4 ex-US *Knox*-class with 1 x 8 ASROC, 1 x
SH-2F hel, 4 x ASTT; plus *Harpoon* (from *ASROC*
launcher), 1 x 127mm gun due to be transferred in
July/August 1993).
PATROL AND COASTAL COMBATANTS: 45:
MISSILE CRAFT: 16:
8 *Do an* (Ge Lürssen-57) PFM with 2 x 4 *Harpoon*
   SSM.
8 *Kartal* (Ge *Jaguar*) PFM with 4 x *Penguin* 2 SSM,
   2 x 533mm TT.
PATROL: 29:
COASTAL: 7: 1 *Girne* PFC, 6 *Sultanhisar* PCC.
INSHORE: 22: 1 *Bora* (US *Asheville*) PFI, 12 AB-25
PCI, 4 AB-21, 5⟨.
MINE WARFARE: 36:
MINELAYERS: 4:
1 *Nusret* (400 mines).
3 *Mordo an* (US LSM) coastal (400 mines).
Note: *Gelibolu* FF, *Bayraktar*, *Sarucabey* and
Çakabey LST have minelaying capability.
MINE COUNTERMEASURES: 32:
12 *Seymen* (US *Adjutant*) MSC.
3 *Trabzon* (Cdn *Bay*) MSC.
6 *Karamürsel* (Ge *Vegesack*) MSC.
4 *Foça* (US *Cape*) MSI.
7 MCM base ships .
AMPHIBIOUS: 7 LST:

2 *Ertu rul* (US *Terrebonne Parish*): capacity 400 tps,
   18 tk.
2 *Bayraktar* (US LST-512): capacity 200 tps, 16 tk.
2 *Sarucabey:* capacity 600 tps, 11 tk.
1 *Çakabey:* capacity 400 tps, 9 tk.
Plus about 59 craft: 35 LCT, 2 LCU, 22 LCM.
SUPPORT AND MISCELLANEOUS: 27:
1 *Akar* AO, 5 spt tankers, 5 depot ships, 3 salvage/
rescue, 2 survey, 3 tpt, 5 tugs, 2 repair, 1 div spt.

NAVAL AVIATION: 21 combat ac, 15 armed hel.
ASW: 1 sqn with 21 S-2A/E/TS-2A *Tracker* ac (Air
Force aircraft, Air Force and Navy crews); 3 AB-
204AS, 12 AB-212 ASW hel.

MARINES: 1 regt (4,000).
HQ, 3 bn, 1 arty bn (18 guns), spt units.

AIR FORCE: 60,000 (30,000 conscripts).
2 tac air forces, 1 tpt, 1 air trg comd.
FGA: 19 sqn:
3 (1 OCU) with F-5A/B (1 incl RF-5A recce);
8 (1 OCU) with F-4E (1 incl RF-4E recce);
6 (1 OCU, 1 converting) with F-16;
2 (1 OCU) with F/TF-104G.
FIGHTER: 2 sqn with F-104S/G, TF-104G.
RECCE: RF-5A, RF-4E (see FGA, above).
ASW: 1 sqn with S-2A/E *Tracker* (see Navy).
TRANSPORT: 6 sqn:
1 with C-130H and C-47;
1 with C-160D;
2 with C-47 (1 ECM/ELINT/SAR/calibration);
2 with CN-235.
2 VIP tpt units with *Viscount* 794, C-47, VC-7.
LIAISON:
3 HQ flt with C-47, AT-11, T-33 ac; UH-1H hel; 10
base flt with C-47, T-33 ac; UH-1H, UH-19B
(Sikorsky S-55) hel.
TRAINING: 3 sqn: 1 with T-34, T-41; 1 with T-33,
SF-260D, T-38; 1 with T-37; trg schools with C-47
ac, UH-1H hel.
SAM: 8 sqn with *Nike Hercules*; 2 *Rapier* sqn.
EQUIPMENT: 539 cbt ac (plus 174 in store), no
attack hel.
AIRCRAFT:
F-16C/D: 126, **-C:** 104; **-D:** 22.
F-5: 137. **-A:** 47 (FGA); **-B:** 10 (6 FGA, 4 recce); **RF-
5A:** 20 (recce); **NF-5A/B:** 60 (FGA); (plus some 44 in
store).
F-4E: 155. 105 (FGA); 30 (OCU); **RF-4E:** 20 (recce);
(plus 30 in store).
F-104G/TF-104G/F104S: 88 (plus some 100 in store).
S-2A/E *Tracker:* 33.
C-130: 13 (tpt). **C-160D:** 19 (tpt). *Viscount:* 1 (VIP).
C-47: 25. *Citation:* **-11:** 4.**CN-235:** 4 (tpt). **SF-260D:** 21
(trg) (VIP tpt). **BN-2A:** 2 (obs) .**T-33:** 75. **T-34:** 16
(trg). **T-37:** 63 trg. **T-38:** 27 (trg). **T-41:** 28 (trg).
HELICOPTERS:
UH-1H: 21 (tpt, liaison, base flt, trg schools).
AS-330: 4.
SAM: 128 *Nike Hercules*, 24 *Rapier*.

FORCES ABROAD:
CYPRUS: 1 corps, (30,000); 300 M-48A5 MBT; 100 M-113, 100 M-59 APC; 144 105mm, 36 155mm, 8 203mm towed; 18 105mm, 6 155mm SP; 114 107mm mor; 84 40mm AA guns; 8 ac, 12 hel.
UN AND PEACEKEEPING
IRAQ/KUWAIT (UNIKOM): 6 Observers.
ITALY (*Deny Flight*) 18 F-16C/D.
SOMALIA (UNOSOM II): 320.

PARAMILITARY:
GENDARMERIE/NATIONAL GUARD: (Ministry of Interior, Ministry of Defence in war) 70,000 active, 50,000 reserve (being reorganised).
COAST GUARD: 1,100: 28 PCI, 8 PCI⟨, plus boats, 2 tpt.

OPPOSITION:
KURDISTAN WORKERS PARTY (PKK): ε11,000.

FOREIGN FORCES:
NATO:
HQ Allied Land Forces South Eastern Europe (LANDSOUTHEAST).
HQ 6 Allied Tactical Air Force (6 ATAF).
OPERATION PROVIDE COMFORT:
US: 2,100. Army (800). Air (1,300): 1 tac, 1 air base gp with some 57 ac (F-15E, F-16, F-111F, EF-111, F-4G).
UK: Air (260): 8 *Harrier*, 2 VC-10 ac.
FRANCE: Air (110): 4 *Mirage* F-1CR, 4 *Jaguar*, 1C-135.

UNITED KINGDOM

GDP	1991: £575.36bn ($1,017.96bn)		
	1992: £593.60bn ($1,048.02bn)		
Growth	1991: -2.3%	1992:	-0.5%
Inflation	1991: 5.9%	1992:	3.7%
Publ Debt	1992: 41%		
Def exp	1991: £24.56bn ($40.43bn)		
Def bdgt	1992: £23.98bn ($42.33bn);		
	1993: £23.52bn ($35.15bn)		
NATO defn	1992: £23.76bn ($41.95bn)		
$1 =	1990: 0.5603	1991:	0.5652
	1992: 0.5664	1993:	0.6657

Population: 57,946,500

	13–17	18–22	23–32
Men	1,832,600	2,014,100	4,567,700
Women	1,740,600	1,917,100	4,414,000

TOTAL ARMED FORCES:
ACTIVE: 274,800 (incl 18,900 women and some 8,000 enlisted outside the UK).

RESERVES: 349,300.
Army: 264,300: Regular 190,100; Territorial Army (TA) 68,500; R Irish Regt (Home Service) 5,700 (3,000 full time). Navy: 33,300: Regular 27,500; Volunteers and Auxiliary Service 5,800.
Marines: 3,900: Regular 2,700; Volunteers and Auxiliary Forces 1,200.
Air Force: 47,800: Regular 46,100; Volunteers and Auxiliary Forces 1,700.

STRATEGIC FORCES: (1,900).
SLBM: 48 msl in 3 SSBN:
3 *Resolution* SSBN each with 16 *Polaris* A-3TK SLBM.
EARLY WARNING
Ballistic Missile Early Warning System (BMEWS) station at Fylingdales.

ARMY: 134,600 (incl 7,600 women and 7,000 enlisted outside the UK, of whom some 6,000 are Gurkhas).
(Note: regt are normally of bn size).
7 Military Districts (6 in UK incl N. Ireland, 1 BAOR).
1 armd div with 3 armd bde, 3 arty, 4 engr, 1 avn, 1 AD regt.
1 div with 2 mech (*Warrior/Saxon*), 1 AB bde, 3 arty, 3 engr, 1 avn, 1 AD regt.
BAOR tps: 1 arty bde (3 MLRS, 2 AD regt), 2 armd recce, 3 engr regt.
1 air mobile bde.
2 inf bde (Berlin, Hong Kong (Gurkha)).
10 inf bde HQ (3 control ops in N. Ireland, remainder mixed regular and TA for trg/administrative purposes only).
3 engr bde HQ.
Summary Combat Arm Units:
9 armd regt (incl 1 trg regt).
2 armd recce regt.
9 mech inf bn (5 FV 432, 4 *Saxon*).
6 armd inf bn (*Warrior*).
30 inf bn (incl 4 Gurkha).
3 AB bn (2 only in para role).
1 SF (SAS) regt.
11 arty regt (3 MLRS, 5 SP, 3 fd (1 cdo, 1 AB, 1 air mobile)).
4 AD regt (2 *Rapier*, 2 *Javelin*).
11 engr regt (incl 1 Gurkha, 1 amph, 5 armd).
6 avn regt.
6 Home Service inf bn (N. Ireland only, some part-time).
RESERVES:
Territorial Army: 1 armd recce, 4 lt recce regt, 36 inf bn, 2 SF (SAS), 2 fd, 3 AD (*Blowpipe*), 9 engr regt, 1 avn sqn.
Hong Kong Regiment. Gibraltar Regiment.
EQUIPMENT:
MBT: 1,126: 426 *Challenger*, some 700 *Chieftain*.
LIGHT TANKS: some 275 FV 101 *Scorpion*.
RECCE: some 315 FV 107 *Scimitar*, 11 *Fuchs* (some

1.000 *Ferret* and 350 *Fox* are to be withdrawn).
AIFV: some 682 *Warrior* (MCV-80), 13 FV 432 *Rarden*.
APC: 3,585: some 2,000 FV 432, some 411 FV 103 *Spartan*, some 611 AT-105 *Saxon*, 313 Humber. (Some 250 FV 603 *Saracen* are to be withdrawn).
TOTAL ARTY: 475.
TOWED ARTY: 293: 105mm: 212 L-118, 140mm: 9 5.5-in; 155mm: 72 FH-70.
SP ARTY: 119: 155mm: 111 M-109A1, 8 AS-90 (plus 200 105mm *Abbot* in store).
MRL: 227mm: some 63 MLRS.
MORTARS: 81mm: some 500 (incl 110 SP).
ATGW: ε1,100 *Milan* (incl 72 FV 103 *Spartan* SP), 87 *Swingfire* (FV 102 *Striker* SP), *TOW*.
RCL: 84mm: *Carl Gustav*.
SAM: *Blowpipe*, some 382 *Javelin* and *Starburst*; 120 *Rapier* (some 40 SP).
AIRCRAFT: 5 BN-2, 19 *Chipmunk* trg.
HELICOPTERS: 30 *Scout*, 159 SA-341, 138 *Lynx* AH-1/-7/-9, 4 A-109.
LANDING CRAFT: 2 *Ardennes*, 9 *Arromanches* log; 4 *Avon*, LCVP ; 3 tugs, 28 other service vessels.

NAVY (RN): 59,300 (incl 6,500 Air, 7,250 Marines, 4,500 women and 300 enlisted outside the UK).
ROYAL FLEET AUXILIARY (RFA): (2,300 civilians) man major spt vessels.
ROYAL MARITIME AUXILIARY SERVICE (RMAS): (1,575 civilians) provides harbour/coastal services.
RESERVES:
ROYAL FLEET RESERVE: (24,000) Ex-regulars, no trg commitment.
ROYAL NAVAL RESERVE (RNR): (4,400) 6 HQ units, 11 Sea Trg Centres (STC), 12 Comms Trg Centres (CTC), 1 MCM sqn: 9 MCMV, 10 PCI.
ROYAL NAVAL AUXILIARY SERVICE (RNXS): (2,600) 72 auxiliary service units; Port HQ, patrols, etc.
BASES: UK: Northwood (HQ Fleet, CINCHAN, CINCEASTLANT), Devonport (HQ), Faslane, Portland, Portsmouth, Rosyth (HQ). Overseas: Gibraltar, Hong Kong.
SUBMARINES: 18:
STRATEGIC SUBMARINES: 3 SSBN (see p. 62).
TACTICAL SUBMARINES: 15:
SSN: 13 (incl 2 in refit):
7 *Trafalgar*, 5 *Swiftsure* all with Mk 24 HWT and *Harpoon* USGW.
1 *Valiant* with Mk 24 HWT and *Harpoon* .
SS: 2:
1 *Upholder* (plus 3 not yet fully op) with Mk 24 HWT and *Harpoon*.
1 *Oberon* with Mk 24 HWT (Nil by 1 October 1993).
PRINCIPAL SURFACE COMBATANTS: 40:
CARRIERS: 2 *Invincible* CVV (plus 1 in long refit); each with **ac:** 8 *Sea Harrier* V/STOL; **hel:** 12 *Sea King:* up to 9 ASW, 3 AEW; plus 1 x 2 *Sea Dart* SAM.

DESTROYERS: 12 DDG (incl 1 in refit):
12 *Birmingham* with 1 x 2 *Sea Dart* SAM; plus 1 *Lynx* hel, 2 x 3 ASTT, 1 x 114mm gun.
FRIGATES: 26 (incl 1 in refit):
4 *Cornwall* (Type 22 Batch 3) with 1 *Sea King* or 2 *Lynx* hel (*Sting Ray* LWT), 2 x 3 ASTT; plus 2 x 4 *Harpoon* SSM, 1 x 114mm gun.
10 *Broadsword* (Type 22 Batch 1/2) with 2 *Lynx* hel (2 with 1 x *Sea King*), 2 x 3 ASTT; plus 4 x MM-38 *Exocet* SSM (4 Batch 1 trg).
6 *Norfolk* (Type 23) with 1 x *Lynx* hel, 2 x 2 ASTT, plus 2 x 4 *Harpoon* SSM, 1 x 114mm gun (incl 1 commissioning by 1 October 1993).
5 *Amazon* with 1 *Lynx* hel, 2 x 3 ASTT; plus 4 x MM-38 *Exocet*, 1 x 114mm gun
1 *Leander* (Batch 2/3A) with 1 *Lynx* hel, 2 x 3 ASTT; plus 4 x MM-38 *Exocet*.
EXTENDED READINESS: (In addition to above): 1 *Leander* (Batch 3A).
PATROL AND COASTAL COMBATANTS: 26:
OFFSHORE: 13 PCO: 1 *Endurance* (ex-*Polar Circle*), 2 *Castle*, 7 *Jersey*, 3 *Peacock*.
INSHORE: 13 PCI: 3 *Kingfisher*, 8 *Archer*, 2 *Ranger*.
MINE WARFARE: 30:
MINELAYER: No dedicated minelayer, but all submarines have limited minelaying capability.
MINE COUNTERMEASURES: 30:
13 *Brecon* MCO.
4 *Sandown* MHC.
10 *Waveney* MSO (9 with RNR).
3 *Ton* MHC.
AMPHIBIOUS: 6:
1 *Fearless* LPD (plus 1 in store) with 4 LCU, 4 LCVP; capacity 400 tps, 15 tk, 3 hel.
1 *Sir Galahad*, 4 *Sir Lancelot* LST: capacity 340 tps, 16 tk (*Sir G*. 18), 1 hel (RFA manned).
Plus 32 craft: 15 LCU, 17 LCVP.
Note: See Army for additional amph lift capability.
SUPPORT AND MISCELLANEOUS: 32:
UNDERWAY SUPPORT: 10:
2 *Fort Victoria*, AOE (not fully op).
3 *Olwen*, 2 *Green Rover* AO, 2 *Fort Grange* AF, 1 *Resource* AEF.
MAINTENANCE/LOGISTIC: 10:
1 AR, 4 AO, 2 AE, 3 AT.
SPECIAL PURPOSE: 7:
1 AVT, 3 trg (1 *Wilton*, 1 *Manly*, 1 chartered), 2 trials/research, 1 Royal Yacht.
SURVEY: 5: 2 *Hecla*, 2 *Bulldog*, 1 *Roebuck* AGHS.
(25 of above civilian manned, either RFA or RMAS).
IN STORE: (not counted above): 1 LPD, 2 MSO

FLEET AIR ARM (FAA): 6,100
FIGHTER/ATTACK: 3 ac sqn with *Sea Harrier* FRS-1.
ASW: 5 hel sqn with *Sea King* HAS-6;
ASW/ATTACK: 2 sqn with *Lynx* HAS-2/-3 (in indep flt).
AEW: 1 hel sqn with *Sea King* AEW-2.
COMMANDO SUPPORT: 3 hel sqn with *Sea King* HC-4.
SAR: 1 hel sqn with *Sea King* HC-4.
1 hel sqn with *Sea King* HAS-5.

TRAINING: 2 sqn: 1 with *Jetstream* ac; 1 with SA-341 *Gazelle* HT-2 hel.
FLEET SUPPORT: *Canberra* T-18/-22, *Hunter* T-7/-8, GA-11, PR-11, 3 *Mystère-Falcon* 20 (civil registration, operated under contract).
TRANSPORT: *Jetstream*, *Sea Heron*, *Sea Devon*.
EQUIPMENT: 42 cbt ac, 153 armed hel.
AIRCRAFT:
Sea Harrier: **FRS-1:** 37 (some being mod to FRS-2).
T-4N: 5* (trg).
Hunter: 12 (spt, trg), (plus 12 in store).
HS-125: 2 (VIP tpt); *Mystère-Falcon* 20: 11 (spt);
Jetstream: 19. **T-2:** 15 (trg); **T-3:** 4 (trg); *Chipmunk:* 14 (trg plus 2 in store).
HELICOPTERS:
Sea King: 119. **HAS-6:** 75, **HC-4:** 36 (cdo), **AEW-2:** 10.
Lynx **HAS-3:** 78.
Gazelle **HT-2/-3:** 26 (trg plus 5 in store).
MISSILES:
ASM: *Sea Skua*, *Sea Eagle*.
AAM: AIM-9 *Sidewinder*.

MARINES (RM): (7,250).
1 cdo bde: 3 cdo; 1 cdo arty regt (Army) + 1 bty (TA); 2 cdo engr sqn (1 Army, 1 TA), 1 log regt (joint service); 1 lt hel sqn.
1 mtn and arctic warfare cadre.
Special Boat Service (SF): HQ: 5 sqn.
1 aslt sqn (6 landing craft).
1 gp (*Commachio*).
EQUIPMENT:
MORTARS: 81mm.
ATGW: *Milan*.
SAM: *Javelin*, *Blowpipe*.
HELICOPTERS: 8 SA-341 (*Gazelle*), 6 *Lynx* AH-1.

AIR FORCE (RAF): 80,900 (incl 6,800 women).
FGA/BOMBER: 8 sqn: (nuclear capable)
6 with *Tornado* GR-1;
2 with *Buccaneer* S-2A/B (maritime attack).
FGA: 5 sqn:
3 with *Harrier*; GR-5/-7.
2 with *Jaguar*.
FIGHTER: 7 sqn, plus 1 flt:
7 with *Tornado* F-3; (1 flt in the Falklands).
RECCE: 2 sqn with *Tornado* GR-1A; 1 photo-recce unit with *Canberra* PR-9, 1 sqn with *Jaguar*.
MR: 3 sqn with *Nimrod* MR-2.
AEW: 1 sqn with *Sentry* E-3D.
ECM/ELINT: 2 sqn: 1 ECM with *Canberra*, 1 ELINT with *Nimrod* R-1.
TANKER: 3 sqn: 1 with *Victor* K-2; 1 with VC-10 K-2/-3; 1 with *Tristar* K-1/KC-1 (tkr/tpt).
TRANSPORT: 5 sqn:
1 strategic with VC-10 C-1.
4 tac with *Hercules* C-1/-1K/-1P/-3P.
LIAISON: 1 comms sqn with HS-125, *Andover* ac; SA-341E hel.
Queen's Flt: 3 BAe-146-100, 2 *Wessex* hel.
CALIBRATION: 2 sqn: 1 with *Andover* E-3/-3A

(Airborne Radio Relay);
1 target facility with *Hawk*.
OCU: 8: *Tornado* GR-1, *Tornado* F-3, *Jaguar* GR-1A/T2A, *Harrier* GR-3/5, *Hercules*, SA-330/CH-47.
1 wpn conversion unit with *Tornado* GR-1.
TRAINING: *Hawk* T-1A, *Jet Provost*, *Jetstream* T-1, *Bulldog* T-1, *Chipmunk* T-10, HS-125 *Dominie* T-1, *Tucano* T-1.
TACTICAL HELICOPTERS: 6 sqn: 1 with CH-47; 1 with CH-47 and SA-330; 2 with *Wessex* HC-2; 2 with SA-330.
SAR: 2 hel sqn; 8 flt: 3 with *Wessex* HC-2; 5 with *Sea King* HAR-3.
TRAINING: *Wessex*, SA-341 *Sea King*.
EQUIPMENT: 688 cbt ac (plus 118 in store), no armed hel.
AIRCRAFT:
Tornado: 307: **GR-1:** 172 (98 strike, 29 recce, 17 in tri-national trg sqn (Cottesmore), 22 in wpn conversion unit, 6 dev); **F-3:** 135 (108 ftr, 24 OCU, 3 dev); plus 33 in store (13 F-2: 5, 20 GR-1).
Buccaneer: 23, plus 4 in store.
Jaguar: 54: **GR-1A:** 44; **T-2A:** 10; (plus 29 in store).
Harrier: 61: **GR-7:** 50 (39 FGA, 11* OCU); **T-4:** 9, **GR-3:** 2 (plus 10 in store).
Hawk: 145 (*82 (T1-A) tac weapons unit *Sidewinder*-capable, 63 trg).
Canberra: 20: **T-4:** 3 (trg); **PR-7:** 2 (trg); **PR-9:** 5 (recce); **T-17:** 10 (ECM); plus 8 in store.
Nimrod: 29: **R-1:** 3 (ECM); **MR-2:** 26* (MR); plus 4 in store.
Sentry (E-3D): 7 (AEW).
Victor: 8 (tkr).
Tristar: 9: **K-1:** 2 (tkr/tpt); **KC-1:** 4 (tkr/cgo); **C-2:** 2 (tpt); **C-2A: 1.**
VC-10: 22: **C-1:** 13 (strategic tpt to be mod to tkr/tpt); **K-2:** 5 (tkr); **K-3:** 4 (tkr) plus 5 undergoing conversion to K-4 (tkr).
Hercules: 62: **C-1:** 26; **C-1K:** 5 (tkr); **C-2:** 1; **C-3:** 30.
Andover: 11 (4 cal, 7 liaison).
HS-125: 24: **T-1:** 12 (trg); **CC-1/-2/-3:** 12 (liaison) plus 7 in store.
BAe-146: 3 (VIP tpt).
Tucano: 129 (trg).
Jetstream: 10 (trg).
Bulldog: 116 (trg).
Chipmunk: 76 (trg).
HELICOPTERS:
Wessex: 65 (38 tac tpt, 10 SAR, 15 OCU, 2 VIP).
CH-47: 31 (25 tac tpt, 6 OCU) plus 3 in store.
SA-330: 41 (36 tac tpt, 5 OCU) plus 1 in store.
Sea King: 16 (14 SAR, 2 OCU) plus 2 in store.
SA-341 (*Gazelle*): 28 (liaison, trg) plus 2 in store.
MISSILES:
ASM: *Martel*, AGM-84D-1 *Harpoon*, *Sea Eagle*.
AAM: AIM-9G *Sidewinder*, *Sky Flash*.
ARM: ALARM.

ROYAL AIR FORCE REGIMENT:
2 wing HQ. 5 fd sqn (with 81mm mortars) 5 SAM sqn with 42 *Rapier* (37 *Scorpion* lt tank, 114 *Spartan* APC in store).

EQUIPMENT:
RESERVES (Royal Auxiliary Air Force Regiment): 6
fd def sqn; 2 lt AA gun sqn with 12 x twin 35mm
Oerlikon and *Skyguard*.

DEPLOYMENT:
ARMY:
United Kingdom Land Forces (UKLF):
Reinforcements for ARRC (declared to
LANDCENT).
Active: 1 div, 1 air-mobile bde, 1 arty regt, 1
avn sqn. Reserve: 2 inf bde, 2 arty regt.
Additional TA units incl 18 inf bn, 2 SAS, 3 AD
(*Blowpipe*) regt.
Allied Command Europe Mobile Force (*Land*)
(AMF(L)): (some 2,300): UK contribution: 1 inf bn,
1 arty bty, 1 sigs sqn, 1 log bn.
HQ Northern Ireland: (some 13,300 plus 5,600
Home Service): 3 inf bde HQ, up to 12 major units
in inf role (6 resident, 6 roulement inf bn), 1 engr, 1
avn regt. 6 Home Service inf bn.
Remainder of Army regular and TA units for Home
Defence.
NAVY:
FLEET: (CinC is also CINCHAN and
CINCEASTLANT).
Regular Forces, with the exception of most Patrol
and Coastal Combatants, Mine Warfare and Support
forces, are declared to EASTLANT.
MARINES: 1 cdo bde (declared to AFNORTH).
AIR FORCE:
STRIKE COMMAND: (CinC is also CINCUKAIR).
Commands all combat air operations other than for
Belize and Falklands: 4 Groups: No. 1 (Strike,
Attack, Transport), No. 2 (Strike, attack-based in
Germany), No. 11 (Air Defence), No 18 (Maritime).
SUPPORT COMMAND: trg, supply and maint spt
of other comds.

OVERSEAS:
ANTARCTICA: 1 ice patrol ship (in summer).
ASCENSION ISLAND: RAF: *Hercules* C-1K det.
BELIZE: 1,500. Army: some 1,200; 1 inf bn, 1 armd
recce tp, 1 fd arty bty, 1 engr sqn, 1 hel flt (3 *Gazelle*
AH-1). RAF: 300; 1 flt (4 *Harrier* GR-3 FGA, 4
Puma hel), 1 *Rapier* AD det (4 fire units) RAF regt.
(force to be withdrawn in 1994).
BRUNEI: Army: some 1,000: 1 Gurkha inf bn, 1 hel
flt (3 hel).
CANADA: Army: trg and liaison unit. RAF:
Tornado det.
CYPRUS: 4,100. Army: 2,600.
2 inf bn, 1 armd recce, 1 engr spt sqn, 1 hel flt.
Navy: 2 PCI.
RAF: 1,500: 1 hel sqn (*Wessex*), det of *Tornado* ac,
1 lt armd sqn RAF regt.
FALKLAND ISLANDS: some 1,600. Army: 1 inf
coy gp, 1 engr sqn (fd, plant). RN: 1 DD/FF, 1 PCO,

1 AO, 1 AR. RAF: 1 *Tornado* F-3 flt, 6 *Hercules* C-
1K, 3 *Sea King* HAR-3, 6 CH-47 hel, 1 sqn RAF
regt (*Rapier* SAM).
GERMANY: 53,600 Army (BAOR declared to
LANDCENT): 39,400; 1 mil district, 1 armd div; 1
arty bde, 1 armd recce, 5 engr regt. Berlin Inf Bde; 2
inf bn, 1 engr sqn. RAF (No. 2 GP RAF), 7,000
(declared to AIRCENT); 6 ac sqn, 4 *Tornado*, 2
Harrier, 1 hel sqn: (SA-330/CH-47 (tpt)), RAF regt:
1 Wing HQ; 2 *Rapier* SAM sqn.
GIBRALTAR: 1,200. Army: 100; Gibraltar regt
(400). Navy/Marines: 800; 2 PCI, Marine det, 2 twin
Exocet launchers (coast defence), base unit. RAF:
300; periodic *Jaguar* ac det.
MEDITERRANEAN: 1 FF/DD
STANAVFORMED.
HONG KONG: 6,500. Army: 5,700 (British 1,600,
Gurkha 4,100). Gurkha inf bde with 1 UK, 2 Gurkha
inf bn, 1 Gurkha engr regt, 1 hel sqn (-) with 10
Scout AH-1, 3 small landing craft, 3 other vessels.
Navy/Marines: 500 (300 locally enlisted); 3 *Peacock*
PCC, (12 patrol boats in local service). RAF: 300; 1
Wessex hel sqn (10 HC-2) (until 1997). Reserves:
Hong Kong regt (1,200).
INDIAN OCEAN
(*Armilla Patrol*): 2 DD/FF, 1 spt ship. Diego Garcia:
1 naval party, 1 Marine det.
NEPAL: Army: 1,200 (Gurkha trg org).
WEST INDIES (see also Belize): 1 DD/FF.
MILITARY ADVISERS: 455 in 30 countries.
UN AND PEACEKEEPING:
ADRIATIC: (*Sharp Guard*) 1 CVV, 2–3 DD/FF, 3–
4 spt ships, 2 *Nimrod* MPA ac.
BOSNIA (UNPROFOR II) 2,281: 1 mech inf bn gp
(incl armd recce sqn), 1 engr sqn.
CAMBODIA (UNTAC): 38 Observers, 70 naval, 13
mine clearance.
CROATIA (UNPROFOR I) 250: 9 Observers, 1
medical unit.
CYPRUS (UNFICYP): 592: 1 inf bn(-), 1 hel flt,
engr and log spt (incl spt for UNIFIL).
FORMER YUGOSLAVIA (*Provide Promise*): 35,
1 C-130 ac.
IRAQ/KUWAIT (UNIKOM): 15 Observers.
ITALY (*Deny Flight*): 400, 8 *Tornado* F3, 2 VC-10
(tkr), 3 E-3D *Sentry*.
(*Disciplined Guard*): 12 *Jaguar*.
SAUDI ARABIA (*Southern Watch*): 150. 6 *Tor-
nado* GR-I.
TURKEY (*Provide Comfort*): 260, 8 *Harrier* GR-7,
2 VC-10 tkr.
WESTERN SAHARA (MINURSO): 15 Observers.

FOREIGN FORCES:
US: 16,800. Navy (2,400). Air (14,400):
1 Air Force HQ, 48 cbt ac.
GERMANY/ITALY: Tri-national *Tornado* trg sqn.

Non-NATO Europe

Political Developments

On 1 January 1993, in what has been described as the 'velvet split', Czechoslovakia divided into the Czech Republic and the Republic of Slovakia. The build-up to, and the implementation of, the split was carried out in an orderly and apparently amicable manner (in particular, agreement over the division of military assets was reached without discord). However, some serious differences have emerged since the division, mainly involving border controls and currency exchange rates. For many years, the demands of the Warsaw Pact and the former Soviet Union had required that the bulk of Czechoslovak forces be deployed in the western part of the country and there is thus little military accommodation and few airfields in the eastern part. Even before the division had been agreed, the authorities were planning to redeploy forces in order to provide a more balanced defensive posture. In general, the armed forces have been split in a ratio of 2:1 in favour of the Czech Republic. However, a considerable quantity of equipment and stores was moved into Slovakia during 1992.

Two latent problems have been intensified by the division: the Hungarian minority in Slovakia, which represented less than 4% of the Czechoslovakian population, now forms 11% of the Slovak population; and the question of the Sudetenland, which the Czech Republic has inherited. Slovakia has also inherited the problem caused by the Gabcikovo dam project, now an outright controversy with Hungary.

Civil War

While the civil war in Bosnia-Herzegovina commands Europe's attention because of its proximity to Western Europe and because of the media coverage it generates, there are several other civil wars being waged in Europe (as defined by the CSCE).

Transcaucasus

The fighting between Armenia and Azerbaijan began some five years ago over the problem of the Nagorno-Karabakh enclave which, while the sovereign territory of Azerbaijan, has a predominantly Armenian population. With the break-up of the Soviet Union, the conflict has become an inter-state war. Armenia has had the military advantage (although not in weapons strength), and by the middle of 1993, had secured virtually all of Nagorno-Karabakh and had gained control of some 20% of Azeri territory outside the enclave. The situation has been complicated by internal Azeri divisions which led to rebel forces ousting President Abulfaz Elchibey and reinstating the former Brezhnevite politburo leader Gaidar Aliyev. The conflict continues to appear irresolvable, despite mediation attempts from Turkey, Russia and the US.

Georgia is caught in two complicated internal political struggles. The Abkhaz and South Ossetian ethnic minority groups have taken up arms against the central Georgian leadership. The South Ossetian dispute resulted in an uneasy truce in June 1992 when a tripartite Russian–Georgian–South Ossetian peacekeeping force was introduced into the region. The Abkhaz conflict, ignited in August 1992, has not found a similar resolution and Georgian and Abkhaz forces continue a low-intensity war in the north-western corner of Georgia. This internal instability has fractured the central Georgian leadership. President Eduard Shevardnadze has so far failed to overcome the internal divisions within it and has had constantly to struggle with other independent figures, such as the Defence Minister Tengiz Kitovani and the guerrilla leader Dzhaba Iosseliani. The previous president, Zviad Gamsakhurdia, also continues to have a sizeable following in the country.

Former Yugoslavia

The situation in the former Yugoslavia, and in Bosnia-Herzegovina in particular, has deteriorated further over the last 12 months. In Croatia, the situation has more or less been stabilised, but the UN protection force (UNPROFOR I) has been unable to fulfil its mandate because the United Nations Protected Areas (UNPAs) have not been fully demilitarised. In January 1993, Croatian forces launched a counter-attack aimed at widening the narrow corridor which linked northern and southern Croatia to allow the rebuilding of the vital road bridge at Maslenica and to open the airfield at Zadar. Serbian militia recovered their heavy weapons from UN-monitored parks and halted the Croat advance. After a cease-fire had been established, both sides agreed to pull back, leaving UNPROFOR I to monitor a demilitarised zone, but Croat forces have not yet done so.

On 13 August 1992 the UN Security Council adopted Resolution 770; it called on states to take 'all measures necessary to facilitate the delivery of humanitarian assistance' in Bosnia-Herzegovina. It was only in October 1992, however, that a NATO force (UNPROFOR II) was deployed. Initially, fighting in Bosnia was either between Serbs and Muslims or Serbs and Croats. By June 1993, however, attacks by Croats and Muslims against each other had become common. Although sorely tested, UNPROFOR II has managed throughout to maintain its essential neutrality. In December 1992, the Serbs mounted a major offensive in eastern Bosnia and soon surrounded a number of Muslim-inhabited towns, prevented aid from reaching them and subjected them to intermittent bombardment. On 6 May 1993 UN Security Council Resolution 824 declared six towns and their surroundings to be 'safe areas' free from armed attack. The withdrawal of Bosnian Serb forces to a distance at which they ceased to constitute a menace was required, as was free and unimpeded access for UNPROFOR II and humanitarian agencies. The resolution has achieved only limited success and UN reinforcements are still awaited. An offer from seven Muslim countries of over 20,000 troops has been greeted with some alarm by both contributors to UNPROFOR and the Bosnian Serbs. However, an air force has been assembled in Italy to provide air support for UN troops should they come under 'persistent and continuous attack'.Throughout the conflict, a debate has raged concerning the moral obligation of other countries to intervene with force to halt the fighting. More recently, this debate has focused on the related topics of supplying arms to the Muslims and providing them with a degree of air cover. Thus far the argument has always been won by the advocates of caution and non-intervention in a civil war (despite the precedent this could set to others considering the use of force). In early July 1993 the Serbs indicated they would no longer allow CSCE monitors in Kosovo, Vojvodina or Sandzak.

The Baltic Republics

All three Baltic Republics have given the highest priority to obtaining firm agreements on the withdrawal of Russian forces from their territory. Only Lithuania has so far secured a date – 31 August 1993 – for the withdrawal to be completed. Negotiations were made easier by the Lithuanian offer to build 10,000 homes for soldiers in Kaliningrad in exchange for two torpedo craft and two other naval boats. In the other two republics negotiations and troop withdrawals have been suspended as a result of the crisis regarding the status of Russians living there. The situation in Estonia is more severe as the 500,000 Russians living there are concentrated in the Narva province. An unofficial referendum was held in Narva and Sillamae in mid-July 1993 resulting in an overwhelming majority vote in favour of autonomy; the Estonian government considers the referendum illegal and is ignoring its result as only about 50% of the electorate voted. There are over 900,000 Russians in Latvia, while Russians living in Lithuania constitute a relatively small minority (less than 10% of the population). Latvia and Estonia are unwilling to grant automatic nationality to Russians, and various criteria (regarding length of residence and knowledge of the language) are being considered. In late June 1993 Estonia passed a law requiring non-citizens to take citizenship within two years (which requires the ability to converse in Estonian), or to apply for residency permits. Russia responded by cutting off gas supplies to Estonia for four days until President Meri suspended application of the law.

Nuclear Forces

Two non-NATO European states have nuclear weapons located on their territory: Belarus and Ukraine. Belarus ratified the START I Treaty on 4 February 1993 and is ready to transfer its 80 mobile

SS-25 ICBM to Russia. As yet, Ukraine has not ratified START I, despite the political commitment
it made in Lisbon in May 1992. There is a growing movement in Ukraine in favour of becoming a
nuclear power. In early July 1993, the Ukrainian parliament declared that Ukraine owned the nuclear
weapons on its territory, but added that it had no intention of using or threatening to use them and
confirmed that it still intended to become a non-nuclear state. Whether Ukraine has the ability to stop
Russian use of ICBM located on its territory, how long it will take Ukraine to be able to fire them
unilaterally or whether it will be able to re-target them, are all open to question. However, Ukraine's
control of strategic or medium-range (but nuclear-capable) bombers, which can be armed with some
600 nuclear ALCM still in the country, is unquestionable. On 16 July it was announced in the Russian
press, and later confirmed by the Ukrainian Minister of Defence, that ten SS-19 ICBM in Ukraine
were being dismantled. The warheads are being retained in Ukraine for the time being.

Conventional Force Developments

Baltic Republics

The three **Baltic Republics** have continued to develop their armed forces but, as yet, have not
acquired much, if any, heavy equipment. **Estonia** has acquired four unarmed inshore patrol craft from
Sweden and Finland; **Latvia** has five inshore patrol craft – one from Sweden and the remainder
converted fishing boats – while the **Lithuanian** Navy has two Soviet-built *Grisha-III*-class frigates.
All three navies expect to receive ships from the disposal of the former East German fleet (Estonia
two *Kondor-I* coastal minesweepers and six *Osa-I* missile craft, Latvia two *Kondor-I* and three *Osa-
I*, Lithuania one *Kondor-I* and three *Osa-I*). So far, only Latvia has started an air wing with transport
aircraft and helicopters. There have been no reports of any tank or artillery acquisitions.

Former Warsaw Pact countries

The former Warsaw Pact countries of Eastern and Central Europe have started the process of
eliminating their equipment in excess of the CFE Treaty limits. Despite the division of Czechoslovakia, perhaps as many as 700 tanks, 1,000 APC and 30 combat aircraft have been eliminated there.
Hungary has disposed of a few tanks, about 100 BTR-series APC and around 250 pieces of towed
artillery (mainly 152mm D-20). **Romania** has made a slow start to the elimination process. **Poland**
has eliminated 300 tanks and its *Scud* launchers. The fourth Military District, the Krakow MD
covering south-east Poland, is now established but will not be fully operational until 1995. It is
planned to station rapid deployment forces in the district. Polish weapons developments include: the
PZL-230F *Skorpion* fighter (the first two aircraft are now being evaluated by the Air Force, which
has ordered four more aircraft for delivery in 1993); and an improved version of the T-72 tank
designated PT-91. It is unlikely that the Army will order this before an export order is secured
(although exports of equipment not bought by the producing country's forces are hard to achieve).
Conscription in the **Czech Republic** was reduced to 12 months from the end of July 1993; this means
that 21,000 men were discharged in July and a further 15,000 will be discharged at the end of
September. It is planned that nearly 50% of the Czech armed forces will be 'career soldiers'.
Conscript service in the **Slovenian** forces is also being reduced to 12 months in July 1993. **Hungary**
has decided to procure 28 MiG-29 (together with spares, ammunition and a training package) from
Russia in lieu of debt repayment.

Transcaucasus Republics

As the Russian Army has withdrawn from the Transcaucasus Republics, so have the national armies
gained in strength, either by being given or taking the equipment of some departing units. **Azerbaijan**
has acquired more equipment than Armenia: some 280 tanks (compared to Armenia's 160), some 480
BMP (200) and 330 pieces of artillery (170). Azerbaijan also has an air force of some 50 combat
aircraft, plus 50 L-29 trainers, which can be armed, and eight Mi-24 attack helicopters. A year ago
Russia had around 120 combat aircraft still stationed in Azerbaijan, while there were no Russian Air

Force units in Armenia. Although very little is known of the equipment holdings in **Georgia**, its Air Force has 40 Su-2 and Su-18 aircraft and a number of helicopters, including a few Mi-24.

Former Yugoslavia

With civil war raging in Bosnia-Herzegovina, and with some 25% of Croatia controlled by Serbian militias, it is not easy to give precise figures on either manpower strengths or equipment holdings, although our estimates this year should be more accurate than those published in *The Military Balance 1992–1993* for the armed forces of the republics of the former Yugoslavia.

In the rump of Yugoslavia, the republics of **Serbia and Montenegro**, the Army has increased the number of its brigades, but it is not yet known whether these are fully established brigades or purely units of much smaller strength given the title 'brigade'. Manpower numbers have not increased, but weapon holdings have decreased – perhaps by 350 tanks, 300 AIFV and about 300 artillery pieces, including 80 MRL. How many of these have been passed to Serbian militias in Bosnia and Croatia is not known.

Belarus and Ukraine

Equipment holdings in both Belarus and Ukraine are larger than those declared at the signing of the CFE Treaty (for those former Soviet military districts inherited by the two states) and thus larger than listed in *The Military Balance 1992–1993*. The additional equipment was redeployed from the Soviet Groups of Forces in Eastern Europe before the break-up of the Soviet Union. The most significant increases in **Belarus** are about 1,400 additional tanks (all of which must be eliminated under the CFE Treaty), 70 additional SP guns and 70 additional MRL which do not bring the artillery total above the CFE limit. Belarus has disbanded all six tank divisions, one motor-rifle division and two SSM brigades, and has formed three mechanised brigades. Two Army HQ have been retitled as Corps HQ. In March 1993 it was reported that the 76th tank division, located at Brest, had ceased to exist as its equipment had been taken to an elimination site. CFE data shows no 76th division at Brest, but an arms and equipment store with a mixture of equipments, which could be the basis for a mobilisation division. There are still three similar stores which could be mobilisation division bases in Belarus. It has now become clear that Russia still has large numbers of aircraft stationed in Belarus. These are mainly medium bombers of the Long-Range Air Force (120 Tu-16, Tu-22, Tu-22H) and a division of Su-24 (80 aircraft). There is also a PVO fighter regiment and a long-range reconnaissance regiment. The additional equipment in Ukraine is mainly some 500 artillery pieces (140 towed guns, 160 SP, 100 MRL, 100 mortars) which still leaves the artillery total below the CFE limit. **Ukraine**, too, is reducing its ground forces and has disbanded one tank division and five SSM brigades. Three motor-rifle divisions have been retitled mechanised divisions (with no apparent change in organisation or equipment holdings) and two mechanised brigades have been formed.

While the Black Sea Fleet remains undivided and under the joint control of Russia and Ukraine, Ukraine has been establishing its own Navy. At present, it only has two ships: one *Krivak-III* built originally for the KGB, which does not have the standard *Krivak* frigate armament (a further ship in this class is expected to be completed shortly); and one *Petya-II* frigate. Ukraine expects to own all new ships completed in the Nicolayev shipyards. When the aircraft carrier *Varjag* is completed, however, there could be further disputes with Russia. Although the Russian/Ukrainian agreement over the Black Sea Fleet division includes naval aviation and shore troops (coastal defence and marines), such forces are already declared by Ukraine and not by Russia in CFE data returns.

Neutral and Non-aligned States

The **Albanian** Army is some 30,000 men stronger than previously reported in *The Military Balance*, and has some 300 more tanks, including some T-62. Albania and Turkey have signed a military cooperation agreement. The **Austrian** Army has taken delivery of 45 more RBS-56 ATGW and 60 *Kuerassier* SP anti-tank guns. The **Cyprus** Army has received 50 more *Leonidas* APC. The higher command structure of the **Finnish** armed forces has been reorganised into three military commands

Arctic Ocean

Atlantic Ocean

North Sea

REP OF IRELAND

UK

NETHERLANDS
BELGIUM

DENMARK

N O R W A Y

S W E D E N

F I N L A N D

Baltic Sea

ESTONIA

LATVIA

LITHUANIA

Kaliningrad

LUXEMBOURG

GERMANY

POLAND

BELARUS

FRANCE

SWITZERLAND

AUSTRIA

CZECH REPUBLIC

SLOVAKIA

RUSSIA

PORTUGAL

S P A I N

Balearic Islands

Corsica

Sardinia

I T A L Y

HUNGARY

U K R A I N E

Mediterranean Sea

Sicily

ALBANIA

ROMANIA

MOLDOVA

BULGARIA

GREECE

Black Sea

Abkhazia

South Ossetia

GEORGIA

ARMENIA

Caspian Sea

T U R K E Y

Crete

Cyprus

Nagorno-Karabakh

AZERBAIJAN

SLOVENIA

CROATIA

Vojvodina

BOSNIA-HERZEGOVINA

Y U G O S L A V I A

SERBIA

Montenegro

Kosovo

MACEDONIA

THE BALKANS

0   300 Kms

0   200 Miles

Red Sea

(seven areas) and two military frontiers (23 districts). The Army has 100 additional T-72 tanks, 70 more BMP-2 AIFV and 90 more A-180 *Sisu* APC. The Navy has commissioned a second *Hämeenmaa*-class and two more *Pansio*-class minelayers. The **Swedish** Army has disbanded one armoured and four infantry mobilisation brigades, and the Air Force one fighter and one FGA squadron and their aircraft placed in store. In **Switzerland**, the result of a referendum over the proposed procurement of 34 F/A-18 aircraft was decisively in favour of the purchase. The Army has taken delivery of an additional M-89 APC (M-113 with 20mm cannon), 70 Pz H6-74 155mm SP guns and 100 MOWAG *Piranha* with *TOW*-2 ATGW.

ALBANIA

GNP	1990ε: leke 28.10bn ($3.24bn)
	1991ε: leke 60.00bn ($2.80bn)
Growth	1990ε: –13% 1991ε: –35%
Inflation	1990: 30% 1991ε: 100%
Debt	1991ε: $500m 1992ε: $600m
Def bdgt	1992ε: leke 2.600bn ($34.7m)
	1993ε: leke 3,300m ($30.0m)
$1 = leke	1990: 6.425 1991: 8.673
	1992: 75.000 1993: 110.000

Population: 3,409,000 (90% Albanian, 8% Greek)

	13–17	18–22	23–32
Men	171,000	161,500	301,000
Women	166,000	154,000	284,000

TOTAL ARMED FORCES:
ACTIVE: 73,000 (22,400 conscripts).
Terms of service: 18 months.
RESERVES: 155,000 (to age 56): Army 150,000, Navy/Air Force 5,000.

ARMY: 60,000 (incl reserves, 20,000 conscripts).
4 Military Districts.
1 tk bde. 11 inf bde.
3 arty regt. 6 lt coastal arty bn.
1 engr regt.
EQUIPMENT:
MBT: 900: T-34, T-54/-59, T-62.
RECCE: 15 BRDM-1.
APC: 90: Ch Type-531.
TOWED ARTY: 122mm: M-1931/37, 120 M-1938, Ch Type-60; 130mm: Ch Type-59-1; 152mm: M-1937, 90 Ch Type-66, D-1.
MRL: 107mm: Ch Type-63.
MORTARS: 82mm: 259; 120mm: 500; 160mm: 100.
RCL: 82mm: T-21.
ATK GUNS: 45mm: M-1942; 57mm: M-1943; 85mm: 61 D-44, Ch Type-56; 100mm: 34 Type-86.
AD GUNS: 23mm: 12 ZU-23-2/ZPU-1; 37mm: 100 M-1939; 57mm: 82 S-60; 85mm: 30 KS-12; 100mm: 56.

NAVY: ε2,000 (ε1,000 conscripts). Additional 400 may serve in coast defence.
BASES: Durrës, Vlorë, Sazan Island.

SUBMARINES:† 2 Sov *Whiskey* with 533mm TT (plus 1 trg, unserviceable).
PATROL AND COASTAL COMBATANTS: † 45:
TORPEDO CRAFT: 29 Ch *Huchwan* PHT with 2 x 533mm TT.
PATROL: 18:
2 Sov *Kronshtadt* PCO; 6 Ch *Shanghai*-II, some 4 Sov PO-2 PFI and some 6 P4 PFI⟨.
MINE WARFARE:† 6: 2 Sov T-43 (in reserve), 4 Sov T-301 MSI;
SUPPORT: 2 Sov *Khobi* harbour tankers.

AIR FORCE: 11,000 (1,400 conscripts); 112 cbt ac†, no armed hel.
FGA: 3 sqn:
1 with 10 J-2; (MiG-15).
2 with 12 J-5, 20 J-6 (MiG-17) (MiG-19).
FIGHTER: 3 sqn:
2 with 50 J-6; (MiG-19).
1 with 20 J-7 (MiG-21).
TRANSPORT: 1 sqn with 10 C-5 (An-2), 3 Il-14M, 6 Li-2 (C-47).
HELICOPTERS: 2 sqn with 28 Ch Z-5 (Mi-4).
TRAINING: 8 CJ-5, 10 MiG-15UTI, 6 Yak-11.
SAM:† some 4 SA-2 sites, 22 launchers.

PARAMILITARY: 16,000.
INTERNAL SECURITY FORCE: (5,000).
PEOPLE'S MILITIA: (3,500).

ARMENIA

GDP	1991ε: r 15.67bn ($9.22bn)
	1992ε: r 236.5bn ($5.99bn)
Growth	1991: -19.3% 1992ε: -45%
Inflation[a]	1991: 175% 1992ε: 1,500%
Debt	1991: $750m
Def bdgt[b]	1991: r 250m ($147.1m)
$1 = r	1991: 1.70 1992: 180
r = rouble	

Population: 3,397,000 (1.5% Russian)

	13–17	18–22	23–32
Men	159,800	141,100	256,500
Women	151,500	132,400	251,000

[a] Year average
[b] Provisional draft budget; 1991 roubles. The war with Azerbaijan is costing each nation an estimated r25–30m a day.

TOTAL ARMED FORCES: some 20,000.
Terms of service: conscription, 18 months.
RESERVES: Some mobilization reported, possibly
300,000 with military service within 15 years.

ARMY: Some 20,000.
1 Army HQ.
2 MR bde;   1 indep MRR.
1 arty bde;   1 arty regt.
1 MRL regt,   1 ATK regt.
1 indep tk bn.
EQUIPMENT:
MBT: 160: incl 77 T-72.
AIFV: Some 200 BMP-1/-2.
APC: Some 240 BTR-60/-70.
TOTAL ARTY: 257.
TOWED ARTY: 122mm: M-1938, D-30; 152mm: 36
D-20, 24 2A36.
SP ARTY: 122mm: 12 2S1; 152mm: 36 2S3.
MRL: 122mm: 40 BM-21.
ATK GUNS: 85mm: D-44; 100mm: T-12.
ATGW: 18 AT-3 (BRDM), 27 AT-6 (MT-LB).
SAM: SA-4/-8/-9.
AIRCRAFT: ε6 cbt ac reported.
HELICOPTERS: ε9 Mi-8, ε11 Mi-24.

PARAMILITARY:
Ministry of Interior: ε1,000: 4bn.

FOREIGN FORCES:
RUSSIA (Transcaucasus Group of Forces)
Army: 4,500: 1 MRD; 90 MBT, 199 APC, 100 arty.

AUSTRIA

GDP	1991: OS 1,930.10bn ($165.30bn)		
	1992ε: OS 2,022.80bn ($184.07bn)		
Growth	1991: 3.1%	1992: 1.7%	
Inflation	1991: 3.3%	1992: 4.1%	
Publ. Debt	1992: 55.8%		
Def bdgt	1992: OS 18.28bn ($1.66bn)		
	1993: OS 19.02bn ($1.66bn)		
$1 = OS	1990: 11.370	1991: 11.676	
	1992: 10.989	1993: 11.452	
OS = schilling			

Population: 7,766,000

	13–17	18–22	23–32
Men	237,000	268,000	644,000
Women	225,000	256,000	627,000

TOTAL ARMED FORCES: (Air Service
forms part of the Army):
ACTIVE: some 52,000 (ε20–30,000 conscripts;

some 66,000 reservists a year undergo refresher
training, a proportion at a time).
Terms of service: 6 months recruit trg, 60 days
reservist refresher trg during 15 years (or 8 months
trg, no refresher); 60–90 days additional for officers,
NCO and specialists.
RESERVES: 119,000 ready (72 hrs) reserves;
960,000 with reserve trg but no commitment, all
ranks to age 50.

ARMY: 46,000 (19,500 conscripts).
3 Corps
2 with 1 engr bn, 1 recce, 1 arty regt, 3 Provincial
mil comd, 6 inf regt
1 with 3 mech inf bde (1 tk, 1 mech inf, 1 SP arty
bn), 1 engr, 1 recce bn, 1 arty regt, 2 Provincial mil
comd, 2 inf regt.
1 Provincial mil comd with 1 inf regt, 1 guard bn
On mob inf regt convert to bde.
EQUIPMENT:
MBT: 169 M-60A3.
APC: 465 Saurer 4K4E/F.
TOWED ARTY: 105mm: 108 IFH (M-2A1);
155mm: 24 M-114.
SP ARTY: 155mm: 54 M-109A2.
FORTRESS ARTY: 155mm: 24 SFK M-2.
MRL: 128mm: 18 M-51.
MORTARS: 81mm: 700; 107mm: 102 M-2; 120mm:
274 M-43.
ATGW: 118 RBS-56 *Bill*.
RCL: 74mm: *Miniman*; 84mm: *Carl Gustav*; 106mm:
446 M-40A1.
ATK GUNS:
SP: 105mm: 285 *Kuerassier* JPz SK.
TOWED: 85mm: 220 M-52/-55;
STATIC: 90mm: some 60 M-47 tk turrets;
105mm: some 200 L7A1 (*Centurion* tk);
AD GUNS: 20mm: 560; 35mm: 74 GDF-002 twin
towed; 40mm: 38 M-42A1 twin SP.
MARINE WING (under School of Military Engineer-
ing): 2 river patrol craft(; 10 unarmed boats.

AIR FORCE: 6,000 (2,400 conscripts)
54 cbt ac, no armed hel.
1 air div HQ; 3 air regt; 3 AD bn.
FGA: 1 regt with 30 SAAB 105Oe.
FIGHTER: 1 regt with 24 J-35Oe.
HELICOPTERS:
RECCE: 12 OH-58B, 12 AB-206A.
TRANSPORT: (med): 23 AB-212; (lt): 8 AB-204 (9
in store).
SAR: 24 A-316 B *Alouette*.
LIAISON: 1 sqn with 2 *Skyvan* 3M, 15 O-1 (10 -A, 5 -
E), 11 PC-6B.
TRAINING: 16 PC-7.
AD: 3 bn with 36 20mm, 18 M-65 twin 35mm AA
guns; *Super-Bat* and *Skyguard* AD, *Goldhaube*,
Selenia MR(S-403) 3-D radar systems.

FORCES ABROAD:
UN AND PEACEKEEPING:
CAMBODIA (UNTAC): 17 Observers, 19 civ pol.
CYPRUS (UNFICYP): 1 inf bn (347).
EL SALVADOR (ONUSAL): 3 civ pol.
IRAQ/KUWAIT (UNIKOM): 7 Observers.
MIDDLE EAST (UNTSO): 13.
SYRIA (UNDOF): 1 inf bn (451).
WESTERN SAHARA (MINURSO): 1 Observer.

AZERBAIJAN

GDP	1991: r 22.41bn ($13.18bn)		
	1992ε: r 315.98bn ($10.28bn)		
Growth	1991: -0.7%	1992ε: -21.8%	
Inflation[a]	1991: 87.3%	1992ε: 1,350%	
Debt	1991: $1.30bn		
Def bdgt	1991: r 514.3m ($302.5m)		
	1992: r 2.85 bn ($189.86m)		
$1[b] = r	1991: 1.70	1992: 180	
r = rouble			

Population: 7,383,600 (7.9% Russian)

	13–17	18–22	23–32
Men	360,000	328,500	608,800
Women	316,700	307,000	607,100

[a] Year average
[b] In 1992, the manat = r10 was introduced to replace the rouble.

TOTAL ARMED FORCES:
ACTIVE: 42,600.
Terms of service: 17 months.
RESERVES: Some mob 560,000 with military service within 15 years.

ARMY: 38,900.
2 Corps HQ.
1 tk bde.
9 mech bde (incl 2 trg).
1 mech regt (cadre).
2 arty bde, 2 arty regt.
EQUIPMENT:
MBT: 286 T-72.
AIFV: 480 BMP.
APC: 161 BTR, 201 MT-LB.
TOTAL ARTY: 330.
TOWED ARTY: D-30.
MRL: BM-21.
MORTARS: ε130, incl some PM38.
SAM: SA-4/-9/-13.
HELICOPTERS: 15 Mi-2/-8, 8 Mi-24.

NAVY: 2,100.
BASE: Baku
About 15 naval units from ex-Sov Caspian Flotilla and Border Guards, incl 1 *Petya-II* FF and some 6 *Stenka* PFI.

AIR FORCE: 1,600: 47 cbt ac:
AIRCRAFT: 7 MiG-21, 28 MiG-25, 2 Su-17, 9 Su-24, 1 Su-25, 52 L-29 (trg).

PARAMILITARY:
Militia (Ministry of Internal Affairs): 20,000+.
Popular Front: Karabakh People's Defence: up to 12,000 claimed.

OPPOSITION:
Armed forces of Nagorno-Karabakh: ε20,000, incl ε8,000 volunteers from Armenia. Eqpt reported incl 13 MBT, 120 APC, 16 arty.

BELARUS

GDP	1991: r 71.6bn ($42.12bn)		
	1992ε: r 730.32bn ($36.22bn)		
Growth[a]	1991: -3.1%	1992ε: -15%	
Inflation[b]	1991: 80.3%	1992ε: 1,100%	
Debt	1991: $3.40bn		
Def bdgt[c]	1992ε: r 17bn ($944m)		
	1993ε: r 56.2 bn ($660m)		
$1 = r[d]	1991: 1.70	1992: 180	
	1993ε: 800		
r = rouble			

Population: 10,438,000 (13.2% Russian)

	13–17	18–22	23–32
Men	388,800	364,800	706,500
Women	376,900	357,700	712,900

[a] NMP growth
[b] Year average
[c] Excl procurement; with arms purchases the 1992 defence budget may be as high as r28bn. ($1,647.0m); 1993 bdgt is provisional.
[d] Belarus introduced the rubel = 10 roubles in June 1992. All figures for 1991, 1992 are in roubles.

TOTAL ARMED FORCES
ACTIVE: 102,600 (reducing to 90,000 by 1995) incl about 600 MoD staff and 21,800 in centrally controlled units.
Terms of service: 18 months.
RESERVES: Some 289,500 with military service within 5 years.

STRATEGIC NUCLEAR FORCES: (Russian-controlled forces on Belarus territory).
ICBM: 80
SS-25 *Sickle* (RS-12m): 80 (mobile, single warhead msl; 2 bases with 9 units of 9).

ARMY: (50,500)
1 army, 1 corps HQ.

2 motor div (1 trg).
3 mech bde.
1 ABD; 1 AB bde.
1 arty div.
3 SSM bde.
2 ATK bde/regt.
1 *Spetsnaz* bde.
7 SAM bde.
EQUIPMENT:
MBT: 3,287: 280 T-54, 443 T-55, 459 T-62, 300 T-64, 1,800 T-72, 5 T-80.
LIGHT TANKS: 9 PT-76.
AIFV: 2,514: 938 BMP-1, 1,300 BMP-2, 160 BRM, 116 BMD.
APC: 1,195: 348 BTR-60, 405 BTR-70, 192 BTR-80, 117 BTR-D, 133 MT-LB.
TOTAL ARTY: some 1,594 incl:
TOWED ARTY: 440: 122mm: 190 D-30; 152mm: 6 M-1943 (D-1), 58 D-20, 136 2A65, 50 2A36.
SP ARTY: 588: 122mm: 239 2S1; 152mm: 168 2S3, 120 2S5; 152mm: 13 2S19; 203mm: 48 2S7.
COMBINED GUN/MORTAR: 120mm: 54 2S9.
MRL: 428: 122mm: 277 BM-21, 18 9P138; 130mm: 1 BM-13; 220mm: 84 9P140; 300mm: 48 9A52.
MORTARS: 84; 120mm: 78 2S12, 6 PM-38.
SSM: 60 *Scud*, 36 *FROG*/SS-21.

AIR FORCE: 14,100.
1 air army, 341 cbt ac, 95 attack hel.
FGA/BOMBERS: 1 regt with 9 Su-17, 30 Su-24, 20 MiG-27.
FGA: 2 regt with 99 Su-25.
FIGHTER: 2 regt: 15 MiG-23, 33 MiG-25, 84 MiG-29.
RECCE: 19 MiG-25, 12 Su-24, 20 Yak-28.
HELICOPTER: 4 regt, 4 sqn: 26 Mi-2, 32 Mi-6, 143 Mi-8, 95* Mi-24, 15 Mi-26.
TRANSPORT: 29 Il-76, 6 An-12, 7 An-24, 1 An-26, 1 Tu-134.

AIR DEFENCE: 15,600
1 PVO army, 76 cbt ac.
FIGHTER: 2 regt with 38 MiG-23, 13 MiG-25, 25 Su-27.
SAM: 650 SAM.

PARAMILITARY:
Border Guards (Ministry of Interior): 8,000

FOREIGN FORCES:
Russian Air Force, 272 cbt ac, 3 air div.
1 bbr div with 3 regt with 82 Su-24.
1 hy bbr div; 2 regt with 55 Tu-22, 1 regt with 20 Tu-22M and 15 Tu-16.
1 hy bbr div; 2 regt with 32 Tu-22M.
1 ftr regt with 40 MiG-25
1 recce regt with 28 Tu-22

BOSNIA-HERZEGOVINA

GDP	1991ε: $10.95bn
Growth	1991ε: -32%

Population: 4,508,000 (39.5% 'Muslims', 32% Serbs, 18.4% Croats)

The fighting in Bosnia and the lack of accurate information make it impossible to follow the standard layout.

TOTAL ARMED FORCES:
ACTIVE: some 60,000.
RESERVES: some 120,000.

ARMY: 60,000.
5 'Corps' HQ.

Some 59 inf 'bde'.	4 mech 'bde'.
Some 7 mtn 'bde'.	1 SF 'bde'.
1 arty 'bde'.	Some 2 AD regt.

EQUIPMENT:
MBT: ε20 incl T-55.
APC: ε30.
ARTY: some, incl a few 203mm, 120mm mor.
AD GUNS: 20mm, 30mm.

DEPLOYMENT (manpower incl some reserves).
1 Corps: Sarajevo: up to 40,000 and up to 20 'bde'.
2 Corps: Tuzla: up to 10,000 and up to 21 'bde'.
3 Corps: Zenica: up to 30,000 and up to 20 'bde'.
4 Corps: Mostar: 5,000 plus and up to 8 'bde'.
5 Corps: Bihac: up to 25,000 and up to 8 'bde'.

OTHER FORCES:
CROAT (Croatian Defence Council (HVO)):
ε50,000 (incl Croatian Forces HV and HOS).
Some 30 'bde'.
1 SF 'bde'.
EQUIPMENT:
MBT: ε50, incl T-34, T-55.
ARTY: ε500.

SERB (Army of the Serbian Republic of Bosnia and Herzegovina) up to 80,000.
7 'Corps' HQ.

Some 44 inf 'bde'.	2 mech inf 'bde'.
2 mtn 'bde'.	2 armd 'bde'.
1 arty 'bde'.	

EQUIPMENT:
MBT: ε330, incl M-84, T-72.
APC: 400.
ARTY: 800 (incl mortars): towed: 122mm: D-30, M-1938 (M-30); 130mm: M-46; 152mm: D-20.
SSM: *Frog* 7.
AD GUNS: incl 20mm, 23mm, ZSU 23-4, 30mm: M53/59SP; 90mm.

SAM: SA-2/-6/-8/-9/-14.
AIRCRAFT: 5 MiG-21, 12 *Jastreb*, some 20 G-4 *Super Galeb* and *Orao* 1.
HELICOPTERS: 12 Mi-8, 25 SA-341 *Gazela*.

DEPLOYMENT:
1 Krajina Corps: Banja Luka: up to 9 'bde'.
2 Krajina Corps: Bihak: 5 'bde'.
3 Krajina Corps: Doboj: up to 9 'bde'.
Tuzla Corps: Bijeljina: up to 9 'bde'.
Drina Corps: 6 'bde'.
Sarajevo Corps: up to 7 'bde'.
Herzegovina Corps: 5 'bde'.

FOREIGN FORCES:
CROATIA: HOS 1,000.
UNITED NATIONS (UNPROFOR II): Some 2,000, incl 4 inf bn for Sarajevo. Some 7,500 incl 4 inf bn gps (some armd recce and engr spt) for aid distribution and 'safe area' protection.

BULGARIA

GDP	1991ε: leva 138.40bn ($25.72bn)		
	1992ε: leva 214.00bn ($20.83bn)		
Growth	1991: –23%	1992ε: –17%	
Inflation	1991: 380%	1992: 80%	
Debt	1990: $11.05bn	1991: $12.30bn	
Def bdgt*a*	1992: leva 8.11bn ($1.31bn)		
	1993: leva 8.79bn ($1.18bn)		
$1 = leva	1990: 0.80	1991: 16.0	
	1992: 23.6	1993: ε26.0	

a Dollar values are estimated.

Population: 8,763,000

	13–17	18–22	23–32
Men	316,000	316,000	580,000
Women	300,000	297,000	550,000

TOTAL ARMED FORCES:
ACTIVE: 99,400 (ε60,000 conscripts). Incl about 20,000 centrally controlled, 2,600 Ministry of Defence staff but excl some 10,000 construction tps.
Terms of service: 18 months.
RESERVES: 303,000. Army 250,500; Navy (to age 55, officers 60 or 65) 7,500; Air (to age 60) 45,000.

ARMY: 52,000 (ε33,300 conscripts).
3 Military Districts/Army HQ:
1 with 1 tk bde;
1 with 1 MRD, 1 Regional Training Centre (RTC), 1 tk bde;
1 with 2 MRD, 2 RTC, 2 tk bde;
Army tps: 4 *Scud*, 1 SS-23, 1 SAM bde, 3 arty, 3 AD arty, 1 SAM regt.
1 AB regt.
EQUIPMENT:
MBT: 2,209: 599 T-34, 1,277 T-55, 333 T-72.

ASSAULT GUN: 167 SU-100.
RECCE: 60 BRDM-1/-2.
AIFV: 114 BMP-23.
APC: 780 BTR-60, 1,142 MT-LB.
TOTAL ARTY: 2,081.
TOWED: 695: 100mm: 16 M-1944 (BS-3); 122mm: 344 M-30, 25 M-1931/37 (A-19); 130mm: 72 M-46; 152mm: 32 M-1937 (ML-20), 206 D-20.
SP: 122mm: 692 2S1.
MRL: 122mm: 222 BM-21.
MORTARS: 472: 120mm: 18 2B11, 61 B-24, 359 *Tundzha* SP; 160mm: 34 M-160.
SSM: launchers: 28 *FROG*-7, 36 *Scud*, 8 SS-23.
ATGW: 200 AT-3 *Sagger*.
ATK GUNS: 85mm: 150 D-44; 100mm: 200 T-12.
AD GUNS: 400: 23mm: ZU-23, ZSU-23-4 SP; 57mm: S-60; 85mm: KS-12; 100mm: KS-19.
SAM: 20 SA-3, 27 SA-4, 20 SA-6.

NAVY: 3,000 (2,000 conscripts).
BASES: coastal: Varna (HQ), Atiya, Sozopol, Balchik. Danube: Vidin (HQ).
SUBMARINES: 2 *Pobeda* (Sov *Romeo*) class with 533mm TT.
FRIGATES: 1.
1 *Smeli* (Sov *Koni*) with 1 x 2 SA-N-4 SAM, 2 x 12 ASW RL; plus 2 x 2 76mm guns.
PATROL AND COASTAL COMBATANTS: 23:
CORVETTES: 9: 6 *Poti* ASW with 2 x ASW RL, 4 x ASTT.
1 *Tarantul II* ASUW with 2 x 2 SS-N-2C *Styx*, 2 x 4 SA-N-5 *Grail* SAM; plus 1 x 76mm gun.
2 *Pauk I* with 1 SA-N-5 SAM, 2 x 5 ASW RL; plus 4 x 406mm TT.
MISSILE CRAFT: 6 *Osa* PFM with 4 x SS-N-2A/B *Styx* SSM.
PATROL INSHORE: about 8 *Zhuk* PFI
MINE WARFARE: 28:
MINELAYERS: 10 *Vydra*.
MCMV: 18:
4 *Sonya* MSC.
14 MSI: 4 *Vanya*, 4 *Yevgenya*, 6 *Olya*.
AMPHIBIOUS: 2:
2 Sov *Polnocny* LSM, capacity 150 tps, 6 tk.
SUPPORT AND MISCELLANEOUS: 7:
2 AOT, 2 AGHS, 1 AGI, 1 trg, 1 AT.
NAVAL AVIATION: 10 armed hel.
HELICOPTERS: 1 SAR/ASW sqn with 9 Mi-14 (ASW), 1 Ka-25.
COASTAL ARTY:
2 regt, 20 bty:
GUNS: 100mm: ε150; 130mm: 4 SM-4-1.
SSM: SS-C-1b *Sepal*, SSC-3 *Styx*.
NAVAL GUARD: 3 coy.

AIR FORCE: 21,800 (16,000 conscripts);
275 cbt ac, 44 attack hel.
2 air div, 1 mixed air corps, 6 cbt regt.
FGA: 1 regt with 39 Su-25.
1 regt with 37 MiG-23.

FIGHTER: 3 regt with some 22 MiG-23; 108 MiG-21PFM, 22 MiG-29.
RECCE: 1 regt with 26 MiG-21, 21 Su-22.
TRANSPORT: 1 regt with 2 Tu-134, 3 An-24, 4 An-26, 5 L-410, 3 Yak-40 (VIP).
SURVEY: 1 An-30.
HELICOPTERS: 2 regt with 14 Mi-2, 25 Mi-17, 44 Mi-24 (attack).
TRAINING: 3 trg regt with 120 L-29, 70 L-39.
MISSILES:
ASM: AS-7 *Kerry*.
AAM: AA-2 *Atoll*, AA-7 *Apex*, AA-8 *Aphid*.
SAM: SA-2/-3/-5/-10 (20 sites, some 110 launchers).

FORCES ABROAD:
UN AND PEACEKEEPING:
CAMBODIA (UNTAC): 808: 1 inf bn, plus 16 Observers, 74 civ pol.

PARAMILITARY:
BORDER GUARDS (Ministry of Interior): 12,000; 12 regt.
Some 50 craft including 12 Sov PO2 PCI⟨.
SECURITY POLICE: 4,000.
RAILWAY AND CONSTRUCTION TROOPS: 18,000.

CROATIA

GDP	1991ε: D 851.5bn ($22.5bn)		
	1992ε: $18.0bn		
Growth	1991ε: -30%	1992ε: - 20%	
Inflation	1991: 65%	1992ε: 850%	
Debt	1991: $3.10bn		
Def bdgt	1992: CD 393.0m ($5.61bn)		
	1993: CD 1.66bn		

Population: 4,743,000 (75% Croats, 11% Serb)

	13-17	18-22	23-32
Men	166,700	164,600	338,000
Women	157,000	156,600	324,000

$1 = D, Croatian Dinar, Kruma

TOTAL ARMED FORCES:
ACTIVE: ε103,300
Terms of Service: 10 months.
RESERVES: Army: 180,000. Home Defence: 10,000.

ARMY: ε95,000.
4 op zone (OZ) (Zagreb, Split, Osijek, Gospic;
1 indep. op comd (OC) (South Croatia);
Some 30 HV 'bde';
7 National Guard (ZNG) 'bde';
1 SF bde.
RESERVES: 13 Home Def regt.

EQUIPMENT
MBT: 200: 170 T-54/-55, 30 M-84.
RECCE: BRDM-2.
AIFV: M-80/-83.
APC: BTR-40/-50, M-60.
TOWED ARTY: 76mm: ZIS-3; 85mm; 100mm; 105mm; 122mm: 2S1; 130mm; 152mm; 203mm: 12 M-115.
MRL: 122mm: BM-21, RM-70; 128mm: M-77.
MORTARS: 82mm; 120mm: UBM-120.
ATGW: AT-3 *Sagger*, AT-4 *Spigot*.
RL: 90mm: M-79.
AD GUNS: 600+: 14.5mm: ZPU-2/-4; 20mm: BOV-1 SP, M-55; 30mm: M-53/59, BOV-3SP.
SAM: SA-7 (2,000), SA-9, SA-13, SA-14.

AIR FORCE: ε300: some 20 ac and hel, incl 2 MiG-21, *Galeb*, *Jastreb* FGA ac, An-2, An-26 tpt ac; Mi-8 hel.

AIR DEFENCE: 4,000
no details available.

NAVY: ε4,000.
BASES: Split, Pula, Sibenik, Ploce.
Minor facilities: Lastovo, Vis.
SUBMARINES: 1: *Una* SSI for SF ops.
PATROL AND COASTAL COMBATANTS: 11:
CORVETTES: 1 *King Petar Kresimir IV* (*Kobra*-class).
MISSILE CRAFT: 3:
1 *Rade Koncar* PFM with 2 x SS-N-2B *Styx*.
2 *Mitar Acev* (Sov *Osa-I*) PFM with 4 x SS-N-2A.
TORPEDO CRAFT: 3:
3 *Topcider* (Sov *Shershen*) with 4 x 533mm TT.
PATROL: 4:
COASTAL: 1 *Morar* ASW with 4 x ASW RL.
INSHORE: 3 *Mirna*
MINE WARFARE: 3
MINELAYERS: 1: *Cetina* (*Silba*-class), 94 mines.
Also DTM-211 and DSM-501 LCT can lay 100 mines – see amph forces.
MCM: 2:
1 *Vukov Klanac* MHC.
1 UK *Ham* MSI.
AMPHIBIOUS: craft only; 12: 4 DTM-211 and 1 DSM-501 LCT, about 7 LCM.
SUPPORT AND MISCELLANEOUS: 5:
1 *Spasilac* salvage, 1 Sov *Moma* survey, 1 AE, 2 tugs.
MARINES: 7 indep inf coy.
COAST DEFENCE:
Some 16 coast arty bty.

PARAMILITARY:
Police: 40,000 armed.
HOS (military wing of Croatian Party of Rights (HSP)) 1,000 (deployed in Bosnia).

OTHER FORCES:
SERBIAN ARMY OF SERBIAN KRAJINA (SASK) 40–50,000.
6 'Corps' HQ (North Dalmatia, Lika, Kordun, Banija, Baranja/Slavonia, West Slavonia). Some 25 'bde'.
1 SF bde.
EQUIPMENT:
MBT: ε200: T-34, T-54/-55.
APC: ε100.
ARTY: ε500.

PARAMILITARY: 24,000.
BORDER POLICE: 8,000, 4 bde (mech inf).
INTERIOR POLICE: 16,000, 8 bde (lt inf).

FOREIGN FORCES:
UN (UNPROFOR I): 15,400: 11 inf bn, plus spt units from 18 countries.

CYPRUS

GDP	1991: £C 2.65bn ($5.75bn)		
	1992: £C 3.01bn ($6.68bn)		
Growth	1991: 0.9%	1992: 7.7%	
Inflation	1991: 5.1%	1992: 6.4%	
Publ. Debt	1992: 52.5%		
Def bdgt	1992: £C 214.8m ($477.1m)		
	1993: £C 249.0m ($518.8m)		
$1 = 1C	1990: 0.457	1991: 0.461	
	1992: 0.450	1993: 0.483	

Population: 719,400

	13–17	18–22	23–32
Men	28,200	26,700	58,700
Women	26,500	25,200	54,900

TOTAL ARMED FORCES:
ACTIVE: 10,000 (incl 400 women).
Terms of service: conscription, 26 months, then reserve to age 50 (officers 65).
RESERVES: 88,000: 45,000 first-line (age 20–34); 43,000 second-line (age 35–50).

NATIONAL GUARD: 10,000.
1 Army, 2 div HQ.
2 bde HQ.
1 armd bde (-).
13 inf bn (incl 4 reserve).
1 SF bn.
1 ATK bn.
7 arty bn.
EQUIPMENT:
MBT: 52 AMX-30B-2.
RECCE: 126 EE-9 *Cascavel*, ε36 EE-3 *Jararaca*.
AIFV: 27 VAB-VCI.

APC: 92 *Leonidas*, 116 VAB (incl variants).
TOWED ARTY: 196: 75mm: 4 M-116A1 pack; 76mm: 54 M-42; 88mm: 18 25-pdr; 100mm: 36 M-1944; 105mm: 72 incl M-101, M-56; 155mm: 12 TR F1.
SP: 155mm: 12 F3.
MRL: 128mm: 24 Yug M-63 (YMRL-32).
MORTARS: 81mm: 72 incl SP; 82mm: 80 M-41/-43 some SP; 107mm: 12 M-2; 120mm: 114 RT61.
ATGW: *Milan* (24 on EE-3 *Jararaca*), *HOT* (18 on VAB).
RL: 89mm: 450 M-20.
RCL: 57mm: 216 M-18; 106mm: 144 M-40A1.
AD GUNS: 155: 20mm: M-55; 35mm: 8 GDF-005 with *Skyguard*; 40mm; 94mm: 3.7-in.
SAM: 24 SA-7, 18 *Mistral*.
MARINE: 1 *Salamis* PFI .
AIRCRAFT: 1 BN-2A *Maritime Defender*, 2 PC-9, 1 PA-22.
HELICOPTERS: 2 Bell 206, 1 MD-500, 4 SA-342 *Gazelle* (with *HOT*).

PARAMILITARY:
ARMED POLICE: 3,700; Shorland armd cars, 6 PCI .
MARITIME POLICE: 3 PFI : 2 *Evagoras* and 1 *Kinon* PFI .

FOREIGN FORCES:
GREECE: 950 (ELDYK) (Army) 2 inf bn, plus ε1,300 officers/NCO seconded to Greek-Cypriot National Guard.
UNITED KINGDOM: (in Sovereign Base Areas) 4,100: Army: 2 inf bn, 1 armd recce sqn. Air Force: 1 hel sqn, plus ac on det.
UNITED NATIONS:
UNFICYP: some 964; 2 inf bn (Austria, UK).

'Turkish Republic of Northern Cyprus'

Data presented here represents the *de facto* situation in the island. It in no way implies recognition, or IISS approval.

Def bdgt	1987ε:	TL 5.20bn ($6.07m)	
	1988:	TL 8.00bn ($5.62m)	
$1 = TL	(1987): 857	(1988): 1,422	
TL = Turkish lira			

TOTAL ARMED FORCES:
ACTIVE: some 4,000.
Terms of service: conscription, 24 months, then reserve to age 50.
RESERVES: 11,000 first-line; 10,000 second-line; 5,000 third-line.

ARMY:
7 inf bn.
MARITIME: 3 patrol boats.

FOREIGN FORCES:
TURKEY: 30,000; 1 corps, 300 M-48A5 MBT; 100
M-113, 100 M-59 APC; 144 105mm, 36 155mm, 8
203mm towed; 18 105mm, 6 155mm SP; 114
107mm mor, 84 40mm AA guns; 8 ac, 12 hel.

THE CZECH REPUBLIC

GDP	1991:	[Kcs 977.76bn ($33.17bn)]	
	1992ε:	Kcs 717.05bn ($25.37bn)	
Growth	1991:	[-14%] 1992ε: -8%	
Inflation	1991:	[57%]	1992: 12.3%
Debt	1990:	$8.1bn	1991: $9.3bn
Def exp^a	1990:	[Kcs 29.70bn ($1,654m)]	
	1991:	[Kcs 27.90bn ($946.4m)]	
Def bdgt^a	1992:	[Kcs 26.96bn ($954.0m)]	
	1993:	Kcs 22.99bn ($794.1m)	
$1 = Kcs	1990:	17.950	1991: 29.480
	1992:	28.260	1993: 28.840

Kcs = koruny
^{a} Data in [ ] refer to Czechoslovakia.

Population: 10,302,000

	13–17	18–22	23–32
Men	424,000	399,000	725,000
Women	410,000	385,000	701,000

TOTAL ARMED FORCES:
ACTIVE: 106,500 (40,400 conscripts) incl about
29,000 MOD and rear services staff).
Terms of service: 12 months.

ARMY: 41,900 (25,900 conscripts).
2 Command HQ:

2 armd div (-)	3 mech div.
1 mot inf div.	1 inf div.
2 arty bde.	1 SSM regt.

4 engr bde (incl 1 pontoon).
2 indep armd, 2 ATK, 1 rapid reaction bn.
EQUIPMENT:
MBT: 1,543: T-54/-55, T-72M.
RECCE: some 200 BRDM, OT-65.
AIFV: 780 BVP-1, BMP-2, BRM-1K.
APC: 1,200 OT-62A/B, OT-64A/C, OT-90, OT-810.
TOWED: 100mm: 150 M-53; 122mm: M-1938, 150
D-30; 130mm: M-46; 152mm: M-1937 (ML-20).
SP: 122mm: 100 2S1; 152mm: 275 *Dana* (M-77);
203mm: 2S7.
MRL: 122mm: 150 RM-70; 130mm: 200 RM-130
(M-51).
MORTARS: 120mm: 400; 240mm: 2S4.
SSM: 10–14: *FROG*-7, SS-21, *Scud*, SS-23.

ATGW: AT-3 *Sagger*, AT-5 *Spandrel*.
AD GUNS: 30mm: M-53/-59; 57mm: S-60.
SAM: SA-7, SA-9/-13.

AIR FORCE: 35,600 (14,500 conscripts);
226 cbt ac (plus 50 MiG-21, 12 Su-7 in store), 36
attack hel.
FGA: 3 regt: 1 with 35 Su-22; 1 with 31 MiG-23 BN,
16 MiG-21; 1 with 25 Su-25.
FIGHTER: 2 regt, 1 sqn: 1 regt with 33 MiG-23, 1 regt
with 10 MiG-29, 33 MiG-21, 1 sqn with 21 MiG-21.
TRANSPORT: 1 regt with 1 Tu-134, 1 Tu-154, 1 An-
12, 4 An-24, 4 An-26, 11 L-410.
HELICOPTERS: 1 regt (attack) with 36 Mi-24, 1 regt
(assault/tpt) with 51 M-2, 24 Mi-8, 3 Mi-8PPA
(ECM), 1 Mi-9, 33 Mi-17.
TRAINING: 1 regt with *22 MiG-21 U/MF, 10 L-29,
13 L-39C, 2 L-59 (L-39MS).
AAM: AA-2 *Atoll*, AA-7 *Apex*, AA-8 *Aphid*, AA-10
Alamo, AA-11 *Archer*.
AD: 2 AD div (7 AD units), SA-2, SA-3, SA-5, SA-6.

FORCES ABROAD:
UN AND PEACEKEEPING:
CROATIA (UNPROFOR I): 503: 1 inf bn, 19
Observers.
MOZAMBIQUE (ONUMOZ): 20 Observers.

PARAMILITARY:
BORDER GUARDS: ε7,000.
INTERNAL SECURITY FORCES: ε2,000.
CIVIL DEFENCE TROOPS: ε2,000.

ESTONIA

GDP	1991:	r 16.75bn ($9.85bn)	
	1992ε:	Kn 14.54bn ($6.70bn)	
Growth	1991:	-12.0%	1992: -26.3%
Inflation	1991:	211.8%	1992ε: 1,076.4%
Debt	1991:	$496m	
Def bdgt	1992:	r 63.4m ($37.3m)	
	1993:	Kn 124.4m ($27.6m)	
$1 = r, kn^a	1991:	1.70	1992: 4.9
	1993:	13.0	

r = rouble
Kn = Kroon
^{a} Estonia introduced the Kroon in June 1992 to replace the
rouble.

Population: 1,613,000

	13–17	18–22	23–32
Men	59,000	57,800	114,600
Women	57,100	55,600	109,900

TOTAL ARMED FORCES:
ACTIVE: 2,500.

Terms of service: 12 months.
RESERVES: some 6,000 militia.

ARMY: 2,500.
3 inf, 1 guard, 1 AD bn.
RESERVES:
Militia: 16 Def League units.

NAVY: 2: Formed 1 July 1993:
Base: Tallinn

PARAMILITARY:
BORDER GUARD (Ministry of Interior): 2,000
(1,200 conscripts).
MARITIME BORDER GUARD: 4 PCI: 3 Finnish
Koskelo-class PCI⟨, 1 ex-Sw coast guard PCI⟨.
COAST GUARD: 3 PCI⟨ (converted fishing boats).

FOREIGN FORCES:
RUSSIA: ε7,000:
Army: 1 MRD, (40 MBT, 160 AIFV, 130 APC, 60
arty/MRL/mor).

FINLAND

GDP	1991: m 503.65bn ($124.54bn)		
	1992ε: m 490.76bn ($109.56bn)		
Growth	1991: -6.4%	1992: -3.6%	
Inflation	1991: 4.1%	1992: 2.6%	
Debt	1991: $69.7bn	1992: $73.9bn	
Def exp	1991: m 8.90bn ($2.20bn)		
	1992: m 9.30bn ($2.08bn)		
Def bdgt	1992: m 9.50bn ($2.12bn)		
	1993: m 8.96bn ($1.51bn)		
$1 = m	1990: 3.8235	1991: 4.0444	
	1992: 4.4794	1993: 5.9208	
m = markka			

Population: 5,037,600

	13–17	18–22	23–32
Men	163,500	163,400	366,300
Women	154,900	155,200	349,400

TOTAL ARMED FORCES:
ACTIVE: 32,800 (24,100 conscripts).
Terms of service: 8–11 months (11 months for
officers, NCOs and soldiers with special duties).
Some 30,000 a year do conscript service.
RESERVES (all services): some 700,000; some
30,000 reservists a year do refresher trg: total
obligation 40 days (75 for NCO, 100 for officers)
between conscript service and age 50 (NCO and
officers to age 60).
Total strength on mob some 500,000, with 300,000 in

general forces (bde etc) and 200,000 in local defence
forces, (Army 460,000, Navy 12,000, Air Force 30,000)
plus 200,000 unallocated as replacements etc.

ARMY: 27,300 (21,600 conscripts).
3 Military comd; 12 Military Provinces:
1 armd trg bde (1 armd, 1 mech inf, 1 ATK bn, 1 arty
regt, 1 AA bty).
8 inf trg bde (each 3 inf bn; 3 with 1 arty regt, 1 with
1 arty bn).
2 indep inf bn.
1 arty bde.
Coast arty: 2 regt; 3 indep bn (1 mobile).
4 AD regt (incl 1 SAM bn with SAM-79).
2 engr bn.
(All units have a primary trg role).
RESERVES:

2 armd bde.	10 *Jaeger* bde.
14 inf bde.	1 coast bde.
Some 50 indep bn.	200 local defence units.

EQUIPMENT:
MBT: 70 T-55, 160 T-72.
LIGHT TANKS: 15 PT-76.
AIFV: 40 BMP-1, 110 BMP-2.
APC: 50 BTR-50P, 110 BTR-60, 310 XA-180 *Sisu*,
220 MT-LB.
TOWED ARTY: 105mm: 252 H 61-37; 122mm: 276 H
63 (D-30); 152mm: 72 H 55 (D-20), 47 H 88-40, H
88-37 (ML-20), H 38 (M-10); 155mm: 36 M-74 (K-
83).
SP ARTY: 122mm: PsH 74 (2S1); 152mm: 18 *Telak*
91 (2S5).
COAST ARTY: 100mm: D-10T (tank turrets);
122mm: M-60; 130mm: 170 M-54; (static).
COAST SSM: some RBS-15.
MRL: 122mm: Rak H 76 (BM-21), Rak H 89 (RM-
70).
MORTARS: 81mm: 880; 120mm: 614.
ATGW: 24 M-82 (AT-4 *Spigot*), 12 M-83 (BGM-71D
TOW 2), AT-5 *Spandrel*.
RL: 112mm: *APILAS*.
RCL: 55mm: M-55; 66mm: 66 KES, 75 (M-72A3);
95mm: 100 SM-58-61.
AD GUNS: 23mm: 100+ ZU-23; 30mm; 35mm: GDF-
005, *Marksman* GDF-005 SP; 57mm: 12 S-60 towed,
12 ZSU-57-2 SP.
SAM: SAM-78 (SA-7), SAM-79 (SA-3),
SAM-86 (SA-16), SAM-90 (*Crotale* NG).

NAVY: 2,500 (1,000 conscripts).
BASES: Upinniemi (Helsinki), Turku.
4 functional sqn (gunboat, missile, patrol, mine
warfare). Approx 50% of units kept fully manned.
Others in short-notice storage, rotated regularly.
PATROL AND COASTAL COMBATANTS: 23:
CORVETTES: 2 *Turunmaa* with 1 x 120mm gun, 2 x
5 ASW RL.
MISSILE CRAFT: 11:
4 *Helsinki* PFM with 4 x 2 MTO-85 (Sw RBS-15SF)
SSM.

3 *Tuima* (Sov *Osa-II*) with 4 MTO-66 (Sov SS-N-2B) SSM.
4 *Rauma* PFM with 2 x 2 and 2 x 1 MTO-85 (Sw RBS-15SF) SSM.
PATROL CRAFT: inshore: 10:
2 *Rihtniemi* with 2 ASW RL.
3 *Ruissalo* with 2 ASW RL.
5 *Nuoli* PFI .
MINE WARFARE: 13:
MINELAYERS: 7
2 *Hämeenmaa*, 150–200 mines, plus 1 x 6 MATRA *Sidal* SAM.
1 *Pohjanmaa*, 100–150 mines; plus 1 x 120mm gun and 2 x 5 ASW RL
3 *Pansio* aux minelayer, 50 mines.
1 *Tuima* (ex-PFM), 20 mines.
MCM: 6 *Kuha* MSI .
(plus 7 *Kiiski*-class minesweeping boats)
AMPHIBIOUS: craft only; 3 *Kampela* LCU tpt, 3 *Kala* LCU.
SUPPORT AND MISCELLANEOUS: 14:
4 *Valas* coastal tpt (can be used for minelaying).
Plus about 10 civilian-manned ships:
1 *Aranda* AGOR (Min of Trade control).
9 icebreakers (Board of Navigation control).

AIR FORCE: 3,000 (1,500 conscripts);
112 cbt ac, no armed hel.
3 AD areas: 3 fighter wings.
FIGHTER: 3 wings:
1 with 15 MiG-21bis; 10 *Hawk* Mk 51.
2 with 41 J-35, 20 *Hawk* Mk 51.
OCU: 4* MiG-21U/UM, 5* SAAB SK-35C.
RECCE: some *Hawk* Mk 51 and MiG-21 bis (incl in ftr sqn).
SURVEY: 3 *Learjet* 35A (survey, ECM trg, target-towing).
TRANSPORT: 1 ac sqn with 3 F-27.
1 hel flt with 2 Hughes 500, 7 Mi-8 (tpt/SAR).
TRAINING: 17 *Hawk** Mk 51, 28 L-70 *Vinka*.
LIAISON: 15 Piper (9 *Cherokee Arrow*, 6 *Chieftain*), 10 L-90 *Redigo*.
AAM: AA-2 *Atoll*, AIM-9 *Sidewinder*, RB-27, RB-28 (*Falcon*), MATRA *Mistral*.

FORCES ABROAD:
UN AND PEACEKEEPING:
CROATIA (UNPROFOR I): 296: construction tps.
CYPRUS (UNFICYP): 4.
INDIA/PAKISTAN (UNMOGIP): 5.
IRAQ/KUWAIT (UNIKOM): 6.
LEBANON (UNIFIL): 519: 1 inf bn.
MACEDONIA (UNPROFOR M): elm inf bn (135), 8 Observers.
MIDDLE EAST (UNTSO): 17.
SYRIA (UNDOF): 355: 1 inf bn.

PARAMILITARY:
FRONTIER GUARD (Ministry of Interior): 4,400

(on mob 24,000); 4 frontier, 3 coast guard districts, 1 air comd; 2 offshore, 3 coastal, 7 inshore patrol craft;

GEORGIA

(Not a member of the Commonwealth of Independent States)

GDP	1991: r 23.47bn ($13.81bn)	
	1992ε: r 362.5bn ($10.36bn)	
Growth	1991: -8.1%	1992ε: -30%
Inflation	1991: 80%	1992ε: 1,100%
Debt	1991: $1.30bn	
Def bdgt	1992ε: r 6bn ($333.3m)	
$1 = r	1991: 1.70	1992: 230
r = roubles		

Population: 5,554,400 (12.8% Russian)

	13–17	18–22	23–32
Men	218,900	212,100	405,800
Women	211,000	202,800	403,100

TOTAL ARMED FORCES:
Terms of service: conscription, 2 years.
RESERVES: Possibly up to 500,000 with military service in last 15 years.

ARMY: Armed forces of up to 20,000 planned, incl National Guard.
2 Corps HQ.
Some 6 bde (incl border guard).
EQUIPMENT:
MBT: 120 T-55.
AIFV/APC: 180.
TOTAL ARTY: 60.
SAM: SA-2/-3.

NAVY: 100
BASE: Poti
Formal transfer of some Black Sea units pending.

AIR FORCE:
Some 40 Su-25 and Su-15 ac, some 15 Mi-2, Mi-6, Mi-8 and Mi-24 hel.

PARAMILITARY:
National Guard: ε15,000 (being incorporated into national army).

OPPOSITION FORCES:
ABKHAZIA: 4,000.
SOUTH OSSETIA: No details known.
OTHERS: 1,500 (Forces loyal to former President Zviad Gamsakhurdia).

FOREIGN FORCES:
RUSSIA (Transcaucasus Group of Forces): Army: 20,000, 1 Corps HQ, 2 MRD. Air Force: 1 tpt/hel regt. Some 35 tpt ac and hel incl An-2, An-72 and Mi-8.
PEACEKEEPING: 1 AB regt, 1 air aslt bn (Russia).

HUNGARY

GDP	1991: f 2,308.4bn ($30.89bn)			
	1992ε: f 2,641.8bn ($33.44bn)			
Growth	1991: −10.0%		1992ε: −5.0%	
Inflation	1991: 35.0%		1992: 23.0%	
Debt	1991: $21.40bn		1992: $21.44bn	
Def exp[a]	1991: f 54.44bn ($1.24bn)			
	1992: f 60.80bn ($1.18bn)			
Def bdgt[a,b,c]	1992: f 59.60bn ($1.16bn)			
	1993: f 66.50bn ($1.16bn)			
$1 = f	1990: 63.206		1991: 74.735	
	1992: 78.988		1993: 88.000	

f = forint
[a] Incl. internal police and sy budget.
[b] Does not incl costs incurred by Yugoslav crisis est at f150–200m a month.
[c] Dollar values are estimated.

Population: 10,396,000

	13–17	18–22	23–32
Men	388,000	391,000	688,000
Women	370,000	370,000	656,000

TOTAL ARMED FORCES:
ACTIVE: 78,000 (52,000 conscripts).
Terms of service: 12 months.
RESERVES: 195,000: Army: 183,600; Air: 11,400 (to age 50).

LAND FORCES: 60,500 (40,000 conscripts).
4 Military District Corps/HQ:
1 with 2 tk, 2 mech bde, 1 MRL, 1 ATK, 1 AD arty, 1 engr regt.
1 with 1 tk, 3 mech, 2 arty, 1 ATK bde, 1 ATK, 1 engr regt.
1 with 4 mech, 1 arty, 1 AD arty, 1 engr bde, 1 engr regt.
1 (Budapest) with 1 guard, 1 engr regt, 1 rivercraft bde.
RESERVES:
1 Home Defence bde.
EQUIPMENT:
MBT: 1,331 (439 in store): 58 T-34 (in store), 61 T-54 (44 in store), 1,074 T-55 (323 in store), 138 T-72.
LIGHT TANKS: 7 PT-76.
RECCE: 42 FUG D-442.
AIFV: 493 BMP-1, 7 BRM-1K.
APC: 1,182: 148 BTR-80, 1,004 PSZH D-944, 30 MT-LB. (Plus some 836 'look alike' types).
TOTAL ARTY: 787:
TOWED: 328: 122mm: 230 M-1938 (M-30) (147 in store); 152mm: 49 M-1943 (D-1), 49 D-20.
SP: 156: 122mm: 151 2S1 (3 in store); 152mm: 5 2S3.
MRL: 122mm: 56 BM-21.
MORTARS: 247: 120mm: 3 2B11, 244 M-120.
ATGW: 329: 117 AT-3 *Sagger*, 30 AT-4 *Spigot* (incl BRDM-2 SP), 182 AT-5 *Spandrel*.
ATK GUNS: 85mm: 69 D-44; 100mm: 101 MT-12.
AD GUNS: 23mm: 14 ZSU-23-4 SP; 57mm: 144 S-60.
SAM: 240 SA-7, 54 SA-14.
Rivercraft bde:
MCMV: 6 *Nestin* MSI (riverine); some 45 mine disposal/patrol boats (about 20 in reserve).

AIR FORCE: 17,500 (12,000 conscripts);
91 cbt ac, plus 43 in store, 39 attack hel.
2 air corps:
FIGHTER:
3 regt with 50 MiG-21bis/MF, 9 MiG-23MF. (Plus 43 MiG-21 bis/MF in store.)
RECCE: 1 sqn with 11 Su-22.
TRANSPORT: 2 An-24, 9 An-26, 3 L-410.
HELICOPTERS: 3 regt.
1 ATK/tpt.
  2 sqn with 39 Mi-24.
  1 sqn with 23 Mi-8/-17;
1 tpt with 25 Mi-8
1 liaison with 35 Mi-2
TRAINING: 15 *MiG-21U, 3 *MiG-23, 3 *Su-22.
AAM: AA-2 *Atoll*.
AD: some 16 sites
1 bde: 18 SA-4
5 regt: 82 SA-2/-3/-5, 40 SA-6, 28 SA-9, 4 SA-13.

FORCES ABROAD:
UN AND PEACEKEEPING:
ANGOLA (UNAVEM II): 5 Observers.
CAMBODIA (UNTAC): 97 civ pol.
IRAQ/KUWAIT (UNIKOM): 6 Observers.
MOZAMBIQUE (ONUMOZ): 18 Observers.

PARAMILITARY:
BORDER GUARDS: (Ministry of Interior) 15,900 (8,900 conscripts); 11 districts.
CIVIL DEFENCE TROOPS: 2,000.
INTERNAL SECURITY TROOPS: 1,500.

IRELAND

GDP	1991: £I 26.98bn ($43.59bn)		
	1992ε: £I 28.06bn ($47.86bn)		
Growth	1991: 2.5%	1992: 2.3%	
Inflation	1991: 3.2%	1992: 3.1%	

Publ. Debt   1992: 96.8%
Def exp   1990: £I 306.43m ($508.21m)
              1991: £I 317.45m ($512.84m)
Def bdgt   1992: £I 328.5m ($560.20m)
              1993ε:£I 339.0m ($529.72m)
$1 = £I   1990: 0.6030   1991: 0.6190
              1992: 0.5864   1993: 0.6400

Population: 3,500,000

	13–17	18–22	23–32
Men	167,900	165,200	275,100
Women	159,000	155,000	262,000

TOTAL ARMED FORCES:
ACTIVE: 13,000 incl 100 women.
Terms of service: voluntary, 3-year terms to age 60,
officers 56–65.
RESERVES: 16,100 (obligation to age 60, officers
57–65). Army: first-line 1,000, second-line 14,800.
Navy 350.

ARMY: 11,200.
4 Territorial Commands.
1 inf force (2 inf bn).
4 inf bde:
2 with 2 inf bn, 1 with 3, all with 1 fd arty regt, 1 cav
recce sqn, 1 engr coy;
1 with 2 inf bn, 1 armd recce sqn, 1 fd arty bty.
Army tps: 1 lt tk sqn, 1 AD regt, 1 Ranger coy.
(Total units: 11 inf bn; 1 UNIFIL bn *ad hoc* with elm
from other bn, 1 tk sqn, 4 recce sqn (1 armd), 3 fd
arty regt (each of 2 bty); 1 indep bty, 1 AD regt (1
regular, 3 reserve bty), 3 fd engr coy, 1 Ranger coy).
RESERVES:
4 Army Gp (garrisons), 18 inf bn, 6 fd arty regt,
3 cav sqn, 3 engr sqn, 3 AA bty.
EQUIPMENT:
LIGHT TANKS: 14 *Scorpion.*
RECCE: 19 AML-90, 32 AML-60.
APC: 60 Panhard VTT/M3, 10 *Timoney,* 2 A-180
Sisu.
TOWED ARTY: 88mm: 48 25-pdr; 105mm: 12 lt.
MORTARS: 81mm: 400; 120mm: 72.
ATGW: 21 *Milan.*
RCL: 84mm: 444 *Carl Gustav;* 90mm: 96 PV-1110.
AD GUNS: 40mm: 24 L/60, 2 L/70.
SAM: 7 RBS-70.

NAVY: 1,000.
BASE: Cork.
PATROL AND COASTAL COMBATANTS: 7:
7 PCO:
1 *Eithne* with 1 *Dauphin* hel;
3 *Emer,* 1 *Deirdre.*
2 *Orla* (UK *Peacock*).

AIR FORCE: 800.
16 cbt ac, 15 armed hel.

3 wings (1 trg):
COIN: 1 sqn with 5 CM-170-2 *Super Magister.*
COIN/TRAINING: 1 sqn with 7 SF-260WE,
1 SF-260 MC ac, 2 SA-342L trg hel.
MR: 2 *Super King Air* 200, 1 CN 235.
TRANSPORT: 1 HS-125, 1 *Super King Air* 200, 1
Gulfstream IV.
LIAISON: 1 sqn with 6 Reims Cessna F-172H,
1 F-172K.
HELICOPTERS: 3 sqn.
1 Army spt with 8 SA-316B (*Alouette*).
1 Navy spt with 2 SA-365 (*Dauphin*).
1 SAR with 3 SA-365.

FORCES ABROAD:
UN AND PEACEKEEPING:
ANGOLA (UNAVEM II): 2 Observers.
CAMBODIA (UNTAC): 11 Observers.
CROATIA (UNPROFOR I): 6.
CYPRUS (UNFICYP): 9.
EL SALVADOR (ONUSAL): 2 Observers.
IRAQ/KUWAIT (UNIKOM): 6.
LEBANON (UNIFIL): 679: 1 bn; 4 AML-90 armd
cars, 10 *Sisu* APC, 4 120mm mor.
MIDDLE EAST (UNTSO): 18.
WESTERN SAHARA (MINURSO): 6.

LATVIA

GDP   1991: r 28.67bn ($13.76bn)
           1992ε: Lr^a 182.5bn ($7.35bn)
Growth   1991: -8%   1992: -32.0%
Inflation 1991: 124.5%   1992ε: 1,000%
Debt   1991: $912m
Def bdgt   1992ε: r 796m ($39.8m)
           1993ε: Lr 1,800m
$1 = r   1991: 1.70   1992: 140
           1993: 0.68

Lr/r = roubles, Latvian rouble, Lats
[a] Latvia introduced the Latvian rouble in May 1992 as an
interim measure until its regular currency, the Lats, could
be restored. The Lats was introduced in March 1993. $1 =
0.68 lati.

Population: 2,733,000

	13–17	18–22	23–32
Men	97,000	92,600	193,300
Women	94,200	90,200	188,500

TOTAL ARMED FORCES:
ACTIVE: 5,000 incl Border Guard
Terms of service: 18 months.
RESERVES: 16,000 Home Guard.

ARMY:
1 inf bn.

1 recce bn.
RESERVES: Home Guard.

NAVY: 300
BASE: Liepaja, Riga.
5 PCI: 1 ex-Sw coast guard PCI⟨, 4 converted fishing boats⟨.

AIR FORCE:
Some An-2, L-410 ac; Mi-2, Mi-8 hel.

PARAMILITARY:
Border Guard.

FOREIGN FORCES:
RUSSIA: 17,000
Army: 1 MR bde, 1 attack hel regt, (53 MBT, 50 AIFV, 50 arty/MRL/mor, 24 attack hel), Air Force: 1 FGA, 1 recce regt (90 cbt ac), 1 tpt hel regt (20 Mi-8), Air Defence: 1 ftr regt (40 cbt ac, 25 SA-10).

LITHUANIA

GDP	1991: r 32.81bn ($19.30bn)		
	1992ε: t 280.87bn ($7.80bn)		
Growth[a]	1991: -13.4%	1992ε: 1,165%	
Inflation	1991: 224%	1992ε: 1,165%	
Debt	1991: $1.13bn		
Def bdgt	1992ε: r 1.60bn ($55.17m)		
	1993ε[b]: t 6.05bn ($=?)		
$1 = r,t	1991: 1.70	1992: 240	
	1993ε: 500		

rc = rouble
t = talonas
[a] NMP growth 1991, GNP growth 1992
[b] Incl Civil Defence.
[c] Lithuania was planning to introduce the Lita = r10 in 1992, to replace the rouble, but in the meantime is using the talonas (coupons) as legal tender $1 = 390 t (end 1992).

Population: 3,833,000

	13–17	18–22	23–32
Men	140,600	138,100	293,600
Women	136,900	135,200	285,800

TOTAL ARMED FORCES:
ACTIVE: 9,800 (incl Border Guard).
Terms of service: 12 months.
RESERVES: 11,000.

ARMY: 4,300 (incl conscripts).
Rapid reaction bde (7 bn).

EQUIPMENT:
APC: 7 BTR-60.
RESERVES:
National Guard; Territorial Guard.

NAVY: ε250.
Lithuania is currently creating a Navy which will also fulfil function of coast guard.
BASE: Klaipeda.
FRIGATES: 2 ex-Sov 2 *Grisha-III*, with 2 x 12 ASW RL, 4 x 533mm TT.
PATROL AND COASTAL COMBATANTS: About 7: 1 ex-Sw coast guard PCI, 2 ex-Sov *Turya* PHT (no TT), 4 converted civilian craft.

AIR FORCE: 250: no cbt ac.
4 L-39, 2 L-410.

PARAMILITARY:
Border Guard: 5,000.

FOREIGN FORCES:
RUSSIA: 2,400 (to withdraw by end of August 1993)

MACEDONIA

Macedonia considers itself independent.

GDP	1991ε: D 191.69bn ($3.82bn)		
Growth[a]	1992ε: -140%		
Inflation	1992ε: 9,000+%		
[a] National Income			
$1 = Dinar	1991: 37.85	1992: 865	

Population: 2,124,500 (67% Macedonians, 20% Albanians, 4.5% Turks, 2% Serbs, 2% 'Muslims', 2.4% Gypsies).

TOTAL ARMED FORCES
ACTIVE: 10,400 (8,000 conscripts).
RESERVES: 100,000 planned.

ARMY:
3 Corps HQ (cadre)
3 indep bde (planned).
EQUIPMENT: No hy wpn, former Territorial Defence Force: mors, RCL, AD guns, man-portable SAM.
AIR FORCE: 50: no ac. only hel planned.

PARAMILITARY:
Police: 7,500 (some 4,500 armed).

MALTA

GDP	1991: LM 797.37m ($2.47bn)
	1992: LM 849.19m ($2.67bn)
Growth	1991: 6.1%	1992: 4.9%
Inflation	1991: 2.6%	1992: 1.6%
Debt	1991: $140.4m	1992: $146.3m
Def exp	1990: LM 6.72m ($21.19m)
	1991: LM 7.03m ($21.79m)
Def bdgt	1992: LM 9.61m ($30.24m)
	1993: LM 9.17m ($26.20m)
$1 = LM	1990: 0.3172	1991: 0.3226
	1992: 0.3178	1993: 0.3500

LM = lira

Population: 357,200

	13–17	18–22	23–32
Men	14,500	13,400	26,900
Women	13,600	12,800	25,700

TOTAL ARMED FORCES:
ACTIVE: 1,650.

'ARMED FORCES OF MALTA':
Comd HQ, spt tps.
No. 1 Regt (inf bn) with:
3 rifle, 1 spt coy.
No. 2 Regt (composite regt):
1 air sqn with 3 SA-316, 2 Breda Nardi Hughes, 1 AB-206A, 3 AB-47G, 1 Bell 47G hel and 5 O–1 (*Bird Dog*) ac.
1 maritime sqn (160) with:
2 ex-GDR *Kondor-II* PCC, 4 PCI plus boats.
1 AD bty; 14.5mm: 50 ZPU-4; 40mm: 40 Bofors.
No. 3 Regt (Depot Regt) with:
1 engr sqn.
1 workshop, 1 ordnance, 1 airport coy.

MOLDOVA

GDP[a]	1991: r 22.25bn ($13.09bn)
	1992ε: r 211.85bn ($10.70 bn)
Growth[a]	1991: -11.9%	1992ε: -26.8%
Inflation[b]	1991: 98%	1992ε: 2,198.0%
Debt	1991: $1.10bn
Def bdgt[c]	1991: r 1.43bn ($875.5m)
	1992: r 4.1bn ($227.8m)
$1 = r	1991: 1.70	1992: 180
	1993: 800

[a] NMP growth.
[b] Year average.
[c] Incl national security.

Population: 4,445,000 (12.8% Russian)

	13–17	18–22	23–32
Men	192,800	174,200	295,000
Women	217,100	153,800	271,100

TOTAL ARMED FORCES: 9,400, incl about 3,500 MOD and rear services staff.
Terms of service: up to 18 months.
RESERVES: some 300,000 with military service within last 5 years.

ARMY: 3,800.
3 mech bde.
1 arty bde.
1 recce/assault bn.
EQUIPMENT:
AIFV: 52 BMD.
APC: 12 BTR-80, 20 BTR-D, 3 BTR-60PB.
TOWED ARTY: 122mm: 18 M-30; 152mm: 32 D-20, 21 2A36.
COMBINED GUN/MORTAR: 120mm: 9 2S9.
MRL: 220mm: 28 9P140 *Uragan*.

AIR FORCE: 2,100 (incl AD).
1 ftr regt with 31 MiG-29, 3 Mi-8 hel.
5 tpt ac incl An-72.
SAM: 25 SA-3/-5.

PARAMILITARY:
Internal troops (Ministry of Interior): 2,500.
OPON (riot police) (Ministry of Interior): 900

OPPOSITION FORCES:
Dniestr 10,000: incl Republican Guard (Dniestr bn), e1,000 Cossacks.

FOREIGN FORCES
RUSSIA (14th Army)
1 army HQ (Dniestr), 1 MRD (Dniestr), 1 SSM bde (Moldova), 1 hel unit, 120 MBT, 180 ACV, 120 arty/MRL/mors, 12 *Scud*, 10 attack hel.
PEACEKEEPING: 6 AB bn (Russia), 2 inf bn (Ukraine), 2 bn (Moldova).

POLAND

GDP	1991: z 940,425.3bn ($92.44bn)
	1992: z 1,139,000.0bn ($83.59bn)
Growth	1991: −18%	1992: 0%
Inflation	1992: 70.3%	1992: 43%
Debt	1991: $48.4bn	1992: $47.0bn
Def exp	1992: z 26,236.0bn ($1.93bn)
Def bdgt	1992: z 25,643.5bn ($1.88bn)
	1993: z 37,487.3bn ($2.25bn)
$1 = z	1990: 9,500.0	1991: 10,576.0
	1992: 13,626.0	1993: 16,650.0

z = zlotys

Population: 38,655,000

	13–17	18–22	23–32
Men	1,614,000	1,440,000	2,730,000
Women	1,533,000	1,372,000	2,603,000

TOTAL ARMED FORCES:
ACTIVE: 287,500 (162,400 conscripts).
Terms of service: All services 18 months.
RESERVES: 465,500. Army 375,000; Navy 20,500 (to age 50); Air Force 70,000 (to age 60).

ARMY: 188,500 (106,700 conscripts) (incl
centrally controlled staffs (2,100); trg (24,100) and log units (20,800)).
4 Military Districts/Army HQ:
1 (Pomerania) with 3 mech div, 1 coast def, 1 arty, 1 *Scud*, 1 engr bde, 1 SA-6 regt.
1 (Silesia) with 4 mech div, 2 arty, 1 *Scud*, 2 engr, 2 SA-4 bde, 2 ATK, 1 SA-6 regt.
1 (Warsaw) with 2 mech div, 1 engr bde, 1 arty, 1 SA-6 regt.
1 (Krakow) with 2 mech div, 1 air aslt, 1 mtn inf bde.
Div tps: 8 SA-6/-8 regt.
RESERVES: 1 mob mech div.
EQUIPMENT:
MBT: 2,545: 1,758 T-55, 787 T-72.
LIGHT TANKS: 30 PT-76.
RECCE: 561 FUG/BRDM-2.
AIFV: 1,409 BMP-1, 62 BMP-2.
APC: 642: 582 OT-64, 60 OT-62, plus some 693 'look alike' types.
TOTAL ARTY: 2,321:
TOWED: 877: 122mm: 715 M-1938 (M-30); 152mm: 162 D-20.
SP: 635: 122mm: 516 2S1; 152mm: 111 *Dana* (M-77); 203mm: 8 2S7.
MRL: 261: 122mm: 231 BM-21, 30 RM-70.
MORTARS: 120mm: 548 M-120.
SSM: launchers: 40 *FROG*.
ATGW: 410: 270 AT-3, 115 AT-4 *Spigot*, 18 AT-5 *Spandrel*, 7 AT-6 *Spiral*.
ATK GUNS: 85mm: 722 D-44.
AD GUNS: 969: 23mm: ZU-23-2, ZSU-23-4 SP; 57mm: S-60.
SAM: 1,280: SA-6/-7/-8/-9/-13.

NAVY: 19,200 incl Naval Aviation (3,000).
(10,400 conscripts).
BASES: Gdynia, Hel, Swinoujscie; Kolobrzeg (border/coast guard).
SUBMARINES: 3:
1 *Orzel* SS (Sov *Kilo*) with 533mm TT.
2 *Wilk* (Sov *Foxtrot*) with 533mm TT.
PRINCIPAL SURFACE COMBATANTS: 2:
DESTROYERS: 1 *Warszawa* DDG (Sov mod *Kashin*) with 2 x 2 SA-N-1 *Goa* SAM, 4 x SS-N-2C *Styx* SSM, 5 x 533mm TT, 2 x ASW RL.
FRIGATES: 1 *Kaszub* with 2 x ASW RL, 4 x 533mm TT, 76mm gun.

PATROL AND COASTAL COMBATANTS: 21:
CORVETTES: 4 *Gornik* (Sov *Tarantul I*) with 2 x 2 SS-N-2C *Styx* SSM.
MISSILE CRAFT: 8 Sov *Osa*-I PFM with 4 SS-N-2A SSM.
PATROL: 9:
COASTAL: 1 *Sassnitz*.
INSHORE: 8 *Obluze* PCI
MINE WARFARE: 22:
MINELAYERS: None, but submarines, *Krogulec* MSC and *Lublin* LSM have capability.
MINE COUNTERMEASURES: 22:
6 *Krogulec* MSC.
13 *Goplo* (*Notec*) MSI,
1 *Mamry* (*Notec*) MHI.
2 *Leniwka* MSI.
AMPHIBIOUS: 5:
5 *Lublin* LSM, capacity 135 tps, 9 tk.
Plus craft: 3 *Deba* LCU.
(None of the above are employed in amph role.)
SUPPORT AND MISCELLANEOUS: 12:
1 cmd ship, 2 AGI, 4 spt tankers, 2 survey, 2 trg, 1 research.

NAVAL AVIATION: (3,000):
36 cbt ac, 14 armed hel.
2 regt, 2 sqn.
FIGHTER: 1 regt, 36 MiG-21 BIS/U.
1 special naval regt with 15 TS-11, 8 An-2.
1 ASW/SAR sqn with 5 Mi-2, 14 Mi-14 (ASW).
1 sqn SAR/liaison sqn: 2 An-28, 6 W-3 Sokol.

COAST DEFENCE: (3,100 incl in Army total).
6 arty bn with M-1937 152mm.
3 SSM bn with SS-C-2B.

AIR FORCE: 79,800 (incl AD tps) (45,300
conscripts);
468 cbt ac, (plus 88 in store for sale), 30 attack hel. 2 air div:
FGA: 4 regt:
4 with 20 Su-20, 104 Su-22.
FIGHTER: 3 Air Defence Corps: 8 regt with 213 MiG-21/U; 37 MiG-23MF; 12 MiG-29U.
RECCE: 29 MiG-21R/U, plus 7 in store.
TRANSPORT: 2 regt with: Ac: 10 An-2, 1 An-12, 10 An-26, 10 Yak-40, 1 Tu-154, 2 Il-14. Hel: 4 Mi-8, 1 Bell 412.
HELICOPTERS: 2 attack regt: 30 Mi-24 (attack), 107 Mi-2, 1 tpt hel regt with 37 Mi-8, 3 Mi-17.
TRAINING: 53* Su-22, 150 TS-11 *Iskra*, 5 PZL I-22.
IN STORE: 28 MiG-17, 53 MiG-21.
AAM: AA-2 *Atoll*, AA-8 *Aphid*.
ASM: AS-7 *Kerry*.
SAM: 4 bde; 1 indep regt with 50 sites with about 250 SA-2/-3/-5.

FORCES ABROAD:
UN AND PEACEKEEPING:
CAMBODIA (UNTAC): 665:1 inf bn, 17 Observers, 30 civ pol.

CROATIA (UNPROFOR I): 973: 1 inf bn, 20 Observers.
IRAQ/KUWAIT (UNIKOM): 7.
KOREA (NNSC): Staff.
LEBANON (UNIFIL): 78.
SYRIA (UNDOF): 134. Log spt.
WESTERN SAHARA (MINURSO): 2 Observers.

PARAMILITARY:
BORDER GUARDS (Ministry of Interior): 16,000: 14 Provincial Comd: 14 units.
MARITIME BORDER GUARD: About 28 patrol craft: 2 PCC, some 9 PCI and 17 PC1-10 .
PREVENTION UNITS OF POLICE: (OPP): 7,400 (1,400 conscripts).

FOREIGN FORCES:
RUSSIA: Military Mission to supervise transit arrangement for tps withdrawing from Germany.

ROMANIA

GNP^a 1991ε: lei 2,109.7bn ($38.80bn)
                1992ε: lei 7,560.0bn ($32.59bn)
Growth   1991ε: -16%   1992ε: -18.2%
Inflation   1991: 180%   1992: 212%
Debt   1991: $2.50bn   1992: $2.44bn
Def bdgt^a 1992: lei 221.19bn ($955m)
                1993: lei 297.85bn ($851m)
$1 = lei   1990: 22.432   1991: 76.390
                1992: 307.95   1993: 595.4
^{a} Dollar values are estimated.

Population: 22,759,000

	13–17	18–22	23–32
Men	929,500	944,500	1,660,000
Women	887,300	903,500	1,596,000

TOTAL ARMED FORCES:
ACTIVE: 203,100 (125,000 conscripts).
Terms of service: Army, Air Force: 12 months; Navy: 18 months.
RESERVES: 427,000: Army 400,000; Navy 6,000; Air 21,000.

ARMY: 161,000 (105,000 conscripts).
4 Army Areas:
1 with 1 TD, 1 MRD, 1 mtn bde, 1 AB regt;
1 with 2 MRD, 1 mtn, 1 AD bde, 1 AB, 1 arty, 1 ATK regt.
1 with 2 MRD, 1 tk, 1 mtn, 1 AD bde, 1 AB, 1 arty, 1 ATK regt.
1 with 1 TD, 2 MRD, 2 mtn, 1 AD bde, 1 AB, 1 arty, 1 ATK regt.
MOD tps:
2 *Scud*, 2 arty bde; 2 AA regt.

EQUIPMENT:
MBT: 2,869, incl 1,053 T-34, 756 T-55, 30 T-72, 617 TR-85, 413 TR-580.
ASSAULT GUN: 412: 326 SU-76, 66 SU-100, 20 ISU-152.
RECCE: 139 BRDM-2, 8 TAB-80.
AIFV: 154 MLI-84.
APC: 2,630, incl variants: 26 BTR-40, 35 BTR-50, 50 BTR-60, 155 TAB-77, 441 TABC-79, 1,870 TAB-71, 53 MLVM.
TOTAL ARTY: 3,707.
TOWED: 1,546: 100mm: 267 Skoda (various models); 105mm: 87 Schneider; 122mm: 458 M-1938 (M-30), 2 M-1931/37 (A-19); 130mm: 144 Gun 82; 150mm: 128 Skoda (Model 1934), 6 Ceh (Model 1937); 152mm: 84 D-20, 54 Gun-How 85, 61 Model 1938, 255 Model 81.
SP: 48: 122mm: 6 2S1, 42 Model 89.
MRL: 446: 122mm: 116 APR-21, 294 APR-40; 130mm: 36 R-2.
MORTARS: 1,667: 120mm: 1,002 M-120, 603 Model 1982; 160mm: 50 M-160; 240mm: 12 M-240.
SSM: launchers: 13 *Scud*, 12 *FROG*.
ATGW: 534: AT-1 *Snapper*, AT-3 *Sagger* (incl BRDM-2).
ATK GUNS: 1,450: 57mm: M-1943; 85mm: D-44; 100mm: 829 Gun 77, 75 Gun 75.
AD GUNS: 1,118: 30mm; 37mm; 57mm; 85mm; 100mm.
SAM: 62 SA-6/-7.

NAVY: ε19,000 incl Naval inf (ε5,000). (10,000 conscripts). 1 maritime div, 1 patrol boat bde, 1 river bde, 1 maritime/river bde, 1 nav inf div.
BASES: Coastal: Mangalia, Constanţa; Danube: Braila, Giurgiu, Tulcea.
SUBMARINE: 1 Sov *Kilo* SS with 533mm TT.
PRINCIPAL SURFACE COMBATANTS: 6:
DESTROYER: 1 *Marasesti* (ex-*Muntenia*) DDG with 4 x 2 SS-N-2C *Styx* SSM, plus SA-N-5 *Grail* SAM, 2 IAR-316 hel, 2 x 3 533mm TT.
FRIGATES: 5 *Tetal* with 2 x ASW RL, 4 x ASTT.
PATROL AND COASTAL COMBATANTS: 88:
CORVETTES: 6:
3 Sov *Poti* ASW with 2 x ASW RL, 3 x 533mm TT.
3 *Tarantul I* with 2 x 2 SS-N-2C *Styx*, 1 x 4 SA-N-5 *Grail* SAM; plus 1 x 76mm gun.
MISSILE CRAFT: 6 Sov *Osa*-I PFM with 4 x SS-N-2A *Styx*.
TORPEDO: 38:
12 *Epitrop* PFT with 4 x 533mm TT.
26 Ch *Huchuan* PHT with 2 x 533mm TT (incl ε8 non-op).
PATROL: 38:
OFFSHORE: 4 *Democratia* (GDR M-40) PCO.
COASTAL: 2 Sov *Kronshtadt* PCC†.
INSHORE: 8: 4 Ch *Shanghai* PFI, 4 Ch *Huchuan*.
RIVERINE: 24: Some 6 *Brutar* with 1 x 100mm gun, 18⟨.
MINE WARFARE: 34:
MINELAYERS: 2 *Cosar*, capacity 100 mines.
MCM: 32:

4 *Musca* MSC.
3 T.301 MSI (plus some 9 non-op).
25 VD141 MSI(.
SUPPORT AND MISCELLANEOUS: 10:
2 *Constanta* log spt with 1 *Alouette* hel, 3 spt tankers, 2 AGOR, 1 trg, 2 tugs.
HELICOPTERS: 2 1AR-316.
NAVAL INFANTRY: (Marines): (some5,000).
1 inf div (3 inf, 1 arty regt).
1 indep inf bde. 1 indep tk regt.
EQUIPMENT:
MBT: 294: 107 T-34, 187 TR-580.
ASSAULT GUN: 36 SUC-76, 20 ISU-152.
APC: 193 TAB-71, 46 TABC-79, 8 TAB-77, 3 TAB-80, 5 BTR-50.
TOWED ARTY: 100mm: 54 Gun 77; 122mm: 36 M-1938 (M-30); 152mm: 36 Model 81.
MRL: 122mm: 18 APR-21, 18 APR-40.
MORTARS: 120mm: 36 Model 1982, 104 M-120.

COASTAL DEFENCE (1,000): HQ Constanţa.
4 sectors:
4 coastal arty bty with 32 130mm.
10 AA arty bty: 3 with 18 30mm; 5 with 30 37mm; 2 with 12 57mm.

AIR FORCE: 23,100 (10,000 conscripts); 469 cbt ac, 219 armed hel.
Air Force comd, plus 2 air div: 8 cbt regt.
FGA: 2 regt with 19 MiG-17, 61 IAR-93, 70 MiG-15.
FIGHTER: 19 sqn with 185 MiG-21, 35 MiG-23, 15 MiG-29.
RECCE: 2 sqn: 1 with 12 Il-28 (recce/ECM), 1 with 10* MiG-21.
TRANSPORT: 1 regt with 9 An-24, 14 An-26, 2 Il-18, 2 Boeing 707, 2 Rombac 1-11, 10 1AR-316B, 7 Mi-8.
SURVEY: 3 An-30.
HELICOPTERS: 5 regt plus 2 sqn with 104 IAR-316B, 82 IAR-330-H, 27 Mi-8, 2 Mi-17, 4 SA-365N.
TRAINING: 32 IAR-823, 10 IAR28, 14 *IAR-93, 45 L-29, 32 L-39, 18* MiG-15, 29 *MiG-21, *1 MiG-29UB, *6 1AR-99. *6 MiG-23DC, 17 An-2, 13 Yak-5.
AAM: AA-2 *Atoll*, AA-7 *Apex*.
AD: 1 div: 20 SAM sites with 120 SA-2.

FORCES ABROAD:
UN AND PEACEKEEPING:
KUWAIT (UNIKOM): 8 Observers.

PARAMILITARY:
BORDER GUARDS: (Ministry of Interior): 12,000 (11,700 conscripts: 6 bde, 7 naval gp; 26 Ch *Shanghai* II PFI).
GENDARMERIE (Ministry of Interior): 10,000: 8 bde; some APC.

NATIONAL GUARD: (Ministry of Defence) 4 regional comd.
CONSTRUCTION TROOPS: 21,000.

SLOVAKIA[a]

GDP[b]	1992:	Kcs 346.0 bn ($12.24bn)	
Growth	1992ε:	-8%	
Inflation	1992ε:	39.8%	
Debt	1992ε:	$3bn	
Def bdgt[a]	1993:	Kcs 8.20bn ($284.34m)	

Kcs = Koruny
Population: 5,487,000 (85% Slovaks, 11% Hungarians)

[a] See entry for Czech Republic for 1991/92 Czechoslovak data
[b] Dollar values are estimated

	13–17	18–22	23–32
Men	225,000	213,000	386,000
Women	218,000	205,000	373,000

TOTAL ARMED FORCES:
ACTIVE: 47,000.
Terms of service: 18 months.

ARMY: 33,000.
1 Command HQ:
1 TD.
1 mech inf div.
1 arty bde.
EQUIPMENT:
MBT: 935 T-72M, T-54/-55.
RECCE: 129 BRDM, 120 OT-65.
AIFV: 476: BVP-1, BMP-2, BPZV, BRM-1K.
APC: 567: OT-90, 476 OT-64A/C.
TOTAL ARTY: 808.
TOWED: 297: 100mm: M-53; 122mm: M-1931/37 (A-19), M-1938, D-30.
SP: 189: 122mm 2S1; 152mm: *Dana* (M-77).
MRL: 243: 122mm: RM-70; 130mm: RM-130 (M-51).
MORTARS: 79: 120mm; 240mm: 2S4.
SSM: 9 *FROG*-7, SS-21, *Scud*, SS-23.
ATGW: AT-3 *Sagger*, AT-5 *Spandrel*.
AD GUNS: 286: 30mm: M-53/-59; 57mm: S-60.
SAM: 437: SA-7, SA-9/-13.

AIR FORCE: 14,000
146 cbt ac, 19 attack hel.
FGA: 41 incl Su-22, Su-25.
FIGHTER: 87 MiG-21, 10 MiG-29.
RECCE: 8 MiG-21 RF.
TRANSPORT: 16 incl An-12, Tu-134, Tu-154, An-24/-26, L410M.
HELICOPTERS:
ATTACK: 19 Mi-24.
ASSAULT TPT: 26 incl Mi-8, Mi-17.

TRAINING: Some 15 L-29, 25 L-39, 4 MiG-21 U/MF.
IN STORE: About 30 incl MiG-21, Su-7.
AAM: AA-2 *Atoll*, AA-7 *Apex*, AA-8 *Aphid*.
AD: SA-2, SA-6.

FORCES ABROAD:
UN AND PEACEKEEPING:
ANGOLA (UNAVEM II): 6 Observers.
CROATIA (UNPROFOR I): 404: 1 engr bn.

PARAMILITARY:
BORDER GUARDS: 600.
INTERNAL SECURITY FORCES: 250.
CIVIL DEFENCE TROOPS: 3,100.

SLOVENIA

GDP	1991ε: D 720.66bn ($19.04bn)
	1992ε: t 426.0bn[a] ($17.52bn)
Growth	1991ε: -9.5% 1992: –8.0%
Inflation:	1991: 80.0% 1992ε: 150%
Debt	1991: $1.66bn 1992: $2.5bn
Def bdgt	1992ε: t 15.0bn ($340.91m)
D= Dinar	
$1 = t[a]	
tolar	1992: 44.0 1993: 120.0

[a] Slovenia introduced the tolar in October 1991 to replace the Dinar.

Population 1,970,000

	13–17	18–22	23–32
Men	76,800	74,700	146,900
Women	71,000	70,200	142,500

TOTAL ARMED FORCES:
ACTIVE: 15,000.
Terms of service: 7 months.
RESERVES: ε85,000.

ARMY: 13,000 (20,000 planned).
7 Military Districts; 26 Military Regions.
1 inf bde.   1 ATK bde.
1 AD bde.   9 indep inf bn (incl 2 cdo).
1 hel unit.
EQUIPMENT
MBT: 150: M-84, T-34, T-55.
APC: ε20
Plus arty, RCL, AD guns and manportable SAM.
HELICOPTERS: some *Gazelle* and 2 AB-412.
MARITIME ELEMENT: less than 100, 2 armed PCI⟨.
RESERVES:
Territorial defence units.

PARAMILITARY
Police: 4,500 armed (plus 5,000 reserve).

SWEDEN

GDP	1990: S kr 1,432.9bn ($236.95bn)
	1991: S kr 1,436.5bn ($246.67bn)
Growth	1991: -0.8% 1992: -1.7%
Inflation	1991: 9.4% 1992: 2.2%
Publ. Debt	1992: 52.9%
Def exp	1991: S kr 39.05bn ($6.46bn)
	1992: S kr 36.31bn ($6.23bn)
Def bdgt	1992: S kr 37.80bn ($6.49bn)
	1993: S kr 37.75bn ($5.24bn)
$1 = kr	1990: 5.9188 1991: 6.0475
	1992: 5.8240 1993: 7.200

kr = kronor

Population: 8,680,000

	13–17	18–22	23–32
Men	258,700	287,800	618,000
Women	244,300	274,100	591,500

TOTAL ARMED FORCES:
ACTIVE: 64,800 (36,600 conscripts);
Terms of service: Army and Navy 7 –15 months, Air Force 8–12 months.
RESERVES[a] (obligation to age 47): 729,000: Army (incl Local Defence and Home Guard) 586,000; Navy 66,000; Air Force 77,000.

ARMY: 43,500 (27,000 conscripts).
3 Military comd; 26 Defence districts.
PEACE ESTABLISHMENT:
38 armd, cav, inf, arty, AA, engr, sig, spt trg units (local defence, cadre for mob, basic conscript plus refresher trg).
WAR ESTABLISHMENT: (630,000 on mob)
Field Army: (280,000).
3 armd bde.
2 mech bde (incl *Gotland* bde).
6 inf, 5 *Norrland* bde.
100 armd, inf, arty and AA arty bn.
1 avn bn.
6 arty avn pl.
Local Defence Units: (250,000)
60 bn, 400 indep coy.
Home Guard: (100,000) incl inf, arty, static arty, AD
EQUIPMENT:
MBT: 338 *Centurion*, 289 Strv-103B.
LIGHT TANKS: 211 Ikv-91.
AIFV: 505 Pbv-302.
TOWED ARTY: 105mm: 489 Type-40; 155mm: 201 FH-77A.
SP ARTY: 155mm: 26 BK-1A.
MORTARS: 81mm: 1,000; 120mm: ε600.
ATGW: RB-55 (*TOW*, incl Pvrbv 551 SP), RB-56 *Bill*.
RL: 84mm: AT-4.
RCL: 84mm: *Carl Gustav*; 90mm: PV-1110.
AD GUNS: 40mm: 600.

SAM: RBS-70 (incl Lvrbv SP), RB-77 (*Improved HAWK*).
HELICOPTERS: 20 Hkp-9A ATK, 16 Hkp-3 tpt, 25 Hkp-5B trg, 19 Hkp-6A utility.

NAVY: 9,800, incl coast defence and naval air (320) (4,100 conscripts).
BASES: Muskö, Karlskrona, Härnösand, Göteborg (spt only).
SUBMARINES: 12:
4 *Västergötland* with TP-617 HWT and TP-613 and TP-43.
1 modernized *Näcken* (AIP) with TP-613 and TP-42.
2 *Näcken*, 5 *Sjöormen*, with TP-613 and TP-42.
PATROL AND COASTAL COMBATANTS: 41:
MISSILE CRAFT: 34 PFM:
4 *Göteborg* with 4 x 2 RBS-15 SSM; plus 4 x 400mm TT, 4 x ASW mor.
2 *Stockholm* with 4 x 2 RBS-15 SSM (or up to 4 additional 533 TT); plus 2 x 533mm, 4 x 400mm TT, 4 x ASW mor.
16 *Hugin* with 6 RB-12 (No *Penguin*) SSM; plus 4 ASW mor.
12 *Norrköping* with 4 x 2 RBS-15 SSM or up to 6 x 533mm TT.
PATROL: 7:
1 PCI, 6 PCI⟨.
MINE WARFARE: 28:
MINELAYERS: 3:
1 *Carlskrona* (200 mines), trg.
2 *Älvsborg* (200 mines).
(mines can be laid by all SS classes).
MINE COUNTERMEASURES: 25:
1 *Utö* MCMV spt.
7 *Landsort* MCC.
3 *Arkö* MSC.
10 MSI, 4 MSI .
AMPHIBIOUS: craft only; 12 LCM.
SUPPORT AND MISCELLANEOUS: 11:
1 AGI, 1 sub rescue/salvage ship, 1 survey, 6 icebreakers, 2 tugs.

COAST DEFENCE:
6 coast arty bde: 12 mobile, 53 static units, incl 2 amph defence bn, arty, barrier bn, minelayer sqn.
EQUIPMENT:
GUNS: 40mm incl L/70 AA, 75mm, 120mm incl CD-80 *Karin* (mobile); 75mm, 120mm *Ersta* (static).
MORTARS: 81mm.
SSM: RBS-17 *Hellfire*, RBS-08A, RBS-15KA, RB-52.
MINELAYERS: 9 inshore, 16 inshore .
PATROL CRAFT: 18 PCI .
AMPHIBIOUS: 10 LCM, 80 LCU, about 60 LCA.

NAVAL AIR: (320): 1 cbt ac, 14 armed hel.
ASW: 1 C-212 ac.
HELICOPTERS: 3 sqn with 14 Hkp-4B/C ASW, 10 Hkp-6 liaison.

AIR FORCE: 11,500 (5,500 conscripts);

390 cbt ac (plus 91 in store), no armed hel.
1 attack staff.
3 Air Commands.
FGA: 4 sqn:
4 with 74 SAAB AJ-37 (plus 13 in store); incl 1 (OCU) with 15 SAAB SK-37 (plus 15 in store).
FIGHTER: 10 sqn:
2 with 44 SAAB J-35 (plus 21 in store), 10 SAAB SK-35C;
8 with 137 SAAB JA-37 (plus 42 in store).
RECCE: 2 sqn with *50 SAAB SH/SF-37.
ECM: 2 *Caravelle*, 13 SAAB 32E.
TRANSPORT: 1 sqn with 8 C-130E/H, 3 *King Air* 200, 2 *Metro* III (VIP), 13 SK-60D/E, 1 SAAB 340B.
TRAINING: 25 SAAB J-32B/D/E (13 -E ECM trg; 5 -D target-towing 7-B), 60 *SK-60B/C (also have lt attack/recce role), 71 SK-61.
SAR: 10 Hkp, 10 *Super Puma*.
3 Hkp 9B (Bo-105 CBS).
UTILITY: 7 Hkp-3.
AAM: RB-24 (AIM-9B/3 *Sidewinder*), RB-27 (*Improved Falcon*), RB-28 (*Falcon*), RB-71 (*Skyflash*), RB-74 AIM 9L (*Sidewinder*).
ASM: RB-04E, RB-05A, RB-15F, RB-75 (*Maverick*).
AD: Semi-automatic control and surveillance system, *Stril* 60, coordinates all AD components.

FORCES ABROAD:
UN AND PEACEKEEPING:
ANGOLA (UNAVEM II): 3 Observers.
CAMBODIA (UNTAC): 36 civ pol.
CROATIA (UNPROFOR I): 97, plus 5 Observers, 6 mil police, 30 civ pol.
CYPRUS (UNFICYP): 21 police (3 mil), 5 staff.
EL SALVADOR (ONUSAL): 2 Observers, 2 civ pol.
INDIA/PAKISTAN (UNMOGIP): 8 Observers.
IRAQ/KUWAIT (UNIKOM): 7 Observers.
KOREA (NNSC): 6 Staff.
LEBANON (UNIFIL): 495: 1 log bn.
MACEDONIA (UNPROFOR M): 153: 1 inf, 1 HQ coy.
MIDDLE EAST (UNTSO): 18 Observers.
MOZAMBIQUE (ONUMOZ): 19 Observers.
SOMALIA (UNOSOM): 155: 1 fd hospital.

PARAMILITARY:
COAST GUARD: (600); 1 *Gotland* PCO and 1 KBV-171 PCC (fishery protection), some 65 PCI; Air Arm: 3 C-212 MR, 1 Cessna 337G, 1 402C ac.
CIVIL DEFENCE: shelters for 6,300,000. All between age 16–25 liable for civil defence duty.
VOLUNTARY AUXILIARY ORGANISATIONS: Some 35,000 volunteers from 10 voluntary auxiliary organisations are provided for army units.

a Each year some 100,000 reservists carry out refresher trg; length of trg depends on rank (officers up to 31 days, NCO and specialists, 24 days, others 17 days). Commitment is 5 exercises during reserve service period, plus mob call-outs.

SWITZERLAND

GDP	1991:	fr 332.70bn ($232.01bn)
	1992:	fr 338.36bn ($240.62bn)
Growth	1991: -0.1%	1992: -0.6%
Inflation	1991: 5.8%	1992: 4.1%
Publ. Debt	1992: 13.7%	
Def bdgt	1992:	fr 5.224bn ($3.72bn)
	1993:	fr 4.93bn ($3.27bn)
$1 = fr	1990: 1.3892	1991: 1.4340
	1992: 1.4062	1993: 1.5073

fr = francs

Population: 6,812,000

	13–17	18–22	23–32
Men	194,000	219,300	521,000
Women	184,700	210,000	507,000

TOTAL ARMED FORCES: (Air Corps forms part of the Army):

ACTIVE: about 1,800 regular, plus recruits (2 intakes (1 of 11,000, 1 of 17,000) each for 17 weeks only).

Terms of service: 17 weeks compulsory recruit trg at age 19–20, followed by 8 refresher trg courses of 3 weeks over a 12-year period between ages 20–32 for *Auszug* (call out), 39 days over a 10-year period (33–42) for *Landwehr* (militia). some 390,000 attend trg each year.

RESERVES (all services): 625,000.

ARMY: 565,000 on mob.

3 fd corps, each 1 mech, 2 inf div, 1 territorial zone, 2–3 border bde.
1 mtn corps with 3 mtn div (each 1 territorial zone, 1 border, 1 redoubt, 1 fortress bde).
Corps Tps:
Each corps with 1 inf, 1 cyclist, 1 engr regt, some arty (fd), indep inf (mtn), 1 hel sqn.
Army Tps:
1 inf, 3 engr regt, 2 sigs (EW) bn.

EQUIPMENT:
MBT: 785: 143 Pz-61, 186 Pz-68, 117 Pz-68/75, 39 Pz-68/88, some 300 Pz-87 (*Leopard* 2).
AIFV: 580 M-63/-73, M-63/-89 (all M-113 with 20mm).
APC: 705 M-63/-73 (M-113) incl variants.
TOWED ARTY: 105mm: 216 Model-35, 420 Model-46.
SP ARTY: 155mm: 540 PzHb-66/-74 (M-109U).
MORTARS: 81mm: 2,750 M-33, M-72; 120mm: 261 M-87, 120 M-74 (M-113).
ATGW: 279 MOWAG *Piranha* with *TOW*-2; 2,700 B/B-77 (*Dragon*).
RL: 83mm: 20,000 M-80.
ATK GUNS: 90mm: 850 Model-50/-57.
AD GUNS: 20mm: 1,700.
SAM: 56 B/L-84 (*Rapier*).
HELICOPTERS: 60 *Alouette* III
MARINE: 12 *Aquarius* patrol boats .

AIR CORPS: 60,000 on mob (incl military airfield guard units).
241 cbt ac, no armed hel.
The Air Corp is an integral part of the Army, structured in 1 Air Force bde, 1 AD, 1 Airbase bde and 1 Comd and control bde.
FGA: 6 sqn with 79 *Hunter* F-58, 7 T-68.
FIGHTER: 9 sqn:
7 with 91 *Tiger* II/F-5E, 12 *Tiger* II/F-5F;
2 with 30 *Mirage* IIIS, 4 -III DS.
RECCE: 1 sqn with 18 *Mirage* IIIRS.
LIAISON/SAR: 1 sqn with 18 PC-6, 2 *Learjet* 36.
HELICOPTERS: 3 sqn with 15 AS-332 M-1, 15 SA-316.
TRAINING: 19 *Hawk* Mk 66, 28 P-3, 39 PC-7, 8 PC-9.
ASM: AGM-65A/B *Maverick*.
AAM: AIM-9 *Sidewinder*, AIM-26 *Falcon*.

AIR DEFENCE:
1 airbase bde:
3 regt x 4 bn, each with 4 bty of 20mm and twin 35mm guns with *Skyguard* fire-control radar.
1 AD bde:
1 SAM regt (2 bn, each of 3 bty; 60 *Bloodhound*);
7 AD arty regt (each with 2 bn of 3 bty; 35mm guns, *Skyguard* fire control).

FORCES ABROAD:
UN AND PEACEKEEPING:
CROATIA (UNPROFOR I): 6 Observers.
KOREA (NNSC): 6 Staff.
MIDDLE EAST (UNTSO): 5 Observers.
WESTERN SAHARA (MINURSO): 1 med unit (42).

PARAMILITARY:
CIVIL DEFENCE: 480,000 (300,000 fully trained).

UKRAINE

GDP	1991:	r 234.0bn ($137.65bn)
	1992ε:	r 3,900bn ($112.9bn)
Growth	1991: -11.2%	1992ε: -18%
Inflation[a]	1991: 84.20%	1992ε: 1,830%
Debt	1991:	$13.40bn
Def bdgt[b]	1992:	r 116bn ($4.32bn)
	1993:	Kar 544.26bn
$1 = r, Kar	1991: 1.70	1992: 180
	1993ε: 3,500+	

r = rouble
Kar = Karbovanet
[a] Year average.
[b] A further Kar 186.52bn have been allocated for conversion of the defence industry.

Population: 52,456,000 (20.3% Russian)

	13–17	18–22	23–32
Men	1,860,000	1,813,500	3,505,500
Women	1,802,000	1,768,000	3,479,000

TOTAL ARMED FORCES:
ACTIVE: 438,000 (excl Strategic Nuclear Forces and Black Sea Fleet) incl 47,000 in central staffs and units not covered below.
Terms of service: 18 months.
RESERVES Some 1m with military service within 5 years.
Forming independent armed forces to include a navy based on former Soviet Union forces. Two-year transition period.

STRATEGIC NUCLEAR FORCES:
(ownership and control disputed)
ICBM: 166
SS-19 *Stiletto* (RS-18): 120 (at two sites).
SS-24 *Scalpel* (RS-22): 46 (silo-based, one site co-located with SS-19).
BOMBERS: 42: 22 Tu-95H (each with 16 AS-15 ALCM), 20 Tu-160 (each with 12 AS-15 ALCM).
TANKERS: 20 Il-78.

GROUND FORCES: 217,000
(former Carpathian, Kiev and Odessa MDs)
MOD tps.
3 MD HQ (to become 2 op comds November 1993).
1 TD (trg).
1 air mobile div (forming).
4 engr bde.
Op Comd.
5 army HQ.
1 corps HQ.
1 arty corps (3 arty, 1 MRL, 2 ATK bde/regt).

2 TD.	11 MRD (2 trg).
3 mech div.	2 mech bde.
2 AB bde (1 trg).	2 SF (*Spetsnaz*) bde.

2 arty div (3 arty, 1 MRL, 1 ATK bde/regt).
6 arty bde/regt (1 trg).
3 MRL bde/regt.
6 ATK bde/regt.

7 SSM bde.	8 SAM bde/regt.
7 engr bde/regt.	7 attack hel regt.

5 spt/tpt hel regt/unit.
EQUIPMENT:
MBT: some 5,700 (incl some 1,400 in store): 1,100 T-54/-55, 400 T-62, 2,500 T-64, 1,300 T-72, 350 T-80.
LIGHT TANKS: 40 PT-76.
RECCE: some 2,000 incl 520 BRM.
AIFV: some 3,450: 1,700 BMP-1, 1,500 BMP-2, 6 BMP-3, 230 BMD.
APC: some 2,600: 630 BTR-60, 1,400 BTR-70, 450 BTR-80, 80 BTR-D, plus 1,500 MT-LB, 3,000 'look alikes'.
TOTAL ARTY: 3,600

TOWED ARTY: 970: 122mm: 390 D-30; 152mm: 150 D-20, 190 2A65, 240 2A36.
SP ARTY: 1,324: 122mm: 660 2S1; 152mm: 500 2S3, 24 2S5, 40 2S19, 203mm: 100 2S7.
COMBINED GUN/MORTAR: 120mm: 85 2S9.
MRL: 640: 122mm: 375 BM-21, 25 9P138; 132mm: 5 BM-13; 220mm: 140 9P140; 300mm: 95 9A52.
MORTARS: 580: 120mm: 330 2S12, 250 PM-38.
SSM: 132 *Scud*, 140 *FROG*/SS-21.
SAM: SA-4/-6/-8/-11/-12A/-15.
HELICOPTERS:
ATTACK: 223 Mi-24, 22 Mi-24R, 21 Mi-24K.
SUPPORT: 36 Mi-6, 250 Mi-8, 9 Mi-24K, 9 Mi-24P.
TRANSPORT: 80 Mi-2, 20 Mi-26.

AIR FORCE (incl Air Defence): 171,000
3 air army, 1 PVO army, some 900 cbt ac, plus 440 in store (MiG-21, MiG-23, MiG-27, MiG-29).
BOMBERS: 2 div HQ, 3 regt (1 trg) with 53 Tu-16, 33 Tu-22, 29 Tu-22M.
FGA/BOMBER: 2 div HQ, 5 regt with 150 Su-24.
FGA: 1 regt with 34 Su-25.
FIGHTER: 2 div (8 regt), 3 PVO div (8 regt) with 125 MiG-23, 80 MiG-25, 194 MiG-29, 60 Su-15, 50 Su-27.
RECCE: 3 regt with 22 Tu-22, 39 Su-17, 26 Su-24.
ECM: 1 regt with 35 Yak-28, 12 Su-24.
TRANSPORT: 174 Il-76, 100 others incl An-12.
TRAINING: 4 centres, 9 regts with 60 Su-24, 500 L-39/L-29.
HELICOPTERS: 20 Mi-6, 114 Mi-8, 8 *Mi-24.
SAM: 2,400: SA-2/-3/-5/-10.

NAVY: ε3,000
BASES: Sevastopol, Odessa
PRINCIPAL SURFACE COMBATANTS: 2: 1 *Krivak-III* PCO, 1 *Petya-II* FF.
OTHER SURFACE SHIPS: 1 *Slavutich* (Sov *Kamchatka*) comd vessel, some 40 coastal, inshore and riverine patrol craft incl *Stenka, Muravey* and *Shemel* classes, 1 or 2 small log spt vessels; 1 large hovercraft: capacity 10 APC, 100 tps.
BLACK SEA FLEET: (ε48,000) (HQ Sevastopol) Since August 1992 the Black Sea Fleet has been controlled jointly by Russia and the Ukraine. Some, mainly minor, units of the Fleet have already been transferred to Ukraine (see above) and Georgia (see page 80).

FORCES ABROAD
UN AND PEACEKEEPING:
BOSNIA (UNPROFOR II): 362: 1 inf bn.

PARAMILITARY FORCES: 72,000.
NATIONAL GUARD: 12,000 (to be 30,000; former MVD eqpt in service).
BORDER GUARD (incl Coast guard): 60,000.

> ## 'Federal Republic of Yugoslavia':
> # SERBIA/MONTENEGRO

GDP[a]   1991ε: ND 5,712.0bn ($19.40bn)
         1992ε: $13.54bn
Growth   1991ε: -19%   1992ε:-26%
Inflation 1991: 117%   1992ε:25,000%
Debt   1990: $17.60bn   1991: $16.40bn
Def bdgt[a] 1991ε: ND 135.00bn ($3.49bn)
         1992ε: ND 245.00bn ($3.76bn)
$1 = ND[a] 1990: 11.318   1991: 37.850
         1992: 180.00   1993: 1,000,000+

ND = New Dinar
[a] Dollar values are estimated.

Population: Serbia 9,893,000 (incl 65% Serbs). Montenegro 643,000 (incl 68% Montenegrins, 13.5% Muslims). A further 2,032,000 Serbs were living in the other Yugoslav republics before the civil war began.

TOTAL ARMED FORCES:
ACTIVE: 136,500 (60,000 conscripts).
Terms of service: 12–15 months.
RESERVES: some 400,000.

ARMY: (JNA) some 100,000 (ε37,000 conscripts);
3 Army, 8 Corps (incl 1 mech).

3 tk bde.	8 mech bde.
28 mot inf bde.	1 mtn bde.
13 inf bde.	1 AB bde.
8 arty bde.	3 arty regt.
3 ATK arty bde.	2 ATK arty regt.
9 AD regt.	5 SAM-6 regt.

EQUIPMENT:
MBT: 640: 390 T-54/-55, some 250 M-84 (T-74; mod T-72) and T-72.
RECCE: 92 M-3A1, 18 M-8, some 130 BRDM-2.
AIFV: 620 M-80.
APC: 143 M-60P, BOV-VP.
TOWED ARTY: 1,130: 105mm: M-56; 122mm: M-1931/37, M-1938, D-30; 130mm: M-46; 152mm: M-1937, D-20, M-84; 155mm: M-59, M-65.
SP ARTY: 105mm: M-7; 122mm: 75 2S1.
MRL: 100: 128mm: M-63, M-77.
MORTARS:[b] 82mm: 1,700; 120mm: 800.
ATGW: 282 AT-3 *Sagger* incl SP (BOV-1, BRDM-1/2).
RCL:[b] 57mm: 1,550; 82mm: 1,000 M-60PB SP; 105mm: 650 M-65.
ATK GUNS:[c] 75mm: 748: M-1943, Pak 40; 90mm: 80 M-36B2 (incl SP); 100mm: 350 T-12.
AD GUNS:[b] 20mm: 475 M-55/-75, 65 BOV-3 SP triple; 30mm: 350 M-53, M-53/-59, 8 BOV-30 SP; 57mm: 54 ZSU-57-2 SP.
SAM: 175: SA-6/-7/-9.

NAVY: ε7,500 (some conscripts).
BASE: Kotor. (Most former Yug bases are now in Croatian hands.)
SUBMARINES: 5:
2 *Sava* SS with 533mm TT
3 *Heroj* SS with 533mm TT
(Plus 5 *Una* SSI for SF ops).
FRIGATES: 4:
2 *Kotor* with 4 x SS-N-2B *Styx* SSM, 2 x 12 ASW RL, 2 x 3 ASTT.
2 *Split* (Sov *Koni*) with 4 SS-N-2B *Styx* SSM, 2 x 12 ASW RL.
PATROL AND COASTAL COMBATANTS: 55:
MISSILE CRAFT: 12:
5 *Rade Koncar* PFM with 2 x SS-N-2B *Styx*.
7 *Mitar Acev* (Sov *Osa-I*) PFM with 4 x SS-N-2A.
TORPEDO CRAFT: 12:
12 *Topcider* (Sov *Shershen*) with 4 x 533mm TT.
PATROL: 31:
COASTAL: 1 *Mornar* ASW with 4 x ASW RL.
INSHORE: 7 *Mirna*
RIVERINE: about 23⟨ (some in reserve).
MINE WARFARE: 12
MINELAYERS: 1: 1 *Sibla*-class, 94 mines.
Also DTM-211 and DSM-501 LCTs can lay 100 mines – see amph forces.
MCM: 11:
3 *Vukov Klanac* MHC
3 UK *Ham* MSI
5 *M-117* MSI.
(plus some 13 riverine MSI⟨).
AMPHIBIOUS: craft only; about 27: 10 DTM-211 and 2 DSM-501 LCT, about 15 LCM.
SUPPORT AND MISCELLANEOUS: 5:
3 PO-91 *Lubin* tpt, 1 trg, 1 river flagship.
MARINES: (900)
2 marine bde (2 regt each of 2 bn).

AIR FORCE: 29,000 (3,000 conscripts); 480 cbt ac, 135 armed hel.
3 air corps each 1 AD div, incl ac, AD arty, SAM.
FGA: 12 sqn with 69 P-2 *Kraguj*, 50 *Jastreb*, 25 *Super Galeb*, 69 *Orao*-2.
FIGHTER: 8 sqn with 98 MiG-21F/PF/M/bis, 10 MiG-21U, 18 MiG-29 (16 -A, 2 -UB).
RECCE: 4 sqn with 12 *Galeb*, 20 *Jastreb* RJ-1, 25 *Orao*-1, 14 MiG-21.
ARMED HEL: 36 Mi-8 (aslt); 99 *Gazela* (attack).
ASW: 1 hel sqn with 4 Mi-14, 4 Ka-25, 2 Ka-27.
TRANSPORT: 2 ac sqn with 2 An-12, 15 An-26, 4 CL-215 (SAR, fire-fighting), 2 *Falcon* 50 (VIP), 2 *Learjet* 25, 6 PC-6, 6 Yak-40.
LIAISON: 46 UTVA-66 ac, 14 *Partizan* hel.
TRAINING: ac: 70 *Super Galeb/Jastreb,* 100 UTVA-75/-76; **hel:** 20 *Gazela*.
AAM: AA-2 *Atoll*, AA-8 *Aphid*, AA-10 *Alamo*, AA-11 *Archer*.
ASM: AGM-65 *Maverick*, AS-7 *Kerry*.
AD: 8 SAM bn, 8 sites with 24 SA-2, 16 SA-3. 15 regt AD arty.

[b] A number of these wpn have been taken over by Bosnia-Herzegovina, Croatia, Macedonia and Slovenia.

Russia

National Overview

Over the year the efforts and energies of President Boris Yeltsin and his ministerial team appear to have been devoted to combating political rivals such as Vice-President Aleksandr Rutskoi, Parliamentary Speaker Ruslan Khasbulatov and hard-line members of the Supreme Soviet over the future constitution of the Russian Federation, the powers of the President and the speed and direction of economic reform. As a result, foreign and security policy have taken second place and a number of internal problems seem to have been ignored by Moscow.

Russia has serious differences with a number of its neighbours: with the Baltic Republics over the status of Russians living there; with Ukraine over the future of the Black Sea Fleet and strategic nuclear forces and also over potential border problems and the cost of oil and gas supplies. In the Transcaucasus Russia apparently backs the 'break-away' ambitions of Abkhazia and South Ossetia from Georgia and is seen as backing Armenia in its conflict with Azerbaijan. Further potential problems lie ahead in Central Asia, in addition to the dispute in Tajikistan where Russia is backing the government. And within the Russian Federation any number of disputes could break out. Already Chechenia, which has split from Ingushetia, has declared itself independent, and more recently the Sverdlovsk Oblast and the Primorskiy Kray have proclaimed themselves autonomous republics. Others are following suit.

Commonwealth of Independent States

Although a number of agreements of a military nature were reached by the Commonwealth of Independent States (CIS) during the last 12 months, the number of republics signing each has significantly decreased since mid-1992. While Marshal Yevgeniy Shaposhnikov has tried to improve CIS military cooperation and the formation of joint armed forces, there has been growing opposition to such policies. At a meeting of CIS defence ministers in May 1993 Russia opposed the formation of CIS forces in peacetime. Russia has also opposed continued CIS control over nuclear forces, claiming that the Lisbon START I protocol established Russia as the sole inheritor of the former USSR's nuclear assets. What may be the penultimate nail in the CIS's military coffin was the decision taken on 15 June 1993 to replace the position of Commander in Chief of CIS joint armed forces with a new post entitled Chief of the Joint Staff for coordinating military cooperation between the CIS states.

In principle, the CIS still has a nominal veto over the use of strategic nuclear forces. However, the fact that only Russia, at present, has the capability to service and maintain warheads and missiles, and to produce firing control codes and targeting instructions, means, in effect, that the other nuclear republics, apart from possibly preventing the use of those on their territory, have little or no control over ICBM. All ballistic missile submarines are already under Russian control. The control of strategic bombers, however, is open to question.

Joint Forces

Command of the Black Sea Fleet is still exercised jointly by Ukraine and Russia; and interminable discussions on how it should be disposed of continue, interspersed with reports of ship defections and the raising of national flags, as opposed to the old Soviet ensign. At a meeting on 17 June 1993 President Yeltsin and Ukrainian President Leonid Kravchuck agreed that the ships of the Fleet should be divided equally between the two states and that Russia would be able to lease facilities in the Crimea, mainly in Sevastopol. The agreement also covers the division of Black Sea Fleet naval aviation and shore-based troops, which, in arms-control treaty terms, have been considered for some time as belonging to Ukraine. Whatever may be decided by Russia and Ukraine may well be frustrated by the officers of the Fleet, many of whom are determined that it should not be split up. On 9 July the Russian parliament voted unanimously to proclaim Russian sovereignty over

Sevastopol, the Black Sea Fleet's main base. They appeared to side with the naval officers over the Fleet's future.

The precise situation regarding other joint forces is less clear. It seemed, a year ago, as if the Central Asian Republics would opt for joint control with Russia of armed forces on their territory. Now, although the situation differs from republic to republic, the only common factor is that air-defence forces (PVO and VVO) remain under Russian command. In Kazakhstan, Kyrgyzstan, Uzbekistan and Tajikistan (with the exception of the 201st Motor-Rifle Division which remains under Russian command) the armed forces are now under national command. Only in Turkmenistan are forces still under joint Russian/Turkmen command. We are only including Central Asian Air Defence Forces, Border Troops, forces in Turkmenistan and the division in Tajikistan in Russian totals.

Withdrawal from Abroad

Russian forces continue to withdraw from Germany and Poland, the three Baltic Republics and from the Transcaucasus. Withdrawal from Mongolia was completed in September 1992, however the Signals Intelligence station remains. The brigade in Cuba was withdrawn in mid-1993, but the troops assigned to the Signals Intelligence station are understood to be remaining. All units have left Poland, but a military mission remains to monitor the transit of stores and equipment to Russia. Withdrawal from Germany has continued as planned and will be completed on schedule by the end of 1994 or earlier. Only 58,000 men remain and only six of the original 19 divisions.

Withdrawal from the Baltic states has proceeded less smoothly. This is partly due to the lack of suitable accommodation for the returning units, partly because of the lack of manpower for labouring jobs (as it had been agreed that no fresh troops could be sent to the republics, and, as conscripts are discharged at the end of their service, units are very much below strength) and partly deliberately to increase pressure on the Estonian and Latvian governments to give full civil rights to the large Russian minorities there. Some 26,000 troops remain in the three republics, of which 17,000 are in Latvia.

Kaliningrad remains a key Russian military base in northern Europe. The Baltic Fleet is dependent on the port of Baltyisk and the significance of the oblast as a whole has increased because of the evacuation from the three Baltic Republics, and of course from Germany and Poland. Kaliningrad is being used as a transit area for troops, weapons and stores withdrawn from Germany but there has not been a significant increase in weapons holdings, as many are being destroyed as part of the CFE agreement. The final force level planned for Kaliningrad is said to be between 40,000 and 60,000 men. While a Lithuanian presidential candidate, Stasys Lozoraitis, has claimed that Kaliningrad should become part of Lithuania, and there have been calls from ethnic Germans elsewhere in Russia that they should be relocated there, there is no serious opposition to continued Russian sovereignty. Nor does Kaliningrad, however strongly armed, really pose a threat to any Baltic nation.

In the Transcaucasus only three out of 11 divisions remain: one in Armenia and two in Georgia; the latter will be withdrawn in 1994, with the total pull-out to be completed by the end of 1995. In all three Transcaucasian states a good deal of Russian equipment has been handed over by departing units or has been stolen by local militias. All air force combat assets have been withdrawn, and both the 34th Air Army and 19th PVO Air Army have been disbanded.

The 14th Army still remains in Moldova, but at a reduced strength of one motor-rifle division and one SSM brigade. It appears to be more and more allied to the insurgent forces in the Dniestr province. As yet no date has been agreed for the withdrawal of the 14th Army, although several rounds of talks have taken place. In June it was ruled that Dniestr citizens could not join the 14th Army (they were doing so in preference to their own forces because of the much higher rate of pay).

Reorganisation

In the last edition of *The Military Balance* we reported that the Volga/Ural Military District (MD) had been split. We assumed that the split was a return to the two original Volga and Ural MDs and

indicated this change on the map of Russian MD boundaries. However, we were wrong: the Volga/
Ural MD has been renamed the Volga MD and its boundaries remain unaltered; and a new Ural MD
has been formed east of the Urals in part of the Siberian MD. The map on page 105 shows the true
situation. Presumably, the Ural MD will act as a reserve area for the MDs west of the Urals, while
the residue of the Siberian MD continues to support the Far East region.

The command level of Strategic Direction (TVD) was abandoned when the Soviet Union broke
up. A new development is the establishment of a joint command in the Far East to which has been
assigned: the Far East MD; 1st Air Force Army; 11th Air Defence Army; and the Border and Internal
Troops in the region. The Transcaucasian MD was retitled the Group of Forces of the Transcaucasus
to reflect its new situation of serving outside Russia. Its strength is much reduced, down to only three
motor-rifle divisions with no supporting air forces.

General Pavel Grachev, the Minister of Defence, has outlined the new basic concept for defence
and the restructuring of the armed forces. There are to be three categories of force: Constant
Readiness Troops which are able to react effectively in local conflicts; Rapid Deployment Forces
(also referred to as Mobile Forces), which are lightly equipped forces with transport aircraft available
to move them at short notice to reinforce Constant Readiness Troops; Strategic Reserves with
missions for large-scale war. This last category of forces would be mobilised before a crisis broke
out, but presumably would normally be kept at a low level of manning. The reorganisation will be
spread over the next ten years. The final organisational structure has not yet been decided upon,
although an increasing number of brigades are being formed (which in past experimental
reorganisations were commanded by Corps), but at the same time several new armies are being
established.

The North Caucasus MD has acquired a new importance as a 'front-line' area, and it is here that
organisational changes at a lower level are most in evidence. A new Army HQ has been formed,
where previously there were only army corps, which commands two newly formed motor-rifle
brigades (others are being formed). The MD has been reinforced with a number of airborne
formations: the 7th division redeployed from Lithuania; an independent brigade withdrawn from
Georgia; and a newly formed brigade. Russia's ability to station large tank and artillery forces in the
MD is constrained by the CFE zonal limits laid down in Article V of the Treaty, and known as the
Flanks Zone. The limit covers numbers in both the Leningrad and North Caucasus MDs and may not
exceed a combined total of 1,300 tanks and 1,680 pieces of artillery. The Defence Minister raised
the question of renegotiating CFE limits with the US Secretary of Defense when they met in June
1993. The Treaty zonal limits were, of course, negotiated on the basis of the Warsaw Pact's
deployment pre-1991 and so there is some justification for the Russian case. However, any minor
readjustment could lead to a more general unravelling of the Treaty and, in any event, is likely to be
opposed by the other republics of the former Soviet Union.

Manpower

That the Russian armed forces are suffering serious manpower shortages is undisputed; assessing
the size of the problem is more difficult. In June 1993 the Defence Minister complained that 'there
are 1,814,000 men of draft age in the country but 1,515,000 of them have legitimate rights to
deferment'. He also said that 50% of those drafted were taken by paramilitary forces (such as Border
and Ministry of Interior troops), leaving only 150,000 conscripts a year for the armed forces. The
situation is made worse by the number of those who are called up but do not report, said to be about
31,000 at the Spring 1993 call-up. The Defence Minister continued 'the forces will be discharging
580,000 men in the Autumn as both those who had completed two years' service and those who need
only serve for the newly revised term of 18 months would be released'. One must assume that he was
putting the worst possible interpretation on the figures. On the other hand, the forces have disbanded
large numbers of units and formations and continue to do so. They have also recruited more than the
planned 100,000 men to serve on short contracts. The number of women in the forces is increasing.
The true picture will not emerge until January 1994 when the next CFE declaration of manpower is

made. In January 1992 Russia declared that it had 1,298,299 men serving west of the Urals. This number did not include men in the Navy nor in the Strategic Rocket Forces.

Nuclear Forces

The Russian Federation parliament ratified the Treaty on the Reduction and Limitation of Strategic Offensive Arms (START) on 4 November 1992, but ratification was accompanied by a statement that it would not effect the exchange of ratification instruments until Belarus, Kazakhstan and Ukraine had acceded to the Nuclear Non-Proliferation Treaty (NPT). On 3 January 1993 President Yeltsin signed the Treaty on Further Reduction and Limitation of Strategic Offensive Arms (START II).

START II bans all ICBM with MIRV warheads (including all heavy ICBM), limits SLBM deployments to 1,750 and limits the total number of warheads held by each side to between 1,700 and 1,750. Further details of START II and its implications for Russia's strategic forces are analysed in the essay 'Nuclear Developments' towards the back of the book.

The Russian Defence Ministry announced on 4 February 1993 that all tactical nuclear weapons had been removed from naval ships (as pledged by President Gorbachev in 1991).

Russia has continued to withdraw older ICBM from service; during the last 12 months 100 SS-11 have been withdrawn. Six SS-18 deployed in Russia have been eliminated. No more SS-25 mobile launchers have been brought into service. One *Delta-I*-class and two *Yankee-I*-class SSBN have been retired, which reduces the number of deployable SLBM by 44. There has been one unconfirmed report that the Tu-95 strategic bombers based in Kazakhstan were being redeployed to Russia; more probably, there has been a rotation of aircraft or some have returned to Russia for major overhaul, so the listing in this respect should be treated with caution.

Once again, we are listing all strategic forces twice: once under Russia, still nominally under CIS control, and also in the country of deployment.

Conventional Forces
Ground Forces

The Russian Army has made more progress in disbanding formations and units than in eliminating TLE as required by the CFE Treaty. To some extent, the reductions appear greater than they are because last year we counted all units under joint control in the Russian totals. Now, a number of republics have formed national armies incorporating some previously joint formations. Nevertheless, within Russia there has been a reduction of three tank divisions and 16 motor-rifle divisions. On the other hand, seven new-style motor-rifle brigades have been formed; in addition to those in the North Caucasus, there are three in the Moscow MD, one being in the newly formed 22nd Army (upgraded from army corps) and another in the Guards Tank Army whose HQ has been redeployed from eastern Germany. As yet, there appears to be no standard equipment holding for these brigades whose manpower establishment is 2,500 and which are likely to include a 31-tank battalion and 24 artillery pieces (most now have the 2S3 152mm SP gun). SSM units are gradually being reduced; since 1990 16 brigades have been disbanded, mainly as they are withdrawn from Germany. How many of the remaining brigades are equipped with SS-21, as opposed to *Scud*, is not clear, but one SS-21 brigade from Germany has joined one of the army corps in the North Caucasus. The status of two airborne divisions is uncertain. The 242nd training division which was based in Lithuania is certainly inoperative and whether it is being relocated or disbanded is not known. The 98th Airborne Division was based in Bolgrad in Ukraine, with one regiment in Moldova. It has been reported in the open press that this regiment has been redeployed to Abakan (south of Krasnoyarsk), and on 9 July the remainder of the division was reported to have left Ukraine and moved to the Ivanovo Oblast (north-west of Moscow). It has been confirmed that, with the agreement of the Ukrainian and Russian governments, the officers of the division have moved to Ivanovo, presumably to re-establish the division there, while Ukraine is forming a new air-mobile division with the troops that did not move.

In *The Military Balance 1991–1992* we pointed to a number of storage units entitled (in CFE data) 'arms and equipment depots' which, judging by the mix of equipments (tanks, APC, artillery and armoured bridge layers) could be divisional mobilisation bases. A report from Belarus by the Interfax news agency (see p. 69) confirms our belief. Of the 15 such depots listed in Russia's 1990 CFE data only five still appear (on the basis of equipment stored) to be divisional mobilisation bases. One is in the Volga MD and four are in the Leningrad MD. There could well be others east of the Urals, possibly in the new Ural MD, but we have no confirmation.

All attack helicopter units are now under army command. Previously attack helicopter training based in the former Volga/Ural MD was under air force control and two regiments in Germany had been temporarily resubordinated to the air force.

Air Forces

The Russian Air Force is having to contend with force reduction, reorganisation and withdrawal from republics of the former Soviet Union and former Warsaw Pact states. A lack of suitable airfield accommodation (rather than any plan to develop a new threat to the Nordic region) accounts for the continued stationing of air force units in Belarus and for the apparent large-scale build-up in the Kola Peninsula.

A number of frontal aviation units have been withdrawn from the Western Group of Forces in Germany in the last six months. Numbers have gone down from ten regiments and 350 combat aircraft to three regiments and 75 combat aircraft. We have no information yet as to where the units have withdrawn (some deployments in Russia will thus be understated).

Despite a reduction in Research and Development funding, a number of new aircraft are being planned. Three new fighters are under development: the MiG-33 is a MiG-29 but with new radar, new infra-red search and tracking system and a more powerful engine; the Su-35 is an advanced version of the Su-27 and has a radar claimed to be capable of tracking at least 15 targets out to 225 nautical miles, and engaging six targets simultaneously. Both have fly-by-wire controls. Mikoyan may also be developing the Type 701, a possible replacement for the MiG-31. A new multirole aircraft project, known as 1-42, is also being developed by Mikoyan and will be the Russian equivalent of the US F-22. Its design is a compromise between the competing demands of low-observable technology (*stealth*) and the aerodynamics necessary to achieve a high degree of agility. Whether Russia can afford such an ambitious development programme is unclear; much will depend on its ability to capture export markets from Western manufacturers.

There has been a growth in the establishment of partnerships with Western firms. For example, two training aircraft, one of which may be chosen to replace Russia's L-29 and L-39 training fleet, are being jointly developed and marketed. The MiG-AT is a Mikoyan/SNECMA (France) venture and Yakovlev and Aermacchi (Italy) are working on the Yak-130. As markets continue to shrink, it is likely that more cooperative ventures will flourish.

Naval Forces

The severe economic restrictions imposed on the Russian Navy for over two years have taken a heavy toll on its operational capability. At the same time the length of conscript service has been reduced to two years, the Baltic Fleet has had to redeploy from its bases in the Baltic Republics, and the Black Sea Fleet has been plagued by the dispute over its future and torn by the demands of both Russia and Ukraine for its loyalty. Widespread publicity was given to the deaths and illness of cadets in the Pacific Fleet from malnutrition which resulted in the dismissal of the Commander-in-Chief and other senior officers. Reports indicate that many ships of the Pacific Fleet, including the aircraft carrier, are unfit to go to sea. Large numbers of decommissioned ships await disposal; most worrying is the problem of disposing of the nuclear reactors which powered many of the submarines and for which there is no apparent method of disposal other than to continue dumping at sea.

The Russian Navy has commissioned a few new ships in the last 12 months but has retired very many more. The sea-worthiness of a number which remain in service must be in doubt. Five new submarines have been commissioned, a tenth *Oscar*-class SSGN, two *Akula*-class SSN and two *Kilo*-class SS, while 35 have been retired (nine SSGN, 11 SSN, three SSG and 12 SS). Neither *Kiev*-class aircraft carrier is considered to be operational. No new cruisers have been commissioned, but four *Kronshtadt*-class have been retired. One *Sovremennyy*-class destroyer has been commissioned, while three destroyers and 15 frigates have been retired. The Northern Fleet appears to be the least affected by the retirement programme.

Defence Industry

When the Soviet Union disintegrated Russia inherited nearly 80% of the defence industry assets, and, with the exception of some components, can continue to produce virtually the whole range of defence equipment requirements. Two major capabilities, both lost to Ukraine, were the aircraft-carrier shipyard at Nikolayev and the Antonov transport aircraft complex. Plants in Ukraine also produced SS-18 and SS-24 ICBM, but both of these are due to be eliminated under START I.

The Russian defence industry has probably been hit far harder than its Western counterparts. It no longer has to meet the large-scale requirements of the Soviet armed forces, nor does it have to provide a wide range of countries with either free or heavily subsidised weapons. On the other hand, the possibility for conversion is much greater than in the West, given the shortage of consumer goods in Russia and Eastern Europe compared with overproduction in the West. However (in Western terms) relatively large numbers of weapons are still being produced but in greatly reduced numbers compared with production two to three years ago. Comparative figures recently put before a US Congressional committee are:

	1990	1992
Tanks	1,300	675
Artillery	1,900	450
Military aircraft	600+	170
Submarines and major surface combatants	20	8

The Russians are putting a great deal of effort into promoting defence exports and are now major participants in events such as the IDEX 93 arms exhibition in Abu Dhabi and the Paris Air Show. A number of export orders have been gained from new customers, the most significant of which is the sale of 18 MiG-29 fighters to Malaysia. Another new customer will be Turkey which signed a protocol on the purchase of Russian armaments in March 1993. Turkish procurement is likely to include helicopters and APC.

The Russian contract to supply India with engines for satellite launch rockets and rocket technology has been interrupted by US claims that it violates the principles of the Missile Technology Control Regime (MTCR) by which Russia has said it will abide. The sale of rocket engines is to go ahead, but the transfer of technology is to be reviewed so that MTCR provisions are complied with. Failure to agree to US demands could have led to the US not giving some intended commercial space-launch business to Russia and to halting discussion on cooperation on a joint space station.

RUSSIA

GNP[a]	1991: r 810.0bn ($476.5bn)
	1992ε: r 14,046.0bn ($400.2bn)
Growth	1991: -11% 1992ε: -19%
Inflation	1991: 89% 1992ε: 2,500%
Debt	1991: $59.10bn 1992: $68.0bn
Def exp	1992ε: r 850.0bn ($47.22bn)
Def bdgt	1992: r 715.7bn ($39.68bn)
	1993ε: r 3,115.51bn ($29.12bn)

$1 = r   1990: 0.6041   1991: 1.70
            1992: 180   1993: 800

r = roubles
[a] Dollar values are estimated.

Population: 150,385,000

	13–17	18–22	23–32
Men	5,584,000	5,212,000	9,981,000
Women	5,428,000	5,073,000	9,745,000

TOTAL ARMED FORCES:
ACTIVE: some 2,030,000 (perhaps 950,000 conscripts) incl about 165,000 MOD staff, centrally controlled units for EW, trg, rear services, but excl 130,000 railway and construction tp.
Terms of service: Army 18 months, Navy 2 years. Women with medical and other special skills may volunteer.
RESERVES: some 2,400,000 with service within last 5 years: Reserve obligation to age 50; total: some 20,000,000.

STRATEGIC NUCLEAR FORCES:
194,000 (incl 29,000 assigned from Air and Navy).

NAVY: (10,000). 788 msl in 52 SSBN.
SSBN: 52: (all based in Russian ports)
6 *Typhoon* with 20 SS-N-20 *Sturgeon* (120 msl).
7 *Delta-IV* with 16 SS-N-23 *Skiff* (112 msl).
14 *Delta-III* with 16 SS-N-18 *Stingray* (224 msl).
4 *Delta-II* with 16 SS-N-8 *Sawfly* (64 msl).
17 *Delta-I* with 12 SS-N-8 *Sawfly* (204 msl).
4 *Yankee-I* with 16 SS-N-6 *Serb* (64 msl).

STRATEGIC ROCKET FORCES: (144,000 incl 70,000 conscripts): 5 rocket armies, org in div, regt, bn and bty, 126 launcher groups, normally 10 silos (6 for SS-18) and one control centre; SS-25 units each 9 launchers; 12 SS-24 trains each 3 launchers, 2 msl test centres.
ICBM: 1,204.
SS-11 *Sego*: 100 mod 2/3 (at 6 fields; all in Russia).
SS-13 *Savage* (RS-12): 40 (at 1 field, all in Russia).
SS-17 *Spanker* (RS-16): 40 (at 1 field; mod 3/4 MIRV; all in Russia).
SS-18 *Satan* (RS-20): 302 (at 6 fields; mostly mod 4/5, 10 MIRV; 198 Russia, 104 Kazakhstan).
SS-19 *Stiletto* (RS-18): 290 (at 4 fields; mostly mod 3, 6 MIRV; 170 Russia, 120 Ukraine).
SS-24 *Scalpel* (RS-22): 92 (deployment complete; 56 silo-based and 36 rail-mobile, 10 MIRV; 10 silo, 36 train Russia, 46 silo Ukraine).
SS-25 *Sickle* (RS-12M): 340+ (mobile, single-warhead msl; 9 bases with some 37 units of 9; 260+ Russia, 80 Belarus).
GROUND DEFENCE: some 1,700 APC, 140 Mi-8 hel declared under CFE. (APC: Russia (West of Urals) 700, Ukraine 416, Belarus 585).

STRATEGIC AVIATION: (19,000)
Long-Range Forces (Moscow).
Western Russia: 1 air army (Smolensk).
Far East: 1 air army (Irkutsk).
BOMBERS: 170, plus 19 trg and test ac.
61 Tu-95B/G (with 1 and 2 AS-4 ASM).
27 Tu-95H6 (with 6 AS-15 ALCM) (Kazakhstan).
62 Tu-95H16 (with 16 AS-15 ALCM) (22 in Ukraine, 13 in Kazakhstan).
11 Tu-95T plus 8 test ac.
20 Tu-160 (with 12 AS-15 ALCM) (in Ukraine).

STRATEGIC DEFENCE: (21,000)
ABM: 100: 36 SH-11 (mod *Galosh*), 64 SH-08 *Gazelle* (Russia).
WARNING SYSTEMS:
SATELLITES: 9 with ICBM/SLBM launch detection capability. Others incl 2 photo-recce, 11 ELINT, 3 recce.
RADARS:
OVER-THE-HORIZON-BACKSCATTER (OTH-B): 3: 2 near Kiev and Komsomolsk (Ukraine), covering US and polar areas; 1 near Nikolayevsk-na-Amure, covering China.
LONG-RANGE EARLY-WARNING:
ABM-ASSOCIATED:
8 long-range phased-array systems at Baranovichi, Skrunda (Latvia), Mukachevo (Ukraine), Olnegorsk (Kola), Lyaki (Azerbaijan), Sary-Shagan (Kazakhstan), Pechora (Urals), Mishelevka (Irkutsk).
11 *Hen House*-series; range 6,000km, 6 locations covering approaches from the west and south-west, north-east and south-east and (partially) south.
Engagement, guidance, battle management:
1 *Pillbox* phased-array at Pushkino (Moscow).

ARMY: 1,000,000 (about 450,000 conscripts).
8 Military Districts (MD), 3 Groups of Forces.
16 Army HQ, 8 Corps HQ.
18 TD (incl 4 trg) (3 tk, 1 motor rifle, 1 arty, 1 SAM regt; 1 armd recce bn; spt units).
61 MRD (incl 6 trg) (3 motor rifle, 1 arty, 1 SAM regt; 1 indep tk, 1 ATK, 1 armd recce bn; spt units).
5 ABD (each 3 para, 1 arty regt; 1 AA bn) (plus 1 trg div, status and location unknown).
7 MG/arty div.
8 arty div incl 1 trg: (no standard org: perhaps 4 bde (12 bn): 152mm SP, 152mm towed and MRL: some will have older eqpt).
Some 39 arty bde/regt. No standard org: perhaps 4 bn: 2 each of 24 152mm towed guns, 2 each of 24 152mm SP guns. 7 hy arty bde (with 4 bn of 12 203mm 2S7 SP guns). Some only MRL.
Some 7 AB bde, (each 4 inf bn; arty, SAM, ATK; spt tps).
8 MR bde (more forming).
5 SF (*Spetsnaz*) bde.
20 SSM bde (incl 3 trg).
15 ATK bde/regt.
14 SAM bde/regt
24 attack hel regt (2 trg).
Other Front and Army tps: engr, pontoon-bridge, pipe-line, signals, EW, CW def, tpt, supply bde/regt/bn.

EQUIPMENT:
MBT: about 25,000 incl: T-54/-55, T-62, T-64A/-B, T-72L/-M and T-80/-M 9, plus some 17,000 in store east of Urals (incl Kazakhstan, Uzbekistan).
LIGHT TANKS: 550 PT-76.
RECCE: 6,000: incl some 2,000 BRDM-2.
AIFV: about 22,000 incl: BMP-1 (73mm gun/AT-3 ATGW), BMP-2 (30mm gun/AT-5 ATGW); some 2,400 BMD (AB), 300 BMP-3.

APC: over 23,000 incl: BTR-50P/-60P/-70/-80/-152, 700 BTR-D; 6,000 MT-LB, plus 'look alikes'.
TOTAL ARTY: 24,000, plus some 21,000, mainly obsolete types, in store east of the Urals.
TOWED ARTY: about 12,500 incl 122mm: 4,500 D-30, 4,000 M-30; 152mm: 1,500 D-20, 1,500 *Giatsint-B* 2A36, 750 *MSTA-B* 2A65; 203mm: 24 B-4M.
SP ARTY: some 6,000 incl 122mm: 2,600 *Gvozdika* 2S1; 152mm: 2,000 *Acatsia* 2S3, 850 *Giatsint-S* 2S5, 130 *MSTA-S* 2S19; 203mm 240 *Pion* 2S7.
COMBINED GUN/MORTAR: about 700: 120mm: 650 *Nona-S* 2S9 SP, 40 *Nona-K* 2B16.
MRL: about 4,500 incl: 122mm: 3,000 BM-21, 30 9P138.
220mm: 1,250 9P140 *Uragan*.
300mm: 100 *Smerch* 9A52.
MORTARS: about 2,000 incl: 120mm: 1,500 2S12, 250 PM-38; 160mm: 50 M-160; 240mm: 100 M-240, 120 *Tulpan* 2S4 SP.
SSM: (nuclear-capable): some 800 launchers, incl about 465 *FROG* (*Luna*)/SS-21 *Scarab* (*Tochka*), 300 *Scud* B/-C mod (R-17).
ATGW: AT-2 *Swatter*, AT-3 *Sagger*, AT-4 *Spigot*, AT-5 *Spandrel*, AT-6 *Spiral*, AT-7 *Saxhorn*, AT-9, AT-10.
ATK GUNS: 57mm: ASU-57 SP; 76mm; 85mm: D-44/SD-44, ASU-85 SP; 100mm: T-12/-12A/M-55 towed.
AD GUNS: 23mm: ZU-23, ZSU-23-4 SP; 37mm; 57mm: S-60, ZSU-57-2 SP; 85mm: M-1939; 100mm: KS-19; 130mm: KS-30.
SAM: SA-4 A/B *Ganef* (twin): (Army/Front weapon).
SA-6 *Gainful* (triple): (div weapon).
SA-7 *Grail* (man-portable).
SA-8 *Gecko* (2 triple): (div weapon).
SA-9 *Gaskin* (2 twin): (regt weapon).
SA-11 *Gadfly* (quad): (replacing SA-4/-6).
SA-12A *Gladiator:* (replacing SA-4).
SA-12B *Giant.*
SA-13 *Gopher* (2 twin): (replacing SA-9).
SA-14 *Gremlin*: (replacing SA-7).
SA-15: (replacing SA-6/SA-8).
SA-16: (replacing SA-7 and some SA-14).
SA-18: replacing SA-7/SA-14.
SA-19 (2S6 SP): (8 SAM plus twin 35mm gun).
HELICOPTERS: some 3,500:
ATTACK: 1,500 Mi-24, Ka-50 *Hokum*.
TRANSPORT: some 1,300, incl 270 Mi-6, 1,000 Mi-8 (some armed), 35 Mi-26 (hy).
EW/ECM: 100 Mi-8.
GENERAL PURPOSE: 580: incl 500 Mi-2, 80 Mi-8 (comms).

AIR FORCE: 170,000 (some 85,000 conscripts) incl 19,000 with Strategic Aviation (see p.99).
7 Air army, 2 MD air forces.
Some 3,600 cbt ac. Forces' strengths vary, mostly org with div of 3 regt of 3 sqn (total 90–135 ac), indep regt (30–60 ac). Regt roles incl AD, interdic-

tion, recce, tac air spt; div roles may be mixed.
LONG RANGE AVIATION:
1 air army, 4 div.
BOMBERS: about 300 incl 30 Tu-16, 65 Tu-22, 180 Tu-26 (22M) (incl 20 trg) plus some 100 Tu-16 in store.
RECCE/ECM: some 100 incl 70 Tu-16, 30 Tu-22, some Il-ZO/22.
TANKERS: 75: 25 Mya-4, 10 Tu-16, 40 Il-78.
FRONTAL AVIATION:
6 air army, 2 MD air forces.
FGA: some 1,800: incl 610 MiG-27, 330 Su-17/-22, 480 Su-24, 340 Su-25.
FIGHTER: some 1,200: incl 510 MiG-23, 110 MiG-25, 430 MiG-29, 140 Su-27.
RECCE: some 345: incl 85 MiG-25 , 100 Su-17, 160 Su-24.
ECM: some 75: incl 40 Yak-28.
TRAINING: some 1,500 L-29, L-39 (not cbt ac).
AAM: AA-2 *Atoll*, AA-7 *Apex*, AA-8 *Aphid*, AA-9 *Amos*, AA-10 *Alamo*, AA-11 *Archer*.
ASM: AS-7 *Kerry*, AS-10 *Karen*, AS-11 *Kilter*, AS-12 *Kegler*, AS-13 *Kingbolt*, AS-14 *Kedge*, AS-16 *Kickback*.
MILITARY TRANSPORT AVIATION (VTA):
3 div, each 3 regt, each 30 ac; some indep regt.
EQUIPMENT: some 350 ac incl: An-12, Il-76M/MD *Candid* B (replacing An-12), An-22, An-124. Additional ac (VTA augmentation force): Tpt ac in comd other than VTA: org in indep regt and sqn: 1,200+: Tu-134, Tu-154, An-2, An-12, An-72, Il-18. Civilian Aeroflot fleet: 1,700 med- and long-range passenger ac, incl some 220 An-12 and Il-76.

AIR DEFENCE TROOPS (VPVO): 230,000 (100,000 conscripts). 5 Air Defence Armies: air regt and indep sqn; AD regt.
AIRCRAFT: (*Aviation of Air Defence* – APVO):
FIGHTER: some 2,200, plus some 300 in store: incl 130 MiG-21 (trg), 860 MiG-23 (6 AAM); 340 MiG-25 (4 AAM); 330 MiG-31 (4 AA-9); 300 Su-15 (2 AAM); 250 Su-27. (Incl some 500 trainer variants, in trg units plus each regt holds 4–5 trainer variants).
TRAINING: 200 L-29, 350 L-39 (not cbt ac).
AEW AND CONTROL: 15 Il-76.
AAM: AA-2 *Atoll*, AA-3 *Anab*, AA-6 *Acrid*, AA-7 *Apex*, AA-8 *Aphid*, AA-9 *Amos*, AA-10 *Alamo*, AA-11 *Archer*.
SAM: some 7,000 launchers in some 900 sites:
SA-2 *Guideline*: 2,000 (being replaced by SA-10).
SA-3 *Goa*: 800 (2 or 4 launcher rails, 200 sites).
SA-5 *Gammon*: 1,800 launchers (110 complexes).
SA-10 *Grumble*: some 2,400 quad.

NAVY: 300,000, (180,000 conscripts), incl 10,000 Strategic forces, 60,000 naval air, 25,000 coastal defence, coastal arty, naval infantry.
SUBMARINES: 219:
STRATEGIC SUBMARINES: 52 (see p. 99).
TACTICAL SUBMARINES: 153:

SSGN: 28:

10 *Oscar* with 24 x SS-N-19 *Shipwreck* USGW (VLS); plus T-65 HWT.

4 *Charlie-II* with 8 x SS-N-9 *Siren* USGW, plus T-53 HWT.

5 *Charlie-I* with 8 x SS-N-7 *Starbright* USGW; plus T-53 HWT.

5 *Echo-II* ε2 with 8 x SS-N-3A *Shaddock*, ε3 with 8 SS-N-12 *Sandbox* SSM; all plus T-53 HWT.

3 *Yankee* 'Notch' with 20+ SS-N-21 *Sampson* SLCM.

1 *Yankee* (trials) with ε12 SS-NX-24 SLCM.

SSN: 50:

10 *Akula* with T-65 HWT; plus SS-N-21.

3 *Sierra* with T-65 HWT; plus SS-N-21.

26 *Victor-III* with T-65 HWT; plus SS-N-15 or -16.

4 *Victor-II* with T-53 HWT; plus SS-N-15 or -16.

7 *Victor-I* with T-53 HWT.

SSG: 5 *Juliet* with 4 x SS-N-3A *Shaddock* SSM.

SS: 70 (all with T-53 HWT): 23 *Kilo*, 18 *Tango*, 26 *Foxtrot*, 3 *Romeo*.

OTHER ROLES: 14:

SSN: 4: 2 *Uniform*, 1 *Alfa*, 1 *Echo* II experimental/ trials.

SS: 10: 1 *Beluga*, 4 *Bravo* wpn targets, 1 *Golf-V* research, 1 *Lima*, 2 *India* rescue, 1 *X-Ray* trials.

IN STORE: 2 *Foxtrot* (not counted in totals).

PRINCIPAL SURFACE COMBATANTS: 169.

CARRIERS: 2:

1 *Kuznetsov* (ex-*Tbilisi*) CVV (65,000t) capacity 25–30 fixed wing ac and 8–10 ASW hel with 12 SS-N-19 *Shipwreck* SSM, 4 x 6 SA-N-9 SAM, 8 CADS-1, 2 RBU-12 (not fully op).

1 *Gorshkov* (ex-*Baku*) (CVV) (38,000t) capacity 15 V/STOL ac, 16 Ka-25/-27 hel (ASW with E-45/-75 LWT/AEW/OTHT/SAR); plus 6 x 2 SS-N-12 *Sandbox* SSM, 4 x 8 SA-N-6 *Grumble* SAM. 2 x 100mm guns.

(Plus 2 *Kiev* (CVV) (38,000t) (both non-op) capacity 15 V/STOL ac, 16 Ka-25/-27 hel; plus 4 x 2 SS-N-12 *Sandbox* SSM, 2 x 2 SA-N-3 SAM, 1 x 2 SUW-N-1).

CRUISERS: 29:

CGN: 3 *Admiral Ushakov* (ex-*Kirov*) (AAW/ASUW) with 12 x 8 SA-N-6 *Grumble*, 20 SS-N-19 *Shipwreck* SSM, 3 Ka-25/-27 hel for OTHT/AEW/ASW; plus 1 with 1 x 2 130mm guns, 1 with 1 x 2 SS-N-14 *Silex* SUGW (LWT or nuc payload), 10 x 533mm TT.

CG: 26:

1 *Moskva* (CGH) (ASW) with 18 Ka-25 hel (E45-75 LWT), 1 x 2 SUW-N-1; plus 2 x 2 SA-N-3 SAM.

3 *Slava* (AAW/ASUW) with 8 x 8 SA-N-6 *Grumble*, 8 x 2 SS-N-12 *Sandbox* SSM, 1 Ka-25/-27 hel; (AEW/ASW); plus 8 x 533mm TT, 1 x 2 130mm guns.

11 *Udaloy* (ASW) with 2 x 4 SS-N-14 *Silex* SUGW, 2 x 12 ASW RL, 8 x 533mm TT, 2 Ka-27 hel; plus 2 x 100mm guns.

7 *Nikolayev* (*Kara*) (ASW) with 2 x 4 SS-N-14 *Silex* SUGW, 10 x 533mm TT, 1 Ka-25 hel; plus 2 x 2 SA-N-3 *Goblet*; (1 (*Azov*) with 3 x 8 SA-N-6, only

1 x SA-N-3 and other differences).

3 *Kronshtadt* (*Kresta-II*) (ASW) with 2 x 4 SS-N-14 SUGW, 1 Ka-25 hel, 10 x 533mm TT; plus 2 x 2 SA-N-3 SAM.

1 *Admiral Zozulya* (*Kresta-I*) (ASUW/ASW) with 2 x 2 SS-N-3b *Shaddock* SSM, 1 Ka-25 hel (OTHT), 10 x 533mm TT.

DESTROYERS: 24:

DDG: 24:

AAW/ASUW: 20:

16 *Sovremennyy* with 2 x 4 SS-N-22 *Sunburn* SSM, 2 x 1 SA-N-7 *Gadfly* SAM, 2 x 2 130mm guns, 1 Ka-25 (B) hel (OTHT); plus 4 x 533mm TT.

2 *Grozny* (*Kynda*) (ASUW) with 2 x 4 SS-N-3b; plus 1 x 2 SA-N-1 *Goa* SAM, 6 x 533mm TT.

2 *Sderzhannyy* (mod *Kashin*) with 4 SS-N-2C *Styx* SSM, 2 x 2 SA-N-1 SAM; plus 5 x 533mm TT.

ASW: 4:

4 *Komsomolets Ukrainyy* (*Kashin*) with 2 x 12 ASW RL, 5 x 533mm TT; plus 2 x 2 SA-N-1 SAM, (1 with trials fit 1 x SA-N-7).

FRIGATES: 114:

11 *Rezvyy* (*Krivak-II*) with 1 x 4 SS-N-14 *Silex* SUGW, 8 x 533mm TT, 2 x 12 ASW RL; plus 2 x 100mm guns.

19 *Bditelnyy* (*Krivak-I*) (weapons as *Rezvyy* but with 2 x twin 76mm guns).

1 *Neustrashimyy* with 2 x 12 ASW RL.

(*Note*: Frigates listed below lie between 1,000 and 1,200 tonnes full-load displacement and are not counted in official releases.)

65 '*Grisha-I, -III, -V*', with 2 x 12 ASW RL, 4 x 533mm TT.

1 *Grisha-IV*, with 2 x 12 ASW RL, 2 x 533mm TT (SA-N-9 trials).

12 '*Parchim-II*' (ASW) with 2 x 12 ASW RL, 4 x 406mm ASTT.

5 '*Petya*' with ASW RL, 5 or 10 x 406mm ASTT.

PATROL AND COASTAL COMBATANTS: 163:

CORVETTES: about 80:

About 44 *Tarantul* (ASUW), 2 -*I*, 18–*II*, both with 2 x 2 SS-N-2C *Styx*; 24 -*III* with 2 x 2 SS-N-22 *Sunburn*.

36 *Nanuchka* (ASUW) -*I*, -*III* and -*IV* with 2 x 3 SS-N-9 *Siren*.

MISSILE CRAFT: 40:

26 *Osa* PFM with 4 x SS-N-2C.

14 *Matka* PHM with 2 x 1 SS-N-2C.

TORPEDO CRAFT: 27:

27 *Turya* PHT with 4 x 533mm TT.

PATROL CRAFT: About 16:

OFFSHORE: About 5 T-58/-43.

COASTAL: 8:

7 *Pauk* PFC (ASW) with 2 x ASW RL, 4 x ASTT.

1 *Babochka* PHT (ASW) with 8 x ASTT.

INSHORE: 3: SO-1 with 2 x ASTT.

MINE WARFARE: About 211:

MINELAYERS: 3 *Pripyat* (*Alesha*), capacity 300 mines.

(*Note*: All submarines and many surface combatants are equipped for minelaying.)

MINE COUNTERMEASURES: About 208:

OFFSHORE: 40:
1 *Gorya* MCO.
34 *Natya-I* and *-II* MSO.
5 T-43 MSO.
COASTAL: About 100:
28 *Yurka* MSC.
2 *Andryusha* MSC (trials).
About 70 *Sonya* MSC
INSHORE: About 68:
18 *Vanya*, about 50 MSI⟨.
AMPHIBIOUS: 75:
LPD: 3 *Ivan Rogov* with 4–5 Ka-27 hel: capacity 520 tps, 20 tk;
LST: 40:
28 *Ropucha*: capacity 225 tps, 9 tk.
12 *Alligator*: capacity 300 tps, 20 tk.
LSM: 32 *Polnocny* (3 types): capacity 180 tps, 6 tk: (some adapted for mine warfare but retain amph primary role)
Plus CRAFT: about 90:
LCU: 9 *Vydra*.
LCM: About 14 *Ondatra*.
LCAC and SES: about 70: incl 7 *Pomornik*, 18 *Aist*, 11 *Tsaplya*, 16 *Lebed*, 2 *Utenok*, 10 *Gus*.
2 *Orlan* 'wing-in-ground-effect' (WIG) experimental.
SUPPORT AND MISCELLANEOUS: about 650
UNDERWAY SUPPORT: 27:
1 *Berezina*, 6 *Chilikin*, 20 other AO.
MAINTENANCE AND LOGISTICS: about 250: incl some 15 AS, 38 AR, 12 general maint/spt, 27 AOT, 18 missile spt/resupply, 70 tugs, 14 special liquid carriers, 13 water carriers, 40 AK.
SPECIAL PURPOSES: about 135: incl some 55 AGI (some armed), 5 msl range instrumentation, 8 trg, about 63 icebreakers (civil manned), 4 AH.
SURVEY/RESEARCH: about 240: incl some
40 naval, 60 civil AGOR.
90 naval, 40 civil AGHS.
10 space-associated ships (civil manned).
MERCHANT FLEET (auxiliary/augmentation): About 2,800 ocean-going vessels (17 in Arctic service), incl 125 ramp-fitted and ro-ro, some with rails for rolling stock, 3 roll-on/float-off, 14 barge carriers, 48 passenger liners, 500 coastal and river ships.

NAVAL AVIATION: (60,000).
Some 913 cbt ac; 239 armed hel.
Four Fleet Air Forces; org in air div, each with 2–3 regt of HQ elm and 2 sqn of 9–10 ac each; recce, ASW, tpt/utility org in indep regt or sqn.
BOMBERS: some 188:
7 regt with some 140 Tu-26 (Tu-22M), (AS-4 ASM).
2 regt with some 33 Tu-16 (AS-5/-6 ASM), 15 Tu-22.
FGA: 325:
115 Su-17.
100 Su-24.
70 Su-25.
40 MiG-23/-27.
TRAINING: Some 225: Tu-16*, Tu-26*, Tu-95*, Su-25*, Su-27*, MiG-29*.
ASW: 175 ac, 239 hel:
AIRCRAFT: 50 Tu-142, 36 Il-38, 89 Be-12.

HELICOPTERS: 63 Mi-14, 88 Ka-25, 88 Ka-27.
MR/EW: some 95 ac, 25 hel:
AIRCRAFT: incl 24 Tu-95, 35 Tu-16 MR/ECM, 6 Tu-22, 20 Su-24, 7 An-12, 3 Il-20.
HELICOPTERS: 25 Ka-25.
MCM: 25 Mi-14 hel.
CBT ASLT: 25 Ka-27 hel.
TANKERS: 6 Tu-16.
TRANSPORT:
AIRCRAFT: Some 110 An-12, An-24, An-26.
HELICOPTERS: 70 Mi-6/-8.
ASM: AS-2 *Kipper*, AS-4 *Kitchen*, AS-5 *Kelt*, AS-6 *Kingfish*, AS-7 *Kerry*, AS-10 *Karen*, AS-11 *Kilter*, AS-12 *Kegler*, AS-13 *Kingbolt*, AS-14 *Kedge*.

COASTAL DEFENCE FORCES (incl
Naval Infantry, Coastal Artillery and Rocket Troops, Coastal Defence Troops):
NAVAL INFANTRY (Marines): (some 12,000).
1 inf div (7,000: 3 inf, 1 tk, 1 arty regt).
4 indep bde (1 reserve) (type: 3,000: 4 inf, 1 tk, 1 arty, 1 MRL, 1 ATK bn).
4 fleet SF bde: 2–3 underwater, 1 para bn, spt elm.
EQUIPMENT:
MBT: 240 T-55.
LIGHT TANKS: 100 PT-76.
RECCE: 60 BRDM-2/*Sagger* ATGW.
APC: some 2,000: BTR-60/-70, some 400 MT-LB.
SP ARTY: 120mm: 160 2S9; 122mm: 144 2S1.
MRL: 122mm: 90 9P138.
COMBINED GUN/MORTAR: 120mm: 160 2S9 SP.
ATGW: 50 AT-3/-5.
AD GUNS: 23mm: 60 ZSU-23-4 SP.
SAM: 250 SA-7, 10 SA-8, 35 SA-9/-13.

COASTAL ARTILLERY AND ROCKET TROOPS: (4,500).
1 coastal arty div (role: protects approaches to naval bases and major ports).
EQUIPMENT:
ARTY: incl SM-4-1 130mm.
SSM: 40 SS-C-1b *Sepal* (similar to SS-N-3), SS-C-3, *Styx*, SS-C-4 reported.

COASTAL DEFENCE TROOPS:
(13,000)
3 Coast Defence div.
2 arty regt.
1 MG/arty bn.
EQUIPMENT:
MBT: 1,080 T-80.
AIFV: 960 BMP.
APC: 480 BTR-60/-70, 790 MT-LB.
TOTAL ARTY: 992.
TOWED ARTY: 872. 100mm: 12 BS-3; 122mm: 290 D-30; 152mm: 144 D-20, 330 2A65, 96 2A36.
SP ARTY: 152mm: 48 2S5.
MRL: 122mm: 72 BM-21.

DEPLOYMENT:
NORTHERN FLEET: (Arctic and Atlantic)
(HQ Severomorsk) (Russia):

BASES: Kola Inlet, Motovskiy Gulf, Gremikha, Polyarnyy, Litsa Gulf.
SUBMARINES: 117: strategic: 32 SSBN; tactical: 78: 19 SSGN, 33 SSN, 26 SS. 7 other roles.
PRINCIPAL SURFACE COMBATANTS: 56: incl: 2 CVV, 9 cruisers, 8 destroyers, 37 frigates.
OTHER SURFACE SHIPS: About 25 patrol and coastal combatants, 40 mine warfare, 12 amph, some 190 spt and misc.
NAVAL AVIATION:
218 cbt ac; 70 armed hel.
BOMBERS: 70: 30 Tu-16, 40 Tu-26.
FIGHTER/FGA: 70: 30 MiG-27, 40 Su-25.
ASW:
AIRCRAFT: 78: 38 Tu-142, 16 Il-38, 24 Be-12;
HELICOPTERS: 55: (afloat): 10 Ka-25, 45 Ka-27.
MR/EW:
AIRCRAFT: 30: 2 An-12, 12 Tu-16, 14 Tu-95, 2 Il-20.
HELICOPTERS: 5 Ka-25.
MCM: 8 Mi-14 hel.
CBT ASLT HEL: 10 Ka-27.
COMMUNICATIONS: 6 Tu-142.
TANKERS: 5 Tu-16.
NAVAL INFANTRY:
2 bde (80 MBT, 110 arty).
COASTAL DEFENCE:
1 Coast Defence div (270 MBT, 790 MT-LB, 150 arty), 1 arty regt (120 arty).

BALTIC FLEET: (HQ Kaliningrad):
BASES: Kronshtadt (Russia), Liepaja (Latvia), Baltiysk (Russia), Tallinn (Estonia).
SUBMARINES: 15: strategic: nil; tactical: 14: 3 SSG, 11 SS; other roles: 1 SS.
PRINCIPAL SURFACE COMBATANTS: 27: incl: 1 cruiser, 2 destroyers, 24 frigates.
OTHER SURFACE SHIPS: About 140 patrol and coastal combatants, 60 mine warfare, 20 amph, some 110 spt and misc.
NAVAL AVIATION:
200 cbt ac, 45 armed hel.
FGA: 180: 5 regts: 80 Su-17, 100 Su-24.
ASW:
AIRCRAFT: 20: 10 Il-38, 10 Be-12;
HELICOPTERS: 35: 3 Ka-25, 22 Ka-27, 10 Mi-14.
MR/EW:
AIRCRAFT 14: 2 An-12, 12 Su-24.
HELICOPTERS: 5 Ka-25.
MCM: 5 Mi-14 hel.
CBT ASLT HEL: 5 Ka-29.
NAVAL INFANTRY:
1 bde, (40 MBT, 60 arty/MRL) (Russia).
COAST DEFENCE:
1 arty regt (120 arty).
1 SSM regt: some 8 SS-C-1b *Sepal*.

BLACK SEA FLEET: ε48,000, incl Naval Air, Naval Inf and Coastal Defence) (HQ Sevastopol) (Ukraine). Under joint Russian/Ukrain-
ian command for 3–5 years, then to be divided between Russia and Ukraine.
BASES: Sevastopol, Odessa (Ukraine).
SUBMARINES: 21: tactical 17: 2 SSG, 15 SS; other roles: 4.
PRINCIPAL SURFACE COMBATANTS: 35: incl: 1 CGH, 4 cruisers, 7 destroyers, 23 frigates.
OTHER SURFACE SHIPS: About 60 patrol and coastal combatants, 30 mine warfare, 16 amph, some 135 spt and misc.
NAVAL AVIATION: 7,600.
some 244 cb ac; 85 cbt hel.
BOMBERS: 1 div, 3 regt with 63 Tu-22M; 29 Tu-16.
FGA: 2 regt: 43 Su-17, 43 Su-25.
FIGHTER: 2 regt: 47 MiG-29, 5 Su-25, 14 Su-27.
ASW: 23 Be-12 ac, 31 Mi-14, 49 Ka-25, 5 Ka-27 hel.
MR/EW: 2 An-12, 12 Tu-16, 6 Tu-22, 1 Il-20 ac, 5 Ka-25 hel.
MCM: 5 Mi-14 hel.
TANKERS: 3 Tu-16.
NAVAL INFANTRY: 2,000.
1 regt: (250 APC, 47 arty (2S1, 2S9)).
COASTAL DEFENCE: 2,100.
1 Coast Defence div (250 MBT, 320 AIFV (BMP-2), 72 arty (D-30)).
1 arty bde (120 arty: D-20, 2A36).

CASPIAN FLOTILLA:
BASES: Astrakan (Russia).
The Caspian Sea Flotilla has been divided between Azerbaijan (about 25%) and Russia, Kazakhstan and Turkmenistan who are operating a joint flotilla under Russian command and currently based at Astrakan.
PRINCIPAL SURFACE COMBATANTS: 2 frigates.
OTHER SURFACE SHIPS: 13 patrol and coastal combatants, 18 mine warfare, some 20 amph ships and craft, about 10 spt.

PACIFIC FLEET (Indian Ocean) (HQ Vladivostok) (Russia):
BASES: Vladivostok, Petropavlovsk, Kamchatskiy, Magadan, Sovetskaya Gavan; abroad: Aden (South Yemen).
SUBMARINES: 66: strategic: 20 SSBN; tactical: 44: 9 SSGN, 17 SSN, 18 SS; other roles: 2 SS.
PRINCIPAL SURFACE COMBATANTS: 49: incl: 14 cruisers, 7 destroyers, 28 frigates.
OTHER SURFACE SHIPS: About 55 patrol and coastal combatants, 70 mine warfare, 15 amph, some 200 spt and misc.
NAVAL AIR (Pacific Fleet Air Force) (HQ Vladivostok): 220 cbt ac, 99 cbt hel.
BOMBERS: 100: 2 regt with 70 Tu-26, 1 with 30 Tu-16 *Badger* C/G.
FGA: 50: 1 regt with 35 Su-17, 15 Su-24.
ASW:
AIRCRAFT 70: 20 Tu-142, 15 Il-38, 35 Be-12.
HELICOPTERS: 89: (afloat): 23 Ka-25, 38 Ka-27; (ashore): 28 Mi-14.
MR/EW:
AIRCRAFT: 62: 2 An-12, 50 Tu-16, 10 Tu-95.

HELICOPTERS: 10 Ka-25.
MCM: 6 Mi-14 hel.
CBT ASLT HEL: 10 Ka-27.
COMMUNICATION: 7 Tu-142.
TANKERS: 10 Tu-16.
NAVAL INFANTRY:
1 div HQ, 3 inf, 1 tk and 1 arty regt:
COAST DEFENCE:
1 Coast Defence div.

DEPLOYMENT:
MILITARY DISTRICTS OF RUSSIA:
LENINGRAD MD (HQ St. Petersburg):
GROUND: 1 army HQ, 2 corps HQ; 6 MRD (1 trg),
1 ABD; plus 1 arty div, 3 arty bde/regt, 2 ATK, 5
Scud (2 trg), 1 AB, 1 *Spetsnaz*, 1 SAM bde, 3 attack
hel regt, 1,600 MBT, 1,900 ACV, 1,500 arty/MRL/
mors, 44 *Scud*, 100 attack hel.
AIR: 1 air army; 2 bbr regt (60: Su-24), 1 recce regt
(35: MiG-25, Su-17).
AIR DEFENCE: 9 regt: 40 MiG-23, 70 MiG-25, 90
MiG-31, 60 Su-15, 70 Su-27.
SAM: 180
MOSCOW MD (HQ Moscow):
GROUND: 2 Army HQ, 3 TD (1 trg), 1 MRD, 1
ABD, plus 1 arty trg div, 5 arty bde/regt, 2 ATK, 2
Scud, 3 indep MR, 1 *Spetsnaz*, 2 SAM bde, 6 attack
hel regt, 2,500 MBT, 3,000 ACV, 1,400 arty/MRL/
mors, 24 *Scud*, 16 *FROG*/SS-21, 300 attack hel.
AIR: 2 ftr regt (100: MiG-23, MiG-29, Su-27), 4 trg
div/centre (405: MiG-21*, MiG-23*, MiG-25*, MiG-
29*, Su-17*, Su-24*, Su-25*, Su-27*; 320 L-29, L-
39).
AIR DEFENCE: 9 regt: 170 MiG-23, 30 MiG-25,
60 MiG-31, 30 Su-15, plus in store 100 Tu-128, 10
MiG-23, 20 Su-15, 1 trg centre: 60 MiG-23, MiG-
25, MiG-31, Su-27 (half are trainer variants).
SAM: 300
VOLGA MD (HQ Kuybyshev (Samarra)):
GROUND: 2 MRD (1 trg), 1 ABD plus 1 arty bde/
regt, 1 indep TR, 1 indep MR, 1 trg *Scud*, 2 SAM
bde, 1 ATK, 3 attack hel regt (2 trg), 1 tpt hel regt.
700 MBT, 1,800 ACV, 350 arty/MRL/mor, 4 *Scud*,
340 attack hel.
AIR: 1 trg regt (110 L-29).
URAL MD (HQ Yekaterinburg):
GROUND:
2 TD (1 trg), 2 MRD, 2 arty bde/regt, 1 ATK bde.
1,900 MBT, 1,900 ACV, 1,000 arty/MRL/mor.
AIR DEFENCE: 3 regt: 80 MiG-23, 40 MiG-25,
plus in store 25 MiG-23, 110 Su-15.
SAM: 60
NORTH CAUCASUS MD (HQ Rostov):
GROUND: 1 Army, 2 corps HQ, 2 MRD, 1 ABD, 2
AB, 2 MR bde plus 1 arty div, 3 arty bde/regt, 3
Scud, 3 SAM bde, 2 ATK regt, 300 MBT, 1,200
ACV, 630 arty/MRL/mor, 24 *Scud*.
AIR: 5 trg div, 14 trg regt, (470: MiG-21*, MiG-
23*, MiG-27*, Su-17*, Su-22*, Su-24*, Su-25*,
800: L-29, L-39).
AIR DEFENCE: 3 regt, 30 MiG-23, 40 MiG-25, 40
Su-27, 2 trg centre: 280: MiG-21, MiG-23, Su-15

(half are trainer variants), 270 L-29/L-39.
SAM: 90
SIBERIAN MD (HQ Novosibirsk):
GROUND: 1 Corps HQ, 8 MRD, 1 arty div, 3 arty
bde/regt, 2 SSM, 1 *Spetsnaz* bde, 1 ATK regt, 2,000
MBT, 2,100 arty/MRL/mor, 24 *Scud*.
AIR: trg units, 275: L-29, L-39.
AIR DEFENCE: 4 regt: 160: MiG-23, Su-15.
TRANSBAYKAL MD (HQ Chita):
GROUND: 3 army HQ, 4 TD (1 trg), 11 MRD (1
trg), plus 2 MG/arty div, 1 arty div, 5 arty bde/regt, 1
AB, 1 *Spetsnaz*, 1 ATK, 3 SAM bde, 2 attack hel
regt, 3,700 MBT, 3,600 ACV, 4,000 arty/MRL/mor,
100 attack hel.
AIR: 1 air army, 2 FGA div, 6 regt (160: MiG-27,
MiG-29, Su-24), 1 ftr div, 2 regt (60: MiG-23, MiG-
29), 1 recce regt (35 MiG-27).
FAR EASTERN MD (HQ Khabarovsk):
GROUND: 4 army, 1 corps HQ, 3 TD (1 trg), 16
MRD (2 trg), plus 5 MG/arty div, 1 arty div, 11 arty
bde/regt, 2 AB, 4 *Scud*, 1 *Spetsnaz*, 4 ATK bde, 6
attack hel regt, 4,400 MBT, 4,950 arty/MRL/mor, 50
Scud, 400 attack hel.
AIR: 3 air army, 3 FGA div, 8 regt (280 MiG-27,
Su-24, Su-25) 1 ftr div, 3 regt (130: MiG-23, MiG-
29, Su-27), 2 recce regt (60: MiG-21, MiG-25, Su-
24).
AIR DEFENCE (Siberian, Transbaykal and Far
Eastern MDs): 15 regt: 180 MiG-23, 100 MiG-25;
90 MiG-31, 90 Su-15.
SAM: 570
GROUPS OF FORCES:
WESTERN GROUP OF FORCES (Germany)
(HQ Zossen-Wünsdorf): (58,400):
GROUND: 2 Army HQ: 4 TD, 2 MRD, plus 1 arty
div; 1 indep MR, 2 arty, 2 SAM regt, 1 attack hel
regt, 1,200 MBT, 1,700 ACV, 1,200 arty/MRL/mors,
55 attack hel plus 1,350 ACV awaiting elimination.
AIR: 1 air army; 1 FGA regt, (40 Su-22); 2 ftr regt
(35 MiG-29); 1 tpt regt (An-12, An-26 ac, Mi-8 hel),
1 assault/tpt regt (60: Mi-6, Mi-8) 3 tpt hel regt (34:
Mi-2, Mi-6, Mi-8).

NORTH-WESTERN GROUP OF FORCES
(HQ Riga):
RUSSIA: (Kaliningrad Oblast) (103,000).
GROUND: 1 army HQ, 2 TD, 2 MRD, plus 1 arty
div (1 bde, 5 regt), 2 *Scud*, 1 AB, 1 SAM bde, 1
MRL, 1 ATK, 1 attack hel regt, 750 MBT, 900 ACV,
600 arty/MRL/mors, 24 *Scud*, 16 SS-21, 48 attack
hel.
AIR DEFENCE:
FIGHTER: 1 regt (35 Su-27).
SAM: 250.
ESTONIA: (7,000)
GROUND: 1 MRD, 40 MBT, 290 ACV, 60 arty/
MRL/mor.
LATVIA: (17,000).
GROUND: 1 MR bde, 1 attack hel regt, 50 MBT, 50
ACV, 80 arty/MRL/mor, 24 attack hel.
AIR: 1 composite regt: ac: An-12, An-26; hel: Mi-8.
LITHUANIA: (2,400) (to be withdrawn by 31
August 1993)

TERRITORY OF THE FORMER SOVIET UNION:
REPUBLIC AND RUSSIAN MILITARY DISTRICT BORDERS

Abbreviations:

WGF   Western Group of Forces

NGF   Northern Group of Forces

NWGF   North Western Group of Forces

Boundaries:

International   —·—·—

Military District   —————

0   500 ml

0   500 km

Ural MD

Leningrad MD

ESTONIA

LATVIA

Volga MD

Moscow MD

KAZAKHSTAN

LITHUANIA

Kaliningrad

BELARUS

WGF

NGF

UKRAINE

MOLDOVA

North Caucasus MD

GEORGIA

AZERBAIJAN

ARMENIA

BELARUS

UKRAINE

MOLDOVA

Leningrad MD

Moscow MD

Transbaykal MD

Ural MD

North Caucasus MD

Volga MD

Far East MD

KAZAKHSTAN

UZBEKISTAN

Siberian MD

TURKMENISTAN

MONGOLIA

CHINA

TAJIKISTAN

KYRGYZSTAN

TRANSCAUCASUS GROUP OF FORCES:
ARMENIA
GROUND: (ε5,000): 1 Army HQ, 1 MRD, 90 MBT, 200 ACV, 100 arty/MRL/mors.
GEORGIA
GROUND (20,000): 1 Corps HQ, 2 MRD, 210 MBT, 300 ACV, 220 arty/MRL/mors.
AIR: 1 composite regt: with some 35 ac: An-12, An-26; hel: Mi-8.

FORCES IN OTHER FORMER SOVIET REPUBLICS:
BELARUS
AIR: 1 bbr div with 3 regt, 82 Su-24, 1 hy bbr div with 2 regt with 55 Tu-22; 1 regt with 20 Tu-22M, 15 Tu-16; 1 hy bbr div with 32 Tu-22M; 1 ftr regt with 40 MiG-25; 1 recce regt with 28 Tu-22.
MOLDOVA (Dniestr) (14th Army): 1 army HQ, 1 MRD 1 *Scud* bde, 120 MBT, 180 ACV, 120 arty/MRL/mor, 12 *Scud*, 10 attack hel.
SAM: 25: SA-3, SA-5.
KAZAKHSTAN
AIR DEFENCE: 2 regt: (35 MiG-21, 45 MiG-31).
SAM: 85: SA-2, SA-3, SA-5.
KYRGYZSTAN
AIR DEFENCE:
SAM: 25: SA-2, SA-3.
TAJIKISTAN
GROUND (8,500): 1 MRD, 200 MBT, 420 ACV, 200 arty/MRL/mors.
AIR DEFENCE:
SAM: 10: SA-2, SA-3.
TURKMENISTAN
JOINT TURKMENISTAN/RUSSIAN FORCES
GROUND (34,000): 1 Corps HQ, 3 MRD (1 trg), 3 arty bde, 900 MBT, 1,700 ACV, 900 arty/MRL/mor, 12 SSM.
AIR: 1 FGA regt (80 Su-17).
AIR DEFENCE: 2 regt: 55 MiG-23, 30 MiG-25.
SAM: 75: SA-2, SA-3, SA-5.
UZBEKISTAN
AIR DEFENCE: 1 regt: (30 Su-27).
SAM: 45: SA-2, SA-3, SA-5

FORCES ABROAD (other than in republics of former USSR or in Groups of Forces):
POLAND: Military mission to monitor transit of tps withdrawn from Germany.
VIETNAM: (500); naval base; 1 Tu-142, 8 Tu-16

MR ac on det; AA, SAM, electronic monitoring station.
OTHER: Algeria 500; Angola 50; Cambodia 500; Congo 20; Cuba some 2,200 (2,100 SIGINT and 100 mil advisers); India 500; Libya 1,000; Mali 20; Mongolia: ε500 SIGINT; Mozambique 25; Peru 50; Syria 500; Yemen 300; Africa (remainder) 100.
UN AND PEACEKEEPING:
CAMBODIA (UNTAC): 52: Naval unit and Observers (47).
CROATIA (UNPROFOR I): 842: 1 AB bn, 12 Observers.
GEORGIA/SOUTH OSSETIA: 1 inf bn.
IRAQ/KUWAIT (UNIKOM): 15 Observers.
MIDDLE EAST (UNTSO): 21 Observers.
MOLDOVA/DNIESTR: 6 AB bn.
MOZAMBIQUE (ONUMOZ): 20 Observers.
WESTERN SAHARA: (MINURSO) 29 Observers.

PARAMILITARY: 220,000.
BORDER TROOPS Committee for the Protection of State Borders (previously KGB): 100,000.
EQUIPMENT:
1,500 ACV (incl BMP, BTR).
90 arty (incl 2S1, 2S9, 2S12).
AIR: some 70 ac: An-2, An-26; hel: some 200+: Mi-8, Mi-24, Mi-26, Ka-17.
PATROL AND COASTAL COMBATANTS: About 212:
OFFSHORE PATROL: About 25:
7 *Krivak-III* with 1 x Ka-27 hel, 1 x 100mm gun. 12 *Grisha-II*, 6 *Grisha-III*.
COASTAL PATROL: About 32: 25 *Pauk*, 7 *Svetlyak*.
INSHORE PATROL: About 155: 110 *Stenka*, 15 *Muravey*, 30 *Zhuk*.
RIVERINE MONITORS: About 126: 19 *Yaz*, 10 *Piyavka*, 7 *Vosh*, 90 *Shmel*.
SUPPORT AND MISCELLANEOUS: About 26:
8 *Ivan Susanin* armed icebreakers, 18 *Sorum* armed ocean tugs.
MVD (*Ministerstvo Vnutrennikh Del*): internal security tps; 1 div, op regt (30,000); special police regt (40,000); guards and escorts (some 50,000) Eqpt incl 1,200 APC, 20 D-30. MVD troops mostly under national control.

OPPOSITION FORCES:
CHECHENIA-INGUSHETIA
National Guard: 62,000
Emergency Volunteer Corps: 300,000.

The Middle East and North Africa

Political and Military Developments

Not a great deal has changed in the last 12 months. The Arab–Israeli peace talks and the *intifada* in the West Bank and Gaza continue. Saddam Hussein is still defying the UN. Iran is perceived by many as the main supporter of Islamic extremism throughout the region, although all Islamic movements have important local roots. Iran continues its military build-up, but its arms acquisition is modest compared to some of the plans of the Gulf Cooperation Council (GCC) states. The GCC has made virtually no progress towards enhancing its collective security.

Arab–Israeli Peace Process

Both the bilateral and multilateral negotiations which make up the Arab–Israeli peace process have continued during the last 12 months. The expectations of substantial progress, engendered by the return to power of the Israeli Labour Party, were not realised; however, a number of positive statements have been made by both Israel and Syria. A major stumbling block to progress was the deportation by Israel of 415 suspected members of *Hamas*, the fundamentalist Palestinian resistance movement, in December 1992. Prime Minister Itzhak Rabin must have thought that he would gain the gratitude of mainstream Palestinians by removing their main competitors for influence in the Territories. His scheme might have worked if there had been fewer deportees, but 415 was too many. The scheme backfired, held up progress in the talks and incurred international censure.

Israel has accepted, for the first time, that UN Security Council Resolutions 242 and 338 apply to the Golan Heights, and Prime Minister Rabin has said that Israel would withdraw on the Golan in return for peace with Syria. So far, Syria, while welcoming this concession, will not meet the Israeli request to spell out exactly what it means by peace. Rabin also stresses that he has only offered withdrawal on, rather than from, the Golan Heights. For their part, the Syrians have said that they are ready for 'total peace' in return for 'total withdrawal' and have talked about a security 'regime' rather than 'arrangements' which is seen as implying a comprehensive and lasting agreement. The US Secretary of State has said that the US would be willing to consider providing security guarantees in the context of an Israeli–Syrian peace treaty. As yet, there has been no commitment to stationing troops on the Golan.

Israeli concessions in the Israeli–Palestinian–Jordanian talks began with the freezing of settlement-building in the Territories. The freeze does not apply to: housing units already started; infrastructure such as roads; the Golan Heights and East Jerusalem; and privately funded development. Thus there are a number of loop-holes. The other main concessions are that: a self-governing authority can be elected for the five-year interim period; a lightly armed police force can be raised (training in Jordan has already begun); any interim agreement will not become permanent; and Faisal Husseini, a leading Palestinian who lives in Jerusalem, may participate directly in the negotiations. Israel has also said that the deportation order on *Hamas* will last only one year.

A wave of murders and attempted murders of Israelis by Palestinians from the Territories provoked the government into first banning and then strictly controlling entry into Israel. In addition to improving security, this measure has opened up jobs for unemployed Israelis and so it is likely to remain in force. To lessen the economic effects on the population Israel has announced a number of initiatives to improve employment prospects in the Territories. At the same time, the border fence, known as the 'Green Line', is being re-erected. It will be interesting to see how far this follows the 1967 Armistice Line or whether it is altered to include some Israeli settlements. In the north, Israel's attempt to halt rocket attacks by *Hizbollah* from South Lebanon, by employing massive artillery fire and air attack (which destroyed a large number of villages and forced several hundred thousand refugees northwards) has received international condemnation but has not, as yet, seriously affected the peace process.

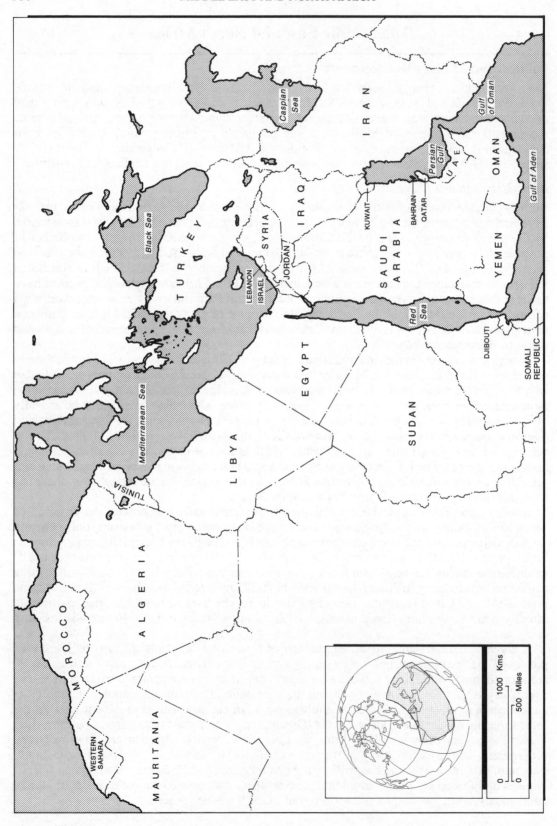

Iraq

The Iraqi situation has changed little. Two zones are still monitored by Coalition aircraft: the Kurdish 'Safe Haven' north of the 36th Parallel; and the air exclusion zone over the Shi'i-populated area south of the 32nd Parallel. On several occasions Coalition aircraft have attacked Iraqi air-defence units in both zones which were seen to be threatening them. The UN Special Commission (UNSCOM) has continued to carry out inspections in an attempt to eliminate Iraq's nuclear, chemical, biological and ballistic missile capability. At ballistic missile test sites in Iraq inspectors were not permitted to install monitoring sensors or to seal test equipment so that it could not be used. In July 1993 the Director of UNSCOM visited Iraq and believed at the time that he had resolved these problems; the sensors are now in place, but no agreement has yet been reached on their use. While UNSCOM knows there are still details of Iraqi programmes, particularly the full list of overseas suppliers of weapons components, which have not been revealed, it seems clear that, apart possibly from some hidden Scud missiles, there is little left of the machinery and plant used in the Iraqi 'weapons of mass destruction' programmes.

Iran

While there is no doubt that Iran is rebuilding its conventional forces, there is no confirmation as yet of its non-conventional forces capability. It is recognised that Iran has a chemical weapons capability but whether it has embarked on a nuclear weapons programme is uncertain and is discussed further in the essay 'Nuclear Developments' towards the back of the book. Iran is known to have ballistic missiles of the Scud variety, possibly with an extended range. There have been strong rumours of possible purchases of Chinese (M-9) and North Korean (improved Scud) missiles. It is suspected that a consignment of North Korean Scud missiles bound for Syria (and which were tracked by intelligence surveillance) was landed in Iran. There are also rumours of Iranian involvement (probably mainly financial) in North Korea's No-dong 1 development programme and the Chinese M-18 programme.

For many years Iran has supported and manipulated the Hizbollah movement in Lebanon and the Palestinian Islamic jihad. More recently, it has funded Hamas which operates mainly in the Gaza Strip. Iran's overseas efforts are now concentrated in the Sudan, to which it has given economic and military aid, as well as more direct military assistance in the form of advisers and training for Sudanese officers in Iran. Other countries in the region, such as Algeria and Egypt, have accused Iran of backing the Islamic extremist movement in their countries, but such movements that exist are mainly home-grown.

The Kurds

The terrorist activity of the Kurdish separatist movements has provoked the governments of Iran and Turkey into taking harsh measures. Iranian forces have carried out several raids into Iraqi territory to attack Iranian Kurdish guerrilla camps. Turkey, too, has made incursions into Iraq in operations against the Partiye Karkaran-e Kurdistan (PKK), but the majority of the fighting between the Turkish Army and the PKK, which has resulted in many casualties, has taken place in eastern Turkey. The PKK have carried out terrorist attacks in Ankara and elsewhere in Turkey, and have also mounted a coordinated campaign of attacks on Turkish targets across Europe.

The majority of the Iraqi Kurds live in the area covered by the Safe Haven. To all intents and purposes they are cut off from the rest of Iraq by a ring of Iraqi forces who both enforce a blockade and constantly nibble away at the edges of the territory. These Kurds are dependent on Turkish goodwill to allow vital supplies to reach them and also to continue to permit allied aircraft, which operate over northern Iraq, to be based in Turkey. They therefore distance themselves from the PKK and have, on occasion, attacked them.

Gulf Cooperation Council

Despite some quite grandiose plans the Gulf Cooperation Council (GCC) has come no closer to achieving a more secure environment in the last 12 months. Although the Damascus Declaration, which aims at achieving Egyptian and Syrian security guarantees for the GCC states, including the stationing of Syrian and Egyptian troops in the region, is not dead, it is probably in an irreversible coma. Nor has the GCC taken any steps towards implementing the Omani proposal for a 100,000-man joint defence force. Surprisingly few new weapons have reached the region so far. Immediately after the Gulf War the US administration reported to Congress that it was planning to sell over $14-bn-worth of arms to Saudi Arabia. Other arms suppliers had equally ambitious plans. A number of large-scale contracts for aircraft, tanks, fighting vehicles and air-defence weapons have been placed, but several are already being reviewed and delivery times extended. There is no coherent regional plan for arms procurement so there will be little compatibility or interoperability. If anything, states appear to have based their procurement plans on buying friendship rather than on the most suitable weapons system. Virtually all states have placed orders with the US, UK and France rather than standardise on one country's tank or aircraft.

Sudan/Somalia

Civil war continues in Sudan with the government forces, backed by Iran, slowly gaining control over the south of the country. The efforts at humanitarian relief made thus far by international aid organisations are being defeated by the civil war. In Somalia, the greater level of media coverage showed up rather dramatically the inability of the initial UN force (UNOSOM) to carry out its mandate. The US therefore, with UN backing, deployed some 30,000 men together with smaller forces from other nations, to ensure that relief aid was delivered throughout the country. In May 1993 the US command withdrew the majority of its troops and handed over responsibility to a new UN force (UNOSOM II). In Mogadishu, UNOSOM was directly challenged by the strongest warlord, General Mohammed Farah Aideed, and his clan. Both UN troops and the civil population have suffered heavier casualties than are expected during UN operations.

Conventional Force Developments

There have been few significant developments in the conventional forces of the region. In **Algeria** the airborne brigade has been expanded to a division, incorporating the independent battalions. The Air Force has retired its 55 MiG-17 FGA/trainers and a number of MiG-23 have been re-roled from the fighter to the FGA role. The overall strength of the forces has dropped by some 17,000 men. The **Moroccan** Navy has acquired two of the Italian-built *Assad*-class corvettes originally intended for the Iraqi Navy. The Army has taken delivery of ten AMX-10P AIFV and 30 155mm FH-70 towed artillery pieces. In **Tunisia,** the National Guard Coastal Patrol has acquired four ex-GDR *Kondor-I*-class patrol craft and five ex-GDR *Bremse*-class inshore patrol craft. The Army reorganisation is complete, with the third mechanised brigade being formed. The brigades now include an artillery and an air-defence regiment which had previously been independent.

The **Libyan** Air Force has 80 more L-39ZO (Czech-built) trainers than had been thought. The **Egyptian** Air Force has taken delivery of 40 F-16C fighters, 26 *Alpha Jet* FGA aircraft and an additional 24 L-29 trainers. The Army inventory has increased by 80 M-1 MBT, 700 M-113 APC, and 200 *Swingfire* ATGW fire units. The Air Defence Command has formed two additional batteries with *Crotale* SAM and two more with *Chaparral*.

The **Israeli** Navy's third *Romat*-class missile craft has been reclassified as a *Hetz*-class which is armed with *Harpoon*, *Gabriel* SSM and *Barak*. Air defences have been improved with the delivery of 45 *Chaparral* SAM. The Army has an additional 70 *Merkava III* MBT. The **Jordanian** Navy has received two ex-GDR *Bremse*-class PCI. The **Lebanese** Army reorganisation continues and a number of new units (including special forces and artillery) have been formed. Increases in equipment holdings are mainly due to bringing weapons, originally held by the militias, into service. Last year we deleted two *Osa*-class missile craft in error from the

Syrian Navy which still has 16 of these craft. It has acquired an additional eight Mi-14 ASW helicopters. The Army inventory has increased by 50 BMP-2 AIFV and 150 122mm 2S1 SP guns.

Saudi Arabia has acquired 17 US Halter-Marine inshore patrol craft both for the Navy and the Coast Guard. The Army has formed a third armoured brigade and has taken delivery of 200 more *Bradley* M-2 AIFV, and its first 12 AH-64 *Apache* attack helicopters. Air Force helicopter numbers have increased too, with 14 more AB-205, 12 more AB-206B and 13 more KV-107. The National Guard has formed two more infantry brigades. The **Kuwaiti** armed forces continue to rebuild, but as yet the Army has received no new equipment in the last year; however, Iraq has returned captured equipment (including tanks, armoured cars, 155mm towed and SP guns) but their value must be doubtful. Most importantly, the Air Force now has 32 F/A-18C FGA aircraft. The Navy has commissioned two Australian-built *Intissar*-class fast patrol craft. **Bahrain**'s Army equipment holdings have been increased by an additional 25 M-60A3 MBT, 115 M-113 APC and 12 105mm light guns. The **Iranian** Navy's second *Kilo*-class submarine has been delivered. The Air Force has taken delivery of ten more Su-24 FGA aircraft. The Army has 150 more BMP-1 AIFV and 30 Chinese 152mm Type 83 towed artillery. The **UAE** Army has taken delivery of 80 BMP-3 AIFV, ten more 105mm light guns, 30 South African G-6 155mm SP guns and 15 *FIROS* MRL. The Air Force has retired its 12 *Mirage* 5 fighters.

ALGERIA

GDP	1991ε: D 735.0bn ($39.79bn)	
	1992ε: D 859.9bn ($38.70bn)	
Growth	1991ε: 2.3%	1992ε: -3.5%
Inflation	1991ε: 30%	1992ε: 40%
Debt	1991: $23.8bn	1992: $26.0bn
Def bdgt	1992: D 23.0bn ($1.05bn)	
	1993: D 29.8bn ($1.19bn)	
Def exp	1990ε: D 17.02bn ($1.91bn)	
$1 = D[a]	1990: 8.958	1991: 18.473
	1992: 21.836	1993: 25.000

D = dinar

[a] The real value of the Dinar is estimated at approximately $1 = D50.

Population: 27,419,000

	13–17	18–22	23–32
Men	1,714,000	1,480,000	2,246,000
Women	1,594,000	1,380,000	2,087,000

TOTAL ARMED FORCES:
ACTIVE: 121,700 (65,000 conscripts).
Terms of service: Army 18 months (6 months basic, 1 year civil projects).
RESERVES: Army: some 150,000, to age 50.

ARMY: 105,000 (65,000 conscripts).
6 Military Regions. Reorganising into div structure.
Numbers of indep bde, regt unclear.
2 armd div (each 3 tk, 1 mech regt).
2 mech div (each 3 mech, 1 tk regt).
5 mot inf bde (4 inf, 1 tk bn).
1 AB div.
7 indep arty, 5 AD bn.
4 engr bn.

EQUIPMENT:
MBT: some 960: 330 T-54/-55, 330 T-62, 300 T-72.
RECCE: 120 BRDM-2.
AIFV: 915: 690 BMP-1, 225 BMP-2.
APC: 460 BTR-50/-60.
TOWED ARTY: 405: 122mm: 25 D-74, 100 M-1931/37, 60 M-30 (M-1938), 190 D-30; 130mm: 10 M-46; 152mm: 20 ML-20 (M-1937).
SP ARTY: 175: 122mm: 150 2S1; 152mm: 25 2S3.
MRL: 126: 122mm: 48 BM-21; 140mm: 48 BM-14-16; 240mm: 30 BM-24.
MORTARS: 82mm: 150 M-37; 120mm: 120 M-1943; 160mm: 60 M-1943.
RCL: 178: 82mm: 120 B-10; 107mm: 58 B-11.
ATK GUNS: 296: 57mm: 156 ZIS-2; 85mm: 80 D-44; 100mm: 10 T-12, 50 SU-100 SP.
AD GUNS: 895: 14.5mm: 80 ZPU-2/-4; 20mm: 100; 23mm: 100 ZU-23 towed, 210 ZSU-23-4 SP; 37mm: 150 M-1939; 57mm: 75 S-60; 85mm: 20 KS-12; 100mm: 150 KS-19; 130mm: 10 KS-30.
SAM: SA-7/-8/-9.

NAVY: ε6,700.
BASES: Mers el Kebir, Algiers, Annaba, Jijel.
SUBMARINES: 2:
2 Sov *Kilo* with 533mm TT.
FRIGATES: 3 *Mourad Rais* (Sov *Koni*) with 2 x 12 ASW RL.
PATROL AND COASTAL COMBATANTS: 22:
CORVETTES: 3 *Rais Hamidou* (Sov *Nanuchka II*) with 4 x SS-N-2C *Styx* SSM.
MISSILE CRAFT: 11 *Osa* with 4 x SS-N-2 SSM.
PATROL: 8
COASTAL: 2 locally-built *Djebel Chinoise*.
INSHORE: about 6 *El Yadekh* PCI.
MINE WARFARE: 1 Sov T-43 MSC.
AMPHIBIOUS: 3:
2 *Kalaat beni Hammad* LST: capacity 240 tps, 10 tk, hel deck.

1 *Polnocny* LSM: capacity 180 tps, 6 tk.
SUPPORT AND MISCELLANEOUS: 3
1 *El Idrissi* AGHS, 1 div spt, 1 *Poluchat* torpedo recovery vessel.

COAST GUARD (under naval control): ε630;
7 Ch *Chui-E* PCC, about 6 *El Yadekh* PCI, 16 PCI⟨, 1 spt.

AIR FORCE: 10,000; 193 cbt ac, 58 armed hel.
FGA: 3 sqn:
1 with 10 Su-24.
2 with 40 MiG-23BN;
FIGHTER: 8 sqn:
6 with 95 MiG-21MF/bis;
1 with 14 MiG-25;
1 with 20 MiG-23B/E.
RECCE: 1 sqn with 3 MiG-25R.
MR: 1 sqn with 2 *Super King Air* B-200T.
TRANSPORT: 2 sqn with 6 An-12, 10 C-130H, 6 C-130H-30, 3 Il-76;
VIP: 2 *Falcon* 900, 3 *Gulfstream* III, 2 F-27.
HELICOPTERS: 5 sqn:
ATTACK HEL: 2 sqn with 38 Mi-24, 1 sqn with 20 Mi-8/-17.
TRANSPORT HEL: (hy): 1 sqn with 15 Mi-8; (med): 1 sqn with 12 Mi-17.
TRAINING: 3* MiG-21U, 5* MiG-23U, 3* MiG-25U, 6 T-34C, 30 L-39, plus 30 ZLIN-142.
AAM: AA-2, AA-6.
AD: GUNS: 3 bde+: 85mm, 100mm, 130mm.
SAM: 3 regt: 1 with SA-3, SA-6, SA-8.

FORCES ABROAD:
UN AND PEACEKEEPING:
CAMBODIA: (UNTAC): 157, plus 16 Observers.

PARAMILITARY:
GENDARMERIE: (Ministry of Interior): 24,000;
44 Panhard AML-60/M-3, 50 *Fahd* APC, 28 Mi-2 hel.
NATIONAL SECURITY FORCES: (Ministry of Interior): 16,000; small arms.
REPUBLICAN GUARD BDE: 1,200; AML-60, M-3 recce.

FOREIGN FORCES:
RUSSIA: 300–500 military advisers.

BAHRAIN

GDP	1991:	D 1.53bn ($4.07bn)	
	1992:	D 1.60bn ($4.24bn)	
Growth	1991:	0.5%	1992ε: 2.5%
Inflation	1991:	0.5%	1992: 1.5%
Debt	1991:	$2.30bn	1992: $2.40bn

Def bdg[a]	1992:	D 89.3m ($237.56m)
	1993:	D 92.0m ($244.10m)
$1 = D	1989–93:	0.3759
D = dinar		

[a] Excl a subsidy from the Gulf Cooperation Council (GCC) of $1.8bn (1984–94) shared between Bahrain and Oman.

Population: 528,200

	13–17	18–22	23–32
Men	23,000	20,600	44,100
Women	23,000	20,400	37,000

TOTAL ARMED FORCES:
ACTIVE: 7,150.

ARMY: 6,000.
1 bde: 2 inf, 1 tk, 1 SF bn, 1 armd car sqn, 2 arty, 2 mor bty.
EQUIPMENT:
MBT: 106 M-60A3.
RECCE: 22 AML-90, 8 *Saladin*, 8 *Ferret*, 8 *Shorland*.
APC: some 10 AT-105 *Saxon*, 110 Panhard M-3, 115 M-113A2.
TOWED ARTY: 155mm: 20 M-198.
MORTARS: 81mm: 9; 120mm: 9.
ATGW: 15 BGM-71A *TOW*.
RCL: 106mm: 30 M-40A1; 120mm: 6 MOBAT.
SAM: 40+ RBS-70, 20+ *Stinger*, *Crotale*.

NAVY: ε500.
BASE: Mina Sulman.
PATROL AND COASTAL COMBATANTS: 10:
CORVETTES: 2 *Al Manama* (Ge Lürssen 62-m) with 2 x 2 MM-40 *Exocet* SSM, 1 x *Dauphin* II hel (AS-15 ASM).
MISSILE CRAFT: 4 *Ahmad el Fateh* (Ge Lürssen 45-m) with 2 x 2 MM-40 *Exocet*.
PATROL: 4: 2 *Al Riffa* (Ge Lürssen 38-m PFI). 2 PFI⟨.
SUPPORT AND MISCELLANEOUS: 1: *Ajeera* LCU-type spt.

AIR FORCE: 650; 24 cbt ac, 12 armed hel.
FGA: 1 sqn with 8 F-5E, 4 F-5F.
FIGHTER: 1 sqn with 8 F-16C, 4 -D.
TRANSPORT: 2 *Gulfstream* (1 -II, 1 -III; VIP).
HELICOPTERS: 1 sqn with 12 AB-212 (8 armed), 4 Bo-105 (armed).
MISSILES:
ASM: AS-11, AS-12.
AAM: AIM-9P *Sidewinder*.

PARAMILITARY: (Ministry of Interior):
COAST GUARD ε400; 1 PCI, about 20 PCI, 3 spt/landing craft, 1 hovercraft.

POLICE 9,000; 2 Hughes 500, 2 Bell 412, 1 Bell 205 hel.

DJIBOUTI

GDP	1989ε: frD 73.04bn ($410.9m)		
	1990: frD 72.00bn ($405.1m)		
Growth:	1989ε: 1%		
Inflation:	1988: 6.4%		1989: 3.7%
Debt	1990: $194.6m		
Def bdgt	1992: frD 4.73bn ($26.60m)		
	1993: frD 4.96bn ($28.15m)		
Def exp	1991: frD 6.91bn ($38.89m)		
	1992: frD 6.74bn ($37.93m)		
FMA	1992: $5.18m (France, US)		
$1 = frD	1988–93: 177.72		

frD = Djibouti francs

Population: 470,800

	13–17	18–22	23–32
Men	25,400	21,500	36,000
Women	25,200	21,000	31,700

TOTAL ARMED FORCES:
ACTIVE: some 3,900, incl 600 Gendarmerie.

ARMY: ε3,000.
3 Comd (North, Central, South).
1 inf bn, incl mor, ATK pl.
1 armd sqn.   1 AB coy.
1 spt bn.   1 arty bty.
1 border cdo bn.
EQUIPMENT:
RECCE: 15 M-11 VBL, 4 AML-60, 20 AML-90, 20 AML-245.
APC: 12 BTR-60.
TOWED ARTY: 105mm: M-56 pack how; 122mm: 6 D-30.
MORTARS: 81mm: 25; 120mm: 20 *Brandt*.
RL: 73mm; 89mm: LRAC.
RCL: 106mm: 16 M-40A1.
AD GUNS: 20mm: 5 M-693 SP; 23mm: 5 ZU-23; 40mm: L/70.

NAVY: 100.
BASE: Djibouti.
PATROL CRAFT, INSHORE: 3 PCI⟨; plus boats.

AIR FORCE: 200; no cbt ac or armed hel.
TRANSPORT: 2 C-212, 2 N-2501F, 2 Cessna U206G, 1 Socata 235GT.
HELICOPTERS: 3 AS-355, 2 SE-3130.
(defected from Ethiopia: some 18 ac and hel incl MiG-23, An-12 ac, Mi-8, Mi-24 hel).

PARAMILITARY:
GENDARMERIE: (Ministry of Defence): 600: 1 bn, 1 patrol boat.
NATIONAL SECURITY FORCE: (Ministry of Interior): ε3,000.

OPPOSITION:
FRONT FOR THE RESTORATION OF UNITY AND DEMOCRACY: ε4,500.

FOREIGN FORCES:
FRANCE: 4,000, incl 1 inf, 1 Foreign Legion regt, 1 sqn: 10 *Mirage* F-1C, 1 C-160 ac, 1 SA-319, 2 AS-355 hel.

EGYPT

GDP	1991: £E 110.44bn ($33.17bn)	
	1992: £E 136.19bn ($40.89bn)	
Growth	1991: 2.3%	1992: 2.8%
Inflation	1991: 19.8%	1992: 13.6%
Debt	1991: $34.7bn	1992: $28.1bn
Def bdgt	1992: £E 8.24bn ($2.47bn)	
	1993ε: £E 9.09bn ($2.73bn)	
FMA[a]	1993: $2,123.8m (US)	
$1 = 1E	1990: 2.000	1991: 3.330
	1992: 3.330	1993: 3.342

[a] Incl $822m as Economic Support.

Population: 55,262,000

	13–17	18–22	23–32
Men	3,043,000	2,616,000	4,477,000
Women	2,870,000	2,452,000	4,189,000

TOTAL ARMED FORCES:
ACTIVE: 430,000 (some 272,000 conscripts).
Terms of service: 3 years (selective).
RESERVES: 304,000. Army 200,000; Navy 14,000; Air Force 20,000; AD 70,000.

ARMY: 310,000 (perhaps 200,000 conscripts).
4 Military Districts, 2 Army HQ:
4 armd div (each with 2 armd, 1 mech bde).
8 mech inf div (each with 2 mech, 1 armd bde).
1 Republican Guard armd bde.
2 indep armd bde.   2 airmobile bde.
3 indep inf bde.   1 para bde.
4 indep mech bde.   7 cdo gp.
15 indep arty bde.   2 hy mor bde.
2 SSM bde (1 with *FROG*-7, 1 with *Scud* B).
EQUIPMENT:[b]
MBT: 3,167: 840 T-54/-55, 200+ *Ramses II* (mod T-54/55), 600 T-62, 1,447 M-60 (700A1, 747A3), 80 M1A1 *Abrams*.
RECCE: 300 BRDM-2.

AIFV: 470: 220 BMP-1, some 250 BMR-600P.
APC: 3,575: 650 *Walid*, 165 *Fahd*, 1,075 BTR-50/
OT-62, 1,685 M-113A2.
TOWED ARTY: 1,108: 122mm: 48 M-31/37, 400 M-
1938, 220 D-30M; 130mm: 440 M-46.
SP ARTY: 155mm: 196 M-109A2.
MRL: 122mm: 75 BM-11, 200 BM-21/*as-Saqr*-10/-
18/-36.
MORTARS: 82mm (some 50 SP); 107mm: some 100
M-30 SP; 120mm: 900 M-43; 160mm: 35 M-160.
SSM (launchers): 12 *FROG*-7, *Sakr*-80 (trials), 9
Scud B.
ATGW: 1,400 AT-3 *Sagger* (incl BRDM-2); 220
Milan; 400 *Swingfire*; 520 *TOW* (incl 52 on M-901
(M-113) SP).
RCL: 82mm: B-10; 107mm: B-11.
AD GUNS: 14.5mm: 600 ZPU-2/-4; 23mm: 550 ZU-
23-2, 117 ZSU-23-4 SP, 45 *Sinai*; 37mm: 150 M-
1939; 57mm: 200 S-60, 40 ZSU-57-2 SP.
SAM: 2,000 SA-7/'*Ayn as-Saqr*, 26 M-54 SP
Chaparral.

NAVY: ε20,000 (ε12,000 conscripts).
BASES: Alexandria (HQ, Mediterranean), Port
Said, Mersa Matruh, Safaqa, Port Tewfig; Hurghada
(HQ, Red Sea).
SUBMARINES: 2:
2 Sov *Romeo* with 533mm TT, (plus 2 non-op and 4
Ch Type-033 undergoing refit in US).
PRINCIPAL SURFACE COMBATANTS: 5:
DESTROYER: 1: *El Fateh* (UK 'Z') (trg) with 4 x
114mm guns, 5 x 533mm TT.
FRIGATES: 4:
2 *El Suez* (Sp *Descubierta*) with 2 x 3 ASTT, 1 x 2
    ASW RL; plus 2 x 4 *Harpoon* SSM.
2 *Al Zaffir* (Ch *Jianghu*-I) with 2 x ASW RL; plus 2
    x CSS-N-2 (HY-2) SSM.
PATROL AND COASTAL COMBATANTS: 39:
MISSILE CRAFT: 21:
6 *Ramadan* with 4 *Otomat* SSM.
4 Sov *Osa-I* with 4 x SS-N-2A *Styx* SSM.
6 *6th October* with 2 *Otomat* SSM (ε3 non-op).
5 Ch *Hegu* (*Komar*-type) with 2 HY-2 SSM.
PATROL: 18:
8 Ch *Hainan* PFC with 4 x ASW RL.
6 Sov *Shershen* PFI; 2 with 4 x 533mm TT and BM-
21 (8-tube) 122mm MRL; 4 with SA-N-5 and 1
BM-24 (12-tube) 240mm MRL.
4 Ch *Shanghai* II PFI.
MINE WARFARE: 8:
MINE COUNTERMEASURES: 8:
4 *Aswan* (Sov *Yurka*) MSC.
4 *Assiout* (Sov T-43 class) MSC.
AMPHIBIOUS: 3 Sov *Polnocny* LSM, capacity 100
tps, 5 tk, plus 11 LCU (some in reserve).
SUPPORT AND MISCELLANEOUS: 19:
6 AOT (small), 5 trg, 6 tugs,
1 diving spt, 1 ex-UK FF trg.

NAVAL AVIATION: 17 armed hel.
HELICOPTERS: 5 *Sea King* Mk 47 (ASW, anti-ship);
12 SA-342 (anti-ship).

COASTAL DEFENCE: (Army tps, Navy
control):
GUNS: 130mm: SM-4-1.
SSM: *Otomat*.

AIR FORCE: 30,000 (10,000 conscripts).[b]
546 cbt ac, 74 armed hel.
FGA: 7 sqn:
2 with 40 *Alpha Jet*.   2 with 40 Ch J-6.
2 with 30 F-4E.   1 with 16 *Mirage* 5E2.
FIGHTER: 16 sqn:
2 with 30 F-16A.   5 with 100 MiG-21.
2 with 80 F-16C.   3 with 54 *Mirage* 5D/E.
3 with 60 Ch J-7.   1 with 16 *Mirage* 2000C.
RECCE: 2 sqn with 6 *Mirage* 5SDR, 14 MiG-21.
EW: 2 C-130H (ELINT), 4 Beech 1900 (ELINT) ac;
4 *Commando* 2E hel (ECM).
AEW: 5 E-2C.
MR: 2 Beech 1900C surveillance ac.
TRANSPORT: 3 sqn with 19 C-130H, 5 DHC-5D, 1
Super King Air.
HELICOPTERS: 15 sqn:
ATTACK: 4 sqn with 74 SA-342K/-L (44 with *HOT*,
30 with 20mm gun).
TACTICAL TRANSPORT: hy: 14 CH-47C; med: 40
Mi-8, 25 *Commando* (5 -1 tpt, 17 -2 tpt, 3 -2B VIP),
2 S-70 (VIP); lt: 12 Mi-4, 17 UH-12E (trg).
TRAINING: incl 4 DHC-5, 54 EMB-312, 6* F-16B,
6* F-16D, 36 *Gumhuria*, 16* JJ-6, 40 L-29, 48 L-39,
24* L-59E, MiG-21U, 5* *Mirage* 5SDD, 3* *Mirage*
2000B.
MISSILES:
ASM: AGM-65 *Maverick*, *Exocet* AM-39, AS-12,
AS-30, AS-30L *HOT*.
ARM: *Armat*.
AAM: AA-2 *Atoll*, AIM-7E/F/M *Sparrow*, AIM-9F/L/
P *Sidewinder*, R-530, R-550 *Magic*.
RPV: 20 R4E-50 *Skyeye*, 27 Teledyne-Ryan 324.

AIR DEFENCE COMMAND: 70,000
(50,000 conscripts).
5 div: regional bde.
100 AD arty bn.
40 SA-2, 53 SA-3, 14 SA-6 bn.
12 bty *Improved HAWK*
12 bty *Chaparral*.
14 bty *Crotale*
EQUIPMENT:
AD GUNS: some 2,000: 20mm, 23mm, 37mm, 57mm,
85mm, 100mm.
SAM: 738: some 360 SA-2, 210 SA-3, 60 SA-6, 72
Improved HAWK, 36 *Crotale*.
AD SYSTEMS: some 18 *Amoun* (*Skyguard*/RIM-7F
Sparrow, some 36 twin 35mm guns, some 36 quad
SAM). *Sinai*-23 short-range AD (Dassault 6SD-20S
radar, 23mm guns, '*Ayn as-Saqr* SAM).

FORCES ABROAD: Advisers in Oman, Saudi
Arabia, Zaire.

UN AND PEACEKEEPING:
BOSNIA (UNPROFOR II): 415: 1 inf bn.
CAMBODIA (UNTAC): 100.
CROATIA (UNPROFOR I): 13 Observers, 17 civ pol.
MOZAMBIQUE (ONUMOZ): 20 Observers.
SOMALIA: 750: 1 inf bn.
WESTERN SAHARA (MINURSO): 9 Observers.

PARAMILITARY:
COAST GUARD: ε2,000.
PATROL, INSHORE: 32:
13 *Timsah* PCI, 10 *Swiftships*, 3 *Nisr*†,
6 *Crestitalia* PFI⟨, plus some 60 boats.
CENTRAL SECURITY FORCES: 300,000.
NATIONAL GUARD: 60,000: *Walid* APC.
BORDER GUARD FORCES: 12,000; 18 Border Guard Regt.

FOREIGN FORCES:
PEACEKEEPING (MFO Sinai): some 2,600.
Contingents from Canada, Colombia, Fiji, France, Italy, Netherlands, New Zealand, Norway, Uruguay and US.

b Most Soviet eqpt now in store, incl MBT and some cbt ac.

IRAN

GDP	1991:	r 46,776.8bn ($68.17bn)	
	1992ε:	r 58,471.0bn ($71.01bn)	
Growth	1991:	10%	1992ε: 8.5%
Inflation	1991:	17.1%	1992: 22.9%
Debt	1991:	$9.01bn	1992: $18.80bn
Def exp*a*	1990ε:	r 895.0bn ($3.18bn)	
	1991ε:	r 1,273.0bn ($5.79bn)	
Def bdgt*a*	1992:	r 413.0bn ($1.80bn)	
	1993:	r 368.0bn ($1.20bn)	
$1 = r*b*	1990:	581.45	1991: 686.20
	1992:	823.4	1993ε: 1,053.9

r = rial
a The 1992 and 1993 def budgets represent official budget figures and do not include arms purchases. The substantial drop in 1993 may reflect the pressing needs of the stabilisation programme of the government which has seen the foreign debt jump from from $9bn in 1991 to $18.8bn in 1992 and an estimated $26.0bn in 1993. Arms purchases have been highlighted in the past and opposition sources claim that Iran spent $19bn on defence in 1991 and $14.5bn in 1992, but these figures do not appear to match the value of weapon deliveries so far.
b Official exchange rate 1993 $1= r 1,600.

Population: 58,942,000

	13–17	18–22	23–32
Men	3,396,000	2,948,000	4,718,000
Women	3,186,000	2,777,000	4,524,000

TOTAL ARMED FORCES:
ACTIVE: 473,000.
Terms of service: 24 months.
RESERVES: Army: 350,000, ex-service volunteers.

ARMY: 320,000 (perhaps 250,000 conscripts).
ε3 Army HQ.
4 armd div (2 of 3, 2 of 4 bde).
7 inf div.
1 AB bde.
1 SF div (4 bde).
Some indep armd, inf bde (incl 'coastal force').
5 arty gps.
RESERVES: '*Qods*' bn (ex-service).
EQUIPMENT:†
MBT: 700+ incl: T-54/-55, Ch T-59, T-62, some T-72, *Chieftain* Mk 3/5, M-47/-48, M-60A1.
LIGHT TANKS: 40 *Scorpion*.
RECCE: 130 EE-9 *Cascavel*.
AIFV: 200 BMP-1.
APC: 700: BTR-50/-60, M-113.
ARTY: 2,300.
TOWED: 105mm: M-101A1; 122mm: D-30, Ch Type-54; 130mm: M-46/Type-59; 152mm: 30 Type-83; 155mm: 50 M-71, 18 FH-77B, ε130 GHN-45, ε50 G-5, 50 M-59; 203mm: some 30 M-115.
SP: 122mm: 20 2S1; 155mm: some 95 M-109; 175mm: 20 M-107; 203mm: 10 M-110.
MRL: 107mm: 40 Ch Type-63; 122mm: 65 BM-21, BM-11; 230mm: *Oghab*; 333mm: *Shahin* 2; 355mm: *Nazeat*; *Iran*-130 reported.
MORTARS: 1,200 incl: 81mm; 107mm: M-30 4.2-in.; 120mm.
SSM: *Frog*-7, 100+ *Scud*-B, some *Scud*-C, local manufacture msl reported under development.
ATGW: *Dragon*, *TOW*, AT-3 *Sagger* (some SP).
RCL: 106mm: M-40.
AD GUNS: 1,500: 23mm: ZU-23 towed, ZSU-23-4 SP; 35mm: 92; 37mm; 57mm: ZSU-57-2 SP.
SAM: SA-7, some HN-5.
AIRCRAFT: incl 40+ Cessna (185, 310, O-2A), 2 F-27, 2 *Falcon* 20, 15 PC-6, 5 *Shrike Commander*.
HELICOPTERS: 100 AH-1J (attack); 31 CH-47C (hy tpt); 100 Bell 214A; 20 AB-205A; 50 AB-206.

REVOLUTIONARY GUARD CORPS
(*Pasdaran Inqilab*): Some 120,000.
GROUND FORCES: some 100,000; 13 Regional Commands: loosely org in bn of no fixed size, grouped into perhaps 12–15 inf, 2–4 armd div and many indep bde, incl inf, armd, para, SF, arty (incl SSM), engr, AD and border defence units, serve indep or with Army; small arms, spt weapons from Army; controls *Basij* (see Paramilitary) when mob.
NAVAL FORCES: some 20,000; five island bases (Al Farsiyah, Halul (oil platform), Sirri, Abu Musa, Larak); some 40 Swedish Boghammar Marin boats armed with ATGW, RCL, machine guns. Italian SSM reported. Controls coast defence elm incl arty

and CSS-N-2 (HY-2) *Silkworm* SSM in at least 3 sites, each 3–6 msl. Now under joint command with Navy.
MARINES: 3 bde reported.

NAVY: 18,000, incl naval air and marines (ε2,000).
BASES: Bandar Abbas (HQ), Bushehr, Kharg, Bandar-e-Anzelli, Bandar-e-Khomeini, Chah Bahar.
SUBMARINES: 2:
2 Sov *Kilo* SS with 6 x 533mm TT.
PRINCIPAL SURFACE COMBATANTS: 8:
DESTROYERS: 3:
1 *Damavand* (UK *Battle*) with 4 x 2 SM-1 (boxed) SSM, 2 x 2 114mm guns; plus 1 x 3 AS mor.
2 *Babr* (US *Sumner*) with 4 x 2 SM-1 SSM (boxed), 2 x 2 127mm guns; plus 2 x 3 ASTT.
FRIGATES: 5:
3 *Alvand* (UK Vosper Mk 5) with 1 x 5 *Sea Killer* SSM, 1 x 3 AS mor, 1 x 114mm gun.
2 *Bayandor* (US PF-103).
PATROL AND COASTAL COMBATANTS: 33:
MISSILE CRAFT: 10 *Kaman* (Fr *Combattante* II) PFM, some fitted for 4 *Harpoon* SSM.
PATROL INSHORE: 23:
3 *Kaivan*, 3 *Parvin* PCI, 1 ex-Iraqi *Bogomol* PFI, 3 N. Korean *Chaho* PFI⟨, plus some 13 hovercraft⟨.
MINE WARFARE: 5:
3 *Shahrokh* MSC (incl 1 in Caspian Sea trg), 2 *Riazi* (US *Cape*) MSI.
(2 *Iran Ajr* LST used for mine-laying).
AMPHIBIOUS: 9:
4 *Hengam* LST, capacity 225 tps, 9 tk, 1 hel.
3 *Iran Hormuz 24* (S. Korean) LST, capacity 140 tps, 8 tk.
2 *Iran Ajr* LST.
Plus craft: 3 LCT.
SUPPORT AND MISCELLANEOUS: 22:
1 *Kharg* AOE with 2 hel, 2 *Bandar Abbas* AOR with 1 hel, 1 repair, 4 water tankers, 7 *Delva*, about 6 *Hendijan* spt vessels, 1 AT.

MARINES: 3 bn.

NAVAL AIR: 9 armed hel.
ASW: 1 hel sqn with ε3 SH-3D, 6 AB-212 ASW.
MCM: 1 hel sqn with 2 RH-53D.
TRANSPORT: 1 sqn with 4 *Commander*, 4 F-27, 1 *Falcon* 20 ac; AB-205, AB-206 hel.

AIR FORCE: 15,000. Some 293 cbt ac (probably less than 50% of US ac types serviceable); no armed hel. (112 cbt ac flew from Iraq to Iran during the Gulf War. They consisted of Su-24, MiG-25, *Mirage* F-1, Su-22, Su-25 and MiG-23. Probably non-op and not incl in these totals.)
FGA: 9 sqn:
4 with some 60 F-4D/E.
1 with 20 Su-24.
4 with some 60 F-5E/F.

FIGHTER: 7 sqn:
4 with 60 F-14.
1 with 25 F-7.
2 with 30 MiG-29.
MR: 5 P-3F, 1 RC-130.
RECCE: 1 sqn (det) with some 5 RF-5, 3 RF-4E.
TANKER/TRANSPORT: 1 sqn with 4 Boeing 707.
TRANSPORT: 5 sqn: 9 Boeing 747F, 11 Boeing 707, 1 Boeing 727, 20 C-130E/H, 3 *Commander* 690, 15 F-27, 5 *Falcon* 20.
HELICOPTERS: 2 AB-206A, 39 Bell 214C, 5 CH-47.
TRAINING: incl 26 Beech F-33A/C, 10 EMB-312, 45 PC-7, 7 T-33, 5* MiG-29B, 5* FT-7, 20* F-5B.
MISSILES:
ASM: AGM-65A *Maverick*, AS-10, AS-11.
AAM: AIM-7 *Sparrow*, AIM-9 *Sidewinder*, AIM-54 *Phoenix*, probably AA-10, AA-11 for MiG-29.
SAM: 12 bn with 150 *Improved HAWK*, 5 sqn with 30 *Rapier*, 15 *Tigercat*, 45 HQ-2J (Ch version of SA-2). Probable SA-5.

FORCES ABROAD:
LEBANON: Revolutionary Guard ε500.
SUDAN: Military advisers.

PARAMILITARY:
BASIJ 'Popular Mobilization Army' volunteers, mostly youths: strength has been as high as 1 million during periods of offensive operations. Org in up to 500 300–350-man 'bn' of 3 coy, each 4 pl and spt; small arms only. Not currently embodied for mil ops.
GENDARMERIE: (45,000 incl border guard elm); Cessna 185/310 lt ac, AB-205/-206 hel, patrol boats: about 90 inshore, 40 harbour craft.
KURDS: Kurdish Democratic Party armed wing *Pesh Merga*, ε12,000.

OPPOSITION:
KURDISH COMMUNIST PARTY OF IRAN (KOMALA): strength unknown.
DEMOCRATIC PARTY OF IRANIAN KURDISTAN (DPIK): perhaps 10,500.
NATIONAL LIBERATION ARMY (NLA): ε4,500. Org in bde, armed with captured eqpt. Perhaps 100+ tanks. Iraq-based.

IRAQ

There is insufficient data on Iraq's economy to produce figures for 1992–1993. The UN embargo on oil exports is believed to have had a serious effect on the economy with industrial production down by 50% and major infrastructure inadequacies, but the Iraqi leadership is still in control.

GDP	1990ε: D 19.66bn ($40.78bn)
	1991ε: $24.5bn
	1992ε: $20bn

Growth	1989:	3.5%	1990ε: -30% to -40%
Inflation	1989:	20.0%	1990ε: 40.0%
Debt	1989:	$80.00bn	1990*a*: $109.67bn
Def bdgt	1990:	D 4.150bn ($8.61bn)	
$1 = D*b*	1990–1993:	0.3109	

D = dinar
a Does not incl any est of war reparations.
b Official exchange rate. The real value of the Iraqi Dinar is estimated at $1 = 50D.
Population: ε18,400,000

TOTAL ARMED FORCES:
ACTIVE: perhaps 382,000.
Terms of service: 18–24 months.
RESERVES: 650,000.

ARMY: ε350,000 (incl perhaps ε100,000 recalled reserves).
6 corps HQ.
22 armd/mech/inf div.
7 Republican Guard Force div (4 armd/mech, 3 inf div).
Presidential Guard/Special Security Force.
15 SF/cdo bde (for COIN ops).
EQUIPMENT:
MBT: perhaps 2,200 incl T-54/-55/M-77, Ch T-59/-69, T-62, T-72, *Chieftain* Mk 3/5, M-60, M-47.
RECCE: perhaps 1,500 incl BRDM-2, AML-60/-90, EE-9 *Cascavel*, EE-3 *Jararaca*.
AIFV: perhaps 700 BMP-1/-2.
APC: perhaps 2,000 incl BTR-50/-60/-152, OT-62/-64, MTLB, YW-531, M-113A1/A2, Panhard M-3, EE-11 *Urutu*.
TOWED ARTY: perhaps 1,500 incl 105mm: incl M-56 pack; 122mm: D-74, D-30, M-1938; 130mm: incl M-46, Type 59-1; 155mm: some G-5, GHN-45, M-114.
SP ARTY: 230 incl 122mm: 2S1; 152mm: 2S3; 155mm: M-109A1/A2, AUF-1 (GCT).
MRL: perhaps 250 incl 107mm; 122mm: BM-21; 127mm: *ASTROS* II; 132mm: BM-13/-16, 262mm: *Ababeel*.
MORTARS: 81mm; 120mm; 160mm: M-1943; 240mm.
ATGW: AT-3 *Sagger* (incl BRDM-2), AT-4 *Spigot* reported, SS-11, *Milan*, *HOT* (incl 100 VC-TH).
RCL: 73mm: SPG-9; 82mm: B-10; 107mm.
ATK GUNS: 85mm; 100mm towed.
HELICOPTERS: ε500 (120 armed) incl.
ATTACK: ε120 Bo-105 with AS-11/*HOT*, Mi-24, SA-316 with AS-12, SA-321 (some with *Exocet*), SA-342.
TRANSPORT: ε350 hy: Mi-6; med: AS-61, Bell 214 ST, Mi-4, Mi-8/-17, SA-330; lt: AB-212, BK-117 (SAR), Hughes 300C, -500D, -530F.
AD GUNS: ε5,500: 23mm: ZSU-23-4 SP; 37mm: M-1939 and twin; 57mm: incl ZSU-57-2 SP; 85mm; 100mm; 130mm.
SAM: SA-2/-3/-6/-7/-8/-9/-13/-14/-16, *Roland*.

NAVY: ε2,000.
BASES: Basra (limited facilities), Az Zubayr, Umm Qasr (currently closed).
FRIGATES: 1: *Ibn Marjid* (ex-*Khaldoum*) (trg) with 2 x ASTT.
PATROL AND COASTAL COMBATANTS: 14:
MISSILE CRAFT: 1 Sov *Osa*-I with 4 SS-N-2A *Styx*.
PATROL INSHORE: 13
1 Sov *Bogomol* PFI, 3 PFI⟨, 6 PCI⟨, 3 SRN-6 hovercraft, plus boats.
MINE WARFARE: 5
2 Sov *Yevgenya*
3 Yug *Nestin* MSI⟨.
SUPPORT AND MISCELLANEOUS: 5:
1 *Aka* (Yug *Spasilac*-class) AR.
3 ro-ro AK with hel deck. Capacity 16 tk, 250 tps. Inactive in foreign ports.
1 Yacht.
Plus 1 *Agnadeen* (It *Stromboli*) AOR laid-up in Alexandria.

AIR FORCE: 30,000 incl 15,000 AD personnel;
Total Iraqi air losses cannot be est. 37 ac were lost in air-to-air cbt, over 100 destroyed on ground, 112 cbt ac flown to Iran; these ac are not included in the totals.
BOMBERS: ε6 incl: H-6D, Tu-16, Tu-22.
FGA: ε130 incl J-6, MiG-23BN, MiG-27, *Mirage* F1EQ5/-200, Su-7, Su-20, Su-25.
FIGHTER: ε180 incl Ch J-7, MiG-21, MiG-25, *Mirage* F-1EQ, MiG-29.
RECCE: incl MiG-25.
AEW: incl Il-76 *Adnan*.
TKR: incl 2 Il-76.
TRANSPORT: incl An-2, An-12, An-24, An-26, Il-76.
TRAINING: incl AS-202, EMB-312, some 40 L-29, some 40 L-39, MB-233, *Mirage* F-1BQ, 25 PC-7, 30 PC-9.
MISSILES:
ASM: AM-39, AS-4, AS-5, AS-11, AS-12, AS-30L, C-601.
AAM: AA-2/-6/-7/-8/-10, R-530, R-550.

PARAMILITARY:
FRONTIER GUARDS: ε20,000
SECURITY TROOPS: 4,800.

OPPOSITION:
KURDISH DEMOCRATIC PARTY (KDP): 25,000 (30,000 more in militia); small arms, some Iranian lt arty, MRL, mor, SAM-7.
KURDISH WORKERS' PARTY: ε20,000; breakaway from KDP, anti-Iran, Syria-based.
PATRIOTIC UNION OF KURDISTAN (PUK): ε12,000 cbt (plus 6,000 spt). Some T-54/-55 MBT; 450 mor (60mm, 82mm, 120mm); 106mm RCL; some 200 12.5mm AA guns; SA-7 SAM.
SOCIALIST PARTY OF KURDISTAN: ε500.
SUPREME ASSEMBLY OF THE ISLAMIC REVOLUTION (SAIRI): ε1 'bde'; Iran-based; Iraqi dissidents, ex-prisoners of war.

FOREIGN FORCES:
UN (UNIKOM): some 300 tps and observers from 29 countries.

ISRAEL

GDP	1991:	NS 134.76bn ($59.13bn)	
	1992:	NS 159.02bn ($64.67bn)	
Growth	1991:	5.9%	1992: 6.4%
Inflation	1991:	18.9%	1992: 11.9%
Debt	1990:	$24.33bn	1991: $23.70bn
Def bdgt	1992:	NS 18.12bn ($7.37bn)	
	1993:	NS 17.79bn ($6.84bn)	
$1 = NS	1990:	2.016	1991: 2.279
	1992:	2,590	1993: 2,600
FMA[a]	1993:	$3,000m (US)	

NS = new sheqalim
[a] Incl $1,200m as Economic Support

Population: 5,117,000 (6,179,000 Jews, 717,000 Muslims, 135,000 Christians, 86,000 Druze).

	13–17	18–22	23–32
Men	257,000	250,000	465,000
Women	244,000	240,000	439,000

TOTAL ARMED FORCES:
ACTIVE: 176,000 (139,500 conscripts).
Terms of service: officers 48 months, men 36 months, women 24 months (Jews and Druze only; Christians, Circassians and Muslims may volunteer). Annual trg as cbt reservists to age 45 (some specialists to age 54) for men, 24 (or marriage) for women.
RESERVES: 430,000: Army 365,000; Navy 10,000; Air Force 55,000. Male commitment until 54 in reserve op units may be followed by voluntary service in the Civil Guard or Civil Defence.

STRATEGIC:
It is widely believed that Israel has a nuclear capability with up to 100 warheads. Delivery means could include ac, *Jericho* 1 SSM (range up to 500km), *Jericho* 2 (tested 1987–9, range ε1,500km) and *Lance*.

ARMY: 134,000 (114,700 conscripts, male and female); some 598,000 on mob.
3 territorial, 1 home front comd.
3 corps HQ
3 armd div (2 armd, 1 arty bde, plus 1 armd, 1 mech inf bde on mob).
2 div HQ (op control of anti-*intifada* units).
3 regional inf div HQ (border def).
4 mech inf bde (incl 1 para trained).
1 *Lance* SSM bn.
3 arty bn with 203mm M-110 SP.

RESERVES:
9 armd div (2 or 3 armd, 1 affiliated mech inf, 1 arty bde).
1 airmobile/mech inf div (3 bde manned by para trained reservists).
10 regional inf bde (each with own border sector).
4 arty bde.
EQUIPMENT:
MBT: 3,960, incl 1,080 *Centurion*, 400 M-48A5, 650 M-60/A1, 750 M-60A3, 100 T-54/-55, 110 T-62, 870 *Merkava* I/II/III.
RECCE: about 400 incl RAMTA RBY, M-2/-3, BRDM-2, ε8 *Fuchs*.
APC: ε6,000 M-113A1/A2, ε80 *Nagmashot*, BTR-50P, ε3,000 M-2/-3 half track.
TOWED ARTY: ε400 incl: 105mm: 60 M-101; 122mm: 70 D-30; 130mm: 80 M-46; 155mm: 40 Soltam M-68/-71, M-839P/-845P.
SP ARTY: 1,284: 105mm: 34 M-7; 155mm: 200 L-33, 100 M-50, 530 M-109A1/A2; 175mm: 200 M-107; 203mm: 220 M-110.
MRL: 100+: 122mm: 40 BM-21; 160mm: LAR-160; 240mm: 30 BM-24; 290mm: MAR-290.
MORTARS: 5,500 incl: 81mm; 120mm: 600; 160mm (some SP).
SSM: 20 *Lance,* some *Jericho* 1/2.
ATGW: 200 *TOW* (incl *Ramta* (M-113) SP), 780 *Dragon*, AT-3 *Sagger*, 25 *Mapats*.
RL: 82mm: B-300.
RCL: 84mm: *Carl Gustav*; 106mm: 250 M-40A1.
AD GUNS: 20mm: 850: incl TCM-20, M-167 *Vulcan*, 35 M-163 *Vulcan*/M-48 *Chaparral* gun/msl systems; 23mm: 100 ZU-23 and 60 ZSU-23-4 SP; 37mm: M-39; 40mm: L-70.
SAM: *Stinger*, 900 *Redeye*, 45 *Chaparral*.

NAVY: 10,000 (3,000 conscripts), 10,000 on mob.
BASES: Haifa, Ashdod, Eilat.
SUBMARINES: 3 *Gal* (UK Vickers) SSC with Mk 37 HWT, *Harpoon* USGW.
PATROL AND COASTAL COMBATANTS: 63:
MISSILE CRAFT: 19 PFM:
2 *Aliya* with 4 *Harpoon*, 4 *Gabriel* SSM, 1 SA-366G *Dauphin* hel (OTHT).
2 *Romat* with 8 *Harpoon*, 8 *Gabriel*.
1 *Hetz* with 8 *Harpoon*, 6 *Gabriel* and *Barak* VLS.
8 *Reshef* with 2–4 *Harpoon*, 4–6 *Gabriel*,
6 *Mivtach/Sa'ar* with 2–4 *Harpoon*, 3–5 *Gabriel*.
PATROL, INSHORE: 44:
About 42 *Super Dvora/Dvora/Dabur* PFI(some with 2 x 324mm TT.
2 Hovercraft.
AMPHIBIOUS: 1:
1 *Bat Sheva* LST type tpt.
Plus craft: 6: 3 *Ashdod* LCT, 3 US type LCM.

MARINES: Naval cdo: 300.

AIR FORCE: 32,000 (21,800 conscripts, mainly in AD), 37,000 on mob; 662 cbt ac (plus perhaps 102 stored), 93 armed hel.

FGA/FIGHTER: 16 sqn:
4 with 112 F-4E (plus 13 in store); (converting 50
  to *Phantom* 2000, some 30 now converted).
2 with 63 F-15 (36 -A, 2 -B, 18 -C, 7 -D);
6 with 209 F-16 (57 -A, 7 -B, 89 -C, 56 -D).
4 with 95 *Kfir* C2/C7 (plus 75 in store);
FGA: 4 sqn with 121 A-4H/N, plus 14 in store.
RECCE: 14 RF-4E.
AEW: 4 E-2C.
EW: 6 Boeing 707 (ELINT/ECM), 1 C-130H, 2 EV-
1E (ECM), 4 IAI-201 (ELINT), 4 RC-12D, 6 RC-
21D (ELINT), 3 RU-21A.
MR: 3 IAI-1124 *Seascan*.
TANKER: 5 Boeing-707, 4 KC-130H.
TRANSPORT: 1 wing: incl 3 Boeing 707, 19 C-47, 24
C-130H, 10 IAI-201, 3 IAI-1124.
LIAISON: 4 *Islander*, 41 Cessna U-206, 2 -172, 2 -
180, 6 Do-27, 9 -28D, 12 *Queen Air* 80.
TRAINING: 6 Cessna 152, 80 CM-170 *Tzukit*, 16* F-
4E, 5* *Kfir* TC2/7, 35 *Super Cub*, 20* TA-4H, 7*
TA-4J.
HELICOPTERS:
ATTACK: 40 AH-1G/S, 35 Hughes 500MD, 18 AH-
64A;
SAR: 2 HH-65A;
TRANSPORT: hy: 32 CH-53 (2 -A, 30 -D); med: 12
UH-1D; lt: 54 Bell 212, 40 Bell 206A.
MISSILES:
ASM: AGM-45 *Shrike*, AGM-62A *Walleye*, AGM-65
Maverick, AGM-78D *Standard*, *Luz*, *Gabriel* III
(mod).
AAM: AIM-7 *Sparrow*, AIM-9 *Sidewinder*, R-530,
Shafrir, *Python* III.
SAM: 17 bty with MIM-23 *Improved HAWK*,
4 bty *Patriot*.

PARAMILITARY:
BORDER POLICE: 6,000; 600 *Walid* 1, BTR-152
APC.
COAST GUARD: ε50; 1 US PBR, 3 other patrol craft.

JORDAN

GDP	1991: D 2.81bn ($4.12bn)	
	1992: D 3.20bn ($4.71bn)	
Growth	1991: 0.5%	1992ε: 10.2%
Inflation	1991: 8.2%	1992: 4.0%
Debt	1991: $8.64bn	1992: $7.68bn
Def bdgt	1992ε: D 357.0m ($525.23m)	
	1993ε: D 373.0m ($541.84m)	
FMA[a]	1993: $91.0m (US)	
$1 = D	1990: 0.664	1991: 0.681
	1992: 0.680	1993: 0.688

D = dinar
[a] Incl $80m as Economic Support.

Population: 4,510,000

	13–17	18–22	23–32
Men	290,000	255,000	388,000
Women	259,000	224,000	337,000

TOTAL ARMED FORCES:
ACTIVE: 100,600.
RESERVES: 35,000 (all services): Army 30,000
(obligation to age 40).

ARMY: 90,000.
2 armd div (each 2 tk, 1 mech inf, 1 arty, 1 AD bde).
2 mech inf div (each 2 mech inf, 1 tk, 1 arty, 1 AD
bde).
1 indep Royal Guards bde.
1 SF bde (3 AB bn).
1 fd arty bde (4 bn).
EQUIPMENT:
MBT: some 1,141: 270 M-47/-48A5 (in store), 218
M-60A1/A3, 360 *Khalid/Chieftain*, 293 *Tariq*
(*Centurion*).
LIGHT TANKS: 19 *Scorpion*.
RECCE: 150 *Ferret*.
AIFV: some 35 BMP-2.
APC: 1,100 M-113, *Saracen*, some 25 EE-11
Urutu.
TOWED ARTY: 123: 105mm: 50 M-102; 155mm: 38
M-114 towed, 10 M-59/M-1; 203mm: 25 M-115
towed (in store).
SP ARTY: 370 incl: 105mm: 30 M-52; 155mm: 20
M-44, 220 M-109A1/A2; 203mm: 100 M-110.
MORTARS: 81mm: 450 (incl 125 SP); 107mm: 50 M-
30; 120mm: 300.
ATGW: 330 *TOW* (incl 70 SP), 310 *Dragon*.
RL: 94mm: 100 LAW-80; 112mm: 900 *APILAS*.
RCL: 106mm: 330 M-40A1.
AD GUNS: 360: 20mm: 100 M-163 *Vulcan* SP;
23mm: 44 ZSU-23-4 SP; 40mm: 216 M-42 SP.
SAM: SA-7B2, 50 SA-8, 50 SA-13, 300 SA-14, 240
SA-16, 250 *Redeye*.

NAVY ε600.
BASE: Aqaba.
PATROL: 5:
3 *Al Hussein* (Vosper 30-m) PFI, 2 Ge *Bremse* PCI⟨
(ex-GDR). Plus 3 Rotork craft (capacity 30 tps) and
other armed boats.

AIR FORCE: 10,000; 106 cbt ac, 24 armed hel.
FGA: 4 sqn with 62 F-5 (55 -E, 7 -F).
FIGHTER: 2 sqn with 32 *Mirage* F-1 (14 -CJ, 16 -EJ,
2 -BJ).
TRANSPORT: 1 sqn with 6 C-130 (2 -B, 4 -H), 3 C-
212A.
VIP: 1 sqn with 2 Boeing 727, 2 *Gulfstream* III, 2
Saberliner 75A, Il-1011 ac; 4 S-76 hel, 2 S-70.
HELICOPTERS: 5 sqn:
ATTACK: 2 sqn with 24 AH-1S (with *TOW* ASM).
TRANSPORT: 1 sqn with 10 S-76, 3 S-70; 1 sqn with
12 AS-332M; 1 sqn with 8 Hughes 500D.
TRAINING: 16 *Bulldog*, 15 C-101, 12 PA-28-161, 6
PA-34-200, *12 F-5A/B.
AD: 2 bde: 14 bty with 126 *Improved HAWK*.

MISSILES:
ASM: AGM-65 *Maverick*, *TOW*.
AAM: AIM-9 *Sidewinder*, R-530, R-550 *Magic*.

FORCES ABROAD:
UN AND PEACEKEEPING:
ANGOLA (UNAVEM II): 6 Observers.
CAMBODIA (UNTAC): 83 civ pol.
CROATIA (UNPROFOR I): 918: 1 inf bn, 31 Observers, 46 civ pol.

PARAMILITARY:
PUBLIC SECURITY DEPARTMENT: (Ministry of Interior) 6,000; some *Scorpion* lt tk, 20 EE-11 *Urutu*, 30 *Saracen* APC.
CIVIL MILITIA 'PEOPLE'S ARMY': 200,000; men 16–65, women 16–45.
PALESTINE LIBERATION ARMY (PLA): 3,000; 1 bde (Palestinians supervised by Jordanian Army).

KUWAIT

GDP	1990: D 5.25bn ($17.87bn)	
	1991: D 3.18bn ($11.21bn)	
	1992: D 6.37bn ($21.73bn)	
Growth	1991: -38%	1992ε: 100%
Inflation	1991ε: 12%	1992ε: 5%
Debt	1991: $12.3bn	1992: $12.7bn
Def exp[a]	1991: D 4.76bn ($16.76bn)	
Def bdgt[b]	1992: D 2.64bn ($9.30bn)	
	1993: D 3.97bn ($13.56bn)	
$1 = D	1990: 0.300	1991: 0.284
	1992: 0.294	1993: 0.300

D = dinar
[a] Incl $7.46bn in off-budget payments for *Operation Desert Storm*. Total war-related expenses are estimated to reach $10.3bn in addition to the $9.3bn defence budget in fiscal 1991–92.
[b] Def budget 1992–93 incl arms procurement costs allocated on 23 August 1992.

Population: 1,481,000 (mid-1991).
Nationals: 620,000. Stateless: 117,000. Foreigners: 744,000.

TOTAL ARMED FORCES:
ACTIVE: 13,700 (ε1,400 conscripts) incl 1,000 central staff.
Terms of service: 2 years.
RESERVES: ε20,000: Obligation to age 40 years. 1 month annual trg.

ARMY: ε9,000.
1 mech bde (-).   1 reserve bde (-)
3 armd bde (-).   1 arty bde (-).
EQUIPMENT:
MBT: 150 M-84.

AIFV: 39 BMP-2.
APC: 37 M-113, 44 *Fahd*.
TOWED ARTY: 105mm: 8 M-101.
SP ARTY: 155mm: 5 M-109A2, 18 GCT.
MORTARS: 81mm; 107mm: 6 M-30 SP.
ATGW: *TOW/Improved TOW* (incl 7 M-901 SP).
RCL: 84mm: 200 *Carl Gustav*.
(Captured eqpt returned by Iraq incl 44 Vickers Mk. 1 MBT, 18 M-109 155mm SP how, 18 AMX-13 155mm SP how. A further 200 Vickers and *Chieftain* tanks are expected. All eqpt is in poor condition.)

NAVY: ε1,200 (incl Coast Guard).
BASE: Ras al Qalaya.
PATROL AND COASTAL COMBATANTS: 4:
MISSILE CRAFT: 2:
1 *Istiqlal* (Ge Lürssen FPB-57) PFM with 2 x MM-40 *Exocet* SSM.
1 *Al Sanbouk* (Ge Lürssen TNC-45) with 2 x MM-40 *Exocet*.
PATROL CRAFT:
INSHORE: 2:
2 *Inttisar* (Aust 31.5m) PFI.
Plus some 55 armed boats.

AIR FORCE: ε2,500
105 cbt ac, 20 armed hel.
FGA: 22 A-4KU/TA-4KU, 40 F-18 (-C 32, -D 8).
FIGHTER: 15 *Mirage* F1CK/BK.
COIN/TRAINING: 1 sqn with 12* *Hawk* 64, 16 Shorts *Tucano*.
TRANSPORT: 3 L-100-30, 1 DC-9.
HELICOPTERS: 3 sqn:
TRANSPORT: 4 AS-332 (tpt/SAR/attack), 9 SA-330.
TRAINING/ATTACK: 16 SA-342 (with *HOT*).

FORCES ABROAD:
UN AND PEACEKEEPING:
SOMALIA (UNOSOM II): ε100.

PARAMILITARY:
NATIONAL GUARD: 5,000 (incl 600 Amiri Guard).

FOREIGN FORCES:
UN (UNIKOM): some 300 tps and Observers from 29 countries.
US: Prepositioned eqpt for 6 coy (3 tk, 3 mech), 1 arty bty, incl 44 MBT, 44 AIFV, 8 arty.

LEBANON

GDP	1991ε: LP 2,543bn ($2.74bn)	
	1992ε: LP 4,831bn ($2.82bn)	
Growth	1991ε: 35%	1992ε: 5.0%

Inflation 1991ε: 45%   1992ε: 90%
Debt   1991: $1.81bn   1992: $2.1bn
Def bdgt[a] 1992: LP 241.69bn ($141.11m)
          1993ε: LP 256.0bn ($146.72m)
Def exp   1992ε: LP 400.0bn ($233.54m)
FMA[b]   1993: $19.6m (US)
$1 = LP   1990: 695.09   1991: 928.2
          1992: 1,712.8   1993: 1,745.0

LP = Lebanese Pound

[a] Def bdgt does not incl aid packages from the West aimed at providing spares and maintenance for existing eqpt worth more than $100m.
[b] Incl $19.1m as Economic Support.

Population: 2,760,000

	13–17	18–22	23–32
Men	150,600	147,200	209,200
Women	147,800	145,700	241,500

Population figures should be treated with caution as available data is scarce and unreliable.

NATIONAL ARMED FORCES:
ACTIVE: 41,300
Terms of Service: 1 year.

ARMY: some 40,000.
11 bde (-) incl Presidential Guard.
1 Ranger, 3 SF regt.
2 arty regt.
1 air aslt regt.
EQUIPMENT:
MBT: some 100 M-48A1/A5, 250 T-54/-55.
LIGHT TANKS: 15 AMX-13 (with 75mm or 105mm guns).
RECCE: 40 *Saladin*, 5 *Ferret*, 60 AML-90, 30 *Staghound*.
APC: 450 M-113, *Saracen*, 60 VAB-VCI, 25 VAB-VTT, 10 AMX-VCI, 50 *Panhard* M3/VTT.
TOWED ARTY: 105mm: 15 M-101A1, 10 M-102; 122mm: 30 M-1938, 10 D-30; 130mm: 25 M-46; 155mm: ε50 incl: some Model 50, 15 M-114A1, 35 M-198.
MRL: 122mm: 5 BM-11, 25 BM-21.
MORTARS: 81mm: 150; 120mm: 130.
ATGW: *ENTAC*, *Milan*, 20 BGM-71A *TOW*.
RL: 85mm: RPG-7; 89mm: M-65.
RCL: 106mm: M-40A1.
AD GUNS: 20mm; 23mm: ZU-23; 40mm: 15 M-42 SP.

NAVY: 500
BASE: Juniye.
PATROL CRAFT: Inshore: 5 PCI⟨, plus about 5 armed boats.
AMPHIBIOUS: Craft only; 2 *Sour* (Fr *Edic*) LCT.

AIR FORCE: Some 800. 3 cbt ac; 5 armed helicopter.

EQUIPMENT: (Numerous ac destroyed 1989–90; op status of remainder is doubtful):
FIGHTERS: 3 *Hunter* (2 F-70, 1 T-66).
HELICOPTERS:
ATTACK: 5 SA-342 with AS-11/-12 ASM;
TRANSPORT: (med): 4 AB-212, 6 SA-330; 2 SA-318, 3 SA-319.
TRAINING: 3 *Bulldog*, 3 CM-170.
TRANSPORT: 1 *Dove*, 1 *Turbo-Commander* 690A.

PARAMILITARY:
INTERNAL SECURITY FORCE (Ministry of Interior): ε9,000 (being reorganised); 30 *Chaimite* APC.
CUSTOMS: 2 *Tracker*, inshore patrol craft .

MILITIAS: Most militias, except *Hizbollah* and the SLA, are being disbanded and hy wpns handed over to the National Army. Reports suggest that large quantities have been placed in hidden stockpiles; these are systematically being seized by govt security forces.
CHRISTIAN:
LEBANESE FORCES MILITIA: ε3,000 (-) (incl The Phalange). Most hy eqpt handed over to the National Army.

MUSLIM:
AMAL (Shi'i, pro-Syria): ε2,000 (-) active; total spt unknown. Most hy eqpt handed over to Syria and the National Army.
HIZBOLLAH ('The Party of God'; Shi'i, fundamentalist, pro-Iranian): ε3,000 (-) active; total spt unknown.
EQUIPMENT incl: APC, arty, RL, RCL, ATGW, (AT-3 *Sagger*) AA guns.

DRUZE:
PROGRESSIVE SOCIALIST PARTY (PSP): several hundred active; total support unknown. Eqpt handed over to the Syrian Army and then to the National Army.

SOUTH LEBANESE ARMY (SLA): ε2,500 active, (mainly Christian, some Shi'i and Druze, trained, equipped and supported by Israel, occupies the 'Security Zone' between Israeli border and area controlled by UNIFIL)
EQUIPMENT:
MBT: 30 T-54/-55.
APC: M-113, BTR-50.
TOWED ARTY: 122mm: D-30; 130mm: M-46; 155mm: M-1950.

FOREIGN FORCES:
UNITED NATIONS (UNIFIL): some 5,400; Contingents from Fiji, Finland, France, Ghana, Ireland, Italy, Nepal, Norway, Poland and Sweden.

SYRIA: 30,000.
BEIRUT: 1 SF div HQ, elm 1 armd bde, elm 6 SF regt.
METN: elm 1 mech bde.
BEKAA: 1 mech div HQ, elm 2 mech inf bde.
TRIPOLI: 2 SF regt.
IRAN: Revolutionary Guards: ε900 incl locally recruited Shi'i Lebanese.
PALESTINIAN GROUPS:
All significant Palestinian factions are listed here irrespective of the countr(ies) in which they are based. The faction leader is given after the full title. Strengths are estimates of the number of active 'fighters'; these could be trebled perhaps to give an all-told figure. In 1991, the Lebanon Armed Forces, backed by the Syrians, entered refugee camps in Southern Lebanon to disarm many Palestinian groups of their heavier weapons, such as tanks, artillery, and armoured personnel carriers.
PALESTINIAN LIBERATION ORGANISATION:
FATAH: Political wing of the PLO.
PLF (Palestine Liberation Front, Al-Abas): ε300–400. Based in Iraq.
PNLA (Palestine National Liberation Army): 7,000. Based in Lebanon, Libya, Jordan, Iraq and elsewhere throughout the region. The PNLA is effectively the military wing of the PLO. Its units in various Middle East countries are closely monitored by host nations' armed forces.
DFLP (Democratic Front for Liberation of Palestine, Hawatmah): ε500–600. Based in Syria, Lebanon, elsewhere.
FATAH (dissidents, Abu Musa): 1,000. Based in Syria and Lebanon.
PFLP (Popular Front for Liberation of Palestine, Habash): ε500. Based in Syria, Lebanon, Occupied Territories.
PFLP (GC) (Popular Front for Liberation of Palestine (General Command, Jibril): ε600. Based in Syria, Lebanon, elsewhere.
PSF (Popular Struggle Front, Ghisha): ε600–700. Based in Syria.
SAIQA (al-Khadi): ε1,000. Based in Syria.

GROUPS OPPOSED TO THE PLO:
FRC (Fatah Revolutionary Council, Abu Nidal Group): 300. Based in Lebanon, Syria, Iraq, elsewhere.
HAMAS ε300. Based in Israeli-occupied territories.
PIJ (Palestine Islamic Jihad): ε350. Based in Israeli-occupied territories.
PLA (Palestine Liberation Army): ε1,100. Based in Syria.

LIBYA

GDP	1991: D 8.60bn ($32.09bn)	
	1992ε: D 8.80bn ($29.24bn)	
Growth	1991ε: 4.7%	1992ε: 4.9%
Inflation	1991ε: 10.2%	1992ε: 10.0%
Debt	1989: $5.38bn	

Def bdgt	1989ε: D 440m ($1.51bn)	
	1990ε: D 490m ($1.82bn)	
$1 = D$ᵃ	1990: 0.270	1991: 0.268
	1992: 0.294	1993: 0.301

D = dinar
ᵃ The real value of the dinar is estimated at approximately $1 = 0.600

Population: 5,088,000

	13–17	18–22	23–32
Men	293,400	244,500	181,000
Women	282,500	234,300	167,800

TOTAL ARMED FORCES:
ACTIVE: 70,000.
Terms of service: selective conscription, 2 years.
RESERVES: People's Militia, some 40,000.

ARMY: 40,000 (ε25,000 conscripts).
6 Military Districts.
33 bde (11 armd, 17 mech, 3 inf, 2 National Guard).

40 tk bn.	45 arty bn.
40 mech inf bn.	14 AD arty bn.
19 para/cdo bn.	
7 SSM bde.	

EQUIPMENT:
MBT: 2,300 (incl 1,200 in store): 1,700 T-54/-55, 350 T-62, 250 T-72.
RECCE: 250 BRDM-2, 380 EE-9 *Cascavel*.
AIFV: 1,000 BMP-1.
APC: 800 BTR-50/-60, 100 OT-62/-64, 40 M-113, 100 EE-11 *Urutu*.
TOWED ARTY: some 720: 105mm: some 60 M-101; 122mm: 270 D-30, 60 D-74; 130mm: 330 M-46.
SP ARTY: some 350: 122mm: 130 2S1; 152mm: 40 2S3, *DANA*; 155mm: 160 *Palmaria*, 20 M-109.
MRL: some 700: 107mm: Type 63; 122mm: BM-21/RM-70, BM-11.
MORTARS: 82mm; 120mm: M-43; 160mm; 240mm: M-240.
SSM launchers: 40 *FROG*-7, 80 *Scud* B.
ATGW: 3,000: *Milan*, AT-3 *Sagger* (incl BRDM SP), AT-4 *Spigot*.
RCL: 106mm: 220 M-40A1.
AD GUNS: 600: 23mm: ZU-23, ZSU-23-4 SP; 30mm: M-53/59 SP; 57mm: 92 S-60.
SAM: SA-7/-9/-13, 24 quad *Crotale*.
DEPLOYMENT:
Aouzou Strip: ε4,000.

NAVY: 8,000, incl Coast Guard.
BASES: Tripoli, Benghazi, Derna, Tobruk, Sidi Bilal, Al Khums.
SUBMARINES: 5 *Al Badr* † (Sov *Foxtrot*) with 533mm and 406mm TT (plus 1 in refit at Riga).
FRIGATES: 3:
1 *Dat Assawari* † (UK Vosper Mk 7) with 2 x 3 ASTT; plus 4 *Otomat* SSM, 1 x 114mm gun.
2 *Al Hani* (Sov *Koni*) with 4 x ASTT, 2 x ASW RL; plus 4 SS-N-2C SSM.

PATROL AND COASTAL COMBATANTS: 39:
CORVETTES: 7:
4 *Assad al Bihar*† (It *Assad*) with 4 *Otomat* SSM;
plus 2 x 3 ASTT (A244S LWT).
3 *Ean al Gazala* (Sov *Nanuchka*-II) with 2 x 2 SS-N-2C *Styx* SSM.
MISSILE CRAFT: 24
9 *Sharaba* (Fr *Combattante* II) with 4 *Otomat* SSM;
12 *Al Katum* (Sov *Osa* II) with 4 SS-N-2C SSM;
3 *Susa* with 8 SS-12M SSM.
PATROL CRAFT: 8:
INSHORE: 8: 4 *Garian*, 3 *Benina*, 1 Sov *Poluchat*.
MINE WARFARE: 8 *Ras al Gelais* (Sov *Natya* MSO).
(*El Temsah* and about 5 other ro-ro tpt have mine-laying capability)
AMPHIBIOUS: 5:
2 *Ibn Ouf* LST, capacity 240 tps, 11 tk, 1 SA-316B hel.
3 Sov *Polnocny* LSM, capacity 180 tps, 6 tk.
Plus craft: 3 LCT.
SUPPORT AND MISCELLANEOUS: 9:
1 log spt/dock, 1 salvage, 1 diving spt, 1 *El Temsah* and about 5 other ro-ro tpt.

NAVAL AVIATION: 30 armed hel.
HELICOPTERS: 2 sqn:
1 with 25 Mi-14 (ASW);
1 with 5 SA-321.

AIR FORCE: 22,000 (incl Air Defence); (some contract Syrian pilots, Russian, N. Korean and Pakistani instructors); 409 cbt ac, 45 armed hel (many ac in store, number n.k.)
BOMBERS: 1 sqn with 5 Tu-22.
FGA: 7 sqn:
40 MiG-23BN, 15 MiG-23U, 22 *Mirage* 5D/DE, 10 *Mirage* 5DD, 8 *Mirage* F-1AD, 16 Su-24, 45 Su-20/-22.
FIGHTER: 9 sqn:
50 MiG-21, 75 MiG-23, 60 MiG-25, 3 -25U, 12 *Mirage* F-1ED, 6 -BD.
COIN: 1 sqn with 30 J-1 *Jastreb*.
RECCE: 1 sqn with 5 *Mirage* 5DR, 7 MiG-25R.
TRANSPORT: 2 sqn:
11 An-26, 12 Lockheed (7 C-130H, 2 L-100-20, 3 L-100-30), 20 G-222, 18 Il-76, 15 L-410.
HELICOPTERS:
ATTACK HEL: 35 Mi-24, 10 Mi-35.
TRANSPORT HEL: hy: 18 CH-47C; **med:** 50 Mi-4, 7 Mi-8; **lt:** 10 Mi-2, 11 SA-316, 5 AB-206.
TRAINING:
89 *Galeb* G-2 ac; 20 Mi-2 hel; other ac incl 2 Tu-22, 150 L-39ZO, 77 SF-260WL.
MISSILES:
ASM: AT-2 *Swatter* ATGW (hel-borne), AS-9.
AAM: AA-2 *Atoll*, AA-6 *Acrid*, AA-7 *Apex*, AA-8 *Aphid*, R-530, R-550 *Magic*.

AIR DEFENCE COMMAND:
'Senezh' AD comd and control system.

3 bde with SA-5A: each 2 bn of 6 launchers, some 4 AD arty gun bn; radar coy.
3 Regions: 2 bde each 18 SA-2; 2–3 bde each 12 twin SA-3; ε3 bde each 20–24 SA-6/-8.

PARAMILITARY:
LIWA HARIS AL-JAMAHIRIYA (Revolution Guard Corps): some 3,000: T-54/-55/-62/-72, armd cars, APC, MRL, ZSU-23-4, SA-8 (Army inventory).
PEOPLE'S CAVALRY FORCE: parade unit.
CUSTOMS/COAST GUARD (Naval control): A few patrol craft incl in naval totals, plus armed boats.

MAURITANIA

GDP	1991: OM 93.05bn ($1.14bn)		
	1992ε: OM 104.22bn ($1.20bn)		
Growth	1991ε: 3.7%	1992: 2.4%	
Inflation	1991: 5.7%	1992ε: 10.9%	
Debt	1990: $2.21bn	1991: $2.3bn	
Def exp	1991: OM 3.24bn ($39.55m)		
	1992ε: OM 3.22bn ($36.98m)		
FMA	1988: $10.13m (US, Fr)		
$1 = OM	1990: 80.609	1991: 81.946	
	1992: 87.082	1993: 113.816	

OM = ouguiyas

Population: 2,138,800

	13–17	18–22	23–32
Men	118,500	103,300	150,600
Women	112,700	98,200	151,300

TOTAL ARMED FORCES:
ACTIVE: ε15,600.
Terms of service: conscription (2 years) authorised.

ARMY: 15,000.
6 Military Regions.

7 mot inf bn.	3 arty bn.
8 inf bn.	4 AD arty bty.
1 para/cdo bn.	1 Presidential sy bn.
2 Camel Corps bn.	1 engr coy.
1 armd recce sqn	

EQUIPMENT:
MBT: 35 T-54/-55.
RECCE: 20 AML-60, 40 -90, 40 *Saladin*, 5 *Saracen*.
TOWED ARTY: 105mm: 35 M-101A1/HM-2; 122mm: 20 D-30, 20 D-74.
MORTARS: 81mm: 70; 120mm: 30.
ATGW: *Milan*.
RCL: 75mm: M-20; 106mm: M-40A1.
AD GUNS: 23mm: 20 ZU-23-2; 37mm: 15 M-1939; 57mm: S-60; 100mm: 12 KS-19.
SAM: SA-7.

NAVY: 400.
BASE: Nouadhibou.
PATROL CRAFT: 6:
1 *N'Madi* (UK *Jura*) PCO (fishery protection).
3 *El Vaiz* (Sp *Barcelo*) PFI†.
1 *El Nasr* (Fr *Patra*) PCI.
1 *Z'Bar* (Ge *Neustadt*) PFI.
Plus 3 armed boats.

AIR FORCE: 150
7 cbt ac, no armed hel.
COIN: 5 BN-2 *Defender*, 2 FTB-337 *Milirole*.
MR: 2 *Cheyenne* II.
TRANSPORT: 2 Cessna F-337, 1 DHC-5D, 1 *Gulfstream* II.

PARAMILITARY:
GENDARMERIE ε3,000; 6 regional coy (Ministry of Interior).
NATIONAL GUARD: (Ministry of Interior) 2,000 plus 1,000 auxiliaries.

MOROCCO

GDP	1991: D 240.76bn ($27.65bn)			
	1992ε: D 242.0bn ($28.34bn)			
Growth	1991: 5.1%		1992ε: -3.0%	
Inflation	1991: 6.5%		1992: 2.8%	
Debt	1991: $21.47bn		1992: $21.20bn	
Def exp[a]	1990ε: D 11.10bn ($1.35bn)			
Def bdgt	1992: D 9.76bn ($1.14bn)			
	1993: D 10.09bn ($1.12bn)			
FMA[b]	1993: $61.1m (US)			
$1 = D	1990: 8.242		1991: 8.707	
	1992: 8.538		1993: 8.979	

D = dirham
[a] Incl border and internal security costs.
[b] Incl $20m as Economic Support.

Population: 27,113,000			
	13–17	*18–22*	*23–32*
Men	1,542,000	1,372,000	2,188,000
Women	1,486,000	1,321,000	2,177,000

TOTAL ARMED FORCES:
ACTIVE: 195,500.
Terms of service: conscription 18 months authorised; most enlisted personnel are volunteers.
RESERVES: Army: 150,000: obligation to age 50.

ARMY: 175,000 (ε100,000 conscripts).
2 Comd (Northern Zone, Southern Zone).
3 mech inf bde.
2 para bde.
1 lt sy bde.

8 mech inf regt.
Independent units:
10 arty bn.   3 mot (camel corps) bn.
1 AD gp.   3 cav bn.
10 armd bn.   1 mtn bn.
37 inf bn.   7 engr bn.
6 cdo units.
ROYAL GUARD: 1,500: 1 bn, 1 cav sqn.
EQUIPMENT:
MBT: 224 M-48A5, 60 M-60A1.
LIGHT TANKS: 5 AMX-13, 100 SK-105 *Kuerassier*.
RECCE: 16 EBR-75, 80 AMX-10RC, 190 AML-90, 38 AML-60-7, 20 M-114.
AIFV: 30 *Ratel* 20, some 30 -90, 45 VAB-VCI, 10 AMX-10P.
APC: 420 M-113, 320 VAB-VTT, some 45 OT-62/-64 may be op.
TOWED ARTY: 105mm: 30 lt (L-118), 20 M-101, 36 M-1950; 130mm: 18 M-46; 155mm: 20 M-114, 30 FH-70.
SP ARTY: 105mm: 5 Mk 61; 155mm: 98 F-3, 44 M-109, 20 M-44.
MRL: 122mm: 37 BM-21.
MORTARS: 81mm: 1,100; 120mm: 600 (incl 20 VAB SP).
ATGW: 440 *Dragon*, 80 *Milan*, 150 *TOW* (incl 42 SP), *HOT*, AT-3 *Sagger*.
RL: 66mm: *LAW*; 89mm: M-20 3.5-in.
RCL: 106mm: 350 M-40A1.
ATK GUNS: 90mm: 28 M-56; 100mm: 8 SU-100 SP.
AD GUNS: 14.5mm: 180 ZPU-2, 20 ZPU-4; 20mm: 40 M-167, 60 M-163 *Vulcan* SP; 23mm: 90 ZU-23-2; 100mm: 15 KS-19 towed.
SAM: 37 M-54 SP *Chaparral*, 70 SA-7.

NAVY: 7,000, incl 1,500 marines.
BASES: Casablanca, Agadir, Al Hoceima, Dakhla, Tangier.
FRIGATE: 1 *Lt Col. Errhamani* (Sp *Descubierta*) with 2 x 3 ASTT (Mk 46 LWT), 1 x 2 375mm AS mor; (fitted for but seldom with 4 x MM-38 *Exocet* SSM).
PATROL AND COASTAL COMBATANTS: 29:
CORVETTES: 2: 2 It *Assad* (ex-Iraqi Navy) with 3 x 2 *Otomat* SSM; plus 2 x3 ASTT (A244S LWT).
MISSILE CRAFT: 4 *Cdt El Khattabi* (Sp *Lazaga* 58-m) PFM with 4 x MM-38 *Exocet* SSM.
PATROL: 23:
COASTAL: 13:
2 *Okba* (Fr PR-72) PFC.
6 *LV Rabhi* (Sp 58-m B-200D) PCC.
5 *El Hahiq* (Dk *Osprey* 55) PCC.
(incl 2 with customs).
INSHORE: 10 *El Wacil* (Fr P-32) PFI⟨.
(incl 4 with customs).
AMPHIBIOUS: 3 *Ben Aicha* (Fr *Champlain BATRAL*) LSM, capacity 140 tps, 7 tk.
Plus craft; 1 LCU.
SUPPORT: 3: 2 log spt, 1 tpt.

MARINES: (1,500). 1 naval inf bn.

AIR FORCE: 13,500; 93 cbt ac, 24 armed hel.
FGA: 2 sqn.
1 with 15 F-5E, 3 F-5F.
1 with 14 *Mirage* F-1EH.
FIGHTER: 1 sqn with 15 *Mirage* F-1CH.
COIN: 2 sqn:
1 with 23 *Alpha Jet*; 1 with 23 CM-170.
RECCE: 1 sqn with 4 OV-10, 2 C-130H (with side-looking radar).
EW: 1 C-130 (ELINT), 1 *Falcon* 20 (ELINT).
TANKER: 1 Boeing 707; 2 KC-130H (tpt/tanker).
TRANSPORT: 11 C-130H, 7 CN-235, 3 Do-28, 3 *Falcon* 20, 1 *Falcon* 50 (VIP), 2 *Gulfstream* II (VIP), 5 *King Air* 100, 3 *King Air* 200.
HELICOPTERS:
ATTACK: 24 SA-342 (12 with *HOT*, 12 with cannon).
TRANSPORT: hy: 7 CH-47; **med**: 27 SA-330, 27 AB-205A; **lt**: 20 AB-206, 3 AB-212.
TRAINING: 10 AS-202, 2 CAP-10, 4 CAP-230, 12 T-34C.
LIAISON: 2 *King Air* 200.
AAM: AIM-9B/D/J *Sidewinder*, R-530, R-550 *Magic*.
ASM: AGM-65B *Maverick* (for F-5E), *HOT*.

DEPLOYMENT:
ARMY:
Northern Zone: 2 para, 1 lt sy bde; 3 inf, 2 cav, 3 armd, 1 arty, 1 camel corps bn.
Southern Zone: 3 mech inf bde; 6 mech inf regt; 34 inf, 1 cav, 7 armd, 1 arty, 2 camel corps bn; 6 cdo units.

FORCES ABROAD:
EQUATORIAL GUINEA: 360: 1 bn.
UAE: some 2,000.
UN AND PEACEKEEPING:
ANGOLA (UNAVEM II): 1 Observer.
CAMBODIA (UNTAC): 98 civ pol.
SOMALIA (UNOSOM II): 1,264: 1 inf regt.

PARAMILITARY: 40,000.
GENDARMERIE ROYALE: 10,000;
1 bde, 2 mobile gp, air sqn, coast guard unit; 18 boats, 2 *Rallye* ac; 3 SA-315, 3 SA-316, 2 SA-318, 6 *Gazelle*, 6 SA-330, 2 SA-360 hel.
FORCE AUXILIAIRE: 30,000 incl Mobile Intervention Corps (5,000).
CUSTOMS/COAST GUARD: 2 PCC, 4 PFI (included in Navy nos) plus boats.

OPPOSITION:
POLISARIO: Military Wing: Sahrawi People's Liberation Army: 9,000 (perhaps 4,000 active) org in bn.
EQUIPMENT: T-55, T-62 tk; BMP-1, 20–30 EE-9 *Cascavel* MICV; D-30/M-30 122mm how; BM-21 122mm MRL; 120mm, 160mm mor; AT-3 *Sagger* ATGW; ZSU-23-2 23mm SP AA guns; SA-6/-7/-9 SAM.
(Captured Moroccan eqpt incl AML-90, *Eland* armd recce, *Ratel* 20, Panhard APC, Steyr SK-105 *Kuerassier* lt tks.)

FOREIGN FORCES:
UN (MINURSO): some 330 in Western Sahara from 26 countries.

OMAN

GDP	1991: R 3.94bn ($10.24bn)		
	1992: R 4.29bn ($11.17bn)		
Growth	1991: -2.6%	1992: 4.0%	
Inflation	1991: 7.2%	1992: 3.5%	
Debt	1991: $2.56bn	1992: $2.48bn	
Def bdg[a]	1992: R 664m ($1.73bn)		
	1993: R 630m ($1.64bn)		
Def exp	1992: R 753m ($1.96bn)		
FMA[b]	1993: $6.1m (US)		
$1 = R	1989–93 0.3845		
R = rial			

[a] Excl $1.8bn military subsidy from GCC between 1984 and 1994, shared with Bahrain.
[b] Incl $5m as Economic Support.

Population: ε1,762,000

	13–17	18–22	23–32
Men	94,200	74,900	124,500
Women	90,200	70,500	106,900

TOTAL ARMED FORCES:
ACTIVE: 36,700 (incl Royal Household tps, and some 3,700 foreign personnel).

ARMY: 20,000. (Regt are of bn size.)
1 div HQ.
2 bde HQ.
2 armd regt (3 tk sqn).
1 armd recce regt (3 armd car sqn).
4 arty (2 fd, 1 med (2 bty), 1 AD (2 bty)) regt.
8 inf regt (incl 3 Baluch).
1 inf recce regt (3 recce coy), 2 indep recce coy.
1 fd engr regt (3 sqn).
1 AB regt.
Musandam Security Force (indep rifle coy).
EQUIPMENT:
MBT: 6 M-60A1, 43 M-60A3, 24 *Qayid al-Ardh* (*Chieftain* Mk 7/-15).
LIGHT TANKS: 37 *Scorpion*, 6 VBC-90.
AIFV: 4 VAB PC.
APC: 2 VAB VCI.
TOWED ARTY: 96: 105mm: 42 ROF lt; 122mm: 30 D-30; 130mm: 12 M-46, 12 Type 59-1.

MORTARS: 81mm; 107mm: 20 M-30 4.2-in.
ATGW: 18 *TOW*, 32 *Milan* (incl 2 VCAC).
AD GUNS: 20mm (incl 2 VAB VD); 23mm: 4 ZU-23-2; 40mm: 12 *Bofors* L/60.
SAM: *Blowpipe*, 28 *Javelin*, SA-7.

NAVY: 3,500.
BASES: Seeb (HQ), Wudam (main base), Raysut, Ghanam Island, Alwi.
PATROL AND COASTAL COMBATANTS: 12:
MISSILE CRAFT: 4 *Dhofar*, 1 with 2 x 3 MM-40, 3 with 2 x 4 MM-40 *Exocet* SSM.
PATROL: 8:
4 *Al Wafi* (Brooke-Marine 37-m) PCI, 4 *Seeb* (Vosper 25-m) PC⟨.
AMPHIBIOUS: 2:
1 *Nasr el Bahr* LST, capacity 240 tps, 7 tk, hel deck (effectively in reserve).
1 *Al Munassir* LST, capacity 200 tps, 8 tk, hel deck (non-op, harbour trg).
Plus craft; 3 LCM, 2 LCU.
SUPPORT: 2: 1 spt, 1 trg with hel deck.

AIR FORCE: 3,500; 45 cbt ac (plus 10 in store), no armed hel.
FGA: 2 sqn with 15 *Jaguar* S(O) Mk 1, 1 GR1, 4 T-2 (plus 10 in store).
FGA/RECCE: 1 sqn with 10 *Hunter* FGA-73, 3 T-67.
COIN/TRAINING: 1 sqn with 12* BAC-167 Mk 82, 7 BN-2 *Defender*.
TRANSPORT: 3 sqn:
1 with 3 BAC-111; 2 with 15 *Skyvan* 3M (7 radar-equipped, for MR), 3 C-130H.
HELICOPTERS: 2 med tpt sqn with 20 AB-205, 3 AB-206, 3 AB-212, 10 AB-214.
TRAINING: 4 AS-202-18.
AD: 2 sqn with 28 *Rapier* SAM, *Martello* radar.
MISSILES:
ASM: *Exocet* AM-39.
AAM: AIM-9P *Sidewinder*.

ROYAL HOUSEHOLD: 6,000.
Royal Guard bde: (4,500).
2 SF regt: (700).
Royal Yacht Squadron (based Muscat): (150);
1 Royal Yacht, 3,800t with hel deck.
1 *Fulk Al Salamah* tps and veh tpt with 2 AS-332C *Puma* hel.
Royal Flight: (250); Boeing-747 SP, 1 DC-8-73CF, 2 *Gulfstream* IV ac, 3 AS-332, 3 SA-330 hel.

PARAMILITARY:
TRIBAL HOME GUARD (*Firqat*): 3,500.
POLICE COAST GUARD: 400: 15 AT-105 APC, 18 inshore patrol craft.
POLICE AIR WING: 1 Boeing 727-100, 2 DHC-5D, 1 Do-228, 2 CASA 235M, 1 *Gulfstream* GII ac, 3 Bell 205A, 6 Bell 214ST.

QATAR

GDP	1991:	R 24.29bn ($6.67bn)	
	1992:	R 25.75bn ($7.07bn)	
Growth	1991:	-9.3%	1992ε: 4.0%
Inflation	1991:	3.0%	1992: 2.0%
Debt	1991:	$1.85bn	1992: $1.89bn
Def bdgt	1991ε:	R 3.4bn ($934.07m)	
$1 =R	1989–93:	3.640	
R = rial			

Population: 481,600

	13–17	18–22	23–32
Men	20,900	18,600	43,400
Women	19,200	15,800	26,200

TOTAL ARMED FORCES:
ACTIVE: 9,500.

ARMY: 8,000.
1 Royal Guard regt.　1 SF 'bn' (coy).
1 tk bn.　1 fd arty regt.
3 mech inf bn.　1 SAM bty with *Rapier*.
EQUIPMENT:
MBT: 24 AMX-30.
AIFV: 30 AMX-10P.
APC: 160 VAB, 22 *Saracen*.
TOWED ARTY: 155mm: 12 G5.
SP ARTY: 155mm: 22 AMX Mk F-3.
MRL: 4 *ASTROS* II.
MORTARS: 81mm (some SP); 120mm: 15.
ATGW: 100 *Milan*, *HOT* (incl 24 VAB SP).
RCL: 84mm: *Carl Gustav*.
SAM: *Blowpipe*, 12 *Stinger*.

NAVY: ε700 (incl Marine Police).
BASE: Doha.
PATROL AND COASTAL COMBATANTS: 9:
MISSILE CRAFT: 3 *Damsah* (Fr *Combattante* III) with 2 x 4 MM-40 *Exocet* SSM.
PATROL, INSHORE: 6:
6 *Barzan* (UK 33-m) PCI.
Plus some 44 small craft operated by marine police.
AMPHIBIOUS: Craft only, 1 LCT.
COAST DEFENCE: 4 x 4 MM-40 *Exocet* bty.

AIR FORCE: 800; 18 cbt ac, 20 armed hel.
FGA: Tac spt unit with 6 *Alpha Jet*.
FIGHTER: 1 AD sqn with 12 *Mirage* F1 (11 -E, 1 -D).
TRANSPORT: 1 sqn with 2 Boeing 707, 1 -727.
HELICOPTERS:
ATTACK: 12 SA-342L (with *HOT*), 8 *Commando* Mk 3 (*Exocet*).
TRANSPORT: 4 *Commando* (3 Mk 2A tpt, 1 Mk 2C VIP).
LIAISON: 2 SA-341G.

MISSILES:
ASM: *Exocet* AM-39, *HOT*.
SAM: 6 *Roland, Rapier*.

SAUDI ARABIA

GDP	1991: R 408.76bn ($109.15bn)
	1992ε: R 458.0bn ($122.30bn)
Growth	1991: 6.6% 1992: 4.5%
Inflation	1991: 4.9% 1992: -0.5%
Debt	1990: $22.50bn 1991: $27.0bn
Def exp[a]	1990ε: R 86.75bn ($23.16bn)
	1991ε: R 132.98bn ($35.51bn)
Def bdgt[b]	1992: R 54.27bn ($14.49bn)
	1993: R 61.64bn ($16.46bn)
$1 = R	1989–93: 3.745
R = rial	

[a] Def exp 1990, 1991 incl costs of contributions to Allies for the Gulf War and costs of arms purchases made during the war.
[b] No budget was announced for 1991, projection for 1991 has been carried over from previous year. The estimated defence expenditure for 1992 may be as high as $35bn if arms purchases and defence construction projects are included.

Saudi population: 12,304,800[c] (72.7% of total)

	13–17	18–22	23–32
Men	556,500	511,000	811,000
Women	483,600	484,000	773,000

[c] Official census statistics (September 1992) put the number of non-Saudi residents as high as 4,624,459 (27.3% of total).

TOTAL ARMED FORCES:
ACTIVE: 101,000 (plus 57,000 active National Guard).

ARMY: 68,000.
3 armd bde (each 3 tk, 1 mech, 1 fd arty, 1 recce, 1 AD, 1 ATK bn).
5 mech bde (each 3 mech, 1 tk, 1 fd arty, 1 AD, 1 spt bn).
1 AB bde (2 AB bn, 3 SF coy).
1 Royal Guard regt (3 bn).
8 arty bn.
EQUIPMENT:
MBT: 696: 290 AMX-30, 406 M-60A3.
RECCE: 235 AML-60/-90.
AIFV: 570+ AMX-10P, 400 M-2 *Bradley*.
APC: 1,700 M-113 (incl variants), 30 EE-11 *Urutu*, 150 Panhard M-3.
TOWED ARTY: 105mm: 100 M-101/-102 (in store); 155mm: 40 FH-70 (in store), 90 M-198, M-114; 203mm: M-115 (in store).
SP ARTY: 170: 155mm: 110 M-109A1B/A2, 60 GCT.
MRL: 60 *ASTROS II*.

MORTARS: 400 incl: 107mm: M-30 4.2-in.; 120mm: Brandt.
SSM: Some 10 Ch CSS-2 (40 msl).
ATGW: BGM-71A *TOW* (incl 200 VCC-1 SP), M-47 *Dragon*, *HOT* (incl 90 AMX-10P SP).
RCL: 84mm: 300 *Carl Gustav*; 90mm: M-67; 106mm: M-40A1.
AVIATION:
HELICOPTERS: 12 AH-64, 11 S-70A-1, 10 UH-60 (tpt, 4 medevac), 6 SA-365N (medevac), 15 Bell 406CS.
SAM: *Crotale, Stinger*, 500 *Redeye*.

NAVY: 11,000 (incl 1,500 marines);
BASES: Riyadh (HQ Naval Forces). Western Fleet: Jiddah (HQ), Yanbu. Eastern Fleet: Al-Jubayl (HQ), Ad-Dammam, Ras al Mishab, Ras al Ghar.
FRIGATES: 8:
4 *Madina* (Fr F.2000) with 4 x 533mm, 2 x 406mm ASTT, 1 x AS-365N hel (AS 15 ASM); plus 8 *Otomat-2* SSM, 1 x 100mm gun.
4 *Badr* (US Tacoma) (ASUW) with 2 x 4 *Harpoon* SSM, 2 x 3 ASTT (Mk 46 LWT).
PATROL AND COASTAL COMBATANTS: 29:
MISSILE CRAFT: 9 *As Siddiq* (US 58-m) PFM with 2 x 2 *Harpoon*.
TORPEDO CRAFT: 3 *Dammam* (Ge *Jaguar*) with 4 x 533mm TT (trg, incl 1 in reserve).
PATROL CRAFT: 17 US Halter Marine PCI⟨ (some with coast guard).
MINE WARFARE: 6:
2 *Al Jawf* (UK *Sandown* MCC).
4 *Addriyah* (US MSC-322) MCC.
AMPHIBIOUS: Craft only; 4 LCU, 4 LCM.
SUPPORT AND MISCELLANEOUS: 7:
2 *Boraida* (mod Fr *Durance*) AO with 1 or 2 hel, 3 ocean tugs, 1 salvage tug, 1 Royal Yacht with hel deck.

NAVAL AVIATION: 20 armed hel.
HELICOPTERS: 24 AS-365N, (4 SAR, 20 with AS-15TT ASM), 12 AS 332B/F (6 tpt, 6 with AM-39 *Exocet*).

MARINES: (1,500): 1 inf regt (2 bn), with 140 BMR-600P.

AIR FORCE: 18,000+; 296 cbt ac, no armed hel.
FGA: 6 sqn:
3 with 51 F-5E;
3 with 48 *Tornado* IDS.
FIGHTER: 3 sqn with 78 F-15C.
2 with 24 *Tornado* ADV.
RECCE: 1 sqn with 10 RF-5E.
AEW: 1 sqn with 5 E-3A.
TANKER: 8 KE-3A (tkr/tpt), 8 KC-130H.
OCU: 2 with 14* F-5B, 21* F-5F, 20* F-15D.
TRANSPORT: 3 sqn:
41 C-130 (7 -E, 34 -H), 5 L-100-30HS (hospital ac), 35 C-212.

HELICOPTERS: 2 sqn: 22 AB-205, 25 AB-206B, 27 AB-212, 20 KV-107 (SAR, tpt).
TRAINING: 32 BAC-167, 30* *Hawk* Mk 65, 30 PC-9, 1 *Jetstream* 31.
ROYAL FLIGHT:
ac: 4 BAe 125, 2 C-140, 4 CN-235, 2 *Gulfstream* III, 2 *Learjet* 35, 6 VC-130H, 1 Cessna 310.
hel: 3 AS-61, AB-212, 1 -S70.
MISSILES:
ASM: AGM-65 *Maverick*, AS-15.
ARM: AGM-45 *Shrike*, ALARM.
AAM: AIM-9J/L/P *Sidewinder*, AIM-7F *Sparrow*, ALARM.

AIR DEFENCE FORCES: 4,000:
33 SAM bty:
16 with 128 *Improved HAWK*;
17 with 68 *Shahine* fire units and AMX-30SA 30mm SP AA guns.
73 *Shahine/Crotale* fire units as static defence.
EQUIPMENT:
AD GUNS: 20mm: 92 M-163 *Vulcan*; 30mm: 50 AMX-30SA; 35mm: 128; 40mm: 150 L/70 (in store).
SAM: 141 *Shahine*, 128 MIM-23B *Improved HAWK*, 40 *Crotale*.

NATIONAL GUARD: (Directly under Royal command) 77,000 (57,000 active; 20,000 tribal levies):
2 mech inf bde, each 4 all arms bn.
6 inf bde.
1 ceremonial cav sqn.
EQUIPMENT:
APC: 1,100 V-150 *Commando*.
TOWED ARTY: 105mm: 40 M-102; 155mm: 30 M-198.
RCL: 106mm: M-40A1.
ATGW: *TOW*.

FORCES ABROAD:
UN AND PEACEKEEPING:
SOMALIA (UNOSOM II): 678: 1 inf bn.

PARAMILITARY:
FRONTIER FORCE: 10,500.
COAST GUARD: (4,500) 4 *Al Jouf* PFI, about 30 PCI(, about 20 hovercraft, 1 trg, 1 Royal Yacht (5,000t) with 1 Bell 206B hel, about 350 armed boats.
GENERAL CIVIL DEFENCE ADMINISTRA-TION UNITS: 10 KV-107 hel.
SPECIAL SECURITY FORCE: 500: UR-416 APC.

FOREIGN FORCES:
PENINSULAR SHIELD FORCE: ε5,000; 1 inf bde (elm from all GCC states).
FRANCE: 130. 9 *Mirage* 2000C, 1 C 135, 1 N-262.
US: Air Force units on rotational det, numbers vary (incl: F-4G, F-15, F-16, F-117, C-130, KC-135, U-2 JSTARS) 1 *Patriot* bn.
UK: 6 *Tornado* GRI, 2 VC-10 (tkr).

SOMALI REPUBLIC

GDP	1989ε: S sh 295.76bn ($601.8m)	
	1990ε: S sh 1,138.80bn ($595.75m)	
Growth	1989: -5%	1990ε: -2%
Inflation	1990ε: 200%	1991ε: 300%
Debt	1991: $2.44bn	1992: $2.17bn
Def exp	1986ε: S sh 6.0bn ($83m)	
Def bdgt	1988ε: S sh 7.92bn ($46m)	
	1989ε: S sh 8.86bn ($18.05m)[a]	
$1 = S sh	1989: 490.68	1990: 1,800
	1991: 3,800	1992: 2,700

S sh = Somali shillings
[a] Incl military and internal sy bdgt.

Population: 6,654,000

	13–17	18–22	23–32
Men	366,800	295,700	449,500
Women	364,500	299,100	466,900

Following the 1991 revolution, no National Armed Forces have yet been formed. The Somali National Movement has declared Northern Somalia as the independent Republic of Somaliland, while in the south, insurgent groups compete for local supremacy. Heavy military equipment which is in a poor state of repair or inoperable is being collected by UNOSOM forces.

CLAN/MOVEMENT GROUPINGS.
'SOMALILAND' (northern Somalia)
UNITED SOMALIA FRONT: Sub-clan Issa:
SOMALIA DEMOCRATIC FRONT: Sub-clan Gadabursi.
SOMALIA NATIONAL MOVEMENT: Clan Isaq, 5–6,000, 3 factions (Tur, Dhegaweyne, Kahin).
UNITED SOMALI PARTY: Sub-clan Dolbuhunta, leader Abdi Hasai.
SOMALIA
SOMALIA SALVATION DEMOCRATIC FRONT: Sub-clan Majerteen, 3,000, leaders 'Colonel' Yusuf, Abshir Musa (loose alliance).
UNITED SOMALI CONGRESS: Clan Hawije
Aideed Faction: leader Mohammed Farah Aideed, 10,000, Habar Gadir sub-clan.
Ali Mahdi Faction: leader Mohammed Ali Mahdi, 10,000(-), Abgal sub-clan.
SOMALI NATIONAL FRONT: Sub-clan Marehan, leaders Mohamed Said Hersi Morgan, Hashi Ganni, Warsame Hashi, 2–3,000.
SOMALI DEMOCRATIC MOVEMENT: Clan Dighil and Rahenwein.

SOMALI PATRIOTIC MOVEMENT: Sub-clan Ogaden, 2–3,000, leaders Ahmed Omar Jess, Aden Nur Gabiyu.

FOREIGN FORCES:
UN AND PEACEKEEPING:
UNOSOM II:16,446 from 24 countries.

SUDAN

GDP   1991: £S 192.66bn ($8.16bn)
             1992ε: £S 443.18bn ($6.38bn)
Growth   1991ε: –8.0%   1992ε: -11%
Inflation[a] 1991: 123.7%   1992: 200%
Debt   1991: $15.91bn 1992: $16.0bn
Def exp   1992e: £S 70.0bn ($1.01bn)
Def bdgt   1992: £S 4.0bn ($736.81m)
             1993: £S 4.1bn ($755.23m)
$1 = £S[b]   1990: 11.066   1991: 23.610

             1992: 69.444   1993: 140.000

[a] Official figures; real inflation is estimated at over 200% for 1991.
[b] Adjusted exchange rates. The Sudanese Pound was floated on 2 February 1992 abandoning the official rate of $1 = £S 5.43. Def bdgt figures in $ are based on the official fixed exchange rate. Def exp 1992 in $ is based on floating exchange rate.

Population: 27,491,000

	13–17	18–22	23–32
Men	1,599,000	1,327,000	2,008,000
Women	1,515,000	1,258,000	1,929,000

TOTAL ARMED FORCES:
ACTIVE: 72,800.
Terms of service: conscription (males 18–30), 3 years.

ARMY: 68,000 (ε10,000 conscripts).
1 armd div.   6 inf div (regional comd).
1 AB div (incl 1 SF bn). 3 mech inf bde.
24 inf bde.   4 arty bde, 3 arty regt.
1 engr div.   6 AD arty bde.
EQUIPMENT:
MBT: 250 T-54/-55, 20 M-60A3, 50 Ch Type-59.
LIGHT TANKS: 70 Ch Type-62.
RECCE: 6 AML-90, 15 *Saladin*, 50 *Ferret*, 60 BRDM-1/-2.
APC: 286: 40 BTR-50/-152, 30 OT-62/-64, 36 M-113, 80 V-100/-150, 100 *Walid*.
TOWED ARTY: 231: 105mm: 18 M-101 pack, 6 Model 56 pack; 122mm: 4 D-74, 24 M-1938, 80 Type-54/D-30; 130mm: 27 M-46/Ch Type 59-1; 152mm: 60 D-20; 155mm: 12 M-114A1.
SP ARTY: 155mm: 6 AMX Mk F-3.

MRL: 122mm: 100 BM-21.
MORTARS: 81mm: 138; 120mm: 12 M-43, 24 AM-49.
ATGW: 4 *Swingfire*.
RCL: 106mm: M-40A1.
ATK GUNS: 76mm: 18 M-1942; 100mm: 20 M-1944.
AD GUNS: 20mm: M-167 towed, M-163 SP; 23mm: ZU-23-2; 37mm: 120 M-1939/Type-63; 40mm: 60 L/60; 85mm: KS-12; 100mm: KS-19 towed.
SAM: SA-7, *Redeye*.

NAVY: ε1,800.
BASES: Port Sudan (HQ), Flamingo Bay, Khartoum.
PATROL CRAFT: 2:
2 *Kadir* PCI⟨, 4 riverine boats, about 10 other armed boats.
AMPHIBIOUS: Craft only; 2 *Sobat* (Yug DTM-221) LCT.

AIR FORCE: 3,000 (incl Air Defence).
51 cbt ac, 2 armed hel.
FGA: 9 F-5 (7 -E, 2 -F), 10 Ch J-5, 9 Ch J-6.
FIGHTER: 8 MiG-21, 3 MiG-23, 6 Ch J-6.
COIN: 1 sqn with 3 BAC-167 Mk 90, 3 *Jet Provost* Mk 55.
MR: 2 C-212.
TRANSPORT: 5 An-24, 5 C-130H, 4 C-212, 3 DHC-5D, 6 EMB-110P, 1 F-27, 2 *Falcon* 20/50.
HELICOPTERS: 1 sqn with 11 AB-412, 8 IAR/SA-330, 4 Mi-4, 5 Mi-8, 2 Mi-24 (armed).
TRAINING: incl 4 MiG-15UTI, 4 MiG-21U, 2 JJ-5, 2 JJ-6.
AD: 5 bty SA-2 SAM (18 launchers).
AAM: AA-2 *Atoll*.

PARAMILITARY:
POPULAR DEFENCE FORCE: ε30–50,000: mil wing of National Islamic Front.

OPPOSITION:
SUDANESE PEOPLE'S LIBERATION ARMY
(SPLA): ε30–50,000: four factions, each org in bn; mainly small arms plus 60mm mor, 14.5mm AA, SA-7 SAM; arty reported; operating mainly in southern Sudan.

FOREIGN FORCES:
IRAN: some mil advisers.

SYRIA

GDP[a]   1991: £S 305.61bn ($16.44bn)
          1992: £S 354.00bn ($15.80bn)
Growth   1991: 8.9%   1992: 6.5%
Inflation 1991ε: 50.0%   1992ε: 60%

Debt[b]   1991: $16.82bn   1992: $16.76bn
Def bdgt[c]   1991: £S 32.68bn ($1.76bn)
               1992: £S 27.12bn ($1.21bn)
Def exp   1991ε: £S 50.83bn ($2.73bn)
$1 = £S[d]   1990: 15.416   1991: 18.589
               1992: 22.405   1993: 25.00

[a] Dollar figures are est, based on exchange rates adjusted for real inflation. Officially inflation is running at 8–12% for 1991–1992.
[b] Most of Syria's foreign debt is military debt to the former USSR in concessional form.
[c] Syria's official defence budget is £S 30bn for 1991/92 but may not include arms purchasing. Dollar figures are adjusted.
[d] Exchange rates adjusted for inflation.

Population: 13,860,000

	13–17	18–22	23–32
Men	821,000	664,000	1,021,000
Women	797,000	647,000	976,000

TOTAL ARMED FORCES:
ACTIVE: 408,000.
Terms of service: conscription, 30 months.
RESERVES (to age 45): 400,000. Army 300,000 active; Navy 8,000.

ARMY: 300,000 (130,000 conscripts, 50,000 reservists).
2 corps HQ:
6 armd div (each 3 armd, 1 mech bde, 1 arty regt).
3 mech div (-) (each 2 armd, 2 mech bde, 1 arty regt).
1 Republican Guard div (-) (2 armd, 1 mech bde).
1 SF div (3 SF regt).
(1 bde in each div at cadre strength).
2 indep mech inf bde.
2 indep inf bde.
2 indep arty bde.
8 indep SF regt.
3 SSM bde (each of 3 bn):
1 with *FROG*; 1 with *Scud*; 1 with SS-21.
1 coastal def SSM bde with SS-C-1B *Sepal* and SS-C-3 *Styx*.
1 Border Guard bde.
1 indep tk regt.
1 indep ATK regt.
RESERVES: 30 inf, arty regt.
EQUIPMENT:
MBT: 4,500: 2,100 T-54/-55, 1,000 T-62M/K, 1,400 T-72/-72M. (Total incl some 1,200 in static positions and in store.)
RECCE: 500 BRDM-2.
AIFV: 2,250 BMP-1, 50 BMP-2.
APC: 1,500 BTR-40/-50/-60/-152.
TOWED ARTY: some 1,500 incl; 122mm: 100 M-1931/-37 (in store), 150 M-1938, 500 D-30; 130mm: 650 M-46; 152mm: 20 D-20, 50 M-1937; 180mm: 10 S23.
SP ARTY: 122mm: 400 2S1; 152mm: 50 2S3.

MRL: 122mm: 280 BM-21.
MORTARS: 82mm; 120mm: 350 M-1943; 160mm: 100 M-1943; 240mm: ε8 M-240.
SSM launchers: 18 *FROG*-7, some 18 SS-21, 20 *Scud* B/-C; SS-C-1B *Sepal*, SS-C-3 coastal.
ATGW: 4,700 AT-3 *Sagger* (incl 4,000 SP), 200 AT-4 *Spigot* and 200 *Milan*.
AD GUNS: some 1,985: 23mm: 600 ZU-23-2 towed, 400 ZSU-23-4 SP; 37mm: 300 M-1939; 57mm: 675 S-60, 10 ZSU-57-2 SP; 100mm: some KS-19.
SAM: SA-7/-9, 20 SA-13.

NAVY: 8,000.
BASES: Latakia, Tartus, Minet el-Baida.
SUBMARINES: 3 Sov *Romeo* † with 533mm TT.
FRIGATES: 2 Sov *Petya-I I* with 4 x ASW RL, 5 x 533mm TT.
PATROL AND COASTAL COMBATANTS: 32:
MISSILE CRAFT: 21: 16 Sov *Osa-I* and *II* PFM with 4 SS-N-2 *Styx* SSM, 5 Sov *Komar*⟨ with 2 SS-N-2 *Styx* SSM.
PATROL: 11:
8 Sov *Zhuk* PFI⟨.
1 Sov *Natya* (ex-MSO).
About 2 *Hamelin* PFI⟨ (ex PLF).
MINE COUNTERMEASURES: 9:
1 Sov T-43, 1 *Sonya* MSC.
2 Sov *Vanya*, 5 *Yevgenya* MSI.
AMPHIBIOUS: 3 *Polnocny* LSM, capacity 100 tps, 5 tk.
SUPPORT AND MISCELLANEOUS: 2: 1 spt, 1 trg.

NAVAL AVIATION: 25 armed hel.
ASW: 20 Mi-14, 5 Ka-25 (Ka-28 to replace) hel.

AIR FORCE: 40,000; 639 cbt ac; 100 armed hel.
(Some may be in store.)
FGA: 10 sqn:
4 with 70 Su-22.
1 with 20 Su-20;
4 with 60 MiG-23 BN.
1 with 20 Su-24.
FIGHTERS: 18 sqn:
8 with 172 MiG-21, 2 with 30 MiG-25, 5 with 80 MiG-23, 3 with 20 MiG-29.
RECCE: 6 MiG-25R.
EW: 10 Mi-8 *Hip* J/K hel.
TRANSPORT: 6 An-12, 4 An-24, civil-registered ac incl: 5 An-26, 2 *Falcon* 20, 4 Il-76, 7 Yak-40, 1 *Falcon* 900.
HELICOPTERS:
ATTACK: 50 Mi-25, 50 SA-342L.
TRANSPORT: 10 Mi-2, 10 Mi-6, 130 Mi-8/-17.
ASW (Navy-assigned): 4 Ka-25, 20 Mi-14.
TRAINING: incl 10 L-29, 90* L-39, 20 MBB-223, 50* MiG-21U, 16* MiG-23UM, 5* MiG-25U.
MISSILES:
ASM: AT-2 *Swatter*, AS-7 *Kerry*, AS-12, *HOT*.
AAM: AA-2 *Atoll*, AA-6 *Acrid*, AA-7 *Apex*, AA-8 *Aphid*, AA-10 *Alamo*.

AIR DEFENCE COMMAND: ε60,000;
22 AD bde (some 95 SAM bty):
11 (some 60 bty) with some 450 SA-2/-3;
11 (27 bty) with some 200 SA-6 and AD arty.
2 SAM regt (each 2 bn of 2 bty) with some
48 SA-5, 60 SA-8.

FORCES ABROAD:
LEBANON: 30,000: 1 mech div HQ, 1 SF div HQ,
elm 1 armd, 3 mech bde, 8 SF, 2 arty regt.

PARAMILITARY:
PALESTINE LIBERATION ARMY: 4,500; 3 bde
(in Syria, some Syrian officers); 60 T-54/-55 MBT;
some arty; MRL; AT-3 *Sagger* ATGW; SA-7 SAM.
GENDARMERIE (Ministry of Interior): 8,000.
BA'TH PARTY: Workers' Militia (People's Army).

FOREIGN FORCES:
UNITED NATIONS (UNDOF): some 1,110,
contingents from Austria, Canada, Finland and
Poland.
RUSSIA: ε500 advisers, mainly in Air Defence.

TUNISIA

GDP	1991: D 12.17bn ($13.16bn)	
	1992: D 13.99bn ($15.82bn)	
Growth	1991: 3.9%	1992: 8.2%
Inflation	1991: 8.2%	1992: 5.4%
Debt	1991: $8.3bn	1992: $8.5bn
Def bdgt	1992: D 467.9m ($529.06m)	
	1993: D 561.7m ($574.69m)	
FMA[a]	1993: $8.2m	
$1 = D	1990: 0.8783	1991: 0.9246
	1992: 0.8844	1993: 0.9774

D = dinar
[a] Incl $5m as Economic Support.

Population: 8,570,000

	13–17	18–22	23–32
Men	483,700	438,200	752,300
Women	460,500	420,600	726,600

TOTAL ARMED FORCES:
ACTIVE: 35,500 (26,400 conscripts).
Terms of service: 12 months selective.

ARMY: 27,000 (25,000 conscripts).
3 mech bde (each with 1 armd, 2 mech inf, 1 arty, 1
AD regt).
1 Sahara bde.
1 SF bde.
1 engr regt.

EQUIPMENT:
MBT: 84: 54 M-60A3, 30 M-60A1.
LIGHT TANKS: 55 SK-105 *Kuerassier.*
RECCE: 24 *Saladin*, 35 AML-90.
APC: 268: 140 M-113A1/-A2, 18 EE-11 *Urutu*,
110 Fiat F-6614.
TOWED ARTY: 117: 105mm: 48 M-101A1/A2;
155mm: 12 M-114A1, 57 M-198.
MORTARS: 81mm: 95; 107mm: 40 4.2-in; 120mm:
18.
ATGW: 65 *TOW* (incl some SP), 500 *Milan.*
RL: 89mm: 300 LRAC-89, 300 M-20 3.5-in.
RCL: 57mm: 140 M-18; 106mm: 70 M-40A1.
AD GUNS: 20mm: 100 M-55; 37mm: 15 Type-55/-
65.
SAM: 48 RBS-70, 25 M-48 *Chaparral.*

NAVY: ε5,000 (ε700 conscripts).
BASES: Bizerte, Sfax, Kelibia.
FRIGATE: 1 *Inkhad* (US *Savage*) with 2 x 3 ASTT
(trg only).
PATROL AND COASTAL COMBATANTS: 20:
MISSILE CRAFT: 6:
3 *La Galite* (Fr *Combattante* III) PFM with 8 MM-
40 *Exocet* SSM;
3 *Bizerte* (Fr P-48) with 8 x SS-12 SSM.
PATROL: 14:
INSHORE: 14: 2 *Gafsah* (Ch *Shanghai*) PFI, 2
Tazarka (UK Vosper 31-m) PCI, some 10 PCI⟨.
SUPPORT AND MISCELLANEOUS: 2: 1 survey/trg,
1 AT.

AIR FORCE: 3,500 (700 conscripts);
32 cbt aircraft, 5 armed hel.
FGA: 15 F-5E/F.
COIN: 1 sqn with 3 MB-326K, 2 MB-326L.
TRANSPORT: 2 C-130H.
LIAISON: 2 S-208M.
TRAINING: 18 SF-260 (6-C, *12-W), 8 MB-326B.
HELICOPTERS:
ARMED: 5 SA-341 (attack).
TRANSPORT: 1 wing with 15 AB-205, 6
AS-350B, 1 AS-365, 6 SA-313, 3 SA-316,
4 UH-1H, 2 UH-1N.
AAM: AIM-9J *Sidewinder.*

FORCES ABROAD:
UN AND PEACEKEEPING:
CAMBODIA (UNTAC): 866, plus 17 Observers, 29
civ pol.
CROATIA (UNPROFOR I): 12 civ pol.
SOMALIA (UNOSOM II): 133.
WESTERN SAHARA (MINURSO): 9 Observers.

PARAMILITARY:
NATIONAL POLICE: 13,000.
NATIONAL GUARD: 10,000; incl Coastal Patrol
with 4 (ex-GDR) *Kondor-I*-class PCC, 5 (ex-GDR)
Bremse-class PCI⟨, plus some 10 other PCI⟨.

UNITED ARAB EMIRATES (UAE)

GDP	1991:	Dh 123.6bn ($33.67bn)	
	1992:	Dh 123.1bn ($33.53bn)	
Growth	1991:	-2.0%	1992ε: -1.0%
Inflation	1991:	2.0%	1992: 3.0%
Debt	1991:	$10.7bn	1992: $9.8bn
Def bdgt	1991:	Dh 5.85bn ($1.59bn)	
	1992ε:	Dh 6.03bn ($1.64bn)	
Def exp[a]	1990:	Dh 9.51bn ($2.59bn)	
	1991:	Dh 17.99bn ($4.90bn)	
$1 = Dh	1989–92: 3.671		
Dh = dirham			

Population: 1,812,000

	13–17	18–22	23–32
Men	75,500	64,400	151,800
Women	71,500	54,200	78,000

[a] Incl $1bn in contributions to UK and US and an est $3.3bn in arms purchases.

TOTAL ARMED FORCES:
The Union Defence Force and the armed forces of the UAE (Abu Dhabi, Dubai, Ras Al Khaimah and Sharjah) were formally merged in 1976; Abu Dhabi and Dubai still maintain a degree of independence.
ACTIVE: 57,500 (perhaps 30% expatriates).

ARMY: 53,000 (incl Dubai: 12,000).
MoD (Dubai); GHQ (Abu Dhabi).
INTEGRATED:
1 Royal Guard 'bde'.   1 armd bde.
1 mech inf bde.   2 inf bde.
1 arty bde.
NOT INTEGRATED:
2 inf bde (Dubai)
EQUIPMENT:
MBT: 125: 95 AMX-30, 30 OF-40 Mk 2 (*Lion*).
LIGHT TANKS: 76 *Scorpion*.
RECCE: 90 AML-90, 50 *Saladin* (in store), 20 *Ferret* (in store).
AIFV: 15 AMX-10P, 80 BMP-3.
APC: 350: 50 VCR (incl variants), 240 Panhard M-3, 60 EE-11 *Urutu*.
TOWED ARTY: 108: 105mm: 70 ROF lt, 18 M-56 pack; 130mm: 20.
SP ARTY: 155mm: 20 Mk F-3, 70 G-6.
MRL: 122mm: 40 *FIROS*-25.
MORTARS: 81mm: 80; 120mm: 21.
ATGW: 230 *Milan, Vigilant*, 25 *TOW, HOT* (incl 20 SP).
RCL: 84mm: *Carl Gustav*; 106mm: 30.
AD GUNS: 20mm: 48 M-3VDA SP; 30mm: 20 GCF-BM2.
SAM: 20+ *Blowpipe*, 10 SA-16.

NAVY: ε2,000.
BASES: Abu Dhabi: Dalma, Mina Zayed; Ajman;
Dubai: Mina Rashid, Mina Jabal 'Ali; Fujairah; Ras al Khaimah: Mina Sakr; Sharjah: Taweela (main base), Mina Khalid, Khor Fakkan.
PATROL AND COASTAL COMBATANTS: 19:
CORVETTES: 2 *Muray Jip* (Ge Lürssen 62-m) with 2 x 2 MM-40 *Exocet* SSM, plus 1 SA-316 hel.
MISSILE CRAFT: 8: 6 *Ban Yas* (Ge Lürssen TNC-45) with 2 x 2 MM-40 *Exocet* SSM.
2 *Mubarraz* (Ge Lürssen 50-m) with 2 x 2 MM-40 *Exocet* SSM, plus 1 x 6 *Sadral* SAM.
PATROL, INSHORE: 9: 6 *Ardhana* (UK Vosper 33-m) PFI, 3 *Kawkab* PCI⟨.
AMPHIBIOUS: Craft only, 2 *Jananah* LCT, 1 LCM.
SUPPORT AND MISCELLANEOUS: 4: 1 div spt, 2 log spt, 1 tug.

AIR FORCE: (incl Police Air Wing): 2,500 (incl Dubai: 700); 79 cbt ac, 19 armed hel.
FGA: 2 sqn:
1 with 9 *Mirage* 2000E;
1 with 14 *Hawk* Mk 63 (FGA/trg).
FIGHTER: 1 sqn with 22 *Mirage* 2000 EAD.
COIN: 1 sqn with 6 MB-326 (4 -KD, 2 -LD), 5 MB-339A.
OCU: *7 *Hawk* Mk 61, *2 MB-339A, *6 *Mirage* 2000 DAD.
RECCE: 8 *Mirage* 2000 RAD.
EW: 4 C-212.
TRANSPORT: incl 1 BN-2, 4 C-130H, 2 L-100-30, 1 G-222.
HELICOPTERS:
ATTACK: 2 AS-332F (anti-ship, with *Exocet* AM-39), 10 SA-342K (with *HOT*), 7 SA-316/-319 (with AS-11/-12).
TRANSPORT: 8 AS-332 (2 VIP), 1 AS-350, 12 Bell (2 -205, 5 -206A, 1 -206L, 4 -214), 11 SA-330.
SAR: 3 Bo-105.
TRAINING: 23 PC-7, 5 SF-260 (4 -TP, 1 -W).
MISSILES:
ASM: *HOT*, AS-11/-12, AS-15TT, *Exocet* AM-39.
AAM: R-550 *Magic*, AIM 9L.
AD:
1 AD bde (3 bn).
5 bty *Improved HAWK*.
12 *Rapier*, 8 *Crotale*, 13 RBS-70 SAM.

FORCES ABROAD:
UN AND PEACEKEEPING:
SOMALIA (UNOSOM II): 639.

PARAMILITARY:
COAST GUARD: (Ministry of Interior): some 40 PCI⟨, plus boats.

FOREIGN FORCES:
MOROCCO: some 2,000; army, gendarmerie and police.

REPUBLIC OF YEMEN

The Yemen Arab Republic and The People's Democratic Republic of Yemen joined to form the Republic of Yemen on 22 May 1990. A major reorganisation of the armed forces continues. The unified Air Forces and Air Defences is now under one command. The Navy has concentrated at Aden.

GDP   1991: R 97.10bn ($7.51bn)
             1992ε: R 121.08bn ($7.57bn)

Growth	1991: -4.8%	1992: -1.5%
Inflation	1991: 45%	1992ε: 70%
Debt	1990: $6.80bn	1991: $7.80bn
Def bdgt	1991: R 12.73bn ($1.06bn)	
	1992: R 11.20bn ($935m)	
$1 = R^a	1990: 12.003	1991: 11.980
	1992: 16.000	1993: 30.000

R = rial

Population:^{b} 12,592,000

	13–17	18–22	23–32
Men	732,700	605,400	828,400
Women	713,600	595,500	883,800

^{a} Official exchange rate.
^{b} Since the end of the Gulf War, an estimated 700,000 Yemenis have returned to the Republic of Yemen swelling the unemployment figures to 30%.

TOTAL ARMED FORCES:
ACTIVE: 64,500 (perhaps ε42,500+ conscripts).
Terms of service: conscription, 2 years.
RESERVES: Army: perhaps 75,000.

ARMY: 60,000 (ε42,500 conscripts).
10 armd bde (-).
23 inf bde.
5 mech bde.
2 AB/cdo bde.
5 militia bde.
7 arty bde.
3 SSM bde.
EQUIPMENT:
MBT: 1,275: 250 T-34, 725 T-54/-55, 250 T-62, 50 M-60A1.
RECCE: 125 AML-90, 60 AML-245, 150 BRDM-2.
AIFV: 300 BMP-1/-2.
APC: 670: 70 M-113, 600 BTR-40/-60/-152.
TOWED ARTY: 477: 85mm: 100 D-44; 105mm: 35 M-101A1; 122mm: 30 M-1931/37, 150 D-30, 50 M-1938; 130mm: 90 M-46; 152mm: 10 D-20; 155mm: 12 M-114.
ASSAULT GUNS: 85mm: 20 SU-85; 100mm: 30 SU-100.
MRL: 122mm: 290 BM-21; 132mm: 15 BM-13; 140mm: 30 BM-14; 240mm: 35 BM-24.
MORTARS: 81mm: 180; 82mm: 250; 120mm: 110; 160mm: 100.

SSM: 6 *Scud* B, 10 SS-21, 12 *FROG*-7.
ATGW: 200 *TOW*, 500 *Dragon*.
RCL: 82mm: 20 B-10; 15 M-43; 106mm: 50 M-40A1.
ATK GUNS: 100mm: 42 M-1944 (BS-3), 40 T-12.
AD GUNS: 20mm: 52 M-167, 20 *Vulcan* SP; 23mm: 200 ZU-23, ZSU-23-4; 37mm: 200 M-1939; 57mm: 120 S-60; 85mm: 40 KS-12; 130mm: 225 KS-30.
SAM: SA-7, SA-9.

NAVY: ε1,500†.
MAIN BASES: Aden, Hodeida
FACILITIES: Al Muka, Perim Island, Al Mukalla, Socotra.
PATROL AND COASTAL COMBATANTS: 16:
CORVETTES: 2 *Tarantul-I* with 1 x 2 SA-N-4, 2 x 12 ASW RL; plus 2 x 2 76mm gun.
MISSILE CRAFT: 6 Sov *Osa-II* with 4 x SSN-2B *Styx* SSM.
PATROL CRAFT, INSHORE: 8:
3 *Sana'a* (US *Broadsword* 32-m) PFI,
5 Sov *Zhuk*⟨.
MINE COUNTERMEASURES: 9:
2 Sov *Natya* MSO.
1 Sov *Sonya* MSC.
6 Sov *Yevgenya* MSI.
AMPHIBIOUS: 4:
2 Sov *Polnocny* LSM, capacity 100 tps, 5 tk.
2 Sov *Ondatra* LCM, plus 2 LCVP.
SUPPORT AND MISCELLANEOUS: 2: 2 small tankers (1,300 tons).

AIR FORCE: 3,000;
109 cbt ac, 10 armed hel.
FGA: 4 sqn:
1 with 11 F-5E;
3 with 35 Su-20/-22.
FIGHTER: 4 sqn with 47 MiG-21.
TRANSPORT: 3 An-12, 1 An-24, 10 An-26, 2 C-130H, 4 C-47, 3 *Twin Otter*, 2 F-27, 2 *Skyvan* 3M.
HELICOPTERS: 5 AB-212, 3 AB-214, 40 Mi-8, 10 Mi-24 (attack).
TRAINING: *8 F-5B, 8* MiG-21U, 15 Yak-11.
AD: 30 SAM bty: 20 with SA-2; 5 with SA-3; 5 with SA-6, SA-9.
ASM: AS-7, AS-9, AT-2, AT-6.
AAM: AA-2 *Atoll*, AIM-9 *Sidewinder*.

PARAMILITARY:
CENTRAL SECURITY ORGANISATION: 20,000.
TRIBAL LEVIES: at least 20,000.
Customs service some 6 PFI⟨.

FOREIGN FORCES:
RUSSIA: some advisers.

Central and Southern Asia

Regional Overview

The emergence of independent states in the former Soviet Central Asia, the continuing civil war in Afghanistan and the impact these had on both South Asia and certain areas in the Middle East have blurred the geopolitical boundaries between these three regions. Here we summarise separately the principal developments in Central and Southern Asia, while recognising that politics overlaps in these regions.

Central Asia

After the failure of the August 1991 coup in Moscow, the traditional communist-dominated government in Tajikistan came increasingly under threat from the mixed democrat–Islamic opposition. By the middle of 1992, it seemed that opposition forces had taken control of the capital, Dushanbe. However, with the help of Russian and Uzbek troops, the ruling regime staged a comeback and regained power by the beginning of 1993. In the process, however, over half a million Tajiks were made refugees (many crossed the border into Afghanistan), and thousands more were killed. Using Afghan territory as sanctuary, the opposition forces have carried out numerous attacks on border posts, thus provoking a Russian reaction. The Russians have claimed the right to attack dissident forces across the border in Afghanistan, which could, in turn, provoke greater Afghan support for the Tajik rebels.

The other states of Central Asia watched the descent into anarchy in Tajikistan with considerable concern. There was widespread fear that the Tajik events might be a prelude to increased instability and disintegration in the region. However, Uzbekistan, Turkmenistan, Kyrgyzstan and Kazakhstan managed to avoid Tajikistan's fate and have been attempting to implement the economic reforms so critical for their future. With Russia's help, they are also starting to develop their indigenous armed forces to protect them from those which so destabilised Tajikistan.

In Afghanistan, no sooner had the *Mujaheddin* ousted the government of Mohammed Najibullah than they began falling out amongst themselves in an ever-changing series of coalitions and alliances. Bitter rivals, although members of the same government, maintained their quite separate ambitions. Kabul initially fell to Ahmed Shah Masud, a commander of Tajik descent, who immediately found himself opposed by another Islamic fundamentalist leader, Gulbuddin Hekmatyar, a Pashtun. Masud formed a joint military command with Abdul Rashid Dostam, commander of the pro-Najibullah government Uzbek militia. Eventually Burhanuddin Rabbani, leader of the only non-Pashtun faction based in Pakistan – the fundamentalist Islamic Society – was appointed President. After heavy fighting in and around Kabul, Hekmatyar and Rabbani agreed a cease-fire and a meeting was held in Islamabad in March 1993 where eight faction leaders signed an accord which set out a programme and timetable for establishing an elected government. Neither Masud nor Dostam were included in the Islamabad talks. Hekmatyar was then appointed Prime Minister, while Masud remained Minister of Defence. However, most power, in military terms, is held by Dostam, who was appointed a general and who managed to hold the Northern Corps of the army together and formed a secular movement called the National Islamic Movement of Afghanistan (FIM). Pakistan, Saudi Arabia and Iran, while sensitive to each other's influence in the region, appear to be keeping their options open by providing backing for both Hekmatyar and Dostam with the official Afghan government losing out.

South Asia

India continues to be beset by internal problems. The rise of Hindu fundamentalism risks creating a greater Hindu/Muslim split and threatens, to some degree, the existence of India as a secular democracy. Differences with Pakistan are no nearer a solution, and negotiations between the countries are influenced by Pakistan's own internal political squabbles. Although the Indian government criticised the US decision not to place Pakistan on the list of states which support state terrorism, others believe that, had Pakistan been included, the Indian government would have found it hard not to react militarily next time there was serious terrorist activity in the Punjab. In Sri Lanka the civil war continues as clashes between government forces and Tamil Tiger rebels occur with monotonous regularity and with heavy casualties.

Nuclear Forces

Kazakhstan has ratified the START I Treaty but has not yet joined the Nuclear Non-Proliferation Treaty (NPT). It plans to use its SS-18 missiles as transport in space-research projects in order to earn hard currency. A launch is forecast for October 1993; whether this means a number of SS-18 will have been disarmed by then is not known.

For the third year running the US President has been unable to certify to Congress that **Pakistan** does not have unsafeguarded, military-capable nuclear facilities. The Pressler Amendment to the Foreign Assistance Act will bar economic and military aid to Pakistan. In December 1992 the Minister of Defence Production stated that Pakistan was able to manufacture nuclear weapons. A former Pakistani Chief of Staff has denied that he told a reporter that Pakistan had laboratory-tested a nuclear weapon in 1987. India and Pakistan are still unwilling to join the NPT.

Conventional Military Developments

Most **Central Asian** former republics of the Soviet Union have now formed their own armed forces, based primarily on the units and equipment of the Soviet forces that had been stationed there. Only in **Turkmenistan** are the armed forces still considered to be under joint Russian/Turkmen control; this is due more to Turkmenistan's inability to organise and fund armed forces than to any other cause. However, for the moment, Air Defence forces appear to be coordinated across the region and we consider them still to be under Russian control. Likewise Border Troops are still under Russian control, certainly along the borders with Iran, Afghanistan and China. The Central Asian Republics will rely on Russia for military support, particularly in the training and equipment procurement areas, for some years. In **Afghanistan** the armed forces, with the exception of the units of the Northern Corps under the command of General Dostam, have disintegrated. Most of the soldiers, along with their heavy equipment, have been incorporated into their local militia, while a number of officers have gone north and joined Dostam.

The **Indian** Ministry of Defence announced in June 1993 that it had carried out a successful test-firing of a production-batch *Prithvi* SSM. No information has been released on how *Prithvi* units will be organised or where they will be deployed. It can be expected that deployment would be made to match that of Pakistan's *Hatf* SSM. *Prithvi* has a 250-km range with a 1,000-kilogram payload. (*Hatf*-1 has an 80-km range and 500-kg payload, *Hatf*-2 300-km and 500-kg). The Army has now accepted the *Arjun* MBT for service, but there are contradictory reports regarding its introduction; one claims two regiments will be equipped over the next 12 months; the other that production will be delayed for some years for financial reasons. The Navy has taken delivery of ten Do-228 maritime reconnaissance aircraft. A number of older ships are being retired but kept in preservation. The **Pakistani** Army order of battle shows some small changes: the two additional artillery brigades have now formed, as have one more infantry and one more air-defence brigade. A French *Eridon*-class coastal minehunter has been commissioned and two more have been ordered. The US is not renewing the leases on eight frigates in service with the Pakistani Navy and they will be returned as the five-year leases run out. To replace these, Pakistan is buying six UK *Amazon*-class frigates, as they become available. The first was handed over in July 1993. It is not clear yet what the implications will be of Pakistan's decision not to pay the next tranche due on the contracts for 71 F-16 aircraft being built in the US. The **Sri Lankan** Army has been reorganised, eliminating the task-force level of command and making no distinction between brigades. Manpower levels have risen in all three services. The Air Force has taken delivery of four FMA IA 58A *Pucará* COIN aircraft. The Navy has acquired several more locally-built armed boats for use in anti-terrorist operations, principally in the Jaffna Lagoon.

AFGHANISTAN

GDP   1987: Afs 198.31bn ($3.92bn)
                1988: Afs 187.22bn ($3.70bn)
Growth   1988: 2.3%   1989: 0%
Inflation   1990: 42%   1991: 57%
Debt   1986ε: $30bn
Def bdgt   1985: Afs 14.50bn ($286.56m)
FMAε: 1990: $3.5–$4.5bn
$1 = Afs 1987–92: 50.60
Afs = afghanis

Population: ε21,320,000
                13–17   18–22   23–32
Men   1,240,300   1,049,000   1,625,000
Women   1,193,400   1,005,900   1,552,000

Following the fall of the Najibullah government in April 1992 the bulk of the armed forces broke up with only the Northern corps retaining its structure, the rest appear to have transferred their allegiance to their local *Mujaheddin* group.

EQUIPMENT:
It is not possible to show how ground forces equipment has been divided between the different factions. The list below represents weapons known to be in the country in April 1992.
MBT: 1,200: T-54/-55, T-62.
LIGHT TANKS: 60 PT-76.
RECCE: 250 BRDM-1/-2.
AIFV: 550 BMP-1/-2.
APC: 1,100 BTR-40/-60/-70/-80/-152.
TOWED ARTY: 2,000+: 76mm: M-1938, M-1942; 85mm: D-48; 100mm: M-1944; 122mm: M-30, D-30; 130mm: M-46; 152mm: D-1, D-20, M-1937 (ML-20).
MRL: 122mm: BM-21; 140mm: BM-14; 220mm: BM-22.
MORTARS: 1,000+: 82mm: M-37; 107mm; 120mm: 100 M-43.
SSM: 30: *Scud, FROG*-7 launchers.
ATGW: AT-1 *Snapper*, AT-3 *Sagger*.
RCL: 73mm: SPG-9; 82mm: B-10.
AD GUNS: 600+ 14.5mm; 23mm: ZU-23, 20 ZSU-23-4 SP; 37mm: M-1939; 57mm: S-60; 85mm: KS-12; 100mm: KS-19.
SAM: SA-7/-13.

AIR FORCES:
Air Force organisation and loyalty following the fall of the government is uncertain. The majority are controlled either by the Defence Minister, Ahmed Shah Masud, or by General Dostam. The inventory shows aircraft in service in April 1992. Serviceability is doubtful.
FGA: 30 MiG-23, 80 Su-7/-17/-22.
FIGHTER: 80 MiG-21F.
ARMED HELICOPTERS: 25 Mi-8, 35 Mi-17, 20 Mi-25.

TRANSPORT:
AIRCRAFT: 2 Il-18D; 50 An-2, An-12, An-26, An-32.
HELICOPTERS: 12 Mi-4.
TRAINING: 25 L-39*, 18 MiG-21*.
AIR DEFENCE:
SAM: 115 SA-2, 110 SA-3, guns 37mm, 85mm, 100mm.

MUJAHEDDIN GROUPS:
Afghan insurgency was a broad national movement, united only against the Najibullah government.

GROUPS ORIGINALLY BASED IN PESHAWAR
TRADITIONALIST MODERATE:
NATIONAL LIBERATION FRONT (*Jabha't-Nija't-Milli'*): ε15,000. Sibghatullah Modjaddi (enclaves in Kandahar, Zabol provinces, eastern Konar) Pashtun.
NATIONAL ISLAMIC FRONT (*Mahaz-Millin Isla'mi*): ε15,000. Sayyed Amhad Gailani (eastern Paktia, astride Vardak/Lowgar border) Pashtun.
ISLAMIC REVOLUTIONARY MOVEMENT (*Haraka't-Inqila'b-Isla'mi*): ε25,000. Mohammed Nabi Mohammed (Farah, Zabol, Paktika, southern Ghazni, eastern Lowgar, western Paktia, northern Nimruz, northern Helmand, northern Kandahar) Pashtun.
ISLAMIC FUNDAMENTALIST:
ISLAMIC PARTY (*Hizbi-Isla'mi-Kha'lis*): ε40,000. Yu'nis Kha'lis (Central Paktia, Nangarhar, south-east Kabul) Pashtun.
ISLAMIC PARTY (*Hizbi-Isla'mi-Gulbaddin*): ε50,000. Gulbuddin Hekmatyar (north and southern Kabul, Parvan, eastern Laghman, northern Nangarhar, south-east Konar, large enclave junction Badghis/Ghowr/Jowzjan, western Baghlan, enclaves in Farah, Nimruz, Kandahar, Oruzgan and Zabol) Pashtun/Turkoman/Tajik.
ISLAMIC UNION (*Ittiha'd-Isla'mi Barai Azadi*): ε18,000. Abdul Rasul Sayyaf (east of Kabul) Pashtun.
ISLAMIC SOCIETY (*Jamia't Isla'mi*): ε60,000. Burhanuddin Rabbani (eastern and northern Farah, Herat, Ghowr, Badghis, Faryab, northern Jowzjan, northern Balkh, northern Kondoz, Takhar, Baghlan, Kapisa, northern Laghman, Badakhshan) Turkoman/Uzbek/Tajik.

GROUPS ORIGINALLY BASED IN IRAN:
Shia groups have now formed an umbrella party known as the *Hezbi-Wahdat* (Unity Party).
Sazman-e-Nasr (some 50,000) (Bamian, northern Oruzgan, eastern Ghowr, southern Balkh, southern Samangan, south-west Baghlan, south-east Parvan, northern Vardak) Hazara.
Harakat-e-Islami (20,000) (West of Kabul, enclaves in Kandahar, Ghazni, Vardak, Samangan, Balkh) Pashtun/Tajik/Uzbek.
Pasdaran-e-Jehad (8,000).
Hizbollah (4,000).

Nehzat (4,000).
Shura-Itifaq-Islami (some 30,000+) (Vardak, eastern Bamian) Hazara
NATIONAL ISLAMIC MOVEMENT (NIM)
Formed March 1992 by Uzbek militia commander, Abdul Rashad Dostam, mainly from troops of former Northern Command of the Afghan Army. Predominantly: Uzbek, Tajik, Turkomen, Ismaeli and Hazara Shia. Strength ε65,000 (120–150,000 in crisis). 2 Corps HQ, 5–7 inf div, some indep bde.

BANGLADESH

GDP	1991: Tk 802.22bn ($21.92bn)	
	1992ε: Tk 839.9bn ($21.56bn)	
Growth	1991: 3.3%	1992ε: 3.7%
Inflation	1991: 7.2%	1992: 4.8%
Debt	1991: $11.92bn	1992: $12.26bn
Def bdgt	1990: Tk 11.12bn ($321.68m)	
	1991: Tk 11.10bn ($303.31m)	
Def exp	1990: Tk 11.30bn ($326.90m)	
$1 = Tk	1990: 34.569	1991: 36.596
	1992: 38.950	1993: 38.800
Tk = Taka		

Population: 113,209,900

	13–17	18–22	23–32
Men	7,084,000	6,107,000	9,338,000
Women	6,722,500	5,802,500	8,878,000

TOTAL ARMED FORCES:
ACTIVE: 107,000.

ARMY: 93,000.
7 inf div HQ.
18 inf bde (some 26 bn).
1 armd bde (2 armd regt).
1 armd regt.
3 arty bde (6 arty regt).
6 engr bn.
EQUIPMENT:†
MBT: some 40 Ch Type-59/-69, 30 T-54/-55.
LIGHT TANKS: some 40 Ch Type-62.
TOWED ARTY: 105mm: 30 Model 56 pack, 50 M-101; 122mm: 20 Ch Type-54; 130mm: 40+ Ch Type-59.
MRL: 122mm: reported.
MORTARS: 81mm; 82mm: Ch Type-53; 120mm: 50 Ch Type-53.
RCL: 106mm: 30 M-40A1.
ATK GUNS: 57mm: 18 6-pdr; 76mm: 50 Ch Type-54.
AD GUNS: 37mm: 16; 57mm.

NAVY:† ε7,500.
BASES: Chittagong (HQ), Dhaka, Khulna, Kaptai.
FRIGATES: 4:
1 *Osman* (Ch *Jianghu I*) with 2 x 5 ASW mor, plus 2

x 2 CSS-N-2 *Hai Ying*-2 (HY-2) SSM, 2 x 2 100mm guns.
1 *Umar Farooq* (UK *Salisbury*) with 1 x 3 *Squid* ASW mor, 1 x 2 114mm guns.
2 *Abu Bakr* (UK *Leopard*) with 2 x 2 114mm guns.
PATROL AND COASTAL COMBATANTS: 39:
MISSILE CRAFT: 8:
4 *Durdarsha* (Ch *Huangfeng*) with 4 x HY-2 SSM.
4 *Durbar* (Ch *Hegu*) PFM⟨ with 2 x HY-2 SSM.
TORPEDO CRAFT: some 8 Ch *Huchuan* PFT⟨ with 2 x 533mm TT.
PATROL, COASTAL: 5:
2 *Durjoy* (Ch *Hainan*) with 4 x 5 ASW RL.
2 *Meghna* fishery protection.
1 *Shahjalal*.
PATROL, INSHORE: 13:
8 *Shahead Daulat* (Ch *Shanghai II*) PFI.
2 *Karnaphuli*, 2 *Padma*, 1 *Bishkali* PCI.
RIVERINE: 5 *Pabna*⟨.
AMPHIBIOUS: 1 *Shahamanat* LCU; plus craft: 4 LCM, 3 LCVP.
SUPPORT AND MISCELLANEOUS: 4:
1 trg, 1 coastal tanker, 1 repair, 1 ocean tug.

AIR FORCE:† 6,500;
70 cbt ac, no armed hel.
FGA: 3 sqn with 18 J-6/JJ-6 (F-6/FT-6), 13 Q-5 (A-5 *Fantan*), 12 Su-7BM (ex-Iraqi ac).
FIGHTER: 2 sqn with 17 J-7 (F-7M), 4 MiG-21MF, 2 MiG-21U.
TRANSPORT: 1 sqn with 1 An-24, 4 An-26, 1 DHC-3.
HELICOPTERS: 3 sqn with 2 Bell 206L, 10 -212, 7 Mi-8, 4 Mi-17, 3 UH-1N.
TRAINING: 20 Ch CJ-6, 8 CM-170, 4* JJ-7 (FT-7), 4 MiG-15UTI, 3 Su-7U.

FORCES ABROAD:
UN AND PEACEKEEPING:
CAMBODIA (UNTAC): 922: 1 inf bn, 20 Observers, 220 civ pol.
CROATIA (UNPROFOR I): 24 Observers, 44 civ pol.
IRAQ/KUWAIT (UNIKOM): 7 Observers.
MOZAMBIQUE (ONUMOZ): 1,371: 1 inf bn plus spt, 20 Observers.
WESTERN SAHARA (MINURSO): 1 Observer.

PARAMILITARY:
BANGLADESH RIFLES: 30,000 (border guard); 37 bn.
ARMED POLICE: 5,000.
ANSARS (Security Guards): 20,000.

OPPOSITION:
SHANTI BAHINI (Peace Force), Chakma tribe Chittagong Hills, ε5,000.

INDIA

GDP	1991:	Rs 6,095.0bn ($268.01bn)
	1992ε:	Rs 6,991.0bn ($269.73bn)
Growth	1991: 1.3%	1992: 4.2%
Inflation	1991: 13.9%	1992: 11.7%
Debt	1991: $73.51bn	1992: $77.03bn
Def exp	1990:	Rs 176.84bn ($10.1bn)
	1991ε:	Rs 183.55bn ($8.07bn)
Def bdgt	1992:	Rs 175.0bn ($6.75bn)
	1993:	Rs 191.8bn ($6.33bn)
$1 = Rs	1990: 17.504	1991: 22.742
	1992: 25.914	1993: 30.295

Rs = rupees

Population: 897,759,000

	13–17	18–22	23–32
Men	48,206,000	44,183,000	75,790,000
Women	44,866,000	40,702,000	69,068,000

TOTAL ARMED FORCES:
ACTIVE: 1,265,000.
RESERVES: Army 300,000 (first-line reserves within 5 years of full-time service, a further 650,000 have a commitment until the age of 50); Territorial Army (volunteers) 160,000; Air Force 140,000; Navy 55,000.

ARMY: 1,100,000.
HQ: 5 Regional Comd (= Fd Army), 11 Corps.
2 armd div (each 2/3 armd, 1 SP arty (2 SP fd, 1 med regt) bde).
1 mech div (each 3 mech (4/6 mech bn), 3 armd regt, 1 arty bde).
22 inf div (each 2–5 inf, 1 arty bde; some have armd regt).
10 mtn div (each 3–4 bde, 1 or more arty regt).
14 indep bde: 5 armd, 7 inf, 1 mtn, 1 AB/cdo.
3 indep arty bde.
6 AD bde.
4 engr bde.
These formations comprise:
55 tk regt (bn).
355 inf bn (incl 25 mech, 9 AB/cdo).
290 arty regt (bn) reported: incl 1 hy, 1 SSM, 5 MRL, 50 med (11 SP), 69 fd (3 SP), 39 mtn, 29 AD arty regt; perhaps 10 SAM gp (3–5 bty each).
Army Aviation:
14 hel sqn: 6 ATK, 8 air obs.
EQUIPMENT:
MBT: 3,400: some 800 T-55, 1,400 T-72/-M1, 1,200 *Vijayanta*, plus 500 in store.
LIGHT TANKS: 100 PT-76.
RECCE: BRDM-2.
AIFV: 900 BMP-1/-2 (*Sarath*).
APC: 400 OT-62/-64, 50 BTR-60.
TOWED ARTY: 3,325 incl: 75mm: 900 75/24 mtn, 215 Yug M-48; 105mm: some 1,200 IFG Mk I/II, 50 M-56; 130mm: 550 M-46; 155mm: 410 FH-77B.

SP ARTY: 105mm: 80 *Abbot*; 130mm: 100 mod M-46.
MRL: 122mm: 80 BM-21.
MORTARS: 81mm: L16A1; 120mm: 1,000 incl M-43, *Brandt*, E1; 160mm: 200 M-160.
SSM: some *Prithvi*.
ATGW: *Milan*, AT-3 *Sagger*, AT-4 *Spigot*, AT-5 *Spandrel*.
RCL: 57mm: M-18; 84mm: *Carl Gustav*; 106mm: 1,000+ M-40A1.
AD GUNS 2,510: 20mm: *Oerlikon* (reported); 23mm: 140 ZU 23-2, 75 ZSU-23-4 SP; 30mm: 50 2S6 SP (reported); 40mm: 1,245 L40/60, 1,000 L40/70.
SAM: 100 SA-6, 620 SA-7, 48 SA-8A/-B, 200 SA-9, 50 SA-11, 45 SA-13, 200 SA-16.
HELICOPTERS: 200 *Chetak*, *Cheetah*, *Krishnar* Mk II.
RESERVES: Territorial Army: 25 inf bn, plus 31 'departmental' units.
DEPLOYMENT:
North – 2 Corps with 7 inf, 1 mtn div.
West – 3 Corps with 1 armd, 8 inf div.
Central – 1 Corps with 1 armd, 2 inf div, plus 1 inf, 1 mtn div.
East – 3 Corps with 8 mtn div.
South – 2 Corps with 1 mech, 3 inf div.

NAVY: 55,000, incl 5,000 Naval Aviation and 1,000 Marines.
PRINCIPAL COMMANDS: Western, Eastern, Southern.
Sub-Commands: Submarine, Naval Air.
BASES: Bombay (HQ Western Cmd), Goa (HQ Naval Air), Lakshadweep (Laccadive Is), Karwar (under construction); Cochin (HQ Southern Cmd), Visakhapatnam (HQ Eastern and Submarines), Calcutta, Madras, Port Blair (Andaman Is), Arakonam (Naval Air).
FLEETS: Western (based Bombay), Eastern (based Visakhapatnam).
SUBMARINES: 15:
SS: 15:
8 *Sindhughosh* (Sov *Kilo*) with 533mm TT.
3 *Shishumar* (Ge T-209/1500) with 533mm TT.
4 *Kursura* (Sov *Foxtrot*) with 533mm TT trg.(Plus 2 non-op).
PRINCIPAL SURFACE COMBATANTS: 24:
CARRIERS: 2:
1 *Viraat* (UK *Hermes*) (29,000t) CVV.
1 *Vikrant* (UK *Glory*) (19,800t) CVV.
Air group typically:
ac: 8 *Sea Harrier* fighter/attack.
hel: 6 *Sea King* ASW/ASUW (*Sea Eagle* ASM).
DESTROYERS: 5:
5 *Rajput* (Sov *Kashin*) DDG with 2 x 2 SA-N-1 *Goa* SAM; plus 4 SS-N-2C *Styx* SSM, 5 x 533mm TT, 2 x ASW RL, 1 Ka-25 or 27 hel (ASW).
FRIGATES: 17:
3 *Godavari* FFH with 2 x *Sea King* hel, 2 x 3 324mm ASTT; plus 4 x SS-N-2C *Styx* SSM and 1 x 2 SA-N-4 SAM.
6 *Nilgiri* (UK *Leander*) with 2 x 3 ASTT, 4 with 1 x 3 *Limbo* ASW mor, 1 *Chetak* hel, 2 with 1 *Sea King*, 1 x 2 ASW RL; plus 2 x 114mm guns.

4 *Kamorta* (Sov *Petya*) with 4 ASW RL, 3 x 533mm
TT.
4 *Khukri* (ASUW) with 2 or 4 SS-N-2C (*Styx*), hel
deck.
Additional in store: some 2 ex-UK FF and 4
Kamorta FF.

PATROL AND COASTAL COMBATANTS: 40:
CORVETTES: 15:
3 *Vijay Durg* (Sov *Nanuchka* II) with 4 x SS-N-2B
Styx SSM.
5 *Veer* (Sov *Tarantul*) with 4 x *Styx* SSM.
3 *Vibhuti* (similar to *Tarantul*) with 4 x *Styx* SSM.
4 *Abhay* (Sov *Pauk-II*) (ASW) with 4 x ASTT, 2 x
ASW mor.
MISSILE CRAFT: 6 *Vidyut* (Sov *Osa* II) with 4 x *Styx*.
PATROL, OFFSHORE: 7 *Sukanya* PCO.
PATROL, INSHORE: 12:
12 SDB Mk 2/3.
MINE WARFARE: 20:
MINELAYERS: None, but *Kamorta* FF and
Pondicherry MSO have minelaying capability.
MINE COUNTERMEASURES: 20:
12 *Pondicherry* (Sov *Natya*) MSO.
2 *Bulsar* (UK 'Ham') MSI.
6 *Mahé* (Sov *Yevgenya*) MSI⟨.
AMPHIBIOUS: 9:
1 *Magar* LST, capacity 200 tps, 12 tk, 1 hel.
8 *Ghorpad* (Sov *Polnocny* C) LSM, capacity 140
tps, 6 tk.
Plus craft: 7 *Vasco da Gama* LCU.
SUPPORT AND MISCELLANEOUS: 22:
2 *Deepak* AO, 1 *Amba* (Sov *Ugra*) sub
spt, 1 div spt, 2 ocean tugs, 5 small AO, 6
Sandhayak and 4 *Makar* AGHS, 1 *Tir* trg.

NAVAL AVIATION: (5,000);
64 cbt ac, 75 armed hel.
ATTACK: 1 sqn with 23 *Sea Harrier* FRS Mk-51,
2 T-60 trg.
ASW: 6 hel sqn with 26 *Chetak*, 7 Ka-25, 10 Ka-28,
32 *Sea King* Mk 42A/B.
MR: 3 sqn: 6 Il-38, 10 Tu-142M *Bear* F, 10 Do-228,
13 BN-2 *Defender*.
COMMUNICATIONS: 1 sqn with 5 BN-2 *Islander*, 2
Do-228 ac; 3 *Chetak* hel.
SAR: 1 hel sqn with 6 *Sea King* Mk 42C.
TRAINING: 2 sqn: 6 HJT-16, 8 HPT-32 ac; 2 *Chetak*,
4 Hughes 300 hel.
MISSILES:
AAM: R-550 *Magic* I and II.
ASM: *Sea Eagle*, *Sea Skua*.

MARINES: (ε1,000);
1 regt (2nd forming).

AIR FORCE: 110,000;
707 cbt ac, 36 armed hel. 5 Air Comd.
FGA: 23 sqn:
5 with 80 *Jaguar* IS.
9 with 144 MiG-21 MF/PFMA.
3 with 54 MiG-23 BN/UM.
6 with 96 MiG-27.

FIGHTER: 17 sqn:
4 with 74 MiG-21 FL/U.
6 with 108 MiG-21 bis/U.
2 with 26 MiG-23 MF/UM.
3 with 59 MiG-29/UB.
2 with 36 *Mirage* 2000H/TH.
MARITIME ATTACK: 8 *Jaguar* with *Sea Eagle*.
ATTACK HELICOPTERS: 2 sqn:
1 with 18 Mi-25;
1 with 18 Mi-35.
RECCE: 2 sqn:
1 with 8 *Canberra* PR-57; 4 HS-748.
1 with 6 MiG-25R, 2 MiG-25U;
MR/SURVEY: 2 Gulfstream IV SRA, 2 *Learjet* 29.
TRANSPORT:
AIRCRAFT: 11 sqn:
6 with 105 An-32 *Sutlej*;
1 with 16 BAe-748;
2 with 30 Do-228;
2 with 24 Il-76 *Gajraj*;
HELICOPTERS: 11 sqn with 80 Mi-8, 50 Mi-17, 10
Mi-26 (hy tpt).
VIP: 1 HQ sqn with 2 Boeing 707-337C, 4 Boeing
737, 7 BAe-748.
LIAISON: flt and det: 16 BAe-748.
TRAINING: 24 BAe-748, 7 *Canberra* T-4/-13/-67,
120 *Kiran* I, 56 *Kiran* II, 88 HPT-32, 30 HT-2, 20
Hunter T-66, 6* *Jaguar* IB, 5 MiG-29UB, 44 TS-11
Iskara ac; 20 *Chetak*, 2 Mi-24, 2 Mi-35 hel.
MISSILES:
ASM: *Akash*, AM-39 *Exocet*, AS-7 *Kerry*, AS-11B
(ATGW), AS-12, AS-30, *Sea Eagle*.
AAM: AA-2 *Atoll*, AA-7 *Apex*, AA-8 *Aphid*, AA-10
Alamo, AA-11 *Archer*, R-550 *Magic*, *Super* 530D.
SAM: 30 bn: 280 *Divina* V75SM/VK (SA-2), SA-3,
SA-5.

FORCES ABROAD:
UN AND PEACEKEEPING:
ANGOLA (UNAVEM II): 4 Observers.
CAMBODIA (UNTAC): 1,335: 1 inf bn, 17
Observers, 421 civ pol.
EL SALVADOR (ONUSAL): 2 Observers.
IRAQ/KUWAIT (UNIKOM): 6 Observers.
MOZAMBIQUE (ONUMOZ): 670, (HQ coy, engr,
log) plus 19 Observers.
SOMALIA (UNOSOM): 173.

PARAMILITARY:
NATIONAL SECURITY GUARDS: 7,500: anti-
terrorism contingency deployment force. Comprises
elm of the Armed Forces, CRPF, Border Guard.
CENTRAL RESERVE POLICE FORCE (CRPF):
(Ministry of Home Affairs) 125,000; 70 bn, internal
security duties.
BORDER SECURITY FORCE: (Ministry of
Home Affairs) 171,000; some 147 bn, small arms,
some lt arty, tpt/liaison air spt.
ASSAM RIFLES: (Ministry of Home Affairs)
35,000; 31 bn, security within north-eastern states.

INDO-TIBETAN BORDER POLICE: (Ministry of Home Affairs) 29,000; 28 bn.
SPECIAL FRONTIER FORCE: 10,000.
CENTRAL INDUSTRIAL SECURITY FORCE: (Ministry of Home Affairs) 74,000.
DEFENCE SECURITY CORPS: 31,000.
RAILWAY PROTECTION FORCES: 70,000.
PROVINCIAL ARMED CONSTABULARY: 400,000.
NATIONAL RIFLES: (being formed, to be 10,000).
HOME GUARD: 464,200
COAST GUARD: 5,300;
PATROL CRAFT: 40:
9 *Vikram* PCO, 11 *Tara Bai* PCC, 5 *Rajhans* PFI, 7 *Jija Bai* PCI, 8⟨.
AVIATION: 3 air sqn with 20 Do-228, 2 Fokker F-27 ac, 4 *Chetak* hel.

KAZAKHSTAN

GDP[a]	1991:	r 76.68bn ($45.10bn)	
	1992:	r 613.60bn ($39.24bn)	
Growth	1991:	-6.8%	1992: -15%
Inflation	1991:	82.9%	1992: 750%
Debt	1991:	$3.1bn	
Def bdgt	1992:	r 22.2bn ($1.48bn)	
	1993:	r 69.3bn ($707m)	
$1 = r	1991:	1.70	
r = rouble	1992:	180	1993: 800

[a] Dollar values are estimated.

Population: 17,242,000 (38% Russian)

	13–17	18–22	23–32
Men	817,000	740,000	1,292,000
Women	799,000	719,000	1,258,000

STRATEGIC NUCLEAR FORCES:
(Russian-controlled forces on Kazakhstan territory).
ICBM: 104
SS-18 *Satan* (RS-20), 104 at 2 sites.
BOMBERS: 40
40 Tu-95H (ALCM-equipped).

ARMY: (44,000)
1 TD
3 MRD (1 trg).
1 AB bde.
2 arty bde
1 ATK bde.
1 *Spetsnaz* bde.
1 attack hel regt.
EQUIPMENT:
Some 1,400 MBT, 2,000 arty/MRL/mor, 12 SSM, 50 attack hel, plus over 3,000 MBT in store (probably Russian-controlled).

NAVY: None, however Caspian Sea Flotilla (see Russia) is operating as a joint Russian, Kazakhstan

and Turkmenistan flotilla under Russian command and based at Astrakan.

AIR FORCE:
FGA/FIGHTER: 140 including MiG-23, MiG-27, Su-24.
RECCE: 2 regt with 55 MiG-25, Su-17.
TRAINING: 95 incl MiG-23, L-29, L-39.

FOREIGN FORCES:
RUSSIA:
AIR DEFENCE:
FIGHTER: 2 regt: 35 MiG-21, 45 MiG-31.
SAM: 85 SA-2, SA-3, SA-5.

KYRGYZSTAN

GDP[a]	1991:	r 15.83bn ($8.92bn)	
	1992:	r 134.55bn ($7.02bn)	
Growth	1991:	-3.6%	1992: -25.0%
Inflation	1991:	88.2%	1992: 870%
Debt	1991:	$700m	1992: $760m
Def bdgt	1992:	r 800m ($47.06m)	
$1 = r	1991:	1.70	1992: 180
	1993:	800	

[a] Dollar values are estimated
r = roubles

Population: 4,612,000 (21.5% Russian)

	13–17	18–22	23–32
Men	241,000	208,400	341,800
Women	237,000	205,500	339,000

Terms of service: 18 months.

ARMY: (12,000).
1 MRD.
1 mtn bde.
EQUIPMENT: 240 MBT, 415 ACV, 240 arty/MRL/mor.

AIR FORCE:
1 trg centre: 200+ incl MiG-21, L-29, L-39.

FOREIGN FORCES:
RUSSIA:
AIR DEFENCE:
SAM: 26 SA-2, SA-3.

MYANMAR (BURMA)

GDP	1991ε:	K 217.11bn ($10.94bn)	
	1992ε:	K 282.0bn ($11.57bn)	
Growth	1991:	3.7%	1992ε: 4%
Inflation	1991:	29%	1992: 26%

Debt	1991: $4.8bn	1992: $4.9bn

Def bdgt 1991ε: K 7.9bn ($398.19m)
1992ε: K 8.7bn ($356.15m)

$1 = K^a	1990: 6.339	1991: 6.284
	1992: 6.300	1993: 6.200

K = kyats
^{a} Official rate. Black market rate may be as high as $1 = K 220–250.

Population: 44,491,000

	13–17	18–22	23–32
Men	2,436.000	2,264,000	3,702,000
Women	2,355,000	2,203,000	3,765,000

TOTAL ARMED FORCES:
ACTIVE: ε286,000.

ARMY: 265,000.
10 lt inf div (each 3 tac op comd (TOC)).
10 Regional Comd (8 with 3 TOC, 2 with 4 TOC).
32 TOC with 145 garrison inf bn.
Summary of cbt units:
223 inf bn.
3 armd bn.
7 arty bn.
1 AA arty bn.
EQUIPMENT:†
MBT: 26 *Comet*, 30 Ch T-69II.
LIGHT TANKS: 30 Type-63.
RECCE: 45 *Ferret*, 40 *Humber*, 30 *Mazda* (local manufacture).
APC: 20 *Hino* (local manufacture).
TOWED ARTY: 76mm: 100 M-1948; 88mm: 50 25-pdr; 105mm: 96 M-101; 140mm: 5.5-in.
MRL: 122mm: Type-63 reported.
MORTARS: 81mm; 82mm; 120mm: 80 Soltam.
RCL: 84mm: 500 *Carl Gustav*; 106mm: M40A1.
ATK GUNS: 60: 57mm: 6-pdr; 76.2mm: 17-pdr.
AD GUNS: 37mm: 24 Type-74; 40mm: 10 M-1; 57mm: 12 Type-80.

NAVY:† 12,000–15,000 (incl 800 Naval Infantry).
BASES: Bassein, Mergui, Moulmein, Seikky, Rangoon (Monkey Point), Sittwe.
PATROL AND COASTAL COMBATANTS: 52:
CORVETTES: 2:
1 *Yan Taing Aung* (US PCE-827)
1 *Yan Gyi Aung* (US *Admirable* MSF).
PATROL: 50:
COASTAL: 8: *Yan Sit Aung* (Ch *Hainan*).
INSHORE: 13: 10 US PGM-401/412, 3 Yug PB-90 PFI⟨.
RIVERINE: 29: 2 *Nawarat*, 2 imp Yug Y-301 and 10 Yug Y-301, about 15⟨, plus some 25 boats.
AMPHIBIOUS: 5:
5 LCU, plus craft: 10 LCM.
SUPPORT: 4: 1 coastal tpt, 2 AGHS, 1 PC/div spt.
NAVAL INFANTRY: 800: 1 bn.

AIR FORCE: 9,000;
43 cbt ac, 10 armed hel.
FIGHTERS: 1 sqn: 10 F-7, 2 FT-7.
COIN: 2 sqn: 15 PC-7, 4 PC-9, 12 *Super Galeb* G4.
TRANSPORT: 1 F-27, 4 FH-227, 5 PC-6A/-B, 2 Y-8D.
LIAISON: 6 Cessna 180, 1 -550.
HELICOPTERS: 4 sqn: 12 Bell 205, 6 -206, 9 SA-316, 10 Mi-2 (armed), 12 PZL W-3 *Sokol*.

PARAMILITARY:
PEOPLE'S POLICE FORCE: 50,000.
PEOPLE'S MILITIA: 35,000.
PEOPLE'S PEARL AND FISHERY MINISTRY: ε250: 11 patrol boats (3 *Indian* (Dk *Osprey*) PCC, 3 US *Swift* PGM PCI, 5 Aust *Carpentaria* PCI⟨).

OPPOSITION:
Numerous rebel groups with loose and varying alliances. Only main groups listed.
NATIONAL DEMOCRATIC FRONT (NDF): Some 20,000: coalition of numerous ethnic gp, mainly in border areas incl Kachin (8,000), Shan and Karen (5,000) groups.
ROHINGYA SOLIDARITY ORGANISATION: ε6,000.
ARAKAN ROHINGYA ISLAMIC FRONT: ε500.
PRIVATE ARMIES (mainly narcotics linked)
Mong Tai Army (formerly Shan United Army) Chang Shee Fu 'Khun Sa' (narcotics warlord): 2,100. Kan Chit: 450. United Revolutionary Army: ε1,000; Kuomintang-linked. Loi Maw Rebels/Army: ε3,000.

NEPAL

GDP	1991: NR 105.30bn ($2.83bn)	
	1992: NR 130.69bn ($3.06bn)	
Growth	1991: 5.6%	1992: 3.1%
Inflation	1991: 15.5%	1992: 17.5%
Debt	1991: $1.69bn	1992: $1.90bn
Def bdgt	1992ε: NR 1.50bn ($35.0m)	
	1993ε: NR 1.95bn ($40.5m)	
$1 = NR	1990: 29.369	1991: 37.255
	1992: 42.700	1993: 48.000

NR = Nepalese rupees

Population: 20,463,000

	13–17	18–22	23–32
Men	1,152,000	980,000	1,519,000
Women	1,085,000	913,700	1,436,000

TOTAL ARMED FORCES:
ACTIVE 35,000 (to be 40,000).
RESERVES none.

ARMY: 34,800
1 Royal Guard bde: incl 1 cav sqn, 1 garrison bn.
5 inf bde.
1 spt bde: incl AB bn, arty regt, engr bn, armd recce sqn.
1 log bde.
EQUIPMENT:
RECCE: 25 *Ferret*.
TOWED ARTY: 75mm: 6 pack; 94mm: 5 3.7-in mtn;
105mm: 6 pack.
MORTARS: 81mm; 120mm: 18.
AD GUNS: 14.5mm: 30 Ch; 40mm: 2 L/60.

AIR FORCE: 200
No cbt ac, or armed hel.
TRANSPORT:
AIRCRAFT: 1 BAe-748, 2 *Skyvan*, 1 *Twin Otter*.
HELICOPTERS: 2 AS-332 (Royal Flight), 1 Bell
206L, 3 *Chetak*, 2 SA-330.

FORCES ABROAD:
UN AND PEACEKEEPING:
CAMBODIA (UNTAC): 85 civ pol.
CROATIA (UNPROFOR 1): 897: 1 inf bn, 6
Observers, 45 civ pol.
LEBANON (UNIFIL): 721: 1 inf bn.

PARAMILITARY:
POLICE FORCE: 28,000.

PAKISTAN

GDP	1991:	Rs 992.65bn ($41.71bn)		
	1992:	Rs 1,155.4bn ($46.06bn)		
Growth	1991:	4.7%	1992:	7.8%
Inflation	1991:	11.8%	1992:	9.6%
Debt	1991:	$22.3bn	1992:	$23.3bn
Def exp	1991:	Rs 76.96bn ($3.23bn)		
	1992:	Rs 89.10bn ($3.55bn)		
Def bdgt	1992:	Rs 82.15bn ($3.28bn)		
	1993:	Rs 92.01bn ($3.45bn)		
$1 = Rs	1990:	21.707	1991:	23.801
	1992:	25.000	1993:	26.700
Rs = rupees				

Population: 122,638,000 (excl Afghan refugees)

	13–17	18–22	23–32
Men	7,209,000	6,290,000	10,081,000
Women	6,509,000	5,597,000	8,984,000

TOTAL ARMED FORCES:
ACTIVE: 577,000.
RESERVES: 313,000; Army 300,000: obligation to
ages 45 (men) or 50 (officers); active liability for 8
years after service. Navy 5,000. Air 8,000.

ARMY: 510,000.
9 Corps HQ, 1 area comd.
2 armd div.
19 inf div.
6 indep armd bde.
9 indep inf bde.
9 corps arty bde.
8 AD arty bde.
7 engr bde.
3 armd recce regt.
1 SF gp (3 bn).
Avn: 15 sqn: 7 ac, 8 hel, 1 VIP, 1 obs flt.
EQUIPMENT:
MBT: 1,890+: 120 M-47, 280 M-48A5, 50 T-54/-55,
1,200 Ch Type-59, 200 Ch Type-69, 40 T-85
reported.
APC: 800 M-113.
TOWED ARTY: 1,805: 85mm: 200 Ch Type-56;
88mm: 200 25-pdr; 105mm: 300 M-101, 50 M-56
pack; 122mm: 200 Ch Type-60, 400 Ch Type-54;
130mm: 200 Ch Type-59-1; 140mm: 45 5.5in;
155mm: 30 M-59, 60 M-114, 100 M-198; 203mm:
20 M-115.
SP ARTY: 240: 105mm: 50 M-7; 155mm: 150 M-
109A2; 203mm: 40 M-110A2.
MRL: 122mm: 45 BM-11.
MORTARS: 81mm: 500; 120mm: 225 AM-50, M-61.
SSM: 18 *Hatf*-1, *Hatf*-2 (op status uncertain).
ATGW: 800: *Cobra*, *TOW* (incl 24 on M-901 SP), Ch
Red Arrow.
RL: 89mm: M-20 3.5-in.
RCL: 75mm: Type-52; 106mm: M-40A1.
AD GUNS: 2,000+ incl: 14.5mm; 35mm: 200 GDF-
002; 37mm: Ch Type-55/-65; 40mm: M1, 100 L/60;
57mm: Ch Type-59.
SAM: 350 *Stinger*, *Redeye*, RBS-70, 500 *Anza*.
AVIATION:
AIRCRAFT:
SURVEY: 1 *Commander* 840.
LIAISON: 1 Cessna 421, 2 *Commander* 690, 80
Mashshaq.
OBSERVATION: 40 O-1E, 50 *Mashshaq*.
HELICOPTERS:
ATTACK: 20 AH-1F (*TOW*).
TRANSPORT: 7 Bell 205, 10 -206B, 16 Mi-8, 6 IAR/
SA-315B, 23 IAR/SA-316, 35 SA-330, 5 UH-1H.

NAVY: 22,000 (incl Naval Air and maritime
security agency).
BASE: Karachi (Fleet HQ).
SUBMARINES: 6:
2 *Hashmat* (Fr *Agosta*) with 533mm TT (F-17
HWT), *Harpoon* USGW.
4 *Hangor* (Fr *Daphné*) with 533mm TT (L-5 HWT),
Harpoon USGW.
Plus 3 SX-756 SSI SF insertion craft.
PRINCIPAL SURFACE COMBATANTS: 14.
DESTROYERS: 3:
1 *Babur* (UK *Devonshire*) DDH with 1 x *Sea King*
Mk-45 hel (ASW/ASUW), plus 2 x 2 114mm guns
(trg).

2 *Alamgir* (US *Gearing*) (ASW) with 1 x 8 *ASROC*; plus 2 x 3 ASTT, 2 x 2 127mm guns, 3 x 2 *Harpoon* SSM and hel deck.
(Plus 1 *Alamgir* alongside trg and 1 in store).
FRIGATES: 11:
FFG: 5:
4 *Badr* (US *Brooke*) with 1 x SM-1 MR SAM, 1 x 8 *ASROC*, 2 x 3 ASTT, 1 x 127mm gun and equipped for SA-316B hel (on 5-yr lease expiring 1993–94).
1 *Tariq* (UK *Amazon*) with 1 hel, 2 x 3 ASTT; plus 4 x MM-38 *Exocet*, 1 x 114mm gun.
FF: 6:
2 *Shamsher* (UK *Leander*) with SA-316 hel, 1 x 3 ASW mor, plus 2 x 114mm guns.
4 *Saif* (US *Garcia*) with 1 x 8 *ASROC*, 2 x 3 ASTT, plus 2 x 127mm guns, equipped for SA-316 hel (on 5-yr lease expiring 1993–94).
PATROL AND COASTAL COMBATANTS: 18:
MISSILE CRAFT: 8:
4 Ch *Huangfeng* with 4 x *Hai Ying 2* SSM.
4 Ch *Hegu* with 2 x *Hai Ying 2*.
PATROL: 10:
COASTAL: 3 *Baluchistan* (Ch *Hainan*) PFC with 4 x ASW RL.
INSHORE: 7:
6 *Quetta* (Ch *Shanghai*) PFI (some in reserve).
1 *Rajshahi* PCI.
MINE WARFARE: 3: 1 *Munsif* (Fr *Eridan*) MHC, 2 *Mahmood* (US-MSC 268) MSC.
SUPPORT AND MISCELLANEOUS: 5:
1 *Nasr* (Ch *Fuqing*) AO, 1 *Dacca* AO, 1 AGOR, 1 ocean tug, 1 repair.

NAVAL AIR:
4 cbt ac, 10 armed hel.
ASW/MR: 1 sqn with 4 *Atlantic* (operated by Air Force).
ASW/SAR: 2 hel sqn: 1 with 4 SA-316B (ASW), 6 *Sea King* Mk 45 (ASW).
COMMUNICATIONS: 3 Fokker F-27 ac (Air Force).
ASM: *Exocet* AM-39.

AIR FORCE: 45,000; 393 cbt ac, (plus 48 *Mirage* IIIO in store), no armed hel.
FGA: 7 sqn:
1 with 18 *Mirage* (15 IIIEP (some with AM-39 ASM), 3 IIIDP (trg));
3 (1 OCU) with 58 *Mirage* 5 (54 -5PA/PA2, 4 -5DPA/DPA2);
3 with 50 Q-5 (A-5 *Fantan*).
FIGHTER: 9 sqn:
4 with 100 J-6/JJ-6,(F-6/FT-6);
3 (1 OCU) with 35 F-16A/B.
2 (1 OCU) with 75 J-7 (F-7P).
RECCE: 1 sqn with 12 *Mirage* IIIRP.
ASW/MR: 1 sqn with 4 *Atlantic*.
TRANSPORT: 12 C-130 (5 -B, 7 -E), 1 L-100; 3 Boeing 707, 3 *Falcon* 20, 2 F-27-200 (1 with Navy), 2 Beech (1 *Travel Air*, 1 *Baron*).
SAR: 1 hel sqn with 6 SA-319.

TRANSPORT HEL: 1 sqn with 12 SA-316, 4 SA-321, 12 SA-315B *Lama*.
TRAINING: 12 CJ-6A (PT-6A), 30 JJ-5 (FT-5), *45 MFI-17B *Mashshaq*, 6 MiG-15UTI, 10 T-33A, 44 T-37B/C.
AD: 7 SAM bty:
6 each with 24 *Crotale*;
1 with 6 CSA-1 (SA-2).
MISSILES:
ASM: AM-39 *Exocet*.
AAM: AIM-7 *Sparrow*, AIM-9 *Sidewinder*, R-530, R-550 *Magic*.

FORCES ABROAD:
UN AND PEACEKEEPING:
CAMBODIA (UNTAC): 1,087: 1 inf bn, 17 Observers, 197 civ pol.
IRAQ/KUWAIT (UNIKOM): 7 Observers.
SOMALIA (UNOSOM): 4,436: 1 inf bde.
WESTERN SAHARA (MINURSO): 1 Observer.

PARAMILITARY:
NATIONAL GUARD: 185,000; incl Janbaz Force; National Cadet Corps; Women Guards.
FRONTIER CORPS: (Ministry of Interior) 65,000, 45 UR-416 APC.
PAKISTAN RANGERS: (Ministry of Interior) 23,000.
MARITIME SECURITY AGENCY: (ε2,000)
1 *Alamgir* (US *Gearing* DD) (no *ASROC* or TT), 6 *Barakat* PCC.
COAST GUARD: Some 23 PFI, plus boats.

SRI LANKA

GDP	1991: Rs 372.59bn ($9.01bn)			
	1992: Rs 423.29bn ($9.69bn)			
Growth	1991: 4.3%		1992: 5.9%	
Inflation	1991: 12.2%		1992: 11.4%	
Debt	1991: $6.1bn		1992: $6.4bn	
Def bdgt	1991ε: Rs 18.62bn ($450.06m)			
	1992ε: Rs 20.71bn ($474.04m)			
Def exp	1992: Rs 23.90bn ($547.19m)			
$1 = Rs	1990: 40.063		1991: 41.372	
	1992: 43.678		1993: 48,000	
Rs = rupees				

Population: 17,592,000

	13–17	18–22	23–32
Men	907,000	835,500	1,577,000
Women	871,000	809,000	1,512,500

TOTAL ARMED FORCES: some 110,800 incl recalled reservists.
ACTIVE: ε75,000.
RESERVES: some 10,600; Army 1,100; Navy

1,000; Air 8,500. Obligation: 7 years post-Regular service.

ARMY: 90,000, incl recalled reservists.
3 div, 1 area comd HQ.
1 armd bde.
20 inf bde.
1 indep SF bde (1 cdo, 1 SF regt).
3 recce regt (bn).
4 fd arty (1 reserve), 4 fd engr regt (1 reserve).
EQUIPMENT:
MBT: 25 T-54/-55.
RECCE: 24 *Saladin*, 20 *Ferret*, 12 Daimler *Dingo*.
APC: 24 Ch Type-85, 10 BTR-152, 37 *Buffel*, 73 *Unicorn*, 8 Shorland, 9 *Hotspur*, 30 *Saracen*.
TOWED ARTY: 76mm: 12 Yug M-48; 85mm: 12 Ch Type-56; 88mm: 24 25-pdr; 130mm: 12 Ch Type-59-1.
MORTARS: 81mm: 176; 82mm: 36; 120mm: 36 M-43.
RCL: 105mm: 20 M-65; 106mm: 40 M-40.
AD GUNS: 40mm: 7 L-40; 94mm: 3 3.7-in.

NAVY: 10,100.
BASES: Colombo (HQ), Trincomalee (main base): Karainagar, Tangalle, Kalpitiya, Galle, Kochchikade, Welisara.
PATROL AND COASTAL COMBATANTS: 44:
PATROL, COASTAL: 2 *Jayesagara* PCC.
PATROL, INSHORE: 42:
5 *Sooraya*, 3 *Rana* (Ch *Shanghai* II) PFI.
12 Is *Dvora* PFI⟨.
3 S. Korean PFI⟨.
19 PCI⟨, plus some 30 boats.
AMPHIBIOUS: craft only; 4 LCM (1 non-op), 2 fast personnel carrier.
SUPPORT AND MISCELLANEOUS: 3:
3 *Abheetha* spt/cmd.

AIR FORCE: 10,700;
31 cbt ac, 17 armed hel.
FGA: 4 F-7M.
COIN: 8 SF-260TP, 4 FMA IA58A *Pucará*.
ATTACK HELICOPTERS: 13 Bell 212, 4 -412.
MR: 1 sqn with 6 Cessna 337 ac; 2 SA-365 hel.
TRANSPORT: 1 sqn with 5 BAe 748, 1 Cessna 421C, 1 *Super King Air*, 1 Ch Y-8, 9 Y-12.
HELICOPTERS: 7 Bell 206, 3 Mi-17.
TRAINING: incl 6 Cessna 150, 4 DHC-1, 2* FT-5, 1* FT-7, 12* SF-260 MB, 4 *Chipmunk*.
RESERVES: Air Force Regt, 3 sqn; Airfield Construction Regt, 1 sqn.

PARAMILITARY:
POLICE FORCE: (Ministry of Defence) 40,000 active, incl 1,000 women. (22,000 reserves, increase to 28,000 planned.) Total incl Special Task Force: 3,000-man anti-guerrilla unit.

NATIONAL GUARD: ε15,000.
HOME GUARD: 15,200.

OPPOSITION:
LIBERATION TIGERS OF TAMIL EELAM (LTTE): Leader: Veluppillai Prabaharan: ε7,000.

TAJIKISTAN

GDP[a]	1991: r 13.0bn ($7.65bn)	
	1992ε: r 104.0bn ($5.51bn)	
Growth	1991: -8.7%	1992ε: -32%
Inflation	1991: 103%	1992ε: 800%
Debt	1992: $660m	
Def bdgt	1992: r 3.25bn ($202.8m)	
$1 = r	1991: 1.70	1992: 180
	1993: 800 .	

r = rouble
[a] Dollar values are estimated

Population: 5,748,000 (10.4% Russian)

	13–17	18–22	23–32
Men	318,500	261,600	415,800
Women	311,000	256,400	420,000

TOTAL ARMED FORCES
ACTIVE: some 2–3,000
Tajikistan has not yet been able to form any military units. A number of potential officers are under training at the Higher Army Officers and Engineers College in Dushanbe. It is planned to form an air force squadron.

FOREIGN FORCES:
RUSSIA:
ARMY: (8,500)
1 MRD
EQUIPMENT: 200 MBT, 420 ACV, 200 arty/MRL/mors.
AIR DEFENCE:
SAM: 10. SA-2/-3.

TURKMENISTAN

GDP	1991: r 18.60bn ($10.94bn)[a]	
	1992ε r 111.6bn ($8.97bn)	
Growth	1991: –0.6%	1992: –18%
Inflation	1991: 90.4%	1992: 550%
Debt	1992: $560m	
Def bdgt	1992: r 5.00bn ($433.3m)	
$1 = r	1991: 1.70	1992: 180
	1993: 800	

r = rouble
[a] Dollar values are estimated.

Population: 3,908,000 (12.6% Russian)

	13–17	18–22	23–32
Men	213,000	184,000	303,500
Women	209,000	180,000	302,500

FORCES UNDER JOINT CONTROL:
Turkmenistan/Russia:
ARMY: (28,000)
1 Army HQ.
4 MRD (1 trg).
3 arty bde.
EQUIPMENT:
900 MBT, 1,800+ ACV, 900 arty/MRL/mor, 12 SSM.

NAVY: None at present. Has announced intention to form a Navy/Coast Guard. However, Caspian Sea Flotilla (see Russia) is operating as a joint Russian, Kazakhstan and Turkmenistan Flotilla under Russian command and based at Astrakan.

AIR FORCE:
1 FGA regt with 80 Su-17.

AIR DEFENCE:
FIGHTER: 2 regt: 55 MiG-23, 30 MiG-25.
SAM: 75. SA-2/-3/-5.

UZBEKISTAN

GDP	1991: r 56.30bn ($33.12bn)[a]	
	1992ε: r 394.0bn ($27.49bn)	
Growth	1991: -0.9%	1992ε: -20%
Inflation	1991: 82.2%	1992: 570%
Debt	1992: $2.62bn	
$1 = r	1991: 1.70	1992: 180
	1993: 800	

[a] Dollar values are estimated
r = rouble

Population: 21,871,000 (10.8% Russian)

	13–17	18–22	23–32
Men	1,203,000	1,014,000	1,668,000
Women	1,178,500	999,000	1,677,000

TOTAL ARMED FORCES: 40,000.
ACTIVE:
Terms of Service: conscription 18 months.

ARMY: some 38,000.
1 Corps HQ.
1 MRD.
1 ABD (cadre).
1 arty bde.
1 attack hel regt.
EQUIPMENT:
210 MBT, 160 ACV, 685 arty/MRL/mors,
8 SSM, 32 attack hel, plus 5,000 MBT, 1,800 ACV,
800 arty in store (probably Russian-controlled).

AIR FORCE: some 2,000.
FGA: 70 Su-17, Su-24, Su-25.
FIGHTER: 30 MiG-29.
TRANSPORT: 20 An-2.

PARAMILITARY:
National Guard: 1 bde 700.

FOREIGN FORCES:
RUSSIA
AIR DEFENCE:
FIGHTER: 1 regt, 32 Su-27.
SAM: 45: SA-2/-3/-5.

East Asia and Australasia

Regional Overview

The countries of the region see an American presence as essential for their continued stability. There are a number of latent issues, which in the absence of any regional security or arms control arrangements, could escalate into war. These include: disputed ownership of the Spratly and Paracel Islands; the status of Taiwan and its relationship with China; and the possible development of nuclear weapons by North Korea. Other destabilising issues in the region include: the possibility and problems of Korean reunification; Japanese ambitions to recover the Kuril islands from Russia; the first deployment of Japanese troops overseas since 1946, albeit in a restricted UN peacekeeping role; and the emergence of China as a potential superpower. There have also been some positive developments. In Cambodia the results of the UN-monitored election have been accepted and progress has been made in forming a government composed of three of the four factions, in the demobilisation of forces and creating a national army. The UN has announced its plan to withdraw its troops. However, the *Khmer Rouge* still remain a major threat to peace in Cambodia.

ASEAN Regional Forum

On 25 July 1993 the foreign ministers of the six ASEAN countries (Brunei, Indonesia, Malaysia, Philippines, Singapore and Thailand), meeting with their seven dialogue partners at an informal dinner in Singapore, announced the formation of an ASEAN Regional Forum. Invitations for membership have been sent to the dialogue partners: Australia, Canada, European Community, Japan, New Zealand, South Korea and the United States, and to five other regional states, China, Laos, Papua New Guinea, Russia and Vietnam. The 18-member ministerial-level forum will meet once a year. The first meeting is scheduled for Bangkok in 1994 to coincide with the next ASEAN Ministerial Meeting; it will be preceded by a meeting of senior officials from the states involved. The Forum is intended to provide an opportunity for ASEAN and regional states to hold talks on regional political and security issues. It will be the first group of this kind in the region.

At the annual ASEAN Ministerial Meeting from 23 to 24 July 1993 it was agreed to continue the intra-ASEAN dialogue on security cooperation involving ASEAN foreign and defence ministry officials which first met in Manila in June 1992. They are scheduled to meet next in Bangkok in late January or early February 1994.

Armaments in the Region

It would be incorrect to say that there is an arms race in the region, but it is true that the majority of states in East Asia, and in southern Asia too, have been expanding and improving the quality of their armed forces for some years. The most worrying aspect is the fact that most of the improvements to capability that have been achieved and that are planned involve naval and air forces which are the most suitable for projecting military force in a region where distances are great. This edition of *The Military Balance* includes a loose wall-map of the area from Pakistan in the west to Australia and Japan in the east, giving details of weapons holdings today and in 1984, and of defence expenditure over the last ten years. A number of states plan naval and air force enhancements in the future. Major naval orders have been placed or are being planned by Australia (eight ANZAC frigates, six submarines and a new minehunter class). Indonesia (corvettes, mine countermeasures vessels, amphibious craft and possibly submarines), Japan (two submarines, five destroyers and frigates), South Korea (ten KDX, two more *Ulsan* frigates and eight more T-209 submarines), Malaysia (two British-built frigates), Taiwan (submarines and French frigate hulls) and Thailand (two more Chinese frigates, perhaps some coastal submarines and one, possibly two, helicopter carriers). Air Force orders have been placed or are being planned by: Brunei (*Hawk* COIN aircraft), China (more Su-27 and locally produced variant of MiG-31), Indonesia (more F-16, 24 *Hawk* trainers), Malaysia

(28 *Hawk*, 18 MiG-29, 8 F/A-180), Singapore (10 F-16), Taiwan (150 F-16, 60 *Mirage* 2000-5, *Ching-Kuo* fighters) and Thailand (18 F-16).

The region also contains the two countries which are contributing most to the spread of ballistic missiles across the world – China and North Korea. China has already supplied short- and medium-range missiles to Iran, Iraq and Saudi Arabia. Although China has publicly announced its intention to abide by the rules of the Missile Technology Control Regime (MTCR), it is now being accused of violating these by the export of M-11 SSM components to Pakistan. Proving such an accusation is not easy, but US sources point to the movement of 'suspicious crates'; there is a branch of intelligence expertise known as 'cratology'. China has claimed that it would honour contracts signed before its statement on the MTCR, and also that the M-11 does not fall within the MTCR parameters as its range of 280km is below the MTCR's trigger of 300. For some years North Korea has been manufacturing and exporting an improved version of the *Scud* SSM. A consignment thought to be destined for Syria (which is also thought to be procuring Chinese M-9 missiles) was tracked in transit and appears to have been landed in Iran. North Korea, possibly in collaboration with Iran, has developed and tested the *No-dong 1* missile which is credited with a range of 1,500km. China, but not North Korea, made a declaration regarding its arms exports to the United Nations Register of Conventional Arms but as the missile category includes any missile with a range of 25 kilometres or over it is not necessarily helpful. In any event, China only declared missile exports to Thailand.

Nuclear Developments

The Military Balance has reviewed its listing of **Chinese** nuclear delivery means. We have felt for sometime that we have been understating the numbers deployed and so have revised our figures upwards. We must emphasise that there has not been a recent dramatic increase. It is, of course, a subject shrouded in secrecy but none of our commentators have objected to our revised figures. There have been other assessments which show much higher numbers still. Despite China's accession to the Nuclear Non-Proliferation Treaty (NPT) in 1992, it has still not signed a safeguard agreement with the IAEA.

North Korea is strongly suspected of pursuing a nuclear weapons programme. Its behaviour over compliance with IAEA safeguard requirements, only shortly after entering into the agreement, has only increased international suspicion. Further details on North Korea's nuclear programme are given in the essay 'Nuclear Developments' towards the back of the book.

Recent Japanese statements show that the once unthinkable topic of Japanese nuclear weapons is being thought about. The outgoing Foreign Minister has said that Japan must have the will to build nuclear weapons if necessary in the event of a nuclear threat from North Korea.

The US is said to be reviewing its policy towards the South Pacific nuclear-free zone and the plan by ASEAN to create a similar zone. In the past, the US has opposed such zones, arguing that they would weaken the concept of global nuclear deterrence. ASEAN officials have stressed that a treaty would preserve all existing rights of passage through international sea-lanes and airspace.

Conventional Military Force Developments

The **Australian** Army has increased its holdings of artillery and armed helicopters by: 40 *Hamel* 105mm towed guns (UK light gun produced under licence); 19 armed UH-14 and 18 AS-350B helicopters. The **Brunei** Army has formed its first Special Forces unit and is forming its first artillery battery. In **Cambodia** the *Khmer Rouge* have not demobilised but the numbers of men in three of the four factions have dropped significantly: Government Forces by 33,000; the Khmer People's National Liberation Armed Forces (KPNLAF) (Son Sann) by 13,000; Armée Nationale Sihanoukiste (ANS) (Sihanouk) by 10,000.

In **China** the long-term effects of population control are now evident; the numbers of males in the age groups 13–17 and 18–22 have both dropped by approximately 1 million. The number of females has dropped by roughly the same amount. The Army appears to continue to reorganise, with the loss of some divisions and units; how these affect the deployment by military regions is still unclear. The

Navy has commissioned its sixth improved *Ming*-class submarine, its first *Luhu*-class destroyer (armed with four twin C-801 SSM launchers and embarking two helicopters), the second *Jiangwei*-class GW frigate which also embarks a helicopter, while one *Chengdu* frigate has been retired. Three more *Houxin*-class missile craft have joined the fleet, while the numbers of coastal patrol craft have been reduced by 12 Soviet 24 *Kronshtadt*-class which have been retired. There are three more *Wosao*-class coastal minesweepers. There is no doubt that China is planning to buy both weapons and weapons-technology from Russia, but the true extent of its plans is unconfirmed. Reports include: procurement of a total of 72 Su-27 fighters; the manufacture under licence of 300 MiG-31 interceptors; and orders for SA-10 SAM for which an anti-ballistic missile capability is claimed. There have been numerous allusions to Chinese ambitions to acquire an aircraft carrier: the *Varyag* still under construction in the Ukraine is often mentioned; more recently they feature the transfer of an aircraft carrier from the Russian Pacific Fleet. There has also been talk of building two 40–50,000-tonnes aircraft carriers in Chinese shipyards. Whichever, if any, of these options are followed it will be several years before China could have an operational aircraft carrier and air wing. There has been no confirmation yet of a reported plan to abolish Military Regions and to divide the country into three Military Zones.

The **Indonesian** Navy has commissioned two ex-Soviet T-43 coastal minesweepers and added ten AS-332L armed helicopters to its air wing. Over the next two years the Navy will take delivery of the bulk of the remaining ships of the former East German Navy, including corvettes, mine countermeasure vessels and tank landing ships. Indonesia has recently ordered a total of 24 *Hawk* 100 series FGA and single-seat 200 series multirole aircraft.

The **Japanese** Ground Self-Defense Force continues to modernise its equipment inventory, albeit relatively slowly. Some 26 Type-90 tanks have replaced a similar number of Type-61 and small numbers of Type-87 reconnaissance vehicles, Type-89 AIFV, and Type-82 APC have been added. A further 33 FH-70 155mm towed artillery have been procured. The Maritime Self-Defense Force has commissioned two more *Harushio*-class submarines and (with two more being built) two *Uzushio*-class have been retired (one operational and one training boat). The first *Kongo*-class destroyer has commissioned, three more will be built, it is armed with a *Harpoon* and a VLS for SM-2MR SAM and *ASROC* and incorporates a helicopter deck. The last two (of six) *Abukuma*-class frigates have been commissioned.

We have listed a *Scud* SSM brigade in the **North Korean** army for the first time, although this unit may have been formed some time ago; the number of *Scud* launchers has been doubled to 30. We have reassessed tank holdings and believe these are 700 larger than previously thought. The SA-16, the more modern version of SA-7 (both hand-held Soviet made SAM), has been brought into service. Naval strength has been increased by six missile craft: three *Soju* and three *Sohung*-class. A reassessment of weapon holdings shows that the **South Korean** Army has 2,000 KIFV (AIFV) and not 1,000, some 400 more SP guns but 500 less towed artillery. 80 UH-60P *Black Hawk* and 20 Hughes 500 utility helicopters have been procured. In October the first South Korean-built submarine was launched. **Malaysia** is, after much deliberation, to procure both Russian MiG-29 and US F/A-18 aircraft. During the year the Navy took delivery of six more *Wasp* HAS-1 armed helicopters.

The **Mongolian** Army is building up its strength. Manpower has been increased by some 6,000; and an artillery and an air-defence brigade have been formed, as has an airborne battalion. Russian troops, with the exception of a large signals intelligence listening station, were withdrawn by the end of 1992. The **Philippines** Navy has increased its aviation inventory with three more BN-2A *Defender* maritime reconnaissance aircraft, while the Air Force now has seven more Bell UH-1H/M and five more AUH-76 (armed) helicopters, and three more RT-33A reconnaissance aircraft. The US completed its withdrawal from Subic Bay in October 1992. The **Singapore** Army has taken delivery of 36 French LG1 105mm towed guns, the Navy has acquired a British *Sir Lancelot*-class LST and the Air Force has increased its armed helicopter force by 14 more AS 550A2/C2 helicopters. The strength of the **Taiwanese** Army has been understated for some years and is some 50,000 stronger at 312,000 than previously thought. Tank strength has increased by 50 M-48H tanks. The

Navy has commissioned its first *Cheng Kung*-class (Taiwanese-built) GW frigate which embarks a helicopter; five more ships in this class and two of a larger class are planned, and two ex-US *Knox*-class frigates. Two *Po Yang* (US-*Sumner*-class) destroyers and two *Tien Shau* (US *Lawrence*-class) frigates have been retired. Taiwan, and its suppliers have risked hostile Chinese reaction by ordering 150 F-16 fighters and four E-2T *Hawkeye* aircraft from the US and 60 *Mirage* 2000-5 multirole aircraft from France. Taiwan is also developing its own defensive fighter, the *Ching-Kuo*. Ten aircraft are being tested and the eventual order is to be for 250 to 300 aircraft to replace F-5 and F-104 fighters. The **Thai** Navy has commissioned a second Chinese-built *Jianghu*-IV-class frigate and improved its maritime reconnaissance and ASW capability with the procurement of three P-3A *Orion* aircraft. The **Vietnamese** Air Force has retired its Su-17 FGA aircraft and has increased by 25 to 65 the number of Su-22. There are 50 more MiG-21 fighters than was originally thought.

AUSTRALIA

GDP	1991: $A 380.73bn ($US 296.63bn)	
	1992: $A 392.88bn ($US 288.90bn)	
Growth	1991: -1.1%	1992: 2.2%
Inflation	1991: 3.2%	1992: 1%
Public Debt	1992: 29.4%	
Def bdgt	1992: $A 9.44bn ($US6.94bn)	
	1993: $A 9.89bn ($US6.96bn)	
Def exp	1992: $A 9.36bn ($US6.89bn)	
$US 1 = $A	1990: 1.279	1991: 1.284
	1992: 1.360	1993: 1.420
$A = Australian dollars		

Population: 17,873,000

	13–17	18–22	23–32
Men	672,000	711,000	1,521,000
Women	631,000	678,000	1,463,000

TOTAL ARMED FORCES:
ACTIVE: 63,200 (incl 7,500 women).
RESERVES: 29,400. Army: 26,200; Navy: 1,600; Air: 1,600.

ARMY: 28,600 (incl 3,000 women).
LAND COMD: 6 military districts, 1 northern comd.
Comd tps:
1 AD regt +
1 avn regt.
1 SF regt (3 sqn)
1 inf div:
1 mech bde (1 armd, 1 mech, 1 para inf bn)
2 inf bde (1 of 2, 1 of 3 inf bn)
1 recce regt +
1 APC regt
3 arty regt (1 med, 2 fd)
1 engr regt +
1 avn regt (3 hel, 1 ac sqn).
(2 reserve inf bde see below)
RESERVES:
1 div HQ, 7 bde HQ, 2 recce regt, 1 APC regt, plus 2 APC sqn, 14 inf bn, 1 cdo, 5 arty (1 med, 4 fd) regt, 1 fd arty bty, 4 engr (2 fd, 2 construction) regt, 3 regional surveillance units.

EQUIPMENT:
MBT: 103 *Leopard* 1A3.
AIFV: 47 M-113 with 76mm gun.
APC: 724 M-113 (incl variants, 119 in store), 15 LAV.
TOWED ARTY: 105mm: 216 M2A2/L5, 105 *Hamel*; 155mm: 34 M-198.
MORTARS: 81mm: 302.
ATGW: 10 *Milan*
RCL: 84mm: 608 *Carl Gustav*; 106mm: 67 M-40A1.
SAM: 19 *Rapier*, 19 RBS-70.
AIRCRAFT: 22 GAF N-22B *Missionmaster*.
HELICOPTERS: 38 S-70 A-9 (Army/Air Force crews), 44 OH-58 *Kalkadoon*, 25 UH-1H (armed), 18 AS-35OB.
MARINE: 15 LCM, 53 LARC-5 amph craft.

NAVY: 15,300 (incl 750 Fleet Air Arm, 1,400 women).
Maritime Command, Support Command, 6 Naval Area cmd.
BASES: Sydney, NSW. (Maritime Command HQ). Base for: 4 SS, 3 DDG, 6 FF, 1 patrol, 1 LST, 1 AOR, 1 AGT, 2 LCT. Cockburn Sound, WA. Base for: 2 SS, 3 FF, 3 patrol, 1 survey, 1 AOR. Cairns, Qld: 5 patrol. 1 survey, 2 LCT Darwin, NT: 6 patrol, 1 LCT.
SUBMARINES: 5 *Oxley* (mod UK *Oberon*) (2 in refit) with Mk 48 HWT and *Harpoon* SSM.
PRINCIPAL SURFACE COMBATANTS: 11: incl 2 at 14 days notice for ops.
DESTROYERS: 3 *Perth* (US *Adams*) DDG with 1 SM-1 MR SAM/*Harpoon* SSM launcher; plus 2 x 3 ASTT (Mk 46 LWT), 2 x 127mm guns.
FRIGATES: 8:
5 *Adelaide* (US *Perry*) FFG, with S-70B-2 *Sea Hawk*, 2 x 3 ASTT; plus 1 x SM-1 MR SAM/*Harpoon* SSM launcher. 6 by end of 1993)
2 *Swan*, 1 *Paramatta* FF with 2 x 3 ASTT; plus 2 x 114mm guns.
PATROL AND COASTAL COMBATANTS: 18:
INSHORE: 18:
15 *Fremantle* PFI, 2 *Attack* PCI (Reserve trg).
1 *Banks* PCC (Reserve trg).
MINE WARFARE: 5:
2 *Rushcutter* MHI.
2 *Bandicoot* and 1 *Brolga* auxiliary MSI.

AMPHIBIOUS: 1:
1 *Tobruk* LST, capacity 22 tk, 378 tps, hel deck. Plus craft; 6 LCT, capacity 3 tk (incl 1 in store).
SUPPORT AND MISCELLANEOUS: 12:
1 *Success* (mod Fr *Durance*), 1 *Westralia* AO, 1 *Protector* sub trials and safety, 1 trg/log spt (ex-ferry), 2 AGHS, 4 small AGHS, 2 tugs.

FLEET AIR ARM: (750);
no cbt ac, 15 armed hel.
ASW: 1 hel sqn with 7 *Sea King* Mk 50/50A (ASW), 1 hel sqn with 16 S-70B-2 (ASW/trg).
UTILITY/SAR: 1 sqn with 6 AS-350B, 3 Bell 206B; 1 with 2 BAe-748 (EW trg), 1 F-27 (survey).

AIR FORCE: 19,300 (incl 3,100 women); 157 cbt ac, no armed hel.
FGA/RECCE: 2 sqn with 18 F-111C, 4 RF-111C.
FIGHTER/FGA: 3 sqn with 52 F-18 (50 -A, 2 -B).
TRAINING: 2 sqn with 46* MB-326H.
MR: 2 sqn with 19 P-3C.
OCU: 1 with 18* F-18B.
FAC: 1 flt with 4 CA-25 *Winjeel*.
TANKER: 4 Boeing 707-32OC.
TRANSPORT: 7 sqn:
2 with 24 C-130 (12 -E, 12 -H);
1 with 5 Boeing 707 (4 fitted for air-to-air refuelling);
2 with 19 DHC-4;
1 VIP with 5 *Falcon*-900.
1 with 10 HS-748 (8 for navigation trg, 2 for VIP tpt).
TRAINING: 64 PC-9.
SUPPORT: 4 *Dakota*, 2 *Nomad*.
MISSILES:
ASM: AGM-84A.
AAM: AIM-7 *Sparrow*, AIM-9L/M *Sidewinder*.
AD: *Jindalee* OTH radar: 1 experimental, 3 planned.
3 control and reporting units (1 mobile).

FORCES ABROAD:
MALAYSIA: Army: 1 inf coy (on 3-month rota-tional tours). Air Force: det with 2 P-3C ac.
PAPUA NEW GUINEA: 100; trg unit, 2 engr unit, 75 advisers.
Advisers in Fiji, Indonesia, Solomon Is., Thailand, Vanuatu, Tonga, W. Samoa and Kiribati.
UN AND PEACEKEEPING:
CAMBODIA (UNTAC): 611, plus 11 civ pol.
CROATIA (UNPROFOR I): 1 Observer
CYPRUS (UNFICYP): 20 civ pol.
EGYPT (MFO): 10 Observers.
MIDDLE EAST (UNTSO): 13 Observers.
SOMALIA (UNOSOM): 30.
WESTERN SAHARA (MINURSO): 43, plus 2 Observers.

PARAMILITARY:
BUREAU OF CUSTOMS: 10 GAF N-22B *Searchmaster* MR ac; about 6 boats.

FOREIGN FORCES:
US: 400: Air Force: 300; Navy: 100, joint facilities at NW Cape (until October 1993), Pine Gap and Nurrungar.
NEW ZEALAND: Air Force: 50: 6 A-4K/TA-4K (providing trg for Australian Navy).
SINGAPORE: (250) Flying Training School with 30-S-211 ac.

BRUNEI

GDP	1991:	$B 7.52bn ($US 4.30bn)	
	1992ε:	$B 8.00bn ($US 4.97bn)	
Growth	1990:	2.1%	1991: 5.1%
Inflation	1990:	2.0%	1991: 1.5%
Def bdgt	1992:	$B 636.9m ($US 395.6m)	
$US 1 = $B	1990:	1.867	1991: 1.750
	1992:	1.610	1993: 1.642

$B = Brunei dollars

Population: 280,600

	13–17	18–22	23–32
Men	13,200	12,400	28,500
Women	13,500	12,300	20,700

TOTAL ARMED FORCES: (all services form part of the Army): (Malays only eligible for service.)
ACTIVE: 4,400, incl 250 women.
RESERVES: Army: 700.

ARMY: 3,400.
3 inf bn.
1 armd recce sqn.
1 SAM bty: 2 tps with *Rapier*.
1 SF sqn.
1 engr sqn.
EQUIPMENT:
LIGHT TANKS: 16 *Scorpion*.
APC: 24 Sankey AT-104, 26 VAB.
MORTARS: 81mm: 24.
SAM: 12 *Rapier* (with *Blindfire*).
RESERVES: 1 bn (forming).

NAVY: 700.
BASE: Muara.
PATROL AND COASTAL COMBATANTS: 6†:
MISSILE CRAFT: 3 *Waspada* PFM with 2 x MM-38 *Exocet* SSM.
PATROL: 3 *Perwira* PFI⟨.
RIVERINE: Boats only.
AMPHIBIOUS: Craft only; 2 LCM⟨.

AIR FORCE: 300;
4 cbt ac, 7 armed hel.

COIN: 1 sqn with 7 Bo-105 armed hel.
HELICOPTERS: 1 sqn with 10 Bell 212, 1 -214 (SAR).
SULTAN'S FLIGHT: 1 A-320 *Airbus*, 2 A-340 *Airbus*.
1 B747-400, 1 B727-200, 2 *Gulfstream II*.
VIP tpt: 2 S-70 hel, 2 Bell 214ST.
TRAINING: *4 SF-260W (COIN, trg) ac, 2 Bell 206B hel.

FORCES ABROAD:
UN AND PEACEKEEPING:
CAMBODIA (UNTAC): 3 Observers, 12 civ pol.

PARAMILITARY:
GURKHA RESERVE UNIT: 2,300+: 2 bn.
ROYAL BRUNEI POLICE: 1,750, 3 PCI⟨, boats.

FOREIGN FORCES:
UK: some 1,000. (Army) 1 Gurkha inf bn, 1 hel flt.
SINGAPORE: some 500: trg school incl hel det (5 UH-1).

CAMBODIA

GNP	1991ε: r 1,335.9bn ($US 1.07bn)	
	1992ε: r 2,558.0bn ($1.15bn)	
Growth	1991ε: 7.6%	1992ε: 8.0%+
Inflation	1991ε: 81.0%	1992ε: 96.0%
Def exp[a]	1991: r 47.0bn ($42.73m)	
	1992: r 122.0bn ($58.10m)	
FMA[b]	1993: $12m (US)	
$1 = riel	1990: 580.0	1991: 780
	1992: 846.6	1993: 3,800.0

R = Riel

[a] All dollar figures are adjusted.
[b] Security assistance to the Cambodian resistance as Economic Support.

Population: 9,068,000

	13–17	18–22	23–32
Men	323,700	352,400	829,800
Women	326,500	351,300	807,000

TOTAL ARMED FORCES:
ACTIVE: some 102,000 incl provincial forces.
Terms of service: conscription, 5 years; ages 18 to 35. Militia serve 3 to 6 months with Regulars.

ARMY: some 50,000.
5 Military Regions.
7 inf div.
3 indep inf bde.
9 indep inf regt.
3 armd regt.
Some indep recce, arty, AD bn.

EQUIPMENT:
MBT: 150 T-54/-55/-59.
LIGHT TANKS: 10 PT-76.
APC: 210 BTR-60/-152, M-113.
TOWED ARTY: some 490: 76mm: M-1942; 122mm: M-1938, D-30; 130mm: Type 59.
MRL: 107mm: Type-63; 122mm: 8 BM-21; 132mm: BM-13-16; 140mm: 20 BM-14-16.
MORTARS: 82mm: M-37; 120mm: M-43; 160mm: M-160.
RCL: 82mm: B-10; 107mm: B-11.
AD GUNS: 14.5mm: ZPU 1/-2/-4; 37mm: M-1939; 57mm: S-60.
SAM: SA-7.

NAVY: ε1,000.
PATROL AND COASTAL COMBATANTS: 10:
2 Sov *Turya* PFI (no TT).
2 Sov *Stenka* PFI (no TT), about 6⟨.
AMPHIBIOUS: Craft only: 2 Sov LCVP.

AIR FORCE: ε1,000.
21 cbt ac; no armed hel.
FIGHTER: 21 MiG-21.
TRANSPORT: 3 An-24, Tu-134.
HELICOPTERS: 5 Mi-8/-17.

PROVINCIAL FORCES: some 50,000.
Reports of at least 1 inf regt per province: with varying number of inf bn with lt wpn.

PARAMILITARY:
MILITIA: Some 220,000 local forces, org at village level for local defence. ε10–20 per village. Not all armed.

OTHER FORCES: UN to monitor demobilisation, incl government forces to form united army.
KHMER ROUGE (National Army of Democratic Kampuchea) some 25,000 org in 25 'bde', plus 2 indep regt.
KHMER PEOPLE'S NATIONAL LIBERATION ARMED FORCES (KPNLAF): some 7,000 org in 5 div and 3 indep bde.
ARMEE NATIONALE SIHANOUKISTE (ANS): perhaps 7,000 org in 5 div.
EQUIPMENT: T-54, Type-62 tk; 122mm: M-1938; 130mm arty; 60mm, 82mm mor; RPG-7 RL, RCL, SA-7 SAM.

FOREIGN FORCES:
UNITED NATIONS (UNTAC): some 16,000, plus 3,540 civ pol from 45 countries incl inf bn from Bangladesh, Bulgaria, France, Ghana, India, Indonesia, Malaysia, Netherlands, Pakistan, Tunisia and Uruguay. Air Assets: 3 C-160, 2 C-130, 1 *Beechcraft* ac, 21 Mi-17, 12 Mi-26, 6 Bell-212, 9 Bell 206, 6 *Puma* hel.

CHINA

GNP	1991:	Y 1,975.9bn ($371.20bn)
	1992:	Y 2,393.8bn ($434.08bn)
Growth	1991: 6.8%	1992: 12.8%
Inflation	1991: 6.0%	1992: 10.4%
Debt	1991: $53bn	1992: $60.56bn
Def exp	1991ε: Y 100bn ($18.79bn)	
	1992ε: Y 120bn ($21.76bn)	
Def bdgt[a]	1992: Y 37bn ($6.71bn)	
	1993: Y 41.8bn ($7.31bn)	
$1 = yuan	1990: 4.783	1991: 5.323
	1992: 5.515	1993: 5.711

Y = yuan
[a] Official budget.

Population: 1,184,360,000

	13–17	18–22	23–32
Men	52,242,000	60,413,000	117,001,000
Women	48,826,000	56,590,000	108,747,000

TOTAL ARMED FORCES:
ACTIVE: some 3,030,000 (perhaps 1,275,000 conscripts, some 136,000 women), being reduced.
Terms of service: selective conscription; Army, Marines 3 years; Navy, Air Force 4 years.
RESERVES: 1,200,000+ militia reserves being formed on a province-wide basis.

STRATEGIC MISSILE FORCES:
OFFENSIVE (Strategic Rocket Units): (90,000).
MISSILES: org in 6 bases (army level) with bde/regt incl 1 msl testing and trg regt; org varies by msl type.
ICBM: some 14:
4 CSS-4 (DF-5); mod tested with MIRV.
10+ CSS-3 (DF-4).
IRBM: some 90+
60+ CSS-2 (DF-3), some updated.
SUBMARINES: 1:
SSBN: 1 *Xia* with 12 CSS-N-3 (J-1).
DEFENSIVE:
(a) Tracking stations: Xinjiang (covers Central Asia) and Shanxi (northern border).
(b) Phased-array radar complex. Ballistic missile early warning.

ARMY: 2,300,000 (perhaps 1,075,000 conscripts), (reductions continue).
7 Military Regions (MR), 28 Military Districts, 3 Garrison Comd.
24 Integrated Group Armies (GA, equivalent to Western corps) org varies, normally with 3 inf div, 1 tk, 1 arty, 1 AAA bde or 3 inf, 1 tk div, 1 arty, 1 AAA bde, cbt readiness category varies.
Summary of Combat units:
78 inf div (incl 2 mech 'all arms').
10 armd div (normally 3 regt, 323 MBT).
5 field arty div.
2 indep armd, 5 indep fd arty, 5 indep AA bde.
30 indep engr regt.
6 Rapid Deployment Force bn.
Avn: 3 group hel bn (2 more forming); some hel regt, 1 hel trg regt.
AB (manned by Air Force):
1 corps of 3 div.
Spt tps.

EQUIPMENT:
MBT: some 7,500–8,000: 700 T-34/85, some T-54, 6,000 Type-59, 200 T-69 (mod Type-59), some Type-79, Type-80, Type-85 II reported.
LIGHT TANKS: 1,200 Type-63 amph, 800 Type-62.
AIFV: WZ-501, YW-307/-309.
APC: 2,800 Type-531 C/-D/-E, YW-534, Type-85 (YW-531H), Type-55 (BTR-40), -56 (BTR-152), -63, Type-77-1/-2 (Sov BTR-50PK amph); Type-523.
TOWED ARTY: 14,500:
100mm: Type-59 (fd/ATK), Type-86; 122mm: 6,000: Type-54, Type-60, Type-83, D-30; 130mm: 1,000 Types-59/-59-1; 152mm: Type-54, 1,400 Type-66, Type-83; 155mm: ε30 WAC-21.
SP ARTY: 122mm: Type-54-1 (Type-531 chassis), Type-85; 152mm: Type-83.
MRL: 3,800: 107mm: Types-63 towed /-81 SP (being replaced by 122mm); 122mm: Type-81, Type-83; 130mm: Type-63, Type-70 SP, Type-82, Type-85; 140mm: BM-14-16; 273mm: Type-83; 284mm: Type-74 minelayer; 320mm: WS-1; 425mm: Type-762 mine clearance.
MORTARS: 82mm: Type-53 (incl SP); 120mm: Type-55 (incl SP); 160mm: Type-56.
SSM: M-9 (CSS-6/DF-15) (range 500km); M-11 (CSS-7/DF-11) (range 120–150km).
ATGW: HJ-73 (*Sagger*-type), HJ-8 (*TOW/Milan*-type).
RCL: 75mm: Type-52, Type-56; 82mm: Type-65.
RL: 90mm: Type-51.
ATK GUNS: 57mm: Type-55; 76mm: Type-54; 100mm: Type-73, Type-86.
AD: GUNS: 15,000: incl 23mm: (ZSU-23 type); 37mm: Types-55/-65/-74, -63 twin SP; 57mm: Types-59, -80 SP; 85mm: Type-56; 100mm: Type-59.
SAM: HN-5, HN-5A/-C (SA-7 type); HQ-61 twin SP.
HELICOPTERS: 30 Z-9, 8 SA-342 (with *HOT*), 24 S-70.
RESERVES: (undergoing major reorganisation on a provincial basis) perhaps 700,000: ε60 inf div.

NAVY: ε260,000 incl Coast Defence (25,000), Naval Air (25,000) and Marines (5,000) (some 40,000 conscripts);
SUBMARINES: 47:
STRATEGIC SUBMARINES: 1 SSBN.
TACTICAL SUBMARINES: 45:
SSN: 5 *Han* with 533mm TT.

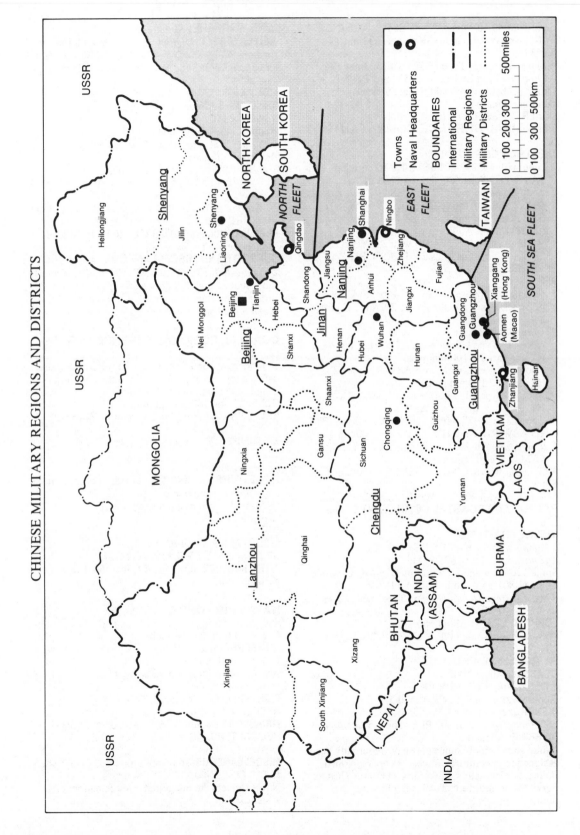

CHINESE MILITARY REGIONS AND DISTRICTS

SSG: 1 modified *Romeo* (Type ES5G), with 6 C-801 (YJ-6, *Exocet* derivative) SSM; plus 533mm TT.
SS: 39:
6 *Improved Ming* (Type ES5E) with 533mm TT.
33 *Romeo* (Type ES3B)† with 533mm TT.
(Note: probably about additional 50 *Romeo*-class non-operational).
OTHER ROLES: 1 *Golf* (SLBM trials)
PRINCIPAL SURFACE COMBATANTS:
56:
DESTROYERS: 18 DDG:
1 *Luhu* with 4 x 2 C-801 SSM, 1 x 100mm gun, 2 Z-9A (Fr *Dauphin*) hel, plus 2 x 3 ASTT.
2 modified *Luda*, 1 with 2 x 3 CSS-N-2 *Hai Ying-2* (HY-2 *Styx* derivative) and 1 with 4 x 2 C-801) SSM, 1 x 2 130mm guns, 2 Z-9A (Fr *Dauphin*) hel (OTHT), 2 x 3 ASTT.
15 *Luda* (Type-051) (ASUW) with 2 x 3 HY-2 SSM, 2 x 2 130mm guns; plus 2 x 12 ASW RL
FRIGATES: 38:
FFG: 33:
2 *Jiangwei* with possibly 2 x 3 C-801 SSM, 2 x 5 ASW RL, 1 x 2 100mm gun, 1 Z-9A (Fr *Dauphin*) hel.
27 *Jianghu*; 4 variants:
    About 13 Type I, with 4 x 5 ASW RL, plus 2 x 2 HY-2 SSM, 2 x 100mm guns.
    About 9 Type II, with 2 x 5 ASW RL, plus 2 x 2 HY-2, 2 x 2 100mm guns.
    About 3 Type III, with 8 x C-801 SSM, 2 x 2 100mm guns; plus 4 x 5 ASW RL.
    About 2 Type IV, with 1 Z-9A hel, 2 x 3 ASTT, 2 x 5 ASW RL, 2 x 2 HY-2 SSM, 1 x 100mm gun.
1 *Jiangdong* with 2 x 5 ASW RL, 2 x 2 CSA-NX-2 SAM, 2 x 2 100mm guns.
3 *Chengdu* with 1 x 2 HY-2 SSM, 3 x 100mm guns.
FF: 5.
5 *Jiangnan* with 2 x 5 ASW RL, 3 x 100mm guns.
PATROL AND COASTAL COMBATANTS: About 870:
MISSILE CRAFT: 215:
1 *Huang* with 6 x C-801 SSM.
4 *Houxin* with 4 x C-801 SSM.
Some 120 *Huangfeng/Hola* (Sov *Osa-I*-type) with 6 or 8 x C-801 SSM; some with 4 x HY-2.
About 90 *Hegu/Hema*⟨ (*Komar*-Type) with 2 x HY-2 or 4 x C-801 SSM.
TORPEDO CRAFT: About 160:
100 *Huchuan*, some 60 P-6, all ⟨ with 2 x 533mm TT.
PATROL: About 495:
COASTAL: About 100:
4 *Haijui* with 3 x 5 ASW RL.
About 96 *Hainan* with 4 x ASW RL.
INSHORE: About 350:
300 *Shanghai*, 5 *Huludao* PFI, about 45 *Shantou*⟨.
RIVERINE: About 45⟨.
(Note: some minor combatants have reportedly been assigned to paramilitary forces – People's Armed Police, border guards, the militia and to the Customs Service – or into store. Totals therefore may be high.)

MINE WARFARE: About 126:
MINELAYERS: 1 *Beleijan* reported. In addition *Luda*, *Anshan*, *Jiangnan*, *Chengdu* class DD/FF, *Hainan*, and *Shanghai* PC and T-43 MSO have minelaying capability.
MCM: About 125:
35 Sov T-43 MSO.
5 *Wosao* MSC.
About 80 *Lienyun* aux MSC.
5 *Fushun* MSI; plus about 60 drone MSI⟨.
AMPHIBIOUS: 51:
3 *Yukan* LST, capacity about 200 tps, 10 tk.
13 *Shan* (US LST-1) LST, capacity about 150 tps, 16 tk.
30 *Yuliang*, 1 *Yuling*, 4 *Yudao* LSM, capacity about 100 tps, 3 tk.
Plus about 400 craft: 320 LCU, 40 LCP, 10 LCT and some hovercraft.
SUPPORT AND MISCELLANEOUS: About 164:
2 *Fuqing* AO, 33 AOT, 14 AF, 10 submarine spt, 1 sub rescue, 2 repair, 9 *Qiong Sha* tps tpt, 30 tpt, 33 survey/research/experimental, 4 icebreakers, 25 ocean tugs, 1 trg.

COASTAL REGIONAL DEFENCE FORCES:
(25,000).
ε35 indep arty and SSM regt deployed in 25 coastal defence regions to protect naval bases, offshore islands and other vulnerable points.
GUNS: 85mm, 100mm, 130mm.
SSM: CSS-C-2 (*Hai Ying 2* variant, '*Silkworm*').

MARINES: (Naval Infantry): (some 5,000).
1 bde.
Special recce units.
RESERVES: On mob to total 8 div (24 inf, 8 tk, 8 arty regt), 2 indep tk regt.
(3 Army div also have an amph role.)
EQUIPMENT:
MBT: T-59.
LIGHT TANKS: T-60/-63, PT-76.
APC: Type-531, LVT; some Type-77.
ARTY: how: 122mm: Type-54 (incl -54-1 SP).
MRL: Type-63.

NAVAL AIR FORCE: (25,000);
880 shore-based cbt ac, 65 armed hel.
Org in 3 bbr, 6 ftr div, incl:
BOMBERS: some 30 H-6, some H-6D reported with C-601 anti-ship ALCM.
About 130 H-5 torpedo-carrying lt bbr.
FGA: some 100 Q-5.
FIGHTER: some 600, incl J-5/-6/-7/-8.
RECCE: H-5.
MR/ASW: 15 ex-Sov Be-6 *Madge*, 5 PS-5 (SH-5).
HELICOPTERS: ASW: 15 SA-321, 40 Z-5, 10 Z-9.
MISCELLANEOUS: some 60 lt tpt ac; JJ-5/-6 trg ac.
ALCM: FL-1/C-601.
Naval fighters are integrated into the national AD system.

DEPLOYMENT AND BASES:

NORTH SEA FLEET: Coastal defence from Korean border (Yalu River) to south of Lianyungang (approx 35°10'N); equates to Shenyang, Beijing and Jinan Military Regions; and to seaward.
BASES: Qingdao (HQ), Dalian (Luda), Huludao, Weihai, Chengshan.
9 coastal defence districts.
FORCES: 2 submarine, 3 escort, 1 mine warfare, 1 amph sqn; plus Bohai Gulf trg flotillas. About 300 patrol and coastal combatants.
EAST SEA FLEET: Coastal defence from south of Lianyungang to Dongshan (35°10'N to 23°30'N approx); equates to Nanjing Military Region, and to seaward:
BASES: Shanghai (HQ), Wusong, Dinghai, Hangzhou.
7 coastal defence districts.
FORCES: 2 submarine, 2 escort, 1 mine warfare, 1 amph sqn. About 250 patrol and coastal combatants.
Marines: 1 cadre div.
Coastal Regional Defence Forces: Nanjing Coastal District.
SOUTH SEA FLEET: Coastal defence from Dongshan (approx 23°30'N) to Vietnam border; equates to Guangzhou Military Region, and to seaward (including Paracel and Spratly Islands).
BASES: Zhanjiang (HQ), Shantou, Guangzhou, Haikou, Yulin, Beihai, Huangpu; plus outposts on Paracel and Spratly Is.
9 coastal defence districts.
FORCES: 2 submarine, 2 escort, 1 mine warfare, 1 amph sqn. About 300 patrol and coastal combatants.
Marines: 1 bde.

AIR FORCE: 470,000, incl strategic forces and 220,000 AD personnel (160,000 conscripts); some 4,970 cbt ac, few armed hel.
7 Military Air Regions, HQ Beijing.
Combat elm org in armies of varying numbers of air div (each with 3 regt of 3 sqn of 3 flt of 4–5 ac, 1 maint unit, some tpt and trg ac).
Tpt ac in regt only.
BOMBERS:
MEDIUM: 120 H-6 (some may be nuclear-capable). Some carry C-601 ASM.
LIGHT: Some 350 H-5 (some with C-801 ASM).
FGA: 500 Q-5.
FIGHTER: ε4,000, incl 400 J-5, some 60 regt with about 3,000 J-6/B/D/E, 500 J-7, 100 J-8, 20 Su-27, 4 Su-27B.
RECCE: ε40 HZ-5, 150 JZ-5, 100 JZ-6 ac.
TRANSPORT: some 600, incl 18 BAe *Trident* 1E/2E, 30 Il-14, 10 Il-18, 10 Il-76, 50 Li-2, 300 Y-5, 25 Y-7, 25 Y-8, 15 Y-11, 2 Y-12.
HELICOPTERS: some 400: incl 6 AS-332, 4 Bell 214, 28 Mi-17, 20 S-70C-2, 30 Mi-8, 250 Z-5, 100 Z-6, 15 Z-8, 50 Z-9.
TRAINING: incl CJ-5/-6, HJ-5, J-2, JJ-2, JJ-4/-5/-6.
MISSILES:
AAM: PL-2/-2A, PL-5B *Atoll*-type, PL-7.
ASM: HOT: C-601 subsonic ALCM (anti-ship, perhaps HY-2 SSM derivative); C-801 surface skimmer.
AD ARTY:
16 div: 16,000 35mm, 57mm, 85mm and 100mm guns; 28 indep AD regts (100 SAM units with HQ-2/-2B, -2J (CSA-1), -61 SAM).

FORCES ABROAD:
UN AND PEACEKEEPING:
CAMBODIA (UNTAC): 402 (engrs), plus 45 Observers and engrs.
MIDDLE EAST (UNTSO): 5 Observers.
IRAQ/KUWAIT(UNIKOM): 15 Observers.
WESTERN SAHARA (MINURSO): 19 Observers.

PARAMILITARY: some 1,200,000, Ministry of Defence: People's Armed Police: 1.2 million: 60 div, duties incl border and internal security (returned to PLA control June 1993).

FIJI

GDP	1991:	$F 1.81bn ($US 1.23bn)
	1992ε:	$F 2.29bn ($US 1.52bn)
Growth	1991: -0.1%	1992: 2.8%
Inflation	1991: 6.5%	1992: 4.9%
Debt	1991:	$US 350.0m
	1992:	$US 356.0m
Def exp	1991:	$F 47.8m ($US 32.39m)
Def bdgt	1992:	$F 34.7m ($US 23.09m)
	1993:	$F 39.9m ($US 25.91m)
$US 1 = $F	1990: 1.481	1991: 1.476
	1992: 1.503	1993: 1.540

$F = Fiji dollar

Population: 766,800

	13–17	18–22	23–32
Men	44,100	37,900	63,400
Women	41,900	36,400	63,500

TOTAL ARMED FORCES:
ACTIVE: 3,900 (incl recalled reserves).
RESERVES: some 5,000 (to age 45).

ARMY: ε3,600 (incl reserves).
7 inf bn (incl 4 cadre).
1 engr bn.
EQUIPMENT:
MORTARS: 81mm: 12.

NAVY: 300.
BASE: Suva.
PATROL AND COASTAL COMBATANTS: 6:
4 *Vai* (Is *Dabur*) PCI⟨.
2 *Levuka* PCI⟨.

SUPPORT AND MISCELLANEOUS: 2: 1 *Kiro* (US *Redwing*-class) trg.
1 *Cagidonu* presidential yacht.

AIR WING:
1 AS-350 F-2, 1 SA-365N.

FORCES ABROAD: about 1,000.
UN AND PEACEKEEPING:
CAMBODIA (UNTAC): 50 civ pol.
EGYPT (MFO): 350. 1 inf bn(-).
IRAQ/KUWAIT (UNIKOM): 6 Observers.
LEBANON (UNIFIL): 647; 1 inf bn.

INDONESIA

GDP	1991:	Rp 227,163.0bn ($116.48bn)	
	1992:	Rp 258,950.0bn ($127.58bn)	
Growth	1991:	6.6%	1992: 5.7%
Inflation	1991:	9.2%	1992: 7.5%
Debt	1991:	$73.63bn	1992: $77.90bn
Def exp	1992:	Rp 3,742.0bn ($1.84bn)	
Def bdgt	1992:	Rp 3,596.0bn ($1.77bn)	
	1993:	Rp 4,040.0bn ($1.95bn)	
$1 = Rp	1990:	1,842.8	1991: 1,950.3
	1992:	2,029.9	1993: 2,075.0

Rp = rupiahs

Population: 186,846,000

	13–17	*18–22*	*23–32*
Men	10,699,000	9,300,000	15,029,000
Women	10,288,000	9,309,000	15,253,000

TOTAL ARMED FORCES:
ACTIVE: 270,900.
Terms of service: 2 years selective conscription authorised.
RESERVES: 400,000: Army (planned): cadre units; numbers, strengths unknown, obligation to age 45 for officers.

ARMY: 202,900.
Strategic Reserve (KOSTRAD): (9,400).
2 inf div HQ.
3 inf bde (9 bn).
3 AB bde (9 bn).
2 fd arty regt (6 bn).
1 AD arty regt (2 bn).
2 engr bn.
10 Military Area Comd (KODAM): (190,000): (Provincial (KOREM) and District (KORIM) comd)
65 inf bn (incl 4 AB).
8 cav bn.
8 fd arty, 8 AD bn.
8 engr bn.
1 composite avn sqn, 1 hel sqn.
SF (KOPASSUS): (3,500): 2 SF gp (each 2 bn).

EQUIPMENT:
LIGHT TANKS: some 125 AMX-13, 30 PT-76 .
RECCE: 60 *Saladin*, 45 *Ferret*.
APC: 200 AMX-VCI, 45 *Saracen*, 200 V-150 *Commando*, 20 *Commando Ranger*, 140 BTR-40, 25 BTR-50.
TOWED ARTY: 76mm: M48; 105mm: 170 M-101, 10 M-56.
MORTARS: 81mm: 800; 120mm: 75 Brandt.
RCL: 90mm: 90 M-67; 106mm: 45 M-40A1.
RL: 89mm: 700 LRAC.
AD GUNS 20mm: 125; 40mm: 90 L/70; 57mm: 200 S-60.
SAM: 50 *Rapier*, 40 RBS-70.
AIRCRAFT: 1 BN-2 *Islander*, 2 C-47, 4 NC-212, 2 Cessna 310, 2 *Commander* 680, 18 *Gelatik* (trg).
HELICOPTERS: 10 Bell 205, 15 Bo-105, 4 NB-412, 10 Hughes 300C (trg).

NAVY: ε44,000, incl ε1,000 Naval Air and 12,000 Marines.
PRINCIPAL COMMANDS:
WESTERN FLEET (HQ Tanjung Priok (Jakarta)):
BASES: Jakarta, Tanjung Pinang (Riau Is.), Sabang, Belawan (Sumatra).
EASTERN FLEET (HQ Surabaya);
BASES: Surabaya, Manado (Celebes), Ambon (Moluccas), Ujung Pandang.
MILITARY SEALIFT COMMAND: (KOLINLAMIL): Controls some amph and tpt ships used for inter-island comms and log spt for Army and Navy (assets incl in Navy and Army listings).
SUBMARINES: 2 *Cakra* (Ge T-209/1300) with 533mm TT (Ge HWT).
FRIGATES: 17:
3 *Ahmad Yani* (Nl *Van Speijk*) with 1 *Wasp* hel (ASW) (Mk 44 LWT), 2 x 3 ASTT; plus 2 x 4 *Harpoon* SSM.
3 *Fatahillah* with 2 x 3 ASTT (not *Nala*), 1 x 2 ASW mor, 1 *Wasp* hel (*Nala* only); plus 2 x 2 MM-38 *Exocet*, 1 x 120mm gun.
3 *M.K. Tiyahahu* (UK *Ashanti*) with 1 *Wasp* hel, 1 x 3 *Limbo* ASW mor; plus 2 x 114mm guns.
4 *Samadikun* (US *Claud Jones*) with 2 x 3 ASTT, (probably 3 in store).
1 *Hajar Dewantara* (Yug) (trg) with 2 x 533mm TT, 1 ASW mor; plus 2 x 2 MM-38 *Exocet*.
PATROL AND COASTAL COMBATANTS: 45:
MISSILE CRAFT: 4 *Mandau* PFM with 4 x MM-38 *Exocet* SSM.
TORPEDO CRAFT: 2 *Singa* (Ge Lürssen 57-m (NAV I)) with 2 x 533mm TT and 1 x 57mm gun.
PATROL: 39:
COASTAL: 9:
2 *Pandrong* (Ge Lürssen 57-m (NAV II)) PFC, with 1 x 57mm gun.
3 *Barakuda* (Sov *Kronshtadt*)†.
4 *Kakap* (Ge Lürssen 57-m (NAV III)) PFC, with 40mm gun and hel deck.
INSHORE: 30:
3 Yug *Kraljevica* (in reserve), 8 *Sibarau* (Aust

Attack) PCI, 1 *Bima Samudera* PHM, 18⟨.
MINE WARFARE: 4:
2 *Pulau Rengat* (mod Nl *Tripartite*) MCC (mainly used for coastal patrol).
2 *Pulau Rani* (Sov T-43) MCC (mainly used for coastal patrol).
AMPHIBIOUS: 14:
6 *Teluk Semangka* LST, capacity about 200 tps, 17 tk, 4 with 3 hel (2 fitted as comd ships and 1 as hospital ship).
1 *Teluk Amboina* LST, capacity about 200 tps, 16 tk.
7 *Teluk Langsa* (US LST-512) and 2 *Teluk Banten* (mod US LST-512) LST, capacity: 200 tps, 16 tks).
(3 LST assigned to Mil Sealift Comd.)
Plus about 80 craft: 4 LCU, some 45 LCM.
SUPPORT AND MISCELLANEOUS: 21:
1 *Sorong* AOR, 1 *Arun* AO (UK *Rover*), 2 Sov *Khobi* AOT, 1 cmd/spt/replenish, 1 repair, 8 tpt (Mil Sea Lift Comd), 1 ocean tug, 6 survey/research.
(The following ships have been purchased from Germany and delivery is expected over next 2 years: 16 *Parchim* corvettes; 9 *Kondor-II* MCMV; 12 *Frosch I* LST; 2 *Frosch II* spt ships.)

NAVAL AIR: (ε1,000); 18 cbt ac, 25 armed hel.
ASW: 9 *Wasp* HAS-1 hel, 10 AS-332L.
MR: 12 N-22 *Searchmaster* B, 6 *Searchmaster* L, 6 CN-235-100 IPTN/CASA.
OTHER:
 AIRCRAFT: incl 4 *Commander*, 4 NC-212; 2 *Bonanza* F33 (trg), 6 PA-38 (trg).
HELICOPTERS: 4 NAS-332F, *6 NBo-105, 2 SA-313.

MARINES: (12,000);
2 inf bde (6 bn);
1 SF bn(-).
1 cbt spt regt (arty, AD)
EQUIPMENT:
LIGHT TANKS: 80 PT-76 .†
RECCE: 20 BRDM.
AIFV: 10 AMX-10 PAC-90.
APC: 100: 25 AMX-10P, 75 BTR-50P.
TOWED ARTY: 122mm: 40 M-38.
MRL: 140mm: BM-14.
AD GUNS: 40mm, 57mm.

AIR FORCE: 24,000;
80 cbt ac, no armed hel.
2 Air Operations Areas:
FGA: 2 sqn with 28 A-4 (26 -E, 2 TA-4H).
1 with 12 F-16 (8 -A, 4 -B).
FIGHTER: 1 sqn with 14 F-5 (10 -E, 4 -F).
COIN: 2 sqn:
1 with 14 *Hawk* Mk 53 (COIN/trg);
1 with 12 OV-10F.
MR: 1 sqn with 3 Boeing 737-200, 1 C-130H-MP.
TANKER: 2 KC-130B.
TRANSPORT:
19 C-130 (9 -B, 3 -H, 7 -H-30), 1-L100-30.

1 Boeing 707, 5 Cessna 401, 2 -402, 7 F-27-400M, 1 F-28-1000, 10 NC-212, 1 *Skyvan* (survey), 30 CN-235M.
HELICOPTERS: 3 sqn:
1 with 12 S-58T;
2 with 2 Bell 204B, 2 -206B, 10 Hughes 500, 12 NBo-105, 13 NSA-330, 3 SE-3160.
TRAINING: 4 sqn with 40 AS-202, 2 Cessna 172, 5 -207 (liaison), 23 T-34C, 10 T-41D.
AIRFIELD DEFENCE: 5 bn *Rapier*.

FORCES ABROAD:
UN AND PEACEKEEPING:
CAMBODIA (UNTAC): 1,795 (inf), plus 17 Observers, 224 civ pol.
IRAQ/KUWAIT (UNIKOM): 6 Observers.

PARAMILITARY:
POLICE (POLRI): some 215,000: incl Police 'Mobile bde' (BRIMOB) org in coy: some 8,000 incl Police COIN unit (GEGANA); 3 *Commander*, 1 Beech 18, 7 lt ac; 10 Bo-105, 3 Bell 206 hel.
MARINE: About 10 PCC and 9 PCI and 6 PCI⟨ (all armed).
KAMRA (People's Security): 1.5m: some 300,000 a year get 3 weeks' basic trg. Part-time police auxiliary.
WANRA (People's Resistance): part-time local military auxiliary force under comd of Regional Military Commands (KOREM).
CUSTOMS: About 72 PFI⟨, armed.
SEA COMMUNICATIONS AGENCY: (Responsible to Department of Transport) 5 *Kujang* PCI, 4 *Golok* PCI (SAR) plus boats.

OPPOSITION:
FRETILIN (Revolutionary Front for an Independent East Timor): some 100 incl spt; small arms.
FREE PAPUA MOVEMENT (OPM): perhaps 500–600 (100 armed).
FREE ACEH MOVEMENT (Gerakan Aceh Merdeka): 750 armed reported.

JAPAN

GDP	1991:	¥ 450,795bn ($3,346.5bn)		
	1992:	¥ 464,933bn ($3,666.2bn)		
Growth[a]	1991:	4.5%	1992ε:	1.3%
Inflation[b]	1991:	3.3%	1992:	1.7%
Public Debt	1992:	66.2%		
Def bdgt	1992:	¥ 4,551.8bn ($35.94bn)		
	1993:	¥ 4,640.6bn ($39.71bn)		
$1 = ¥	1990:	144.79	1991:	134.71
	1992:	126.65	1993:	116.87

¥ = yen
[a] GNP
[b] Real inflation is higher, national accounting not considering housing costs which are substantial.

Population: 124,834,000

	13–17	18–22	23–32
Men	4,414,000	4,808,000	8,778,000
Women	4,192,000	4,572,000	8,448,000

TOTAL ARMED FORCES:
ACTIVE: 237,700, incl 160 Central Staffs (reducing), 8,000 women.
RESERVES: Army 44,600; Navy 1,100; Air 800.

ARMY: (Ground Self-Defense Force): 149,900
(incl 5,200 women).
5 Army HQ (Regional Commands).
1 armd div.
12 inf div (5 at 7,000, 7 at 9,000 each).
2 composite bde.
1 AB bde.
1 arty bde; 2 arty gp.
2 AD bde; 3 AD gp.
4 trg bde; 2 trg regt.
5 engr bde.
1 hel bde.
2 ATK hel pl, 1 more forming.
EQUIPMENT:
MBT: 1,200: some 271 Type-61 (retiring), some 873 Type-74, 56 Type-90.
RECCE: 75 Type-87.
AIFV: some 26 Type-89.
APC: 300 Type-60, 300 Type-73, some 186 Type-82.
TOWED ARTY: 590: 105mm: 290 M-101; 155mm: 260 FH-70; 203mm: 40 M-115.
SP ARTY: 302: 105mm: 20 Type-74; 155mm: 200 Type-75; 203mm: 82 M-110A2.
MRL: 130mm: some 120 Type-75 SP.
MORTARS: 1,900 incl 81mm: 820 (some SP); 107mm: 560 (some SP).
SSM: 50 Type-30, 24 Type-88 coastal.
ATGW: 170 Type-64, 133 Type-79, 102 Type-87.
RL: 89mm: 70 3.5-in M-20.
RCL: 3,370: 75mm; 84mm: *Carl Gustav*; 106mm (incl Type 60 SP).
AD GUNS: 140: 35mm: 70 twin; 37mm SP; 40mm SP.
SAM: 180 *Stinger*, some 90 Type 81, 200 *Improved HAWK*.
AIRCRAFT: 18: 16 LR-1, 2 TL-1 (trg).
HELICOPTERS:
ATTACK: 72 AH-1S;
TRANSPORT: 3 AS-332L (VIP), 28 CH-47J, 72 KV-107, 180 OH-6D/J, 131 UH-1B/H, 33 TH-55 (trg).

NAVY: (Maritime Self-Defense Force): 43,100
(incl ε12,000 MSDF air).
BASES: Yokosuka, Kure, Sasebo, Maizuru, Ominato.
Fleet: Surface units org into 4 escort flotillas, of 6–8 DD/FF each; based at Yokosuka (2), Sasebo and Maizuru. Submarines org into 2 flotillas based at Kure and Yokosuka. Remainder assigned to 10 regional/district units.
SUBMARINES: 17:
TACTICAL SUBMARINES: 15:
4 *Harushio* with 533mm TT (Jap Type-89 HWT) with *Harpoon* USGW.
1 *Uzushio* with 533mm 77 (Mk 37 HWT).
10 *Yuushio* with 533mm TT (US Mk 37, GRX-2 HWT), 7 with *Harpoon* USGW.
OTHER ROLES: 2: 1 *Uzushio* (trg).
PRINCIPAL SURFACE COMBATANTS: 62:
DESTROYERS: 7 DDG:
1 *Kongo* with 2 x VLS Mk 41 SM-2-MR, *Standard* SAM and *ASROC* SUGW; plus 2 x 4 *Harpoon* SSM, 2 x 3 ASTT and hel deck.
2 *Hatakaze* with 1 x SM-1-MR Mk 13 SAM; plus 2 x 4 *Harpoon* SSM, 1 x 8 *ASROC* SUGW (Mk 46 LWT) 2 x 3 ASTT, 2 x 127mm guns.
3 *Tachikaze* with 1 x SM-1-MR; plus 1 x 8 *ASROC*, 2 x 3 ASTT, 8 x *Harpoon*, 2 x 127mm guns.
1 *Amatsukaze* with 1 x SM-1-MR; plus 1 x 8 *ASROC*, 2 x 3 ASTT.
FRIGATES: 55: (incl 2 trg):
FFH: 24:
2 *Shirane* with 3 x SH-60J *Sea Hawk* ASW hel, 1 x 8 *ASROC*, 2 x 3 ASTT; plus 2 x 127mm guns.
2 *Haruna* with 3 x *Sea King* hel, 1 x 8 *ASROC*, 2 x 3 ASTT; plus 2 x 127mm guns.
8 *Asagiri* with 1 *Sea King* hel, 1 x 8 *ASROC*, 2 x 3 ASTT; plus 2 x 4 *Harpoon* SSM.
12 *Hatsuyuki* with 1 *Sea King*, 1 x 8 *ASROC*, 2 x 3 ASTT; plus 2 x 4 *Harpoon* SSM.
FF: 31:
6 *Abukuma* with 1 x 8 *ASROC*, 2 x 3 ASTT; plus 2 x 4 *Harpoon* SSM.
2 *Takatsuki* with 1 x 8 *ASROC*, 2 x 3 ASTT, 1 x 4 ASW RL; plus 2 with 2 x 4 *Harpoon* SSM, 1 x 127mm gun; 2 with 2 x 127mm guns.
4 *Yamagumo* with 1 x 8 *ASROC*, 2 x 3 ASTT, 1 x 4 ASW RL.
3 *Minegumo* with 1 x 8 *ASROC*, 2 x 3 ASTT, 1 x 4 ASW RL.
2 *Yubari* with 2 x 3 ASTT, 1 x 4 ASW RL; plus 2 x 4 *Harpoon* SSM
1 *Ishikari* with 2 x 3 ASTT, 1 x 4 ASW RL; plus 2 x 4 *Harpoon* SSM.
11 *Chikugo* with 1 x 8 *ASROC*, 2 x 3 ASTT.
1 *Isuzu* (trg) with 1 x 4 ASW RL; plus 4 x 2 76mm gun.
1 *Katori* (trg) with 2 x 3 ASTT, 1 x ASW RL.
PATROL AND COASTAL COMBATANTS: 8:
MISSILE CRAFT: 2
2 It *Sparviero* type PHM with 4 *Mitsubishi* SSM-1B.
TORPEDO CRAFT: 1 *Juichi-go* PFT with 4 x 533mm TT.
PATROL: 5 *Jukyu-go* PCI⟨.
MINE WARFARE: 38:
MINELAYERS: 1:
1 *Souya* (460 mines) plus hel deck, 2 x 3 ASTT, also MCM spt/comd.
MINE COUNTERMEASURES: 37:
1 *Hayase* MCM cmd with hel deck, 2 x 3 ASTT, plus minelaying capacity (116 mines).

26 *Hatsushima* MCC.
2 *Yaeyama* MSO
3 *Takami* MCC.
4 *Nana-go* MSI⟨.
1 *Fukue* coastal MCM spt.
AMPHIBIOUS: 6:
3 *Miura* LST, capacity 200 tps, 10 tk.
3 *Atsumi* LST, capacity 130 tps, 5 tk.
Plus craft; 4 LCT, 15 LCM, 21 LCVP.
SUPPORT AND MISCELLANEOUS: 20:
3 *Towada* AOE, 1 *Sagami* AOE (all with hel deck);
2 sub depot/rescue, 2 *Akizuki* and 2 *Yamagumo* trg, 2
trg spt, 7 survey/experimental, 1 icebreaker.

MSDF AIR ARM: (12,000);
93 cbt ac (plus 15 in store), 75 armed hel.
7 Air Groups.
MR: 10 sqn:
9 (1 trg) with 87 P-3C (plus 15 in store);
1 with 6 P-2J.
ASW: 6 hel sqn (1 trg) with 75 HSS-2B, plus 24 in
store.
MCM: 1hel sqn with 10 MH-53E.
EW: 1 sqn with 2 EP-3C.
TRANSPORT: 1 sqn with 4 YS-11M.
TEST: 1 sqn with 3 P-3C ac;
2 HSS-2B, 2 SH-60J hel.
SAR: 1 sqn with 7 US-1A.
3 rescue sqn with 10 S-61 hel, 3UH-60J.
TRAINING:6 sqn with 13 KM-2, 10* P-3C, 24 T-5,
23 TC-90/UC-90, 10 YS-11T ac; 10 HSS-2B, 12
OH-6D/J hel.

AIR FORCE: (Air Self-Defense Force): 44,700;
438 cbt ac (plus 54 in store), no armed hel.
7 cbt air wings; 1 cbt air unit; 1 recce gp; 1 AEW unit.
FGA: 4 sqn.
3 with 73 F-1.
1 with 21 F-4EJ (anti-ship).
FIGHTER: 10 sqn:
7 with 158 F-15J/DJ.
3 with 72 F-4EJ (being upgraded); 50 more in store.
RECCE: 1 sqn with 10 RF-4EJ. 4 more in store.
AEW: 1 sqn with 12 E-2C.
EW: 1 flt with 1 C-1, 4 YS-11.
AGGRESSOR TRAINING: 1 sqn with 20 T-2, 2 T-33.
TRANSPORT: 5 sqn:
3 with 30 C-1, 15 C-130H, 10 YS-11;
2 heavy-lift hel sqn with 20 CH-47J.
Plus 2 747-400 (VIP).
SAR: 1 wing (10 det) with 30 MU-2 ac; 22 KV-107,
6 CH-47J hel, 1 UH-60J. (UH-60J hel, being
delivered.)
CALIBRATION: 1 wing with 2 MU-2J, 1 YS-11, 3 U-
125-800.
TRAINING: 5 wings: 10 sqn: 40* T-1A/B, 64* T-2, 40
T-3, 64 T-4, 10 T-33A (to be replaced by T-4).
LIAISON: 11 *Queen Air* 65, 126 T-33.
TEST: 1 wing with C-1, 3 F-4EJ, F-15J.
MISSILES:
ASM: ASM-1.

AAM: AAM-1, AIM-7 *Sparrow*, AIM-9 *Sidewinder*.
AIR DEFENCE:
Ac control and warning: 4 wings; 30 radar sites.
SAM: 6 AD msl gp (18 sqn) with 180 *Nike*-J (*Patriot*
replacing).
Air Base Defense Gp with 20mm *Vulcan* AA guns,
Type 81 *Tan*, *Stinger* SAM.

FORCES ABROAD:
UN AND PEACEKEEPING:
CAMBODIA (UNTAC): 602 (engrs), plus 8
Observers, 66 civ pol.
MOZAMBIQUE (ONUMOZ): 53 (movement
control).

PARAMILITARY:
MARITIME SAFETY AGENCY: (Coast Guard)
(Ministry of Transport, no cbt role) 12,000:
PATROL VESSELS: Some 335:
OFFSHORE: (over 1,000 tons): 48, incl 1 *Shikishima*
with 2 *Super Puma* hel, 2 *Mizuho* with 2 Bell 212, 8
Soya with 1 Bell 212 hel and 2 *Izu* and 28 *Shiretoko*.
COASTAL: (under 1,000 tons): 36.
INSHORE: about 250 patrol craft most⟨
MISCELLANEOUS: about 90 service, 80 tender/trg
vessels;
AIRCRAFT: 5 NAMC YS-11A, 2 Short *Skyvan*, 16
King Air, 1 Cessna U-206G.
HELICOPTERS: 32 Bell 212, 4 Bell 206, 2 Hughes
369.

FOREIGN FORCES:
US: 43,100 Army (1,900): 1 Corps HQ; Navy
(7,300) bases at Yokosuka (HQ 7th Fleet) and
Sasebo; Marines (18,300): 1 MEF in Okinawa; Air
(15,600): 1 Air HQ, 78 cbt ac.

KOREA: DEMOCRATIC PEOPLE'S REPUBLIC (NORTH)

GNP	1991ε: won 49.2bn ($22.90bn)	
	1992ε: won 45.9bn ($21.10bn)	
Growth	1991ε: -5.2%	1992ε: -6.7%
Inflation	1991ε: 2%	1992ε: 3%
Debt	1991: $9.28bn	1992: $9.72bn
Def exp	1992: won 11.80bn ($5.54bn)	
Def bdgt	1992: won 4.48bn ($2.06bn)	
	1993ε: won 4.70bn ($2.19bn)	
$1 = won	1989: 2.23	1990: 2.14
	1991: 2.15	1992: 2.13

Population: 22,728,000

	13–17	18–22	23–32
Men	1,057,000	1,265,000	2,408,000
Women	1,035,000	1,242,000	2,374,000

TOTAL ARMED FORCES:
ACTIVE: 1,127,000.
Terms of service: Army 5–8 years; Navy 5–10 years; Air Force 3–4 years, followed by compulsory part-time service in the Pacification Corps to age 40. Thereafter service in the Worker/Peasant Red Guard to age 60.
RESERVES: Army 500,000, Navy 40,000. Mob claimed in 12 hours; up to 6,000,000 have some Reserve/Militia commitment. See Paramilitary.

ARMY: 1,000,000.
16 Corps (1 armd, 4 mech, 8 inf, 1 arty, 1 capital defence, 1 Special Purpose).
26 inf/mot inf div.
14 armd bde.
23 mot/mech inf bde.
5 indep inf bde.
Special Purpose Corps: 3 cdo, 4 recce, 1 river crossing regt, 3 amph, 3 AB bn, 22 lt inf bn. 'Bureau of Reconnaissance SF' (8 bn).
Arty:
Army tps: 8 hy arty bde (incl MRL), 1 indep *Scud* SSM regt.
Corps tps: 14 bde incl 122mm, 152mm SP, MRL.
RESERVE: Pacification Corps: some 1.2m. 23 inf div, 6 inf bde.
EQUIPMENT:
MBT: some 3,700: T-34, T-54/-55, T-62, Type-59.
LIGHT TANKS: 500 PT-76, M-1985.
APC: 2,500 BTR-40/-50/-60/-152, Ch Type-531, N. Korean Type M-1973.
TOWED ARTY: 2,300: 122mm: M-1931/-37, D-74, D-30; 130mm: M-46; 152mm: M-1937 M-1938, M-1943.
SP ARTY: Some 4,500: 122mm: M-1977, M-1981, M-1985; 130mm: M-1975; 152mm: M-1974, M-1977; 170mm: M-1978, M-1989.
MRL: 2,280: 107mm: Type-63; 122mm: BM-21, BM-11; 240mm: M-1989.
MORTARS: 9,000: 82mm: M-37; 120mm: M-43; 160mm: M-43.
SSM: 54 *FROG*-3/-5/-7; some 30 *Scud* B/-C (Korean improved).
ATGW: AT-1 *Snapper*, AT-3 *Sagger*.
RCL: 82mm: 1,500 B-10.
AD GUNS: 8,800: 14.5mm: ZPU-1/-2/-4 SP, M-1983 SP; 23mm: ZU-23, ZSU-23-4 SP; 37mm: M-1939; 57mm: S-60; 85mm: KS-12; 100mm: KS-19.
SAM: 10,000 SA-7/-16.

NAVY: 45,000.
BASES: East Coast: Toejo (HQ), Changjon, Munchon, Songjon-pardo, Mugye-po, Mayang-do, Chaho Nodongjagu, Puam-Dong, Najin.
West Coast: Nampo (HQ), Pipa Got, Sagon-ni, Chodo-ri, Koampo, Tas-ri.
2 Fleet HQ.
SUBMARINES: 25:
21 Ch Type-031/Sov *Romeo* with 533mm TT.

4 Sov *Whiskey* with 533mm and 406mm TT.
(Plus some 50 midget submarines mainly used for SF ops, but some with 2 x TT).
FRIGATES: 3:
1 *Soho* with 4 x ASW RL, plus 4 x SS-N-2 *Styx* SSM, 1 x 100mm gun and hel deck.
2 *Najin* with 2 x 5 ASW RL, plus 2 SS-N-2 *Styx* SSM, 2 x 100mm guns.
PATROL AND COASTAL COMBATANTS: 387:
CORVETTES: 3 *Sariwon* with 1 x 100mm gun.
MISSILE CRAFT: 45:
14 *Soju*, 8 Sov *Osa*, 4 Ch *Huangfeng* PFM with 4 x SS-N-2 *Styx*.
9 *Sohung*, 10 Sov *Komar* PFM with 2 x SS-N-2.
TORPEDO CRAFT: 173:
3 Sov *Shershen* with 4 x 533mm TT.
Some 170 with 2 x 533mm TT.
PATROL: 166:
COASTAL: 18 PFC: 6 *Hainan* with 4 x ASW RL, 12 *Taechong* with 2 x ASW RL.
INSHORE: some 148:
13 SO-1, 12 *Shanghai* II, 3 *Chodo*, some 120.
MINE WARFARE: About 23 MSI⟨.
AMPHIBIOUS: craft only; 24 LCM, 7 LCU, about 100 *Nampo* LCVP , plus about 100 hovercraft.
SUPPORT AND MISCELLANEOUS: 7: 2 ocean tugs, 1 AS, 1 ocean and 3 inshore survey.
COAST DEFENCE: SSM: 2 regt: *Silkworm* in 6 sites;
GUNS: 122mm: M-1931/-37; 130mm: SM-4-1; 152mm: M-1937.

AIR FORCE: 82,000;
730 cbt ac, 50 armed hel.
BOMBERS: 3 lt regt with 80 H-5.
FGA: 7 regt:
3 with 160 J-5 (MiG-17);
2 with 120 J-6 (MiG-19);
1 with 40 Q-5 (*Fantan*);
1 with 14 Su-7, 36 Su-25.
FIGHTER: 10 regt:
2 with 80 J-5 (MiG-17);
2 with 60 J-6 (MiG-19);
1 with 40 J-7 (MiG-21);
3 with 120 MiG-21;
1 with 46 MiG-23;
1 with 14 MiG-29.
ATTACK HELICOPTERS: 50 Mi-24.
TRANSPORT:
AIRCRAFT: 162 An-2, 6 An-24, 5 Il-14, 2 Il-18, 4 Il-62M, 2 Tu-134, 4 Tu-154, 120 Y-5.
HELICOPTERS: 1 Hughes 300C, 80 -500D, 6 -500E, 140 Mi-2, 15 Mi-8/-17, 48 Z-5.
TRAINING: incl 10 CJ-5, 170 CJ-6.
AAM: AA-2 *Atoll*, AA-7 *Apex*.
SAM: 240 SA-2, 36 SA-3, 24 SA-5.

FORCES ABROAD: Advisers in some 12 African countries.

PARAMILITARY:

SECURITY TROOPS (Ministry of Public Security): 115,000, incl Border guards.
WORKER/PEASANT RED GUARD: some 3.8m. Org on a provincial/town/village basis. Comd structure is bde – bn – coy – pl. Small arms with some mor and AD guns (but many units unarmed).

KOREA: REPUBLIC OF (SOUTH)

GDP	1991:	won 208,201bn ($289.90bn)	
	1992:	won 231,727bn ($296.84bn)	
Growth	1991: 8.4%		1992: 4.8%
Inflation	1991: 9.7%		1992: 6.2%
Debt	1991: $38.2bn		1992: $42.6bn
Def bdgt	1992:	won 8,738bn ($11.19bn)	
	1993:	won 9,597bn ($12.06bn)	
$1 = won	1990: 707.76		1991: 733.35
	1992: 780.7		1993: 795.0

Population: 43,966,000

	13–17	18–22	23–32
Men	2,083,000	2,232,000	4,350,600
Women	1,929,000	2,066,000	4,074,000

TOTAL ARMED FORCES:
ACTIVE: 633,000.
Terms of service: conscription, Army 26 months, Navy and Air Force 30 months, then First Combat Forces (Mobilisation Reserve Forces) or Regional Combat Forces (Homeland Defence Forces) to age 33.
RESERVES: 4,500,000; being reorganised.

ARMY: 520,000.
HQ: 3 Army, 9 Corps.
3 mech inf div (each 3 bde: 3 mech inf, 3 tk, 1 recce, 1 engr bn; 1 fd arty bde).
19 inf div (each 3 inf regt, 1 recce, 1 tk, 1 engr bn; 1 arty regt (4 bn)).
2 indep inf bde.
7 SF bde.
3 counter-infiltration bde.
3 SSM bn with NHK-I/-II (*Honest John*).
3 AD arty bde.
3 *HAWK* bn (24 sites), 2 *Nike Hercules* bn (10 sites).
1 avn comd.
RESERVES: 1 Army HQ, 23 inf div.
EQUIPMENT:
MBT: 1,800: 450 Type 88, 400 M-47, 950 M-48.
AIFV: some 2,000 KIFV.
APC: some 1,550 incl 300 M-113, 275 Fiat 6614/ KM-900/-901.
TOWED ARTY: some 3,500: 105mm: 1,700 M-101, KH-178; 155mm: M-53, M-114, KH-179; 203mm: M-115.

SP ARTY: 900: 155mm: M-109A2; 175mm: M-107; 203mm: M-110.
MRL: 130mm: 140 *Kooryong* (36-tube).
MORTARS: 6,000: 81mm: KM-29; 107mm: M-30.
SSM: 12 NHK-I/-II.
ATGW: *TOW*.
RCL: 57mm, 75mm, 90mm: M67; 106mm: M40A2.
ATK GUNS: 76mm: 8 M-18; 90mm: 50 M-36 SP.
AD GUNS: 600: 20mm: incl 60 M-167 *Vulcan*; 35mm: 20 GDF-003; 40mm: 80 L60/70, M-1.
SAM: 350 *Javelin*, 60 *Redeye*, 130 *Stinger*, 110 *HAWK*, 200 *Nike Hercules*.
AIRCRAFT: 5 O-1A.
HELICOPTERS:
ATTACK: 65 AH-1F/-J, 68 Hughes 500 MD.
TRANSPORT: 15 CH-47D.
UTILITY: 195 Hughes 500, 125 UH-1H, 30 UH-23, 90 UH-60P.

NAVY: 60,000 (ε19,000 conscripts) incl 25,000 Marines.
BASES: Chinhae (HQ), Cheju, Inchon, Mokpo, Mukho, Pukpyong, Pohang, Pusan.
3 Fleet Commands.
SUBMARINES: 4:
1 *Chang Bogo* (Ge T-209/1400) with 8 x 533 TT.
3 KSS-1 *Dolgorae* SSI (175t) with 2 x 406mm TT.
PRINCIPAL SURFACE COMBATANTS: 38:
DESTROYERS: 9:
7 *Chung Buk* (US *Gearing*) with 2 or 3 x 2 127mm guns; plus 2 x 3 ASTT; 5 with 2 x 4 *Harpoon* SSM, 1 *Alouette* III hel (OTHT), 2 with 1 x 8 ASROC.
2 *Dae Gu* (US *Sumner*) with 3 x 2 127mm guns; plus 2 x 3 ASTT, 1 *Alouette III* hel.
FRIGATES: 29:
7 *Ulsan* with 2 x 3 ASTT (Mk 46 LWT); plus 2 x 4 *Harpoon* SSM.
22 *Po Hang* with 2 x 3 ASTT; some with 2 x 1 MM-38 *Exocet*.
PATROL AND COASTAL COMBATANTS: 120:
CORVETTES: 4 *Dong Hae* (ASW) with 2 x 3 ASTT.
MISSILE CRAFT: 11:
8 *Pae Ku-52*, 3 with 4 *Standard* (boxed) SSM, 5 with 2 x 2 *Harpoon* SSM.
1 *Pae Ku-51* (US *Asheville*), with 2 x *Standard* SSM.
2 *Kilurki-71* (*Wildcat*) with 2 x MM-38 *Exocet* SSM.
PATROL, INSHORE: 105:
78 *Kilurki-11* ('Sea Dolphin') 37-m PFI.
27 *Chebi-51* ('Sea Hawk') 26-m PFI((some with 2 x MM-38 *Exocet* SSM).
MINE WARFARE: 11:
3 *Kan Keong* (mod It *Lerici*) MHC.
8 *Kum San* (US MSC-268/289) MSC.
AMPHIBIOUS: 14:
7 *Un Bong* (US LST-511) LST, capacity 200 tps, 16 tk.
7 *Ko Mun* (US LSM-1) LSM, capacity 50 tps, 4 tk.
Plus about 36 craft; 6 LCT, 10 LCM, about 20 LCVP.

SUPPORT AND MISCELLANEOUS: 11:
1 AOE, 2 spt tankers, 2 ocean tugs, 2 salv/div spt, about 4 survey (civil manned, Ministry of Transport funded).

NAVAL AIR: 15 cbt ac; 47 armed hel.
ASW: 2 sqn:
1 ac with 15 S-2E; 1 hel with 25 Hughes 500MD (maritime patrol).
1 flt with 10 SA-316 hel (maritime patrol), 2 Bell 206 (liaison), 12 *Lynx* (ASW).
Lynx being delivered, to replace SA-316.

MARINES: (25,000).
2 div, 1 bde.
Spt units.
EQUIPMENT:
MBT: 60 M-47.
APC: 60 LVTP-7.
TOWED ARTY: 105mm, 155mm.
SSM: *Harpoon* (truck-mounted).

AIR FORCE: 53,000;
445 cbt ac (plus 52 in store), no armed hel. 7 cbt, 2 tpt wings.
FGA: 8 sqn:
2 with 48 F-16 (36 -C, 12 -D),
6 with 190 F-5 (60-A, 130 -E). Plus 16 in store.
FIGHTER: 4 sqn with 96 F-4D/E. Plus 36 in store.
COIN: 1 sqn with 23 A-37B.
FAC: 10 O-2A, 20 OA-37B.
RECCE: 1 sqn with 18 RF-4C, 10 RF-5A.
SAR: 1 hel sqn with 15 Bell UH-1B, 2 UH-1N.
TRANSPORT: 3 sqn:
AIRCRAFT: 2 BAe 748 (VIP), 1 Boeing 737-300 (VIP), 9 C-54, 1 C-118, 15 C-123J/K, 10 C-130H, 3 *Commander*.
HELICOPTERS: 7 Bell 212, 3 -412, 5 UH-1D/H.
TRAINING: 25* F-5B, 35* F-5, 25 T-33A, 35 T-37, 20 T-41D.
MISSILES:
ASM: AGM-65A *Maverick*.
AAM: AIM-7 *Sparrow*, AIM-9 *Sidewinder*.

PARAMILITARY:
CIVILIAN DEFENCE CORPS (to age 50): 3,500,000.
COAST GUARD: (ε4,500).
PATROL CRAFT: 75:
PATROL CRAFT, OFFSHORE: 13:
1 *Mazinger* (HDP-1000) (CG flagship).
6 *Han Kang* (HDC-1150)
6 *Sea Dragon/Whale* (HDP-600)
COASTAL: 24:
22 *Sea Wolf/Shark*
2 *Bukhansan*
INSHORE: 38: 18 *Seagull*; about 20‹, plus numerous boats.
SUPPORT AND MISCELLANEOUS: 2 salvage.
HELICOPTERS: 9 Hughes 500D.

FOREIGN FORCES:
US: 35,500. Army (26,000): 1 army HQ, 1 inf div. Air Force (9,500): 1 Air Force HQ: 2 wings: 84 cbt ac.

LAOS

GDP	1991ε: kip 1,062.9bn ($1.49bn)	
	1992ε: kip 1,193.8bn ($1.68bn)	
Growth	1991: 4.0%	1992ε: 7.1%
Inflation	1991: 10.4%	1992: 9.5%
Debt	1990: $1.07bn	1991: $1.12bn
Def bdg*a*	1992: kip 72.54bn ($102.17m)	
$1 = kip	1990: 726.44	1991: 714.00
	1992: 710.0	1993: 720.0

a Incl Public Security budget.

Population: 4,604,000

	13–17	18–22	23–32
Men	241,300	204,500	326,100
Women	237,800	202,400	324,300

TOTAL ARMED FORCES:
ACTIVE: 37,000.
Terms of service: conscription, 18 months minimum.

ARMY: 33,000.
4 Military Regions	5 arty, 9 AD arty bn.
5 inf div	65 indep inf coy.
7 indep inf regt	1 lt ac liaison flt.
3 engr (2 construction) regt.	

EQUIPMENT:
MBT: 30 T-54/-55, T-34/85.
LIGHT TANKS: 25 PT-76.
APC: 70 BTR-40/-60/-152.
TOWED ARTY: 75mm: M-116 pack; 105mm: 25 M-101; 122mm: 40 M-1938 and D-30; 130mm: 10 M-46; 155mm: M-114.
MORTARS: 81mm; 82mm; 107mm: M-2A1, M-1938; 120mm: M-43.
RCL: 57mm: M-18/A1; 75mm: M-20; 106mm: M-40; 107mm: B-11.
AD GUNS: 14.5mm: ZPU-1/-4; 23mm: ZU-23, ZSU-23-4 SP; 37mm: M-1939; 57mm: S-60.
SAM: SA-3, SA-7.

NAVY: (Army Marine Section) ε500.
PATROL CRAFT, river: some 12 PCI‹, 4 LCM, plus about 40 boats.

AIR FORCE: 3,500;
31 cbt ac; no armed hel.
FGA: 1 regt with some 29 MiG-21.
TRANSPORT: 1 sqn with 5 An-24, 2 An-26, 2 Yak-40.

HELICOPTERS: 1 sqn with 2 Mi-6, 10 Mi-8.
TRAINING: *2 MiG-21U.
AAM: AA-2 *Atoll.*

PARAMILITARY:
MILITIA SELF-DEFENCE FORCES: 100,000+:
village 'homeguard' org for local defence.

OPPOSITION:
Numerous factions/groups. Total armed strength
ε2,000. Largest group United Lao National Liberation Front (ULNLF).

MALAYSIA

GDP	1991:	$M 123.9bn ($US 45.05bn)
	1992ε:	$M 140.3bn ($US 55.08bn)
Growth	1991: 8.8%	1992: 8.6%
Inflation	1991: 4.4%	1992: 4.7%
Debt	1991: $US 14.9bn	1992: $US 14.5bn
Def exp	1992: $M 6.80bn ($US 2.67bn)
Def bdgt	1992: $M 5.00bn ($US1.96bn)
	1993ε: $M 5.06bn ($US1.96bn)
$US1 = $M	1990: 2.705	1991: 2.750
	1992: 2.547	1993: 2.580

$M = ringgit

Population: 19,223,000

	13–17	18–22	23–32
Men	1,001,000	905,600	1,583,000
Women	955,000	871,000	1,577,000

TOTAL ARMED FORCES:
ACTIVE: 114,500.
RESERVES: 58,300: Army 55,000; Navy 2,700;
Air 600.

ARMY: 90,000 (reducing to 85,000).
2 Military Regions, 1 corps, 5 div HQ.
10 inf bde, consisting of 36 inf bn (1 APC, 2 AB), 4
armd, 5 fd arty, 1 AD arty, 5 engr regt.
1 SF regt (3 bn).
RESERVES: 1 bde HQ; 12 inf regt; 4 highway sy
bn.
EQUIPMENT:
LIGHT TANKS: 26 *Scorpion* (90mm).
RECCE: 156 SIBMAS, 140 AML-60/-90,
92 *Ferret* (60 mod).
APC: 184 V-100/-150 *Commando*, 25 *Stormer*, 460
Condor, 32 M-3 *Panhard.*
TOWED ARTY: 105mm: 150 Model 56 pack, 40 M-
102A1 († in store); 155mm: 9 FH-70.
MORTARS: 81mm: 300.
ATGW: SS-11.
RL: 89mm: M-20.

RCL: 84mm: *Carl Gustav*; 106mm: 150 M-40.
AD GUNS: 35mm: 16 Oerlikon; 40mm: 36 L40/70.
SAM: 48 *Javelin*, 12 *Rapier.*
ASSAULT CRAFT: 165 Damen.

NAVY: 12,000 incl Naval Air (160).
Two Regional Commands: plus Fleet.
Area 1: Malayan Peninsula (west of 109°E).
Area 2: Borneo Area (east of 109°E).
BASES: Area 1: Lumut (Fleet HQ).
Tanjong Gelang (Area HQ), Kuantan; Woodlands
(Singapore), trg base.
Area 2: Labuan (Area HQ), Sungei Antu (Sarawak).
FRIGATES: 4:
2 *Kasturi* (FS-1500) with 2 x 2 ASW mor, deck for
  Wasp hel; plus 2 x 2 MM-38 *Exocet* SSM, 1 x
  100mm gun.
1 *Hang Tuah* (UK *Mermaid*) with 1 x 3 *Limbo* ASW
  mor, hel deck for *Wasp*; plus 1 x 2 102mm gun
  (trg).
1 *Rahmat* with 1 x 3 ASW mor, 1 x 114mm gun hel
  deck.
PATROL AND COASTAL COMBATANTS: 37:
MISSILE CRAFT: 8
4 *Handalan* (Sw *Spica*) with 4 MM-38 *Exocet* SSM.
4 *Perdana* (Fr *Combattante* II) with 2 *Exocet* SSM.
PATROL: 29:
OFFSHORE: 2 *Musytari* with 1 x 100mm gun,
hel deck.
INSHORE: 27: 6 *Jerong* PFI, 3 *Kedah*, 4 *Sabah*, 14
Kris PCI.
MINE WARFARE: 5:
4 *Mahamiru* (mod It *Lerici*) MCO.
1 diving tender (inshore).
AMPHIBIOUS: 2:
2 *Sri Banggi* (US LST-511) LST, capacity 200
tps, 16 tk (but usually employed as tenders to
patrol craft).
Plus 33 craft: 5 LCM, 13 LCU, 15 LCP.
SUPPORT AND MISCELLANEOUS: 3:
2 log/fuel spt, 1 survey.

NAVAL AIR: (160)
No cbt ac, 12 armed hel.
HELICOPTERS: 12 *Wasp* HAS-1.

AIR FORCE: 12,500;
77 cbt ac, no armed hel; 4 Comd.
FGA: 2 sqn: with 33 A-4 (27 A-4PTM, 6 TA-4);
FIGHTER: 1 sqn with 13 F-5E, 4 -F.
RECCE: 1 recce/OCU sqn with 2 RF-5E, 2 F-5F.
MR: 1 sqn with 3 C-130HMP, 4 B200T.
TRANSPORT:
AIRCRAFT: 4 sqn:
1 with 5 C-130H;
2 with 14 DHC-4;
1 with 2 BAe-125 (VIP), 1 *Falcon*-900 (VIP), 2 HU-
16 (1 tpt, 1 VIP), 12 Cessna 402B ac; 1 NAS-332
hel.
HELICOPTERS: 4 sqn with 30 S-61A, 20 SA-316A/B

(liaison), 3 AS-332.
TRAINING: 4 trg units:
AIRCRAFT: 11* MB-339, 40 PC-7 (12* wpn trg);
HELICOPTERS: 8 SE-316, 5 Bell 47, 4 S-61.
AAM: AIM-9 *Sidewinder*.
AIRFIELD DEFENCE TROOPS: 1 sqn.

FORCES ABROAD:
UN AND PEACEKEEPING:
CAMBODIA (UNTAC): 1,063 (inf), plus 29
Observers, 223 civ pol.
IRAQ/KUWAIT (UNIKOM): 6 Observers.
MOZAMBIQUE (ONUMOZ): 21 Observers.
SOMALIA: (UNOSOM II): 850: 1 inf bn, 5 hel.
WESTERN SAHARA (MINURSO): 1 Observer.

PARAMILITARY:
POLICE FIELD FORCE: 18,000; 4 bde HQ: 21 bn
(incl 2 Aboriginal, 1 cdo) 4 indep coy; *Shorland*
armd cars, 140 AT-105 *Saxon*, SB-301 APC.
MARINE POLICE: 48 inshore patrol craft:
15 *Lang Hitam* (38-m) PFI
6 *Sangitan* (29-m) PFI
27 PCI⟨, plus boats.
POLICE AIR WING: 4 Cessna 206, 7 PC-6 ac, 1
Bell 206L3, 2 AS-355F2.
AUXILIARY POLICE FIELD FORCE: (Area
Security Units), 3,500 men in 89 units.
BORDER SCOUTS (in Sabah, Sarawak): 1,200.
PEOPLE'S VOLUNTEER CORPS (RELA):
168,000.
CUSTOMS SERVICE: 56 patrol craft: 6 *Perak*
(Vosper 32-m) armed PFI, about 50 craft⟨.

FOREIGN FORCES:
AUSTRALIA: Army: 1 inf coy. Air Force: det with
2 P-3C ac.

MONGOLIA

GDP	1991: t 18.91bn ($450.24m)	
	1992: t 42.87bn ($357.25m)	
Growth	1991: -9.9%	1992: -7.6%
Inflation	1991: 120%	1992: 450%
Debt	1990ε: $2.00bn	1991: $2.5bn
Def exp[a]	1992: t 1.11bn ($20.5m)	
Def bdgt[a]	1992: t 1.12bn ($21.42m)	
	1993: t 3.50bn ($23.33m)	
$1 = t[b]	1990: 3.35	1991: 42.0
	1992: 120.0	1993: 150+

t = tugrik

[a] Defence bdgt incl budgets for border troops and civil
defence.
[b] Several devaluations in 1991 brought official rate down
to $1 = t5.6 at beginning of 1991. Black market rates as
high as $1 = t120.

Population: 2,304,600

	13–17	18–22	23–32
Men	128,900	114,400	183,300
Women	123,900	110,800	181,400

TOTAL ARMED FORCES:
ACTIVE: 21,250 (perhaps 12,350 conscripts).
Terms of service: Conscription: males 18–28 years, 2
years.
RESERVES: Army 140,000.

ARMY: 20,000 (perhaps 12,000 conscripts).
4 MRD (understrength).
1 arty bde.
1 AD bde.
1 AB bn.
EQUIPMENT:
MBT: 650 T-54/-55/-62.
RECCE: 135 BRDM-2.
AIFV: 420 BMP-1.
APC: 300 BTR-40/-60/-152.
TOWED ARTY: 300: 122mm: M-1938/D-30;
130mm: M-46; 152mm: M-1937.
MRL: 122mm: 135+ BM-21.
MORTARS: 140: 82mm, 120mm, 160mm.
ATK GUNS: 100mm: T-12.
AD GUNS: 100: 14.5mm: ZPU-4;
37mm: M-1939; 57mm: S-60.
SAM: 300 SA-7.

AIR FORCE: 1,250 (350 conscripts);
15 cbt ac; 12 armed hel.
FIGHTER: 1 sqn with 12 MiG-21.
ATTACK HELICOPTERS: 12 Mi-24.
TRANSPORT: at least 2 sqn:
15 An-2, 18 An-24, 3 An-26, 1 Tu-154.
HELICOPTERS: 1 sqn with 10 Mi-4, 4 Mi-8.
TRAINING: 2 MiG-15U, 3* MiG-21U, 3 PZL-104, 6
Yak-11, Yak-18.

PARAMILITARY:
MILITIA (Ministry of Public Security):
10,000: internal security troops, frontier guards;
BTR-60/-152 APC.

FOREIGN FORCES:
RUSSIA: ε500 (SIGINT station).

NEW ZEALAND

GDP	1991: $NZ 73.21bn ($US 42.39bn)	
	1992: $NZ 78.22bn ($US 42.10bn)	
Growth	1991: -2.0%	1992ε: 3.1%
Inflation	1991: 2.6%	1992: 1.1%

Debt 1991: $US 31.0bn 1992: $US 35.0bn
Def exp 1989: $NZ 1.37bn ($US 818.17m)
1990: $NZ 1.38bn ($US 826.27m)
Def bdgt 1992: $NZ 1.22bn ($US 656.62m)
1993ε: $NZ 1.21bn ($US 643.75m)
$US 1 = $NZ 1990: 1.675 1991: 1.727
1992: 1.858 1993: 1.877
$NZ = New Zealand dollars

Population: 3,479,000

	13–17	18–22	23–32
Men	135,100	146,200	292,000
Women	126,400	137,000	277,600

TOTAL ARMED FORCES:
ACTIVE: 10,800 incl 1,300 women.
RESERVES: 8,500. *Regular* 2,900: Army 1,650, Navy 1,050, Air 200. *Territorial* 5,600: Army 4,600, Navy 600, Air 400.

ARMY: 4,800 (incl 400 women).
2 inf bn.
1 lt armd sqn.
1 fd arty bty.
2 SF sqn (incl reserves).
RESERVES: Territorial Army: 6 inf bn, 6 fd, 1 med arty bty, 2 armd sqn (1 APC, 1 lt recce).
EQUIPMENT:
LIGHT TANKS: 26 *Scorpion*.
APC: 76 M-113 (incl variants).
TOWED ARTY: 105mm: 20 M-101A1 (8 in store), 24 *Hamel*.
MORTARS: 81mm: 72.
RL: *LAW*.
RCL: 84mm: 61 *Carl Gustav*; 106mm: 13 M-40A1.

NAVY: 2,300 (incl 300 women).
BASE: Auckland (Fleet HQ).
FRIGATES: 4 *Waikato* (UK *Leander*) with 1 *Wasp* hel, 2 x 3 ASTT and 3 with 2 x 114mm guns.
PATROL AND COASTAL COMBATANTS: 4:
4 *Moa* PCI (reserve trg).
SUPPORT AND MISCELLANEOUS: 4:
1 *Endeavour* AO, 1 *Monowai* AGHS, 1 AGOR, 1 diving spt.

NAVAL AIR:
No cbt ac, 6 armed hel.
HELICOPTERS: 6 *Wasp* (plus 2 in store) see Air Force.

AIR FORCE: 3,700 (incl 600 women);
38 cbt ac, no armed hel.
OPERATIONAL GROUP:
FGA: 2 sqn with 15 A-4K, 5 TA-4K.
MR: 1 sqn with 6 P-3K *Orion*.
LIGHT ATTACK/TRG: 1 sqn for ab initio and ftr lead-in trg with 12 MB-339C.

ASW: 6 *Wasp* HAS-1 (Navy-assigned) (plus 2 in store).
TRANSPORT: 3 sqn:
AIRCRAFT: 2 sqn:
1 with 5 C-130H, 2 Boeing 727;
1 with 9 *Andover*.
HELICOPTERS: 1 with 11 UH-1H.
SUPPORT GROUP:
TRAINING: 1 wing with 18 CT-4 ac; 5 Bell 47 hel.
MISSILES:
ASM: AGM-65 *Maverick*.
AAM: AIM-9H *Sidewinder*.

FORCES ABROAD:
AUSTRALIA: 50: 6 A-4*K*/TA-4K.
SINGAPORE: 20: spt unit.
UN AND PEACEKEEPING:
CAMBODIA (UNTAC): 88 (comms and Navy).
CROATIA (UNPROFOR I): 9 Observers.
EGYPT (MFO): 25.
MIDDLE EAST (UNTSO): 5 Observers.
SOMALIA: (UNOSOM II): 22.

PAPUA NEW GUINEA

GDP 1991: K 3.61bn ($3.79bn)
1992: K 4.08bn ($4.23bn)
Growth 1991: 9.6% 1992: 8.9%
Inflation 1991: 6.9% 1992: 4.7%
Debt 1991: $3.38bn 1992: $3.60bn
Def exp 1989: K 39.0m ($45.57m)
1990: K 47.6m ($49.82m)
Def bdgt 1992: K56.5m ($58.55m)
1993: K54.4m ($55.92m)
$1 = K 1990: 0.955 1991: 0.952
1992: 0.965 1993: 0.973
K = kina

Population: 4,223,000

	13–17	18–22	23–32
Men	241,800	219,700	351,900
Women	224,800	200,300	304,500

TOTAL ARMED FORCES:
ACTIVE: about 3,800.

ARMY: 3,200.
2 inf bn.
1 engr bn.

NAVY: 500.
BASES: Port Moresby (HQ), Lombrum (Manus Is.) Forward bases at Kieta and Alotau.
PATROL AND COASTAL COMBATANTS: 4:
4 *Tarangau* (Aust *Pacific Forum* 32-m) PCI
AMPHIBIOUS: craft only: 2 *Salamaua* (Aust

Balikpapan) LCT plus 6 other landing craft. (4 civilian-manned and operated by Dept of Defence).

AIR FORCE: 100. 2 cbt ac, no armed hel.
MR: 2 N-22B *Searchmaster* B.
TRANSPORT: 2 N-22B *Missionmaster*, 2 CN-235, 3 IAI-201 *Arava*, †5C-47.
HELICOPTERS: 4 UH-1H.

OPPOSITION FORCES:
Bougainville Revolutionary Army: 2,000+.

FOREIGN FORCES:
AUSTRALIA: 100; 2 engr unit, 75 advisers.

PHILIPPINES

GDP	1991:	P 1,244.0bn ($45.27bn)	
	1992:	P 1,342.5 bn ($52.62 bn)	
Growth	1991:	-0.7%	1992: 0.1%
Inflation	1991:	18.7%	1992: 8.9%
Debt	1991:	$31.9bn	1992: $29.8bn
Def exp	1992:	P 19.5bn ($764.35m)	
Def bdgt	1992:	P 29.1bn ($1.14bn)	
	1993:	P 29.9bn ($1.17bn)	
FMA[a]	1993:	$42.3m(US)	
$1 = P	1990:	24.311	1991: 27.479
	1992:	25.512	1993: 25.600

P = pesos
[a] Incl $25m as Economic Support.

Population: 65,246,000

	13–17	18–22	23–32
Men:	3,796,000	3,326,000	5,369,000
Women:	3,583,000	3,140,000	5,332,000

TOTAL ARMED FORCES:
ACTIVE: 106,500.
RESERVES: 131,000. Army 100,000 (some 75,000 more have commitments); Navy 15,000; Air 16,000 (to age 49).

ARMY: 68,000.
5 Area Unified Comd (joint service).
8 inf div (each with 3 inf bde).
1 lt armd bde ('regt').
1 scout ranger regt.
3 engr bde; 1 construction bn.
8 arty bn.
1 SF regt.
1 Presidential Security Group.
EQUIPMENT:
LIGHT TANKS: 41 *Scorpion*.
AIFV: 85 YPR-765 PRI.
APC: 100 M-113, 20 *Chaimite*, 165 V-150.

TOWED ARTY: 105mm: 230 M-101, M-102, M-26 and M-56; 155mm: 12 M-114 and M-68.
MORTARS: 81mm: M-29; 107mm: 40 M-30.
RCL: 75mm: M-20; 90mm: M-67; 106mm: M-40 A1.

NAVY: † 23,000 (incl 8,500 Marines). 6 Naval Districts .
BASES: Sangley Point/Cavite, Zamboanga, Cebu.
FRIGATES: 1:
1 *Datu Siratuna* (US *Cannon*) with ASW mor.
PATROL AND COASTAL COMBATANTS: 33:
PATROL OFFSHORE: 10:
2 *Rizal* (US *Auk*) with hel deck.
7 *Miguel Malvar* (US PCE-827).
1 *Magat Salamat* (US-MSF).
INSHORE: 23:
2 *Aguinaldo*, 3 *Kagitingan* and about 18 PCI.
AMPHIBIOUS: 9:
1 US *F.S. Beeson*-class LST, capacity 32 tk plus 150 tps.
Some 8 *Agusan del Sur* (US LST-1/511/542) LST, capacity: either 16tk or 10tk plus 200 tps.
Plus about 39 craft; 30 LCM, 3 LCU, some 6 LCVP.
SUPPORT AND MISCELLANEOUS: 11:
2 AOT (small), 1 repair ships, 3 survey/research, 3 spt, 2 water tankers.

NAVAL AVIATION: 8 cbt ac, no armed hel.
MR/SAR: 8 BN-2A *Defender*, 1 *Islander*; 11 Bo-105 (SAR) hel.

MARINES: (8,500):
4 bde (10 bn).
EQUIPMENT:
APC: 30 LVTP-5, 55 LVTP-7.
TOWED ARTY: 105mm: 150 M-101.
MORTARS: 4.2-in. (107mm): M-30.

AIR FORCE: 15,500;
53 cbt ac, some 106 armed hel.
FIGHTER: 1 sqn with 7 F-5 (5 -A, 2 -B).
COIN:
AIRCRAFT: 1 sqn with 23 OV-10 *Broncos*.
HELICOPTERS: 3 sqn with 62 Bell UH-1H/M, 16 AUH-76 (S-76 gunship conversion), 28 Hughes 500/520MD.
MR: 2 F-27M.
RECCE: 6 RT-33A.
SAR: 4 HU-16 ac, 10 Bo-105C hel.
PRESIDENTIAL AIRCRAFT WING:
AIRCRAFT: 1 F-27, 1 F-28.
HELICOPTERS: 2 Bell 212, 2 S-70A, 2 SA-330.
TRANSPORT: 3 sqn:
AIRCRAFT:
1 with 3 C-130H, 3 L-100-20; 3 C-47, 7 F-27.
2 with 20 BN-2 *Islander*, 14 N-22B *Nomad Missionmaster*.
HELICOPTERS: 2 sqn with 55 Bell 205, 17 UH-1H.
LIAISON: 7 Cessna 180, 2 -210, 1 -310, 5 DHC-2, 12 U-17A/B.

TRAINING: 4 sqn:
1 with 6 T-33A, 3 RT-33.
1 with 20 T-41D.
1 with 14 SF-260MP, 9* -WP.
1 with 14* S-211.
AAM: AIM-9B *Sidewinder*.

FORCES ABROAD:
UN AND PEACEKEEPING:
CAMBODIA (UNTAC): 127 (naval), plus 224 civ pol.

PARAMILITARY:
PHILIPPINE NATIONAL POLICE (Department of Interior and Local Government): 40,500; 62,000 active auxiliary; 12 Regional, 73 Provincial Comd.
COAST GUARD: 2,000. (No longer part of Navy.)
EQUIPMENT:
1 *Kalinga* PCO, 4 *Basilan* (US PGM-39/42 PCI, 2 *Tirad Pass* PCI (SAR), 4 ex-US Army spt ships, plus some 50 patrol boats, 2 lt ac.
CITIZEN ARMED FORCE GEOGRAPHICAL UNITS (CAFGU): Militia: 60,000, 56 bn. Part-time units which can be called up for extended periods.

OPPOSITION:
NEW PEOPLE'S ARMY (NPA; Communist): 13,000 (ε10,000 armd).
BANGSA MORO ARMY (armed wing of Moro National Liberation Front (MNLF), Muslim): ε3,300.
MORO ISLAMIC LIBERATION FRONT (breakaway from MNLF; Muslim): 3,400.
MORO ISLAMIC REFORMIST GROUP (breakaway from MNLF): 900.

SINGAPORE

GDP	1991:	S 69.45bn ($40.19bn)	
	1992:	S 74.96bn ($46.03bn)	
Growth	1991: 6.7%		1992: 5.8%
Inflation	1991: 3.4%		1992: 2.2%
Def bdgt	1990:	S 3.08bn ($1.70bn)	
	1991:	S 3.68bn ($2.13bn)	
$1 = S	1990: 1.813		1991: 1.728
	1992: 1.629		1993: 1.620

S = $ Singapore

Population: 3,132,000

	13–17	18–22	23–32
Men	116,000	124,600	297,300
Women	108,700	118,700	286,300

TOTAL ARMED FORCES:
ACTIVE: 55,500 (34,800 conscripts).
Terms of service: conscription 2 years.
RESERVES: Army 250,000 (incl ε30,000 People's Defence Force); annual trg to age 40 for men, 50 for officers. Navy ε4,500. Air Force ε7,500.

ARMY: 45,000 (30,000 conscripts).
1 combined arms div: 2 inf bde (each 3 inf bn), 1 mech bde, 1 recce, 2 arty, 1 AD, 1 engr bn.
1 cdo bn.
1 arty, 1 SP mor bn.
1 engr bn.
RESERVES:
4 div (2 combined arms, 2 op reserve), 1 mech, 6 inf bde HQ; 18 inf, 1 cdo, 10 arty, 2 AD arty, 3 engr bn. People's Defence Force: some 30,000; org in 2 comd, 7 bde gp, ε21 bn.
EQUIPMENT:
LIGHT TANKS: ε350 AMX-13SM1.
RECCE: 22 AMX-10 PAC 90.
APC: 720 M-113, 30 V-100, 250 V-150/-200 *Commando*, 22 AMX-10P.
TOWED ARTY: 105mm: 36 LG1; 155mm: 38 Soltam M-71, 16 M-114A1 (may be in store), M-68 (may be in store), 52 FH88.
MORTARS: 81mm (some SP); 120mm: 50 (some SP in M-113); 160mm: 12 Tampella.
ATGW: 30 *Milan*.
RL: *Armbrust*; 89mm: M-20 3.5-in.
RCL: 84mm: *Carl Gustav*; 106mm: 90 M-40A1 (in store).
AD GUNS: 20mm: 30 GAI-CO1 (some SP).
SAM: RBS-70 (some SP in V-200).

NAVY: 4,500 (1,800 conscripts).
BASE: Pulau Brani (Singapore).
PATROL AND COASTAL COMBATANTS: 30:
CORVETTES: 6 *Victory* (Ge Lürssen 62-m) with 8 x *Harpoon* SSM, 2 x 3 ASTT.
MISSILE CRAFT: 6 *Sea Wolf* (Ge Lürssen 45-m) PFM with 2 x 2 *Harpoon*, 2 x *Gabriel* SSM.
PATROL, INSHORE: 18:
6 *Independence/Sovereignty* (33-m) (incl 4 with marine police).
12 *Swift*(, plus boats.
MINE WARFARE: Nil (*Mercury* (US *Bluebird*) MSC and *Jupiter* have mine-hunting capability).
AMPHIBIOUS: 5:
1 *Perseverance* (UK *Sir Lancelot*) LST capacity: 340 tps, 16 tk, 1 hel.
4 *Endurance* (US LST-511) LST, capacity 200 tps, 16 tk.
Plus craft; 8 LCM, 1 hovercraft and boats.
SUPPORT AND MISCELLANEOUS: 3: 1 *Jupiter* and 1 *Mercury* div spt and salvage, 1 trg.

AIR FORCE: 6,000 (3,000 conscripts);
193 cbt ac, 20 armed hel.
FGA: 5 sqn:
3 with 62 A-4S/SI, 13 TA-4S/SI.
1 with 20 *Hunter* F-74, 4 T-75.
1 with 6 F-16 (2 -A, 4 -B).

FIGHTER: 2 sqn with 29 F-5E, 9 F-5F.
RECCE: 8 RF-5E.
AEW: 1 sqn with 4 E-2C.
ARMED HELICOPTERS: 1 sqn with 20 AS 550A2/C2.
TRANSPORT:
AIRCRAFT: 2 sqn:
1 with 4 C-130B (tkr/tpt), 6 C-130H/H-30.
1 with 6 *Skyvan* 3M (tpt/SAR).
HELICOPTERS: 3 sqn:
1 with 6 AS350B.
1 with 5 Bell 205;
1 with 20 AS-332M (incl 3 SAR).
TRAINING: 3 sqn:
2 with 30* SIAI S-211;
1 with 26 SF-260 (14 -MS, 12* -WS).
AD: 3 bn: 2 SAM, 1 arty:
1 with 10 *Rapier* (with *Blindfire*);
1 with 12 *Improved HAWK.*
1 with 35mm Oerlikon (towed) guns.
AIRFIELD DEFENCE: 1 field defence sqn (reservists).
AAM: AIM-9 J/P *Sidewinder.*

FORCES ABROAD:
AUSTRALIA: (250) Flying trg school with 30 S-211 ac.
BRUNEI: (500); trg school, incl hel det (with 5 UH-1).
TAIWAN: 4 trg camps.
UNITED STATES: 100, 9 F-16A/B leased from USAF at Luke AFB.
UN AND PEACEKEEPING:
ANGOLA (UNAVEM II): 8 Observers.
CAMBODIA: (UNTAC): 75 civ pol.
IRAQ/KUWAIT (UNIKOM): 9 Observers.

PARAMILITARY:
POLICE/MARINE POLICE: 11,600; incl some 750 Gurkhas, some 4 PCI and about 80 boats.
CIVIL DEFENCE FORCE: ε100,000 (incl regulars, conscripts, ε34,000 former army reservists). 1 construction bde (2,500 conscripts).

FOREIGN FORCES:
NEW ZEALAND: 20: spt unit.
US: 140: Navy (100); Air Force (40).

TAIWAN

GNP	1991:	$NT 4,821.2bn ($US 178.83bn)
	1992:	$NT 5,307bn ($US 208.13bn)
Growth	1991: 7.2%	1992: 6.1%
Inflation	1991: 3.6%	1992: 4.5%
Debt	1990: $US 950m	1991: $US 1,146m
Def exp	1992: $NT 255.8bn ($US10.03bn)	
Def bdgt	1992: $NT 262.3bn ($US 10.29bn)	
	1993: $NT 274.9bn ($US 10.45bn)	
$1 = $NT	1990: 26.86	1991: 26.96
	1992: 25.50	1993: 26.30
$NT = New Taiwan dollars		

Population: 20,856,000

	13–17	18–22	23–32
Men	988,000	435,000	1,899,000
Women	933,000	881,800	1,809,000

TOTAL ARMED FORCES:
ACTIVE: 442,000.
Terms of service: 2 years.
RESERVES: 1,657,500. Army: 1,500,000 have some Reserve obligation to age 30. Navy 32,500, Marines 35,000, Air 90,000.

ARMY: 312,000 (incl mil police).
3 Army, 1 AB Special Ops HQ.
13 inf div.
2 mech inf div.
2 AB bde.
6 indep armd bde.
2 tk gp.
22 fd arty bn.
5 SAM bn: 2 with *Nike Hercules*, 3 with *HAWK*.
2 avn gp, 6 avn sqn.
RESERVES: 7 lt inf div.
EQUIPMENT:
MBT: 309 M-48A5, some M-48A3, 200+ M-48H.
LIGHT TANKS: 230 M-24 (90mm gun), 675 M-41/ Type 64.
AIFV: 225 M-113 with 20/30mm cannon.
APC: 650 M-113, 300 V-150 *Commando.*
TOWED ARTY: 105mm: 650 M-101 (T-64); 155mm: M-44, 90 M-59, 250 M-114 (T-65); 203mm: 70 M-115.
SP ARTY: 105mm: 100 M-108; 155mm: 45 T-69, 110 M-109A2; 203mm: 60 M-110.
MRL: 117mm: KF VI; 126mm: KF III/IV towed and SP.
MORTARS: 81mm: M-29 (some SP); 107mm.
ATGW: 1,000: *TOW* (some SP).
RCL: 90mm: M-67; 106mm: 500 M-40A1/Type 51.
AD GUNS: 40mm: 400 (incl M-42 SP, Bofors).
SAM: 40 *Nike Hercules*, 100 *HAWK*, some *Chaparral.*
AVIATION:
AIRCRAFT: 20 O-1.
HELICOPTERS: 100 UH-1H, 12 KH-4.
DEPLOYMENT:
QUEMOY: 55,000,
MATSU: 18,000.

NAVY: 60,000 incl 30,000 Marines.
3 Naval Districts.
BASES: Tsoying (HQ), Makung (Pescadores), Keelung.
SUBMARINES: 4:
2 *Hai Lung* (Nl mod *Zwaardvis*) with 533mm TT.
2 *Hai Shih* (US *Guppy* II) with 533mm TT (trg only).
PRINCIPAL SURFACE COMBATANTS: 33:
DESTROYERS: 22:
DDG: 8 *Chien Yang* (US *Gearing*), (*Wu Chin* III

conversion) with 10 x SM-1 MR SAM (boxed), plus 1
x 8 *ASROC*, 2 x 3 ASTT, plus 1 *Hughes* MD-500 hel.
DD: 14.
6 *Fu Yang* (US *Gearing*) (ASW); 5 with 1 *Hughes*
MD-500 hel, 1 with 1 x 8 *ASROC*, all with 2 x 3
ASTT; plus 1 or 2 x 2 127mm guns, 3 or 5 *Hsiung
Feng-I (HF-1)* (Is *Gabriel*) SSM.
4 *Po Yang* (US *Sumner*) with 1 or 2 x 2 127mm
guns; plus 2 x 3 ASTT; 5 or 6 HF-1 SSM, 2 with 1
Hughes MD-500 hel.
4 *Kun Yang* (US *Fletcher*) with 2 or 3 x 127mm
guns; 1 x 76mm gun; plus 2 x 3 ASTT with 5 *HF-
1* SSM.
FRIGATES: 11:
FFG: 1 *Cheng Kung* with 1 x SM-1 MR SAM, 1 S-
70C hel, 2 x 3 ASTT plus 2 x 4 *Hsiung Feng-II*.
FF: 10:
7 *Tien Shan* (US *Lawrence/Crosley*), some with 2 x
3 ASTT; plus 2 x 127mm guns (fishing protection
and transport 160 tps).
1 *Tai Yuan* (US *Rudderow*) with 2 x 3 ASTT; plus 2
x 127mm guns.
2 ex-US *Knox* with 1 x 8 *ASROC*, 1 x SH-2F hel, 4 x
ASTT; plus *Harpoon* (from *ASROC* launchers), 1
x 127mm gun (3rd by Oct 1993).
PATROL AND COASTAL COMBATANTS: 98:
MISSILE CRAFT: 52:
2 *Lung Chiang* PFM with 2 x *HF-1* SSM
50 *Hai Ou* (mod Is *Dvora*)⟨ with 2 x *HF-1* SSM
PATROL, OFFSHORE: 1 *Ping Jin* (US *Auk* MSF) with
1 x 3 ASTT plus 2 x 76mm guns.
INSHORE: 45: 22 Vosper-type 32-m PFI,
7 PCI and about 16 PCI⟨.
MINE WARFARE: 15:
MINELAYERS: Nil but *Tai Yuan* and 1 *Ping Jin* have
capability.
MINE COUNTERMEASURES: 15
11 *Yung Chou* (US *Adjutant*) MSC.
4 MSC converted from oil rig spt ships.
AMPHIBIOUS: 26:
1 *Kao Hsiung* (US LST 511) amph comd.
20 *Chung Hai* (US LST 511) LST, capacity 16 tk,
200 tps.
4 *Mei Lo* (US LSM-1) LSM, capacity about 4 tk.
1 *Cheng Hai* (US *Cabildo*) LSD, capacity 3 LCU or
18 LCM.
Plus about 400 craft; 22 LCU, some 260 LCM, 120
LCVP.
SUPPORT AND MISCELLANEOUS: 25:
4 spt tankers, 2 repair/salvage, 1 *Wu Yi* combat spt
with hel deck, 2 *Yuen Feng* and 5 *Wu Kang* attack tpt
with hel deck, 3 tpt, 1 survey/research, 7 ocean tugs.
COASTAL DEFENCE: 1 SSM coastal def bn with
Hsiung Feng (*Gabriel* type).

NAVAL AIR: 32 cbt ac; 34 armed hel.
MR: 1 sqn with 32 S-2 (25 -E, 7 -G).
HELICOPTERS: 1 sqn with 12 Hughes 500MD ASW
Defender, 12 SH-2F, 10 S-70B.

MARINES: 30,000.
2 div, spt elm.

EQUIPMENT:
APC: LVT-4/-5.
TOWED ARTY: 105mm, 155mm.
RCL: 106mm.

AIR FORCE: 70,000;
484 cbt ac, no armed hel. 5 cbt wings.
FGA/FIGHTER: 14 sqn with 8 F-5B, 215 -E, 54 -F, 8
F-104D/DJ, 81 -G, 20 -J, 32 TF-104G,
10 *Ching-Kuo* (testing).
RECCE: 1 sqn with 6 RF-104G.
SAR: 1 sqn with 8 HU-16B ac, 12 S-70, 12 UH-1H
hel.
TRANSPORT: 8 sqn:
AIRCRAFT: 2 with 8 C-47, 2 C-54, 1 C-118B,
1 DC-6B;
3 with 30 C-119G, 10 C-123B/K;
1 with 12 C-130H.
1 with 12 Beech 1900.
1 VIP with 1 Boeing 707-720B, 4 -727-100.
HELICOPTERS: 5 CH-34, 3 CH-47C, 1 S-62A (VIP),
14 S-70.
TRAINING: ac incl 60* AT-3, 20 T-38A, 42 T-34C,
30 T-CH-1, hel; 12 Bell 47G/OH-13, 9 Hughes
500.
MISSILES:
ASM: AGM-65A *Maverick*.
AAM: AIM-4D *Falcon*, AIM-9J/P *Sidewinder*,
Shafrir.

PARAMILITARY:
SECURITY GROUPS 25,000: National Police
Administration (Ministry of Interior). Bureau of
Investigation (Ministry of Justice). Military Police
(Ministry of Defence).
MARITIME POLICE: ε800 with about 38 armed
patrol boats.
CUSTOMS SERVICE (Ministry of Finance) 650; 4
PCO, 2 PCC, 1 PCI, 5 PCI⟨; most armed.

FOREIGN FORCES:
SINGAPORE: 4 trg camps.

THAILAND

GDP	1992ε: b 2,570bn ($101.18bn)	
Growth	1991: 7.5%	1992: 7.0%
Inflation	1991: 5.7%	1992: 4.1%
Debt	1991: $27.4bn	1992: $29.1bn
Def bdgt	1992: b 68.81bn ($2.71bn)	
	1993: b 79.60bn ($3.16bn)	
FMA	1993: $2m (US)	
$1 = b	1990: 25.585	1991: 25.571
	1992: 25.40	1993: 25.200
b = baht		

Population: 57,697,000

	13–17	18–22	23–32
Men	3,099,000	3,038,000	5,419,000
Women	2,999,000	2,943,000	5,299,000

TOTAL ARMED FORCES:
ACTIVE: 295,000.
Terms of service: conscription 2 years.
RESERVES: 500,000.

ARMY: 190,000 (80,000 conscripts).
4 Regional Army HQ, 2 Corps HQ.
1 armd div.
1 cav (lt armd) div (2 cav, 1 arty regt).
2 mech inf div.
6 inf div (incl Royal Guard, 5 with 1 tk bn)
(1 to be mech, 1 to be lt).
2 SF div.
1 arty div, 1 AD arty div (6 AD arty bn).
19 engr bn.
1 indep cav regt.
8 indep inf bn.
4 recce coy.
Armd air cav regt with 3 air-mobile coy.
Some hel flt.
RESERVES: 4 inf div HQ.
EQUIPMENT:
MBT: 50+ Ch Type-69 (in store), 100 M-48A5, 53 M-60.
LIGHT TANKS: 154 *Scorpion*, 250 M-41, 106 *Stingray*.
RECCE: 32 *Shorland* Mk 3.
APC: 340 M-113, 150 V-150 *Commando*, 450 Ch Type-85 (YW-531H).
TOWED ARTY: 105mm: 200 M-101/-101 mod, 12 M-102, 32 M-618A2 (local manufacture); 130mm: 15 Ch Type-59; 155mm: 56 M-114, 62 M-198, 32 M-71.
MORTARS: 81mm, 107mm.
ATGW: *TOW*, 300 *Dragon*.
RL: M-72 *LAW*.
RCL: 75mm: M-20; 106mm: 150 M-40.
AD GUNS: 20mm: 24 M-163 *Vulcan*, 24 M-167 *Vulcan*; 37mm: 122 Type-74; 40mm: 80 M-1/M-42 SP, 28 L/70; 57mm: 24.
SAM: *Redeye*, some *Aspide*.
AVIATION:
TRANSPORT: 1 Beech 99, 4 C-47, 10 Cessna 208, 1 Short 330, 1 *Beech King Air*.
LIAISON: 63 O-1A, 17 -E, 5 T-41A, 13 U-17A.
TRAINING: 16 T-41D.
HELICOPTERS:
ATTACK: 4 AH-1F.
TRANSPORT: 10 Bell 206, 9 -212, 6 -214, 70 UH-1H.
TRAINING: 36 Hughes 300C, 3 OH-13, 7 TH-55.

NAVY: 62,000 incl Naval Air (1,150), Marines (20,000), Coastal Defence and Coast Guards. 25,000 conscripts.

3 Naval Area Commands:
  1: East Thai Gulf
  2: West Thai Gulf.
  3: Andaman Sea.
2 Naval Air Wings.
BASES: Bangkok, Sattahip (Fleet HQ), Songkhla, Phang Nga, Nakhon Phanom (HQ Mekong River Operating Unit), Trat.
FRIGATES: 9:
FFG: 4:
2 *Chao Phraya* (Ch *Jianghu*-III) with 8 x C-801 SSM, 2 x 2 100mm guns; plus 2 x 5 ASW RL
2 *Kraburil* (Ch *Jianghu*-IV type) with 8 x C-801 SSM, 1 x 2 100mm guns; plus 2 x 5 ASW RL and *Bell* 212 hel.
FF: 5.
1 *Makut Rajakumarn* with 2 x 3 ASTT (*Sting Ray* LWT); plus 2 x 114mm guns.
2 *Tapi* (US PF-103) with 2 x 3 ASTT (Mk 46 LWT).
2 *Tachin* (US *Tacoma*) with 2 x 3 ASTT (1 trg, 1 CG).
PATROL AND COASTAL COMBATANTS: 63:
CORVETTES: 5:
2 *Rattanakosin* with 2 x 3 ASTT (*Sting Ray* LWT); plus 2 x 4 *Harpoon* SSM.
3 *Khamronsin* with 2 x 3 ASTT; plus 1 x 76mm gun.
MISSILE CRAFT: 6:
3 *Ratcharit* (It Breda 50-m) with 4 x MM-38 *Exocet* SSM.
3 *Prabparapak* (Ge Lürssen 45-m) with 5 *Gabriel* SSM.
PATROL: 52:
COASTAL: 12:
3 *Chon Buri* PFC, 6 *Sattahip*, 3 *Sarasin* (US PC-461) PCC.
INSHORE: 40: 10 T-11 (US PGM-71), about 30 PCI⟨.
MINE WARFARE: 7:
2 *Bang Rachan* (Ge Lürssen T-48) MCC.
4 *Ladya* (US 'Bluebird' MSC) MSC.
1 *Thalang* MCM spt with minesweeping capability.
Plus some 5 MSB.
AMPHIBIOUS: 8:
2 *Sichang* (Fr PS-700) LST, capacity 14 tk, 300 tps with hel deck.
4 *Angthong* (US LST-511) LST, capacity 16 tk, 200 tps (1 trg).
2 *Kut* (US LSM-1) LSM, capacity about 4 tk.
Plus about 50 craft: 9 LCU, about 24 LCM, 1 LCG, 2 LSIL, 3 hovercraft, 12 LCVP.
SUPPORT AND MISCELLANEOUS: 11:
1 *Chula* AO, 4 small tankers, 3 survey, 3 trg (incl 1 *Pin Klao* (US *Cannon*) FF.

NAVAL AIR: (1,150); 29 cbt ac; 8 armed hel.
MR/ASW: 3 P-3A *Orion*, 1 sqn with 3 Do-228, 3 F-27 MPA, 5 N-24A *Searchmaster* L.
ASW HELICOPTERS: 8 Bell 212 ASW.
MR/SAR: 1 sqn with 2 CL-215.
MR/ATTACK: 10 Cessna T-337 *Skymasters*.
SAR: 1 hel sqn with 8 Bell 212, 2 -214, 4 UH-1H.
ASM: AGM-84 *Harpoon* (for F-27MPA).

MARINES: (20,000)
1 div HQ, 6 inf regt, 1 arty regt (3 fd, 1 AA bn);
1 amph aslt bn; recce bn.
EQUIPMENT:
APC: 33 LVTP-7.
TOWED ARTY: 155mm: 18 GC-45.
ATGW: *TOW*, *Dragon*.

AIR FORCE: 43,000;
156 cbt ac, no armed hel.
FGA: 1 sqn with 8 F-5A, 4 -B.
14 F-16A, 4 -B.
FIGHTER: 2 sqn with 38 F-5E, 6 -F.
COIN: 7 sqn:
1 with 15 A-37B;
1 with 7 AC-47;
3 with 24 AU-23A;
2 with 30 OV-10C.
ELINT: 1 sqn with 3 IAI-201.
RECCE: 3 RF-5A, 3RT-33A.
SURVEY: 1 *Commander* 690, 3 *Learjet* 35A, 2
Merlin IVA, 2 *Queen Air*.
TRANSPORT: 4 sqn:
1 with 3 C-130H, 3 C-130H-30, 3 DC-8-62F.
1 with 10 C-123B/-K, 6 BAe-748.
1 with 10 C-47.
1 with 20 N-22B *Missionmaster*.
VIP: Royal flight: 1 Boeing 737-200, 1 *King Air* 200,
3 *Merlin* IV ac; 2 Bell 412 hel.
TRAINING: 24 CT-4, 31 *Fantrainer*-400, 16
Fantrainer -600, 16 SF-260, 10 T-33A, 20 PC-9, 13
T-37B, 6 -C, 11 T-41.
LIAISON: 3 *Commander*, 2 *King Air* E90, 30 O-1
Bird Dog.
HELICOPTERS: 2 sqn:
1 with 18 S-58T.
1 with 21 UH-1H.
AAM: AIM-9B/J *Sidewinder*.
AD: *Blowpipe* and *Aspide* SAM. 1 AA arty bty: 4
Skyguard, 1 *Flycatcher* radars, each with 4 fire units
of 2 x 30mm Mauser guns.

FORCES ABROAD:
UN AND PEACEKEEPING:
CAMBODIA (UNTAC): 720: 1 engr bn.
CROATIA (UNPROFOR I): 4 Observers.
IRAQ/KUWAIT (UNIKOM): 7 Observers.

PARAMILITARY:
THAHAN PHRAN ('Hunter Soldiers'): 18,500
volunteer irregular force; 27 regt of some 200 coy.
NATIONAL SECURITY VOLUNTEER CORPS:
43,000.
MARINE POLICE: 1,700; 1 PCO, 2 PCC, 3 PFI,
some 60 PCI⟨.
POLICE AVIATION: 500; 1 *Airtourer*, 3 AU-23, 1
C-47, 2 Cessna 310, 1 CT-4, 3 DHC-4, 1 Do-28, 4
PC-6, 1 Short 330 ac; 27 Bell 205A, 14 -206, 3 -212,
6 UH-12, 5 KH-4, 1 S-62 hel.

BORDER PATROL POLICE: 28,000.
PROVINCIAL POLICE: ε50,000 incl Special
Action Force (ε500).

VIETNAM

GDP[a]	1991ε: d 19,100bn ($15.60bn)	
	1992ε: d 20,100bn ($15.95bn)	
Growth	1991: 3.8%	1992ε: 5.3%
Inflation	1991: 78.9%	1992ε: 25.0%
Debt	1991: $15.30bn	1992: $16.40bn
Def bdgt	1991ε:$1.87bn	1992ε:$1.75bn
$1 = d	1990: 8,700.0	1991: 11,000.0
	1992: 11,145.1	1993: 10,500.0

d = dong
[a] $ figures est as conversion, although the official rate of
exchange is meaningless.

Population: 71,122,000

	13–17	18–22	23–32
Men	4,020,000	3,667,000	6,120,000
Women	3,879,000	3,498,000	6,132,000

TOTAL ARMED FORCES:
ACTIVE: 857,000 (referred to as 'Main Force').
Terms of service: 2 years, specialists 3 years, some
ethnic minorities 2 years.
RESERVES 'Strategic Rear Force' some 3–4m
manpower potential, see also Paramilitary.

ARMY: 700,000.
8 Military Regions, 2 special areas.
14 Corps HQ.
50 inf div.[b]
3 mech div.
10 armd bde.
15 indep inf regt.
SF incl AB bde, demolition engr regt.
Some 10 fd arty bde.
8 engr div.
10–16 economic construction div; 20 indep engr bde.
EQUIPMENT:
MBT: 1,300: T-34/-54/-55, T-62, Ch Type-59, M-
48A3.
LIGHT TANKS: 600 PT-76, Ch Type-62/63.
RECCE: 100 BRDM-1/-2.
AIFV: 300 BMP.
APC: 1,100 BTR-40/-50/-60/-152, YW-531, M-113.
TOWED ARTY: 2,300: 76mm; 85mm; 100mm: M-
1944, T-12; 105mm: M-101/-102; 122mm: Type-54,
Type-60, M-1938, D-30, D-74; 130mm: M-46;
152mm: D-20; 155mm: M-114.
SP ARTY: 152mm: 30 2S3; 175mm: M-107.
COMBINED GUN/MORTAR: 120mm: 2S9 reported.
ASSAULT GUNS: 100mm: SU-100; 122mm: ISU-
122.
MRL: 107mm: 360 Type 63; 122mm: 350 BM-21;
140mm: BM-14-16.

MORTARS: 82mm, 120mm: M-43; 160mm: M-43.
ATGW: AT-3 *Sagger*.
RCL: 75mm: Ch Type-56; 82mm: Ch Type-65, B-10; 87mm: Ch Type-51.
AD GUNS: 12,000: 14.5mm; 23mm: incl ZSU-23-4 SP; 30mm; 37mm; 57mm; 85mm; 100mm.
SAM: SA-7/-16.

NAVY: ε42,000 (incl 30,000 Naval Infantry). Four Naval Regions.
BASES: Hanoi (HQ): Cam Ranh Bay, Da Nang, Haiphong, Ha Tou, Ho Chi Minh City, Can Tho, plus several smaller bases.
FRIGATES: 7:
1 *Phan Ngu Lao* (US *Barnegat*) (ASUW), with 2 x SS-N-2 *Styx* SSM, 1 x 127mm gun.
5 Sov *Petya-II* with 4 x ASW RL, 3 x 533mm TT.
1 *Dai Ky* (US *Savage*) with 2 x 3 ASTT (trg).
PATROL AND COASTAL COMBATANTS: 55:
MISSILE CRAFT: 8 Sov *Osa -I I* with 4 x SS-N-2 SSM.
TORPEDO CRAFT: 19:
3 Sov *Turya* PHT with 4 x 533mm TT.
16 Sov *Shershen* PFT with 4 x 533mm TT.
PATROL: 28:
INSHORE: 28:
8 Sov SO-1, 3 US PGM-59/71, 11 *Zhuk*⟨, 4⟨.
2 Sov *Turya* (no TT).
MINE WARFARE: 11:
2 *Yurka* MSC, 4 *Sonya* MSC, 2 Ch *Lienyun* MSC, 1 *Vanya* MSI, 2 *Yevgenya* MSI , plus 5 K-8 boats.
AMPHIBIOUS: 7:
3 US LST-510-511 LST, capacity 200 tps, 16 tk.
3 Sov *Polnocny* LSM, capacity 180 tps, 6 tk.
1 US LSM-1 LSM, capacity about 50 tps, 4 tk.
Plus about 30 craft; 12 LCM, 18 LCU.
SUPPORT AND MISCELLANEOUS: 30+ incl:

1 survey, 4 small tankers, about 12 small tpt, 2 ex-Sov Floating Docks and 3 div spt.
NAVALANTRY: (30,000) (amph, cdo).

AIR FORCE: 15,000; 240 cbt ac, 28 armed hel (plus many in store). 4 Air Div.
FGA: 1 regt:
1 with 65 Su-22.
FIGHTER: 5 regt with 175 MiG-21bis/PF.
ATTACK HELICOPTERS: 20 Mi-24.
MR: 4 Be-12.
ASW HEL: 8 Ka-25.
SURVEY: 2 An-30.
TRANSPORT: 3 regt: incl 12 An-2, 4 An-24, 30 An-26, 8 Tu-134, 14 Yak-40.
HELICOPTERS: some 80 hel incl Mi-4, Mi-6, Mi-8.
TRAINING: 3 regt with 53 ac incl L-39, *MiG-21U.
AAM: AA-2 *Atoll*.

AIR DEFENCE FORCE: 100,000.
14 AD div:
SAM: some 66 sites with SA-2/-3/-6;
4 AD arty bde: 37mm, 57mm, 85mm, 100mm, 130mm; plus People's Regional Force: ε1,000 units.
6 radar bde: 100 sites.

PARAMILITARY:
LOCAL FORCES: Some 4–5m. Incl People's Self Defence Force (urban units), People's Militia (rural units). Comprise: static and mobile cbt units, log spt and village protection pl. Some arty, mor and AD guns. Acts as reserve.

[b] Inf div strengths vary from 5,000 to 12,500.

Caribbean and Latin America

Political Developments

Events in Latin America, while receiving little attention in the international press, are nonetheless as important to those involved as more publicised events elsewhere. In the last 12 months there have been both positive and negative developments in the region. On the whole, it has been a more encouraging year than those that immediately preceded it.

In **El Salvador**, the military provisions of the cease-fire signed by the government and the Farabundo Martí National Liberation Front (FMLN) have proceded relatively smoothly. The FMLN completed its demobilisation under UN supervision on 1 December 1992. The El Salvador army has reduced its strength by 12,000 men to 28,000. Both former rebels and soldiers are being enlisted in the new National Civilian Police. The distribution of land to both former rebels and soldiers is, however, well behind schedule.

In September 1992 the World Court issued its ruling on the El Salvador–Honduras border dispute. Both presidents have stated their determination to put the ruling into effect.

In **Colombia** the government launched a major campaign against the rebel groups which form the Coordinadora Nacional Guerrillera Simon Bolívar (CNGSB) and has achieved a high degree of success. Some 700 guerrillas have been killed, 1,600 captured and already more than 100 have surrendered, with more expected to engage in 'dialogue' with the government. A group thought to number up to 800 men, a faction of the Ejército de Liberación Nacional, are expected to demobilise in July 1993. In **Peru** the government of Alberto Fujimori captured a number of guerrilla leaders who have claimed that the Movimiento Revolucionario Tupac Amarú (MRTA) could be defeated within months; over 300 MRTA men have opted to surrender to the government. The much larger *Sendero Luminoso* (Shining Path) movement has suffered far less, despite the capture of its leader in September 1992. Overall, however, the level of terrorist activity is much reduced.

In **Nicaragua** there has been a resurgence of dissident activity. In early 1993 there were clashes between government forces and former Contras in the north of the country in which 65 people were killed. Up to 1,400 men are said to have taken up arms again. Also in the north a dissident group of Sandinistas has emerged, calling itself the Rural Workers Revolutionary Front, which occupied the town of Estelí until driven out by government troops in July 1993.

On 13 May 1993 the British government announced that it would be pulling out the bulk of its 1,500-strong force from **Belize** in 1994, leaving behind only a training team to assist indigenous forces and a training camp for the British Army. The Belizean Prime Minister then called an election which he lost. The new government has not yet asked the UK to reverse its decision but has said it will suspend the legislation implementing the agreement reached with Guatemala in 1991 (which led to the British withdrawal decision). The new government is opposed to the access route to the Atlantic granted to Guatemala. Quite independently of all this, the President of **Guatemala**, Jorge Serrano Elias assumed dictatorial powers in May 1993. A week later he was out of office. Soon after, the Defence Minister was dismissed, to be replaced by a general, considered to be a hardliner, but who is believed, somewhat paradoxically, to want to keep the army out of politics. On 3 August 1993, the Vice-President said that recognition of Belize should be withdrawn.

There have been both progress and setbacks in the continuing dialogue between **Argentina** and the UK over the Falkland Islands. In May 1993, it was agreed that, in view of their improved relations, the confidence-building measure which required the advance notification of naval or air force activity would be changed, and the distance from coastlines at which notification of activity was necessary was consequently reduced from 80 to 55 nautical miles. Notification of ground force exercises of more than 1,000 troops was discarded. The UK has extended its 12-mile fishing exclusion zone around South Georgia and the Sandwich Islands to 200 miles in order to conserve the stock. Argentina has reiterated its annual claim to the Falklands at the meeting of the UN Committee on Decolonisation.

On 16 June 1993 the UN Security Council adopted Resolution 841 which imposed an oil and arms embargo on **Haiti**, and ordered the freezing of Haiti's overseas funds. Meanwhile, the US and UN have been negotiating with the Haitian military dictator for the return of the ousted President, Jean-Bertrand Aristide. Agreement was reached for Aristide's return, together with US and other international aid and assistance in re-forming and training the security forces. A Prime Minister is to be nominated by Aristide and confirmed by the legally reconstituted parliament; the UN will then consider lifting sanctions.

Military Developments

The reorganisation of the **Argentinian** Army appears to have been completed. Contrary to expectations the divisional level of command has not been retained; although the three regional commands are still named as Corps, they are, in effect, of divisional strength. One infantry brigade has been reclassified as mechanised, another as a training brigade, and there is no longer a 'jungle brigade'. Little new equipment has been procured: three ASH-3H ASW helicopters for the Navy, and six MS-760 COIN aircraft for the Air Force. A change in US policy will allow Argentinian purchases of US weapons in the future; so far 36 A-4 *Skyhawk* FGA aircraft have been ordered, and 20 OV-1 *Mohawk* for training, observation and civil tasks (drug enforcement and survey) are to be delivered. The **Chilean** Army has formed an eighth division, but only one additional regiment has been raised. There is now an airborne battalion. Naval acquisitions include: the first of probably four *Micalvi*-class 500-ton patrol craft built in Chile; six Israeli *Dabur*-class inshore patrol craft (transferred in 1991); the first of seven P-3 *Orion* maritime reconnaissance aircraft; and we believe there are a total of 21 ASW helicopters as opposed to 12. The Air Force has ten more COIN aircraft (6 A-37B and 4 A-36) and its first airborne early-warning aircraft, an Israeli converted 707 (*Phalcon*). The **Brazilian** Air Force has taken delivery of 15 AS-350 helicopters (not HB-350 as forecast last year). The Navy has commissioned its third *Inhauma*-class frigate which is armed with *Exocet* and embarks a helicopter. The last remaining US *Guppy*-class submarine which had a training role has been retired. The Air Force has increased its inventory with five more AMX FGA and 14 AMX-T trainers.

The **Bolivian** Air Force has a further four PC-7 COIN aircraft. The **Colombian** Air Force has three AC-47 COIN aircraft more than previously listed. The largest air force increase has been in **Venezuela** which has an additional 13 EMB-312 *Tucano* and 19 T-2D *Buckeye* COIN aircraft.

The **Guatemalan** Army field force has been reorganised into two brigades, and a second airborne battalion has been formed. The **Panamanian** Navy has recommissioned, following refit, a second Vosper (UK). The **Mexican** Navy has also added to its force of patrol craft with two *S.J. Holzinger* (Mexican-built) offshore craft, one US *Cape Higgon*-class and three US *Point* inshore craft.

ARGENTINA

GDP[a]   1991: P 5.86bn ($97.60bn)
1992: P 6.36bn ($106.05bn)
Growth 1991: 8.9% 1992: 8.6%
Inflation 1991: 171.7% 1992: 24.9%
Debt 1991: $75.05bn 1992: $70.36bn
Def exp[b] 1991: P 2.6bn ($2.72bn)
Def bdgt 1992: P 2.00bn ($2.02bn)
1993: P 2.06bn ($2.08bn)
FMA 1992: $1.2m (US)
$1 = A 1990: 4,876.0 1991: 0.9536
$1 = P 1992: 0.9906 1993: 0.9906
A = Australes. P = Pesos

[a] On 1 January 1992, the Peso Argentino, equal to 10,000 Australes, was introduced. All GDP figures are in 1985 prices and exchange rates and have been converted into Pesos.
[b] Def bdgt and exp are in current prices and exchange rates.

Population: 33,374,000

	13–17	18–22	23–32
Men	1,575,000	1,413,000	2,422,000
Women	1,527,000	1,375,000	2,371,000

TOTAL ARMED FORCES:
ACTIVE: 70,800 (18,100 conscripts).
Terms of service: all services up to 14 months; conscripts may actually serve less than 7 months.
RESERVES: 377,000: Army 250,000 (National Guard 200,000; Territorial Guard 50,000); Navy 77,000; Air 50,000.

ARMY: 40,400 (13,400 conscripts).
3 Corps:
1 with 1 armd, 1 mech bde, 1 trg bde.
1 with 1 inf, 1 mtn bde.

1 with 1 armd, 2 mech, 1 mtn bde.
Corps tps: 1 lt armd cav regt (recce), 1 arty, 1 AD arty, 1 engr bn in each Corps.
Strategic Reserve:
1 AB bde.
1 mech bde.
Army tps:
1 mot inf bn (Army HQ Escort Regt).
1 mot cav regt (Presidential Escort).
1 SF coy, 3 avn bn.
1 AD arty bn, 2 engr bn.

EQUIPMENT:
MBT: 266: 96 M-4 *Sherman*, 170 TAM.
LIGHT TANKS: 60 AMX-13, 106 SK-105 *Kuerassier*.
RECCE: 50 AML-90.
AIFV: 30 AMX-VCI, some 160 *TAM* VCTP.
APC: ε75 M-3 half-track, 240 M-113, 80 MOWAG *Grenadier* (mod *Roland*).
TOWED ARTY: 250: 105mm: 150 M-56; 155mm: 100 CITEFA Models 77/-81.
SP ARTY: 125: 155mm: Mk F3, L33.
MRL: 105mm: SLAM *Pampero*; 127mm: SLAM SAPBA-1.
MORTARS: 81mm: 1,000; 120mm: 130 *Brandt* (some SP in VCTM AIFV).
ATGW: 600 SS-11/-12, *Cobra (Mamba)*, 2,100 *Mathogo*.
RCL: 75mm: 75 M-20; 90mm: 100 M-67; 105mm: 150 M-968.
AD GUNS: 20mm: 130; 30mm: 40; 35mm: 15 GDF-001; 40mm: 80 L/60, 15 L/70; 90mm: 20.
SAM: *Tigercat*, *Blowpipe*, *Roland*, SAM-7.
AIRCRAFT: 5 Cessna 207, 5 *Commander* 690, 2 DHC-6, 3 G-222, 1 *Merlin* IIIA, 4 -IV, 3 *Queen Air*, 1 *Sabreliner*, 5 T-41, 12 OV-1D.
HELICOPTERS: 6 A-109, 3 AS-332B, 5 Bell 205, 4 FH-1100, 4 SA-315, 3 SA-330, 10 UH-1H, 8 UH-12.

NAVY: 21,500, incl naval aviation (3,000) and marines (4,000) (incl 3,500 conscripts).
3 Naval Areas: Centre: from River Plate to South: from 42° 45' S to Cape Horn; and Antarctica.
BASES: Buenos Aires, Ezeiza (Naval Air), La Plata, Rio Santiago (Submarine base), Puerto Belgrano (HQ Centre), Punta Indio (Naval Air), Mar del Plata (submarine base), Ushuaia (HQ South).
SUBMARINES: 2:
2 *Santa Cruz* (Ge TR-1700) with 533mm TT (SST-4 HWT).
Plus 2 non-op *Salta* (Ge T-209/1200) with 533mm TT (SST-4 HWT) (both in major refit/modernisation).
PRINCIPAL SURFACE COMBATANTS: 13:
DESTROYERS: 6:
2 *Hercules* (UK Type 42) with 1 x 2 *Sea Dart* SAM; plus 1 SA-319 hel (ASW), 2 x 3 ASTT, 4 x MM-38 *Exocet* SSM, 1 x 114mm gun.
4 *Almirante Brown* (Ge *MEKO-360*) ASW with 2 x SA-316 hel, 2 x 3 ASTT; plus 8 x MM-40 *Exocet* SSM, 1 x 127mm gun.
FRIGATES: 7:
4 *Espora* (Ge *MEKO-140*) with 2 x 3 ASTT, hel deck; plus 8 x MM-40 *Exocet*.
3 *Drummond* (Fr A-69) with 2 x 3 ASTT; plus 4 x MM-38 *Exocet*, 1 x 100mm gun.
ADDITIONAL IN STORE: 1 carrier: 1 *Veinticinco de Mayo* CVS (UK *Colossus*).
PATROL AND COASTAL COMBATANTS: 13:
TORPEDO CRAFT: 2 *Intrepida* (Ge Lürssen 45-m) PFT with 2 x 533mm TT (SST-4 HWT)
PATROL CRAFT: 11:
OFFSHORE: 7:
1 *Teniente Olivieri* (ex-US oilfield tug).
2 *Irigoyen* (US *Cherokee* AT).
2 *King* (trg) with 3 x 105mm guns.
2 *Sorbral* (US *Sotoyomo* AT).
INSHORE: 4 *Baradero* PCI(.
MINE WARFARE: 6:
4 *Neuquen* (UK 'Ton') MSC.
2 *Chaco* (UK 'Ton') MHC.
AMPHIBIOUS: 1 *Cabo San Antonio* LST (hel deck), capacity 600 tps, 18 tk.
Plus 20 craft; 4 LCM, 16 LCVP.
SUPPORT AND MISCELLANEOUS: 9:
1 AGOR, 3 tpt, 1 ocean tug, 1 icebreaker, 2 trg, 1 research.

NAVAL AVIATION: (3,000);
42 cbt ac, 13 armed hel.
ATTACK: 1 sqn with 12 *Super Etendard*.
MR/ASW: 1 sqn with 3 L-188, 6 S-2E.
EW: 2 L-188E.
HELICOPTERS: 2 sqn: 1 ASW/tpt with 7 ASH-3H (ASW) and 4 AS-61D (tpt); 1 spt with 6 SA-316/-319 (with SS-11).
TRANSPORT: 1 sqn with 1 BAe-125, 3 F-28-3000, 3 L-188, 4 *Queen Air* 80, 9 *Super King Air*, 4 US-2A.
SURVEY: 3 PC-6B (Antarctic flt).
TRAINING: 2 sqn:
7* EMB-326, 9* MB-326, 5* MB-339A, 10 T-34C.
MISSILES:
ASM: AGM-12 *Bullpup*, AM-39 *Exocet*, AS-12, *Martín Pescador*.
AAM: AIM-9 *Sidewinder*, R-550 *Magic*.

MARINES: (4,000).
Fleet Forces: 2: each 2 bn, 1 amph recce coy, 1 fd arty bn, 1 ATK, 1 engr coy.
Amph spt force: 1 marine inf bn.
1 AD arty regt (bn).
2 indep inf bn.
EQUIPMENT:
RECCE: 12 ERC-90 *Lynx*.
APC: 19 LVTP-7, 15 LARC-5, 6 MOWAG *Grenadier*, 24 Panhard.
TOWED ARTY: 105mm: 15 M-101/M-56; 155mm: 6 M-114.
MORTARS: 81mm: 20.
RL: 89mm: 60 3.5-in M-20.
ATGW: 50 *Bantam*, *Cobra (Mamba)*.
RCL: 105mm: 30 M-1968.
AD GUNS: 30mm: 10 HS-816.
SAM: *Tigercat*.

AIR FORCE: 8,900 (1,200 conscripts):
180 cbt ac, 11 armed hel, 9 air bde, 10 AD arty
bty, SF (AB) coy.
AIR OPERATIONS COMMAND (9 bde):
BOMBERS: 1 sqn with 4 *Canberra* B-62, 2 T-64.
FGA/FIGHTER: 4 sqn:
2 (1 OCU) with 20 *Mirage* IIIC (17 -CJ, 1 -BE, 2 -
BJ), 15 *Mirage* IIIEA; 2 with 8 *Mirage* 5P, 23 *Dagger*
(*Nesher* ; 20 -A, 3 -B).
FGA: 4 sqn with 16 A-4B/C.
COIN: 3 sqn:
2 with 36 IA-58A, 16 IA-63, 30 MS-760;
1 armed hel with 11 Hughes MD500, 3 UH-1H.
MR: 1 Boeing 707.
SURVEY: 3 *Learjet* 35A, 4 1A-50.
TANKER: 2 Boeing 707, 2 KC-130H.
SAR: 4 SA-315 hel.
TRANSPORT: 5 sqn with:
AIRCRAFT: 5 Boeing 707, 6 C-47, 2 C-130E, 5 -H, 1 L-
100-30, 6 DHC-6, 12 F-27, 4 F-28, 15 IA-50, 2 *Merlin*
IVA. Antarctic spt unit with 1 DHC-6, 1 LC-47.
HELICOPTERS: 5 Bell 212, 2 CH-47C, 1 S-61R.
CALIBRATION: 1 sqn with 2 Boeing 707, 3 IA-50, 2
Learjet 35, 1 PA-31.
LIAISON: 1 sqn with 20 Cessna 182, 1 -320, 7
Commander, 1 *Sabreliner*.
AIR TRAINING COMMAND:
28 EMB-312, 10* MS-760, 30 T-34B ac.
4 Hughes 500D hel.
MISSILES:
ASM: ASM-2 *Martín Pescador*.
AAM: AIM-9B *Sidewinder*, R-530, R-550, *Shafrir*.

FORCES ABROAD:
UN AND PEACEKEEPING:
ANGOLA (UNAVEM II): 3 Observers, 6 civ pol.
CAMBODIA (UNTAC): 2.
CROATIA (UNPROFOR I): 895: 1 inf bn, plus 30
civ pol.
EL SALVADOR (ONUSAL): 7.
IRAQ/KUWAIT (UNIKOM): 6 Observers.
MIDDLE EAST (UNTSO): 6 Observers.
MOZAMBIQUE (ONUMOZ): 40 plus 8 Observers.
WESTERN SAHARA (MINURSO): 7 Observers.

PARAMILITARY:
GENDARMERIE (Ministry of Defence): 18,000; 5
Regional Comd.
EQUIPMENT: *Shorland* recce, 40 UR-416; 81mm
mor; ac: 3 Piper, 5 PC-6; hel: 5 SA-315.
PREFECTURA NAVAL (Coast Guard): (13,000); 7
comd.
EQUIPMENT: 6 PCO: 5 *Mantilla*, 1 *Delfin*; 4 PCI⟨, 19;
5 C-212, 4 Short *Skyvan* ac; 3 SA-330, 6 MD-500 hel.

THE BAHAMAS

GDP   1991: $B 2.73bn ($US 2.73bn)
            1992ε: $B 2.84bn ($US 2.84bn)

Growth   1991: -2.5%   1992ε: -1%
Inflation 1991: 7.10%   1992: 5.8%
Debt   1991ε: $US 412.0m 1992ε: $US 438.0m
Sy bdgt[a] 1992: $B 65.0m ($US 65.0m)
$US1 = $B 1987–93: 1.0
$B = Bahamian dollars
[a] Incl Police allocation.

Population: 268,800

	13–17	18–22	23–32
Men	15,500	16,000	25,500
Women	14,200	15,000	25,700

TOTAL SECURITY FORCES:
ACTIVE: 2,550: Police (1,700); Defence Force (850).

NAVY: 850 (50 women).
(ROYAL BAHAMIAN DEFENCE FORCE)
BASE: Coral Harbour, New Providence Island.
PATROL AND COASTAL COMBATANTS: 15:
INSHORE: 3 *Yellow Elder* PFI, 1 *Marlin*, 6 *Fenrick
Sturrup* (ex-USCG *Cape Higgon* Cl) PCI, 5 PCI⟨,
plus some ex-fishing vessels and boats.
MISCELLANEOUS: 2: 1 converted LCM (ex USN), 1
small auxiliary.
AIRCRAFT: 1 Cessna 404, 1 Cessna 421, 1 *Black
Hawk* hel.

BELIZE

GDP[a]   1991: $BZ 791.2m ($US 395.6m)
           1992: $BZ 854.5m ($US 427.3m)
Growth   1991: 2%   1992: 6%
Inflation 1991: 5.6%   1992: 2.8%
Debt   1990: $US 150.9m 1991: $US167.1m
Def bdgt   1989ε: $BZ 19.88m ($US 9.94m)
           1990ε: $BZ 19.36m ($US 9.68m)
$US1 = $BZ 1987–93: 2.0
$BZ = $ Belize

[a] Confirmation that the 1,500 British troops will be
withdrawn by mid-1994 is expected to have a major impact
on Belize's economy. Army spending in the country is
estimated at almost 20% of GDP.

Population: 204,200

	13–17	18–22	23–32
Men	12,300	11,800	17,000
Women	12,300	11,800	17,000

TOTAL ARMED FORCES:
ACTIVE: 660.
RESERVES (militia): 700: 300 reserve, 400 volun-
teers.

ARMY: 600.
1 inf bn (3 inf, 1 spt, 1 trg, 3 Reserve coy).

EQUIPMENT:
MORTARS: 81mm: 6.
RCL: 84mm: 8 *Carl Gustav*.

MARITIME WING: 50.
PATROL: 2 PCI⟨, plus some 6 armed boats.

AIR WING: 15: 2 cbt ac, no armed hel.
MR/TRANSPORT: 2 BN-2B *Defender*.

FOREIGN FORCES:
UNITED KINGDOM: 1,500. Army: some 1,200; 1 inf bn + spt elm (incl *Rapier*). RAF: 300; 1 *Harrier* (FGA) flt, *Puma* hel flt (to be withdrawn).

BOLIVIA

GDP	1991:	B 21.69bn ($6.06bn)	
	1992:	B 24.29bn ($6.23bn)	
Growth	1991:	4%	1992: 3.8%
Inflation	1991:	17.8%	1992: 10.7%
Debt	1991:	$4.08bn	1992: $4.06bn
Def bdgt	1992:	B 433m ($111.01m)	
	1993:	B 503m ($122.21m)	
Def exp	1992:	B 458m ($117.42m)	
FMA	1992:	$87.9m (US)	
$1 = B	1990:	3.173	1991: 3.581
	1992:	3.910	1993: 4.120

B = Bolivianos
[a] Mostly Economic support. Incl. $17m as anti-narcotics assistance.

Population: 7,754,000

	13–17	18–22	23–32
Men	450,000	375,000	570,000
Women	449,000	380,000	593,000

TOTAL ARMED FORCES:
ACTIVE: 33,500 (some 20,000 conscripts).
Terms of service: 12 months, selective.

ARMY: 25,000 (some 18,000 conscripts).
HQ: 9 Military Regions.
Army HQ direct control:
2 armd bn.
1 mech cav regt.
1 Presidential Guard inf regt.
10 'div'; org, composition varies; comprise:
8 cav gp (5 horsed, 2 mot, 1 aslt); 1 mot inf 'regt' with 2 bn. 22 inf bn (incl 5 inf aslt bn); 1 armd bn; 1 arty 'regt' (bn); 5 arty gp (coy); 1 AB 'regt' (bn); 6 engr bn.
EQUIPMENT:
LIGHT TANKS: 36 SK-105 *Kuerassier*.
RECCE: 24 EE-9 *Cascavel*.
APC: 108: 50 M-113, 10 V-100 *Commando*,

24 MOWAG *Roland*, 24 EE-11 *Urutu*.
TOWED ARTY: 75mm: 70 incl M-116 pack, ε10 Bofors M-1935; 105mm: 30 incl M-101, FH-18.
MORTARS: 81mm: 50; 107mm: M-30.
RCL: 90mm: 30.
AVIATION: 2 C-212, 1 *King Air* B90, 1 *Super King Air* 200 (VIP).

NAVY: 4,500 (incl 2,000 marines).
6 Naval Districts; covering Lake Titicaca and the rivers; each 1 Flotilla.
BASES: Riberalta (HQ), Tiquina (HQ), Puerto Busch, Puerto Guayaramerín (HQ), Puerto Villaroel, Trinidad (HQ), Puerto Suárez (HQ) Cobija (HQ).
RIVER PATROL CRAFT: some 10⟨; plus some 15 US *Boston* whalers.
SUPPORT: Some 20 riverine craft/boats.

NAVAL AVIATION:
AIRCRAFT: 1 Cessna 206, 1 402.
MARINES: 6 bn (1 in each District).

AIR FORCE: 4,000 (perhaps 2,000 conscripts); 52 cbt ac, 10 armed hel.
FIGHTER: 1 sqn with 12 AT-33N, 4 F-86F (ftr/trg).
COIN: 16 PC-7.
SPECIAL OPS: 1 sqn with 10 Hughes 500M hel.
SAR: 1 hel sqn with 4 HB-315B, 2 SA-315B, 1 UH-1.
SURVEY: 1 sqn with 5 Cessna 206, 1 210, 1 402, 3 *Learjet* 25.
TRANSPORT: 3 sqn:
1 VIP tpt with 1 L-188, 1 *Sabreliner*, 2 *Super King Air*.
2 tpt with 9 C-130, 4 F-27-400, 1 IAI-201, 2 *King Air*, 4 C-47.
LIAISON:
AIRCRAFT: 9 Cessna 152, 2 -185, 13 -206, 2 -402.
HELICOPTERS: 2 Bell 212, 22 UH-1H.
TRAINING: 1 Cessna 152, 2 172, 11* PC-7, 4 SF-260CB, 15 T-23, 9* T-33A, 1 Lancair 320.
1 air-base defence regt (Oerlikon twin 20mm, some truck-mounted guns).

PARAMILITARY:
NATIONAL POLICE: some 30,000.
NARCOTICS POLICE: some 600.

BRAZIL

GDP[a]	1991:	Cr 1,544.0bn ($249.6bn)	
	1992ε:	Cr 1,525.0bn ($246.2bn)	
Growth	1991:	1.2%	1992: -1.4%
Inflation	1991:	460%	1992: 1,156%
Debt	1991:	$116.5bn	1992: $120.0bn
Def bdgt	1991ε:	Cr 935.20bn ($2.30bn)	
	1992:	Cr 7,423.0bn ($2.12bn)	

$1 = Cr   1990: 68.30   1991: 406.61
           1992ε 4,513   1993: 40,000
Cr = Cruzeiro
a All GDP figures are in 1985 prices and exchange rates.

Population: 159,075,000

	13–17	18–22	23–32
Men	8,164,000	7,446,000	13,459,000
Women	8,117,000	7,451,000	13,512,000

TOTAL ARMED FORCES:
ACTIVE: 296,700 (133,500 conscripts).
Terms of service: 12 months (can be extended by 6 months).
RESERVES: Trained first-line 1,115,000; 400,000 subject to immediate recall. Second-line 225,000.

ARMY: 196,000; (126,500 conscripts).
HQ: 7 Military Comd, 12 Military Regions;
8 div (3 with Region HQ).
1 armd cav bde (2 mech, 1 armd, 1 arty bn).
3 armd inf bde (each 2 inf, 1 armd, 1 arty bn).
4 mech cav bde (each 3 inf, 1 arty bn).
12 motor inf bde (26 bn).
1 mtn bde.
2 'jungle' bde (7 bn).
1 frontier bde (6 bn).
1 AB bde (3 AB, 1 SF bn).
2 coast and AD arty bde.
3 cav guard regt.
28 arty gp (4 SP, 6 med, 18 fd).
2 engr gp each 4 bn; 10 bn (incl 2 railway) (to be increased to 34 bn).
Avn: hel bde forming, to comprise 50 hel per bn.
EQUIPMENT:
LIGHT TANKS: some 520, some 150 M-3, some 80 X-1A, 40 X-1A2 (M-3 mod); 250 M-41B.
RECCE: 300 EE-9 *Cascavel*, 250 EE-3 *Jararaca*, 30 M-8.
APC: 845: 225 EE-11 *Urutu*, 20 M-59, 600 M-113.
TOWED ARTY: 538: 105mm: 370 M-101/-102, 18 Model 56 pack; 155mm: 150 M-114.
SP ARTY: 105mm: 60 M-7/-108.
COAST ARTY: some 240 incl 57mm, 75mm, 120mm, 150mm, 152mm, 305mm.
MRL: 108mm: SS-06; 180mm: SS-40; 300mm: SS-60 incl SP; 4 *ASTROS* II.
MORTARS: 81mm; 107mm: M-30; 120mm: 180.
ATGW: 300 *Cobra*.
RCL: 57mm: 240 M-18A1; 75mm: 20; 105mm; 106mm: M-40A1.
AD GUNS: 20mm; 35mm: 50 GDF-001; 40mm: 60 L-60/-70 (some with BOFI).
SAM: 4 *Roland* II.
HELICOPTERS: 36 SA-365, 15 AS-350.

NAVY: 50,000 (2,000 conscripts) incl 700 naval aviation and 15,000 marines.
5 Oceanic Naval Districts plus 1 Riverine; 1 Comd.

BASES: OCEAN: Rio de Janeiro (HQ I Naval District), Salvador (HQ II District), Natal (HQ III District), Belém (HQ IV District), Rio Grande do Sul (HQ V District).
RIVERINE: Ladario (HQ VI District), Manaus.
SUBMARINES: 4:
1 *Tupi* (Ge T-209/1400) with 533mm TT (UK *Tigerfish* HWT).
3 *Humaita* (UK *Oberon*) with 533mm TT (*Tigerfish* HWT).
(Plus 1 *Bahia* (US *Guppy* II) with 533mm TT (restricted trg only)).
PRINCIPAL SURFACE COMBATANTS: 20:
CARRIER: 1 *Minas Gerais* (UK *Colossus*) CVS (ASW), capacity 20 ac: typically 7–8 S-2E ASW ac, 8 ASH-3H hel.
DESTROYERS: 6:
2 *Marcilio Dias* (US *Gearing*) ASW with 1 *Wasp* hel (Mk 46 LWT), 1 x 8 *ASROC*, 2 x 3 ASTT; plus 2 x 2 127mm guns.
4 *Mato Grosso* (US *Sumner*) ASW, 4 with 1 *Wasp* hel, all with 2 x 3 ASTT; plus 3 x 2 127mm guns.
FRIGATES: 13:
4 *Para* (US *Garcia*) with 1 x 8 *ASROC*, 2 x 3 ASTT, 1 x *Lynx* hel; plus 2 x 127mm guns.
4 *Niteroi* ASW with 1 *Lynx* hel, 2 x 3 ASTT, *Ikara* SUGW, 1 x 2 ASW mor; plus 2 x MM-40 *Exocet* SSM, 1 x 114mm gun.
2 *Niteroi* GP; weapons as ASW, except 4 x MM-40 *Exocet*, 2 x 114mm guns, no *Ikara*.
3 *Inhauma*, with 1 *Lynx* hel, 2 x 3 ASTT, plus 4 x MM-40 *Exocet*, 1 x 114mm gun.
PATROL AND COASTAL COMBATANTS: 28:
9 *Imperial Marinheiro* PCO.
6 *Piratini* (US PGM) PCI,
3 *Aspirante Nascimento* PCI (trg).
4 *Tracker* PCI〈.
6 Riverine patrol: 3 *Roraima* and 2 *Pedro Teixeira*, 1 *Parnaiba*.
MINE WARFARE: 6: 6 *Aratü* (Ge *Schütze*) MSI.
AMPHIBIOUS: 3:
2 *Ceara* (US *Thomaston*) LSD capacity 350 tps, 38 tk.
1 *Duque de Caxais* (US *de Soto County* LST), capacity 600 tps, 18 tk.
Plus some 39 craft; 3 LCU, 6 LCM, 30 LCVP.
SUPPORT AND MISCELLANEOUS: 22:
1 *Almirante G. Motta* AO, 1 repair ship, 1 submarine rescue, 4 tpt, 9 survey/oceanography, 1 *Brasil* trg, 5 ocean tugs.

NAVAL AVIATION: (700); 13 armed hel.
ASW: 1 hel sqn with 7 ASH-3A.
ATTACK: 1 with 6 *Lynx* HAS-21.
UTILITY: 2 sqn with 5 AS-332, 8 AS-350B, 9 AS-355.
TRAINING: 1 hel sqn with 15 TH-57.
ASM: AS-11, AS-12, *Sea Skua*.

MARINES: (15,000).
Fleet Force:
1 amph div (1 comd, 3 inf bn, 1 arty gp).
Reinforcement Comd:
5 bn incl 1 engr, 1 special ops.

Internal Security Force:
8+ regional gp.
EQUIPMENT:
RECCE: 5 EE-9 Mk IV *Cascavel*.
AAV: 12 LVTP-7A1
APC: 15 M-113, 5 EE-11 *Urutu*.
TOWED ARTY: 105mm: 12 M-101, 10 L118; 155mm:
6 M-114.
RL: 89mm: 3.5-in. M-20.
RCL: 106mm: M-40A1.
AD GUNS: 40mm: 6 L/70 with BOFI.

AIR FORCE: 50,700; (5,000 conscripts) 326 cbt
ac, 8 armed hel.
AD COMMAND: 1 Gp
FIGHTER: 2 sqn with 14 F-103E (*Mirage* IIIEBR), 4
F-103D (*Mirage* IIIDBR).
TACTICAL COMMAND: 10 Gp.
FGA: 3 sqn with 49 F-5E, 4 -B, 4 -F, 20 AMX.
COIN: 3 sqn with 48 AT-26.
COIN/TRG: 30 T-27.
RECCE: 2 sqn with 4 RC-95, 20 RT-26, 3 *Learjet* 35,
3 RC-130E.
LIAISON/OBSERVATION: 7 sqn: 1 ac with 8 T-27; 1 hel
with 8 UH-1H (armed), 5 ac/hel with 31 U-7 ac and
30 UH-1H hel.
MARITIME COMMAND: 4 Gp.
ASW (afloat): 1 sqn with 11 S-2A/E.
MR/SAR: 3 sqn with 11 EMB-110B, 10 EMB-111.
TRANSPORT COMMAND: 6 Gp (6 sqn), 7 regional
indep sqn:
HEAVY: 2 sqn:
1 with 8 C-130;
1 with 2 KC-130H, 4 Boeing 707-320C tpt.
MED/LT: 2 sqn:
1 with 12 C-91;
1 with 23 C-95A/B/C.
TACTICAL: 1 sqn with 12 C-115.
VIP: 1 sqn with 1 VC-91, 10 VC/VU-93, 2 VC-96, 5
VC-97, 5 VU-9, ac; 3 VH-4 hel.
REGIONAL: 7 sqn with 7 C-115, 82 C-95A/B/C, 6 EC-
9 (VU-9).
HELICOPTERS: 9 AS-332, 13 AS-355, 2 Bell 206, 6
SA-330, 30 SA-350, 6 SH-1H.
LIAISON: 50 C-42, 3 Cessna 208, 30 U-42.
TRAINING COMMAND:
AIRCRAFT: 50* AT-26, 70 EMB-110, 25 T-23, 98 T-
25, 78* T-27, 14* AMX-T.
HELICOPTERS: 4 OH-6A, 25 OH-13.
CALIBRATION: 1 unit with 2 C-95, 1 EC-93, 4 EC-95,
1 U-93.
AAM: AIM-9 *Sidewinder*, R-530, *Magic* 2.

FORCES ABROAD:
UN AND PEACE-KEEPING:
ANGOLA (UNAVEM II): 7 Observers, 8 civ pol.
CROATIA (UNPROFOR I): 13 Observers.
EL SALVADOR (ONUSAL): 17 Observers.
MOZAMBIQUE (ONUMOZ): 19 Observers.

PARAMILITARY:
PUBLIC SECURITY FORCES (R): some 243,000
in state military police org (State Militias) under Army
control and considered an Army Reserve.

CHILE

GDP	1991:	pCh 10,939.2bn ($31.31bn)		
	1992:	pCh 13,739.6bn ($37.89bn)		
Growth	1991:	6.0%	1992:	10.4%
Inflation	1991:	21.9%	1992:	15.6%
Debt	1991:	$17.9bn	1992:	$17.7bn
Def bdgt	1992:	pCh 369bn ($1.02bn)		
	1993:	pCh 405bn ($1.0bn)		
$1 = pCh	1990:	305.06	1991:	349.37
	1992:	362.59	1993:	405.00

pCh = pesos Chilenos

Population: 13,751,000

	13–17	18–22	23–32
Men	632,700	620,600	1,217,000
Women	609,800	602,500	1,195,800

TOTAL ARMED FORCES:
ACTIVE: 91,800 (31,000 conscripts).
Terms of service: Army 1 year, Navy and Air Force 2
years.
RESERVES: Army 50,000.

ARMY: 54,000 (27,000 conscripts).
7 Military Regions, 2 Corps HQ.
7 div:
1 with 3 mot inf, 1 armd cav, 1 arty, 1 engr regt;
1 with 1 mot inf, 1 inf, 5 mtn, 1 armd cav, 1 arty, 1
engr regt;
1 with 1 inf, 5 mtn, 1 armd cav, 1 mot arty regt;
1 with 1 inf, 2 mtn, 3 armd cav, 2 mot arty, 1 engr
regt;
1 with 2 mtn, 2 armd cav, 1 arty, 1 engr regt;
1 with 2 mtn, 1 engr regt.
1 with 1 mot inf, 1 cdo regt.
1 bde with 1 armd cav, 1 mtn regt.
Army tps: 1 avn, 1 engr regt, 1 AB bn.
EQUIPMENT:
MBT: 171: 150 M-51, 21 AMX-30.
LIGHT TANKS: 157: 60 M-24, 50 M-41, 47 AMX-13
(in store).
RECCE: 200 EE-9 *Cascavel*.
AIFV: 20 MOWAG *Piranha* with 90mm gun.
APC: 60 M-113, 180 Cardoen/MOWAG *Piranha*, 300
EE-11 *Urutu*.
TOWED ARTY: 150: 105mm: 120 incl M-101, Model
56; 155mm: 30 M-68.
SP ARTY: 155mm: 10 Mk F3.
MORTARS: 81mm: 300 M-29; 107mm: 15; 120mm:
110 ECIA (incl 50 SP).
ATGW: *Milan/Mamba*.
RL: 89mm: 3.5-in. M-20.

RCL: 150 incl: 57mm: M-18; 75mm; 106mm: M-40A1.
AD GUNS: 20mm: some SP (Cardoen/MOWAG).
SAM: *Blowpipe*, *Javelin*.
AIRCRAFT:
TRANSPORT: 6 C-212, 1 *Citation* (VIP), 3 CN-235, 4 DHC-6, 3 PA-31, 8 PA-28 Piper *Dakota*.
TRAINING: 16 Cessna R-172.
HELICOPTERS: 2 AB-206, 3 AS-332, 15 Enstrom 280 FX, 5 Hughes 530F (armed trg), 10 SA-315, 9 SA-330.

NAVY: ε25,000 (3,000 conscripts), incl naval aviation (500), marines (3,000) and Coast Guard (ε1,500).
DEPLOYMENT AND BASES:
3 main commands: Fleet (includes DD and FF), Submarine Flotilla, Transport. Remaining forces allocated to 4 Naval Zones:
1st Naval Zone (26ºS – 36ºS approx).
Valparaiso (HQ), Vina Del Mar.
2nd Naval Zone (36ºS – 43ºS approx).
Talcahuano, (HQ), Puerto Montt.
3rd Naval Zone (43ºS to Cape Horn), Punta Arenas, (HQ), Puerto Williams.
4th Naval Zone (north of 26ºS approx) Iquique (HQ).
SUBMARINES: 4:
2 *O'Brien* (UK *Oberon*) with 533mm TT (Ge HWT).
2 *Thompson* (Ge T-209/1300) with 533mm TT (HWT).
PRINCIPAL SURFACE COMBATANTS: 10:
DESTROYERS: 6:
2 *Prat* (UK *Norfolk*) DDG with 1 x 2 *Seaslug-2* SAM, 4 x MM-38 *Exocet* SSM, 1 x 2 114mm guns, 1 SA-365 hel.
2 *Blanco Encalada* (UK *Norfolk*) DDH with 4 x MM-38, 1 x 2 114 mm guns, 2 SA-332 hel. (*Cochrane* in refit).
2 *Almirante Riveros* (ASUW) with 4 x MM-38 *Exocet* SSM, 4 x 102mm guns; plus 2 x 3 ASTT (Mk 44 LWT), 2 x 3 ASW mor.
FRIGATES: 4 *Condell* (mod UK *Leander*) with 2 x 3 ASTT, 1 hel; plus 2 x 2 MM-40 (1 with 4 x MM-38) *Exocet*, 1 x 2 114mm guns.
PATROL AND COASTAL COMBATANTS: 17:
MISSILE CRAFT: 4:
2 *Casma* (Is *Reshef*) PFM with 4 *Gabriel* SSM.
2 *Iquique* (Is *Sa'ar*) PFM with 6 *Gabriel* SSM.
TORPEDO CRAFT: 4 *Guacolda* (Ge Lürssen 36-m) with 4 x 533mm TT.
PATROL: 9:
1 PCO (ex-US tug).
1 *Micalvi* PCC.
1 *Papudo* PCC (ex-US PC-1638).
6 *Grumete Diaz* (Is *Dabur*) PCI⟨.
AMPHIBIOUS: 3:
3 *Maipo* (Fr *BATRAL*) LSM, capacity 140 tps, 7 tk.
Plus craft; 2 *Elicura* LCT.
SUPPORT AND MISCELLANEOUS: 12:
1 *Almirante Jorge Montt* (UK '*Tide*') AO, 1 *Araucano* AO, 1 submarine spt, 1 tpt, 1 survey, 1 *Uribe* trg, 1 Antarctic patrol, 5 tugs/spt.

NAVAL AVIATION: (500);
7 cbt ac, 21 armed hel. 4 sqn.
MR: 1 sqn with 6 EMB-111N, 2 *Falcon* 200, 1 P-3 *Orion* (7 more to be delivered).
ASW HEL: 6 SA-316, 3 AS-332, 3 Bo-105, 6 Bell-47G, 3 AB-206AS.
LIAISON: 1 sqn with 3 C-212A, 3 EMB-110N, 2 IAI-1124, 1 PA-31.
HELICOPTERS: 1 sqn with 4 AB-206, 3 SH-57.
TRAINING: 1 sqn with 10 PC-7.
MARINES: (ε3,000).
4 gp: each 1 inf bn (+), 1 cdo coy, 1 fd arty, 1 AD arty bty.
1 amph bn.
EQUIPMENT:
APC: 40 MOWAG *Roland*, 30 LVTP-5.
TOWED ARTY: 105mm: 16 M-101; 155mm: 36 M-114.
COAST GUNS: 155mm: 16 GPFM-3.
MORTARS: 60mm: 50; 81mm: 50.
RCL: 106mm: ε30 M-40A1.
SAM: *Blowpipe*.

COAST GUARD: (ε1,500)
PATROL CRAFT: 17:
2 PCC (Buoy Tenders), 1 *Castor* PCI, 2 *Alacalufe* PCI, 12 PCI⟨, plus about 12 boats.

AIR FORCE: 12,800 (1,000 conscripts);
117 cbt ac, no armed hel. 5 Air Bde: 5 wings.
FGA: 2 sqn:
1 with 32 *Hunter* (17 F-71, 8 FGA-9, 4 FR-71, 3 T-72);
1 with 16 F-5 (13 -E, 3 -F).
COIN: 2 sqn with 30 A-37B, 24 A-36.
FIGHTER/RECCE: 1 sqn with 15 *Mirage* 50 (8 -FCH, 6 -CH, 1 -DCH).
RECCE: 2 photo units with 2 *Canberra* PR-9, 1 *King Air* A-100, 2 *Learjet* 35A.
AEW: 1 IAI-707 *Phalcon*.
TRANSPORT: 1 sqn with:
AIRCRAFT: 4 Boeing 707, 2 C-130H, 2 C-130B, 9 Beech 99 (ELINT, tpt, trg), 14 DHC-6 (5 -100, 9 -300).
HELICOPTERS: 5 SA-315B.
LIAISON HELICOPTERS: 6 Bo-105CB, 4 UH-1H.
TRAINING: 1 wing, 3 flying schools:
AIRCRAFT: 16 PA-28, 50 T-35A/B, 20 T-36, 26 T-37B/C, 8 T-41D.
HELICOPTERS: 10 UH-1H.
MISSILES:
ASM: AS-11/-12.
AAM: AIM-9B *Sidewinder*, *Shafrir*.
AD: 1 regt (5 gp) with: 20mm: S-639/-665, GAI-CO1 twin; 35mm: 36, K-63 twin; *Blowpipe*, 12 *Cactus* (*Crotale*), MATRA *Mistral*.

FORCES ABROAD:
UN AND PEACEKEEPING:
CAMBODIA (UNTAC): 52.
EL SALVADOR (ONUSAL): 26 civ pol.

INDIA/PAKISTAN (UNMOGIP): 3 Observers.
MIDDLE EAST (UNTSO): 3 Observers.

PARAMILITARY:
CARABINEROS: 31,000: 8 zones, 38 districts.
EQUIPMENT:
APC: MOWAG *Roland*.
MORTARS: 60mm, 81mm.
AIRCRAFT: 1 *Metro*.
HELICOPTERS: 2 Bell 206, 12 Bo-105.

OPPOSITION:
**FRENTE PATRIOTICO MANUEL RODRIGUEZ/
DISSIDENT (FPMR/D):** ε800; leftist.
**MOVEMENT OF THE REVOLUTIONARY LEFT
(MIR):** some 500.

COLOMBIA

GDP	1991:	pC 26,393.3bn ($41.69bn)			
	1992:	pC 34,047.4bn ($44.84bn)			
Growth	1991:	2.2%	1992:	3.5%	
Inflation	1991:	30.4%	1992:	27%	
Debt	1991:	$17.4bn	1992:	$17.35bn	
Def bdgt	1992ε:	pC 825.3bn ($1.09bn)			
	1993ε:	pC 1,045.3bn ($1.23bn)			
FMA[a]	1993:	$53.6m (US)			
$1 = pC	1990:	502.26	1991	633.05	
	1992:	759.28	1993:	850.00	

pC = pesos Colombianos
[a] Redirected to the Police Forces from the military. Incl.
$25m for anti-narcotics assistance.

Population: 33,982,000

	13–17	18–22	23–32
Men	1,889,000	1,777,000	3,161,000
Women	1,806,000	1,715,000	3,123,000

TOTAL ARMED FORCES:
ACTIVE: 140,000 (some 40,400 conscripts).
Terms of service: 1–2 years, varies (all services).
RESERVES: 116,900: Army 100,000; Navy 15,000;
Air 1,900.

ARMY: 120,000 (38,000 conscripts).
4 div HQ.
12 inf bde (Regional) each with: 3 inf, 1 arty bn, 1
engr gp, 1 mech or horsed cav gp;
Army Tps:
3 COIN bde (9 bn incl 1 SF, 1 AB bn).
1 trg bde.
1 mech regt.
1 Presidential Guard bn.
1 AD arty bn.

EQUIPMENT:
LIGHT TANKS: 12 M-3A1.
RECCE: 4 M-8, 120 EE-9 *Cascavel*.
APC: 80 M-113, 76 EE-11 *Urutu*.
TOWED ARTY: 105mm: 130 M-101.
MORTARS: 81mm: 125 M-1; 107mm: 148 M-2;
120mm: 120 Brandt.
ATGW: *TOW*.
RCL: 75mm: M-20; 106mm: M-40A1.
AD GUNS: 40mm: 30 Bofors.

NAVY: 13,000 (incl 8,000 marines) (some 500
conscripts).
BASES: OCEAN: Cartagena (main), Buenaventura,
Malala (Pacific).
RIVER: Puerto Leguízamo, Puerto Orocué, Puerto
Carreño, Leticia.
SUBMARINES: 2:
2 *Pijao* (Ge T-209/1200) with 533mm TT (Ge HWT).
Plus 2 *Intrepido* (It SX-506) SSI (SF delivery).
FRIGATES: 5:
4 *Almirante Padilla* with 1 x Bo-105 hel (ASW), 2 x 3
   ASTT; plus 8 x MM-40 *Exocet* SSM.
1 *Boyaca* (US *Courtney*) with 2 x 3 324mm TT, 2 x
   76mm gun; plus hel deck (used HQ ship).
PATROL AND COASTAL COMBATANTS: 26:
PATROL:
OFFSHORE: 3 *Pedro de Heredia* (ex-US tugs).
INSHORE: 9: 2 *Quito Sueno* (US *Asheville*) PFI.
1 *Castillo Y Rada* (Swiftships 32-m) PCI.
6 PCI⟨.
RIVERINE: 14: 3 *Arauca*, 11⟨.
SUPPORT AND MISCELLANEOUS: 4:
1 tpt, 2 research, 1 trg.

MARINES: (8,000); 2 bde: (8 bn).
No hy eqpt (to get EE-9 *Cascavel* recce, EE-11 *Urutu*
APC).

NAVAL AVIATION: 500
AIRCRAFT: 3 *Commander*, 3 PA-28, 2 PA-31, 4* A-
37B.
HELICOPTERS: 4 Bo-105.

AIR FORCE: 7,000 (some 1,900 conscripts);
92 cbt ac, 61 armed hel.
AIR COMBAT COMMAND:
FGA: 2 sqn:
1 with 15 *Mirage* 5 (11 -COA, 2 -COD trg, 2 -COR
recce);
1 with 13 *Kfir* (11 -C2, 2 -TC2).
COIN: 4 AC-47, 10 AT-33A, 3 IA-58A, 8 A-37B, 17
OA-37B, 18 OV-10, 4 OA-37B ac; 6 UH-1B, 25 -H
(armed hel).
TACTICAL AIR SUPPORT COMMAND:
COIN: 1 sqn hel with 12 OH-6/Hughes 500D, 18
Hughes 500MG/530MG hel.
RECCE: 1 sqn with:
AIRCRAFT: 3 RT-33A;
HELICOPTERS: 5 Hughes 300C, 4 -500D, 2-E.

MILITARY AIR TRANSPORT COMMAND:
AIRCRAFT: 1 BAe 748, 1 Boeing 707, 8 C-47, 4 C-54, 2 C-130B, 1 -E, 2 -H-30, 2 Cessna 310, 1 -340, 4 -404, 1 *Commander* 560A, 4 DC-6, 10 DHC-2, 2 F-28, 2 IAI-201, 2 PA-31, 1 PA-32, 1 PA-34, 1 PA-44, 5 PC-6B, 4 *Queen Air*, 2 EMB 110P (VIP).
HELICOPTERS: 10 Bell 205, 3 212, 2 412, 8 UH-60.
AIR TRAINING COMMAND:
AIRCRAFT: 20 T-34A/B, 30 T-41D, 14 EMB 312 *Tucano*.
HELICOPTERS: 2 Hughes 500C, 8 OH-13, 6 TH-55.
AAM: AIM-7 *Sparrow*, R-530.

FORCES ABROAD:
UN AND PEACEKEEPING:
CAMBODIA (UNTAC): 144 civ pol.
CROATIA (UNPROFOR I): 4 Observers, plus 46 civ pol.
EGYPT (MFO): 500.
EL SALVADOR (ONUSAL): 5 Observers, 14 civ pol.

PARAMILITARY:
NATIONAL POLICE FORCE: 85,000; 35 ac, 25 hel.
COAST GUARD: 1,500
PATROL CRAFT: 2 PCI.

OPPOSITION:
COORDINADORA NACIONAL GUERRILLERA SIMON BOLIVAR (CNGSB): loose coalition of guerrilla gp incl: Revolutionary Armed Forces of Colombia (FARC): some 3–4,000 active; National Liberation Army (ELN): ε1,000, pro-Cuban.

COSTA RICA

GDP	1991:	C 689.85bn ($5.63bn)	
	1992:	C 878.28bn ($6.53bn)	
Growth	1991:	2.3%	1992: 7.3%
Inflation	1991:	28.7%	1992: 18.2%
Debt	1991:	$4.04bn	1992: $4.25bn
Sy bdgt[a]	1991:	C 6.77bn ($55.31m)	
	1992ε:	C 8.19bn ($60.70m)	
FMA[b]	1992:	$22.59m (US)	
$1 = C	1990:	91.580	1991: 122.430
	1992:	134.510	1993: 138.200

C = colones
[a] No armed forces. Figures are for sy and Police.
[b] Incl $20m as Economic Support.

Population: 3,135,000

	13–17	18–22	23–32
Men	156,600	145,000	278,000
Women	153,000	140,000	272,000

TOTAL SECURITY FORCES:
ACTIVE (Paramilitary): 7,500.

CIVIL GUARD: 4,300.
6 Border Sy Comd (4 North, 2 South)
Presidential Guard: 1 bn, 7 coy.
MARINE: (400)
PATROL, INSHORE: 6:
1 *Isla del Coco* (US *Swift* 32-m) PFI, 1 *Astronauta Franklin Chang* (US *Cape Higgon*) PCI, 4 PFI⟨; plus about 10 boats.
AIRCRAFT: 4 Cessna 206, 1 *Commander* 680, 3 O-2 (surveillance), 2 PA-23, 3 PA-28, 1 PA-31, 1 PA-34.
HELICOPTERS: 2 Hughes 500E, 1 Hiller FH-1100.

RURAL GUARD: (Ministry of Government and Police): 3,200; small arms only.

CUBA

GSP[a]	1991ε: $16.51bn	
	1992ε: $13.21bn	
Growth	1991ε: -25%	1992ε: -28%
Inflation	1989ε: 4.0%	1990ε: 3.5%
Debt[b]	1989: $6.80bn	1990ε: $6.40bn
Def bdgt	1990ε: pC 1.36bn ($1.69bn)	
	1991ε: pC 1.16bn ($1.16bn)	
$1 = pC	1989: 0.762	1990: 0.804
	1991ε: 0.890	1992ε: 1.000

pC = pesos Cubanos
[a] Gross Social Product: excl the so-called 'non-productive' service sectors of the economy, such as education and housing which are included in GDP. GSP figures in dollars are exaggerated by the official exchange rate. The actual size of the economy is estimated to be up to 30% smaller in real dollar terms.
[b] Excl debt to socialist countries. Cumulative debt to CMEA ε $35–40bn.

Population: 10,906,000

	13–17	18–22	23–32
Men	431,000	530,000	1,086,000
Women	405,000	498,000	1,039,000

TOTAL ARMED FORCES:
ACTIVE: 173,500 incl ε15,000 Ready Reserves, (74,500 conscripts).
Terms of service: 2 years.
RESERVES: Army: 135,000 Ready Reserves (serve 45 days per year) to fill out Active and Reserve units; See also Paramilitary.

ARMY:
145,000 (incl ε15,000 Ready Reservists). (ε60,000 conscripts)
HQ: 4 Regional Command; 3 Army, 1 Isle of Youth.

1 armd div (Cat A).
13 mech inf div (3 mech inf, 1 armd, 1 arty, 1 AD arty regt) (Cat B).
9 inf div (3 inf, 1 arty, 1 AD arty regt) (Cat B/C).
1 indep armd bde.
AD: AD arty regt and SAM bde (Cat varies: SAM εCat A, AD arty B or C).
1 AB bde (Cat A).
Forces combat readiness system: Cat A div fully manned by active tps; Cat B: partial manning augmented by reservists on mob; Cat C: Active cadre, full manning by reservists on mob.

EQUIPMENT:
MBT: 1,575: 75 T-34 (in store), 1,100 T-54/-55, 400 T-62.
LIGHT TANKS: 50 PT-76.
RECCE: 100 BRDM-1/-2.
AIFV: 400 BMP-1.
APC: 1,200 BTR-40/-50/-60/-152.
TOWED ARTY: 620: 76mm: M-1942; 122mm: M-1931/37, D-74; 130mm: M-46; 152mm: M-1937, D-20, D-1.
SP ARTY: 40: 122mm: 2S1; 152mm: 2S3.
MRL: 300: 122mm: BM-21; 140mm: BM-14.
MORTARS: 82mm: 120: M-41/-43; 120mm: M-38/-43.
STATIC DEFENCE ARTY: some 15 JS-2 (122mm) hy tk, T-34 (85mm), SU-100 (100mm) SP guns.
ATGW: AT-1 *Snapper*, AT-3 *Sagger*.
ATK GUNS: 350: 85mm: D-44; 100mm: SU-100 SP.
AD GUNS: 1,600 incl 23mm: ZU-23, ZSU-23-4 SP; 30mm: M-53 (twin)/BTR-60P SP; 37mm: M-1939; 57mm: S-60 towed, ZSU-57-2 SP; 85mm: KS-12; 100mm: KS-19.
SAM: 12 SA-6, SA-7/-8/-9/-13/-14.

NAVY: 13,500 (8,500 conscripts).
3 Naval Districts, 4 Operational Flotillas.
BASES: Cienfuegos, Cabanas, Havana, Mariel, Punta Movida, Nicaro.
SUBMARINES: 3 Sov *Foxtrot* with 533mm and 406mm TT (incl 1 in refit).
FRIGATES: 3 Sov *Koni* with 2 x ASW RL.
PATROL AND COASTAL COMBATANTS: 28:
MISSILE CRAFT: 18:
18 Sov *Osa-I/-II* with 4 x SS-N-2 *Styx* SSM.
TORPEDO CRAFT: some of 9 *Turya* listed below have 4 x 533mm TT.
PATROL: 10:
COASTAL: 1:
1 Sov *Pauk* II PFC with 2 x ASW RL, 4 x ASTT.
INSHORE: 9:
9 Sov *Turya* PHI (incl 2 in reserve).
MINE WARFARE: 15:
3 Sov *Sonya* MSC
12 Sov *Yevgenya* MSI.
AMPHIBIOUS: 2 Sov *Polnocny* LSM, capacity 6 tk, 180 tps.
SUPPORT AND MISCELLANEOUS: 5:
1 AOT, 1 AGI, 1 survey, 2 trg.

NAVAL INFANTRY: (550+).
2 amph aslt bn.

COASTAL DEFENCE:
ARTY: 122mm: M-1931/37; 130mm: M-46; 152mm: M-1937.
SSM: 2 SS-C-3 systems.

AIR FORCE: ε15,000+, incl AD (6,000 conscripts);
140 cbt ac, 85 armed hel.
FGA: 2 sqn:
2 with 20 MiG-23BN.
FIGHTER: 4 sqn:
2 with 30 MiG-21F;
1 with 50 MiG-21bis;
1 with 20 MiG-23MF.
6 MiG-29.
ATTACK HELICOPTERS: 20 Mi-8, 40 Mi-17, 20 Mi-25.
ASW: 5 Mi-14 hel.
TRANSPORT: 4 sqn: 8 An-2, 3 An-24, 21 An-26, 2 An-32, 4 Yak-40, 2 Il-76 (Air Force ac in civilian markings).
HELICOPTERS: 60 Mi-8/-17.
TRAINING: 25 L-39, 15 MiG-15, 15 MiG-15UTI, 8* MiG-21U, 4* MiG-23U, 2* MiG-29UB, 20 Z-326.
MISSILES:
ASM: AS-7.
AAM: AA-2, AA-8, AA-10, AA-11.
AD: 200+ SAM launchers: SA-2, SA-3.
Civil Airline: 10 Il-62, 7 Tu-154, 12 Yak-42 used as troop tpt.

PARAMILITARY:
YOUTH LABOUR ARMY: 100,000:
CIVIL DEFENCE FORCE: 50,000:
TERRITORIAL MILITIA (R): 1,300,000.
STATE SECURITY (Ministry of Interior): 15,000.
BORDER GUARDS (Ministry of Interior): 4,000.
About 30 Sov *Zhuk* and 3 Sov *Stenka* PFI⟨, plus boats.

FOREIGN FORCES:
US: 2,300: Navy: 1,900; Marine: 400: 1 reinforced coy at Guantánamo Bay.
RUSSIA: 1,100: SIGINT personnel (1,000); mil advisers (ε100).

DOMINICAN REPUBLIC

GDP	1991:	$RD 91.40bn ($US 7.20bn)		
	1992:	$RD 99.81bn ($US 7.81bn)		
Growth	1991:	-0.6%	1992ε:	7.7%
Inflation	1991:	53.9%	1992ε:	6%
Debt	1991:	$US 4.80bn	1992:	$US 4.70bn
Def bdgt	1993:	$RD 1,371.0m ($US 108.81m)		
$US 1 = $RD	1990:	8.290	1991:	12.692
	1992:	12.774	1993:	12.600

$RD = pesos República Dominicana

Population: 7,455,000

	13–17	18–22	23–32
Men	417,700	388,000	671,000
Women	404,700	377,000	654,000

TOTAL ARMED FORCES:
ACTIVE: 23,200.

ARMY: 15,000.
5 Defence Zones.
4 inf bde (with 10 inf, 1 SF bn).
1 armd, 1 Presidential Guard, 1 arty, 1 engr bn.
EQUIPMENT:
LIGHT TANKS: 2 AMX-13 (75mm), 12 M-41A1 (76mm).
RECCE: 8 V-150 *Commando*.
APC: 20 M-2/M-3 half-track.
TOWED ARTY: 105mm: 22 M-101.
MORTARS: 81mm: M-1; 120mm: 24 ECIA.

NAVY: 4,000.
BASES: Santo Domingo (HQ), Las Calderas.
PATROL AND COASTAL COMBATANTS: 19:
OFFSHORE: 9:
1 *Mella* (Cdn *River*) (comd/trg)
3 *Cambiaso* (US *Cohoes*).
3 armed ocean tugs (ex USCG *Argo*-class).
2 *Prestol* (US *Admirable*).
INSHORE: 10: 1 *Betelgeuse* (US PGM-71), 1 *Capitan Alsina* (trg), 8⟨ .
AMPHIBIOUS: craft only;
1 LCU.
SUPPORT AND MISCELLANEOUS: 4:
1 AOT (small harbour), 3 ocean tugs.

AIR FORCE: 4,200; 10 cbt ac, no armed hel.
COIN: 1 sqn with 8 A-37B.
TRANSPORT: 1 sqn with 3 C-47, 1 *Commander* 680, 1 MU-2.
LIAISON: 1 Cessna 210, 4 O-2A, 2 PA-31, 3 *Queen Air* 80, 1 *King Air*.
HELICOPTERS: 8 Bell 205, 1 OH-6A, 2 SA-318C, 1 SA-365 (VIP), 1 SA-365.
TRAINING: 2* AT-6, 6 T-34B, 3 T-41D.
AB: 1 AB sqn.
AD: 1 bn with 4 20mm guns.

PARAMILITARY:
NATIONAL POLICE: 15,000.

ECUADOR

GDP	1991: ES 12,149.0bn ($11.61bn)
	1992ε: ES 18,830.9bn ($12.28bn)
Growth	1991: 3.8% 1992: 3.5%

Inflation	1991: 48.7%	1992: 60.2%
Debt	1991: $12.47bn	1992: $12.35bn
Def bdgt	1990: ES 193.0bn ($251.38m)	
	1991ε: ES 273.0bn ($260.92m)	
$1 = ES	1990: 767.75	1991: 1,046.30
	1992: 1,534.0	1993: 1,900.0

ES = Ecuadorean sucres

Population: 10,968,000

	13–17	18–22	23–32
Men	633,400	568,200	919,600
Women	615,800	553,800	900,400

TOTAL ARMED FORCES:
ACTIVE: 58,000.
Terms of service: conscription 1 year, selective.
RESERVES: 100,000; ages 18–55.

ARMY: 50,000.
4 Defence zones.
1 div with 1 armd, 2 inf bde.
2 inf bde.
3 jungle bde.
Army tps:
1 SF (AB) bde (2 gp).
1 AD arty gp.
1 avn gp.
3 engr bn
EQUIPMENT:
LIGHT TANKS: 45 M-3, 108 AMX-13.
RECCE: 27 AML-60/-90, 22 EE-9 *Cascavel* 10 EE-3 *Jararaca*.
APC: 20 M-113, 60 AMX-VCI, 20 EE-11 *Urutu*.
TOWED ARTY: 105mm: 50 M2A2; 155mm: 10 M-198.
SP ARTY: 155mm: 10 Mk F3.
MORTARS: 300: 81mm: M-29; 107mm: 4.2-in M-30; 160mm: 12 Soltam.
RCL: 90mm: 380 M-67; 106mm: 24 M-40A1.
AD GUNS: 20mm: 20 M-1935; 35mm: 30 GDF-002 twin; 40mm: 30 L/70.
SAM: 75 *Blowpipe*.
AVIATION:
AIRCRAFT:
SURVEY: 1 Cessna 206, 1 *Learjet* 24D.
TRANSPORT: 1 CN-235, 1 DHC-5, 3 IAI-201, 1 *King Air* 200, 3 PC-6.
LIAISON/TRG/OBS: 1 Cessna 172, 1 -182.
HELICOPTERS:
SURVEY: 3 SA-315B.
TRANSPORT/LIAISON: 10 AS-332, 4 AS-350B, 1 Bell 214B, 3 SA-315B, 3 SA-330, 30 SA-342.

NAVY: 4,500, incl 250 naval aviation and 1,500 Marines.
BASES: Guayaquil (main base), Jaramijo, Galápagos Islands.
SUBMARINES: 2 *Shyri* (Ge T-209/1300) with 533mm TT (Ge SUT HWT).
PRINCIPAL SURFACE COMBATANTS: 2:

FRIGATES: 2 *Presidente Eloy Alfaro* (ex-UK *Leander Batch II*) with 1 206B hel, plus 4 x MM-38 *Exocet* SSM.
PATROL AND COASTAL COMBATANTS: 12:
CORVETTES: 6 *Esmeraldas* with 2 x 3 ASTT, hel deck; plus 2 x 3 MM-40 *Exocet* SSM.
MISSILE CRAFT: 6:
3 *Quito* (Ge Lürssen 45-m) with 4 x MM-38 *Exocet*.
3 *Manta* (Ge Lürssen 36-m) with 4 x *Gabriel* II SSM.
AMPHIBIOUS: 1:
1 *Hualcopo* (US LST-511) LST, capacity 200 tps, 16 tk.
SUPPORT AND MISCELLANEOUS: 8:
1 survey, 1 ex-GDR depot ship, 1 AOT (small), 1 *Calicuchima* (ex UK *Throsk*) armament carrier, 1 water carrier, 2 armed ocean tugs, 1 trg.

NAVAL AVIATION: 250:
AIRCRAFT:
LIAISON: 1 *Citation* I, 1 *Super King Air*, 1 CN-235.
TRAINING: 2 Cessna 172, 3 -337, 3 T-34C.
HELICOPTERS: 5 Bell 206.

MARINES: (1,500): 3 bn: 2 on garrison duties, 1 cdo (no hy weapons/veh).

AIR FORCE: 3,500; 83 cbt ac, no armed hel.
OPERATIONS COMMAND: 2 wings, 5 sqn:
FGA: 2 sqn:
1 with 8 *Jaguar* S, 1 -B;
1 with 9 *Kfir* C-2, 1 TC-2.
FIGHTER: 1 sqn with 13 *Mirage* F-1JE, 1 F-1JB.
COIN: 1 sqn with 20 A-37B.
COIN/TRAINING: 1 sqn with 7 *Strikemaster* Mk 89.
MILITARY AIR TRANSPORT GROUP:
2 civil/military airlines:
TAME: 4 Boeing 727, 2 BAe-748, 2 C-130H, 3 DHC-6, 1 F-28, 1 L-100-30.
ECUATORIANA: 3 Boeing 707-720, 4 -707, 1 DC-10-30.
LIAISON: 1 *King Air* E90, 1 *Sabreliner*.
LIAISON/SAR hel flt: 2 AS-332, 1 Bell 212, 6 Bell-206B, 6 SA-316B, 1 SA-330, 2 UH-1B, 24 UH-1H.
TRAINING: incl 23* AT-33, 20 Cessna 150, 5 -172, 19 T-34C, 4 T-41.
AAM: R-550 *Magic*, *Super* 530, *Shafrir*.
1 AB sqn.

FORCES ABROAD:
UN AND PEACEKEEPING:
EL SALVADOR (ONUSAL): 8 Observers.

PARAMILITARY:
COAST GUARD 200:
PATROL INSHORE: 6:
2 *25 de Julio*, 2 *5 de Agosta*, 2 PCI⟨, plus some 15 boats.

EL SALVADOR

GDP	1991:	C 47.79bn ($5.91bn)	
	1992:	C 54.76bn ($5.97bn)	
Growth	1991:	3.5%	1992: 4.6%
Inflation	1991:	14.4%	1992: 11.2%
Debt	1991:	$2.17bn	1992: $2.35bn
Def bdgt	1992:	C 917.1m ($100.01m)	
	1993:	C 886.5m ($101.78m)	
FMA[a]	1993:	$122.2m (US)	
$1 = C	1990:	8.03	1991: 8.08
	1992:	9.17	1993: 8.71

C = colones
[a] Incl $110m as Economic Support.

Population: 5,507,000

	13–17	18–22	23–32
Men	357,700	310,700	402,000
Women	346,000	303,700	428,000

TOTAL ARMED FORCES:
ACTIVE: 30,500.
Terms of service: selective conscription, 2 years: all services.
RESERVES: ex-soldiers registered.

ARMY: 28,000 (some conscripts).
6 Military Zones (14 Departments).
6 inf bde (12 inf bn).
1 special sy bde (3 mil police bn).
8 inf det (8 bn).
1 engr comd (1 engr, 1 inf bn).
1 arty bde (3 fd, 1 AD bn).
1 mech cav regt (2 bn).
2 indep bn (1 presidential guard, 1 sy).
1 special ops gp (1 para, 1 naval inf, 1 SF coy).
EQUIPMENT:
RECCE: 15 AML-90.
APC: 54 M-37B1 (mod), 14 M-113, 8 UR-416.
TOWED ARTY: 105mm: 36 M-101/102, 14 M-56.
MORTARS: 81mm: incl 300 M-29; 120mm: 60 UB-M52, M-74.
RL: *LAW*.
RCL: 90mm: 400 M-67; 106mm: 20+ M-40A1 (some SP).
AD GUNS: 20mm: 24 Yug M-55, 4 SP.
SAM: some captured SA-7 may be in service.

NAVY: ε500 (plus some 120 naval infantry and sp forces).
BASES: La Uníon, La Libertad, Acajutla and El Triunfo.
PATROL AND COASTAL COMBATANTS: 5:
PATROL INSHORE: 3 Camcraft 30-m, 2 PCI⟨, plus boats.
AMPHIBIOUS: Craft only, 2 LCM, plus boats.
NAVAL INFANTRY: (marines):
1 Marine coy (110).

AIR FORCE: 2,000 (incl AD); ε500 conscripts.
21 cbt ac, 18 armed hel.
COIN:
AIRCRAFT: 1 sqn with 10 A-37B, 2 AC-47, 3 O-2A.
HELICOPTERS: 1 sqn with 10 Hughes (armed: 3 MD
500D, 7 -E), 15 UH-1M (armed), 35 UH-1H (tpt).
TRANSPORT: 1 gp:
4 C-47, 2 C-47 Turbo-67, 1 C-123K, 1 *Commander*,
1 DC-6B, 3 IAI-201, 1 *Merlin* IIIB, 9 *Rallye*.
LIAISON: 6 Cessna 180, 1 Cessna 182, 1 Cessna 185
ac.
TRAINING: 6* CM-170 (COIN/trg;), 3 T-41C/D.

PARAMILITARY:
NATIONAL CIVILIAN POLICE: Forming with
former FMLN rebels, soldiers and police.

FOREIGN FORCES:
UNITED NATIONS (ONUSAL): 71 Observers, plus
302 civ pol from 17 countries.

GUATEMALA

GDP	1991:	q 46.99bn ($9.34bn)	
	1992ε:	q 53.57bn ($10.35bn)	
Growth	1991:	3.2%	1992: 4.6%
Inflation	1991:	33.2%	1992: 10.1%
Debt	1991:	$2.90bn	1992: $2.70bn
Def bdgt	1992:	q 565.0m ($109.16m)	
	1993:	q 530.0m ($94.64m)	
FMA[a]	1993:	$10.9m (US)	
$1 = q	1990:	4.486	1991: 5.029
	1992:	5.176	1993: 5.600

q = quetzales
[a] Incl $10.5m as Economic Support.

Population: 10,052,000

	13–17	18–22	23–32
Men	601,500	500,800	742,000
Women	584,900	488,000	731,000

TOTAL ARMED FORCES: (National Armed
Forces are combined; the Army provides log spt for
Navy and Air Force).
ACTIVE: 43,900.
Terms of service: Conscription; selective, 30 months.
RESERVES: Army ε35,000 (trained), Navy (some),
Air 200.

ARMY: 42,000 (30,000 conscripts).
19 Military Zones (39 inf, 1 trg bn, 6 armd sqn).
2 Strategic Reserve bde (6 inf, 1 lt armd bn, 1 recce
sqn, 2 arty bty).
1 SF gp (2 bn).

2 AB bn.
1 mil police bn.
1 engr bn.
EQUIPMENT:
LIGHT TANKS: 10 M-41A3.
RECCE: 8 M-8, 10 RBY-1.
APC: 9 M-113, 7 V-100 *Commando*, 30 *Armadillo*.
TOWED ARTY: 75mm: 10 M-116; 105mm: 4 M-101, 8
M-102, 56 M-56.
MORTARS: 81mm: 55 M-1; 107mm: 12 M-30;
120mm: 18 ECIA.
RL: 89mm: 3.5-in. M-20.
RCL: 57mm: M-20; 105mm.
AD GUNS: 20mm: 16 M-55, 20 GA1-DO1;
RESERVES: ε20 inf bn.

NAVY: ε1,200 incl some 700 marines.
BASES: Santo Tomás de Castilla (Atlantic), Puerto
Quetzal (Pacific).
PATROL CRAFT, INSHORE 9:
1 *Kukulkan* (US *'Broadsword'* 32-m) PFI, 8 PCI⟨,
plus boats.

MARINES: Some 700: 2 under strength bn.

AIR FORCE: 700; 20 cbt ac, 8 armed hel.
Serviceability of ac is less than 50%.
COIN: 1 sqn with 8 Cessna A-37B, 8 PC-7, 4 IAI-201.
ATTACK HELICOPTERS: 6 Bell 212, 2 Bell 412.
TRANSPORT: 1 sqn with 3 C-47, 3 T-67 (mod C-47
Turbo), 3 F-27, 1 *Super King Air* (VIP).
LIAISON: 1 sqn with 3 Cessna 206, 1 -310.
HELICOPTERS: 1 sqn with 9 Bell 206, 5
UH-1D/-H, 3 S-76.
TRAINING: 6 T-41.

PARAMILITARY:
NATIONAL POLICE: 10,000.
TREASURY POLICE: 2,500.
TERRITORIAL MILITIA (R) (CVDC): ε500,000.

OPPOSITION:
**UNIDAD REVOLUCIONARIA NACIONAL
GUATEMALTECA** (URNG): some 800–1,100;
coalition of 3 main groups: Ejército Guerrillero de los
Pobres (EGP): 300–400. Fuerzas Armadas Rebeldes
(FAR): ε300–400. Organización del Pueblo en Armas
(ORPA): 200–300.

GUYANA

GDP	1991:	$G 38.39bn ($US 343.34m)	
	1992:	$G 46.80bn ($US 374.37m)	
Growth	1991:	6.1%	1992: 7.8%
Inflation	1991:	80.2%	1992: 15.0%
Debt	1991:	$1.9bn	1992: $2.0bn

Def bdgt 1986: $G 277.71m ($US 65.00m)
          1988: $G 138.1m ($US 14.4m)
$US 1 = $G 1990: 39.533   1991: 111.800
          1992: 125.000   1993: 126.000
$G = $ Guyanese

Population: 810,000
            13–17   18–22   23–32
Men   43,700   44,000   77,800
Women   41,900   42,000   75,400

TOTAL ARMED FORCES: (Combined
Guyana Defence Force):
ACTIVE: 1,700.
RESERVES: some 3,000 People's Militia.
(see Paramilitary).

ARMY: 1,500.
1 inf, 1 guard, 1 SF, 1 spt wpn, 1 engr bn.
EQUIPMENT:
RECCE: 3 *Shorland* .
TOWED ARTY: 130mm: 6 M-46.
MORTARS: 81mm: 12 L16A1; 82mm: 18 M-43;
120mm: 18 M-43.

NAVY: 100;
BASES: Georgetown, New Amsterdam.
About 4 boats.

AIR FORCE: 100; No cbt ac, no armed hel.
TRANSPORT:
AIRCRAFT: 4 BN-2A, 1 *Super King Air* B-200 (VIP),
2 *Skyvan*.
HELICOPTERS: 1 Bell 206, 1 -212, 1 -412, 2 Mi-8.

FORCES ABROAD:
UN AND PEACEKEEPING:
EL SALVADOR (ONUSAL): 10 civ pol.

PARAMILITARY:
GUYANA PEOPLE'S MILITIA (GPM): some 3,000.
GUYANA NATIONAL SERVICE (GNS): 1,500.

HAITI

GDP   1991: G 12.86bn ($2.57bn)
          1992ε: G 13.12bn ($2.20bn)
Growth   1991: -0.8%   1992ε: -12%
Inflation 1990: 21.5%   1991: 15.4%
Debt   1990: $874.0m   1991: $747.0m
Def bdgt 1991: G 147.0m ($29.40m)
          1992ε: G 275.0m ($55.0m)
$1 = G   1987–93: 5.0
G = gourdes

Population: 6,882,000
            13–17   18–22   23–32
Men   380,000   338,000   532,000
Women   374,000   334,000   540,000

TOTAL ARMED FORCES:
ACTIVE: 7,400.

ARMY: 7,000 (has police/gendarmerie, fire-
fighting, immigration, etc, roles).
1 defence unit (4 inf coy).
9 military departments (27 coy).
EQUIPMENT:
APC: 5 M-2, 6 V-150 *Commando*.
TOWED ARTY: 75mm: 5 M-116; 105mm: 4 M-101.
MORTARS: 60mm: 36 M-2; 81mm: M-1.
ATK GUNS: 37mm: 10 M-3A1; 57mm: 10 M-1.
RCL: 57mm: M-18; 106mm: M-40A1.
AD GUNS: 20mm: 6 TCM-20, 4 other; 40mm: 6 M-1.

NAVY: ε250 (Coast Guard).
BASE: Port au Prince
PATROL CRAFT: Boats only.

AIR FORCE: 150; 2 cbt ac, no armed hel.
TRANSPORT: 1 *Baron*, 1 DHC-6, 2* Cessna 337.
TRAINING: 3 Cessna 150, 1 -172, 5 SF-260TP, 1 *Twin
Bonanza*.

HONDURAS

GDP   1991: L 16.07bn ($2.98bn)
          1992: L 18.17bn ($3.12bn)
Growth   1991: 3.1%   1992: 4.3%
Inflation 1991: 33.9%   1992: 8.8%
Debt   1991: $3.18bn   1992: $3.22bn
Def exp[a] 1990: L 276.0m ($45.74m)
Def bdgt 1992: L 247.5m ($42.45m)
          1993: L 262.7m ($43.78m)
FMA[b]   1993: $12.3m (US)
$1 = L   1990: 2.00   1991: 5.40
          1992: 5.83   1993: 6.00
L = lempiras
[a] Adjusted to floating exchange rates.
[b] Incl $9.7m as Economic Support.

Population: 5,594,000
            13–17   18–22   23–32
Men   335,600   290,600   430,000
Women   324,500   281,700   423,800

TOTAL ARMED FORCES:
ACTIVE: 16,800; (13,200 conscripts).
Terms of service: conscription, 24 months.
RESERVES: 60,000 ex-servicemen registered.

ARMY: 14,000 (12,000 conscripts).
10 Military Zones:
2 inf bde (each with 3 inf, 1 arty bn).
1 inf bde (incl special tac gp) with 2 inf bn, 1 ranger
gp, 1 arty, 1 engr bn, 2 trg units.
1 territorial force (2 inf, 1 SF, 1 AB bn).
1 armd cav regt (2 bn).
1 arty, 1 engr bn.
RESERVES:
3 inf bde.
EQUIPMENT:
LIGHT TANKS: 12 *Scorpion*.
RECCE: 3 *Scimitar*, 1 *Sultan*, 50 *Saladin*, 12 RBY Mk 1.
TOWED ARTY: 105mm: 24 M-102; 155mm: 4 M-198.
MORTARS: 400 60mm; 81mm; 120mm: 60 Brandt;
160mm: 30 *Soltam*.
RL: 84mm: 120 *Carl Gustav*.
RCL: 106mm: 80 M-40A1.

NAVY: 1,000, incl 400 marines (500 conscripts).
BASES: Puerto Cortés, Puerto Castilla (Atlantic),
Amapala (Pacific).
PATROL CRAFT: 11:
INSHORE: 11:
3 *Guaymuras* (US Swiftships 31-m) PFI, 2 *Copan*
(US Lantana 32-m) PFI⟨, 6 other PCI⟨, plus boats.
AMPHIBIOUS: craft only; 1 *Punta Caxinas* LCT; plus
some 3 ex-US LCM.

MARINES: (400); 1 bn.

AIR FORCE: some 1,800 (700 conscripts);
46 cbt ac, no armed hel.
FGA: 2 sqn:
1 with 13 A-37B;
1 with 10 F-5E, 2 -F.
FIGHTER: 1 sqn with 8 *Super Mystère* B2 (non
operational).
TRANSPORT: 9 C-47, 1 C-123, 4 C-130A, 2
DHC-5, 1 L-188, 2 IAI-201, 1 IAI-1123, 1 -1124.
LIAISON: 1 sqn with 1 *Baron*, 3 Cessna 172,
2 -180, 2 -185, 4 *Commander*, 1 PA-31, 1
PA-34.
HELICOPTERS: 9 Bell 412, 4 Hughes 500, 5
TH-55, 8 UH-1B, 7 UH-1H, 1 S-76.
TRAINING: 4* C-101BB, 6 U-17A, 11* EMB-312, 5
T-41A.

FORCES ABROAD:
UN AND PEACEKEEPING:
WESTERN SAHARA (MINURSO): 14 Observers.

PARAMILITARY:
PUBLIC SECURITY FORCES (Ministry of Public
Security and Defence) 5,500: 11 regional comd.

FOREIGN FORCES:
US: Army: 800.

JAMAICA

GDP	1991:	$J 42.37bn ($US 3.50bn)	
	1992:	$J 59.31bn ($US 2.58bn)	
Growth	1991:	0.2%	1992: 2%
Inflation	1991:	51.1%	1992: 41.5%
Debt	1991:	$US 4.3bn	1992: $US 4.4bn
Def bdgt	1991:	$J 298m ($US 24.60m)	
	1992:	$J 444.5m ($US 19.36m)	
$US 1 = $J	1990:	7.184	1991: 12.116
	1992:	22.960	1993: 22.190

$J = $ Jamaican

Population: 2,480,000

	13–17	18–22	23–32
Men	135,800	135,000	222,900
Women	130,400	131,000	230,000

TOTAL ARMED FORCES (all services form
combined Jamaica Defence Force):
ACTIVE: some 3,350.
RESERVES: some 870: Army 800; Coast guard: 50;
Air wing: 20.

ARMY: 3,000.
2 inf bn, 1 spt bn.
EQUIPMENT:
APC: 14 V-150 *Commando*.
MORTARS: 81mm: 12 L16A1.
RESERVES: 800: 1 inf bn.

COAST GUARD: ε150.
BASE: Port Royal
PATROL CRAFT: 4 inshore:
1 *Fort Charles* PFI, (US 34-m), 3 PFI⟨, plus boats.

AIR WING: 170; no cbt ac, no armed hel.
AIRCRAFT: 2 BN-2A, 1 Cessna 210, 1 Cessna 337, 1
King Air.
HELICOPTERS: 3 Bell-205, 1 Bell-205A, 4 Bell-206, 3
Bell-212.

MEXICO

GDP	1991:	Np 865.2bn ($286.63bn)	
	1992ε:	Np 1,003.6bn ($324.29bn)	
Growth	1991:	3.6%	1992: 2.7%
Inflation	1991:	22.7%	1992: 15.5%
Debt	1991:	$101.74bn	1992: $102.0bn
Def bdgt	1992:	Np 4,713.0bn ($1.52bn)	
$1ᵃ = Np	1990:	2.813	1991: 3.018
	1992:	3.095	1993: 3.100

Np = New Pesos
[a] On 1 January 1993 the new peso equal to 1,000 pesos was
introduced.

Population: 91,354,000

	13–17	18–22	23–32
Men	5,273,000	5,068,000	8,036,000
Women	5,093,000	4,931,000	8,008,000

TOTAL ARMED FORCES:
ACTIVE: 175,000 (60,000 conscripts).
Terms of service: 1 year conscription (4 hours per week) by lottery.
RESERVES: 300,000.

ARMY: 130,000 regular (incl ε60,000 conscripts).
36 Zonal Garrisons: incl 1 armd, 19 mot cav, 1 mech inf, 3 arty regt, 80 inf bn.
1 armd bde (3 armd, 1 mech inf regt).
1 Presidential Guard bde (4 inf, 1 arty bn).
3 inf bde (each 3 inf bn, 1 arty bn).
1 AB bde (3 bn).
AD, engr and spt units.
EQUIPMENT:
RECCE: 50 M-8, 120 ERC-90F *Lynx*, 40 M-11 VBL, 70 DN-3/-5 *Caballo*, 30 MOWAG, 40 Mex-1.
APC: 40 HWK-11, 30 M-3 halftrack, 40 VCR/TT.
TOWED ARTY: 75mm: 18 M-116 pack; 105mm: 16 M-2A1/M-3, 60 M-101, 24 M-56.
SP ARTY: 75mm: 5 M-8.
MORTARS: 81mm: 1,500; 120mm: 20 *Brandt*.
ATGW: *Milan* (incl 8 M-11 VBL).
ATK GUNS: 37mm: 30 M-3.
AD GUNS: 12.7mm: 40 M-55.

NAVY: 37,000, incl 500 naval aviation and 8,000 Marines.
6 Navy regions covering 2 Areas:
Gulf: 6 Naval Zones.
Pacific: 11 Naval Zones.
BASES: Gulf: Vera Cruz (HQ), Tampico, Chetumal, Ciudad del Carmen, Yukalpetén, Lerna, Frontera, Coatzacoalcos, Isla Mujéres.
Pacific: Acapulco (HQ), Ensenada, La Paz, San Blas, Guaymas, Mazatlán, Manzanillo, Salina Cruz, Puerto Madero, Lázaro Cárdenas, Puerto Vallarta.
DESTROYERS: 3:
2 *Quetzalcoatl* (US *Gearing*) ASW with 1 x 8 ASROC, 2 x 3 ASTT; plus 2 x 2 127mm guns, hel deck.
1 *Cuitlahuac* (US *Fletcher*) with 5 x 533mm TT, 5 x 127mm guns.
PATROL AND COASTAL COMBATANTS: 102.
PATROL, OFFSHORE: 44:
4 *S.J. Holzinger* (ex *Uxmal*) (imp *Uribe*) with Bo-105 hel.
6 *Cadete Virgilio Uribe* (Sp '*Halcon*') with Bo-105 hel.
1 *Comodoro Manuel Azueta* (US *Edsall*) (trg).
3 *Zacatecas* (US *Lawrence/Crosley*) with 1 x 127mm gun.
17 *Leandro Valle* (US *Auk* MSF).
1 *Guanajuato* with 2 x 102mm gun.

12 D-01 (US *Admirable* MSF).
PATROL, INSHORE: 37:
31 *Quintana Roo* (UK *Azteca*) PCI.
3 ex-US *Cape Higgon* PCI.
3 ex-US *Point* PCI〈.
PATROL, RIVER: 21〈.
AMPHIBIOUS:
2 *Panuco* (US-511) LST.
SUPPORT AND MISCELLANEOUS: 19:
1 *V. Guerrero* PCI spt, 4 log spt, 6 ocean tugs, 5 survey, 1 *Durango* tpt, plus 2 other tpt.

NAVAL AVIATION: (500);
9 cbt ac, no armed hel.
MR: 1 sqn with 9 C-212, 6 HU-16 (SAR).
MR HEL: 12 Bo-105 (8 afloat).
TRANSPORT: 1 C-212, 2 Cessna 180, 3 -310, 1 DHC-5, 4 FH-227, 1 *King Air* 90, 1 *Learjet* 24.
LIAISON: 3 Cessna 150, 2 -337, 2 -402.
HELICOPTERS: 3 Bell 47, 4 SA-319, 2 UH-1H, 4 MD-500 (trg).

MARINES: (8,000).
3 bn (incl 1 Presidential Guard).
15 gp.
EQUIPMENT:
AMPH VEH: 25 VAP-3550.
TOWED ARTY: 105mm: 8 M-56.
MORTARS: 100 incl 60mm, 81mm.
RCL: 106mm: M-40A1.

AIR FORCE: 8,000 (incl 1,500 AB bde);
101 cbt ac, 25 armed hel.
FIGHTER: 1 sqn with 9 F-5E, 2 -F.
COIN: 5 sqn:
3 with 40 PC-7;
1 with 15 AT-33;
1 hel with 5 Bell 205, 5 -206, 15 -212.
RECCE: 1 photo sqn with 10 *Commander* 500S.
SAR: 1 sqn with 5 IAI-201.
TRANSPORT: 5 sqn with 2 BN-2, 12 C-47, 1 C-54, 10 C-118, 9 C-130A, 5 *Commander* 500, 1 -680, 5 DC-6 *Skytrain*, 2 F-27.
HELICOPTERS: 4 Bell-205, 12 Bell-206, 15 Bell-212, 3 SA-330.
PRESIDENTIAL TRANSPORT:
AIRCRAFT: 7 Boeing 727, 2 Boeing 737, 1 L-188, 3 FH-227, 2 *Merlin*.
HELICOPTERS: 1 AS-332, 2 SA-330.
LIAISON/UTILITY: 2 *King Air*, 1 *Musketeer*, 40 *Beech Bonanza* F-33A, 10 *Beech, Musketeer*.
TRAINING:
AIRCRAFT: 20 CAP-10, 10 *Musketeer*, 20 PC-7, 5 T-39 *Sabreliner*, 35* AT-33.
HELICOPTERS: 10 MD 530F (SAR/paramilitary/trg).

FORCES ABROAD:
UN AND PEACEKEEPING:
EL SALVADOR (ONUSAL): 107 civ pol.

PARAMILITARY:
RURAL DEFENCE MILITIA (R): 14,000.

NICARAGUA

GDP	1991:	Co 6,628.8m ($1.55bn)		
	1992ε:	Co 8,286.0m ($1.51bn)		
Growth	1991:	-0.7%	1992ε:	-0.5%
Inflation	1991:	450%	1992:	9.9%
Debt	1991:	$10.45bn	1992:	$10.10bn
Def bdgt	1992ε:	$214.50m		
	1993ε:	$210.0m		
FMA[a]	1993:	$151.8m (US)		
$US 1 = Co	1990:	0.141	1991:	4.270
	1992:	5.500	1993:	6.000

$C = Co = Cordoba oro
[a] All Economic Support.

Population: 4,244,000

	13–17	18–22	23–32
Men	252,700	212,000	320,600
Women	245,400	231,200	333,700

TOTAL ARMED FORCES:
ACTIVE: 15,200.
Terms of service: voluntary, 18–36 months.
RESERVES: numbers/details not yet known.

ARMY: ε13,500.
Reorganisation in progress.
6 Regional Commands; 2 Military Det.
1 mot inf bde.   2 armd bn.
1 mech inf bn   3 arty bn.
10 inf coy.
EQUIPMENT :
MBT: some 130 T-55.
LIGHT TANKS: 22 PT-76.
RECCE: 80 BRDM-2.
APC: 19 BTR-60, 100 BTR-152.
TOWED ARTY: 122mm: 36 D-30, 300 *Grad* 1P (single tube rocket launcher); 152mm: 60 D-20.
MRL: 107mm: 30 Type-63; 122mm: 30 BM-21.
MORTARS: 82mm: 500; 120mm: 20 M-43; 160mm: some M-160.
ATGW: AT-3 *Sagger* (12 on BRDM-2).
ATK GUNS: 57mm: 325 ZIS-2; 76mm: 84 Z1S-3; 100mm: 24 M-1944 (BS-3).
SAM: 500+ SA-7/-14/-16.

NAVY: ε500.
BASES: Corinto, Puerto Cabezzas, El Bluff.
PATROL AND COASTAL COMBATANTS: 16:
PATROL, INSHORE: 16:
2 Sov *Zhuk* PFI⟨, 8 N. Korea *Sin Hung* PFI⟨, 6 PCI⟨.
MINE COUNTERMEASURES: 5:
2 Sov *Yevgenya*, 3 K-8 MSI⟨.

AIR FORCE: 1,200;
16 cbt ac, 2 armed hel.
COIN: 1 sqn with 6 Cessna 337†, 6 L-39ZO†, 4 SF-260 WL†
ATTACK HELICOPTERS: 2 Mi-25.
TRANSPORT: 8 An-2, 5 An-26.
HELICOPTERS: 19 Mi-8/-17.
UTILITY/TRAINING:
1 Cessna -172, 1 Cessna -185, 1 Cessna -404, 2 *Piper* PA-18, 2 *Piper* PA-28.
hel: 5 Mi-2.
ASM: AT-2 *Swatter* ATGW.
AD GUNS: 800: 14.5mm: ZEU-1, ZPU-1/-2/-4; 23mm: ZU-23-2; 37mm: M-1939; 57mm: S-60; 100mm: KS-19.

OPPOSITION:
FRENTE NORTE: ε1,400 (former Contra rebels) perhaps 500 armed.

PANAMA

GDP	1991:	B 5.49bn ($5.49bn)		
	1992ε:	B 6.04bn ($6.04bn)		
Growth	1991:	9.3%	1992:	8%
Inflation	1991:	1.0%	1992:	1.8%
Debt	1991:	$6.79bn	1992:	$7.12bn
Def bdgt	1991:	B 75.0m ($75.0m)		
	1992:	B 75.0m ($75.0m)		
FMA[a]	1993:	$6.3m (US)		
$1 = B	1987–93:	1.00		

B = balboas
[a] All Economic Support

Population: 2,548,500

	13–17	18–22	23–32
Men	137,700	132,500	227,900
Women	131,700	127,700	222,000

TOTAL PUBLIC FORCES:
ACTIVE: 11,800.

NATIONAL POLICE FORCE: 11,000.
No hy mil eqpt, small arms only.

NATIONAL MARITIME SERVICE: ε400.
BASES: Amador (HQ), Balboa, Colón.
PATROL CRAFT:
INSHORE: 4:
2 *Panquiaco* (UK Vosper 31.5-m), 1 *Tres de Noviembre* (ex-USCG *Cape Higgon*), 1⟨, (plus about 4 other ex-US patrol/spt craft().
AMPHIBIOUS: craft only; 6 LCM.

NATIONAL AIR SERVICE: 400.

TRANSPORT: 1 CN-235-2A, 1 BN-2B, 1 PA-34, 3 CASA-212M *Aviocar*.
TRAINING: 9 T-35D.
HELICOPTERS: 2 Bell 205, 3 -212, 1 UH-H, 1-N.

FOREIGN FORCES:
US: 10,500. Army: 7,700; 1 inf bde and spt elm.
Navy: 500. Marines: 200. Air Force; 2,100; 1 air div.

PARAGUAY

GDP	1991:	Pg 7,545.3bn ($5.64bn)	
	1992:	Pg 8,828.0bn ($5.88bn)	
Growth	1991:	2.5%	1992: 1.5%
Inflation	1991:	24.3%	1992: 15.1%
Debt	1991:	$2.10bn	1992: $1.25bn
Def bdgt	1991:	Pg 141.8bn ($107.0m)	
	1992:	Pg 173.9bn ($115.9m)	
$1 = Pg	1990:	1,229.8	1991: 1,325.2
	1992:	1,500.3	1993: 1,680

Pg = guaranies

Population: 4,719,000

	13–17	18–22	23–32
Men	254,200	224,600	385,100
Women	245,200	216,300	369,900

TOTAL ARMED FORCES:
ACTIVE: 16,500 (10,800 conscripts).
Terms of service: 12 months; Navy 2 years.
RESERVES: some 45,000.

ARMY: 12,500 (8,600 conscripts).
3 corps HQ.
9 div HQ (6 inf, 3 cav).
6 inf regt (bn).   2 cav regt (horse).
20 frontier det.   2 arty gp (bn).
1 armd cav regt.   5 engr bn.
1 mech cav regt.
EQUIPMENT:
MBT: 5 M-4A3.
LIGHT TANKS: 18 M-3A1.
RECCE: 5 M-3, 30 EE-9 *Cascavel*.
APC: 10 EE-11 *Urutu*.
TOWED ARTY: 75mm: 20 Model 1927/1934;
105mm: 15 M-101; 152mm: 6 Mk V 6-in (anti-ship).
MORTARS: 81mm: 80.
RCL: 75mm: M-20.
AD GUNS: 20mm: 20 Bofors; 40mm: 10 M-1A1.

NAVY: 3,000 (ε1,500 conscripts) (incl Marines, Harbour and River Guard).
BASES: Asunción (Puerto Sajonia), Bahía Negra, Ciudad Del Este.
PATROL AND RIVERINE COMBATANTS: 7:

COASTAL: 5
2 *Paraguay* with 4 x 120mm guns.
3 *Nanawa* (Arg *Bouchard* MSO)
RIVERINE: 2:
1 *Capitan Cabral* (built 1908).
1 *Itaipu*.
SUPPORT AND MISCELLANEOUS: 6:
1 tpt, 1 *Boqueron* spt (ex-US LSM with hel deck), 1 trg/tpt, 1 survey⟨, 2 LCT.

MARINES: 500 (200 conscripts)).
1 marine bn.
1 cdo bn.

NAVAL AVIATION: (100). 2 cbt ac, no armed hel.
COIN: 2 AT-6G.
TRANSPORT: 1 C-47.
LIAISON: 3 Cessna 150, 3 -206, 1 -210.
HELICOPTERS: 2 HB-350, 1 OH-13, 2 UH-12E.

AIR FORCE: 1,000 (700 conscripts);
17 cbt ac, no armed hel.
COMPOSITE SQN: .
COIN: 5 AT-6, 7 EMB-326.
LIAISON: 1 Cessna 185, 2 -206, 1 -337, 1 -402, 2 T-41.
HELICOPTER: 3 HB-350, 1 UH-1B, 4 UH-12, 4 Bell 47G.
TRANSPORT: 1 sqn with 5 C-47, 4 C-212, 3 DC-6B, 1 DHC-6 (VIP).
TRAINING: 5* EMB-312, 6 T-6, 10 T-23, 5 T-25, 15 T-35, 1 T-41.

PARAMILITARY:
SPECIAL POLICE SERVICE: 8,000.

PERU

GDP	1991:	NS 34.770 tr ($44.96bn)	
	1992ε:	NS 56.000 tr ($44.95bn)	
Growth	1991:	2.7%	1992: -2.8%
Inflation	1992:	73.5%	
Debt	1991:	$20.71bn	1992: $21.58bn
Def bdgt	1991:	NS 541.520bn ($701.0m)	
	1992:	NS 975.000m ($782.63m)	
FMA[a]	1993:	$147.9m (US)	
$1,000 = NS	1990:	187.9	1991: 772.5
	1992:	1,245.8	1993: 2,000

NS = New Sol
[a] Incl. $129.7m as Economic Support.
Population: 23,141,000

	13–17	18–22	23–32
Men	1,274,000	1,164,000	1,935,000
Women	1,269,000	1,162,000	1,939,000

TOTAL ARMED FORCES:
ACTIVE: 115,000 (65,500 conscripts).

Terms of service: 2 years, selective.
RESERVES: 188,000 (Army only).

ARMY: 75,000 (50,000 conscripts).
5 Military Regions:
Army Troops:
1 AB 'div' (bde: 3 cdo, 1 para bn, 1 arty gp).
1 Presidential Escort regt.
1 AD arty gp.
Regional Troops:
3 armd div (bde, each 2 tk, 1 armd inf bn,
1 arty gp, 1 engr bn).
1 armd gp (3 indep armd cav, 1 fd arty, 1 AD arty, 1
engr bn).
1 cav div (3 mech regt, 1 arty gp).
7 inf div (bde, each 3 inf bn, 1 arty gp).
1 jungle div.
2 med arty gp; 2 fd arty gp.
1 indep inf bn.
1 indep engr bn.
3 hel sqn.
EQUIPMENT:
MBT: 300 T-54/-55 (ε50 serviceable).
LIGHT TANKS: 110 AMX-13 (ε30 serviceable).
RECCE: 60 M-8/-20, 10 M-3A1, 50 M-9A1, 15 Fiat
6616, 30 BRDM-2.
APC: 130 M-113, 130 UR-416.
TOWED ARTY: 105mm: 20 Model 56 pack, 130 M-
101; 122mm: 30 D-30; 130mm: 30 M-46.
SP ARTY: 155mm: 12 M-109A2, 12 Mk F3.
MRL: 122mm: 14 BM-21.
MORTARS: 81mm: incl some SP; 107mm: incl some
140 M-106 SP; 120mm: 300 Brandt, ECIA.
RCL: 106mm: M40A1.
AD GUNS: 23mm: 50 ZSU-23-2, 35 ZSU-23-4 SP;
40mm: 45 M-1, 80 L60/70.
SAM: SA-7.
AVIATION:
AIRCRAFT: 1 Cessna 182, 2 -U206, 1 -337, 1 *Queen
Air* 65, 3 U-10, 3 U-17.
HELICOPTERS: 2 Bell 47G, 2 Mi-6, 28 Mi-8, 14 Mi-
17, 6 SA-315, 5 SA-316, 3 SA-318, 2 *Agusta* A-109.

NAVY: 25,000 (13,500 conscripts) incl some 700
naval air, marines (300).
3 Naval Force Areas: Pacific, Lake Titicaca, Amazon
River.
BASES: ocean: Callao, San Lorenzo Island, Paita,
Talara. lake: Puno. river: Iquitos, Puerto Maldonado.
SUBMARINES: 9:
6 *Casma* (Ge T-209/1200) with 533mm TT (It A184
HWT).
3 *Abtao* (US *Mackerel*) with 533mm TT.
(Plus 1 *Pedrera* (US *Guppy* I) with 533mm TT (Mk
37 HWT) alongside trg only).
PRINCIPAL SURFACE COMBATANTS: 12:
CRUISERS: 2:
1 *Almirante Grau* (Nl *De Ruyter*) with 4 x 2 152mm
guns, 8 *Otomat* SSM.
1 *Aguirre* (Nl *De 7 Provincien*) with 3 x SH-3D *Sea

King hel (ASW/ASUW) (Mk 46 LWT/AM-39
Exocet), 2 x 2 152mm guns.
DESTROYERS: 6:
2 *Palacios* (UK *Daring*) with 4 x 2 MM-38 *Exocet*, 3
x 2 114mm guns, hel deck.
4 *Bolognesi* (Nl *Friesland*) with 4 x 120mm guns, 2 x
4 ASW RL.
FRIGATES: 4 *Carvajal* (mod It *Lupo*) with 1 AB-212
hel (ASW/OTHT), 2 x 3 ASTT; plus 8 *Otomat* SSM,
2 x 20 105mm MRL, 1 x 127mm gun.
PATROL AND COASTAL COMBATANTS: 7:
MISSILE CRAFT: 6 *Velarde* PFM (Fr PR-72 64-m)
with 4 x MM-38 *Exocet*.
PATROL: 1 *Unanue* (ex-US *Sotoyomo*) PCC (Antarctic
ops).
AMPHIBIOUS: 4 *Paita* (US *Terrebonne Parish*) LST,
capacity 395 tps, 16 tk.
SUPPORT AND MISCELLANEOUS: 9:
2 AO, 3 AOT, 1 tpt, 2 survey, 1 ocean tug (SAR).
RIVER AND LAKE FLOTILLAS: 8:
Some 4 gunboats, 4 patrol⟨.

NAVAL AVIATION: 7 cbt ac, 14 armed hel.
ASW/MR: 4 sqn with:
AIRCRAFT: 7* S-2, 6 *Super King Air* B
200T.
HELICOPTERS: 6 AB-212 ASW, 8 SH-3D (ASW).
TRANSPORT: 2 C-47.
LIAISON: 4 Bell 206B, 6 UH-1D hel, 2 SA-319, 3 Mi-
8.
TRAINING: 1 Cessna 150, 5 T-34C.
ASM: *Exocet* AM-39 (on SH-3 hel).

MARINES: (3,000).
1 Marine bde (5 bn, 1 recce, 1 cdo coy).
EQUIPMENT:
RECCE: V-100.
APC: 15 V-200 *Chaimite*, 20 BMR-600.
RCL: 84mm: *Carl Gustav*, 106mm: M-40A1.
MORTARS: 81mm; ε18 120mm.
AD GUNS: twin 20mm SP.

COAST DEFENCE: 3 bty with 18 155mm how.

AIR FORCE: 15,000 (2,000 conscripts);
96 cbt ac, 15 armed hel.
BOMBERS:
1 Gp (2 sqn) with 13 *Canberra* (5 serviceable).
FGA: 2 Gp: 6 sqn:
3 with 30 Su-22 (incl 4* Su-22U);
3 with 25 Cessna A-37B.
FIGHTER: 3 sqn:
1 with 10 *Mirage* 2000P, 2 -DP;
2 with 14 *Mirage* 5P, 2 -DP.
ATTACK HELICOPTERS: 1 hel sqn with 15 Mi-25
RECCE: 1 photo-survey unit with 2 *Learjet* 25B, 2 -
36A.
TANKER: 1 Boeing KC 707-323C.
TRANSPORT: 3 Gp (7 sqn):
AIRCRAFT: 14 An-32, 4 C-130A, 6 -D, 5 L-100-20, 2
DC-8-62F, 12 DHC-5, 8 DHC-6, 1 FH-227, 9 PC-6, 6
Y-12.

PRESIDENTIAL FLT: 1 F-28, 1 *Falcon* 20F.
HELICOPTERS: 3 sqn with 8 Bell 206, 15 -212, 5 -214, 1 -412, 10 Bo-105C, 5 Mi-6, 5 Mi-8, 5 SA-316.
LIAISON: 2 Beech 99, 3 Cessna 185, 1 -320, 15 *Queen Air* 80, 3 *King Air* 90, 1 PA-31T.
LIAISON HELICOPTERS: 8 UH-1D.
TRAINING: 2 Cessna 150, 25 EMB-312, 13 MB-339A, 20 T-37B/C, 15 T-41A/-D.
TRAINING HELICOPTERS: 12 Bell 47G.
MISSILES:
ASM: AS-30.
AAM: AA-2 '*Atoll*', R-550 *Magic*.
AD: 3 SA-2, 6 SA-3 bn with 18 SA-2, 24 SA-3 launchers.

PARAMILITARY:
NATIONAL POLICE: 60,000 (amalgamation of Guardia Civil, Republican Guard and Policia Investigacionara Peruana); MOWAG *Roland* APC.
COAST GUARD: 600; 5 *Rio Nepena* PCC, 3 PCI, 7 riverine PCI⟨.
RONDAS CAMPESINAS (peasant self-defence force): perhaps 2,000 *rondas* 'groups', up to pl strength, some with small arms. Deployed mainly in emergency zone.

OPPOSITION:
SENDERO LUMINOSO (Shining Path): some ε5–8,000; maoist.
MOVIMIENTO REVOLUCIONARIO TUPAC AMARU (MRTA): ε500; mainly urban gp.

FOREIGN FORCES:
RUSSIA: 50.

SURINAME

GDP	1990:	gld 3.06bn ($1.71bn)	
Growth	1989:	1.5%	1990: 0.4%
Inflation	1989:	15%	1990: 14%
Debt	1989:	$123m	1990: $123m
Def exp	1990:	gld 162.0m ($90.76m)	
Def bdgt	1991:	gld 134.0m ($75.07m)	
	1992:	gld 110.0m ($61.62m)	
$1 = gld	1987–93: 1.785		
gld = guilders			

Population: 477,600

	13–17	18–22	23–32
Men	22,800	23,200	45,300
Women	22,200	22,700	45,300

TOTAL ARMED FORCES:
(all services form part of the Army):
ACTIVE: 1,800.

ARMY: 1,400.
1 inf bn (4 inf coy).
1 mech cav sqn.
1 Military Police 'bde' (bn).
EQUIPMENT:
RECCE: 6 EE-9 *Cascavel*.
APC: 9 YP-408, 15 EE-11 *Urutu*.
MORTARS: 81mm: 6.
RCL: 106mm: M-40A1.

NAVY: 240.
BASE: Paramaribo.
PATROL CRAFT: 5 inshore:
3 S-401 (Nl 32-m), 2⟨, plus boats.

AIR FORCE: ε150; 5 cbt ac, no armed hel.
COIN: 3 BN-2 *Defender*, 2 PC-7.
LIAISON: 1 Cessna U206.
HELICOPTERS: 2 SA-316, 1 AB-205.

TRINIDAD & TOBAGO

GDP	1991:	$TT 22.42bn ($US 5.28bn)	
	1992:	$TT 23.77bn ($US 5.59bn)	
Growth	1991:	3.1%	1992: 0.0%
Inflation	1991:	3.8%	1992: 6.5%
Debt	1991:	$US 2.40bn	1992: $US 2.30bn
Def bdgt	1989:	$TT 250.75m ($59.0m)	
	1992ε:	$TT 314.50m ($74.0m)	
$US 1 = $TT	1989–93 4.25		
$TT = $ Trinidad & Tobago			

Population: 1,275,000

	13–17	18–22	23–32
Men	62,600	56,700	106,200
Women	61,500	56,200	111,200

TOTAL ARMED FORCES:
(all services are part of the Army):
ACTIVE: 2,550.

ARMY: 2,000.
2 inf bn.
1 spt bn.
EQUIPMENT:
MORTARS: 60mm: ε40; 81mm: 6 L16A1.
RL: 82mm: 13 B-300.
RCL: 84mm: *Carl Gustav*.

COAST GUARD: 550 (incl 50 Air Wing).
BASE: Staubles Bay (HQ), Hart's Cut, Point Fortin, Tobago.
PATROL CRAFT: Inshore: 9: (some non-op).
2 *Barracuda* PFI (Sw *Karlskrona* 40-m).
7 PCI⟨, plus boats and 3 ex-marine police spt vessels.

AIR WING:
AIRCRAFT: 1 Cessna 310, 1 -402, 1 Cessna 172.

PARAMILITARY:
POLICE: 4,800.

URUGUAY

GDP	1991:	pU 19,793bn ($9.80bn)	
	1992:	pU 34,523bn ($11.41bn)	
Growth	1991:	2.9%	1992: 7.4%
Inflation	1991:	102%	1992: 54.3%
Debt	1991:	$4.19bn	1992: $4.09bn
Def exp	1990:	pU 210.78bn ($180.0m)	
	1991:	pU 524.88bn ($240.8m)	
$1 = pU	1990:	1,171.0	1991: 2,180.0
	1992:	3,027.0	1993: 3,800.0

pU = pesos Uruguayos

Population: 3,143,800

	13–17	18–22	23–32
Men	136,700	129,700	225,400
Women	131,900	125,900	227,800

TOTAL ARMED FORCES:
ACTIVE: 24,700.

ARMY: 17,200.
4 Military Regions/div HQ.
5 inf bde (4 of 3 inf bn, 1 of 1 mech, 1 mot, 1 para bn).
1 engr bde (3 bn).
3 cav bde (10 cav bn (4 horsed, 3 mech, 2 mot, 1 armd)).
1 arty bde (2 arty, 1 AD arty bn).
3 arty, 4 cbt engr bn.
EQUIPMENT:
LIGHT TANKS: 17 M-24, 28 M-3A1, 22 M-41A1.
RECCE: 20 FN-4-RM-62, 25 EE-3 *Jararaca*,
10 EE-9 *Cascavel*.
APC: 15 M-113, 50 *Condor*, 18 EE-11 *Urutu*.
TOWED ARTY: 75mm: 12 Bofors M-1902; 105mm: 50 M-101A/M-102; 155mm: 5 M-114A1.
MORTARS: 81mm: 50 M-1; 107mm: 8 M-30.
ATGW: 5 *Milan*.
RCL: 57mm: 30 M-18; 106mm: 30 M-40A1.
AD GUNS: 20mm: 6 M-167 *Vulcan*; 40mm: 11 L/60.

NAVY: 4,500 incl 300 naval air, 500 naval infantry, 2,000 Prefectura Naval (coast guard).
BASES: Montevideo (HQ), La Paloma Y Fray Bentos.
FRIGATES: 3:
3 *General Artigas* (Fr *Cdt. Rivière*) with 2 x 3 ASTT,

1 x 2 ASW mor, 2 x 100mm guns.
PATROL AND COASTAL COMBATANTS: 8:
OFFSHORE: 1:
1 *Campbell* (US *Auk* MSF) PCO (Antarctic patrols).
INSHORE: 7:
2 *Colonia* PCI (US *Cape*).
3 *15 de Noviembre* PFI (Fr *Vigilante* 42-m).
1 *Salto* PCI, 1 *Paysandu* PCI⟨.
MINE WARFARE: 4:
4 *Temerario* MSC (Ge *Kondor II*).
AMPHIBIOUS: craft only; 4 LCM, 2 LCVP.
SUPPORT AND MISCELLANEOUS: 4:
1 trg, 2 salvage, 1 ocean tug.

NAVAL AVIATION: (300); 6 cbt ac, no armed hel.
ASW: 1 flt with 3 S-2A, 3 -G.
MR: 1 *Super King Air* 200T.
TRAINING/LIAISON: 1 *Super Cub*, 2 T-28, 2 T-34B, 2 T-34C, 1 PA-34-200T, 1 C-182 *Skylane*.
HELICOPTERS: 2 Wessex 60, 1 Bell 47G, 1 Bell 222, 2 SH-34J.

NAVAL INFANTRY: (500); 1 bn.

AIR FORCE: 3,000; 37 cbt ac, no armed hel.
COIN: 2 sqn:
1 with 12 A-37B, 6 AT-33.
1 with 6 IA-58B, 6 T-33A.
SURVEY: 1 EMB-110B1.
SAR: 1 sqn with: 2 Bell 212, 2 UH-1B, 3 UH-1H hel.
TRANSPORT: 3 sqn with 3 C-212 (tpt/SAR), 3 EMB-110C, 1 F-27, 1 FH-227.
LIAISON: 2 Cessna 182, 4 *Queen Air* 80, 4 U-17.
TRAINING: *7 AT-6A, 7 T-33, 30 T-34A/B, 6 T-41D.

FORCES ABROAD:
UN AND PEACEKEEPING:
CAMBODIA (UNTAC): 930, plus 10 Observers.
EGYPT (MFO): 64.
INDIA/PAKISTAN (UNMOGIP): 1 adviser.
IRAQ/KUWAIT (UNIKOM): 6 Observers.
MOZAMBIQUE (ONUMOZ): 844, plus 10 Observers.

PARAMILITARY:
METROPOLITAN GUARD: 700.
REPUBLICAN GUARD: 500.
COAST GUARD: The Prefectura Naval (PNN) is part of the Navy.

VENEZUELA

GDP	1991:	Bs 3,036.3bn ($53.44bn)	
	1992:	Bs 4,180.3bn ($61.14bn)	
Growth	1991:	10.3%	1992: 7.3%
Inflation	1991:	34.2%	1992: 31.4%

Debt	1991:	$34.37bn	1992:	$34.71bn
Def exp	1991:	Bs 107.95bn ($1.89bn)		
Def bdgt	1992:	Bs 52.80bn ($772.20m)		
	1993:	Bs 72.74bn ($826.63m)		
$1 = Bs	1990:	46.900	1991:	56.816
	1992:	68.376	1993:	88.000

Bs = bolivares

Population: 21,160,000

	13–17	18–22	23–32
Men	1,157,000	1,034,000	1,786,000
Women	1,116,000	1,001,000	1,738,000

TOTAL ARMED FORCES:
ACTIVE: 75,000 incl National Guard (ε18,000 conscripts).
Terms of service: 2 years 6 months (Navy 2½ years) selective, varies by region for all services.
RESERVES: Army: ε8,000.

ARMY: 34,000 (incl conscripts).
6 inf div.
1 armd bde.
1 cav bde.
7 inf bde (18 inf, 1 mech inf, 4 fd arty bn).
1 AB bde.
1 Ranger bde (6 Ranger bn).
1 avn regt.
RESERVES: ε10 inf bn.
EQUIPMENT:
MBT: 70 AMX-30.
LIGHT TANKS: 75 M-18, 36 AMX-13, ε50 *Scorpion*.
RECCE: 10 AML-245, 25 M-8.
APC: 25 AMX-VCI, 100 V-100, 30 V-150, 100 *Dragoon* (some with 90mm gun), 35 EE-11 *Urutu*.
TOWED ARTY: 105mm: 40 Model 56, 40 M-101; 155mm: 12 M-114.
SP ARTY: 155mm: 5 M-109, 10 Mk F3.
MRL: 160mm: 20 LAR SP.
MORTARS: 81mm: 165; 120mm: 65 Brandt.
ATGW: AT-4, AS-11, 24 *Mapats*.
RCL: 84mm: *Carl Gustav*; 106mm: 175 M-40A1.
AVIATION:
AIRCRAFT: 3 IAI-202, 2 Cessna 182, 2 -206, 2 -207.
ATTACK HEL: 6 A-109 (ATK);
TRANSPORT HEL: 4 AS-61A, 3 Bell 205, 6 UH-1H.
LIAISON: 2 Bell 206.

NAVY: 11,000, incl naval aviation (2,000), marines (6,000) and coast guard (ε750) (ε4,000 conscripts).
5 Commands: Fleet, Marines, Naval Avn, Coast guard, Fluvial (River Forces).
5 Fleet sqn: submarine, frigate, patrol, amph, service.
BASES: Caracas (HQ), Puerto Cabello (submarine, frigate, amph and service sqn), Punto Fijo (patrol sqn).

Minor bases: Puerto de Hierro, Puerto La Cruz, El Amparo (HQ Arauca River), Maracaibo, La Guaira, Ciudad Bolivar (HQ Fluvial Forces).
SUBMARINES: 2:
2 *Sabalo* (Ge T-209/1300) with 533mm TT. (SST-4 HWT); (1 refitting in Germany).
FRIGATES: 6 *Mariscal Sucre* (It *Lupo*) with 1 AB-212 hel (ASW/OTHT), 2 x 3 ASTT (A-244S LWT); plus 8 *Teseo* SSM, 1 x 127mm gun, 1 x 8 *Aspide* SAM.
PATROL AND COASTAL COMBATANTS: 6:
MISSILE CRAFT: 6: 3 *Constitución* PFM (UK Vosper 37-m), with 2 x *Teseo*.
3 *Constitución* PFI with 4 x *Harpoon* SSM.
AMPHIBIOUS: 5:
4 *Capana* LST, capacity 200 tps, 12 tk.
1 *Amazonas* (US-1152) LST, capacity 395 tps, 16 tk.
Plus craft; 2 LCU (river comd), 11 LCVP.
SUPPORT AND MISCELLANEOUS: 3:
1 log spt, 1 trg, 1 *Punta Brava* AGHS.

NAVAL AVIATION: (2,000);
4 cbt ac, 8 armed hel.
ASW: 1 hel sqn (afloat) with 8 AB-212.
MR: 1 sqn with 4 C-212.
TRANSPORT: 2 C-212, 1 DHC-7, 1 *Rockwell Commander* 680.
LIAISON: 1 Cessna 310, 1 -402, 1 *King Air* 90.
HELICOPTERS: 2 Bell 47J.

MARINES: (6,000).
4 inf bn.
1 arty bn (3 fd, 1 AD bty).
1 amph veh bn.
1 river patrol, 1 engr, 2 para/cdo unit.
EQUIPMENT:
AAV: 11 LVTP-7 (to be mod to -7A1).
APC: 25 EE-11 *Urutu*, 10 *Fuchs/Transportpanzer* 1.
TOWED ARTY: 105mm: 18 Model 56.
AD GUNS: 40mm: 6 M-42 twin SP.

COAST GUARD: (ε750).
BASE: La Guaira; operates under Naval Command and Control, but organisationally separate.
PATROL, OFFSHORE: 3:
2 *Almirante Clemente* (It FF type),
1 *Miguel Rodriguez* (ex-US ocean tug).
PATROL INSHORE: 6: 2 *Petrel* (USCG *Point*-class) PCI⟨, 4 (riverine) PCI⟨, plus boats.

AIR FORCE: 7,000 (some conscripts);
141 cbt ac, 27 armed hel.
FIGHTER/FGA: 3 Air Gp: 1 with 15 CF-5A/B, 19 T-2D; 1 with 2 *Mirage* IIIEV, 5 *Mirage* 50EV; 1 with 18 F-16A, 6 -B.
COIN: 1 Air Gp with 25 EMB-312, 25 OV-10E, 19 T-2D *Buckeye*.
ATTACK HELICOPTERS: 1 Air Gp with 10 SA-316, 12 UH-1D, 5 UH-1H.

TRANSPORT: 7 C-123, 6 C-130H, 8 G-222, 2 HS-748, 2 B-707 (tkr).
TRANSPORT HELICOPTERS: 3 Bell 214, 4 -412, 5 AS-332B, 2 UH-1N.
PRESIDENTIAL FLT: 1 Boeing 737, 3 *Falcon* 20, 1 *Gulfstream* II, 1 -III, 1 *Learjet* 24D.
LIAISON: 9 *Cessna* -182, 1 *Citation* I, 1 -II, 2 *Queen Air* 65, 5 *Queen Air* 80, 5 *Super King Air* 200, 9 SA-316B *Alouette III*.
TRAINING: 1 Air Gp: 28 EMB-312, *7 F-5 (1 CF-5D, 6 NF-5B), 20 T-34.
AAM: R-530 *Magic*, AIM-9P *Sidewinder*.
AD GUNS: 110: 20mm: some Panhard M-3 SP; 35mm; 40mm: Bofors L/70 towed, Breda towed.
SAM: 10 *Roland*.

NATIONAL GUARD: *Fuerzas Armadas de*

Cooperación: 23,000 (internal sy, customs).
8 regional commands.
EQUIPMENT: 25 UR-416 AIFV, 204 Fiat-6614 APC, 100 60mm mor, 50 81mm mor.
AIRCRAFT: 1 *Baron*, 1 BN-2A, 2 Cessna 185, 5 -U206, 4 IAI-201, 1 *King Air* 90, 1 *King Air* 200C, 2 *Queen Air* 80.
HELICOPTERS: 4 A-109, 20 Bell 206.
PATROL CRAFT: inshore: 22 ; some 60 boats.

FORCES ABROAD:
UN AND PEACEKEEPING:
CROATIA (UNPROFOR I): 3 Observers.
EL SALVADOR (ONUSAL): 16 Observers.
IRAQ/KUWAIT (UNIKOM): 7 Observers.
WESTERN SAHARA (MINURSO): 15 Observers.

Sub-Saharan Africa

Regional Overview

For the last 12 months, Sub-Saharan Africa has been the region most plagued by conflict and instability. There is a growing feeling amongst Africans that their problems are considered to be less serious than those elsewhere in the world. While the UN has devoted some attention to the problems of Angola, Mozambique, Rwanda and Somalia, 'peacekeeping' efforts have not resulted in definitive conflict resolution. The Organisation of African Unity (OAU) has revived discussions about creating its own peacekeeping forces and working directly with the UN to solve regional conflict, but this (with the exception of Rwanda) has not yet borne fruit.

Civil War

The elections in **Angola,** which were won by the governing Movimento Popular para a Libertaçao de Angola (MPLA), were declared as fair and valid by the UN and other international monitors. However, the number of monitors was insufficient and they were not provided with enough transport to allow them to observe more than a percentage of the polling stations. The MPLA and the União Nacional para a Independência Total de Angola (UNITA) were set to form a coalition government, demobilisation of forces had begun, and a joint army was being formed when Jonas Savimbi, the UNITA leader, rejected the election result. As UNITA had not declared the true state of its armed forces nor demobilised as large a proportion of them as had the government, it was able to take control of several provincial capitals and threaten Luanda. Since then, the civil war has continued unabated but with a difference. The MPLA can no longer call on the support of Cuban forces, nor does UNITA any longer enjoy the support of the US (which has recognised the MPLA government) or of South Africa (although there are suspicions that the latter has provided some military supplies). The UN peacekeeping force has been reduced to less than 100 military and police observers, and international aid missions are severely hampered by the renewed fighting.

On 4 October 1992 Joachim Chissano, the President of **Mozambique**, and Alfonso Dhlakama, the leader of the Resistência Nacional Moçambicana (Renamo), signed a peace agreement which ended the 14-year civil war. The two sides called on the UN for assistance in monitoring the cease-fire, demobilising forces, protecting infrastructure (including the land corridors) and collecting and destroying weapons. They also asked for technical and monitoring assistance for elections and coordination of humanitarian aid. The UN special representative and a small team of military observers arrived in Mozambique in mid-October 1992, but the main elements of the UN force, ONUMOZ, only deployed between March and May 1993. This was mainly due to delays in preparing contingents from the contributing countries. There have been several violations of the cease-fire, and the training programme to be run by the British Army in Zimbabwe for officers of the new joint army has been delayed as no students had been provided by Renamo until August 1993 when a pilot course, with 25 students each from the government army and Renamo, began.

The **Liberian** civil war may be nearing an end, following successful talks in Cotonou, Benin. The civil war, which broke out in 1989, has been between the National Patriotic Front of Liberia (NPFL), led by Charles Taylor, and the United Liberation Movement for Democracy in Liberia (ULIMO), led by Alhaji Koromah. At one stage the issue was complicated by a third faction – Prince Johnson's Independent National Patriotic Front. Until early 1993, the two rebel factions controlled the greater part of the country, while the interim president, Amos Sawyer, backed by the peacekeeping force established by the Economic Organisation of West African States (ECOWAS), but in fact manned largely by Nigeria, controlled only the area around the capital Monrovia. In mid-1993 ECOWAS forces succeeded in recapturing territory previously controlled by Taylor; this affected the tenor of later talks. However, it will be some time before genuine and lasting peace is brought to the country.

The civil war in **Rwanda**, which began in October 1990, has been formally ended with the signing of an agreement between the government and the Rwandan Patriotic Front. A transitional government will take office and multiparty elections will take place in June 1995. The OAU has been asked to expand its neutral military observer group until an international force can be deployed. A UN Observer Mission is being deployed to monitor the Rwanda–Uganda border.

Political Developments

The presidential election held in **Nigeria** on 12 June 1993 was expected to be the final step in the transition from military to civil rule. The election was won, albeit with a very low turnout, by the Social Democratic Party candidate, Moshood Abiola, a Muslim from the Yoruba tribe. Most Nigerians and international observers consider the elections to have been free and fair. However, on 16 June, before the full results had been announced, the National Electoral Commission suspended the election after the losing party, the National Republican Convention, had complained of large-scale vote-rigging. The military government of General Babangida annulled the election on 23 June, promised new elections and that 27 August would remain the date as planned, for the handover of civil rule. As yet no date has been set for the second election; instead, an interim government of military officers and civilians chosen by the present administration is to be formed, which could provide a cover for continued military rule. Riots and civil disobedience in Lagos and the south-west of the country have been countered by the Army. The situation is tense and many non-indigenous people are returning to their tribal homes. Both Britain and the US have condemned the military government's actions and have begun to restrict military cooperation and the provision of military aid. There is evidence that the Army is not fully behind Babangida.

In **South Africa** progress towards ending apartheid and forming a coalition government of national unity, in which the ANC leader, Nelson Mandela, is likely to be President, has continued in fits and starts. An election is planned for April 1994, but progress is being severely threatened by the terrorist activities of both black and white extremists and of the Zulu Inkatha Freedom Party. There have been murderous attacks on white country clubs and farms and most recently on a church congregation. A leading ANC activist, Chris Hani, was murdered on 10 April 1993, and in June the Afrikaner Volksfront Movement stormed the World Trade Centre in Johannesburg where the multiparty constitutional talks were taking place. Some 2,000 armed men are reported to have taken part in the break-in which was not resisted by the police who, it is reported, were influenced by the sight of snipers positioned on neighbouring roofs. Eugene Terre'Blanche, leader of the Afrikaner Resistance Movement (AWB), has forecast the Third Boer War. A 'Committee of Generals' has been formed to coordinate pro-apartheid groups some of which are campaigning for the establishment of an all-Afrikaner state. The majority of the many deaths occur in clashes between ANC supporters and the Zulu *impis* of Inkatha, who also aim for a Zulu state. There is a growing tendency to attack the security forces sent to restore law and order, and there has been an increased use of firearms in these attacks.

On 23 April 1993 **Eritrea** cast a virtually unanimous vote, in a UN-monitored referendum, in favour of independence from Ethiopia. Independence was declared on 25 May and the new state has been recognised by the US, UK, Italy, Egypt and others, but has not yet been admitted to the United Nations. Eritrea participated in the OAU summit meeting. Before the referendum, Eritrea had assured Ethiopia of guaranteed access to the sea, principally through the port of Assab. In July 1993 the two countries agreed to cooperate in the education, energy, transport, defence and security fields, to use their resources jointly and not to interfere in each other's internal affairs.

Instability and violence have rocked other African countries. States of Emergency were declared in **Congo** (July 1992) and **Zambia** (March 1993). Belgian and French troops were sent to Zaire to assist in the evacuation of their nationals following clashes between loyal troops and those opposed to President Mobuto. Chad, Kenya, Mali, Niger, Senegal and Togo have all suffered ethnically or politically motivated outbreaks of violence. The International Monetary Fund (IMF) has insisted on deep cuts in defence spending in Kenya, Zambia and Zimbabwe, if they are to receive aid. This will mean a large reduction in manpower in these forces.

Military Developments

There are few military developments to report. The general state of African economies means there is little or no cash available for arms purchases and the days of free or highly subsidised arms hand-outs are over.

A number of African countries are taking part in UN peacekeeping operations for the first time. **Botswana** has contributed troops to both ONUMOZ and UNOSOM; **Zambia** and **Cape Verde** contribute to ONUMOZ, and **Namibia** and **Cameroon** to UNTAC. Nigeria has provided contingents for UNTAC, UNOSOM and UNPROFOR I, but the battalion deployed to Croatia has now been withdrawn.

In **Angola** some 70 aircraft, or about half the Air Force strength, are no longer in service. **Botswana** has acquired a small number of UK-made *Javelin* SAM. **Guinea-Bissau** has acquired one ex-GDR *Kondor-I*-class inshore patrol craft. **Cape Verde** no longer maintains a Navy; there is no information available regarding the disposal of the five inshore patrol craft with which the Navy was credited. **Kenya** has formed its first airborne battalion. The **Niger** Army has increased its strength by about 2,000 men and has formed two more reconnaissance squadrons, another infantry and a second airborne battalion. An additional 70 AML-90 armoured reconnaissance vehicles have also been acquired. The **Nigerian** Army has taken delivery of some 75 EE-9 *Cascavel* armoured reconnaissance vehicles. The **Zimbabwe** Air Force has taken delivery of six more *Hawk* Mk 60 COIN aircraft. Zimbabwe is reported to be planning large-scale defence cuts following pressure from the World Bank and the IMF who are backing an economic reform programme. Considerable savings should be made following the withdrawal of Zimbabwean troops from Mozambique; along with troops from Malawi (who have also been withdrawn) they were guarding the land transit routes. **Zambia**, too, is under similar pressure to reduce its defence spending.

In **South Africa** the overall strength of the armed forces has dropped by some 5,000 men. Fresh information has allowed us to revise the weapons inventory, but the changes listed may have taken place over several years. New equipment in service includes: 100 *Rooikat* wheeled armoured cars mounting a 76mm gun, 160 *Mamba* – a wheeled APC (which looks like an armoured land rover and has bullet-proof windows) – and some 155mm G-4. There are 60 *Valkiri* SP MRL with 24 tubes (number unknown earlier). The number of helicopters has been revised considerably: there are only a total of 37 SA-316 and SA-330 and not 63 of each as we listed previously. The reorganisation of the Citizen Force mentioned last year appears to have been completed. There are now three divisions (instead of two) and the brigade level of command has been eliminated.

ANGOLA

| GDP | 1991ε: K 995.4bn ($4.31bn) |
| | 1992ε: K 1,839.1bn ($3.45bn) |

Growth	1991: 0.6%	1992ε: -7%
Inflation	1991ε: 180.0%	1992ε: 220%
Debt	1991: $8.36bn	1992: $8.60bn
Def exp	1989ε: K 81.75bn ($2.69bn)	
$1 = K	1990: 29.9	1991: 60.0
	1992: 585.0	1993: 4,000.0

K = kwanza

Population: 10,929,000

	13–17	18–22	23–32
Men	602,000	505,000	763,000
Women	606,000	511,000	785,000

TOTAL ARMED FORCES:
ACTIVE: ε45,000.

ARMY: ε35,000.
Current structure unknown.
EQUIPMENT:†
MBT: 100 T-34†, 100 T-54/-55, some T-62.
LIGHT TANKS: some 10 PT-76.
AIFV: 50+ BMP.
RECCE: some 40+ BRDM-2.
APC: 100 BTR-60/-152.
TOWED ARTY: 300: incl 76mm: M-1942 (ZIS-3); 85mm: D-44; 122mm: D-30; 130mm: M-46.
ASSAULT GUNS: SU-100.
MRL: 122mm: 50 BM-21, some BM-24.
MORTARS: 82mm: 250; 120mm: 40+ M-43.
ATGW: AT-3 *Sagger*.
RCL: 500: 82mm: B-10; 107mm: B-11.
AD GUNS: 200+: 14.5mm: ZPU-4; 23mm: ZU-23-2, 20 ZSU-23-4 SP; 37mm: M-1939; 57mm: S-60 towed, 40 ZSU-57-2 SP.
SAM: SA-7/-14.

NAVY:† ε4,000.
BASES: Luanda (HQ), Lobito, Namibe.
PATROL AND COASTAL COMBATANTS: 13:
MISSILE CRAFT: 6 Sov *Osa*-II† with 4 x SS-N-2 *Styx* SSM.
TORPEDO CRAFT: 4 *Shershen*† with 4 x 533mm HWT.
PATROL, INSHORE 3: 2 Sov *Poluchat*†, 1 Sov *Zhuk*⟨†.
MINE WARFARE: 2 Sov *Yevgenya* MHI.
AMPHIBIOUS: 3 Sov *Polnocny* LSM, capacity 100 tps. 6 tk.
Plus craft; 1 LCT, about 5 LCM.
COASTAL DEFENCE: SS-C-1 *Sepal* at Luanda.

AIR FORCE/AIR DEFENCE: ε6,000;
81 cbt ac, 40 armed hel.†
FGA: 20 MiG-23, 19 Su-22, 10 Su-25.
FIGHTER: 15 MiG-21 MF/bis.
COIN/RECCE: 6 PC-7/-9.
MR: 2 EMB-111, 1 F-27MPA.
ATTACK HELICOPTERS: 28 Mi-25/35, 6 SA-365M (guns), 6 SA-342 (*HOT*).
TRANSPORT: 2 sqn with 12 An-12, 20 An-26, 6 BN-2, 3 C-47, 5 C-212, 2 L-100-20, 4 PC-6B, 7 BN-2A *Islander*.
HELICOPTERS: 2 sqn with 30 IAR-316, 10 SA-316, 16 Mi-8, 13 Mi-17, 1 SA-315, 10 SA-365.
LIAISON: 5 An-2, 5 Do-27.
TRAINING: 3 Cessna 172, 3 MiG-15UTI, 6 MiG-21U, 5* Su-22, 6 Yak-11.
AD: 5 SAM bn†. 10 bty; with 40 SA-2, 12 SA-3, 25 SA-6, 15 SA-8, 20 SA-9, 10 SA-13.
MISSILES:
ASM: *HOT*.
AAM: AA-2 *Atoll*.

PARAMILITARY:
INTERNAL SECURITY POLICE: ε20,000.

OPPOSITION:
UNITA (*Union for the Total Independence of Angola*): ε40,000.
EQUIPMENT: captured T-34/-85, 70 T-55 MBT reported, misc APC (not in service); BM-21 122mm MRL; 75mm, 76mm, 122mm, 130mm fd guns; 81mm, 82mm, 120mm mor; 85mm RPG-7 RL; 75mm RCL; 12.7mm hy machine guns; 14.5mm, 20mm, ZU-23-2 23mm AA guns; *Stinger*, SAM-7.
FLEC (*Front for the Liberation of the Cabinda Enclave*): (claims 5,000, actual strength ε600); small arms only.

FOREIGN FORCES:
UNITED NATIONS (UNAVEM II): 75 military observers and 28 civ pol from 16 countries.

BENIN

GDP	1991:	fr 535.5bn ($1.90bn)		
	1992:	fr 575.6bn ($2.17bn)		
Growth	1991:	3%	1992:	4.7%
Inflation	1991:	3.6%	1992:	3.5%
Debt	1991:	$1.31bn	1992:	$1.30bn
Def bdgt	1991ε:	fr 5.77bn ($20.47m)		
	1992ε:	fr 7.20bn ($27.20m)		
$1 = fr	1990:	272.26	1991:	282.11
	1992:	264.7	1993:	272.0

fr = francs CFA (Communauté financière africaine)
Benin's economy is to a large extent subsidised by the French government which is covering part of the country's bdgt deficit through economic aid (fr 61.31bn CFA for 1993).

Population: 5,194,800

	13–17	18–22	23–32
Men	293,000	233,000	343,000
Women	308,000	250,000	375,000

TOTAL ARMED FORCES:
ACTIVE: 4,300.
Terms of service: conscription (selective), 18 months.

ARMY 3,800.
3 inf, 1 AB/cdo, 1 engr bn, 1 armd sqn, 1 arty bty.
EQUIPMENT:
LIGHT TANKS: 20 PT-76.
RECCE: 9 M-8, 14 BRDM-2, 10 VBL M-11.
TOWED ARTY: 105mm: 4 M-101.
MORTARS: 81mm.
RL: 89mm: LRAC.

NAVY:† ε150.
BASE: Cotonou.
PATROL AND COASTAL COMBATANTS: 1:
PATROL, INSHORE: 1 *Patriote* PFI (Fr 38-m)⟨.
SUPPORT AND MISCELLANEOUS: 1: 1 tug.
In store: 4 Sov *Zhuk*⟨ PFI.

AIR FORCE:† 350; no cbt ac, 1 armed hel.
AIRCRAFT: 3 An-2, 2 An-26, 2 C-47, 1 *Commander* 500B, 2 Do-128.
HELICOPTERS:
ATTACK: 1 SA-355M.
TRANSPORT: 2 AS-350B, 1 Ka-26, 1 SE-3130.

PARAMILITARY:
GENDARMERIE: 2,000; 4 mobile coy.
PUBLIC SECURITY FORCE.
PEOPLE'S MILITIA: 1,500–2,000.

BOTSWANA

GDP	1991: P 6.99bn ($3.22bn)		
	1992: P 7.87bn ($3.70bn)		
Growth	1991: 8.7%	1992: 5.8%	
Inflation	1991: 11.7%	1992: 15%	
Debt	1991: $542.8m	1992: $550m	
Def bdgt	1989ε: P 221.40m ($110.01m)		
	1990ε: P 243.54m ($130.94m)		
FMA	1991: $1.4m		
$1 = P	1990: 1.860	1991: 2.175	
	1992: 2.133	1993: 2.345	

P = pula

Population: 1,364,000

	13–17	18–22	23–32
Men	83,000	65,700	95,000
Women	85,000	67,500	105,000

TOTAL ARMED FORCES:
ACTIVE: 6,100+.

ARMY: 6,000+.
2 bde:
4 inf bn; 2 fd arty, 2 AD arty, 1 engr regt,
1 cdo unit.
EQUIPMENT:
RECCE: 10 *Shorland*, 12 V-150 *Commando* (11 with 90mm gun).
APC: 30 BTR-60†.
TOWED ARTY: 105mm: 12 lt, 4 Model 56 pack.
MORTARS: 81mm; 120mm: 6 M-43.
ATGW: *TOW* reported.
RCL: 84mm: 30 *Carl Gustav*.
AD GUNS: 20mm: M-167.
SAM: 12 SA-7, 5 *Javelin*.

AIR FORCE: 100+. 20 cbt ac, no armed hel.
COIN: 1 sqn with 8 BAC-167 Mk 83, 5 BN-2 *Defender*.
TRANSPORT: 1 sqn with 2 *Defender*, 2 CN-235, 2 *Skyvan* 3M, 1 BAe 125-800 (VIP).
LIAISON/TRG: 1 sqn with 1 Cessna 152, 7* PC-7.
HEL: 1 sqn with 2 AS-350L, 5 Bell 412 (VIP).

FORCES ABROAD:
UN AND PEACEKEEPING:
MOZAMBIQUE (ONUMOZ): 747: 1 inf bn(-).
SOMALIA (UNOSOM II): 202.

PARAMILITARY:
POLICE MOBILE UNIT: 1,000.

BURKINA FASO

GDP	1991: fr 839.0bn ($2.97bn)		
	1992: fr 881.0bn ($3.33bn)		
Growth	1991: 4.8%	1992ε: 4.0%	
Inflation	1990: –0.5%	1991ε: 3.1%	
Debt	1990: $834m	1991: $865m	
Def bdgt	1991ε: fr 28,160.0m ($108.10m)		
	1992ε: fr 37,800.0m ($138.97m)		
FMA	1992: fr (Fr) 5.7m (France)		
$1 = fr	1990: 272.26	1991: 282.11	
	1992: 264.7	1993: 272.0	

fr = francs CFA (Communauté financière africaine)

Population: 9,827,000

	13–17	18–22	23–32
Men	552,600	453,000	717,000
Women	542,000	462,500	711,000

TOTAL ARMED FORCES:
ACTIVE: 8,700 (incl Gendarmerie).

ARMY: 7,000.
6 Military Regions.
5 inf 'regt': HQ, 3 'bn' (each 1 coy of 5 pl).
1 AB 'regt': HQ, 1 'bn', 2 coy.
1 tk 'bn': 2 pl.
1 arty 'bn': 2 tps.
1 engr 'bn'.
EQUIPMENT:
RECCE: 83: 15 AML-60/-90, 24 EE-9 *Cascavel*, 10 M-8, 4 M-20, 30 *Ferret*.
APC: 13 M-3.
TOWED ARTY: 105mm: 8 M-101.
MRL: 107mm: Ch Type-63.
MORTARS: 81mm: Brandt.
RL: 89mm: LRAC, M-20.
RCL: 75mm: Ch Type-52.
AD GUNS: 14.5mm: 30 ZPU.
SAM: SA-7.

AIR FORCE: 200; 18 cbt ac, no armed hel.
FIGHTER: 1 sqn with 8 MiG-21.
COIN: 4 SF-260W, 6 SF-260WP.
TRANSPORT: 2 C-47, 1 *Commander* 500B, 2 HS-748, 2 N-262.
LIAISON: 3 MH-1521M, 2 SA-316, 2 SA-365.
HELICOPTERS: 2 SA-316B, 2 SA-365N.

PARAMILITARY: 1,750:
GENDARMERIE: 1,500; 6 coy (2 mobile).
SECURITY COMPANY (CRG): 250.
PEOPLE'S MILITIA(R): 45,000 trained.

BURUNDI

GDP   1990: fr 189.14bn ($1.10bn)
             1991: fr 210.26bn ($1.16bn)
Growth   1990: 3.5%   1991: 5.0%
Inflation   1991: 8.7%   1992: 4.7%
Debt   1990: $905m   1991: $961m
Def bdgt   1987: fr 3,910.0m ($31.64m)
             1988: fr 4,500.0m ($32.05m)
$1 = fr   1990: 171.36   1991: 181.51
             1992: 208.30   1993: 245.00
fr = Burundi francs

Population: 5,981,000

	13–17	18–22	23–32
Men	324,000	272,000	444,000
Women	321,000	271,000	447,000

TOTAL ARMED FORCES:
ACTIVE: ε7,150 (incl Gendarmerie).

ARMY: 5,500.
2 inf, 1 AB, 1 cdo bn.
1 armd car coy.
EQUIPMENT:
RECCE: 6 AML-60, 12 -90, 7 *Shorland*.
APC: 29: 9 M-3, 20 BTR-40 and *Walid*.
MORTARS: 82mm: 18 M-43.
RL: 83mm: *Blindicide*.
RCL: 75mm: 15 Ch Type-52.
AD GUNS: 14.5mm: 15 ZPU-4.

AIR: 150. 3 cbt ac, no armed hel.
COIN: 3 SF-260W.
TRANSPORT: 1 C-47.
HELICOPTERS: 3 SA-316B, 4 SA-342L.
LIAISON: 3 Reims-Cessna 150, 1 Do-27Q.
TRAINING: 7 SF-260 (3 -C, 4 -TP).

PARAMILITARY:
GENDARMERIE: ε1,500. Incl Marine Police: ε50:
Base: Bujumbura, patrol boats river: ε2.

CAMEROON

GDP   1990ε: fr 3,130.9bn ($11.50bn)
             1991ε: fr 3,270.0bn ($11.37bn)
Growth   1991ε: -3.2%   1992ε: -3.5%
Inflation   1991ε: 3%   1992ε: 2%
Debt   1990: $6.02bn   1991: $6.28bn
Def bdgt   1990: fr 51,977bn ($190.9m)
             1992ε: fr 35,490bn ($134.08m)
FMA   1988: $8.28m (Fr, US)

$1 = fr   1990: 272.26   1991: 282.11
             1992: 264.690   1993: 272.0
fr = francs CFA (Coopération financière en Afrique centrale)

Population: 12,827,000

	13–17	18–22	23–32
Men	760,000	583,000	856,000
Women	757,000	584,000	867,000

TOTAL ARMED FORCES:
ACTIVE: 12,100 (incl Gendarmerie).

ARMY: 6,600.
3 Military Regions; 7 Military Sectors: coy gp under cmd.
Presidential Guard: 1 guard, 1 armd recce bn, 3 inf coy.
1 AB/cdo bn.
5 inf bn (1 trg).
1 engr bn.
1 arty bn (5 bty).
1 AA bn (6 bty).
EQUIPMENT:
RECCE: 8 M-8, *Ferret*, 8 V-150 *Commando* (20mm gun), 5 VBL M-11.
AIFV: 12 V-150 *Commando* (90mm gun).
APC: 29 V-150 *Commando*, 12 M-3 half-track.
TOWED ARTY: 22: 75mm: 6 M-116 pack; 105mm: 16 M-101.
MORTARS: 81mm (some SP); 120mm: 16 Brandt.
ATGW: *Milan*.
RL: 89mm: LRAC.
RCL: 57mm: 13 Ch Type-52; 106mm: 40 M-40A2.
AD GUNS: 14.5mm: 18 Ch Type-58; 35mm: 18 GDF-002; 37mm: 18 Ch Type-63.

NAVY: ε1,200.
BASES: Douala (HQ), Limbe, Kribi.
PATROL AND COASTAL COMBATANTS: 2:
MISSILE CRAFT: 1 *Bakassi* (Fr P.48) PFM with 2 x 4 MM-40 *Exocet* SSM.
PATROL, INSHORE: 1 *L'Audacieux* (Fr P.48) PFI.
RIVERINE: Boats only, some 30 US Swiftsure-38, 6 SM 30/36 types.
AMPHIBIOUS: craft only: 2 LCM, 5 LCVP.

AIR FORCE: 300; 16 cbt ac, 4 armed hel.
1 composite sqn.
1 Presidential flt.
FGA/COIN: 5 *Alpha Jet*, 11 CM-170.
MR: 2 Do-128D-6.
ATTACK HEL: 4 SA-342L (with *HOT*).
TRANSPORT: 3 C-130H/-H-30, 1 DHC-4, 4 DHC-5D, 1 IAI-201, 2 PA-23.
HEL: 3 Bell 206, 3 SE-3130, 1 SA-318, 4 SA-319.

FORCES ABROAD:
UN AND PEACEKEEPING:
CAMBODIA (UNTAC): 14 Observers, plus 73 civ pol.

PARAMILITARY:
GENDARMERIE: 4,000: 10 regional groups.
PATROL BOATS: about 10 US Swiftsure-38 (incl in Navy entry).

CAPE VERDE

GDP 1991ε: CV E 28.52bn ($399.5m)
1992ε: CV E 29.95bn ($440.3m)
Growth 1991: 3.3% 1992ε: 1%
Inflation 1991: 9.4% 1992: 3.3%
Debt 1990: $152.9m 1991: $158.3m
Def bdgt 1991: CV E 261.51m ($3.66m)
1992: CV E 242.05m ($3.56m)
$1 = CV E 1990: 70.031 1991: 71.408
1992: 68.020 1993: 75.000
CV E = Cape Verde escudos

Population: 408,800
	13–17	18–22	23–32
Men	22,500	20,000	33,500
Women	23,000	20,600	36,400

TOTAL ARMED FORCES:
ACTIVE: 1,100.
Terms of service: conscription (selective).

ARMY: 1,000 (Popular Militia).
2 bn.
EQUIPMENT:
RECCE: 10 BRDM-2.
TOWED ARTY: 75mm: 12; 76mm: 12.
MORTARS: 82mm: 12; 120mm: 6 M-1943.
RL: 89mm: 3.5-in.
AD GUNS: 14.5mm: 18 ZPU-1; 23mm: 12 ZU-23.
SAM: 50 SA-7.

NAVY: No naval forces exist at present.

AIR FORCE: under 100; no cbt ac.
MR: 1 Do-228.

FORCES ABROAD:
UN AND PEACEKEEPING:
MOZAMBIQUE (ONUMOZ): 15 Observers.

CENTRAL AFRICAN REPUBLIC

GDP 1990: fr 363.7bn ($1.34bn)
1991: fr 362.0bn ($1.28bn)
Growth 1990: 1.9% 1991ε: 0.1%
Inflation[a] 1991: -2.2% 1992ε: 0.2%
Debt 1990: $766m 1991: $884m
Def bdgt 1992ε: fr 7,4.000m ($27.96m)
$1 = fr 1990: 272.260 1991: 282.11
1992: 264.69 1993: 272.0
fr = francs CFA (Coopération financière en Afrique centrale)
[a] Inflation figures represent the consumer price index (CPI) for African households.

Population: 3,280,000
	13–17	18–22	23–32
Men	176,000	163,000	232,000
Women	178,000	159,000	234,000

TOTAL ARMED FORCES:
ACTIVE: 6,500 incl Gendarmerie.
Terms of service: conscription (selective), 2 years; Reserve obligation thereafter, term unknown.

ARMY: 3,500.
1 Republican Guard regt (2 bn).
1 territorial defence regt (bn).
1 combined arms regt (1 mech, 1 inf bn).
1 spt/HQ regt.
1 Presidential Guard bn.
EQUIPMENT:†
MBT: 4 T-55.
RECCE: 10 *Ferret.*
APC: 4 BTR-152, some 10 VAB, 25+ ACMAT.
MORTARS: 81mm; 120mm: 12 M-1943.
RL: 89mm: LRAC.
RCL: 106mm: 14 M-40.
RIVER PATROL CRAFT: 9⟨.

AIR FORCE: 300; No cbt ac, no armed hel.
TRANSPORT: 2 C-47, 2 Cessna 337, 1 DC-4.
LIAISON: 8 AL-60, 6 MH-1521.
HELICOPTERS: 1 AS-350, 1 SE-3130.

PARAMILITARY:
GENDARMERIE: 2,700;
3 Regional Legions, 8 'bde'.

FOREIGN FORCES:
FRANCE: 1,200. 1 inf bn gp, 1 armd cav sqn, 1 arty bty. 5 *Jaguar*, 3 C-160.

CHAD

GDP   1990ε: fr 334.40bn ($1.23bn)
           1991ε: fr 364.0bn ($1.29bn)
Growth   1991ε: 11.4%
Inflation 1990: 0.6%   1991ε: 7.6%
Debt   1990: $504.7m   1991: $606.3m
Def bdgt   1992ε: fr 9,354.2m ($35.34m)
FMA   1991: $2.4m (US); fr 5bn (France)
$1 = fr   1990: 272.26   1991: 282.11
           1992: 264.69   1993: 272.0
fr = francs CFA (Coopération financière en
Afrique centrale).

Population: 6,146,000

	13–17	18–22	23–32
Men:	315,000	270,000	436,000
Women:	317,000	273,000	445,000

TOTAL ARMED FORCES:
ACTIVE: some 25,200.
Terms of service: conscription, 3 years.

ARMY: ε25,000.
7 Military Regions.
EQUIPMENT:
AFV: some 63: 4 Panhard ERC-90, some 50 AML-60/-90, 9 V-150 with 90mm.
TOWED ARTY: 105mm: 5 M-101.
MORTARS: 81mm; 120mm: AM-50.
ATGW: *Milan*.
RL: 89mm: LRAC.
RCL: 106mm: M-40A1; 112mm: *APILAS*.
AD GUNS: 20mm, 30mm.

AIR FORCE: 200; 4 cbt ac, no armed hel.
COIN: 2 PC-7, 2 SF-260W.
TPT: 3 C-47, 1 C-130A, 2 -B, 1 -H, 1 C-212, 2 DC-4.
HELICOPTERS: 4 SA-330, 1 SA-341.
LIAISON: 2 PC-6B, 5 Reims-Cessna FTB 337.

PARAMILITARY:
GENDARMERIE: 4,500.

OPPOSITION:
WESTERN ARMED FORCES: strength unknown.
MOVEMENT FOR DEVELOPMENT AND DEMOCRACY: strength unknown.

FOREIGN FORCES:
FRANCE: 750. 2 inf coy, AD arty units; 3 C-160.

CONGO

GDP   1991: fr 821.0bn ($2.91bn)
           1992ε: fr 880.0bn ($3.32bn)
Growth   1991: -1.9%   1992ε: 0.8%
Inflation 1990: 2.1%   1991ε: 6.4%
Debt   1990: $4.82bn   1991: $4.74bn
Def bdgt   1992ε: fr 33.25bn ($125.63m)
$1 = fr   1990: 272.260   1991: 282.11
           1992: 264.69   1993: 272.0
fr = francs CFA (Coopération financière en Afrique
centrale)

Population: 2,515,000

	13–17	18–22	23–32
Men:	138,000	119,000	182,000
Women:	137,000	119,000	185,000

TOTAL ARMED FORCES:
ACTIVE: 10,800.

ARMY: 10,000.
2 armd bn.
2 inf bn gp (each with lt tk tp, 76mm gun bty).
1 inf bn.
1 arty gp (how, MRL).
1 engr bn.
1 AB/cdo bn.
EQUIPMENT:†
MBT: 25 T-54/-55, 15 Ch Type-59 (some T-34 in store.)
LIGHT TANKS: 10 Ch Type-62, 3 PT-76.
RECCE: 25 BRDM-1/-2.
APC: M-3, 80 BTR (30 -50, 30 -60, 20 -152).
TOWED ARTY: 76mm: M-1942; 100mm: 10 M-1944; 122mm:10 D-30; 130mm: 5 M-46; 152mm: some D-20.
MRL: 122mm: 8 BM-21; 140mm: BM-14-16.
MORTARS: 82mm; 120mm: 10 M-43.
RCL: 57mm: M-18.
ATK GUNS: 57mm: 5 M-1943.
AD GUNS: 14.5mm: ZPU-2/-4; 23mm: ZSU-23-4 SP; 37mm: 28 M-1939; 57mm: S-60; 100mm: KS-19.

NAVY:† ε300.
BASE: Point Noire.
PATROL AND COASTAL COMBATANTS: 6:
PATROL, INSHORE: 6:
3 *Marien N'gouabi* PFI (Sp *Barcelo* 33-m).
3 Sov *Zhuk* PFI⟨.
RIVERINE: Boats only.

AIR FORCE:† 500. 22 cbt ac, no armed hel.
FGA: 10 MiG-17, 12 MiG-21.
TPT: 5 An-24, 1 An-26, 1 Boeing 727, 1 N-2501.
TRG: 4 L-39, 1 MiG-15UTI.
HELICOPTERS: 2 SA-316, 2 SA-318, 1 SA-365.

FORCES ABROAD:
UN AND PEACEKEEPING:
ANGOLA (UNAVEM II): 6 Observers.

PARAMILITARY: 6,100:
GENDARMERIE: 1,400; 20 coy.
PEOPLE'S MILITIA: 4,700.

FOREIGN FORCES:
RUSSIA: 20 military advisers.

CÔTE D'IVOIRE

GDP	1991: fr 2,615.0bn ($9.27bn)		
	1992ε: fr 2,719.6bn ($10.27bn)		
Growth	1991: -2%	1992ε: 0.7%	
Inflation	1991: 1.3%	1992: 4.3%	
Debt	1990: $18.08bn	1991: $18.85bn	
Def bdgt	1992ε: fr 21.39bn ($80.8m)		
FMA	$4.0m (Economic Support, US)		
$1 = fr	1990: 272.26	1991: 282.11	
	1992: 264.69	1993: 272.0	

fr = francs CFA (Communauté financière africaine)

Population: 13,284,000

	13–17	18–22	23–32
Men	754,000	603,000	933,000
Women	761,000	604,000	895,000

TOTAL ARMED FORCES:
ACTIVE: 7,100.
Terms of service: conscription (selective), 6 months.
RESERVES: 12,000.

ARMY: 5,500.
4 Military Regions:
1 armd, 3 inf bn, 1 arty gp.
1 AB, 1 AA, 1 engr coy.
EQUIPMENT:
LIGHT TANKS: 5 AMX-13.
RECCE: 7 ERC-90 *Sagaie*, ε16 AML-60/-90.
APC: 16 M-3, 13 VAB.
TOWED ARTY: 105mm: 4 M-1950.
MORTARS: 81mm; 120mm: 16 AM-50.
RL: 89mm: LRAC.
RCL: 106mm: M-40A1.
AD GUNS: 20mm: 16 incl 6 M-3 VDA SP;
40mm: 5 L/60.

NAVY: 700.
BASE: Locodjo (Abidjan).
PATROL AND COASTAL COMBATANTS: 4:
MISSILE CRAFT: 2:

2 *L' Ardent* (Fr *Auroux* 40-m) with 4 x SS-12 SSM.
PATROL: 2 *Le Vigilant* (Fr SFCN 47-m) PCI.
AMPHIBIOUS: 1 *L'Eléphant* (Fr *BATRAL*) LSM,
capacity 140 tps, 7 tk, hel deck, plus some 8 craft.

AIR FORCE: 900; 6 cbt ac, no armed hel.
FGA: 1 sqn with 6 *Alpha Jet*.
TRANSPORT: 1 hel sqn with 1 SA-318, 1 SA-319, 1
SA-330, 4 SA-365C.
PRESIDENTIAL FLIGHT:
AIRCRAFT: 1 F-28, 1 *Gulfstream* IV, 1 Fokker 100.
HELICOPTERS: 1 SA-330.
TRAINING: 6 Beech F-33C, 2 Reims Cessna 150H.
LIAISON: 1 Cessna 421, 2 *Super King Air* 200.

PARAMILITARY: 7,800:
PRESIDENTIAL GUARD: 1,100.
GENDARMERIE: 4,400; VAB APC, 4 patrol boats.
MILITIA: 1,500.
MILITARY FIRE SERVICE: 800.

FOREIGN FORCES:
FRANCE: 500: 1 marine inf regt; 1 AS-355 hel.

EQUATORIAL GUINEA

GDP	1990ε: fr 43.06bn ($158.14m)	
	1991ε: fr 40.60bn ($143.92m)	
Growth	1990: 2.9%	1991ε: -2.6%
Inflation[a]	1990: 1.1%	1991: -3.2%
Debt	1990: $237.6m	1991: $249.3m
$1 = fr	1990: 272.26	1991: 282.11
	1992: 264.69	1993: 272.0

fr = francs CFA (Coopération financière en Afrique
centrale)
[a] Inflation figures represent the CPI of African households.

Population: 446,400

	13–17	18–22	23–32
Men:	21,700	19,200	32,000
Women:	22,200	19,800	32,500

TOTAL ARMED FORCES:
ACTIVE: 1,300.

ARMY: 1,100. 3 inf bn.
EQUIPMENT:
RECCE: 6 BRDM-2.
APC: 10 BTR-152.

NAVY†: 120.
BASES: Malabo (Santa Isabel), Bata.
PATROL COMBATANTS: 3 PFI⟨, 1 PCI⟨.

AIR FORCE: 100; no cbt ac or armed hel.
TRANSPORT: 1 Yak-40, 3 C-212, 1 Cessna-337.

PARAMILITARY:
GUARDIA CIVIL: 2 coy.

FOREIGN FORCES:
MOROCCO: 360: 1 bn.

ERITREA

Population: ε3,000,00

	13–17	18–22	23–32
Men	167,000	139,000	210,000
Women	161,000	134,000	203,000

Eritrea declared itself independent from Ethiopia on 27 April 1993. Est strength of Eritrean forces is some 80,000. No information is available on division of eqpt of former Ethiopian government. It is likely that Eritrea, which cuts Ethiopia off from the sea, has inherited any naval assets which are listed below. Army and Air Force assets shown under Ethiopia.

BASES: Massawa, Assab.
FRIGATES: 2 *Zerai Deres* (Sov *Petya-II*) with 2 x ASW RL, 10 x 406mm TT.
PATROL AND COASTAL COMBATANTS: 15:
MISSILE CRAFT: 4 Sov *Osa* with 4 x SS-N-2 *Styx* SSM.
TORPEDO CRAFT: 4: 2 Sov *Turya* PHT, 2 *Mol* PFT all with 4 x 533mm TT.
PATROL INSHORE: 7 PFI: 3 US Swiftships 32-m, 4 Sov *Zhuk*⟨.
AMPHIBIOUS: 2 Sov *Polnocny* LSM, capacity 100 tps, 6 tk.
Plus craft: 3 LCT (1 Fr EDIC and 2 *Chamo* (Ministry of Transport)), 4 LCM.
SUPPORT AND MISCELLANEOUS: 2: 1 AOT (sm), 1 trg.

ETHIOPIA

GDP	1990ε: EB 12.53bn ($5.86bn)	
	1991ε: EB 13.40bn ($5.39bn)	
Growth	1990: -6.0%	1991ε: -8.0%
Inflation	1991: 35.8%	1992: 10.6%
Debt	1990: $3.26bn	1991: $3.48bn
Def bdgt	1989ε: EB 1,110.15m ($536.30m)	
	1990: EB 2,691.00m ($1.31bn)	
$1 = EB[a]	1990: 2.05	1991: 2.1
	1992: 5.0	1993: 5.0

EB = birr
[a] Official rate fixed at $1 = EB 2.07 until 1991, $1 = EB 5.0 thereafter. Figures in $ est but even at the old fixed exchange rate the per capita income of Ethiopia has dropped to $90 or less.

Population: ε50,000,000

	13–17	18–22	23–32
Men	2,783,000	2,309,000	3,489,000
Women	2,674,000	2,221,000	3,386,000

Following the declaration of independence by Eritrea in April 1993, est strength of Ethiopian armed forces some 100,000. Most are former members of the Tigray People's Liberation Front (TPLF) with maybe 10–15,000 from the Oromo Liberation Front which is showing increasing signs of opposition to the government. No information on division of military assets between Ethiopia and Eritrea is available. We list all ground and air force assets under Ethiopia and naval assets under Eritrea. Est numbers in service must be treated with caution.

ARMY:†
MBT: ε350 T-54/-55, T-62.
RECCE/AIFV/APC: ε200 incl: BRDM, BMP, BTR-60/-152.
TOWED ARTY: 76mm: ZIS-3; 85mm: D-44; 122mm: D-30/M-30; 130mm: M-46.
MRL: BM-21.
MORTARS: 82mm: M-1937; 120mm: M-1938.
ATGW: AT-3 *Sagger*.
RCL: 82mm: B-10; 107mm: B-11.
AD GUNS: 23mm: ZU-23, ZSU-23-4 SP; 37mm: M-1939; 57mm: S-60.
SAM: 20 SA-2, 30 SA-3, 300 SA-7, SA-9.

AIR FORCE:† 38 cbt ac, 18 armed hel.
The Air Force is essentially grounded. Air Force activity is believed to be limited to reorganisation, some ground crew training and maintenance. Types and numbers of remaining ac are assessed as follows:
FGA: 20 MiG-21MF; 18 MiG-23BN
TPT: 6 An-12, 2 DH-6, 2 L-100-30 (liaison), 1 Yak-40 (VIP), 2 Y-12.
TRG: 14 L-39.
ATTACK HEL: 18 Mi-24.
TPT HEL: 1 IAR-330, 25 Mi-8, 1 UH-1, 2 Mi-14.

GABON

GDP	1991ε: fr 1,269.1bn ($4.50bn)	
	1992ε: fr 1,256.4bn ($4.75bn)	
Growth	1991: 1.4%	1992ε: 1.0%
Inflation[a]	1991ε: -5.8%	1992ε: -3.7%
Debt	1990: $3.64bn	1991: $3.84bn
Def bdgt	1988ε: fr 45,800.0m ($153.77m)	
	1989ε: fr 46,510.0m ($145.79m)	
$1 = fr	1990: 272.260	1991: 282.11
	1992: 264.69	1993: 272.0

fr = francs CFA (Communauté financière africaine)
[a] Inflation figures represent the consumer price index of African households.

Population: 1,236,000

	13–17	18–22	23–32
Men	57,400	50,700	89,800
Women	58,900	52,400	88,300

TOTAL ARMED FORCES:
ACTIVE: 4,750.

ARMY: 3,250.
Presidential Guard bn gp (1 recce/armd, 3 inf coy, arty, AA bty) (under direct Presidential control). 8 inf, 1 AB/cdo, 1 engr coy.
EQUIPMENT:
RECCE: 16 EE-9 *Cascavel*, 24 AML-90, 6 ERC-90 *Sagaie*, 12 EE-3 *Jararaca*, 14 VBL M-11.
AIFV: 12 EE-11 *Urutu* with 20mm gun.
APC: 9 V-150 *Commando*, Panhard M-3, 12 VXB-170.
TOWED ARTY: 105mm: 4 M-101.
MRL: 140mm: 8 *Teruel*.
MORTARS: 81mm: 35; 120mm: 4 Brandt.
ATGW: 4 *Milan*.
RL: 89mm: LRAC.
RCL: 106mm: M40A1.
AD GUNS: 20mm: 4 ERC-20 SP; 23mm: 24 ZU-23-2; 37mm: 10 M-1939; 40mm: 2 Bofors.

NAVY: ε500.
BASE: Port Gentil (HQ).
PATROL AND COASTAL COMBATANTS: 3:
MISSILE CRAFT: 1 *General Nazaire Boulingu* PFM (Fr 42-m) with 4 SS-12 SSM.
PATROL COASTAL: 2 *General Ba'Oumar* (Fr P.400 55-m).
AMPHIBIOUS: 1 *President Omar Bongo* (Fr *BATRAL*) LSM, capacity 140 tps, 7 tk.
Plus craft; 1 LCM.

AIR FORCE: 1,000. 19 cbt ac, 7 armed hel.
FGA: 9 *Mirage* 5 (2 -G, 4 -GII, 3 -DG).
MR: 1 EMB-111.
TRANSPORT: 1 C-130H, 1 L-100-20, 2 L-100-30, 2 EMB-110, 2 YS-11A.
HELICOPTERS:
ATTACK: 2 AS-350, 5 SA-342.
TRANSPORT: 3 SA-330C/-H.
LIAISON: 3 SA-316/-319.
PRESIDENTIAL GUARD:
COIN: 6 CM-170, 4 T-34.
TRANSPORT: ac 1 ATR-42F, 1 EMB-110, 1 *Falcon* 900, 1 *Gulfstream* III, 1 AS-332 hel.

PARAMILITARY:
COAST GUARD: ε2,800; boats only.
GENDARMERIE: 2,000; 3 'bdes', 11 coy, 2 armd sqn, air unit.

FOREIGN FORCES:
FRANCE: 500: 1 marine inf regt; 1 AS-355 hel, 1 C-160, 1 *Atlantic* ac.

THE GAMBIA

GDP	1991:	D 2,689m ($305.51m)	
	1992ε:	D 3,046.6m ($342.78m)	
Growth	1991:	4.0%	1992ε: 2.0%
Inflation	1991:	8.6%	1992: 9.5%
Debt	1990:	$352.2m	1991: $350.7m
Def bdgt	1988:	D 20.10m ($3.00m)	
$1 = D	1990:	7.883	1991: 8.803
	1992:	8.888	1993: 8.980

D = dalasi

Population: 956,600

	13–17	18–22	23–32
Men	50,200	41,400	66,500
Women	49,500	41,700	68,500

TOTAL ARMED FORCES:
ACTIVE: 800.

GAMBIAN NATIONAL ARMY (GNA):
1 inf bn (4 coy), engr sqn.
MARINE UNIT: About 70.
BASE: Banjul.
PATROL, INSHORE: 3:
2 *Gonjur* (Ch *Shanghai-II*) PFI, 1 PFI‹, boats.

FOREIGN FORCES:
NIGERIA: 70+ trg team.

GHANA

GDP	1991:	C 2,438.0bn ($6.63bn)	
	1992ε:	C 2,700.0bn ($6.18bn)	
Growth	1991:	5.3%	1992ε: 3.9%
Inflation	1991:	18.0%	1992: 10.0%
Debt	1991:	$3.76bn	1992: $4.21bn
Def bdgt	1992ε:	C 20,700m ($47.36m)	
$1 = C	1990:	326.33	1991: 367.83
	1992:	437.10	1993: 560.00

C = cedi

Population: 16,359,000

	13–17	18–22	23–32
Men	940,000	774,000	1,153,000
Women	933,000	773,000	1,169,000

TOTAL ARMED FORCES:
ACTIVE: 6,850.

ARMY: 5,000.
2 Command HQ:
2 bde (comprising 6 inf bn (incl 1 trg, 1 UNIFIL, 1 ECOMOG), spt units).
1 recce regt (2 sqn).
1 AB force (incl 1 para coy).
1 arty 'regt' (mor bn).
1 fd engr regt (bn).
EQUIPMENT:
RECCE: 3 Saladin, 3 EE-9 Cascavel.
AIFV: 50 MOWAG Piranha.
MORTARS: 81mm: 50; 120mm: 28 Tampella.
RCL: 84mm: 50 Carl Gustav.

NAVY: ε850 Commands: Western and Eastern.
BASES: Sekondi (HQ, West), Tema (HQ, East).
PATROL AND COASTAL COMBATANTS: 4:
COASTAL: 2 Achimota (Ge Lürssen 57-m) PFC.
INSHORE: 2 Dzata (Ge Lürssen 45-m) PCI.

AIR FORCE: 1,000. 18 cbt ac, no armed hel.
COIN: 1 sqn with 4 MB-326K†, 2 MB-339.
TRANSPORT:
3 Fokker (2 F-27, 1 F-28) (VIP); 3 F-27, 1 C-212, 1 with 6 Skyvan.
HELICOPTERS: 2 Bell 212 (VIP), 2 Mi-2, 4 SA-319.
TRAINING: 1 sqn with 10 Bulldog 122†, 12* L-29, 6 MB 326F.

FORCES ABROAD:
LIBERIA: about 1,000 forming part of ECOMOG.
UN AND PEACEKEEPING:
CAMBODIA: (UNTAC): 892, plus 20 Observers and 218 civ pol.
CROATIA (UNPROFOR I): 17 Observers.
IRAQ/KUWAIT (UNIKOM): 6 Observers.
LEBANON (UNIFIL): 781: 1 inf bn.
WESTERN SAHARA (MINURSO): 1 Observer.

PARAMILITARY:
PEOPLE'S MILITIA: 5,000: part-time force with police duties.
PRESIDENTIAL GUARD: 1 inf bn.

GUINEA

GDP	1991: G fr 2,346.0bn ($2.96bn)	
	1992ε: G fr 2,833.0bn ($3.49bn)	
Growth	1991: 2.4%	1992ε: 3.5%
Inflation	1991: 12.2%	1992: 16.0%
Debt	1991: $2.48bn	1992: $2.63bn
Def exp	1989ε: $27m	
$1 = G fr	1990: 660.3	1991: 792.6
	1992: 812.6	1993: 810.0

G fr = Guinean franc

Population: 6,212,000

	13–17	18–22	23–32
Men	348,000	289,000	440,000
Women	358,000	296,000	452,000

TOTAL ARMED FORCES:
ACTIVE: 9,700 (perhaps 7,500 conscripts).
Terms of service: conscription, 2 years.

ARMY: 8,500.
1 armd bn.
1 cdo bn.
5 inf bn.
1 SF bn.
1 arty bn.
1 engr bn.
1 AD bn.
EQUIPMENT:†
MBT: 30 T-34, 8 T-54.
LIGHT TANKS: 20 PT-76.
RECCE: 25 BRDM-1/-2, 2 AML-90.
APC: 40 BTR (16 -40, 10 -50, 8 -60, 6 -152).
TOWED ARTY: 76mm: 8 M-1942; 85mm: 6 D-44; 122mm: 12 M-1931/37.
MORTARS: 82mm: M-43; 120mm: 20 M-1938/43.
RCL: 82mm: B-10.
ATK GUNS: 57mm: M-1943.
AD GUNS: 30mm: twin M-53; 37mm: 8 M-1939; 57mm: 12 S-60, Ch Type-59; 100mm: 4 KS-19.
SAM: SA-7.

NAVY: 400.
BASES: Conakry, Kakanda.
PATROL AND COASTAL COMBATANTS: 9:
PATROL: 9:
1 Kaba Sov T-58C PCO.†
Some 3 Sov Bogomol PFI.
2 Sov Zhuk, 1 US Swiftships-77, 2 other PCI, all⟨.

AIR FORCE:† 800; 11 cbt ac, no armed hel.
FGA: 4 MiG-17F, 7 MiG-21.
TRANSPORT: 2 An-12, 4 An-14.
TRAINING: 3 L-29, 2 MiG-15UTI, 6 Yak-18.
HELICOPTERS: 1 IAR-330, 4 Mi-4, 1 SA-316B, 1 SA-330, 1 SA-342K.

FORCES ABROAD:
UN AND PEACEKEEPING:
LIBERIA: some 600, forming part of ECOMOG.
WESTERN SAHARA (MINURSO): 1 Observer.

PARAMILITARY:.
PEOPLE'S MILITIA: 7,000.
GENDARMERIE: 1,000.
REPUBLICAN GUARD: 1,600.

GUINEA-BISSAU

GDP   1991ε: pG 650.0bn ($194.32m)
           1992ε: pG 950.0bn ($189.9m)
Growth   1991ε: 2.2%   1992ε: 0.5%
Inflation 1991ε: 21.2%   1992ε: 46%
Debt   1990: $595.8m   1991: $653.3m
Def bdgt   1989: pG 8,027.0m ($4.43m)
$1 = pG   1990: 2,230.0   1991: 3,345.0
           1992: 5,003.0   1993: 4,977.0

pG = Guinea pesos

Population: 1,038,000

	13–17	18–22	23–32
Men	59,600	52,200	75,200
Women	55,800	48,500	76,800

TOTAL ARMED FORCES: (all services incl
Gendarmerie are part of the Army):
ACTIVE: 9,200.
Terms of service: conscription (selective).

ARMY: 6,800.
1 armd 'bn' (sqn).
5 inf, 1 arty bn, 1 recce, 1 engr coy.
EQUIPMENT:
MBT: 10 T-34.
LIGHT TANKS: 20 PT-76.
RECCE: 10 BRDM-2.
APC: 35 BTR-40/-60/-152, 20 Ch Type-56.
TOWED ARTY: 85mm: 8 D-44; 122mm: 18 M-1938/D-30.
MORTARS: 82mm: M-43; 120mm: 8 M-1943.
RL: 89mm: M-20.
RCL: 75mm: Ch Type-52; 82mm: B-10.
AD GUNS: 23mm: 18 ZU-23; 37mm: 6 M-1939; 57mm: 10 S-60.
SAM: SA-7.

NAVY: 300.
BASE: Bissau.
PATROL AND COASTAL COMBATANTS: 10:
PATROL INSHORE: 10:
1 ex-Ge *Kondor-I* PCI, 2 Sov *Bogomol*, 2 Ch *Shantou* PFI, some 5 PCI⟨ (incl 1 customs service).

AIR FORCE: 100. 3 cbt ac, no armed hel.
FIGHTER: 3 MiG-17.
HELICOPTERS: 1 SA-318, 2 SA-319.

FORCES ABROAD:
UN AND PEACEKEEPING:
ANGOLA (UNAVEM II): 6 Observers.

PARAMILITARY:
GENDARMERIE: 2,000.

KENYA

GDP   1991: sh 227.24bn ($8.26bn)
           1992ε: sh 290.87bn ($9.03bn)
Growth   1991: 2.2%   1992ε: 0.4%
Inflation 1991: 19.8%   1992: 27.5%
Debt   1990: $7.01bn   1991: $7.01bn
Def bdgt   1993ε: sh 10.37bn ($148.1m)
Def exp   1991ε: sh 6.13bn ($223.0m)
           1992ε: sh 8.26bn ($256.2m)
FMA   1991: $5.1m (US)
$1 = sh   1990: 22.915   1991: 27.508
           1992: 32.200   1993: 70.000

sh = Kenyan shillings

Population: 26,916,000

	13–17	18–22	23–32
Men:	1,653,000	1,311,000	1,849,000
Women:	1,655,000	1,318,000	1,871,000

TOTAL ARMED FORCES:
ACTIVE: 24,400.

ARMY: 20,500.
1 armd bde (3 armd bn).
2 inf bde (1 with 2, 1 with 3 inf bn); 1 indep inf bn.
1 arty bde (2 bn).
1 engr bde.
1 AB bn.
1 AD arty bn.
2 engr bn.
1 indep air cav bn.
EQUIPMENT:
MBT: 80 Vickers Mk 3.
RECCE: 52 AML-60/-90, 12 *Ferret*, 8 *Shorland*.
APC: 52 UR-416, 10 Panhard M-3.
TOWED ARTY: 105mm: 40 lt, 8 pack.
MORTARS: 81mm: 50; 120mm: 12 Brandt.
ATGW: 40 *Milan*, 14 *Swingfire*.
RCL: 84mm: 80 *Carl Gustav*.
AD GUNS: 20mm: 50 TCM-20, 11 *Oerlikon*; 40mm: 13 Bofors.

NAVY: 1,400.
BASE: Mombasa.
PATROL AND COASTAL COMBATANTS: 10:
MISSILE CRAFT 6:
2 *Nyayo* (UK Vosper 57-m) PFM, with 4 *Otomat* II SSM.
1 *Mamba*, 3 *Madaraka* (UK Brooke Marine 37-m/32-m) PFM with 4 x *Gabriel* II SSM.
PATROL, INSHORE: 4: 3 *Simba* (UK Vosper 31-m) PCI, 1 PCI⟨ (all in reserve).
SUPPORT AND MISCELLANEOUS: 1 tug.

AIR FORCE: 2,500: 32 cbt ac, 34 armed hel.
FGA: 10 F-5 (8 -E, 2 -F).

COIN: 1 *Strikemaster* Mk 87, 9 *Hawk* Mk 52, 12 *Tucano*.
TRANSPORT: 7 DHC-5D, 7 Do-28D, 1 PA-32, 3 DHC-8.
TRAINING: 7 *Bulldog* 103/127.
ATTACK HEL: 11 Hughes 500MD (with TOW), 8 500ME, 15 500M.
TRANSPORT HEL: 9 IAR-330, 4 SA-330, 1 SA-342.
TRAINING: 2 Hughes 500D.
MISSILES:
ASM: AGM-65 *Maverick*, *TOW*.
AAM: AIM-9 *Sidewinder*.

FORCES ABROAD:
UN AND PEACEKEEPING:
CAMBODIA (UNTAC): 100 civ pol.
CROATIA (UNPROFOR I): 935: 1 inf bn, 36 Observers, 44 civ pol.
IRAQ/KUWAIT (UNIKOM): 6 Observers.
WESTERN SAHARA (MINURSO): 10 Observers.

PARAMILITARY:
POLICE GENERAL SERVICE UNIT: 5,000.
POLICE AIR WING: 7 Cessna lt ac, 3 Bell hel (1 206L, 2 47G).
CUSTOMS/POLICE NAVAL SQN: about 5 PCI〈 (2 Lake Victoria), some 12 boats.

LESOTHO

GDP	1991:	M 1,643.8m ($596.44m)
	1992:	M 2,116.2m ($717.36m)
Growth	1991ε: 4%	1992ε: 8%
Inflation	1991: 17.7%	1992ε: 12.0%
Debt	1990: $390.0m	1991: $427.7m
Def exp	1992ε: M 111.40m ($37.78m)	
$1 = M	1990: 2.586	1991: 2.756
	1992: 2.950	1993: 3.100

M = maloti

Population: 1,921,000

	13–17	*18–22*	*23–32*
Men	106,000	88,500	135,080
Women	105,000	87,500	138,000

TOTAL ARMED FORCES:
ACTIVE: 2,000.
ARMY:
7 inf coy.
1 spt coy (incl recce/AB, 81mm mor).
1 air sqn.
EQUIPMENT:
RECCE: 10 Is RAMTA, 8 *Shorland*.
TOWED ARTY: 105mm: 2.
MORTARS: 81mm: some.

AIRCRAFT: 2 C-212 *Aviocar* 300.
HELICOPTERS: 2 Bo-105, 1 Bell 47, 3 Bell 412.

LIBERIA

GDP	1991ε: $L 2,800.0m ($ 1,142.8m)	
	1992ε: $L 5,040.0m ($ 1,029.0m)	
Growth	1991ε: -10%	
Inflation	1991ε: 75%	1992ε: 100%
Debt	1990: $US 3.5bn	1991ε: $US 3.5bn
Def bdgt	1993ε: $L 35.34m ($US 14.43m)	
$1 = $L[a]	1986–93: 1.00	

[a] $1 = $L fluctuates on parallel market; unofficial estimate $1 = $L8–10.

Population: 2,811,000

	13–17	*18–22*	*23–32*
Men	160,000	134,000	208,000
Women	156,000	129,000	198,000

As a result of civil war the Armed Forces of Liberia (AFL) with a cbt strength of ε2,000 are now confined to the capital Monrovia. Eqpt held by the AFL has been destroyed or is unserviceable. The area west of Monrovia, up to the Sierra Leone border is controlled by the United Liberation Movement for Democracy in Liberia (ULIMO) with a cbt strength of ε3–4,000. Both are opposed by the National Patriotic Forces of Liberia (NPFL) who control most of the country with a cbt strength of ε5,000. A 3-nation peacekeeping force (ECOMOG) provided by the Economic Community of West African States (ECOWAS) is deployed within the country and is composed of forces from:
Ghana – ε1,000; Guinea – ε600; Nigeria – ε10,000.

MADAGASCAR

GDP	1991: fr 4,906.4bn ($2.67bn)	
	1992ε: fr 5,249.4bn ($2.75bn)	
Growth	1991: -1.0%	1992ε: 1.4%
Inflation	1991: 12.8%	1992: 14.5%
Debt	1990: $3.63bn	1991: $3.72bn
Def bdgt	1991: fr 58,600.0m ($31.93m)	
	1992ε: fr 59,175.0m ($30.98m)	
FMA	1988: $2.88m (Fr, US)	
$1 = fr	1990: 1,494.10	1991: 1,835.4
	1992: 1,910.0	1993: 1,792.3

fr = Malagasy francs

Population: 12,763,000

	13–17	*18–22*	*23–32*
Men	717,000	598,000	922,000
Women	701,000	587,000	915,000

TOTAL ARMED FORCES:
ACTIVE: 21,000.

Terms of service: conscription (incl for civil purposes), 18 months.

ARMY: some 20,000.

2 bn gp.	1 service regt.
1 engr regt.	7 construction regt.
1 sigs regt.	

EQUIPMENT:
LIGHT TANKS: 12 PT-76.
RECCE: 8 M-8, ε20 M-3A1, 10 *Ferret*, ε35 BRDM-2.
APC: ε30 M-3A1 half-track.
TOWED ARTY: 76mm: 12 ZIS-3; 105mm: some M-101; 122mm: 12 D-30.
MORTARS: 82mm: M-37; 120mm: 8 M-43.
RL: 89mm: LRAC.
RCL: 106mm: M-40A1.
AD GUNS: 14.5mm: 50 ZPU-4; 37mm: 20 Type 55.

NAVY: 500 (incl some 100 marines).

BASES: Diégo-Suarez, Tamatave, Fort Dauphin, Tuléar, Majunga.
PATROL CRAFT: 1 *Malaika* (Fr PR48-m) PCI.
AMPHIBIOUS: 1 *Toky* (Fr *BATRAM*) LSM, with 8 x SS-12 SSM, capacity 30 tps, 4 tk.
Plus craft; 1 LCT (Fr EDIC), 1 LCA, 3 LCVP.
SUPPORT AND MISCELLANEOUS: 1 tpt/trg.

AIR FORCE: 500; 12 cbt ac, no armed hel.

FGA: 1 sqn with 4 MiG-17F, 8 MiG-21FL.
TRANSPORT: 4 An-26, 3 BN-2, 2 C-212, 2 Yak-40 (VIP).
HELICOPTERS: 1 sqn with 6 Mi-8.
LIAISON: 1 Cessna 310, 2 -337, 1 PA-23.
TRAINING: 4 Cessna 172.

PARAMILITARY:

GENDARMERIE: 7,500, incl maritime police with some 5 PCI⟨.

MALAWI

GDP	1991: K 6.14bn ($2.19bn)		
	1992: K 6.52bn ($1.81bn)		
Growth	1991: 7.8%	1992: -7.9%	
Inflation	1991: 12.7%	1992: 22.0%	
Debt	1991: $1.63bn	1992: $1.83bn	
Def bdgt	1992ε: K 70.0m ($19.43m)		
	1993ε: K 90.8m ($20.42m)		
FMA	1991: $1.25m (US)		
$1 = K	1990: 2.729	1991: 2.803	
	1992: 3.603	1993: 4.450	

K = kwacha

Population: 9,436,000

	13–17	18–22	23–32
Men:	515,000	427,000	640,000
Women:	514,000	439,000	682,000

TOTAL ARMED FORCES: (all services form part of the Army):

ACTIVE: 10,400.
RESERVES: Army: 10,000 (militia).

ARMY: 10,000.

3 inf bn; 1 spt bn (incl 1 recce sqn).
EQUIPMENT:
RECCE: 20 *Fox*, 10 *Ferret*, 13 *Eland*.
TOWED ARTY: 105mm: 9 lt.
MORTARS: 81mm: 8 L16.
RL: 89mm: M-20.
RCL: 57mm: M-18.
AD GUNS: 14.5mm: 50 ZPU-4.
SAM: 15 *Blowpipe*.

MARINE: 200.

BASE: Monkey Bay (Lake Nyasa).
PATROL CRAFT: 1 PCI⟨, 2 LCVP, some boats.

AIR: 200; No cbt ac, 4 armed hel.

TRANSPORT: 1 sqn with 4 Do-228, 2 C-47, 1 HS-125-800 (VIP), 1 *King Air* C90
HELICOPTERS:
ATTACK: 4 AS-350.
TRANSPORT: 3 SA-319, 3 SA-330, 1 SA-365.

PARAMILITARY:

MOBILE POLICE FORCE: (MPF): 1,500: 8 Shorland armd car; 3 BN-2T *Defender* (border patrol), 1 *Skyvan* 3M, 4 Cessna ac; 2 AS-350 hel.

MALI

GDP	1991ε: fr 607.06bn ($2.15bn)		
	1992ε: fr 570.67bn ($2.16bn)		
Growth	1991: -0.2%	1992ε: -4.0%	
Inflation	1991: 1.8%	1992: -6.2%	
Debt	1990: $2.43bn	1991: $2.53bn	
Def bdgt	1992ε: fr 17,360m ($65.59m)		
	1993ε: fr 16,320m ($60.00m)		
$1 = fr	1990: 272.26	1991: 282.11	
	1992: 264.69	1993: 272.0	

fr = francs CFA (Communauté financière africaine)

Population: 9,244,000

	13–17	18–22	23–32
Men	533,000	452,000	629,000
Women	531,000	451,000	645,000

TOTAL ARMED FORCES: (all services form part of the Army):

ACTIVE: 7,350.
Terms of service: conscription (incl for civil purposes), 2 years (selective).

ARMY: 6,900.
2 tk, 4 inf, 1 AB, 2 arty, 1 engr, 1 SF bn, 2 AD, 1
SAM bty.
EQUIPMENT:†
MBT: 21 T-34.
LIGHT TANKS: 18 Type 62.
RECCE: 20 BRDM-2.
APC: 30 BTR-40, 10 BTR-60, 10 BTR-152. •
TOWED ARTY: 85mm: 6 D-44; 100mm: 6 M-1944;
122mm: 8 D-30.
MRL: 122mm: 2 BM-21.
MORTARS: 82mm: M-43; 120mm: 30 M-43.
AD GUNS: 37mm: 6 M-1939; 57mm: 6 S-60.
SAM: 12 SA-3.

NAVY:† About 50.
BASES: Bamako, Mopti, Segou, Timbuktu.
RIVER PATROL CRAFT: 3⟨.

AIR FORCE: 400; 16† cbt ac, no armed hel.
FGA: 5 MiG-17F.
FIGHTER: 11 MiG-21.
TRANSPORT: 2 An-2, 2 An-24, 2 An-26.
TRAINING: 6 L-29, 1 MiG-15UTI, 4 Yak-11, 2 Yak-18.
HELICOPTERS: 2 Mi-4, 1 Mi-8.

PARAMILITARY:
GENDARMERIE: 1,800; 8 coy.
REPUBLICAN GUARD: 2,000.
MILITIA: 3,000.
NATIONAL POLICE: 1,000.

FOREIGN FORCES:
RUSSIA: 20 military advisers.

MAURITIUS

GDP	1991: R 42.74bn ($2.73bn)		
	1992: R 47.23bn ($3.03bn)		
Growth	1991: 4.1%	1992: 5.8%	
Inflation	1991: 7.0%	1992: 4.6%	
Debt	1990: $946m	1991: $991m	
Def and Sy bdgt	1992ε: R 163.0m ($10.47m)		
	1993ε: R 179.0m ($10.59m)		
$1 = R	1990: 14.863	1991: 15.652	
	1992: 15.563	1993: 16.900	

R = Rupees

Population: 1,202,000

	13–17	18–22	23–32
Men	54,500	52,300	104,600
Women	54,100	51,800	105,700

PARAMILITARY FORCES
SPECIAL MOBILE FORCE: 1,300.
6 rifle, 2 mobile, 1 engr coy, spt tp.
EQUIPMENT:
APC: 10 VAB.
MORTARS: 81mm: 2.
RL: 89mm: 4 LRAC.
COAST GUARD: ε500.
1 *Amar* PCI, 2 Sov *Zhuk* PCI⟨, plus boats.
AIR ARM:
MR: 1 Do-228-101, 1 BN-2T *Defender*.
POLICE AIR WING: 2 *Alouette* III.

MOZAMBIQUE

GDP	1991:	M 1,871.0bn ($1.06bn)	
	1992ε:	M 2,525.8bn ($998.0bn)	
Growth	1991:	-2.3%	1992ε: -2.4%
Inflation	1991:	35.2%	1992ε: 46.0%
Debt	1990:	$4.74bn	1991: $4.70bn
Def bdgt[a]	1992ε:	M 256.75bn ($100.69m)	
	1993ε:	M 349.6bn ($112.77m)	
$1 = M	1990:	930.25	1991: 1,764.0
	1992:	2,550.0	1993: 3,100.0

M = meticais
[a] Incl sy. Demob programme est $50m.

Population: 17,167,000

	13–17	18–22	23–32
Men	941,000	787,000	1,220,000
Women	956,700	803,000	1,258,000

Following the end of the civil war the Mozambique
government and its opponent Resistência Nacional
Moçambicana (Renamo) have agreed to merge their
armed forces to form a new 30,000-strong National
Army. Details outlined below reflect the general
situation and estimated status as of early 1993.

TOTAL ARMED FORCES:
ACTIVE: 50,000.
Terms of service: conscription (selective, blacks
only), 2 years (incl women), extended during
emergency.

ARMY: ε45,000 (perhaps 85% conscripts; all units
well under strength.)
10 Provincial Commands.
1 tk bde.
7 inf bde.
1 lt inf bde.
Many indep cbt and cbt spt bn and sy units.
6 AA arty bn.
EQUIPMENT:†
MBT: some 100 T-54/-55 (300+ T-34, T-54/-55 non-op).
RECCE: 30 BRDM-1/-2.

AIFV: 20 BMP-1.
APC: 150+ BTR-60, 100 BTR-152.
TOWED ARTY: 100+: 76mm: M-1942; 85mm: 150+: D-44, D-48, Type-56; 100mm: 24 M-1944; 105mm: M-101; 122mm: M-1938, D-30; 130mm: 24 M-46; 152mm: 20 D-1.
MRL: 122mm: 30 BM-21.
MORTARS: 82mm: M-43; 120mm: M-43.
RCL: 75mm; 82mm: B-10; 107mm: B-11.
AD GUNS: 400: 20mm: M-55; 23mm: 90 ZU-23-2; 37mm: 100 M-1939; 57mm: 90: S-60 towed, ZSU-57-2 SP.
SAM: SA-7.
(All eqpt est to be at 10% or less serviceability).

NAVY†: ε1,000.
BASES: Maputo (HQ), Beira, Nacala, Pemba, Inhambane, Quelimane (ocean); Metangula (Lake Nyasa) where 3 PCI⟨ (non-op) are based.
PATROL AND COASTAL COMBATANTS: 12:
INSHORE: 12†:
2 Sov SO-1, 3 *Zhuk* PFI⟨.
some 7 PCI⟨.
MINE WARFARE: 2 Sov *Yevgenya* MSI.
AMPHIBIOUS: craft only; 2 LCU†.

AIR FORCE: 4,000 (incl AD units);
43 cbt ac†, 4 armed hel.†
FGA: 5 sqn with 43 MiG-21.
TRANSPORT: 1 sqn with 5 An-26, 2 C-212, 2 Cessna 152, 1 -172.
HELICOPTERS:
ATTACK: 4 Mi-24.
TRANSPORT: 5 Mi-8.
TRAINING: 4 Cessna 182, 4 PA-32.
AD SAM:† SA-2, 10 SA-3.

PARAMILITARY:
PROVINCIAL MILITIA: 9 bn; 1 bn (less Nyasa) per province. To be disbanded in 1993.

OPPOSITION:
MOZAMBIQUE NATIONAL RESISTANCE:
(MNR or RENAMO): 20,000, ε10,000+ trained. 8 bn (active).
EQUIPMENT:
RCL: 82mm B-10, RPG-7.
MORTARS: 60mm, 82mm, 120mm M-1943.
AD GUNS: 12.7mm and 14.5mm.

FOREIGN FORCES:
UNITED NATIONS:
ONUMOZ: 5,900 to be 7,500; 5 inf bn (Bangladesh, Botswana, Italy, Uruguay, Zambia), 1 engr bn, plus spt units; 250 (to be 350) Observers.

NAMIBIA

GDP	1991:	R 5.44bn ($2.17bn)	
	1992ε:	R 6.64bn ($2.27bn)	
Growth	1991:	2.5%	1992ε: 3.0%
Inflation	1991:	11.8%	1992: 17.9%
Debt	1991:	$273.0m	1992: $449.0m
Def bdgt	1992:	R 189.00m ($64.64m)	
	1993:	R 187.34m ($58.86m)	
Def exp	1992:	R 191.00m ($65.32m)	
FMA[a]	1991:	$5.18m (US)	
$ 1 = R	1990:	2.586	1991: 2.583
	1992:	2.924	1993: 3.183

R = rand
[a] Incl $5m as Economic Support.

Population: 1,953,000

	13–17	18–22	23–32
Men	111,200	90,600	136,800
Women	111,700	91,100	138,000

TOTAL ARMED FORCES:
ACTIVE: 8,100.

ARMY: 8,000.
1 Presidential Guard bn.
4 mot inf bn.
1 arty bn.
1 AD arty bn.
1 ATK bn.
EQUIPMENT:
RECCE: BRDM-2.
APC: some *Casspir, Wolf*, BTR-152.
MRL: 122mm: 5 BM-21.
MORTARS: 81mm; 82mm.
RCL: 82mm: B-10.
ATK GUNS: 57mm; 76mm.
AD GUNS: 14.5mm: ZPU-4; 23mm: 15 ZU-23.
SAM: SA-7.

MARINE: ε100.
BASE: Walvis Bay.
PATROL: Boats only.

FORCES ABROAD:
UN AND PEACEKEEPING:
CAMBODIA (UNTAC): 43.

NIGER

GDP	1991ε:	fr 670.8bn ($2.37bn)	
	1992ε:	fr 625.3bn ($2.36bn)	
Growth	1991:	-1.4%	1992ε: -6.8%
Inflation	1991:	5.8%	1992ε: -6.1%
Debt	1990:	$1.83bn	1991: $1.65bn

Def bdgt	1991:	fr 6,150m ($21.80m)	
	1992	fr 6,176m ($23.33m)	
FMA	1991:	$0.8m (US)	
$1 = fr	1990: 272.26	1991: 282.11	
	1992: 264.69	1993: 272.00	

fr = francs CFA (Communauté financière africaine)

Population: 8,443,000

	13–17	18–22	23–32
Men:	463,000	377,000	580,000
Women:	469,000	385,000	592,000

TOTAL ARMED FORCES:
ACTIVE: 5,300.
Terms of service: selective conscription (2 years).

ARMY: 5,200.
3 Military Districts.
4 armd recce sqn.
7 inf, 2 AB, 1 engr coy.
EQUIPMENT:
RECCE: 90 AML-90, 9 AML-60, 6 VBL.
APC: 22 M-3.
MORTARS: 81mm: 19 Brandt; 82mm: 17; 120mm: 4 Brandt.
RL: 89mm: 36 LRAC.
RCL: 75mm: 6 M-20; 106mm: 8.
ATK GUNS: 85mm; 90mm.
AD GUNS: 20mm: 39 incl 10 M-3 VDA SP.

AIR FORCE: 100; no cbt ac or armed hel.
TRANSPORT: 2 C-130H, 1 Do-228, 1 Boeing 737-200 (VIP).
LIAISON: 2 Cessna 337D, 2 Do-28D.

PARAMILITARY:
GENDARMERIE: 1,400.
REPUBLICAN GUARD: 2,500.
NATIONAL POLICE: 1,500.

NIGERIA

GDP	1991:	N 288.56bn ($29.12bn)	
	1992:	N 455.52bn ($26.33bn)	
Growth	1991: 4.5%	1992: 4.3%	
Inflation	1991: 13.0%	1992: 44.6%	
Debt	1991: $34.5bn	1992: $26.7bn	
Def exp	1990:	N 2,285m ($284.27m)	
Def bdgt[a]	1992:	N 3,060.0m ($176.9m)	
	1993:	N 4,550.0m ($197.8m)	
$1 = N	1990: 8.038	1991: 9.909	
	1992: 17.298	1993: 23.000	

N = naira
[a] Excl Police and Police Affairs Dept, and Internal Affairs Ministry.

Population: 90,491,000

	13–17	18–22	23–32
Men	5,006,000	4,095,000	6,046,000
Women	4,993,000	4,110,000	6,152,000

TOTAL ARMED FORCES:
ACTIVE: 78,800.
RESERVES: planned; none organised.

ARMY: 62,000.
1 armd div (2 armd bde).
1 composite div (incl 1 mot inf,
1 amph bde, 1 AB bn).
2 mech div (each 1 mech, 1 mot inf bde).
1 AD bde.
Div tps: each div 1 arty, 1 engr bde, 1 recce bn.
EQUIPMENT:
MBT: 157: 60 T-55†, 97 Vickers Mk 3.
LIGHT TANKS: 100 *Scorpion*.
RECCE: 20 *Saladin*, ε120 AML-60, 60 AML-90, 55 *Fox*, 75 EE-9 *Cascavel*.
APC: 10 *Saracen*, 300 4K-7FA, 70 MOWAG *Piranha*.
TOWED ARTY: 105mm: 200 M-56; 122mm: 200 D-30/-74; 155mm: 24 FH-77B.
SP ARTY: 155mm: 25 *Palmaria*.
MORTARS: 81mm: 200.
RCL: 84mm: *Carl Gustav*; 106mm: M-40A1.
AD GUNS: 20mm: some 60; 23mm: ZU-23, 30 ZSU-23-4 SP; 40mm: L/60.
SAM: 48 *Blowpipe*, 16 *Roland*.

NAVY: 7,300 (incl Coast Guard).
BASES: Apapa (Lagos; HQ Western Command), Calabar (HQ Eastern Command), Warri, Port Harcourt.
FRIGATES: 2:
1 *Aradu* (Ge *Meko*-360) with 1 *Lynx* hel, 2 x 3 ASTT; plus 8 x *Otomat* SSM, 1 x 127mm gun.
1 *Obuma* with hel deck; plus 1 x 2 102mm guns.
PATROL AND COASTAL COMBATANTS: 53:
CORVETTES: 2
2† *Erinomi* (UK Vosper Mk 9) with 1 x 2 ASW mor.
(Plus 1 *Otobo* (UK Vosper Mk 3) in Italy since 1988, refitting to PCO).
MISSILE CRAFT: 6:
3 *Ekpe* (Ge Lürssen 57-m) PFM with 4 x *Otomat* SSM.
3 *Siri* (Fr *Combattante*) PFM with 2 x 2 MM-38 *Exocet* SSM.
PATROL, INSHORE: 45:
4 *Makurdi* (UK Brooke Marine 33-m), some 41 PCI‹.
MINE WARFARE: 2 *Ohue* (mod It *Lerici*) MCC.
AMPHIBIOUS: 2 *Ambe* (Ge) LST, capacity 220 tps, 5 tk.
SUPPORT AND MISCELLANEOUS: 6: 1 *Lana* AGHS, 4 tugs, 1 nav trg.

NAVAL AVIATION:
HELICOPTERS: 2 *Lynx* Mk 89 MR/SAR.

AIR FORCE: 9,500;
92 cbt ac†, 15 armed hel†.
FGA/FIGHTER: 3 sqn:
1 with 20 *Alpha Jet* (FGA/trg);
1 with †6 MiG-21MF, †4 MiG-21U, †12 MiG-21B/FR.
1 with †15 *Jaguar* (12 -SN, 3 -BN).
COIN/TRAINING: 23 L-39MS, 12 MB-339AN.
ATTACK HELICOPTERS: †15 Bo-105D.
MR/SAR: 1 sqn with:
HELICOPTERS: 4 Bo-105D.
TRANSPORT: 2 sqn with 5 C-130H, 3 -H-30, 3 Do-228 (VIP), 5 G-222.
PRESIDENTIAL FLT: 1 Boeing 727, 1 *Falcon*, 2 *Gulfstream*, 1 BAe 125-700, 1 BAe 125-1000.
LIGHT TPT: 3 sqn with 18 Do-28D, 18 Do-128-6.
HELICOPTERS: incl 4 AS-332, 3 Bo-105CB, 2 SA-330.
TRAINING:
AIRCRAFT:† 25 *Bulldog*.
HELICOPTERS: 14 Hughes 300.
MISSILES:
AAM: AA-2 *Atoll*.

FORCES ABROAD:
LIBERIA: some 10,000; contingent forms major part of ECOMOG.
THE GAMBIA: 70+ trg team.
SIERRA LEONE: 800.
UN AND PEACEKEEPING:
ANGOLA (UNAVEM II): 4 Observers.
CAMBODIA (UNTAC): 150 civ pol.
IRAQ/KUWAIT (UNIKOM): 7 Observers.
SOMALIA: (UNOSOM II) 558: 1 recce bn.
WESTERN SAHARA (MINURSO): 1 Observer.

PARAMILITARY:
COAST GUARD: Incl in Navy entry.
PORT SECURITY POLICE: ε2,000. About 60 boats and some 5 hovercraft.
SECURITY AND CIVIL DEFENCE CORPS (Ministry of Internal Affairs): Police: UR-416, 70 AT-105 *Saxon*† APC; 1 Cessna 500, 3 Piper (2 *Navajo*, 1 *Chieftain*) ac, 4 Bell (2 -212, 2 -222) hel.
NATIONAL GUARD 7,000 (to be 30,000).

RWANDA

GDP	1991: fr 212.9bn ($1.70bn)	
	1992: fr 222.2bn ($1.67bn)	
Growth	1991: -9.1%	1992ε: -4.8%
Inflation	1991: 19.6%	1992: 9.5%
Debt	1990: $736.2m	1991: $844.6m
Def exp	1991ε: fr 14.69bn ($117.39m)	
	1992ε: fr 15.00bn ($112.49m)	
$1 = fr	1990: 82.60	1991: 125.14
	1992: 133.35	1993: 144.00
fr = Rwanda francs		

Population: 8,045,000

	13–17	18–22	23–32
Men	459,000	375,000	542,000
Women	471,000	387,000	566,000

TOTAL ARMED FORCES: (all services form part of the Army):
ACTIVE: 5,200.

ARMY: 5,000.
1 cdo bn.
1 recce, 8 inf, 1 engr coy.
EQUIPMENT:
RECCE: 12 AML-60, 16 VBL M-11.
APC: 16 M-3.
MORTARS: 81mm: 8.
RL: 83mm: *Blindicide*.
ATK GUNS: 57mm: 6.
AVIATION:
TRANSPORT: 2 C-47, 1 Do-27Q-4.
HELICOPTERS: 2 SE-316.

AIR: 200; 2 cbt ac, no armed hel.
COIN: 2 R-235 *Guerrier*.
TRANSPORT: 2 BN-2, 1 N-2501, 1 *Falcon* 50 (VIP).
LIAISON: 5 SA-316, 6 SA-342L hel.

PARAMILITARY:
GENDARMERIE: 1,200.

OPPOSITION:
RWANDA PATRIOTIC FRONT: 12,000.

FOREIGN FORCES:
FRANCE: 400: 2 inf coy.

SENEGAL

GDP	1991ε: fr 1,593.5bn ($5.65bn)	
	1992ε: fr 1,609.4bn ($6.08bn)	
Growth	1991ε: 2.0%	1992ε: 1.1%
Inflation	1991: -1.8%	1992: -0.01%
Debt	1990: $3.74bn	1991: $3.52bn
Def bdgt	1991: fr 31.0bn ($109.9m)	
	1992: fr 33.5bn ($126.7m)	
FMA[a]	1991: $4.53m (US)	
$1 = fr	1990: 272.26	1991: 282.11
	1992: 264.69	1993: 272.00

fr = francs CFA (Communauté financière africaine)
[a] Incl Economic Support of $3.0m.

Population: 8,132,000

	13–17	18–22	23–32
Men	466,000	382,000	564,000
Women	463,000	385,000	572,000

TOTAL ARMED FORCES:
ACTIVE: 9,700.
Terms of service: conscription, 2 years selective.
RESERVE: exists, no details known.

ARMY: 8,500 (mostly conscripts).
4 Military Zone HQ.

1 armd bn.	1 cdo bn.
6 inf bn.	1 arty bn.
1 AB bn.	1 engr bn.
1 Presidential Guard	3 construction coy.
(horsed).	

EQUIPMENT:
RECCE: 10 M-8, 4 M-20, 30 AML-60, 27 -90.
APC: some 16 Panhard M-3, 12 M-3 half-track.
TOWED ARTY: 18: 75mm: 6 M-116 pack; 105mm: 6 M-101/HM-2; 155mm: ε6 Fr Model-50.
MORTARS: 81mm: 8 Brandt; 120mm: 8 Brandt.
ATGW: *Milan.*
RL: 89mm: LRAC.
AD GUNS: 20mm: 21 M-693; 40mm: 12 L/60.

NAVY: 700.
BASES: Dakar, Casamance.
PATROL AND COASTAL COMBATANTS: 10:
PATROL COASTAL: 2:
1 *Fouta* (Dk *Osprey*) PCC.
1 *Njambuur* (Fr SFCN 59-m) PFC.
INSHORE: 8:
3 *Saint Louis* (Fr 48-m) PCI.
3 *Senegal* II PFI⟨.
2 *Challenge* (UK *Tracker*) PCI⟨.
AMPHIBIOUS: craft only; 2 LCT, 2 LCM.

AIR FORCE: 500;
9 cbt ac, no armed hel.
COIN: 1 sqn with 5 CM-170, 4 R-235 *Guerrier.*
MR/SAR: 1 EMB-111.
TRANSPORT: 1 sqn with 6 F-27-400M, 2 MH-1521.
1 PA-23 (liaison), 1 Boeing 727-200 (VIP).
HELICOPTERS: 2 SA-318C, 2 SA-330, 1 SA-341H.
TRAINING: 2 *Rallye* 160, 2 R-235A.

FORCES ABROAD:
UN AND PEACEKEEPING:
CAMBODIA (UNTAC): 2 Observers.
IRAQ/KUWAIT (UNIKOM): 7 Observers.

PARAMILITARY:
GENDARMERIE: 12 VXB-170 APC.
CUSTOMS: 2 PCI⟨, boats.
OPPOSITION:
Casamance Movement of Democratic Forces.

FOREIGN FORCES:
FRANCE: 1,200: 1 marine inf regt, MR *Atlantic* ac.
1 Air tpt unit (1 C-160 ac, 2 SA-316/319 hel).

SEYCHELLES

GDP	1991ε: SR 1,970.0m ($372.45m)	
	1992ε: SR 1,966.0m ($383.85m)	
Growth	1991: -3.0%	1992ε: -3.5%
Inflation	1991: 1.9%	1992: 3.3%
Debt	1990: $199.0m	1991: $201.1m
Def bdgt	1991: SR 84.20m ($15.92m)	
	1992ε: SR 78.00m ($15.23m)	
FMA[a]	$3.40m (US)	
$1 = SR	1990: 5.34	1991: 5.29
	1992: 5.12	1993: 5.16

SR = Seychelles rupees
[a] Incl Economic Support of $3.30m.

Population: 69,800

	13–17	18–22	23–32
Men	4,100	4,000	6,800
Women	4,000	3,600	6,500

TOTAL ARMED FORCES: (all services
form part of the Army):
ACTIVE: 1,100.

ARMY: 1,100 (incl 300 for Presidential sy).
1 inf bn (3 coy).
2 arty tps.
Spt coy.
EQUIPMENT:†
RECCE: 6 BRDM-2, ε8 *Shorland.*
APC: 4 BTR-152.
TOWED ARTY: 122mm: 3 D-30.
MORTARS: 82mm: 6 M-43.
RL: RPG-7.
AD GUNS: 57mm: S-60.
SAM: 10 SA-7.

PARAMILITARY:
NATIONAL GUARD: 1,000.

COAST GUARD: ε300 incl Air Wing (100) and ε80 Marines.
BASE: Port Victoria.
PATROL AND COASTAL COMBATANTS: 3:
INSHORE: 3:

1 *Andromache* (It Pichiotti 42-m) PFI
1 *Zoroaster* (Sov *Turya*, no foils or TT) PCI.
1 *Zhuk* PFI⟨.
AMPHIBIOUS: craft only; 1 LCT.
AIR WING: 1 cbt ac, no armed hel.
MR: 1 BN-2 *Defender*.
LIAISON: 1 *Citation* 5, 1 R-235E.
HELICOPTERS: 1 *Chetak*.
TRAINING: 1 Cessna 152, 1 *Rallye* 235E.

SIERRA LEONE

GDP	1991: Le 150.18bn ($508.48m)		
	1992ε: Le 252.29bn ($505.18m)		
Growth	1991: 2.6%	1992ε: 1.5%	
Inflation	1991: 102.7%	1992: 65.5%	
Debt	1990: $1,177m	1991: $1,291m	
Def exp	1989ε: Le 308.0m ($5.15m)		
$1 = Le	1990: 151.45	1991: 295.34	
	1992: 499.44	1993: 563.00	

Le = leones

Population: 4,461,000

	13–17	18–22	23–32
Men	237,000	202,000	313,000
Women	236,000	202,000	318,000

TOTAL ARMED FORCES:
ACTIVE: 6,150.

ARMY: ε6,000.
4 inf bn.
2 arty bty.
1 engr sqn.
EQUIPMENT:
APC: 10 MOWAG *Piranha*, 4 *Saracen*.
MORTARS: 81mm.
RCL: 84mm: *Carl Gustav*.
SAM: SA-7.

NAVY: ε150.
BASE: Freetown.
PATROL AND COASTAL COMBATANTS: 3:
2 Ch *Shanghai-II* PFI.
1 Swiftships 32-m PFI.
Plus some 3 modern boats.

PARAMILITARY:
1 SF bn (State Security Division).

FOREIGN FORCES:
NIGERIA: 800.

OPPOSITION:
REVOLUTIONARY UNITED FRONT: ε1,000

SOUTH AFRICA

GDP	1991: R 296.67bn ($107.64bn)		
	1992ε: R 326.30bn ($111.59bn)		
Growth	1991: -0.6%	1992ε: -2.1%	
Inflation	1991: 15.3%	1992: 13.9%	
Debt	1991: $19.4bn	1992: $18.0bn	
Def bdgt	1992: R 9.70bn ($3.32bn)		
	1993: R 9.34bn ($2.93bn)		
$1 = R	1990: 2.586	1991: 2.756	
	1992: 2.924	1993: 3.183	

R = rand

Population: 38,569,000

	13–17	18–22	23–32
Men:	1,954,000	1,771,000	3,079,000
Women:	1,935,000	1,759,000	3,049,000

TOTAL ARMED FORCES:
ACTIVE: 67,500 (of the total 6,000 are Medical
Services); (35,400 white conscripts; 4,200 women).
Terms of service: 12 months National Service for
whites, followed by 12 years' part-time service in
Citizen Force (CF) (in any 2-year period of call-up,
duty not to exceed 60 days trg). Thereafter continued
voluntary service in CF (to age 55) or 5 years with
no commitment in Active Citizen Force Reserve.
Then may be allocated to Commandos to age 55 with
annual commitment of 12 days. Races other than
whites volunteer for Full Time Force, National
Service and Commandos but are not conscripted.
Conscription likely to end when new Constitution
comes into effect.
RESERVES:
Citizen Force 360,000; Active Citizen Force Reserve
135,000; Commandos ε140,000.

ARMY: ε47,000. Full Time Force: 18,000 (12,000
White; 4,000 Black and Coloured; 2,000 women).
National Service: ε29,000.
FULL TIME FORCE (FT):
10 area comd (plus Walvis Bay Comd).
(Area comd consist of HQ and a number of unit HQ
but no tps which are provided when necessary by FT
and CF units.)
1 AB bde (1 FT, 2 CF AB bn, 1 CF arty bn (FT bty)
with 120mm mor).
1 indep mech bde (forms from trg units).
SF: 4 recce coy (3 FT, 1 CF)
7 inf bn (2 coloured, 5 black)
Training/Holding Units (incl armd, inf, arty, engr
etc. Cbt role is to provide sub-units either for area
comd for internal sy tasks or for mech bde for ops).

RESERVES:
CITIZEN FORCE (CF):
1 Corps HQ.
3 div (each 2 armd recce, 2 tk, 2 mech inf, 2 mot inf, 3 arty, 2 AD, 1 engr bn).
(Corps and div HQ have skeleton FT staff).
COMMANDOS:
Some 250 inf coy home defence units.
EQUIPMENT:
MBT: some 250 *Olifant* 1A/-B.
RECCE: 1,600 *Eland*-60/-90, 100 *Rooikat*-76.
AIFV: 1,500 *Ratel*-20/-60/-90.
APC: 1,500 *Buffel*, *Casspir*, 160 *Mamba*.
TOWED ARTY: 350 incl: 25-pdr (88mm): 30 G-1 (in store); 5.5-in (140mm): 75 G-2; 155mm: ε75 G-5, some G-4.
SP ARTY: 155mm: ε20 G-6.
MRL: 127mm: 120 *Bataleur* (40 tube), 60 *Valkiri* 22 SP (24 tube); some *Valkiri* 5 towed.
MORTARS: 81mm: 4,000 (incl some SP); 120mm: + 120.
ATGW: ZT-3 *Swift* (some SP), *Milan*.
RL: 92mm: FT-5.
RCL: 106mm: M-40A1.
AD GUNS: 600: 20mm: GAI, *Ystervark* SP; 23mm: 18 *Zumlac* (ZU-23-2) SP; 35mm: 150 GDF-002 twin.
SAM: SA-7/-14.

NAVY: ε4,500 (ε900 conscripts; ε300 women).
Naval HQ: Pretoria.
Three Flotillas: Submarine, Strike, Mine Warfare.
BASES: Simonstown, Durban (Salisbury Island), Walvis Bay (log spt only).
SUBMARINES: 3 *Maria Van Riebeek* (Mod Fr *Daphné*) with 550mm TT.
PATROL AND COASTAL COMBATANTS: 12:
MISSILE CRAFT: 9:
9 *Jan Smuts* (Is *Reshef*) with 6–8 *Skerpioen* (Is *Gabriel*) SSM (3 in reserve).
INSHORE PATROL: 3 PCI‹.
MINE WARFARE: 8:
4 *Kimberley* (UK '*Ton*') MSC.
4 *Umzimkulu* MHC.
SUPPORT AND MISCELLANEOUS: 8:
1 *Drakensberg* AO with 2 hel and extempore amph capability (perhaps 60 tps and 2–4 small landing craft), 1 *Outeniqua* AO with similar capability as *Drakensberg*, 1 AGHS, 1 diving spt, 1 Antarctic tpt with 2 hel (operated by Dept of Economic Affairs), 3 tugs.

AIR FORCE: 10,000 (3,000 conscripts; ε400 women); 245 cbt ac (14 in store), 14+ armed hel.
1 Territorial Area Comd, AD, Tac Spt, Log, Trg Comd.
FGA: 4 sqn.
2 with 75 *Impala* II;
1 with 29 *Mirage* F-1AZ;
1 with 12 *Cheetah* E;
FTR: 14 *Mirage* F-1 CZ (in store);

TKR/EW: 1 sqn with 4 Boeing 707-320 (ELINT/tkr).
MR: 1 sqn with 8 C-47;
TRANSPORT: 3 sqn:
1 with 7 C-130B;
1 (VIP) with 3 HS-125 -400B (civil registration), 2 *Super King Air* 200, 1 *Citation*.
1 with 19 C-47 (being modified to C-4 TP).
HELICOPTERS: 5 sqn with 63 SA-316/-319 (some armed), 63 SA-330C/H/L.
TRAINING COMMAND (incl OCU): 6 schools:
AIRCRAFT: 12 C-47, *14 *Cheetah* D, 130 T-6G *Harvard* IIA/III (80 to be updated), *115 *Impala* I.
HELICOPTERS: 37 SA-316/SA-330.
MISSILES:
ASM: AS-11/-20/-30.
AAM: R-530, R-550 *Magic*, AIM-9 *Sidewinder*, V-3C *Darter*, V-3A/B *Kukri*.
GROUND DEFENCE: *Rhino* APC: 1 regt (South African Air Force Regt).
RADAR: 2 Air Control Sectors, 3 fixed and some mobile radars.
SAM: 2 wings (2 sqn each), some *Bofors* 40mm L/70, 20 *Cactus* (*Crotale*), SA-8/-9/-13.

MEDICAL SERVICE: 6,000 (2,500 conscripts; 1,500 women). A separate service within SADF, organised territorially.

PARAMILITARY:
SOUTH AFRICAN POLICE: 110,000; Police Reserves: 37,000.

OTHER FORCES:
AFRICAN NATIONAL CONGRESS (ANC): combat wing *Umkhonto we Sizwe:* (MK) perhaps 6,000 trained.
PAN AFRICANIST CONGRESS (PAC): Azanian People's Liberation Army: perhaps 200.
INKATHA (Zulu Freedom Party): Has no mil org, although can turn out many demonstrators/rioters.
AFRIKANER VOLKSFRONT MOVEMENT: Coalition of numerous small right-wing groups. No evidence of any mil potential.
AFRIKANER RESISTANCE MOVEMENT (AWB): Despite military uniforms/badges etc. is more rhetoric than substance. Can call on former SADF personnel for armed support.

HOMELANDS
Each homeland has its own armed forces, not incl in South African data. Currency in all cases is the South African Rand.

BOPHUTHATSWANA
Def bdgt 1990: R 97.89m, 1991: R 132.45m
Population: 2,352,000.

ARMED FORCES: ε3,100.
2 inf bn.
1 AB/SF unit (coy-).
2 indep inf coy gp.
EQUIPMENT:
APC: *Buffel, Mamba.*
MORTARS: 81mm.
AIR FORCE: 150, 3 cbt ac, 2 armed hel.
COIN/TRG: 3 PC-7.
LIAISON: 1 CN 235M, 2 C-212 (1-200, 1-300).
HELICOPTERS: 2 BK-117A3, 2 SA-316/-319 (armed 20mm cannon), 1 SA-365N1 (VIP civil registration).

CISKEI
Def bdgt 1989: R 91.2m (incl police).
Population: 1,025,000.
ARMED FORCES: ε1,000:
1 inf bn.
1 AB coy
EQUIPMENT:
APC: *Buffel.*
MORTARS: 81mm.
AIRCRAFT: 3 BN-2, 1 IAI-1124 (VIP), 2 *Skyvan*, 1 Cessna 152.
HELICOPTERS: 3 BK-117, 1 Bo-105.

TRANSKEI
Def bdgt 1989: R 109.2m. 1990: R 120.4m (incl police).
Population: 4,367,000.
ARMED FORCES: ε2,000:
1 inf bn.
1 SF regt: 1 SF coy, AB coy, mounted sqn, marine gp.
Air wing.
EQUIPMENT:
MORTARS: 81mm.
AIRCRAFT: 1 C-212.
HELICOPTERS: 2 BK-117.

VENDA
Def bdgt 1988: R 45.9m (incl police).
Population: 665,000.
ARMED FORCES: ε900:
2 inf bn.
Engr tp.
Air wing.
EQUIPMENT:
APC: *Buffel.*
MORTARS: 81mm.
AIRCRAFT: 1 C-212-200.
HELICOPTERS: 3 BK-117A3, 1 SA-316B.

TANZANIA

GDP	1991:	sh 690.42bn ($3.15bn)		
	1992:	sh 897.52bn ($3.01bn)		
Growth	1991:	3.8%	1992:	4.0%
Inflation	1991:	22.3%	1992:	22.1%
Debt	1990:	$6.13bn	1991:	$6.46bn

Def bdgt	1992:	sh 32.08bn ($107.74m)		
	1993:	sh 32.40bn ($90.00m)		
$1 = sh	1990:	195.060	1991:	219.16
	1992:	297.71	1993:	360.00
sh = Tanzanian shilling				

Population: 26,918,000

	13–17	18–22	23–32
Men	1,488,000	1,240,000	1,789,000
Women	1,560,000	1,306,000	1,972,000

TOTAL ARMED FORCES:
ACTIVE: 49,500.
Terms of service: incl civil duties, 2 years.
RESERVE: 85,000.

ARMY: 45,000.
3 div HQ.   8 inf bde.
1 tk bde.
2 fd arty bn, 2 AA arty bn (6 bty).
2 mor, 2 ATK bn.   1 engr regt (bn).
EQUIPMENT:†
MBT: 30 Ch Type-59, 35 T-54/-55.
LIGHT TANKS: 30 Ch Type-62, 40 *Scorpion.*
RECCE: 40 BRDM-2.
APC: 66 BTR-40/-152, 30 Ch Type-56.
TOWED ARTY: 76mm: 45 ZIS-3; 85mm: 80 Ch Type-56; 122mm: 20 D-30, 100 M-30; 130mm: 40 M-46.
MRL: 122mm: 58 BM-21.
MORTARS: 82mm: 300 M-43; 120mm: 135 M-43.
RCL: 75mm: 540 Ch Type-52.

NAVY:† ε1,000.
BASES: Dar es Salaam, Zanzibar, Mwanza (Lake Victoria – 4 boats).
PATROL AND COASTAL COMBATANTS: 22:
TORPEDO CRAFT: 4 Ch *Huchuan* PHT⟨ with 2 x 533mm TT.
PATROL, INSHORE: 18:
8 Ch *Shanghai* II PFI, some 10 PCI⟨, (4 in Zanzibar) plus boats.

AIR FORCE: 3,500 (incl ε2,500 AD tps); 24 cbt ac, no armed hel†.
FIGHTER: 3 sqn with 3 Ch J-4, 10 J-6, 11 J-7.
TRANSPORT: 1 sqn with 5 DHC-5D, 1 Ch Y-5, 3 HS-748, 2 F-28, 1 HS-125-700.
HELICOPTERS: 4 AB-205.
LIAISON: 7 Cessna 310, 2 -404, 1 -206 ac; 2 Bell 206B hel.
TRAINING: 2 MiG-15UTI, 5 PA-28.
AD GUNS: 14.5mm: 40 ZPU-2/-4; 23mm: 40 ZU-23; 37mm: 120 Ch Type-55.
SAM: 20 SA-3, 20 SA-6, 120 SA-7.

PARAMILITARY:
POLICE FIELD FORCE: 1,400.

POLICE AIR WING: 1 Cessna U-206 ac; 2 AB-206A, 2 -B, 2 Bell 206L hel, 2 Bell 47G.
POLICE MARINE UNIT: (100) boats only.
CITIZENS' MILITIA: 85,000.

TOGO

GDP	1991ε: fr 425.02bn ($1.51bn)		
	1992ε: fr 446.25bn ($1.69bn)		
Growth	1991ε: -1.0%	1992ε: -9.6%	
Inflation	1991: 0.2%	1992ε: 12.0%	
Debt	1990: $1.29bn	1991: $1.36bn	
Def bdgt	1990ε: fr 13.59bn ($49.90m)		
	1991ε: fr 13.38bn ($47.44m)		
$1 = fr	1990: 272.26	1991: 282.11	
	1992: 264.69	1993: 272.00	

fr = francs CFA (Communauté financière africaine)

Population: 4,032,000

	13–17	18–22	23–32
Men:	218,000	178,000	257,000
Women:	230,000	191,000	291,000

TOTAL ARMED FORCES:
ACTIVE: some 5,250.
Terms of service: conscription, 2 years (selective).

ARMY: 4,800.
2 inf regt:
1 with 1 mech bn, 1 mot bn;
1 with 2 armd sqn, 3 inf coy; spt units (trg).
1 Presidential Guard regt: 2 bn (1 cdo), 2 coy.
1 para cdo regt: 3 coy.
1 spt regt: 1 fd arty bty; 2 AD arty bty; 1 log/tpt/engr bn.
EQUIPMENT:
MBT: 2 T-54/-55.
LIGHT TANKS: 9 *Scorpion.*
RECCE: 6 M-8, 3 M-20, 3 AML-60, 7 -90, 36 EE-9 *Cascavel,* 2 VBL M-11.
APC: 4 M-3A1 half-track, 30 UR-416.
TOWED ARTY: 105mm: 4 HM-2.
MORTARS: 82mm: 20 M-43.
RCL: 57mm: 5 ZIS-2; 75mm: 12 Ch Type-52/-56; 82mm: 10 Ch Type-65.
AD GUNS: 14.5mm: 38 ZPU-4; 37mm: 5 M-39.

NAVY: 200 incl marine inf unit.
BASE: Lomé.
PATROL AND COASTAL COMBATANTS: 2
INSHORE: 2 *Kara* (Fr *Esterel*) PFI⟨.

AIR FORCE: 250; 16 cbt ac, no armed hel.
COIN/TRAINING: 5 *Alpha Jet*, 4 CM-170, 4 EMB-326G, 3 TB-30.

TRANSPORT: 2 *Baron*, 2 DHC-5D, 1 Do-27, 1 F-28-1000 (VIP), 1 Boeing 707 (VIP), 2 Reims-Cessna 337.
HELICOPTERS: 1 AS-332, 2 SA-315, 1 SA-319, 1 SA-330.

PARAMILITARY:
GENDARMERIE (Ministry of Interior): 750; 1 trg school, 2 regional sections, 1 mobile sqn.

UGANDA

GDP	1991: N sh 2,103.89bn ($2.87bn)		
	1992ε: N sh 3,366.24bn ($2.97bn)		
Growth	1991: 4.1%	1992ε: 6.8%	
Inflation	1991: 28.0%	1992: 52.4%	
Debt	1990: $2.64bn	1991: $2.83bn	
Def bdgt	1992ε: N sh 98.42bn ($86.81m)		
	1993ε: N sh 107.90bn ($88.59m)		
FMA	1988: $11.15m (US, Fr)		
$1 = N sh	1990: 428.85	1991: 734.00	
	1992: 1,133.8	1993: 1,218.0	

N sh = Ugandan shillings

Population: 18,080,000

	13–17	18–22	23–32
Men	1,073,000	915,000	1,260,000
Women	1,065,000	911,000	1,302,000

TOTAL ARMED FORCES:
ACTIVE: ε60,000 (incl 200 marine, 200 air).

NATIONAL RESISTANCE ARMY
(NRA): 7 'div' (closer to weak bde).
EQUIPMENT:†
MBT: 5 T-54/-55.
LIGHT TANKS: 20 PT-76.
APC: 20 BTR-60, 4 OT-64 SKOT.
TOWED ARTY: 76mm: 60 M-1942; 122mm: 20 M-1938.
MORTARS: 82mm; 120mm: Soltam.
ATGW: 40 AT-3 *Sagger.*
AD GUNS: 14.5mm: ZPU-1/-2/-4; 23mm: ZU-23; 37mm: M-1939.
SAM: 10 SA-7.
AVIATION: 8 cbt ac†, 5 armed hel.
FGA: 4 MiG-17F.
TRAINING: 3 L-39, 4* S-211, 5 SF-260.
HELICOPTERS:
ATTACK: 5 AB-412.
TRANSPORT: 3 Bell 206, 2 Bell 412, 1 Bell 212.
TRANSPORT/LIAISON: 2 AS-202B, 1-L100, 1 *Gulfstream* II.

PARAMILITARY:
POLICE AIR WING:
AIRCRAFT: 1 DHC-2, 1 DHC-4, 1 DHC-6.
HELICOPTERS: 2 Bell 206, 4 Bell 212.
MARINE UNIT: 10 riverine patrol craft⟨.

OPPOSITION:
HOLY SPIRIT MOVEMENT: ε500

ZAIRE

GDP	1990: Z 6,277.0bn ($8.74bn)	
	1991: Z 133,011.0bn ($8.53bn)	
Growth	1991ε: -7.3%	1992ε: -8.0%
Inflation	1991: 2,153.8%	1992: 4,130.0%
Debt	1990: $10.22bn	1991: $10.71bn
Def bdgt	1993ε: Z 633,563.0bn ($234.65m)	
FMA	1991: $3.3m (US)	
$1 = Z[a]	1990: 718.60	1991: 15,587
	1992: 645,500.0	1993: 2,700,000.0

Z = zaires

[a] Est of the value of the Zaire is difficult due to extremely rapid devaluation since 1990.

Population: 41,000,000

	13–17	18–22	23–32
Men:	2,341,000	1,944,000	2,907,000
Women:	2,298,000	1,916,000	2,942,000

TOTAL ARMED FORCES:
ACTIVE: 49,100 (incl Gendarmerie).

ARMY: 25,000.
8 Military Regions.
1 inf div (3 inf bde).
1 Presidential Guard div.
1 para bde (3 para, 1 spt bn) (2nd forming).
1 SF (cdo/COIN) bde.
1 indep armd bde.
2 indep inf bde (each 3 inf bn, 1 spt bn).
EQUIPMENT:
MBT: 20 Ch Type-59, some 40 Ch Type-62.
RECCE:† 30 AML-60, 30 -90.
APC: 12 M-113, 12 YW-531, 60 M-3.
TOWED ARTY: 75mm: 30 M-116 pack; 85mm: 20 Type 56; 122mm: 20 M-1938/D-30, 15 Type 60; 130mm: 8 Type 59.
MRL: 107mm: 20 Type 63; 122mm: 10 BM-21.
MORTARS: 81mm; 107mm: M-30; 120mm: 50 Brandt.
RCL: 57mm: M-18; 75mm: M-20; 106mm: M-40A1.
AD GUNS: 14.5mm: ZPU-4; 37mm: 40 M-1939/Type 63; 40mm: L/60.
SAM: SA-7.

NAVY:† ε1,300 incl marines.
BASES: Banana (coast), Boma, Matadi, Kinshasa (all river), Kalémié (Lake Tanganyika – 4 boats).
PATROL AND COASTAL COMBATANTS: 4:
INSHORE: 2 Ch *Shanghai* II PFI, 2 Swiftships⟨.
Plus about 10 armed boats.
MARINES: 600.

AIR FORCE: 1,800; 22 cbt ac, no armed hel.
FGA/FIGHTER: 1 sqn with 7 *Mirage* 5M, 1 -5DM.
COIN: 1 sqn with 8 MB-326 GB, 6 -K.
TRANSPORT: 1 wing with 1 Boeing 707-320, 1 BN-2, 8 C-47, 5 C-130H, 3 DHC-5.
HELICOPTERS: 1 sqn with 1 AS-332, 4 SA-319, 4 SA-330.
LIAISON: 6 Cessna 310R, 2 Mu-2J (VIP).
TRAINING: incl 12 Cessna 150, 3 -310, 9 SF-260C ac; 6 Bell 47 hel.

PARAMILITARY:
GENDARMERIE: 21,000 (to be 27,000); 40 bn.
CIVIL GUARD: 10,000; some *Fahd* APC.

ZAMBIA

GDP	1991ε: K 219.7bn ($3.56bn)	
	1992ε: K 615.15bn ($3.08bn)	
Growth	1991ε: -1.8%	1992ε: -2.8%
Inflation	1991: 92.6%	1992ε: 207%
Debt	1990: $7.26bn	1991: $7.28bn
Def exp	1989ε: K 1,529.7m ($118.55m)	
	1990ε: K 2,753.4m ($94.99m)	
$1 = K	1990: 28.985	1991: 61.728
	1992: 200.00	1993: 315.00

K = kwacha

Population: 8,950,000

	13–17	18–22	23–32
Men	516,000	416,000	602,000
Women	512,000	426,000	649,000

TOTAL ARMED FORCES:
ACTIVE: 21,600.

ARMY: 20,000 (incl 3,000 reserves).
3 bde HQ.
1 armd regt (incl 1 armd recce bn).
9 inf bn (3 reserve).
1 arty regt.
1 engr bn.
EQUIPMENT:
MBT: 10 T-54/-55, 20 Ch Type-59.
LIGHT TANKS: 30 PT-76.

RECCE: 88 BRDM-1/-2.
APC: 13 BTR-60.
TOWED ARTY: 76mm: 35 M-1942; 105mm:
18 Model 56 pack; 122mm: 25 D-30; 130mm: 18
M-46.
MRL: 122mm: 50 BM-21.
MORTARS: 81mm: 55; 82mm: 24; 120mm: 14.
ATGW: AT-3 *Sagger*.
RCL: 57mm: 12 M-18; 75mm: M-20; 84mm: *Carl
Gustav*.
AD GUNS: 20mm: 50 M-55 triple; 37mm: 40 M-
1939; 57mm: 55 S-60; 85mm: 16 KS-12.
SAM: SA-7.

AIR FORCE: 1,600; 60† cbt ac, some armed
hel.
FGA: 1 sqn with 12 Ch J-6†;
FIGHTER: 1 sqn with 12 MiG-21 MF†.
COIN/TRAINING: 12 *Galeb* G-2, 16 MB-326GB, 8
SF-260MZ.
TRANSPORT: 1 sqn with 4 An-26, 4 C-47, 2 DC-6B,
3 DHC-4, 4 DHC-5D;
VIP: 1 flt with 1 HS-748, 3 Yak-40.
LIAISON: 7 Do-28.
TRAINING: 2-F5T, 2 MiG-21U†.
HELICOPTERS: 1 sqn with 4 AB-205A, 5 AB-212,
12 Mi-8.
LIAISON HELICOPTERS: 12 AB-47G.
MISSILES:
ASM: AT-3 *Sagger*.
SAM: 1 bn; 3 bty: SA-3 *Goa*.

FORCES ABROAD:
UN AND PEACEKEEPING:
MOZAMBIQUE (ONUMOZ): 846: 1 inf bn.

PARAMILITARY:
POLICE MOBILE UNIT (PMU): 700; 1 bn of 4
coy.
POLICE PARAMILITARY UNIT (PPMU): 700; 1
bn of 3 coy.

ZIMBABWE

GDP	1991: $Z 19.00bn ($US 5.54bn)	
	1992ε: $Z 26.61bn ($US 5.22bn)	
Growth	1991ε: 3.6%	1992ε: -8.0%
Inflation	1991: 24.3%	1992: 46.2%
Debt	1991: $US 3.25bn	1992: $US 3.43bn
Def bdgt	1992: $Z 1,145.0m ($US 224.77m)	
	1993: $Z 1,326.0m ($US 208.82m)	
$1 = $Z	1990: 2.448	1991: 3.428
	1992: 5.094	1993: 6.350

Population: 10,638,000

	13–17	18–22	23–32
Men	626,000	530,000	825,000
Women	625,000	532,000	833,000

TOTAL ARMED FORCES:
ACTIVE: 48,200.
Terms of service: conscription, 12 months reported.

ARMY: 47,000.
7 bde HQ (incl 1 Presidential Guard).
1 armd regt.
26 inf bn (incl 3 Guard, 2 mech, 1 cdo, 2 para, 1
mounted).
1 fd arty regt (incl 2 AD bty).
1 engr spt regt.
EQUIPMENT:
MBT: 30 Ch T-59, 10 Ch T-69.
RECCE: 90 EE-9 *Cascavel* (90mm gun),
20 AML-90 *Eland*.
APC: 8 YW-531, ε40 UR-416, 75 *Crocodile*.
TOWED ARTY: 122mm: 18 Ch Type-60, 12 Ch Type-54.
MRL: 107mm: 18 Ch Type-63.
MORTARS: 81mm: L16; 120mm: 4.
RCL: 106mm: 12 M-40A1.
AD GUNS: 14.5mm: ZPU-1/-2/-4; 23mm: ZU-23;
37mm: M-1939.
SAM: SA-7.

AIR FORCE: 1,200; 43 cbt ac, no armed hel.
FGA/COIN: 2 sqn:
1 with 10 *Hunter* FGA-90, 1 T-81;
1 with 12 *Hawk* Mk 60.
FIGHTER: 1 sqn with 12 Ch J-7.
COIN/RECCE: 1 sqn with 8 Reims-Cessna 337 *Lynx*.
TRAINING/RECCE/LIAISON: 1 sqn with 13 SF-260C/
W *Genet*, 5 SF-260TP.
TRANSPORT: 1 sqn with 6 BN-2, 11 C-212-200 (1
VIP), 10 C-47.
HELICOPTERS: 1 sqn with 2 AB-205, 7 SA-316; 10
AB-412.

FORCES ABROAD:
UN AND PEACEKEEPING:
ANGOLA (UNAVEM II): 8 Observers and 7 civ
pol.
SOMALIA (UNOSOM II): 163.

PARAMILITARY:
ZIMBABWE REPUBLIC POLICE FORCE, incl
Air Wing: 15,000.
POLICE SUPPORT UNIT: 2,000.
NATIONAL MILITIA: 4,000.

2

TABLES AND ANALYSES

Comparisons of Defence Expenditure and Military Manpower 1985–1992[a]

Country	Defence Expenditure[b]									Numbers in armed forces (000)		Estimated reservists[c] (000)	Para-military[d] (000)
	$mil. (1985 prices/rates)			$ per capita (1985)			% of GDP/GNP						
	1985	1991	1992	1985	1991	1992	1985	1991	1992	1985	1992	1992	1992
NATO													
Belgium	2,428	2,335	1,866	246	237	189	3.0	2.3	1.8	91.6	80.7	228.8	n.a.
Denmark	1,259	1,299	1,256	246	255	247	2.2	2.1	2.0	29.6	29.2	72.5	n.a.
France	20,780	22,223	21,898	377	393	385	4.0	3.5	3.4	476.6	431.7	374.0	94.6
Germany	19,922	20,122	19,252	262	263	251	3.2	2.5	2.4	478.0	447.0	904.7	25.4
Greece	2,331	1,889	1,903	235	186	186	7.0	5.4	5.6	201.5	159.3	406.0	26.5
Iceland													
Italy	9,733	11,167	10,690	170	195	186	2.3	2.1	2.0	385.1	354.0	584.0	244.8
Luxembourg	38	55	57	104	151	156	0.9	1.2	1.2	0.7	0.8	n.a.	0.6
Netherlands	3,884	3,819	3,818	268	258	257	3.1	2.5	2.4	101.6	89.1	144.3	3.9
Norway	1,797	1,797	2023	433	427	480	3.1	3.1	3.3	37.0	32.7	285.0	0.7
Portugal	654	924	874	64	88	82	3.1	3.2	2.9	73.0	58.3	190.0	49.8
Spain	3,969	3,813	3,735	103	95	93	2.4	1.7	1.7	320.0	217.0	498.0	64.6
Turkey	1,649	3,386	3,423	33	60	59	4.5	5.1	4.7	630.0	560.3	1,107.0	71.1
United Kingdom	23,791	22,330	20,726	421	394	366	5.2	4.3	4.0	327.1	293.5	353.0	n.a.
NATO Europe (Total)	92,235	95,159	91,520	238	239	228	-	-	-	3,151.8	2,753.6	5,147.3	582.0
Canada	7,566	7,559	7,790	298	283	288	2.2	2.0	2.0	83.0	84.0	29.7	n.a.
US	258,165	222,101	242,717	1,079	891	964	6.5	4.9	5.3	2,151.6	1,913.8	1,784.1	68.0
Total NATO	357,966	324,820	342,027	548	481	503	-	-	-	5,386.4	4,751.4	6,961.1	650.0
Russia	n.a.	52,510	39,680	n.a.	443	268	n.a.	11.0	9.9	n.a.	2,720.0	3,000.0	520.0
Other Europe													
Albania[e]	189	103	35	64	31	10	4.1	3.7	2.3	40.4	40.0	155.0	5.0
Armenia[e]	n.a.	n.a.	147	n.a.	n.a.	43	n.a.	n.a.	2.5	n.a.	ε50.0	300.0	30.0
Austria	892	751	725	118	99	96	1.4	0.9	0.9	54.7	52.0	200.0	n.a.
Azerbaijan[e]	n.a.	303	190	n.a.	51	26	n.a.	2.3	1.9	n.a.	ε30.0	500.0	20.0
Belarus[e]	n.a.	n.a.	1,647	n.a.	n.a.	158	n.a.	n.a.	4.5	n.a.	ε125.0	350.0	n.a.
Bosnia[e]	n.a.	n.a.	n.a.	n.a.	n.a.	n.a.	n.a.	n.a.	n.a.	n.a.	ε40.0	n.a.	n.a.
Bulgaria[e]	5,808	1,790	1,310	648	197	144	14.1	7.0	5.7	148.5	107.0	472.5	34.0
Croatia[e]	n.a.	n.a.	4,330	n.a.	n.a.	913	n.a.	n.a.	24.1	n.a.	105.0	100.0	50.0
Cyprus[e]	87	185	279	131	265	395	3.6	5.0	7.1	10.0	8.0	88.0	3.7
Czechoslovakia[f]	4,849	906	789	313	58	50	4.7	2.7	2.2	203.3	145.8	495.0	10.5

Country													
Estonia	n.a.	n.a.	37	n.a.	n.a.	24	n.a.	n.a.	0.6	n.a.	2.0	n.a.	n.a.
Finland	807	1,103	1,140	164	220	226	1.5	1.8	1.9	36.5	32.8	700.0	4.4
Georgia[e]	n.a.	n.a.	333	n.a.	n.a.	60	n.a.	n.a.	3.2	n.a.	3.0	500.0	3.0
Hungary	3,782	1,240	1,180	355	117	112	7.2	4.0	3.5	106.0	80.8	192.0	22.3
Ireland	320	283	283	90	76	75	1.8	1.2	1.2	13.7	13.0	16.1	n.a.
Latvia	n.a.	n.a.	40	n.a.	n.a.	15	n.a.	n.a.	0.5	n.a.	2.6	n.a.	12.0
Lithuania	n.a.	n.a.	55	n.a.	n.a.	15	n.a.	n.a.	0.7	n.a.	7.0	12.5	n.a.
Macedonia	n.a.	n.a.	n.a.	n.a.	n.a.	n.a.	n.a.	0.9	n.a.	n.a.	ε20.0	80.0	n.a.
Malta	14	14	18	39	38	52	1.4	n.a.	1.1	0.8	1.7	n.a.	n.a.
Moldova[e]	n.a.	617	228	n.a.	173	51	n.a.	6.1	2.1	n.a.	12.0	300.0	4.0
Poland[e]	5,760	2,170	2,279	155	57	60	3.0	2.0	2.3	319.0	296.5	435.2	38.0
Romania[e]	1,395	1,150	955	61	51	42	1.4	3.0	2.9	189.5	200.0	593.0	74.8
Slovenia	n.a.	n.a.	341	n.a.	n.a.	177	n.a.	n.a.	1.9	n.a.	15.0	85.0	4.5
Sweden	3,192	3,126	2,861	382	363	330	2.7	2.7	2.5	65.7	60.5	709.0	n.a.
Switzerland	1,930	1,788	1,743	299	275	268	1.9	1.6	1.6	20.0	19.6	625.0	n.a.
Ukraine[e]	n.a.	4,530	4,320	n.a.	108	82	n.a.	3.3	3.8	n.a.	230.0	1,000.0	6.0
Yugoslavia[e]	1,692	3,490	3,760	160	320	342	3.8	18.0	27.8	n.a.	135.0	400.0	n.a.
Middle East													
Algeria	953	1,971	1,599	44	65	59	1.7	2.9	2.7	170.0	139.0	150.0	52.2
Bahrain	151	223	238	362	452	466	3.5	5.4	5.6	2.8	6.2	6.2	9.4
Djibouti	32	31	38	94	76	89	9.2	9.6	n.a.	3.0	3.2	n.a.	1.8
Egypt	4,143	3,587	3,427	85	65	60	8.5	6.7	6.0	445.0	410.0	604.0	374.0
Iran[e]	14,223	4,270	n.a.	319	80	n.a.	8.6	7.1	n.a.	555.0	528.0	350.0	57.0
Iraq[e,g]	12,868	7,490	n.a.	809	381	n.a.	25.9	21.1	11.1	520.0	382.5	650.0	24.8
Israel	5,052	3,331	3,984	1,193	677	783	21.2	9.8	11.2	142.0	175.0	430.0	6.0
Jordan	602	677	586	172	160	133	15.9	14.0	62.4	70.3	99.4	35.0	9.0
Kuwait	1,796	12,815	10,185	1,050	6,500	5,000	9.1	149.7	5.0	12.0	11.7	19.0	5.5
Lebanon	n.a.	20	18	n.a.	7	7	n.a.	5.5	n.a.	17.4	36.8	40.0	7.0
Libya[g]	1,350	1,177	n.a.	249	218	n.a.	6.2	6.3	3.1	73.0	85.0	n.a.	5.5
Mauritania	52	28	25	31	14	14	6.5	3.5	4.0	8.5	9.6	100.0	4.7
Morocco	641	672	692	27	27	27	5.4	3.8	17.5	149.0	195.5	n.a.	40.0
Oman	2,157	1,328	1,498	874	943	874	20.8	16.3	n.a.	21.5	35.7	n.a.	4.0
Qatar	n.a.	781	n.a.	n.a.	1,830	n.a.	n.a.	14.0	11.8	6.0	7.5	n.a.	n.a.
Saudi Arabia	17,693	35,438	14,535	1,830	3,285	1,533	19.6	32.5	n.a.	62.5	157.0	n.a.	11.0
Somali Republic	46	n.a.	9	9	n.a.	9	4.6	n.a.	n.a.	62.7	n.a.	n.a.	n.a.
Sudan	207	n.a.	532	9	n.a.	18	3.4	3.4	15.8	56.6	82.5	n.a.	15.0
Syria	3,483	3,095	n.a.	245	182	n.a.	16.4	16.6	n.a.	402.5	408.0	400.0	12.5
Tunisia	417	323	355	58	34	40	5.0	3.3	3.3	35.1	35.0	n.a.	13.5
UAE[g]	2,043	2,291	4,249	1,363	818	1,363	7.6	7.7	14.6	43.0	54.5	n.a.	n.a.
Yemen	792	910	682	81	52	81	8.9	13.1	9.3	n.a.	63.5	40.0	40.0

| Country | Defence Expenditure[b] | | | | | | | | | Numbers in armed forces (000) | | Estimated reservists[c] (000) | Para-military[d] (000) |
| | $mil. (1985 prices/rates) | | | $ per capita (1985) | | | % of GDP/GNP | | | | | | |
	1985	1991	1992	1985	1991	1992	1985	1991	1992	1985	1992	1992	1992
Central Asia													
Afghanistan	287	n.a.	n.a.	16	n.a.	n.a.	8.7	n.a.	n.a.	47.0	45.0	n.a.	75.0
Bangladesh	169	251	234	2	2	2	1.2	1.5	1.3	91.3	107.0	n.a.	55.0
India	6,263	8,123	7,550	8	10	9	3.0	2.8	2.5	1,260.0	1,265.0	655.0	967.5
Kazakhstan	n.a.	n.a.	1,480	n.a.	n.a.	435	n.a.	n.a.	3.8	n.a.	63.0	n.a.	n.a.
Kyrgyzstan	n.a.	n.a.	47	n.a.	n.a.	11	n.a.	n.a.	0.7	n.a.	8.0	11.0	n.a.
Myanmar (Burma)	228	298	269	6	7	6	3.3	3.6	3.1	186.0	286.0	n.a.	50.3
Nepal	36	35	36	2	2	2	1.5	1.2	1.1	25.0	35.0	n.a.	28.0
Pakistan	2,076	3,056	3,252	22	27	27	6.9	7.8	7.7	482.8	580.0	513.0	268.0
Sri Lanka	228	348	350	14	20	20	3.8	5.0	4.9	37.7	105.9	12.0	30.0
Tajikistan	n.a.	n.a.	203	n.a.	n.a.	39	n.a.	n.a.	3.7	n.a.	6.0	n.a.	n.a.
Turkmenistan	n.a.	n.a.	433	n.a.	n.a.	120	n.a.	n.a.	4.8	n.a.	34.0	n.a.	n.a.
Uzbekistan	n.a.	n.a.	n.a.	n.a.	n.a.	n.a.	n.a.	n.a.	n.a.	n.a.	15.0	n.a.	0.7
East Asia and Australasia													
Australia	4,668	4,207	4,335	296	250	254	3.0	2.4	2.4	70.7	67.9	29.2	n.a.
Brunei	205	n.a.	259	915	n.a.	969	6.0	n.a.	9.8	4.1	4.5	n.a.	2.7
Cambodia	n.a.	43	58	n.a.	5	7	n.a.	3.5	4.8	35.0	135.0	n.a.	n.a.
China	19,850	20,575	22,364	19	18	19	5.1	5.1	5.0	3,900.0	3,030.0	1,200.0	1,200.0
Fiji	14	28	25	20	38	33	1.2	2.6	2.0	2.7	5.0	5.0	n.a.
Indonesia	2,341	1,931	2,003	14	11	11	2.8	1.5	1.4	278.1	283.0	400.0	180.0
Japan	13,151	16,645	16,901	109	134	136	1.0	1.0	1.0	243.0	246.0	48.4	12.0
Korea North	4,156	5,328	5,087	204	231	214	23.0	24.4	25.7	838.0	1,132.0	540.0	115.0
Korea South	4,399	6,440	7,189	107	146	160	5.1	3.6	3.8	598.0	633.0	4,500.0	3.5
Laos	n.a.	n.a.	728	n.a.	n.a.	179	n.a.	n.a.	6.1	53.7	37.0	n.a.	n.a.
Malaysia	1,764	1,670	2,315	113	95	128	5.6	3.8	4.8	110.0	127.5	44.3	22.7
Mongolia	233	264	257	123	121	113	11.0	4.6	5.9	36.5	15.5	200.0	10.0
New Zealand	454	444	295	140	132	116	2.0	1.9	1.6	12.4	10.9	8.5	n.a.
Papua New Guinea	34	40	40	10	10	10	1.5	1.8	1.8	3.2	3.8	n.a.	n.a.
Philippines	474	850	831	9	14	13	1.4	2.2	2.2	114.8	106.5	131.0	90.0
Singapore[g]	1,188	1,370	1,619	464	506	590	6.7	4.9	5.4	55.5	55.5	292.0	111.6
Taiwan	4,136	5,011	5,373	213	240	253	6.6	4.8	4.8	444.0	390.0	1,657.5	25.0
Thailand	1,517	1,726	1,937	29	30	33	4.1	2.6	2.7	235.3	283.0	500.0	80.2
Vietnam	2,400	1,870	1,750	39	27	25	19.4	12.0	11.0	1,027.0	857.0	n.a.	n.a.
Latin America													
Argentina	1,889	1,410	1,427	62	46	43	2.9	1.5	1.7	108.0	65.0	377.0	17.0

Country													
The Bahamas	n.a.	48	45	n.a.	183	167	n.a.	2.4	2.3	0.5	0.9	n.a.	n.a.
Belize[g]	4	9	8	24	47	43	1.8	3.0	2.6	0.6	0.7	0.5	n.a.
Bolivia	127	121	115	20	16	15	2.0	0.7	1.9	27.6	31.5	n.a.	16.2
Brazil	1,731	1,840	1,643	13	7	11	0.8	0.7	0.7	276.0	296.7	1,515.0	243.0
Chile	1,242	791	672	103	61	51	7.8	3.4	2.7	101.0	91.8	45.0	27.0
Colombia	424	1,315	1,162	15	42	36	1.6	2.8	2.4	66.2	139.0	116.9	85.0
Costa Rica	29	48	47	11	16	16	0.7	1.0	0.9	n.a.	n.a.	n.a.	7.5
Cuba[g]	1,597	1,491	1,272	158	140	117	9.6	5.0	5.0	161.5	175.0	1435.0	19.0
Dominican Republic	51	n.a.	59	8	n.a.	8	1.1	n.a.	1.4	22.2	22.2	n.a.	15.0
Ecuador[g]	284	422	401	30	39	35	1.8	2.3	2.2	42.5	57.5	100.0	0.2
El Salvador	252	161	116	53	30	21	4.4	2.4	1.7	41.7	43.7	n.a.	6.0
Guatemala	197	126	144	25	14	15	1.8	1.0	1.1	31.7	44.6	4.7	14.1
Guyana	45	n.a.	n.a.	57	n.a.	n.a.	9.7	n.a.	n.a.	6.6	2.0	2.0	1.5
Haiti	31	21	35	5	3	5	1.5	1.1	2.1	6.9	7.4	n.a.	n.a.
Honduras	72	61	63	16	12	12	2.1	1.5	1.5	16.6	16.8	60.0	5.5
Jamaica	18	19	17	8	8	7	0.9	0.7	0.7	2.1	3.4	0.9	n.a.
Mexico	1,241	n.a.	951	16	n.a.	10	0.7	n.a.	0.5	129.1	175.0	300.0	n.a.
Nicaragua	637	180	165	199	46	56	14.2	11.5	10.9	62.9	14.7	n.a.	n.a.
Panama	97	76	74	44	31	30	2.0	1.4	1.2	12.0	11.7	n.a.	8.0
Paraguay	60	101	108	16	24	25	1.3	1.9	2.0	14.4	16.5	45.0	84.0
Peru	641	561	604	34	27	28	4.5	4.1	3.8	128.0	112.0	188.0	n.a.
Suriname	23	17	13	59	41	29	2.4	4.4	3.4	2.0	1.8	n.a.	4.8
Trinidad and Tobago	73	n.a.	80	62	n.a.	62	1.0	n.a.	1.3	2.1	2.7	n.a.	1.2
Uruguay[g]	128	121	153	42	39	48	2.5	2.2	2.7	31.9	24.7	n.a.	n.a.
Venezuela[g]	824	2,705	1,525	48	136	74	1.3	4.3	3.6	49.0	75.0	8.0	n.a.
Africa													
Angola[g]	1,147	2,732	n.a.	131	280	n.a.	28.4	35.5	n.a.	49.5	e127.5	n.a.	7.0
Benin	21	13	16	5	3	3	1.8	1.1	1.3	3.5	4.4	n.a.	2.0
Botswana[g]	22	108	61	21	88	48	2.5	3.2	3.1	3.0	6.1	n.a.	1.0
Burkina Faso	34	62	83	4	7	9	3.3	3.4	4.3	4.0	7.2	n.a.	1.8
Burundi	35	n.a.	n.a.	7	n.a.	n.a.	3.0	n.a.	n.a.	5.2	5.7	n.a.	1.5
Cameroon	159	94	63	16	8	5	1.9	1.6	0.8	7.3	7.7	n.a.	4.0
Cape Verde	n.a.	2	2	n.a.	5	5	n.a.	0.9	2.0	1.2	1.3	n.a.	n.a.
Central African Republic	37	n.a.	n.a.	n.a.	n.a.	n.a.	5.9	n.a.	n.a.	2.3	3.8	n.a.	2.7
Chad[g]	56	n.a.	16	7	n.a.	4	2.6	n.a.	2.6	12.2	25.2	n.a.	4.5
Congo	76	n.a.	21	30	n.a.	28	1.1	n.a.	3.8	8.7	10.9	n.a.	1.4
Côte d'Ivoire	n.a.	n.a.	62	8	n.a.	3	n.a.	n.a.	0.8	7.7	7.1	12.0	5.5
Equatorial Guinea	n.a.	n.a.	39	n.a.	n.a.	n.a.	n.a.	n.a.	n.a.	2.2	1.3	n.a.	2.0
Ethiopia[g]	447	370	811	11	8	17	9.4	8.9	20.1	217.0	n.a.	n.a.	n.a.
Gabon[g]	79	100	n.a.	79	90	n.a.	2.2	3.7	n.a.	2.4	4.8	n.a.	4.8
The Gambia[g]	2	n.a.	n.a.	3	n.a.	n.a.	1.2	n.a.	n.a.	0.5	0.8	n.a.	n.a.

| Country | Defence Expenditure[b] | | | | | | | | | Numbers in armed forces (000) | | Estimated reservists[c] (000) | Para-military[d] (000) |
| | $mil. (1985 prices/rates) | | | $ per capita (1985) | | | % of GDP/GNP | | | | | | |
	1985	1991	1992	1985	1991	1992	1985	1991	1992	1985	1992	1992	1992
Ghana	63	67	75	5	5	5	1.0	0.7	0.8	15.1	7.2	n.a.	n.a.
Guinea	n.a.	n.a.	n.a.	n.a.	n.a.	n.a.	n.a.	n.a.	n.a.	9.9	9.7	n.a.	2.6
Guinea-Bissau	11	n.a.	n.a.	12	n.a.	n.a.	3.1	n.a.	n.a.	8.6	7.2	n.a.	2.0
Kenya	256	212	236	13	9	9	4.3	2.7	2.8	13.7	24.4	n.a.	5.0
Lesotho	15	n.a.	18	10	n.a.	10	2.4	n.a.	5.3	n.a.	2.0	n.a.	n.a.
Liberia	28	n.a.	n.a.	13	n.a.	n.a.	2.6	n.a.	n.a.	6.8	n.a.	n.a.	n.a.
Madagascar	54	40	35	5	3	3	2.3	1.2	1.1	21.1	21.0	n.a.	7.5
Malawi[g]	21	18	20	3	2	2	1.9	1.1	1.4	5.3	10.8	1.0	6.0
Mali[g]	30	35	35	4	4	4	2.7	2.9	2.9	5.0	7.4	n.a.	4.8
Mauritius[f]	n.a.	7	7	n.a.	6	6	n.a.	0.4	0.4	n.a.	n.a.	n.a.	1.3
Mozambique	239	270	267	17	17	16	9.4	9.5	10.2	15.8	50.2	n.a.	5.0
Namibia	n.a.	50	45	n.a.	40	35	n.a.	3.3	2.9	n.a.	7.5	n.a.	n.a.
Niger	12	16	15	2	2	2	0.8	0.9	1.0	2.2	3.3	n.a.	4.5
Nigeria	1,251	987	912	16	11	10	1.3	0.8	0.7	94.0	76.0	n.a.	12.0
Rwanda	33	109	101	5	16	14	1.7	6.9	6.8	5.2	5.2	n.a.	1.2
Senegal	63	70	75	10	9	9	2.4	1.9	2.1	9.7	9.7	n.a.	2.0
Seychelles	8	10	9	123	152	135	5.0	4.3	4.0	1.2	1.3	n.a.	n.a.
Sierra Leone	5	n.a.	n.a.	1	n.a.	n.a.	0.4	n.a.	n.a.	3.1	6.2	n.a.	n.a.
South Africa	1,951	2,062	1,654	83	80	63	3.6	3.6	3.0	106.4	72.4	360.0	100.0
Tanzania[g]	280	442	365	13	17	14	4.4	4.6	3.6	40.4	46.8	10.0	1.4
Togo	19	28	n.a.	6	8	n.a.	2.6	3.1	n.a.	3.5	5.3	n.a.	0.8
Uganda	53	125	151	4	7	8	2.7	2.6	2.9	18.0	70.0	n.a.	n.a.
Zaire[g]	81	n.a.	235	3	n.a.	8	2.7	n.a.	2.9	26.0	29.1	n.a.	25.0
Zambia[g]	295	71	60	44	9	7	4.1	3.8	2.6	16.2	24.0	n.a.	1.4
Zimbabwe	284	311	214	34	31	20	6.0	6.0	4.3	42.0	48.5	n.a.	17.0

For some countries, 1985 military expenditure and percentage of GDP data are from *ACDA Military Expenditures and Arms Transfers, 1990.*

Notes:

[a] In this edition total defence expenditures and per capita defence expenditures represent national definitions and are given in 1985 prices and in 1985 dollars. Where possible, exchange rates have been taken from the IMF, otherwise published average annual exchange rates have been calculated. The consumer price indices have been taken from the IMF where possible, or, where necessary, constructed from known inflation rates.

[b] Some military expenditures include internal security expenditures; in other cases these and research costs are borne by other ministries' budgets,

[c] Normally, only men within 5 years of their active service period are included,

unless a country entry specifies a different parameter. Home Guard manpower has not been included.

[d] Part-time and reserve paramilitary forces are not included.

[e] The difficulty in calculating suitable exchange rates makes conversion to dollars and international comparison imprecise and unreliable. It is important to refer to individual country entries and to the local-currency figures for defence expenditures and the size of the economy.

[f] Czechoslovakia did not split into the Czech Republic and Slovakia until 1 January 1993. Full data for 1991–93 not available. Data refers to 1990–91.

[g] Full data for 1991–93 not available. Data refers to 1990–91.

Nuclear Developments

This analysis details nuclear developments of an international nature that have taken place over the last 12 months. Changes to national nuclear capability are recorded in the text preceding the relevant regional section.

The most important arms control agreement reached in the last 12 months was the Accord signed on 3 January 1993, by Presidents Bush and Yeltsin on the Treaty on Further Reduction and Limitation of Strategic Offensive Arms (START II). The most important development however, was the failure of Ukraine to ratify the START I treaty. As a result, START I implementation cannot begin nor can START II be considered for ratification.

START I and Ukraine

In May 1992 the US and the four nuclear-armed republics of the former Soviet Union (Russia, Ukraine, Belarus and Kazakhstan) signed a protocol to the START treaty in which the republics agreed to assume the obligations of the USSR under the treaty. In addition Ukraine, Belarus and Kazakhstan undertook to join the Nuclear Non-Proliferation Treaty (NPT) as non-nuclear states as soon as possible.

The Kazakhstan parliament was the first to ratify START I on 2 July 1992 but it has not yet joined the NPT. The US Senate ratified on 1 October 1992; the Russian Federation on 4 November 1992 and Belarus on 4 February 1993. Belarus has also joined the NPT. Only Ukraine has not ratified. The Russian ratification was accompanied by the statement: 'The Russian Federation effects the exchange of ratification instruments following the accession of the Republics of Belarus, Kazakhstan and Ukraine to the treaty on the Non-Proliferation of Nuclear Weapons . . .'

At first it was thought that Ukraine was delaying its ratification as a bargaining chip to obtain more economic aid under the guise of meeting the costs of dismantling and eliminating the nuclear weapons based on its territory. Ukraine also expects to be guaranteed its share of the money raised by the sale of fissile material recovered from nuclear warheads after they have been dismantled. The US has already pledged $175 million towards the cost of eliminating these weapons but Ukraine is claiming that the total cost would be $2.8 billion. The US has also announced that it is prepared to pay some $10bn spread over the next 20 years for 500 tons of highly enriched uranium from all four nuclear republics. No contract has yet been signed, however, as Russia has not yet agreed that Ukraine, Belarus and Kazakhstan should receive an equitable share of the proceeds. When the US Secretary of Defense, Les Aspin, visited Ukraine in June 1993 he did not promise extra money but offered US assistance to build safe and secure storage sites for nuclear warheads in Ukraine to be kept under international supervision until agreement was reached over elimination.

Ukraine is also seeking security guarantees from Russia, the US and UK (as depositories of the NPT). It claims that the three states have already given a similar guarantee to defend Austria and that the US guarantees Japan and South Korea against nuclear attack. Both the US and UK have pointed out their commitment not to use nuclear weapons against non-nuclear states, which would include Ukraine, once it joined the NPT as a non-nuclear state. Russia is not prepared to give separate guarantees to Ukraine beyond those set out in the Commonwealth of Independent States agreements (Alma-Ata protocol of 21 December 1991, Treaty of Collective Security of 15 May 1992).

Ukraine may have thought its continued possession of nuclear weapons was a means of strengthening its hand in the negotiations on the division of the Black Sea Fleet between Ukraine and Russia and perhaps, further in the future, any claim which Russia might make to ownership of the Crimea and other potential border problems. Indeed, Ukraine realises that possession of nuclear weapons gives it a deterrent capability and a degree of diplomatic strength with which it would not otherwise be credited. As the former chair of the British Campaign for Nuclear Disarmament, Bruce Kent, has pointed out, we should not be surprised by Ukrainian policy as it mirrors exactly the belief of British political leaders of all parties that nuclear weapons add to security (by providing a powerful deterrent) and increase influence in the international field; and also the UK government's justification, in the words of the Permanent Under Secretary of the British MOD, Sir Michael Quinlan, that nuclear weapons have 'a unique value in war prevention'.

Whether Ukraine has, or will be able to acquire operational control of the strategic nuclear weapons on its territory is open to question. The Russians have claimed they will be able to do so in six to nine months; it must be only a question of time, however, before Ukraine possesses the ability to prevent them being fired, if they cannot do so already, and over a rather longer period, to be able to fire them themselves. Re-targeting the weapons will prove the most difficult, but this cannot be an insuperable task as Ukraine inherited two of three Soviet plants capable of manufacturing ballistic missile guidance systems. There have been various unconfirmed reports on the serviceability of ICBM in Ukraine. It would be surprising if the SS-24 could not be maintained satisfactorily as they are manufactured in Ukraine.

On 3 July 1993 the Ukrainian parliament proclaimed its ownership of nuclear weapons on its territory. However, it also declared its intention not to use or threaten to use them, and its intention to be a non-nuclear state.

START II

START II, signed by Russia and the US on 3 January 1993 confirms the Joint Understanding signed by Presidents Bush and Yeltsin at the Washington Summit on 17 June 1992. By the year 2003 both countries are to have reduced their strategic warheads to between 3,000 and 3,500. The Treaty in the main uses the rules established for START I for matters such as definitions and procedures for verification and elimination, although there are some important differences.

In addition to reducing the total number of warheads, START II limits submarine-launched ballistic missiles (SLBM) to 1,750 for each side and bans intercontinental ballistic missiles (ICBM) with multiple independently targetable re-entry vehicles (MIRV). The Treaty deadline of 2003 will be brought forward to 2000 if agreement on a programme of assistance for the reduction process (i.e. US aid for the Russian programme) can be reached within one year of the treaty coming into force. There is also an earlier seven-year deadline by which time the overall total of warheads must have been reduced to between 3,800 and 4,250 MIRVed ICBM to 1,200 warheads with only 650 warheads on heavy ICBM (in practice, this means the Soviet SS-18) and SLBM warheads to 2,160.

There are three important changes to START I conditions. The first concerns the counting rules for bombers. In START I bombers not armed with Air Launched Cruise Missiles (ALCM) counted as one warhead (regardless of how many armaments they could carry), 150 US ALCM-equipped bombers counted as ten warheads each and 180 Soviet bombers counted as eight warheads each; ALCM-armed bombers in excess of these numbers would be counted as having the maximum number for which that type of bomber was equipped. The new START II rule is that all bombers will be attributed with the number of warheads that that type of aircraft is equipped to carry. The agreed attributions include: B-52H 20 warheads; B-2 16; *Bear*-H6 six, *Bear*-H16 16.

Another variation to START I regarding bombers is that each side may reorientate to a non-nuclear role up to 100 bombers which have never been specified as ALCM-equipped and thus are not countable. Such bombers are to be based separately from nuclear bombers; nuclear armaments may not be stored closer than 100km from their bases; they may not be used for training in nuclear roles, and they must be distinguishable from nuclear bombers. The US plans to reorient its B-1B force, but there has not yet been a Russian announcement regarding reorientation.

The second change concerns 'downloading', or the formal reduction of the number of warheads carried by a type of ICBM or SLBM. The relevant START I rule allows the 'downloading' of no more than four warheads from any one missile. As START II only allows single-warhead ICBM to be deployed, the Russians would have had to eliminate all their ICBM equipped with six or more warheads. The rule has been relaxed in START II to allow each party to 'download' by not more than five warheads, 105 of one type of existing ICBM. In practice this means that 105 of the 107 Russian SS-19 ICBM, which has six MIRV, can be 'downloaded' rather than scrapped (there are also 130 SS-19 in Ukraine). All Russian and Ukrainian SS-24 and US MX ICBM, both of which have 10 MIRV, must be eliminated. So, too, must all SS-18 ICBM (204 in Russia, 104 in Kazakhstan) as START II bans all heavy ICBM.

The third change concerns the elimination of silo launchers of heavy ICBM which is required by START I. START II allows the conversion of 90 heavy ICBM silo launchers for use as silo launchers for single-warhead ICBM. This will allow Russia to convert mobile SS-25 ICBM into silo-launched ICBM, should it wish to do so, without incurring the added cost of constructing fresh silos.

The US Secretary of Defense has stated in his 'Annual Report to the President and the Congress' that the US post-START II strategic nuclear force will comprise: 500 *Minuteman* II ICBM downloaded from three to one warhead; a fleet of 16 *Trident*-armed SSBN, of which there are now 14 in service and whose SLBM will be downloaded by around 50% of its maximum warhead load; 95 B-52H bombers attributed with 20 ALCM each, and 20 B-2 with 16 warheads each. There have been no Russian announcements about future force posture; however, it can be expected to include 105 downloaded SS-19 ICBM, 340 or more SS-25 mobile ICBM, some of which may be deployed in silos and which include the 80 SS-25 currently deployed in Belarus. Russia can keep its two most modern classes of SSBN in service (6 *Typhoon* each with 20, ten-warhead, SS-N-20 SLBM; and 7 *Delta-IV* with 16, four-warhead, SS-N-23 SLBM) and meet the START II limit of 1,750 SLBM warheads. The air-delivered arm of the strategic forces will probably only comprise Tu-95H *Bear* bombers armed with ALCM; the more modern Tu-160 *Blackjack* bombers may not be handed over by Ukraine. The tables show the strategic forces of the US and former Soviet Union at three stages: today, post-START I and post-START II.

Non-Proliferation

In addition to the five nuclear-declared states – China, France, Russia (and temporarily three other republics of the former Soviet Union), the UK and the US – it is widely recognised that Israel has nuclear weapons and that both India and Pakistan, if they do not already hold nuclear weapons, have the capability to produce them in a short time. None of these three states has signed the Nuclear Non-Proliferation Treaty (NPT). Iraq, which had signed the NPT, was found to have embarked on a wide-scale programme of nuclear weapons development and is now credited with having been within two to three years of being able to produce a crude bomb.

The latest report by the International Atomic Energy Agency (IAEA) to the UN on its monitoring of Iraq's compliance with the requirements for it to dismantle its nuclear capability states: 'renewed resistance by the Iraqi authorities to providing clarification as to their nuclear-material declarations makes impossible a conclusion by the IAEA that all such material has been declared and presented to the IAEA'. Nevertheless, it must be the case that Iraq at present does not have the capability to produce nuclear weapons; and on 30 June 1993 a UNSCOM inspector said, 'From a technical point of view, we don't think there is much left to find'.

This situation could change once UN sanctions are lifted, although those countries whose industrial companies are suspected of having contributed in any way to Iraq's nuclear programme will be extra vigilant in monitoring exports.

On 24 March 1993 President de Klerk of South Africa admitted that his country had made six nuclear warheads between 1974, when the decision to embark on a nuclear programme was taken, and 1990. The first device had been completed in 1980 and all six were eliminated between 1990 and 1991. The surprise lay not so much in the content of the statement but that one had been made at all. Many remember the incident of the 'flash' over the South Atlantic in September 1979 which was strongly suspected to have been, but was never proved to be, a nuclear explosion. There were also strong suspicions that there was Israeli involvement in the South African programme. In his statement President de Klerk categorically denied that there had been any nuclear tests and that any other country had been involved in the weapons development. South Africa joined the NPT in July 1991 and has a safeguard agreement with the IAEA, whose inspectors reported to the IAEA board in September 1992 that nothing had been found to suggest that South Africa's declared inventory of materials and facilities was not complete. South Africa had first been suspected of having a nuclear weapons programme in the late 1970s, when what looked like a weapons test site in the Kalahari Desert was spotted on satellite imagery.

Two signatories of the NPT – North Korea and Iran – are currently strongly suspected of having nuclear weapons programmes. However, no evidence has been found.

North Korea

It can be argued that North Korea had good cause to embark on a nuclear weapons programme. First, in the 1970s it was revealed that South Korea had an embryo nuclear programme which was abandoned at US insistence, while the US continued to station nuclear weapons in South Korea until 1991 when they were withdrawn. Second, it must have been obvious for some time that the relative economic strengths of the two Koreas meant that the North could never match the defence expenditure of the South.

North Korea commissioned an experimental 5-megawatt gas graphite reactor at Yongbyon near Pyongyang in 1985/86, at which time it signed the NPT but did not agree to IAEA safeguards. At maximum efficiency the reactor could have produced between four and seven kilogrammes (kgs) of plutonium a year, but North Korea claims the fuel rods have never been replaced. Two larger reactors are under construction: a 50-megawatt reactor, also at Yongbyon, scheduled to be in operation in 1995 and estimated to produce 40 to 60 kgs of plutonium a year; and a 200-megawatt reactor at Taechon to be completed in 1996 and able to produce 160–200 kgs of plutonium a year. Both these reactors are of old design, employing the gas graphite principle, and lack many of the safety features of light-water reactors which North Korea could have acquired from the Soviet Union. However, they can be more easily operated to produce plutonium. A large plant, described as a 'radiochemical' laboratory but suspected of being a reprocessing plant, is under construction at Yongbyon. It is considered that when complete, in four to five years time, it could handle the spent fuel from all three reactors; it is thought that some reprocessing has already taken place.

North Korea completed an IAEA safeguards agreement in September 1991, but the first IAEA inspection did not take place until June 1992. In December 1991 North and South Korea signed an agreement which committed them not to produce, possess or use nuclear weapons, or to reprocess nuclear fuel. The US agreed to open its military bases for inspection so long as similar inspections were allowed in the North.

At the first IAEA inspection North Korea admitted that it had reprocessed very small quantities of plutonium in 1975 and in 1990. Since then the IAEA has found several discrepancies between North Korean declarations and the findings of the inspections and strongly suspects that more plutonium has been reprocessed than has been declared. Two facilities had been built close to the suspected processing plant at Yongbyon and the IAEA believed the North Koreans were storing spent fuel and treating nuclear waste there. The IAEA invoked its newly established challenge inspection procedure but was refused access – North Korea claimed that the facilities were conventional military sites. In March 1993 North Korea announced its intention of withdrawing from the NPT, for which 90 days' warning must be given. The UN Security Council adopted Resolution 825 on 11 May 1993, calling on North Korea to reconsider its decision and to comply with its IAEA safeguard agreement commitments. After considerable political pressure mainly exerted by the US, North Korea suspended its withdrawal on 11 June but said there would be no change to the monitoring rules.

No conclusions have been reached on North Korea's actions. The simplest, but not necessarily the correct, reason is that the government has something to hide and is perhaps, despite US warnings, far closer to producing a nuclear weapon than had been supposed. Another suggestion is that North Korea, having suspended its nuclear programme, may have thought that it could achieve the permanent cancellation of the US–South Korean annual reinforcement exercise, *Team Spirit* and gain other political advantages. But in that case why refuse access to the disputed sites?

Iran

The second country strongly suspected of embarking on a nuclear weapons programme is Iran. It is certainly re-equipping its armed forces with modern aircraft, submarines and medium-range ballistic missiles. With the example of Iraq in mind, it would not be unreasonable to expect Iran to follow the same course. On 27 March 1992 CIA Director, Robert Gates, reiterated to the US House Armed Services Committee a CIA claim that 'Iran was trying to acquire a nuclear weapons capability'. However, there is, as yet, no published proof of that claim.

The Shah of Iran initiated a nuclear-power programme in the 1960s which forecast the construction of 23 power stations. Iran joined the NPT in 1970 and an IAEA full-scope safeguards agreement came into force in 1974. A US-supplied 5-megawatt reactor started up in 1967. At the time of the revolution in 1979 construction by a West German firm of two 1,300-megawatt reactors was well under way and continued during the Iran–Iraq War, despite several Iraqi air attacks. In 1991, however, the German government decided not to complete the reactors. Iran has secured agreements to purchase a 300-megawatt reactor from China and two 440-megawatt reactors from Russia. The IAEA has made a number of visits to Iran and found no evidence of a military nuclear programme.

There have been numerous press reports of Iranian recruitment of nuclear scientists and engineers from the former Soviet Union, and of attempts to purchase nuclear-related components (in one case the sale of hardware from Argentina was blocked after US pressure). There are even claims that Iran has obtained a number of warheads from former Soviet republics. There are suspicions of nuclear cooperation between Iran and Pakistan. However, none of this can be proved. On the other hand, it can be argued that Iran's reserves of oil and gas do not warrant the proposed investment in nuclear reactors purely to provide energy.

It seems clear, however, that if Iran does have a nuclear weapons programme, it is still in its early stages. In all probability Iran cannot hope to produce its own nuclear weapons before 2000 at the earliest. That said, it is actively procuring weapons systems – aircraft and missiles – capable of delivering nuclear munitions.

Testing

With the exception of China, the nuclear powers are observing a self-imposed moratorium on nuclear testing. Russia was the first to announce a moratorium on 5 October 1991, when President Gorbachev ended Soviet nuclear tests for one year. In October 1992 Russia extended the moratorium until July 1993; in June 1993 the Foreign Minister, Andrei Kozyrev, said that 'Russia would not be the first to end the moratorium, but to expect any nuclear power to refrain from testing if others resumed would be unreasonable'. Russia may find it difficult to carry out tests as its main test site at Semipalatinsk has been closed by the Kazakh authorities. The only other sites are on Novaya Zemlya where any attempt to re-start testing will be bitterly opposed by environmentalists as well as neighbouring states in northern Europe. France announced a moratorium on April 1992 to last until the end of the year. The US moratorium, to last nine months, took effect on 1 October 1992 the day before President Bush signed the Energy and

Water Development Appropriations Act which included a policy for restricting and ending nuclear tests. The Act stipulates that after 30 September 1996 no further tests are to take place unless a foreign state conducts a test after this date. In each of three years until then a maximum of five safety-related and one reliability-related test may take place each year. However, the President must certify that the reliability tests are necessary. The UK, which carries out tests only at the US test-site in Nevada, is barred from testing by the US moratorium. Of the five annual safety-related tests allowed, one may be carried out by the UK. On 3 July 1993 President Clinton extended the moratorium for a further 15 months until 1 October 1994. France also announced that it would maintain its moratorium. The last nuclear test carried out was in May 1992 when China exploded a megaton bomb, a yield far higher than that agreed to in the US–Soviet Threshold Test Ban Treaty which limited their tests to yields of no more than 150 kilotons.

The US President is also required to submit to Congress a plan for negotiating a Comprehensive Test Ban Treaty (CTBT). The UK government has said on several occasions that it supports the long-term goal of a CTBT. Given earlier Soviet statements, Russia is likely also to support a CTBT.

The debate over the need to test nuclear weapons is unlikely to be won outright by either side. Those in favour of testing argue that safety and reliability, both militarily essential, can only be ensured by regular testing while the CTBT lobby claim that scientific evidence shows that safety tests are no longer necessary. Reliability tests only prove that the tested warhead was reliable. The lobby also points out that the non-nuclear countries showed their dissatisfaction over continued testing at the 1990 NPT review conference and further testing could well put renewal of NPT, due in 1995, in jeopardy.

The first session of the NPT Preparatory Meeting took place in New York from 11 to 14 May 1993. It was not a success, agreement was only reached on the dates of future preparatory meetings and of the Review and Extension Conference which will be held from 17 April to 12 May 1995. There is some concern that the US aim of obtaining an indefinite extension of the NPT may not be achieved.

US Strategic Nuclear Forces

	Current Situation: 1 June 1993 — Using START II counting rules			Post /START I — Using START I counting rules					Post/START II[a] — Using START II counting rules			
	Launchers deployed	Warheads/ launchers	Total warheads	Total Launchers deployed	Launcher limit	Warheads/ launchers	Total warheads	Warhead limit	Launchers deployed	Warheads/ launchers	Total warheads	Warhead limit
ICBM												
Minuteman II	261	1	261	–								
Minuteman III	507	3	1,521	500		1–3[b]	944		500	1	500	
MX	50	10	500	50		10	500		–	–	–	
Sub-total ICBM	818		2,282	550			1,444		500		500	
SLBM												
Trident C-4	336	8	2,688	192		8	1,536		192	4	768[c]	
Trident D-5	144	8	1,152	240		8	1,920		240	4	960[c]	
Sub-total SLBM	480		3,840	432			3,456		432		1728	1750
Total Ballistic Missiles	1,298		6,122	982			4,900	4,900	932		2,228	
Bombers												
ALCM-Equipped												
B-52H	94	20	1,880	95		10	950		95	20	1,900	
Non-ALCM												
B-52G	36	12	432	–			–		–		–	
B-1B	94	16	1,504	96		1	96		–		–	
B-2A	2	16	32	20		1	20		20	16	320	
Total Bombers	226		3,848	211			1,066		115		2,220[d]	
GRAND TOTAL	1,524		9,970	1,193	1,600		5,966	6,000	1,047		4,448	3,500

[a] Annual Report to the President and the Congress 1993.
[b] Downloading sufficient to meet treaty limits.
[c] Assumes that all *Trident* SLBM are downloaded to 4 warheads.
[d] Presumably bomber numbers will be reduced to meet START II limits.

Strategic Nuclear Forces: Russia, Belarus, Kazakhstan, Ukraine

		Current Situation: 1 June 1993 (Russia, Belarus, Kazakhstan, Ukraine) Using START II counting rules			Post/START I (a possible Russian deployment) Using START I counting rules					Post/START II (a possible Russian deployment) Using START II counting rules			
		Launchers deployed	Warheads/launchers	Total warheads	Launchers deployed	Launcher limit	Warheads/launchers	Total warheads	Warhead limit	Launchers deployed	Warheads/launchers	Total warheads	Warhead limit
Heavy ICBM	SS-18	302	10	3,020	154	154	10	1,540	1,540	–		–	–
Mobile ICBM	SS-24	36	10	360	36		10	360		–		–	
	SS-25	340	1	340	340		1	340		340	1	340	
Sub-total Mobile ICBM		376		700	376			700	1,100	340		340	
Other ICBM	SS-11	100	1	100	–			–		–		–	
	SS-13	40	1	40	–			–		[40	1	40][a]	
	SS-17	40	4	160	–			–		[40	1	40][a]	
	SS-19	290	6	1,740	152		6	912		105		105	
	SS-24	56	10	560	10		10	100		–		–	
Sub-total ICBM		1,204	–	6,320	692			3,252		525		525	
SLBM	SS-N-6	64	1	64	–			–		–		–	
	SS-N-8	268	1	268	–			–		–		–	
	SS-N-18	224	3	672	–			–		[32	3	96][a]	
	SS-N-20	120	10	1,200	120		10	1,200		120	10	1,200	
	SS-N-23	112	4	448	112		4	448		112	4	448	
Sub-total SLBM		788	–	2,652	232		–	1,648		264		1,744	1,750
Total Ballistic Missiles		1,992		8,972	924	–		4,900	4,900	789		2,269	
Bombers **ALCM-Equipped**	Tu-95H16	62	16	992	40		8	320		40	16	640	
	Tu-95H6	27	6	162	27		8	216		27	6	162	
	Tu-160	20	12	240	–			–		–		–	
Non-ALCM	Tu-95B/G	61	1/2	90	61		1/2	90		61	1/2	90	
Total Bombers		170		1,484	128	–		626		128		892	
GRAND TOTAL		**2,162**		**10,456**	**1,052**	**1,600**	–	**5,526**	**6,000**	**917**		**3,161**	**3,500**

[a] These weapons may already have been eliminated to meet START I requirements. The square brackets [ ] are for emphasis and the figures therein are included in totals.

Nuclear-Capable Delivery Vehicles: NATO, Nuclear-Armed Republics of the Former Soviet Union, and China

Many delivery systems are dual-capable; we show the total number in service, notwithstanding that a high proportion may not be assigned a nuclear role. Maximum aircraft loadings are given, though often fewer weapons may be carried. Some loadings differ from those under SALT/START counting rules. All ground-launched tactical nuclear weapons (SSM and artillery) have been withdrawn to store in Russia and the US. We no longer list delivery systems of other states. All sea-launched weapons (incl SLCM), other than SLBM, have been withdrawn from ships, and air-delivered weapons from ships and shore-based maritime air stations of the US, Russia and NATO. All former Soviet tactical nuclear weapons have been moved to Russia.

Category and type	Year deployed	Range (km)[a]	Throw-weight[b]	CEP (m)[c]	Launcher total	Munition/ warhead	Yield per warhead[d]	Remarks
UNITED STATES								
LAND-BASED								
Strategic								
ICBM								
LGM-30F *Minuteman* II	1966	11,300	8	370	261	Mk 11C; W-56	1.2MT	10 with Emergency Rocket Communications System
LGM-30G *Minuteman* III	1970	14,800	11.5	220	200	3 x Mk 12 MIRV; W-62	170KT	
	1980	12,900	11.5	220	307	3 x Mk 12A MIRV; W-78	335KT	
LGM-118 *Peacekeeper* (MX)	1986	11,000	39.5	100	50	10 x Mk 21 MIRV; W-87	300 or 400KT	In mod *Minuteman* silos
Tactical:[e] All warheads for ground-launched weapons to be destroyed.								
M-109 155mm SP (3 mod)	1963	18/24/30	–	n.k.	2,442	M-454 shell; W-48 under 2KT }	0.1KT	Some 400 warheads remain
M-198 155mm towed	1979	14	–	n.k.	675			
M-114 155mm towed	1940	19.3	–	n.k.	550			
SEA-BASED								
Strategic								
SLBM								
[UGM-73A *Poseidon* C-3	1971	4,600	20	450	128	10 x Mk 3 MIRV; W-68	40KT	Could be installed in 7 non-operational SSBN]
UGM-93A *Trident* C-4	1980	7,400	15	450	336	8 x Mk 4 MIRV; W-76	100KT	Installed in 17 SSBN
UGM-133A *Trident* D-5	1989	12,000	28	90	144	8 x Mk 5 MIRV; W-76/-88	300–475KT	Installed in 6 SSBN (W-88 production halted)
Tactical:[e] (all nuclear warheads withdrawn from ships/submarines)								
SLCM								
BGM-109A *Tomahawk*[g]	1983	2,500	n.k.	80	–	TLAM-N; W-80	200KT	74 submarines, 58 surface combatants have launchers (350 warheads produced)

For notes, see p. 244.

AIR

	Year	Radius of action (km)[a]	Max speed (mach)	Weapon load (000 kg)	Missile total	Max ordnance load[i]	
Strategic							
Long-range bombers[e]							
B-52C/D/E/F	–	–	–	–	–	—	217 awaiting conversion/ elimination
B-52G	1959	4,600	0.95	29.5	36	Internal: 12 bombs (B-61/-83) or 8 *Harpoon*	In conventional role but could re-role. Plus 110 ac awaiting conversion/elimination and 2 test ac
B-52H	1962	6,140	0.95	29.5	94	Internal: 11 bombs (B-61/-83) or 8 SRAM or 8 ALCM. External: 12 ALCM	Plus 1 test ac
B-1B	1986	4,580	1.25	61	94	Internal: 8 ALCM plus 8 SRAM; or 24 SRAM; or 24 B-61 bombs	Plus 2 test ac. Not equipped for ALCM, and to be re-roled as conventional bombers
B-2	1993	5,840	1(–)	ε18	2	Internal: 16 SRAM; or 8 SRAM plus 8 B-61/-83 bombs; or 16 bombs	Plus 6 test aircraft
Tactical[e]							
Land-based							
F-111E/F	1967	1,750	2.2/2.5	13.1	152	3 bombs (B-61)	Plus 172 in store
F-4E	1969	840	2.4	5.9	17	3 bombs (B-61)	Plus some 700 in store
F-16	1979	550/930	2+	5.4	1,685	1 bomb (B-61)	USMCR
A-4M	1970	1,230	0.9	4.5	34	1 bomb (B-61)	
Carrier-borne							
A-6E	1963	1,250	0.9	8.1	342	3 bombs (B-61)	Incl 10 USMC
F/A-18	1982	850	2.2	7.7	762	2 bombs (B-61)	Incl 288 USMC, some in store

	Year	Range (km)[a]	Max speed (mach)	Weapon load (000 kg)	Missile total	Munition/ warhead	Yield per warhead[a]	
ALCM								
AGM-86B[e]	1982	2,400	0.66	–	1,200	W-80	170–200KT	
AGM-129 ACM	1991	3,000	n.k.	–	300	W-80	170–200KT	Production limited to 460
ASM								
AGM-69A (SRAM)	1972	56 (low) 220 (high altitude)	3.5	–	1,000	W-69	170KT	

BOMBS[h]

Type	Yield per warhead[d]	Wpn stockpile	Remarks
B-61 (strategic)	100–500KT(s)	900	In-flight yield selection and fusing, hard target penetration
B-61 (tactical)	1–345KT	1,525	
B-83	1–2MT	650	Replaced B-28, B-53

NATO (excluding US)[j]

Category and type	Year deployed	Range (km)[a] / Radius of action (km)[a]	CEP (m)[c]	Max speed (mach)	Weapon load (000 kg)	Launcher total	Munition/ warhead	Yield per warhead[d]	Remarks
LAND-BASED									
Intermediate-range									
IRBM									
SSBS S-3D	1980	3,500	n.k.			18	TN-61	1MT	Fr
Short-range									
Hadès							AN-51	15 or 25KT	Fr 15 in store
SEA-BASED									
Strategic									
SLBM									
Polaris A-3 TK	1967	4,600	900			48	3 x MRV; W-58 (*Chevaline*)	200KT	UK. In 3 SSBN
M-4	1985	5,000	n.k.			80	6 x MRV; TN-70/-71	150KT	Fr. In 5 SSBN
AIR[e]									
Tactical									
Land-based									
F-104G/S	1958	830		2.2	1.8	106	1 B-61 bomb		It (18), Tu (88)
F-4E/F	1967/73	840		2.4	5.9	339	1 B-61 bomb		Ge (150), Gr (54), Tu (135)
F-16	1982	930		2+	5.4	523	1 B-61 bomb		Be (72), Dk[k] (63), Gr (36), Nl (166), No[k] (60), Tu (126)
Mirage IVP	1986	930		2.2	9.3	15	1 *ASMP*		Fr. Plus 13 in store
Mirage 2000N	1988	690		2.2	6.3	45	1 *ASMP*		Fr

For notes, see p. 244.

Category and type	Year deployed	Radius of action (km)[a]	Max speed (mach)	Weapon load (000 kg)	Launcher total	Max ordnance load	Remarks
Jaguar A	1974	850	1.1	4.75	171	1 or 2 AN-52 bombs	Fr (117) (no longer in nuclear role) UK (54 plus 29 in store)
Tornado IDS UK	1981	1,390	0.92	6.8	441	n.k.	Ge (219), It (79 plus 15 in store), (143 plus 20 in store)
Carrier-borne							
Super Etendard	1980	650	0.98	2.1	38	ASMP	Fr. Plus 19 in store.
Sea Harrier	1980	460/750	0.98	2.3	37	1 (or 2) WE-177 bombs	UK
Maritime							
Buccaneer	1963	1,410	0.85	7.3	23		UK. Plus 4 in store.

		Range (km)[a]			Launcher total	Munition/ warhead	Yield per warhead[a]	Remarks
ASM								
ASMP	1986	100–300	2	n.a.	n.a.		45KT	Fr
Bombs								
AN-22	—	—	—	—	—		15, 300KT	Fr
WE-177	—	—	—	—	—		10, 200, 400KT	UK

NUCLEAR-ARMED FORMER REPUBLICS OF THE SOVIET UNION

Category and type	Year deployed	Throw-weight[b]	CEP (m)[c]	Launcher total	Munition/ warhead	Yield per warhead[a]	Remarks
LAND-BASED							
Strategic							
ICBM							
SS-11 (RS-10) mod 2	1973	13,000 }	12	100	single RV	1MT	Russia
Sego mod 3	1975	10,600			3 x MRV	100–300KT	Russia
SS-13 (RS-12) mod 2	1968	9,400	6	40	single RV	600KT	Russia
Savage							
SS-17 (RS-16) mod 3	1982	10,000	25.5	40	4 x MIRV	500KT	Russia
Spanker							

	Year deployed	Range (km)[a]	Throw-weight[b]	CEP (m)[c]	Launcher total	Munition/ warhead	Yield per warhead[d]	Remarks
SS-18 (RS-20) mod 4	1982	11,000	88	250 }	} 302	10 x MIRV	500KT	104 Kazakhstan, 198 Russia
Satan mod 5	–	ε9,000	88	n.k.		10 x MIRV	750KT	
SS-19 (RS-18) mod 3 *Stiletto*	1982	10,000	43.5	300	290	6 x MIRV	550KT	170 Russia, 120 Ukraine.
SS-24 (RS-22) *Scalpel*	1987/8	10,000	40.5	ε200	92	10 x MIRV	100KT	36 rail-based, Russia, 56 silo-based: 10 Russia, 46 Ukraine
SS-25 (RS-12M) *Sickle*	1985/6	10,500	10	ε200	340	single RV	750KT	Road-mobile. 260 Russia, 80 Belarus
Short-range[e] (All tactical warheads located in Russia)								
SSM								
FROG-7 (Luna)	1965	70	–	400 }	} 465	–	200KT	
SS-21 (Tochka) Scarab	1978	120	–	30		–	100KT	
SS-1c (R-17) *Scud D*[e]	1965	300	–	450	300	–	KT range	
GLCM								
SS-C-1b *Sepal*	1962	450	–	n.k.	40	–	350KT	Coastal defence. Nuclear role doubtful
Artillery[f]								
2A36 152mm towed	1978	27	–	n.k.	1,500	–	2–5KT	
2S5 152mm SP	1980	27	–	n.k.	850	–	2–5KT	
D-20 152mm towed	1955	17.4	–	n.k.	1,500	–	2KT	
2S3 152mm SP	1972	27	–	n.k.	2,000	–	under 5KT	
2S7 203mm SP	1975	18+	–	n.k.	240	–	2–5KT	
2S4 240mm SP mor	1975	12.7	–	n.k.	120	–	n.k.	
SAM								
SH-11 mod *Galosh*	1983/4	320	–	–	36	–	n.k. }	} Deployed Moscow only.
SH-08 *Gazelle*	1984	80	–	–	64	–	10KT	
SA-10 *Grumble*[e]	1981	100	–	–	2,400	–	n.k.	
SA-5 *Gammon*[e]	1967	300	–	–	1,800	–	n.k.	

For notes, see p. 244.

Category and type		Year deployed	Range (km)[a]	Throw-weight[b]	CEP (m)[c]	Launcher total	Munition/warhead	Yield	Remarks
SEA-BASED									
Strategic									
SLBM									
SS-N-6 *Serb*	mod 1	1968	2,400	6.5	1,300	64	single RV	500KT–1MT	In 4 SSBN
	mod 3	1974	3,000	6.5	1,300		2 MRV	ε500KT	
SS-N-8 *Sawfly*	mod 1	1972	7,800	11	1,500	268	single RV	800KT	In 21 SSBN
	mod 2	1973	9,100	11	900		2 MRV	800KT	
SS-N-18	mod 1	1977	6,500	16.5	1,400	224	3 MIRV	20KT	In 14 SSBN
Stingray	mod 2	1977	8,000	16.5	900		single RV	450KT	7 warheads originally attributed in START, now 'downloaded' to 3.
	mod 3	1978	6,500	16.5	900		7 MIRV	100KT	
SS-N-20 *Sturgeon*		1981	8,300	25.5	500	120	10 MIRV	100KT	In 6 SSBN
SS-N-23 *Skiff*		1985	8,300	28	900	112	4 MIRV	100KT	In 7 SSBN
Tactical (all warheads withdrawn from ships/submarines)									
SLCM									
SS-N-3 *Shaddock*[e]		1962	450	–	n.a.	56	–	350KT	In some 7 SSGN/SSG[f], 1 CG, 2 DDG
SS-N-7 *Starbright*[e]		1968	n.a.	–	n.a.	40	–	200KT	In 5 SSGN
SS-N-9 *Siren*[e]		1968/9	100	–	n.a.	248	–	200KT	In 4 SSGN, 36 corvettes
SS-N-12 *Sandbox*[e]		1973	550	–	n.a.	84	–	350KT	In some 3 SSGN[f], 1 CVV, 3 CG
SS-N-19 *Shipwreck*[e]		1980	550	–	n.a.	312	–	500KT	In 10 SSGN, 3 CGN, 1 CVV
SS-N-21 *Sampson*		1987	3,000	–	150	ε112	–	200KT	In 3 SSGN, 13 SSN (ε4 per SSN)
SS-N-22 *Sunburn*[e]		1981	400	–	n.k.	224	–	200KT	In 16 DDG, 24 corvettes
SS-NX-24		–		–	n.k.	ε12	–	n.k.	In trials SSGN
ASW									
SS-N-14 *Silex*[e]		1974	55	–	n.a.	290	–	1 to 5KT	In 1 CGN, 21 CG, 30 frigates
SS-N-15 *Starfish*		1982	45	–	n.k.	n.k.	–	about 5KT	In 30 SSN
SUW-N-1 (FRAS-1)		1975	30	–	n.k.	2	–	5KT	In 1 CGH
Type 53-68 HWT		1970	14	–	–	n.k.	torpedo	20KT	Usable from all 533mm TT
Type 65 HWT		1981	50	–	–	n.k.	torpedo	20KT	Usable from all 650mm TT
Mines		n.k.	–	–	n.k.	–	–	5–20KT	

		Radius of action (km)[a]	Max speed (mach)	Weapon load (000 kg)	Weapon total	Max ordnance load	
AIR							
Strategic							
Long-range bombers							
Tu-95 *Bear B/G*	1956	5,690	0.9	11.3	61	4 bombs/1 and 2 AS-4 ASM	Russia. Plus 8 test ac
Bear H6					27	6 AS-15 ALCM	Kazakhstan
Bear H16					62	16 AS-15 ALCM	13 Kazakhstan, 27 Russia, 22 Ukraine
Tu-160 *Blackjack*	1988	7,300	2.3	16.3	20	12 AS-15 ALCM	Ukraine
Medium-range bombers[e]							
Tu-16 *Badger*	1955	2,180	0.91	9	63	1–2 AS-5/-6 ALCM, 1 bomb	Incl 33 Navy
Tu-22 *Blinder*	1962	1,500	1.4	10	65	1 AS-4 ALCM, 1 bomb	Incl 15 Navy
Tu-26 (Tu-22M) *Backfire*	1974	4,430	1.92	12	320	1–2 AS-4/-16 ALCM, 2 bombs	Incl 140 Navy
Tactical[e]							
Land-based							
MiG-27 *Flogger D/J*	1971	390/600	1.7	4.5	640	2 bombs	
Su-17 *Fitter D/H/K*	1974	430/680	2.1	4	445	2 bombs	
Su-24 *Fencer*	1974	320/1,130	2.3	8	580	2 bombs	
Maritime ASW[e]							
Tu-142 *Bear* F	1972	1,510	0.83	10	50	2 bombs	8 hrs endurance at radius of action.
Il-38 *May*	1970	1,700	0.64	7	36	ε2 bombs	8 hrs endurance at radius of action. Total endurance 15 hrs
Be-12 *Mail*	1965	600	0.5	10	89	2 bombs	8 hrs endurance at radius of action. Total endurance 12 hrs

		Range (km)[a]	Max speed (mach)	Weapon load (000 kg)	Weapon total	Yield[d]	
ALCM							
AS-4 *Kitchen*	1962	300	3.3	n.k.	n.k.	1MT	
AS-6 *Kingfish*	1977	300	3	n.k.	n.k.	350KT–1MT	
AS-15 *Kent*	1984	1,600	0.6	n.k.	n.k.	250KT	
AS-16 *Kickback*	1989	200	n.k.	n.k.	n.k.	350KT	
Bombs	n.k.	–	–	–	n.k.	Strategic: 5, 20, 50MT Tactical: 250, 350KT	
Depth-charges	n.k.	–	–	–	n.k.		Known to exist; no details available

For notes, see p. 244.

	Year deployed	Range (km)[a]	CEP (m)[c]	Launcher total	Munition/warhead	Yield per warhead[d]	Remarks
CHINA							
LAND-BASED							
Strategic							
ICBM							
CSS-4 (DF-5)	1981	15,000	n.k.	4	single RV	5MT	
CSS-3 (DF-4)	1978/9	7,000	n.k.	10	single RV	3MT	
IRBM							
CSS-2 (DF-3)	1970	2,700	n.k.	60	single RV	2MT	
SEA-BASED							
Strategic							
SLBM							
CSS-N-3 (JL-1)	1983/4	2,200–3,000	n.k.	12	–	ε2MT	Installed in 1 SSBN
AIR							
Strategic[g]							
Medium-range bombers		Radius of action (km)[a]	Max speed (mach)	Weapon load (000kg)	Maximum ordnance load		
H-6	1968/9	2,180	0.91	9	up to 120	ε2 bombs	n.k.

Chinese *tactical* nuclear weapons have been reported, but no details are available.

SOURCES: include Cochrane, Arkin and Hoenig, *Nuclear Weapons Databook*, vol. I (Cambridge, MA: Ballinger, 1984); Cochrane, Arkin, Norris and Hoenig, *Nuclear Weapons Databook*, vol. II (Cambridge, MA: Ballinger, 1987); Hansen, *US Nuclear Weapons, The Secret History* (New York: Orion, 1988); *Bulletin of the Atomic Scientists* (various issues); Treaty between the US and USSR on the Reduction and Limitation of Strategic Offensive Arms.

Notes

[a] Ranges and aircraft radii of action in km; for nautical miles, multiply by 0.54. A missile's range may be reduced by up to 25% if max payload is carried. Radii of action for ac are in normal configuration, at optimum altitude, with a standard warload, without in-flight refuelling. When two values are given, the first refers to a low–low-low mission profile and the second to a high-low-high profile.

[b] Throw-weight concerns the weight of post-boost vehicle (warhead(s), guidance systems, penetration aids and decoys). No definition of the term is given in the START Treaty document. Throw-weight is expressed in terms of kg (100s).

[c] CEP (circular error probable) = the radius of a circle around a target within which there is a 50% probability that a weapon aimed at that target will fall.

[d] Yields vary greatly; figures given are estimated maxima. KT range = under 1MT; MT range = over 1MT. Yield, shown as 1–10KT means the yield is between these limits. Yields shown as 1 or 10KT mean that either yield can be selected.

[e] Dual-capable.

[f] Numbers cited are totals of theoretically nuclear-capable pieces. Not all will be certified for nuclear use, and in practice relatively few are likely to be in a nuclear role at any one time. All artillery pieces listed are dual-capable.

[g] It is not possible to give launcher numbers as the vertical launch system (VLS) can mount a variety of missiles in any of its tubes.

[h] All bombs have five option fusing: freefall airburst or surface burst, parachute retarded airburst or surface burst, and retarded delayed surface burst.

[i] External loads are additional to internal loads.

[j] Except for French and UK national weapons, nuclear warheads held in US custody.

[k] No nuclear warheads held on Canadian, Danish, Norwegian, Spanish or Portuguese territory.

[l] Some SSGN/SSG can carry either SS-N-12 *Sandbox* or SS-N-3 *Shaddock*.

Other Arms-Control Developments

The aim of this section is to give a brief update on all arms-control matters other than those concerning nuclear weapons.

Conventional Armed Forces in Europe(CFE) Treaty

The CFE Treaty came into force on 17 July 1992. The 120 days after this date constituted a 'baseline validation period' during which each signatory was required to accept inspections of declared sites equal in number to 20% of its Objects of Verification (OOV). After this period the number of inspections which must be accepted each year is equal to 10% of a state's OOVs.

The table below shows the number of inspections carried out and undergone by each signatory state from July 1992. Most inspections were carried out by multinational teams. The composition of these teams is not limited to NATO or former Warsaw Pact members; any signatory may be invited to join any team. The table shows the number of inspections in which each country participated; as we do not have full details of the composition of each group, it is not possible to analyse who inspected who. Since our data is incomplete, the total number of inspections is not known. In addition to declared site inspections, signatories may carry out inspections (known as reduction inspections) of Treaty Limited Equipment (TLE) being destroyed or converted. Notice of when reduction by destruction is to be carried out must be given to all signatories. There is no limit to the number of reduction inspections which can be made, but no inspected state need accept more than one inspection at each of its reduction sites at any one time. Reduction by destruction can take place without inspection. The table also shows the number of reduction inspections carried out and received.

	Inspections carried out						Inspections undergone		
	During validation period		During remainder of year		Reduction inspections		During validation period	During remainder of year	Reduction inspections
	A	B	A	B	A	B			
Belgium[a]	–	–	–	–	–	–	–	–	–
Canada	3	6	4	4	23	4	1	0	0
Denmark	6	6	4	3	32	2	3	2	0
France	13	14	9	1	12	0	19	5	1
Germany	20	47	12	13	101	40	47	15	12
Greece	0	9	5	4	4	0	13	8	4
Italy	3	7	4	1	4	0	5	4	4
Netherlands	9	11	5	3	26	6	9	0	1
Norway	0	6	0	2	25	0	1	0	0
Portugal	2	3	7	3	3	0	1	0	0
Spain	6	9	7	3	29	8	2	1	0
Turkey	0	15	0	8	0	0	18	5	3
UK	17	27	11	8	103[b]	0	21	7	1
US	16	27	14	2	148[c]	0	23	9	4
Armenia[a]	–	–	–	–	–	–	–	–	–
Azerbaijan[a]	–	–	–	–	–	–	–	–	–
Belarus	0	0	1	3	0	0	17	6	16
Bulgaria	0	15	2	5	0	2	19	5	11
Czech Republic	15	37	15	6	2	11	38	2	51
Georgia[a]	–	–	–	–	–	–	–	–	–
Hungary	2	24	18	6	4	6	12	6	15
Moldova	0	0	3	0	1	0	2	1	0
Poland	9	8	2	3	2	2	19	5	6
Romania	0	10	3	2	0	4	27	8	4
Russia[a]	–	–	–	–	–	–	–	–	–
Slovakia[a]	–	–	–	–	–	–	–	–	–
Ukraine	0	0	4	4	2	0	43	17	34

A = as part of a multinational team. B = as a national team.
[a] No information provided. [b] 21 led by UK. [c] 35 led by US.

The inspection process has been a success. No major treaty violations have been revealed, and any irregularities have been found to have been unintentional. After some initial suspicion, both inspectors and inspected have discovered that inspections are an important confidence-building measure (CBM) that have led to a much improved understanding of each other's problems and military philosophy.

By the date of publication of *The Military Balance 1992–1993* (October 1992) four countries had still not declared their CFE 1A manpower limits. These have now been declared: Azerbaijan: 70,000; Georgia: 40,000; Moldova: 20,000. Armenia has still not declared its manpower limit. The division of Czechoslovakia into the Czech Republic and Slovakia has meant that Czechoslovakia's quota of manpower and TLE has had to be apportioned between the new states. The new quotas are:

	Czech Republic	Slovakia
Manpower	93,333	46,667
Tanks	957	478
Armoured Combat Vehicles	1,367	683
Artillery	767	383
Combat Aircraft	230	115
Attack Helicopters	50	25

A total of 48,610 TLE (18,051 tanks, 8,766 artillery, 19,251 ACV, 225 helicopters and 2,317 aircraft) must be reduced by 17 November 1995. By 17 November 1993, 16 months after the Treaty came into force, each country should have reduced at least 25% of its liability. From the information available to us, it appears that most countries will meet the 16-month reduction target. For example, Germany has already reduced its 10,297 liability by 2,174, and the Czech Republic its 2,969 liability by 1,121. However, Romania has only reduced its liability of 5,175 by 23 TLE. We have no information on the progress of reduction in Russia which has a large reduction liability of 10,678 TLE.

Conference on Security and Cooperation in Europe (CSCE)

At the CSCE meeting held in January and February 1990 the Conference adopted a range of new CBM set out in the 'Vienna Document 1990'. Four of the measures involve visits by military teams.

Notifiable Military Activity: Military activities involving 17,000 or more troops and those which include an amphibious landing or parachute assault of 5,000 or more troops are considered notifiable military activities to which observers must be invited.

Inspection: Inspections of military facilities can be requested subject to the following principles: a state need not accept more than one inspection by the same state each year; a state need accept no more than a total of three inspections each year; an inspection will last 48 hours from the time of arrival of the inspectors at the site; the requesting state must give the reasons for the request.

Evaluation: Information provided in the annual exchange of military information is subject to evaluation, and states must provide the opportunity for evaluation visits to be made; these take place on one working day and can last no more than 12 hours.

Airfield Visits: Each CSCE state is required to arrange visits to its airfields, but it need not arrange more than one visit every five years. Invitations are extended to all CSCE states who may send up to two representatives to each visit.

We have neither the data nor the space to provide a table summarising CSCE activities as we have done for CFE inspections. There have been only five instances of observation at military activity in the last 12 months. Similarly, only five inspections were made. Many more evaluation visits were carried out; in all 40 spread over 22 countries with 18 countries contributing to the evaluation teams. Seven airfield visits were arranged (in Bulgaria, Denmark, Finland, France, Germany, Italy and Norway) and 17 countries took part in most of these.

'Open Skies' Treaty

The Treaty on 'Open Skies', which allows for observation flights to be made over the territory of other treaty signatories, was signed in Helsinki on 24 March 1992. The Treaty enters into force 60 days after 20 instruments of ratification have been deposited. By 1 July 1993 only seven countries had ratified, although 27 had signed the Treaty. Only after the Treaty comes into force may countries, other than NATO members, members of the former Warsaw Pact and republics of the former Soviet Union, join the Treaty. The following countries have signed the 'Open Skies' Treaty; those marked with an asterisk have also ratified the Treaty.

Belarus	Belgium	Bulgaria	Canada*	Czech Republic*
Denmark*	France	Georgia	Germany	Greece*
Hungary*	Iceland	Italy	Kyrgyzstan	Luxembourg
Netherlands	Norway*	Poland	Portugal	Romania
Russia	Slovakia*	Spain	Turkey	Ukraine
UK	US*			

A number of countries have agreed to accept and to carry out trial observation flights. No problems from the trials have been reported.

United Nations Register of Conventional Arms

In December 1991 the United Nations General Assembly adopted Resolution 46/36L entitled 'Transparency in Armaments'. The Resolution requested the Secretary-General to establish and maintain a 'universal and non-discriminatory' Register of Conventional Arms, and called upon member-states to provide data annually on imports and exports of arms. Data on arms transfers for the calendar year 1992 were to be reported to the UN on 30 April 1993. Member-states were also encouraged to provide background information on their own military equipment holdings and procurement through their own national production.

By 1 June 1993, 53 countries had submitted returns, of which 23 had nothing to report. South Africa stated that it was unable to contribute to the Register due to the UN arms embargo imposed by UN Security Council Resolution 418 of 1977. Yugoslavia explained its federal laws governing trade in arms. 28 countries also submitted background information on their arms holdings. The following countries reported to the UN:

Argentina	Australia	Austria	Belarus	Belgium
Brazil	Canada	Chile	China	Croatia*
Cuba*	Czech Republic	Denmark	Finland	France
Georgia*	Germany	Greece	Grenada *	Hungary
Iceland	Ireland*	Italy	Japan	Kazakhstan*
Lesotho*	Libya*	Luxembourg*	Maldives *	Malta
Mexico*	Mongolia*	Namibia *	Netherlands	New Zealand
Nicaragua	Norway	Oman	Panama*	Papua New Guinea*
Paraguay*	Philippines	Poland	Portugal	South Korea
Senegal*	Singapore	Slovakia	Slovenia*	South Africa
Spain	Sweden	Switzerland*	Tunisia*	Turkey
UK	US	Vanuatu *	Yugoslavia	

Countries marked * submitted nil returns, indicating that they had neither imported nor exported armaments subject to the Register. Since 1 June 1993 Russia has reported to the Register.

The following categories of armament are covered by the register:

1) *Battle Tanks*: Tracked or wheeled self-propelled armoured fighting vehicles with high cross-country mobility and a high level of self-protection, weighing at least 16.5 metric tonnes unladen, with a high muzzle velocity direct fire main gun of at least 75 millimetres calibre.

2) *Armoured Combat Vehicles*: Tracked, semi-tracked or wheeled self-propelled vehicles, with armoured protection and cross-country capability, either designed and equipped to transport a squad of four or more infantrymen, or armed with integral or organic weapons of at least 12.5mm calibre or a missile launcher.

3) *Large Calibre Artillery Systems*: Guns, howitzers, artillery pieces, combining the characteristics of a gun or a howitzer, mortars or multiple-launch rocket systems, capable of engaging surface targets by delivering primarily indirect fire, with a calibre of 100mm and above.

4) *Combat Aircraft*: Fixed-wing or variable-geometry wing aircraft, designed, equipped or modified to engage targets by employing guided missiles, unguided rockets, bombs, guns, cannons, or other weapons of destruction, including versions of these aircraft which perform specialised electronic warfare, suppression of air defence or reconnaissance missions. Does not include primary trainer aircraft, unless designed, equipped or modified as described above.

5) *Attack Helicopters*: Rotary-wing aircraft designed, equipped or modified to engage targets by employing guided or unguided anti-armour, air-to-surface, air-to-subsurface, or air-to-air weapons and equipped with an integrated fire control and aiming system for these weapons, including versions of these aircraft which perform specialised reconnaissance or electronic warfare missions.

6) *Warships*: Vessels or submarines armed and equipped for military use with a standard displacement of 750 metric tonnes or above, and those with a standard displacement of less than 750 metric tonnes, equipped for launching missiles with a range of at least 25km or torpedoes with similar range.

7) *Missiles and Missile launchers*: Guided or unguided rockets, ballistic or cruise missiles capable of delivering a warhead or weapon of destruction to a range of at least 25km, and means designed or modified specifically for launching such missiles or rockets, if not covered by categories 1 to 7. For the purpose of the Register, this category also includes remotely-piloted vehicles with the characteristics for missiles as defined above; it does not include ground-to-air missiles.

The definitions of the first five categories are identical to those for the categories of TLE for CFE except that: battle tanks do not have to have a 360 degree traverse to be included; there are no sub-categories of armoured combat vehicle as in CFE, the size of infantry 'squad' has been given as four men (unstated in CFE) and the qualifying armament calibre is 12.5mm (20mm for a CFE AIFV); all combat aircraft including naval aircraft are to be included. Warships and missiles are not covered by CFE.

There is no requirement to give any details beyond the number involved in any transfer, so it is not possible from the Register alone to learn what type, make or model of armament has been transferred. This absence of detail is most worrying in the case of missiles, where no distinction need be made between missiles and missile launchers, or between missile roles: surface-to-surface, air-to-surface, or air-to-air. Nor is any distinction made of range, weight of warhead, type of propulsion or type of guidance.

The Register is to be reviewed in 1994. The review panel will assess the value of the Register and will consider the addition of extra categories of armaments (in-flight refuelling capability, precision-guided ammunition or cluster bombs, for example) and the modification of existing categories (lowering the tonnage threshold for ships and separating missiles by type/range etc).

On balance, the Register can be considered a success, particularly considering it is only in its first year of operation. It is the first globally agreed CBM. It is disappointing but not surprising that a number of countries have not yet reported to the Register. They include: major arms exporters such as Israel and North Korea; major arms importers including, in the Middle East, Egypt, Iran, Kuwait, Qatar, Saudi Arabia and the UAE, and elsewhere India, Pakistan, Taiwan and Thailand.

Arms transfers to the Middle East

In May 1991 President Bush launched a Middle East Arms Control Initiative which included a proposal to establish supplier guidelines for the transfer of armaments to the region. Representatives of the five permanent members of the UN Security Council met in July and September 1991, and in October adopted a set of common guidelines. They agreed to inform each other about transfers of the seven categories of armaments listed in the UN Conventional Arms Register to the Middle Eastern countries. The Initiative is now in limbo following the refusal of the Chinese to cooperate after they had learnt of a US plan to sell 150 F-16 aircraft to Taiwan.

Chemical Weapons Convention (CWC)

The CWC, which was opened for signature in Paris on 13 January 1993 when 130 countries signed, replaces the 1925 Geneva Protocol. It has taken many years to achieve; negotiations began in 1968 but substantive progress was made only after a US–USSR agreement was signed on 2 June 1990. This agreement committed both countries to end CW production and to reduce their CW stocks by destruction to no more than 5,000 metric tons each by the end of 2002. By 9 July 1993, 146 states had signed CWC, and there had been four ratifications.

While the 1925 Protocol bans the use of CW, it did not prohibit development or production; nor were there any provisions for verification. The CWC requires signatories 'never under any circumstances' to undertake:

– to develop, produce, acquire or stockpile CW or transfer it to anyone.
– to use CW.
– to assist or encourage anyone to engage in activity prohibited by the CWC.

They also undertook to destroy all CW stocks and all CW production facilities and not to use riot-control agents in war.

The CWC is of unlimited duration. It will come into force 180 days after the 65th instrument of ratification is deposited, but in any case no earlier than 13 January 1995. CWC established the Organisation for the Prohibition of Chemical Weapons (OPCW) to ensure implementation and to provide a forum for consultation and cooperation.

The organs of OPCW are: the Conference of State Parties; the Executive Council; and the Technical Secretariat. All signatory states are represented on the Conference which is the principal organ of the Organisation. The Conference is responsible for convening CWC review sessions within one year of the fifth and tenth years after entry into force. The Executive Council, elected by the Conference, consists of 41 members with a quota from each region of the world (Africa: nine members, Asia: nine, Eastern Europe: five, Latin America and the Caribbean: seven, Western Europe – and other states designated by states parties located in this region – which covers the US and Canada: ten). Executive decisions on matters of substance require a two-thirds majority. The Technical Secretariat is a full-time body serving the Executive and the Conference and is responsible for carrying out the verification measures provided for in the CWC.

Verification will be implemented at two levels: routine and challenge. Routine verification will be carried out by the Technical Secretariat (in much the same way as the International Atomic Energy Agency (IAEA) operates). Measures include a comprehensive system of information exchange, including details of national production of 43 specific chemicals listed in the CWC, and on-site inspection of chemical industries. Each state party to the Treaty has the right to request on-site challenge inspections of any facility or location of another party, should non-compliance be suspected. While the challenge inspections will be carried out by a Technical Secretariat team, the requesting party, with the agreement of the inspected party, may send an observer with the inspection team. Special provisions have been incorporated into the Treaty to satisfy the inspected nation's security and commercial concerns.

A key element in the verification process is the provision for the collection, handling and analysis of samples. Analysis will be of greater importance in challenge inspections than in routine and especially important in allegations of CW use. It is essential, for the credibility of CWC, that the standard of analysis is beyond criticism. Until OPCW can establish its own laboratories staffed by experienced scientists, it would be better to leave analysis to long-established CW centres, for example in the US, UK or Russia. A Preparatory Commission of OPCW meets regularly to approve reports provided by expert groups on working procedures for OPCW and its organs. A Provisional Technical Secretariat (PTS) was established on 11 February 1993, and by the end of June 1993 43 staff had been recruited. Appointments have been made to the posts of Head PTS and Executive Secretary, Head of Verification, Head of External Relations, and Legal Adviser.

The Australia Group

The Australia Group is an informal grouping of states, formed in 1985, which agree to impose export controls on precursor chemicals from which CW can be produced. It meets twice a year. At its December 1992 meeting agreement was reached on measures to control the export of biological agents and certain equipments that could be used in producing biological weapons. The new control list adds over 60 human and animal pathogens (viruses, rickettsiae, bacteria and toxins) to that of goods prohibited from export. Equipment capable of use in manufacturing chemical and biological agents are also listed for control. Membership of the group has been expanded to 26, new members in the last 12 months being Argentina, Hungary and Iceland. Its members are:

Argentina	Australia	Austria	Belgium	Canada
Denmark	EC	Finland	France	Germany
Greece	Hungary	Iceland	Ireland	Italy
Japan	Luxembourg	Netherlands	New Zealand	Norway
Portugal	Spain	Sweden	Switzerland	UK
US				

Missile Technology Control Regime (MTCR)

The MTCR was formed in April 1987 with seven members (Canada, France, Germany, Italy, Japan, UK and US) to control the transfer of equipment and technology that could contribute to nuclear-capable missiles (with a payload of at least 500kg over a distance of at least 300km). Since then the group has expanded to 25 members, most recently with the addition of Argentina after the handover for destruction of the remaining components of its *Condor* programme. Israel, China and Russia have committed themselves to following the regime's provisions without joining it. A new set of guidelines came into force in January 1993 replacing those of April 1987. These now cover missiles capable of delivering chemical and biological weapons, whereas originally only delivery of nuclear weapons was considered. MTCR partners will next meet in

November 1993 when they will consider future directions for the Regime. Three possible violations of MTCR provisions are currently causing concern: the sale of Chinese M-11 SSM to Pakistan; the sale of rocket engines and associated technology by Russia to India; and the interception in Ukraine of a cargo of rocket fuel in transit from Russia to Libya. In addition, export of the North Korean *No-Dong* SSM, which is still under development and has a range of 1,000km, would seriously undermine the MTCR. Its members are:

Argentina	Australia	Austria	Belgium	Canada
Denmark	Finland	France	Germany	Greece
Hungary	Iceland	Ireland	Italy	Japan
Luxembourg	Netherlands	New Zealand	Norway	Portugal
Spain	Sweden	Switzerland	UK	US

China, Israel, Romania and Russia are all committed to abiding by the provisions of the regime without formally joining it.

Conventional Forces in Europe

Manpower and TLE: current holdings and CFE limits of the forces of the CFE signatories
(current holdings are derived from data declared as at 1 January 1993 and so may differ from The Military Balance listing)

Country	Manpower Holding	Manpower Limit	Tanks[a] Holding	Tanks[a] Limit	ACV[a] Holding	ACV[a] Limit	Arty[a] Holding	Arty[a] Limit	Attack Hel Holding	Attack Hel Limit	Combat Aircraft[b] Holding	Combat Aircraft[b] Limit
Armenia[c]	7,101	–	77	220	189	220	160	285	13	50	3	100
Azerbaijan	52,479	70,000	278	220	338	220	294	285	6	50	50	100
Belarus	143,865	100,000	3,457	1,800	3,947	2,600	1,610	1,615	79	80	389	260
Georgia[d]		40,000	75	220	49	220	24	285	3	50	335	100
Moldova[d]		20,000	0	210	87	210	108	250	0	50	29	50
Russia	1,298,299	1,450,000	8,767	6,400	12,744	11,480	7,946	6,415	989	890	4,387	3,450
Ukraine	509,531	450,000	6,178	4,080	5,393	5,050	3,721	4,040	274	330	1,650	1,090
Bulgaria	99,404	104,000	2,209	1,475	2,232	2,000	2,085	1,750	44	67	335	235
Czech Republic	110,010	93,333	1,703	957	2,462	1,367	1,612	767	37	50	231	230
Hungary	76,226	100,000	1,331	835	1,731	1,700	1,037	810	39	108	143	180
Poland	273,050	234,000	2,807	1,730	2,416	2,150	2,304	1,610	30	130	508	460
Romania	244,807	230,248	2,960	1,375	3,143	2,100	3,928	1,475	15	120	505	430
Slovakia	55,005	46,667	851	478	1,231	683	806	383	18	25	116	115
Belgium	76,088	70,000	362	334	1,267	1,099	378	320	10	46	202	232
Canada[e]	4,077	10,660	76	77	72	277	32	38	0	13	24	90
Denmark	29,256	39,000	499	353	293	316	553	553	12	12	106	106
France	341,988	325,000	1,335	1,306	4,154	3,820	1,392	1,292	352	352	688	800
Germany	401,102	345,000	6,733	4,166	8,626	3,446	4,369	2,705	306	306	946	900
Greece	165,400	158,621	2,276	1,735	1,430	2,534	2,149	1,878	18	18	458	650
Italy	294,900	315,000	1,276	1,348	3,746	3,339	1,955	1,955	142	142	542	650
Netherlands	69,324	80,000	813	743	1,445	1,080	837	607	69	69	175	230
Norway	29,500	32,000	205	170	124	225	544	527	0	0	88	100
Portugal	39,700	75,000	146	300	280	430	354	450	0	26	91	160
Spain	177,078	300,000	896	794	1,057	1,588	1,219	1,310	28	71	175	310
Turkey[f]	575,045	530,000	3,234	2,795	1,862	3,120	3,210	3,523	0	43	355	750
UK	288,626	260,000	1,078	1,015	3,003	3,176	636	636	340	384	717	900
US	175,070	250,000	4,511	4,006	4,800	5,372	1,773	2,492	341	518	334	784

Notes:

[a] Incl TLE with land-based maritime forces (Marines, Naval Inf etc.).
[b] Does not incl land-based maritime aircraft for which a separate limit has been set.
[c] This country has not yet declared its personnel limit.

[d] These countries did not declare their manpower holding at 1 January 1993.
[e] Canada has now withdrawn all its TLE from the ATTU except for the prepositioned stockpile of 6 arty and 14 ACV in Norway
[f] Manpower and TLE is for that in ATTU zone only.

Peacekeeping Operations

UNITED NATIONS

For the second year running the United Nations (UN) has expanded its peacekeeping operations with major commitments in three new areas: Bosnia-Herzegovina; Mozambique and Somalia. In Bosnia-Herzegovina the protection of humanitarian activities required in the first instance a force of some 5,500 troops. There is now also an air-exclusion zone to be enforced and six 'safe areas' to be protected. The additional troops needed for the 'safe areas', who are being found mainly by Muslim states have not yet been deployed; however, the air forces authorised to protect them (should they come under continuous and sustained attacks) have already been assembled in Italy (*Operation Disciplined Guard*). A small 'trip-wire' force (including one US Army detachment) has been deployed to Macedonia. In Mozambique the UN has assembled a 6,000-man force (ONUMOZ) to provide security for the land transit routes and humanitarian aid activities. In Somalia the failure of UNOSOM I to achieve its mandate to protect aid deliveries led the US to volunteer to lead a new type of peacekeeping force: one that was UN-mandated but basically a national operation with troop contributions from other countries (much on the lines of the Coalition formed for the Gulf War). The US force (UNITAF) handed over its responsibilities to UNOSOM II in May 1993. Operations in Mogadishu, mainly against the dominant warlord, General Mohammed Farah Aideed, have gained widespread media coverage. This has highlighted the difficulties the UN faces in undertaking operations which are very different to more traditional peacekeeping missions. Press concentration on events in Mogadishu has meant that the success of the operation elsewhere in Somalia has gone unreported.

The substantial increase in the number of peacekeeping operations undertaken since 1990, and the change in emphasis from traditional operations to Chapter VII operations (those that allow for enforcement action to be taken) with various stages in between, has placed an extraordinary load on the peacekeeping and military advisory staff in UN headquarters in New York. During the year this staff has been increased and now numbers over 40 officers, compared with eight previously, with liaison officers from each major mission. For the first time a 24-hour watch is kept in New York. The internal organisation of the UN Secretariat which separates responsibility for peacekeeping operations on the ground (Department of Peacekeeping Operations (DPKO)) from financial and administrative authority (Field Operations Division of Department of Administrative Management), and which split is replicated in each mission, has led to a degree of extra bureaucracy and, in turn, unnecessary inefficiency.

The increased number of operations has also meant that a large number of countries are providing troops to the UN for the first time. There are therefore not only wide divergences in standards but also in the understanding of the UN command structure so that an increasing number of units refer UN orders to their national authorities at home before obeying them. Countries with conscript armies know they will face domestic political disapproval should their peacekeeping troops suffer casualties (even if they are on a smaller scale than those sustained by Pakistani troops in Somalia). As peacekeeping becomes more complex and more dangerous there will be a growing number of countries who are not prepared to take this risk.

In June 1992 the Secretary-General, Dr Boutros Boutros Ghali, submitted to the Security Council his report entitled 'An Agenda for Peace'. In the report he advocated that member nations form 'peace enforcement' units comprised of volunteers, specially trained and available on call to the Secretary-General. Others have gone further and proposed that the UN should form its own army, possibly along the lines of the French Foreign Legion. There are a number of disadvantages to both proposals. The main problem in providing suitable troops quickly for UN operations is that the growing diversity of tasks precludes training for every eventuality. There is little doubt that troops from the regular peacekeeping contributors (such as Austria, Ireland and the Scandinavian countries) are best suited to traditional peacekeeping tasks. The new more complex operations require professional troops with a high standard of discipline and self-confidence which can only come from comprehensive military training. Such troops are ready for any escalation from peacekeeping to peace enforcement and ultimately to peace imposing. The UN might be better served if member states provided a list of the numbers and types of units that they were prepared to make available (and within what time scale) from which the right mix of infantry and support troops, and of traditional peacekeeping versus high-intensity trained units can be selected. A planning team has been established in the UN Military Adviser's office to examine the principles and problems of establishing UN stand-by forces.

United Nations Truce Supervision Organisation (UNTSO)

Mission: Established in June 1948 to assist the Mediator and the Truce Commission in supervising the observance of the truce in Palestine called for by the Security Council. At present, UNTSO assists and cooperates with UNDOF and UNIFIL in the performance of their tasks; Military Observers are stationed in Beirut, South Lebanon, Sinai, Jordan, Israel and Syria.
Strength: 224
Composition: Observers from Argentina, Australia, Austria, Belgium, Canada, Chile, China, Denmark, Finland, France, Ireland, Italy, Netherlands, New Zealand, Norway, Russia, Sweden, Switzerland, US.

United Nations Military Observer Group in India and Pakistan (UNMOGIP)

Mission: To supervise, in the State of Jammu and Kashmir, the cease-fire between India and Pakistan along the Line of Control.
Strength: 38
Composition: Observers from Belgium, Chile, Denmark, Finland, Italy, Norway, Sweden, Uruguay.

United Nations Peacekeeping Force in Cyprus (UNFICYP)

Mission: Established in 1964 to use its best efforts to prevent the recurrence of fighting and, as necessary, to contribute to the maintenance and restoration of law and order and a return to normal conditions. Since the hostilities of 1974, this has included supervising the cease-fire and maintaining a buffer zone between the lines of the Cyprus National Guard and of the Turkish and Turkish–Cypriot forces.
Strength: 1,000
Composition: Units from Austria (inf), UK (inf, hel, log), Staff Officers from Denmark, Finland, Ireland and Sweden. Civil police detachments from Australia, Sweden.

United Nations Disengagement Observer Force (UNDOF)

Mission: To supervise the cease-fire between Israel and Syria, and to establish an area of separation and verify troop levels, as provided in the Agreement on Disengagement between Israeli and Syrian Forces of 31 May 1974.
Strength: 1,120
Composition: Units from Austria (inf), Canada (log), Finland (inf), Poland (log).

United Nations Interim Force in Lebanon (UNIFIL)

Mission: Established in 1978 to confirm the withdrawal of Israeli forces from southern Lebanon, to restore international peace and security and to assist the government of Lebanon in ensuring the return of its effective authority in the area.
Strength: 5,300
Composition: Units from Fiji (inf), Finland (inf), France (log), Ghana (inf), Ireland (inf, admin), Italy (hel), Nepal (inf), Norway (inf, maint), Poland (medical), Sweden (log).

United Nations Observer Mission in El Salvador (ONUSAL)

Mission: ONUSAL became operational in July 1991 to monitor agreements concluded between the government and the FMLN. A peace agreement was signed between the government and the FMLN in January 1992 under which both sides would report their full strength of troops and weapons to ONUSAL, which would also dispose of FMLN weapons as they were handed over during demobilisation. The UN disbanded ONUCA (UN Observer Group in Central America) in early 1992 and transferred its manpower and equipment to ONUSAL. ONUSAL is to monitor the cease-fire (military observers), monitor human rights violations (civilian observers), and establish a police force on democratic lines.

Strength: 80, plus 300 civil police

Composition: Observers from Argentina, Brazil, Canada, Colombia, Ecuador, India, Ireland, Spain, Sweden and Venezuela.

United Nations Iraq/Kuwait Observer Mission (UNIKOM)

Mission: Established in April 1991 following the recapture of Kuwait from Iraq by Coalition Forces. Its mandate is to monitor the Khor Abdullah and a demilitarised zone (DMZ) extending 10km into Iraq and 5km into Kuwait from the agreed boundary between the two. It is to deter violations of the boundary and to observe hostile or potentially hostile actions.

Strength: 320

Composition: Units from Denmark (Administrative Staff), Norway (Medical). Observers from Argentina, Austria, Bangladesh, Canada, China, Denmark, Fiji, Finland, France, Ghana, Greece, Hungary, India, Indonesia, Ireland, Italy, Kenya, Malaysia, Nigeria, Norway, Pakistan, Poland, Romania, Russia, Senegal, Singapore, Sweden, Thailand, Turkey, UK, Uruguay, US, Venezuela.

United Nations Mission for the Referendum in Western Sahara (MINURSO)

Established in April 1991 to supervise a referendum to choose between independence and integration into Morocco. A transitional period would begin with the coming into effect of a cease-fire and end when the referendum results were announced. Although a cease-fire came into effect on 6 September 1991, the transitional period did not begin as the UN had been unable to complete its registration of eligible voters. It is now apparent that, despite earlier agreements, substantial areas of difference between the two sides remain. MINURSO is therefore currently restricted to verifying the cease-fire.

Strength: 327

Composition: Units from Australia (signals), Canada (movement control), Switzerland (medical). Observers from Argentina, Australia, Austria, Bangladesh, Belgium, Canada, China, Egypt, France, Ghana, Greece, Guinea, Honduras, Ireland, Italy, Kenya, Malaysia, Nigeria, Pakistan, Poland, Russia, Tunisia, UK, US, Venezuela.

United Nations Angola Verification Mission II (UNAVEM II)

Mission: Established June 1991. To verify the cease-fire as set out in the Peace Accords, agreed to by the government of Angola and UNITA, and to monitor the Angolan police as set out in the Protocol of Estoril.

Strength: 75 military and 28 police observers.

Composition: Observers from Argentina, Brazil, Congo, Guinea-Bissau, Hungary, India, Ireland, Jordan, Morocco, Netherlands, Nigeria, Norway, Slovakia, Spain, Sweden, Zimbabwe.

United Nations Transitional Authority in Cambodia (UNTAC)

Mission: A cease-fire in Cambodia entered into effect with the signing of an agreement on a comprehensive political settlement of the Cambodian conflict on 23 October 1991. Prior to the establishment of UNTAC, which became operational on 15 March 1992, the UN had established a small mission, the United Nations Advanced Mission in Cambodia (UNAMIC) to assist the parties in maintaining the cease-fire and provide training in mine clearance.

UNTAC has both civil and military responsibilities. The civil responsibilities include: establishing an environment in which respect for human rights is ensured; establishing an electoral law, registering voters and supervising an election; ensuring law and order and supervising civil police work; organising the repatriation and resettlement of an estimated 350,000 refugees, 170,000 internally displaced persons and 150,000 demobilised troops; coordinating international aid activities. UNTAC also provides a Civil Administration with control of foreign affairs, national defence, finance and public security and information. UNTAC's mandate includes the following military tasks: verification of the withdrawal and non-return of foreign forces; supervision of the cease-fire, the disarmament and demobilisation of troops of all four factions; assistance with mine clearance. Some contingents are being withdrawn.

Strength: 16,000, plus 3,500 police.

Composition: Infantry Battalions from: Bangladesh, Bulgaria, France, Ghana, India, Indonesia, Malaysia, Netherlands, Pakistan, Tunisia and Uruguay. Military Observers from: Algeria, Argentina, Austria, Bangladesh, Belgium, Brunei, Bulgaria, Cameroon, China, France, Ghana, India, Indonesia, Ireland, Japan, Malaysia, Pakistan, Poland, Russia, Senegal, Tunisia, UK, Uruguay and US. Logistic and Support Units: from Australia and New Zealand (comms), China, France, Japan, Poland and Thailand (engr), France and Netherlands (Air), Canada, Chile, New Zealand, Philippines, Russia, UK and Uruguay (Naval), Germany and India (Medical), and Australia, Canada, Netherlands, Pakistan and Poland (log), Namibia (inf and support), Singapore (hel; withdrawn after 31 May 1993).

FORMER YUGOSLAVIA

United Nations Protection Force (UNPROFOR)

Mission: Established in March 1992. UNPROFOR I, which includes military, police and civilian components, is deployed in three United Nations Protected Areas (UNPAs) in Croatia to create the conditions of peace and security required to permit the negotiations of an overall political settlement of the Yugoslav crisis. UNPROFOR I is responsible for ensuring that the UNPAs are demilitarised through the withdrawal or disbandment of all armed forces in them, and that all persons residing in them are protected from fear of armed attack. To this end, UNPROFOR is authorised to control access to the UNPAs, to ensure that they remain demilitarised, and to monitor the functioning of the local police to help ensure non-discrimination and the protection of human rights. Outside the UNPAs, UNPROFOR Military Observers will verify the withdrawal of all Yugoslav National Army (JNA) and Serbian forces from Croatia, other than those disbanded and demobilised there.

Strength: 10,216 (authorised 13,870 military and police, including 12 inf battalions)

Composition: Units and observers from: Argentina (inf bn), Belgium (inf bn), Canada (inf bn and engr), joint Czech Republic/Slovakia (inf bn), Denmark (inf bn), Finland (construction bn), France (inf bn, log bn), Jordan (inf bn), Kenya (inf bn), Luxembourg (inf pl), Nepal (inf bn), Netherlands (signals), Norway (movement control), Poland (inf bn), Russia (inf (airborne) bn), Sweden (HQ/staff coy), UK (medical unit) and observers from Australia, Bangladesh, Brazil, Colombia, Egypt, Finland, Ghana, Ireland, New Zealand, Portugal and Venezuela.

United Nations Protection Force II (UNPROFOR II)

The UN Security Council adopted Resolution 761 on 29 June 1992 which authorised the deployment of additional troops to ensure the security and functioning of Sarajevo airport and the delivery of humanitarian assistance. Initially a Canadian battalion deployed to Sarajevo and was relieved by a small HQ and three battalions of infantry (from Egypt, France and Ukraine). On 13 August 1992 Security Council Resolution 770 was adopted which called on states to take all measures necessary to facilitate the delivery of humanitarian aid. Following the International Conference in London from 26 to 28 August 1992, NATO offered to provide a force with an HQ to protect aid convoys. The offer was accepted and authorised by Resolution 776 adopted on 14 September. UNPROFOR II commenced its deployment in October 1992 and four battalion groups were deployed. In November, UN Resolution 781 authorised 75 observers to monitor flights over Bosnia. Observers would be stationed at airfields in Croatia, Bosnia and the Federal Republic of Yugoslavia.

Resolution 824 adopted on 6 May 1993, after Serbian attacks in eastern Bosnia had left a number of Muslim towns surrounded, declared that: Sarajevo, Tuzla, Zepa, Gorazde, Bihac and Srebrenica would be treated as safe areas; Bosnian Serb units should cease armed attacks there immediately and withdraw to a distance from where they ceased to constitute a menace. The deployment of 50 additional military observers was also authorised. When it was seen that UNPROFOR II was not strong enough to deploy sufficient forces to the safe areas the Security Council adopted Resolution 844 which authorised a reinforcement of 7,600 more troops for their protection. The Resolution reaffirmed the use of air power to protect UNPROFOR troops should this be necessary. So far only one, a French battalion, has reinforced UNPROFOR II.
Strength: 9,480
Composition: Units from Belgium (tpt), Canada (inf bn, spt unit), Denmark (spt unit), France (3 inf bn, engr unit, hel unit), Netherlands (tpt, sigs), Norway (HQ unit), Portugal (medical), Spain (inf bn), UK (inf bn, armd recce sqn, engr sqn) and US (field hospital).

United Nations Protection Force Macedonia Command (UNPROFOR M)

Mission: In late 1992 President Gligorov requested a UN presence in Macedonia. A mission from UNPROFOR visited Macedonia from 28 November to 3 December 1992 and its report was accepted. UN Resolution 795 authorised the deployment of an infantry battalion and observers to monitor Macedonia's borders with Albania and the Federal Republic of Yugoslavia, and also to act as a deterrent to attack on Macedonia. On 18 June 1993 the Security Council authorised the reinforcement of the Macedonian Command by the United States.
Strength: 1,000
Composition: Denmark, Finland, Norway, Sweden (jointly manned inf bn), US (reinforced inf coy gp).

SOMALIA

United Nations Operation in Somalia (UNOSOM)

Mission: The UN Security Council adopted Resolution 733 on 23 January 1992 which called on all parties to cease hostilities, and which imposed a general and complete embargo on the delivery of army and military equipment to Somalia. The UN Security Council, by its Resolution 751 on 21 April 1992, established an operation to monitor the cease-fire and to provide protection for relief supply convoys which comprised 50 observers and a Pakistani infantry battalion.
Composition: Observers from Bangladesh, the Czech Republic, Egypt, Fiji, Finland, Indonesia, Jordan, Morocco, Pakistan, Zimbabwe. Inf bn from Pakistan.

Unified Task Force (UNITAF)

In November 1992 the US administration decided that the tragedy in Somalia, and the apparent failure of UNOSOM to carry out its mandate, required urgent action which could only be successful with the large-scale deployment of US troops. On 3 December 1992 the UN Security Council adopted Resolution 794 which authorised under Chapter VII of the UN Charter 'member states to use all necessary means to establish a secure environment for humanitarian relief operations'. It also authorised the establishment of a unified command. The US deployment, *Operation Restore Hope*, began with a Marine Corps landing overnight on 8–9 December.

The US had always intended that its command of the operation would be of limited length and on 4 May 1993 handed over command and withdrew the bulk of its troops.

Strength: (at its peak) some 35,000, including 28,000 US.

Composition: US: Elements 1st Marine Division, elements 10th Mountain Division, plus supporting elements including special forces, aviation, military police, engineers, public affairs; all told, elements of over 200 army and marine units and sub-units contributed to the force. Countries contributing infantry battalion plus support: Argentina, Australia, Belgium, Canada, Egypt, France, Italy, Morocco, Nigeria, Pakistan, Saudi Arabia. Other force contributions from 18 other countries.

United Nations Operations in Somalia (UNOSOM II)

Mission: On 26 March 1993 the UN Security Council adopted Resolution 814 which authorised, under Chapter VII of the UN Charter, the expansion of UNOSOM and its mandate, initially until 31 October 1993. The resolution 'emphasised the crucial importance of disarmament'. UNOSOM II assumed control of operations in Somalia on 4 May 1993.

Strength: 18,700

Composition: Units (inf or battle group unless specifically stated): Australia, Belgium, Botswana, Egypt, France, Germany, Greece, India, Italy, Kuwait, Malaysia, Morocco, Nigeria, Norway, Pakistan, Saudi Arabia, Sweden, Tunisia, Turkey, UAE, US, Zimbabwe.

United Nations Operations in Mozambique (ONUMOZ)

Mission: Established on 1 March 1993 ONUMOZ's mandate included the following tasks: monitoring and verifying the cease-fire, separation and demobilisation of forces; collection and destruction of weapons; the provision of security for vital national infrastructures and for UN and other international aid activities.

Strength: 6,160

Composition: Units from: Argentina (medical), Bangladesh (inf bn, engr, medical, log), Botswana (inf bn), India (engr, log), Italy (inf bn, aviation, logistics), Japan (movement control), Portugal (comms), Uruguay (inf bn), Zambia (inf bn). Observers from: Argentina, Bangladesh, Brazil, Canada, Cape Verde, Czech Republic, Egypt, Guinea-Bissau, Hungary, India, Malaysia, Russia, Spain, Sweden, Uruguay.

United Nations Observer Mission Uganda–Rwanda (UNOMUR)

Mission: On 22 June 1993 the UN Security Council adopted Resolution 846 which authorised the deployment of a 50-strong observer mission to monitor the Uganda–Rwanda border to verify that no military assistance reached Rwanda.

OTHER MISSIONS

This year we have expanded our listing of peacekeeping missions to include those that are not under UN control. We include details of the European Community Monitoring Mission (ECMM), which plays a useful and successful role in former Yugoslavia, and of the several Conference on Security and Cooperation in Europe (CSCE) missions. We have been unable to obtain sufficient details of the mandates and force composition of either the Economic Community of West Africa States Monitoring Group (ECOMOG) in Liberia or of the Commonwealth of Independent States (CIS) peacekeeping forces in Moldova and Georgia, to justify their inclusion in this analysis. What details are known are shown in the appropriate country entries.

Conference on Security and Cooperation in Europe Missions
Federal Republic of Yugoslavia (FRY)

Mission: Established on 14 August 1992, the mission deployed to Kosovo, Sanjak and Vojvodina on 8 September 1992 with the aim of promoting dialogue and collecting information relevant to human rights violations. The original memorandum of understanding (MOU) signed by the government of the Federal Republic of Yugoslavia was extended until 28 June 1993. The FRY government has now refused to extend the mandate further and the mission had withdrawn by the end of July 1993.
Strength: 40 monitors

Macedonia

Mission: Established and deployed in September 1992 with the task of monitoring developments along the borders of Macedonia with Serbia and other areas which could suffer from the spillover of the conflicts elsewhere in the FRY.
Strength: 8 monitors (plus two ECMM monitors)

Georgia

Mission: Deployed in December 1992, but with an MOU not signed by the government of Georgia until 23 January 1993. Its objective is to 'promote negotiations between the conflicting parties in Georgia which are aimed at reaching a peaceful political settlement'. Separate mandates were agreed for activities in South Ossetia and Abkhazia.
Strength: 11 members

Estonia

Mission: Although the decision to set up the mission was reached in December 1992, deployment did not take place until 15 February 1993. Its aim is to 'promote stability, dialogue and understanding between the communities in Estonia'. Mandate expires on 3 August 1993.
Strength: 6 members

Moldova

Mission: Deployed in April 1993 with the aim of assisting in the achievement of a political settlement of the conflict in the 'left-Bank Dniestr areas of the Republic of Moldova'. The mission's mandate, agreed to in an MOU signed on 7 May 1993, includes investigating specific incidents and providing legal advice, as well as assisting in arranging negotiating meetings. The mandate is to last for six months.
Strength: 8 members

OTHERS
Multinational Force and Observers (MFO)

Mission: Established in August 1981 following the peace treaty between Israel and Egypt and the subsequent withdrawal of Israeli forces from Sinai. Its task is to verify the level of forces in the zones in which forces are limited by the treaty, and to ensure freedom of navigation through the Strait of Tiran.
Strength: 2,600
Composition: Units from Australia (HQ unit), Colombia (inf), Fiji (inf), France (Fixed-Wing Aviation), Italy (naval coastal patrol), Netherlands (sigs and military police), New Zealand (trg), Uruguay (engr and tpt), US (inf and log). Staff Officers from Canada and Norway.

Neutral Nations' Supervisory Commission for Korea (NNSC)

Mission: Established by the Armistice Agreement in July 1953 at the end of the Korean War. The Commission is to supervise, observe, inspect and investigate the Armistice and to report on these activities to the Military Armistice Commission. Today its main role is to maintain and improve relations between both sides and thus keep open a channel of communication.
Composition: Diplomats and military officers from Poland, Sweden and Switzerland.

European Community Monitor Mission (ECMM)

Mission: Established in July 1991 by the Conference for Security and Cooperation in Europe (CSCE) it brings together the 12 EC countries and five CSCE countries (Canada, Sweden, Czech Republic, Slovakia and Poland). Its first task was to monitor and assist with the withdrawal of the Yugoslav National Army (JNA) from Slovenia. Its mandate was later extended to Croatia and then to Bosnia-Herzegovina. The mission attempts to achieve preventive diplomacy, mediation and confidence-building between the parties. All ECMM monitors work unarmed. The Head of the Mission and the senior staff are found by the EC Presidency and rotate every six months.
Strength: 200 monitors (mainly serving or retired military officers or diplomats) and 200 support staff. Italy provides 3 helicopters.

Designations of Aircraft and Helicopters listed
in *The Military Balance*

The use of [square brackets] shows the type from which a variant was derived. 'Q-5 . . . [MiG-19]' indicates that the design of the Q-5 was based on that of the MiG-19.

(Parentheses) indicate an alternative name by which an aircraft is known – sometimes in another version. 'L-188 . . . *Electra* (P-3 *Orion*)' shows that in another version the

Lockheed Type 188 *Electra* is known as the P-3 *Orion*.

Names given in 'quotation marks' are NATO reporting names – e.g. 'Su-27 . . . *'Flanker'*.

When no information is listed under 'Origin' or 'Maker', take the primary reference given under 'Name/designation' and look it up under 'Type'.

Type	Name/designation	Origin	Maker
AIRCRAFT			
A-3	*Skywarrior*	US	Douglas
A-4	*Skyhawk*	US	MD
A-5	*Fantan*	China	Nanchang
A-6	*Intruder*	US	Grumman
A-7	*Corsair* II	US	LTV
A-10	*Thunderbolt*	US	Fairchild
A-36	*Halcón* (C-101)		
A-37	*Dragonfly*	US	Cessna
AC-130	(C-130)		
AC-47	(C-47)		
Airtourer		NZ	Victa
AJ-37	(J-37)		
Ajeet	(Folland *Gnat*)	India/UK	HAL
Alizé		France	Breguet
Alpha Jet		France/Ge	Dassault/Breguet Dornier
AM-3	*Bosbok* (C-4M)	Italy	Aermacchi
An-2	*'Colt'*	Russia	Antonov
An-12	*'Cub'*	Russia	Antonov
An-14	*'Clod'*	Russia	Antonov
An-22	*'Cock'*	Russia	Antonov
An-24	*'Coke'*	Russia	Antonov
An-26	*'Curl'*	Russia	Antonov
An-30	*'Clank'*	Russia	Antonov
An-32	*'Cline'*	Russia	Antonov
An-124	*'Condor'* (*Ruslan*)	Russia	Antonov
Andover	[HS-748]		
Atlantic	(*Atlantique*)	France	Dassault/Breguet
AS-202	*Bravo*	Switz	FFA
AT-3		Taiwan	AIDC
AT-6	(T-6)		
AT-11		US	Beech
AT-26	EMB-326		
AT-33	(T-33)		
AU-23	*Peacemaker* [PC-6B]	US	Fairchild
AV-8	*Harrier* II	US/UK	MD/BAe
Aztec	PA-23	US	Piper
B-1		US	Rockwell
B-52	*Stratofortress*	US	Boeing
BAC-111		UK	BAe
BAC-167	*Strikemaster*	UK	BAe
BAe-146		UK	BAe
BAe-748	(HS-748)		
Baron	(T-42)		
Be-6	*'Madge'*	Russia	Beriev
Be-12	*'Mail'* (*Tchaika*)	Russia	Beriev
Beech 50	*Twin Bonanza*	US	Beech
Beech 95	*Travel Air*	US	Beech
BN-2	*Islander, Defender, Trislander*	UK	Britten-Norman
Boeing 707		US	Boeing
Boeing 727		US	Boeing
Boeing 737		US	Boeing
Boeing 747		US	Boeing
Bonanza		US	Beech
Bronco	(OV-10)		
Buccaneer		UK	BAe
Bulldog		UK	BAe
C-1		Japan	Kawasaki
C-2	*Greyhound*	US	Grumman
C-4M	*Kudu* (AM-3)	S. Africa	Atlas
C-5	*Galaxy*	US	Lockheed
C-7	DHC-7		
C-9	*Nightingale* (DC-9)		
C-12	*Super King Air* (*Huron*)	US	Beech
C-17	*Globemaster III*	US	McDonnell Douglas
C-18	[Boeing 707]		
C-20	(*Gulfstream* III)		
C-21	(*Learjet*)		
C-22	(Boeing 727)		
C-23	(*Sherpa*)	UK	Short
C-42	(Neiva *Regente*)	Brazil	Embraer
C-45	*Expeditor*	US	Beech
C-46	*Commando*	US	Curtis
C-47	DC-3 (*Dakota*) (C-117 *Skytrain*)	US	Douglas
C-54	*Skymaster* (DC-4)	US	Douglas
C-91	HS-748		
C-93	HS-125		
C-95	EMB-110		
C-97	EMB-121		
C-101	*Aviojet*	Spain	CASA
C-115	DHC-5	Canada	De Havilland
C-117	(C-47)		
C-118	*Liftmaster* (DC-6)		
C-119	*Packet*	US	Fairchild
C-123	*Provider*	US	Fairchild
C-127	(Do-27)	Spain	CASA

Type	Name/designation	Origin	Maker	Type	Name/designation	Origin	Maker
C-130	Hercules (L-100)	US	Lockheed	CT-134	Musketeer		
C-131	Convair 440	US	Convair	Dagger	(Nesher)		
C-135	[Boeing 707]			Dakota		US	Piper
C-137	[Boeing 707]			Dakota	(C-47)		
C-140	(Jetstar)	US	Lockheed	DC-3	(C-47)	US	Douglas
C-141	Starlifter	US	Lockheed	DC-4	(C-54)	US	Douglas
C-160		Fr/Ge	Transall	DC-6	(C-118)	US	Douglas
C-212	Aviocar	Spain	CASA	DC-7		US	Douglas
C-235		Spain	CASA	DC-8		US	Douglas
CA-25	Winjeel	Aust	Commonwealth	DC-9		US	MD
Canberra	(B-57)	UK	BAe	Deepak	(HT-32)		
CAP-10		France	Mudry	Defender	BN-2		
CAP-20		France	Mudry	DH-100	Vampire	UK	De Havilland
CAP-230		France	Mudry	DHC-1	Chipmunk	Canada	DHC
Caravelle	SE-210	France	Aérospatiale	DHC-2	Beaver	Canada	DHC
CC-109	(Convair 440)	US	Convair	DHC-3	Otter	Canada	DHC
CC-115	DHC-5			DHC-4	Caribou	Canada	DHC
CC-117	(Falcon 20)			DHC-5	Buffalo	Canada	DHC
CC-132	(DHC-7)			DHC-6	Twin Otter	Canada	DHC
CC-137	(Boeing 707)			DHC-7	Dash-7 (Ranger, CC-132)	Canada	DHC
CC-138	(DHC-6)						
CC-144	CL-600/-601	Canada	Canadair	DHC-8		Canada	DHC
CF-18	F/A-18			Dimona	H-36	Ge	Hoffman
CF-116	F-5			Do-27	(C-127)	Ge	Dornier
Cheetah	[Mirage III]	S. Africa	Atlas	Do-28	Skyservant	Ge	Dornier
Cherokee	PA-28	US	Piper	Do-128		Ge	Dornier
Cheyenne	PA-31T [Navajo]	US	Piper	Do-228		Ge	Dornier
Chieftain	PA-31-350 [Navajo]	US	Piper	E-2	Hawkeye	US	Grumman
Ching-Kuo		Taiwan	AIDC	E-3	Sentry	US	Boeing
Chipmunk	DHC-1			E-4	[Boeing 747]	US	Boeing
Citabria		US	Champion	E-6	[Boeing 707]		
Citation	(T-47)	US	Cessna	E-26	T-35A (Tamiz)	Chile	Enear
CJ-5	[Yak-18]	China		EA-3	[A-3]		
CL-215		Canada	Canadair	EA-6	Prowler [A-6]		
CL-44		Canada	Canadair	Electra	(L-188)		
CL-601	Challenger	Canada	Canadair	EC-130	[C-130]		
CM-170	Magister [Tzukit]	France	Aérospatiale	EC-135	[Boeing 707]		
				EMB-110	Bandeirante		
CM-175	Zéphyr	France	Aérospatiale	EMB-111	Maritime Bandeirante	Brazil	Embraer
CN-235		Sp/Indon	CASA/IPTN				
				EMB-120	Brasilia	Brazil	Embraer
Cochise	T-42			EMB-121	Xingu	Brazil	Embraer
Comanche	PA-24	US	Piper	EMB-312	Tucano	Brazil	Embraer
Commander	Aero-/Turbo-Commander	US	Rockwell	EMB-326	Xavante (MB-326)	Brazil	Embraer
				EMB-810	[Seneca]	Brazil	Embraer
Commodore	MS-893	France	Aérospatiale	EP-3	(P-3 Orion)		
Corvette	SN-601	France	Aérospatiale	Etendard		France	Dassault
CP-3	P-3 Orion			EV-1	(OV-1)		
CP-121	S-2			F-1	[T-2]	Japan	Mitsubishi
CP-140	Aurora (P-3 Orion) Acturas	US	Lockheed	F-4	Phantom	US	MD
				F-5	-A/-B: Freedom Fighter; -E/-F: Tiger II	US	Northrop
CT-4	Airtrainer	NZ	Victa				
CT-39	Sabreliner	US	Rockwell	F-5T	JJ-5	China	Shenyang
CT-114	CL-41 Tutor	Canada	Canadair	F-6	J-6		
CT-133	Silver Star [T-33]	Canada	Canadair	F-7	J-7		
				F-8	J-8		
				F-8	Crusader	US	Republic
				F-14	Tomcat	US	Grumman
				F-15	Eagle	US	MD
				F-16	Fighting Falcon	US	GD

Type	Name/ designation	Origin	Maker	Type	Name/ designation	Origin	Maker
F-18	[F/A-18]			IAR-28		Ro	IAR
F-21	*Kfir*	Israel	IAI	IAR-93	*Orao*	Yug/Ro	SOKO/IAR
F-27	*Friendship*	Nl	Fokker	Il-14	'Crate'	Russia	Ilyushin
F-28	*Fellowship*	Nl	Fokker	Il-18	'Coot'	Russia	Ilyushin
F-35	*Draken*	Sweden	SAAB	Il-20	(Il-18)		
F-84	*Thunderstreak*	US	Lockheed	Il-28	'Beagle'	Russia	Ilyushin
F-86	*Sabre*	US	N.American	Il-38	'May'	Russia	Ilyushin
F-100	*Super Sabre*	US	N.American	Il-62	'Classic'	Russia	Ilyushin
F-104	*Starfighter*	US	Lockheed	Il-76	'Candid' (tpt)	Russia	Ilyushin
F-106	*Delta Dart*	US	Convair		'Mainstay' (AEW)		
F-111		US	GD		'Midas' (tkr)		
F-172	(Cessna 172)	France/ US	Reims- Cessna	*Impala*	[MB-326]	S. Africa	Atlas
				Islander	BN-2		
F/A-18	*Hornet*	US	MD	J-2	[MiG-15]	China	
Falcon	*Mystère-Falcon*			J-5	[MiG-17F]	China	Shenyang
FB-111	(F-111)			J-6	[MiG-19]	China	Shenyang
FH-227	(F-27)	US	Fairchild- Hiller	J-7	[MiG-21]	China	Xian
				J-8	[Sov Ye-142]	China	Shenyang
Flamingo	MBB-233	Ge	MBB	J-32	*Lansen*	Sweden	SAAB
FT-5	JJ-5	China	CAC	J-35	*Draken*	Sweden	SAAB
FT-6	JJ-6			J-37	*Viggen*	Sweden	SAAB
FTB-337	[Cessna 337]			JA-37	(J-37)		
G-91		Italy	Aeritalia	*Jaguar*		Fr/UK	SEPECAT
G-222		Italy	Aeritalia	JAS-39	*Gripen*	Sweden	SAAB
Galaxy	C-5			*Jastreb*		Yug	SOKO
Galeb		Yug	SOKO	*Jet Provost*		UK	BAe
Gardian	(Falcon 20)			*Jetstream*		UK	BAe
Genet	SF-260W			JJ-6	(J-6)		
GU-25	(Falcon 20)			JZ-6	(J-6)		
Guerrier	R-235			KA-3	[A-3]		
Gulfstream Aviation		US	Gulfstream	KA-6	[A-6]		
				KC-10	*Extender* [DC-10]	US	MD
Gumhuria Ac	(Bücker 181)	Egypt	Heliopolis	KC-130	[C-130]		
				KC-135	[Boeing 707]		
H-5	[Il-28]	China	Harbin	KE-3A	[Boeing 707]		
H-6	[Tu-16]	China	Xian	*Kfir*		Israel	IAI
H-36	*Dimona*			*King Air*		US	Beech
Halcón	[C-101]			*Kiran*	HJT-16		
Harrier	(AV-8)	UK	BAe	*Kraguj*		Yug	SOKO
Harvard	(T-6)			*Kudu*	C-4M		
Hawk		UK	BAe	LIM-6	[MiG-17]	Poland	
HC-130	(C-130)			L-4	*Cub*		
HF-24	*Marut*	India	HAL	L-18	*Super Cub*	US	Piper
HFB-320	*Hansajet*	Ge	Hamburger FB	L-19	O-1		
				L-21	*Super Cub*	US	Piper
HJ-5	(H-5)			L-29	*Delfin*	Cz	Aero
HJT-16	*Kiran*	India	HAL	L-39	*Albatros*	Cz	Aero
HPT-32	*Deepak*	India	HAL	L-70	*Vinka*	Finland	Valmet
HS-125	(Dominie)	UK	BAe	L-100	C-130 (civil version)		
HS-748	[Andover]	UK	BAe				
HT-2		India	HAL	L-188	*Electra* (P-3 *Orion*)		US
HU-16	*Albatross*	US	Grumman	Lockheed			
HU-25	(Falcon 20)			L-410	*Turbolet*	Cz	LET
Hunter		UK	BAe	L-1011	*Tristar*	US	Lockheed
HZ-5	(H-5)			*Learjet*	(C-21)	US	Gates
IA-35	*Huanquero*	Arg	FMA	Li-2	[DC-3]	Russia	Lisunov
IA-50	*Guaraní*	Arg	FMA	LR-1	(MU-2)		
IA-58	*Pucará*	Arg	FMA	*Magister*	CM-170		
IA-63	*Pampa*	Arg	FMA	*Marut*	HF-24		
IAI-201/-202	*Arava*	Israel	IAI	*Mashshaq*	MFI-17	Pakistan/ Sweden	PAC/ SAAB
IAI-1124	*Westwind, Seascan*	Israel	IAI				

Type	Name/designation	Origin	Maker	Type	Name/designation	Origin	Maker
Matador	(AV-8)			P-166		Italy	Piaggio
MB-326		Italy	Aermacchi	PA-18	*Super Cub*	US	Piper
MB-339	(*Veltro*)	Italy	Aermacchi	PA-23	*Aztec*		
MBB-233	*Flamingo*			PA-24	*Comanche*	US	Piper
MC-130	(C-130)			PA-28	*Cherokee*	US	Piper
Mercurius	(HS-125)			PA-31	*Navajo*	US	Piper
Merlin		US	Fairchild	PA-34	*Seneca*	US	Piper
Mescalero	T-41			PA-44	*Seminole*	US	Piper
Metro		US	Fairchild	PBY-5	*Catalina*	US	Consolidated
MFI-15	*Safari*	Sweden	SAAB	PC-6	*Porter*	Switz	Pilatus
MFI-17	*Supporter*, (T-17)	Sweden	SAAB	PC-6A/B	*Turbo Porter*	Switz	Pilatus
MH-1521	*Broussard*	France	Max Holste	PC-7	*Turbo Trainer*	Switz	Pilatus
MiG-15	'Midget' trg	Russia	MiG	PC-9		Switz	Pilatus
MiG-17	'Fresco'	Russia	MiG	PD-808		Italy	Piaggio
MiG-19	'Farmer'	Russia	MiG	*Pembroke*		UK	BAe
MiG-21	'Fishbed'	Russia	MiG	*Pillán*	T-35		
MiG-23	'Flogger'	Russia	MiG	PL-1	*Chien Shou*	Taiwan	AIDC
MiG-25	'Foxbat'	Russia	MiG	*Porter*	PC-6		
MiG-27	'Flogger D'	Russia	MiG	PS-5	[SH-5]	China	HAMC
MiG-29	'Fulcrum'	Russia	MiG	PZL-104	*Wilga*	Poland	PZL
MiG-31	'Foxhound'	Russia	MiG	PZL-130	*Orlik*	Poland	PZL
Mirage		France	Dassault	Q-5	'Fantan' [MiG-19]	China	Nanchang
Mission-master	N-22			*Queen Air*	(U-8)		
Mohawk	OV-1			R-160		France	Socata
MS-760	*Paris*	France	Aérospatiale	R-235	*Guerrier*	France	Socata
MS-893	*Commodore*			RC-21	(C-21)		
MU-2		Japan	Mitsubishi	RC-47	(C-47)		
Musketeer	Beech 24	US	Beech	RC-95	(EMB-110)		
Mya-4	'Bison'	Russia	Myasishchev	RC-135	[Boeing 707]		
Mystère-Falcon		France	Dassault	RF-4	(F-4)		
				RF-5	(F-5)		
N-22	*Floatmaster, Missionmaster*	Aust	GAF	RF-35	(F-35)		
				RF-84	(F-84)		
N-24	*Searchmaster B/L*	Aust	GAF	RF-104	(F-104)		
				RF-172	(Cessna 172)	France	Reims-Cessna
N-262	*Frégate*	France	Aérospatiale	RG-8A		US	Schweizer
N-2501	*Noratlas*	France	Aérospatiale	RT-26	(EMB-326)		
Navajo	PA-31	US	Piper	RT-33	(T-33)		
NC-212	C-212	Sp/Indon	CASA/Nurtanio	RU-21	(*King Air*)		
				RV-1	(OV-1)		
NC-235	C-235	Sp/Indon	CASA/Nurtanio	S-2	*Tracker*	US	Grumman
				S-3	*Viking*	US	Lockheed
Nesher	[Mirage III]	Israel	IAI	S-208		Italy	SIAI
NF-5	(F-5)			S-211		Italy	SIAI
Nightingale	(DC-9)			*Sabreliner*	(CT-39)	US	Rockwell
Nimrod		UK	BAe	*Safari*	MFI-15		
O-1	*Bird Dog*	US	Cessna	*Safir*	SAAB-91 (SK-50)	Sweden	SAAB
O-2	(Cessna 337, Skymaster)	US	Cessna	SC-7	*Skyvan*	UK	Short
				SE-210	*Caravelle*		
OA-4	(A-4)			*Sea Harrier*	(*Harrier*)		
OA-37	*Dragonfly*			*Seascan*	IAI-1124		
Orao	IAR-93			*Search-master B/L*	N-24		
Ouragan		France	Dassault				
OV-1	*Mohawk*	US	Rockwell	*Seneca*	PA-34	US	Piper
OV-10	*Bronco*	US	Rockwell		(EMB-810)		
P-2J	[SP-2]	Japan	Kawasaki	*Sentry*	(O-2)	US	Summit
P-3		Switz	Pilatus	SF-37	(J-37)		
P-3	*Orion*	US	Lockheed	SF-260	(SF-260W Warrior)	Italy	SIAI
P-95	EMB-110						
P-149		Italy	Piaggio	SH-37	(J-37)		

Type	Name/ designation	Origin	Maker	Type	Name/ designation	Origin	Maker
Shackleton		UK	BAe	*Travel Air*	Beech 95		
Sherpa	Short 330, C-23			*Trident*		UK	BAe
Short 330		UK	Short	*Trislander*	BN-2		
Sierra 200	(*Musketeer*)			*Tristar*	L-1011		
SK-35	(J-35)	Sweden	SAAB	TS-8	*Bies*	Poland	PZL
SK-37	(J-37)			TS-11	*Iskra*	Poland	PZL
SK-50	(*Safir*)			Tu-16	'Badger'	Russia	Tupolev
SK-60	(SAAB-105)	Sweden	SAAB	Tu-22	'Blinder'	Russia	Tupolev
SK-61	(*Bulldog*)			Tu-26	'Backfire'	Russia	Tupolev
Skyvan		UK	Short	(Tu-22M)			
SM-1019		Italy	SIAI	Tu-28	'Fiddler'	Russia	Tupolev
SN-601	*Corvette*			Tu-95	'Bear'	Russia	Tupolev
SNJ	T-6 (Navy)			Tu-126	'Moss'	Russia	Tupolev
SP-2H	*Neptune*	US	Lockheed	Tu-134	'Crusty'	Russia	Tupolev
SR-71	*Blackbird*	US	Lockheed	Tu-142	'Bear F'	Russia	Tupolev
Su-7	'Fitter A'	Russia	Sukhoi	Tu-154	'Careless'	Russia	Tupolev
Su-15	'Flagon'	Russia	Sukhoi	Tu-160	'Blackjack'	Russia	Tupolev
Su-17/-20/-22	'Fitter'	Russia	Sukhoi	*Turbo Porter*	PC-6A/B		
Su-24	'Fencer'	Russia	Sukhoi	*TwinBonanza*	Beech 50		
Su-25	'Frogfoot'	Russia	Sukhoi	*Twin Otter*	DHC-6		
Su-27	'Flanker'	Russia	Sukhoi	*Tzukit*	[CM-170]	Israel	IAI
Super		France	Dassault	U-2		US	Lockheed
Etendard				U-3	(Cessna 310)	US	Cessna
Super Galeb		Yug	SOKO	U-7	(L-18)		
				U-8	(*Twin Bonanza/*	US	Beech
Super Mystère		France	Dassault		*Queen Air*)		
T-1		Japan	Fuji	U-9	(EMB-121)		
T-1A	*Jayhawk*	US	Beech	U-10	*Super Courier*	US	Helio
T-2	*Buckeye*	US	Rockwell	U-17	(Cessna 180, 185)	US	Cessna
T-2		Japan	Mitsubishi	U-21	(*King Air*)		
T-3		Japan	Fuji	U-36	(*Learjet*)		
T-6	*Texan*	US	N.American	U-42	(C-42)		
T-17	(*Supporter,*			U-93	(HS-125)		
	MFI-17)	Sweden	SAAB	UC-12	(*King Air*)		
T-23	*Uirapurú*	Brazil	Aerotec	UP-2J	(P-2J)		
T-25	Neiva *Universal*	Brazil	Embraer	US-1		Japan	Shin Meiwa
T-26	EMB-326			US-2A	(S-2A, tpt)		
T-27	*Tucano*	Brazil	Embraer	US-3	(S-3, tpt)		
T-28	*Trojan*	US	N.American	UTVA-66		Yug	UTVA
T-33	*Shooting Star*	US	Lockheed	UTVA-75		Yug	UTVA
T-34	*Mentor*	US	Beech	UV-18	(DHC-6)		
T-35	*Pillán* [PA-28]	Chile	Enaer	V-400	*Fantrainer 400*	Ge	VFW
T-36	(C-101)			V-600	*Fantrainer 600*	Ge	VFW
T-37	(A-37)			*Vampire*	DH-100		
T-38	*Talon*	US	Northrop	VC-4	*Gulfstream* I		
T-39	(*Sabreliner*)	US	Rockwell	VC-10		UK	BAe
T-41	*Mescalero*	US	Cessna	VC-11	*Gulfstream* II		
	(Cessna 172)			VC-91	(HS-748)		
T-42	*Cochise* (*Baron*)	US	Beech	VC-93	(HS-125)		
T-43	(Boeing 737)			VC-97	(EMB-120)		
T-44	(*King Air*)			VC-130	(C-130)		
T-47	(*Citation*)			VFW-614		Ge	VFW
TB-20	*Trinidad*	France	Aérospatiale	*Victor*		UK	BAe
TB-30	*Epsilon*	France	Aérospatiale	*Vinka*	L-70		
TBM-700		France	Socata	*Viscount*		UK	BAe
TC-45	(C-45, trg)			VU-9	(EMB-121)		
T-CH-1		Taiwan	AIDC	VU-93	(HS-125)		
Texan	T-6			WC-130	[C-130]		
TL-1	(KM-2)	Japan	Fuji	WC-135	[Boeing 707]	US	Boeing
Tornado		UK/Ge/It	Panavia	*Westwind*	IAI-1124		
TR-1	[U-2]	US	Lockheed	*Winjeel*	CA-25		

Type	Name/ designation	Origin	Maker
Xavante	EMB-326		
Xingu	EMB-121		
Y-5	[An-2]	China	Hua Bei
Y-7	[An-24]	China	Xian
Y-8	[An-12]	China	Shaanxi
Y-12		China	Harbin
Yak-11	'Moose'	Russia	Yakovlev
Yak-18	'Max'	Russia	Yakovlev
Yak-28	'Firebar' ('Brewer')	Russia	Yakovlev
Yak-38	'Forger'	Russia	Yakovlev
Yak-40	'Codling'	Russia	Yakovlev
YS-11		Japan	Nihon
Z-43		Cz	Zlin
Z-226		Cz	Zlin
Z-326		Cz	Zlin
Z-526		Cz	Zlin
Zéphyr	CM-175		

HELICOPTERS

A-109	*Hirundo*	Italy	Agusta
A-129	*Mangusta*	Italy	Agusta
AB-...	(Bell 204/205/206/ 212/214, etc.)	Italy/ US	Agusta/ Bell
AH-1	*Cobra/ Sea Cobra*	US	Bell
AH-6	(Hughes 500/530)	US	MD
AH-64	*Apache*	US	Hughes
Alouette II	SE-3130, SA-318	France	Aérospatiale
Alouette III	SA-316, SA-319	France	Aérospatiale
AS-61	(SH-3)	US/Italy	Sikorsky/ Agusta
AS-332	*Super Puma*	France	Aérospatiale
AS-350	*Ecureuil*	France	Aérospatiale
AS-355	*Ecureuil II*		
AS-365	*Dauphin*	France	Aérospatiale
AS-532	*Super Puma*	France	Aérospatiale
AS-550	*Fennec*	France	Aérospatiale
ASH-3	(*Sea King*)	Italy/US	Agusta/ Sikorsky
AUH-76	(S-76)		
Bell 47		US	Bell
Bell 204		US	Bell
Bell 205		US	Bell
Bell 206		US	Bell
Bell 212		US	Bell
Bell 214		US	Bell
Bell 406		US	Bell
Bell 412		US	Bell
Bo-105	(NBo-105)	Ge	MBB
CH-3	(SH-3)		
CH-34	*Choctaw*	US	Sikorsky
CH-46	*Sea Knight*	US	Boeing-Vertol
CH-47	*Chinook*	US	Boeing-Vertol
CH-53	*Stallion* (*Sea Stallion*)	US	Sikorsky
CH-54	*Tarhe*	US	Sikorsky
CH-113	(CH-46)		

Type	Name/ designation	Origin	Maker
CH-118	Bell 205		
CH-124	SH-3		
CH-135	Bell 212		
CH-136	OH-58		
CH-139	Bell 206		
CH-147	CH-47		
Cheetah	[SA-315]	India	HAL
Chetak	[SA-319]	India	HAL
Commando	(SH-3)	UK/US	Westland/ Sikorsky
EH-60	(UH-60)		
EH-101		UK/ Italy	Westland/ Agusta
FH-1100	(OH-5)	US	Fairchild-Hiller
Gazela	(SA-342)	France/ Yug	Aérospatiale/ SOKO
Gazelle	SA-341/-342		
H-34	(S-58)		
H-76	S-76		
HA-15	Bo-105		
HB-315	*Gavião* (SA-315)	Brazil/ France	Helibras/ Aérospatiale
HB-350	*Esquilo* (AS-350)	Brazil/ France	Helibras/ Aérospatiale
HD-16	SA-319		
HH-3	(SH-3)		
HH-34	(CH-34)		
HH-53	(CH-53)		
Hkp-2	*Alouette* II/ SE-3130		
Hkp-3	AB-204		
Hkp-4	KV-107		
Hkp-5	Hughes 300		
Hkp-6	AB-206		
Hkp-9	Bo-105		
Hkp-10	AS-332		
HR-12	OH-58		
HSS-1	(S-58)		
HSS-2	(SH-3)		
HT-17	CH-47		
HT-21	AS-332		
HU-1	(UH-1)	Japan/US	Fuji/Bell
HU-8	UH-1B		
HU-10	UH-1H		
HU-18	AB-212		
Hughes 269		US	MD
Hughes 300		US	MD
Hughes 369		US	MD
Hughes 500/ 520	*Defender*	US	MD
IAR-316/-330	(SA-316/-330)	Ro/ France	IAR/ Aérospatiale
Ka-25	'Hormone'	Russia	Kamov
Ka-27	'Helix'	Russia	Kamov
Ka-50	*Hokum*	Russia	Kamov
KH-4	(Bell 47)	Japan/US	Kawasaki/ Bell
KH-300	(Hughes 269)	Japan/US	Kawasaki/ MD

Type	Name/designation	Origin	Maker
KH-500	(Hughes 369)	Japan/US	Kawasaki/MD
Kiowa	OH-58		
KV-107	[CH-46]	Japan/US	Kawasaki/Vertol
Lynx		UK	Westland
MD-500/530	*Defender*	US	McDonnell Douglas
MH-6	(AH-6)		
MH-53	(CH-53)		
Mi-1	*'Hare'*	Russia	Mil
Mi-2	*'Hoplite'*	Russia	Mil
Mi-4	*'Hound'*	Russia	Mil
Mi-6	*'Hook'*	Russia	Mil
Mi-8	*'Hip'*	Russia	Mil
Mi-14	*'Haze'*	Russia	Mil
Mi-17	*'Hip'*	Russia	Mil
Mi-24	*'Hind'*	Russia	Mil
Mi-25	*'Hind'*	Russia	Mil
Mi-26	*'Halo'*	Russia	Mil
Mi-28	*'Havoc'*	Russia	Mil
Mi-35	(Mi-25)		
NAS-332	AS-332	Indon/France	Nurtanio/Aérospatiale
NB-412	Bell 412	Indon/US	Nurtanio/Bell
NBo-105	Bo-105	Indon/Ge	Nurtanio/MBB
NH-300	(Hughes 300)	Italy/US	Nardi/MD
NSA-330	(SA-330)	Indon/France	Nurtanio/Aérospatiale
OH-6	*Cayuse* (Hughes 369)	US	MD
OH-13	(Bell 47G)		
OH-23	*Raven*	US	Hiller
OH-58	*Kiowa* (Bell 206)		
OH-58D	(Bell 406)		
PAH-1	(Bo-105)		
Partizan	(*Gazela*, armed)		
PZL-W3	*Sokol*	Poland	Swidnik
RH-53	(CH-53)		
S-55	(*Whirlwind*)	US	Sikorsky
S-58	(*Wessex*)	US	Sikorsky
S-61	SH-3		
S-65	CH-53		
S-70	UH-60		
S-76		US	Sikorsky
S-80	CH-53		
SA-315	*Lama* [*Alouette* II]	France	Aérospatiale
SA-316	*Alouette* III (SA-319)	France	Aérospatiale
SA-318	*Alouette* II (SE-3130)	France	Aérospatiale
SA-319	*Alouette* III (SA-316)	France	Aérospatiale
SA-321	*Super Frelon*	France	Aérospatiale
SA-330	*Puma*	France	Aérospatiale
SA-341/-342	*Gazelle*	France	Aérospatiale
SA-360	*Dauphin*	France	Aérospatiale
SA-365	*Dauphin* II (SA-360)		
Scout	(*Wasp*)	UK	Westland
SE-3130	(SA-318)		
SE-316	(SA-316)		
Sea King	[SH-3]	UK	Westland
SH-2	*Sea Sprite*	US	Kaman
SH-3	(*Sea King*)	US	Sikorsky
SH-34	(S-58)		
SH-57	Bell 206		
SH-60	*Sea Hawk* (UH-60)		
Sioux	(Bell 47)	UK	Westland
TH-55	Hughes 269		
TH-57	*Sea Ranger* (Bell 206)		
UH-1	*Iroquois* (Bell 204/205)		
UH-12	(OH-23)	US	Hiller
UH-13	(Bell 47J)		
UH-19	(S-55)		
UH-34T	(S-58T)		
UH-46	(CH-46)		
UH-60	*Black Hawk* (SH-60)	US	Sikorsky
VH-4	(Bell 206)		
Wasp	(*Scout*)	UK	Westland
Wessex	(S-58)	US/UK	Sikorsky/Westland
Whirlwind	(S-55)	US/UK	Sikorsky/Westland
Z-5	[Mi-4]	China	Harbin
Z-6	[Z-5]	China	Harbin
Z-8	[SA-321]	China	Changhe
Z-9	[SA-365]	China	Harbin